Biographical Memoirs of
Fellows of the British Academy
20

John Gardner, 1965–2019   1
HUGH COLLINS & ANTONY DUFF

Fergus Millar, 1935–2019   25
ALAN BOWMAN & MARTIN GOODMAN

Myles Burnyeat, 1939–2019   51
MALCOLM SCHOFIELD

Trevor Dadson, 1947–2020   75
JEREMY LAWRANCE

Ron Johnston, 1941–2020   89
CHARLES PATTIE, PETER TAYLOR & KELVYN JONES

John Coles, 1930–2020   111
ANTHONY HARDING

Susan Reynolds, 1929–2021   139
DAVID D'AVRAY & JOHN HUDSON

W. Edgar Yates, 1938–2021   165
RITCHIE ROBERTSON

William St Clair, 1937–2021   179
RODERICK BEATON

Christopher Taylor, 1935–2021   201
CHRISTOPHER DYER

Michael Howard, 1922–2019   223
HEW STRACHAN

James Crawford, 1948–2021   245
MARTTI KOSKENNIEMI & GERRY SIMPSON

Andrew Barker, 1943–2021   265
J. L. LIGHTFOOT

Oliver John Braddick, 1944–2022   295
   DOROTHY V. M. BISHOP

John Lucas, 1929–2020   317
   RICHARD SWINBURNE

James Higgins, 1939–2021   335
   STEPHEN M. HART

Simon Gaunt, 1959–2021   357
   BILL BURGWINKLE

Roger Lonsdale, 1934–2022   383
   JAMES McLAVERTY

Peter Linehan, 1943–2020   411
   MALCOLM SCHOFIELD & FRANCISCO HERNÁNDEZ

George Steiner, 1929–2020   433
   EDWARD HUGHES & BEN HUTCHINSON

Corrigendum   453

JOHN GARDNER

John Blair Gardner

23 March 1965 – 11 July 2019

elected Fellow of the British Academy 2013

by

HUGH COLLINS
Fellow of the Academy

ANTONY DUFF
Fellow of the Academy

John Gardner was Professor of Jurisprudence at University College, Oxford, from 2000 to 2016, and a Senior Research Fellow of All Souls College, Oxford, from 2016 to 2019, until his sudden death from cancer aged 54. He was the leading theorist and philosopher of law of his generation. He specialised in theories of criminal law, discrimination law and tort law, as well as contributing to theories of the nature of law in general.

Biographical Memoirs of Fellows of the British Academy, 20, 1–23
Posted 23 March 2021. © British Academy 2021.

JOHN GARDNER

John Gardner was Professor of Jurisprudence at University College, Oxford, from 2000 to 2016, and a Senior Research Fellow of All Souls College, Oxford, from 2016 to 2019, until his sudden death from cancer aged 54. Through his many publications, he became the leading theorist and philosopher of law of his generation. He was also much admired and liked by colleagues and students for his agile, high-octane conversations in which he delighted in clarifying the thoughts of his interlocutors. Often his writing is imagined as a conversation; he typically commences a defence of his analysis by saying 'You may think that…' or 'You may wonder…'. In his professional work, he drew a boundary between the clarificatory analytical philosophy in which he was engaged, and issues of policy and politics to which he contributed only indirectly through his conceptual analysis. Although Gardner did address in his writings some questions of general legal theory such as the nature of law and its relation to morality, his efforts were primarily directed to the elucidation of the concepts and moral principles that underlie particular branches of law. His most sustained and significant contributions are in the fields of criminal law, discrimination law and aspects of private law, especially tort law. In all these fields, his approach was to offer a rigorous scrutiny of standard concepts and assumptions. As he once wrote, 'Uncontroversial ideas need not less but more critical scrutiny, since they generally get such an easy ride.'[1]

I. Life and career

John Gardner was born on 23 March 1965 in Glasgow, Scotland.[2] His father, William Russell Williamson Gardner, was a Senior Lecturer in the German Department of Glasgow University and Chairman of the Goethe Institute in Glasgow. His home was a social and intellectual gathering place for German writers and thinkers. His mother, Sylvia, a secondary school teacher and also a Germanist, and his maternal grandfather, a graduate of Oxford, engaged John at an early age in philosophical conversations. John graduated from Glasgow Academy in 1982, and in 1983 was admitted to New College, Oxford, to study Jurisprudence (law).

At New College, one of the law fellows, Nicola Lacey FBA, became John Gardner's most influential tutor. She steered him towards legal philosophy and encouraged him to study moral philosophy with Jonathan Glover. After graduating with a First Class BA in Jurisprudence, in 1986–7 John studied for the Bachelor of Civil Law, the

---

[1] J. Gardner, *From Personal Life to Private Law* (Oxford, 2018).
[2] This section draws extensively on Annalise Acorn, 'John Gardner 1965–2019', https://www.law.ox.ac.uk/content/john-gardner-1965-2019, which also includes more detail about his life and family.

challenging postgraduate degree in law at Oxford. He thrived in the environment of several weekly seminars on different aspects of legal philosophy, where he could dazzle fellow students and impress his teachers by his capacity to criticise and revise standard conceptual assumptions and frameworks of analysis. During that year, there were two remarkable achievements: he was elected to a Prize Fellowship (now an Examination Fellowship) at All Souls College, Oxford, and he was awarded the prestigious Vinerian Scholarship for the best results in the BCL examinations.

Like most Prize Fellows at All Souls College, John Gardner found it both stimulating and daunting to work as an equal with many brilliant senior colleagues including Gerry Cohen, Tony Honoré, Derek Parfit and Amartya Sen. In conversations with these Fellows and other scholars in the university, he honed his analytical talents on diverse intellectual puzzles. Perhaps his most influential interlocutor in All Souls College was Parfit, who liked to challenge any philosophical distinction with microscopic analysis. In the broader faculty of law, on the basis of the major contributions of H. L. A. Hart, Ronald Dworkin, John Finnis, Joseph Raz and other colleagues in the faculty and their many students, Oxford had become world-leading in the field of legal philosophy. This intellectual milieu provided a fertile environment for Gardner to develop and try out his own ideas through teaching. Under these influences, while he was a Fellow of All Souls College, he developed as a philosopher whilst at the same time, though rather more slowly than he had hoped, completing a DPhil in 1994 under the supervision of Joseph Raz. He also began to teach in a variety of fields. At that time he began a fruitful thirty-year partnership of teaching seminars with Tony Honoré on causation, theories of tort law and legal theory more generally.

On the completion of his Prize Fellowship in 1991, Gardner was appointed to a university lectureship and a tutorial fellowship at Brasenose College, Oxford. In 1996, he was appointed a Reader in Legal Philosophy at King's College, London, where he had particularly fruitful collaborations with his colleague Timothy Macklem.

At the remarkably youthful age of 35, in 2000 he was elected to the chair in Jurisprudence at University College, Oxford, in succession to Ronald Dworkin. In the sixteen years he held the chair, he was a vital leader in the field and an inspiration to colleagues and students alike. When he organised a faculty seminar series, even if it was on a topic that was not on the current syllabus, he would attract not only a substantial number of students, but often an almost equal number of colleagues to hear his sharp analytical responses and his ability to frame issues in unexpected ways. He was gifted at seeing the potential in his students' and others' thoughts, excavating what was of most value and pointing the way to more careful and coherent development of their ideas. He willingly took on substantial administrative burdens, whilst at the same time being extraordinarily conscientious in his care of postgraduate students. In his rooms in Logic

Lane, Gardner carried on the tradition established by Hart and Dworkin of holding weekly philosophical discussions with members of the university and others. He also created, organised and secured funding for the H. L. A. Hart Fellowship at University College for visiting scholars in law and philosophy. During this period he also enjoyed and benefited from visiting appointments abroad, especially at Yale.

In 2016, Gardner was elected to a Senior Research Fellowship at All Souls College. He hoped that a position with few administrative responsibilities and a lighter teaching load would enable him to complete several intellectual projects. Although he was able to bring some of his projects to fruition, mostly in tort law, ambitious plans in the wider theory of private law and discrimination law were cut short by his development of oesophageal cancer. Although initial medical interventions seemed to have been successful, the disease returned and he died in 2019 within a few months of receiving a terminal diagnosis aged 54.

John Gardner was lovingly committed to his second wife, Jenny Kotilaine, a barrister, and devoted to their daughter Audra and his two stepchildren, Henrik and Annika. He drew extensively on his memories of a happy family life in his philosophical discussions. He also believed in enjoying many experiences in life, which included for him playing bass guitar in a rock group and developing his culinary skills and posting innovative recipes on his always interesting and popular personal website.[3] The website contains hundreds of memorials from John's friends, colleagues, former students and lots of others who barely knew him but admired him greatly as a scholar and a person.

II. Criminal law

Most of Gardner's published work on criminal law appeared between 1990 and 2007, when he published a collection of sixteen of his papers on criminal law, along with a substantial 'Reply to Critics'[4]; his interest in criminal law was sparked and sustained by his intellectual friendships with his fellow graduate students Jeremy Horder and Stephen Shute (with whom he co-authored a much-discussed paper on what makes rape so serious a wrong).[5] Although his 'philosophical positions', he insisted, were

---

[3] https://johngardnerathome.info/.

[4] J. Gardner, *Offences and Defences: Selected Essays in the Philosophy of Criminal Law* (Oxford, 2007). He later published a further reply to critics: 'In defence of *Offences and Defences*' (2012) 4 *Jerusalem Review of Legal Studies* 110.

[5] J. Gardner and S. Shute, 'The wrongness of rape', in Gardner, *Offences and Defences*, p. 1 (originally in J. Horder (ed.), *Oxford Essays in Jurisprudence* (4th Series; Oxford, 2000), p. 193); for later clarification and defence, see J. Gardner, 'The opposite of rape' (2018) 38 *Oxford Journal of Legal Studies* 48.

'not driven by any comprehensive vision',[6] a vision of criminal law's essential character emerges from his work; and although no one could accuse him of simplifying (let alone over-simplifying) the issues or the institutions with which he dealt, at the core of that conception of criminal law lies a deceptively simple thought—that criminal law

> is primarily a vehicle for the public identification of wrongdoing ... and for responsible agents, whose wrongs have been thus identified, to answer for their wrongs by offering justifications and excuses for having committed them.[7]

By unpacking this thought, we can identify the central elements of Gardner's quite distinctive conception of criminal law.

The first point to note is that this is not a justificatory account, according to which criminal law's purpose, what makes it worth maintaining such an institution, is the public identification of wrongdoings and the calling to account of wrongdoers. To say that this is criminal law's peculiar activity is certainly to espouse some version of 'legal moralism', but Gardner is not the kind of legal moralist who thinks that the justifying purpose of criminal law is to call wrongdoers to account (or to punish them).[8] That is what criminal law does; that is what gives it its distinctive character as a legal institution: but whether it is worth maintaining such an institution, what valuable ends it can serve, and what its scope and limits should be, are further questions that this account does not purport to answer. When we turn to those further questions we must, Gardner insists, recognise what a harmful institution criminal law is. It

> wreaks such havoc in people's lives, and its punitive side is such an extraordinary abomination, that it patently needs all the justificatory help it can get. If we believe it should remain a fixture in our legal and political system, we cannot afford to dispense with or disdain any of the various things ... which can be said in its favour.[9]

The things that 'can be said in its favour' are, Gardner also argues, primarily instrumental:[10] what can justify maintaining such a havoc-wreaking practice is that it can help to secure various goods or to avert various evils, including such things as the prevention of wrongdoing (both the kinds of wrongdoing that are themselves

---

[6] J. Gardner, 'As inconclusive as ever' (2019) 19 *Jerusalem Review of Legal Studies* 204, 223. The key word here is 'driven': Gardner would not resist a 'comprehensive vision' if that was where the arguments led him.
[7] J. Gardner, 'In defence of defences', in *Offences and Defences*, p. 80 (originally in P. Asp *et al.* (eds.), *Flores Juris et Legum: Festskrift till Nils Jareborg* (Uppsala, 2002), p. 251).
[8] Contrast e.g. M. S. Moore, *Placing Blame: a Theory of Criminal Law* (Oxford, 1997).
[9] J. Gardner, 'Crime: in proportion and in perspective', in *Offences and Defences*, pp. 214–15 (originally in A. J. Ashworth and M. Wasik (eds.), *Fundamentals of Sentencing Theory* (Oxford, 1998), p. 31).
[10] See J. Gardner and J. Edwards, 'Criminal law', in H. LaFolette (ed.), *International Encyclopedia of Ethics* (Oxford, 2013; https://doi.org/10.1002/9781444367072.wbiee640) on 'the instrumental principle'.

criminalised, and further wrongdoings, such as private acts of revenge, that may flow from them) and the prevention of harm. Harm prevention is also one of the 'constraints' that limit the scope of the criminal law—that limit the range of wrongdoings that it should seek publicly to identify or to call agents to answer for committing. Gardner does not espouse what is perhaps the more familiar version of the Harm Principle, according to which conduct is a candidate for criminalisation only if it is itself harmful: as he and Shute applied the principle in their explanation of why even 'pure' cases of rape that might cause no harm should be criminalised, criminalisation itself can be justified only if it serves to prevent harm.[11] The rationale for this constraint is that criminalisation is itself such a harmful and havoc-wreaking enterprise that it can be justifiably invoked only if it can be expected to prevent more harm than it causes.

The second point to note is that this account of criminal law puts responsible agents and their agency at the very centre of the picture: indeed, although Gardner officially espouses, as we have just seen, the instrumental principle that criminal law must be justified by its beneficial effects, he also shows the intrinsic, non-instrumental value of a practice that engages us as responsible agents. A responsible agent, for Gardner, is one who has 'an ability to offer justifications and excuses … the ability to explain oneself, to give an intelligible account of oneself, to answer for oneself, as a rational being'.[12] The 'intelligible account' that we can, as responsible agents, give of ourselves is an account of the reasons that guided us—reasons that guided our actions, but also our beliefs and emotions; it is in terms of such reasons that we can justify or excuse our actions. Furthermore, rational agents will want to be able thus to answer for themselves—'as rational beings we cannot but want our lives to have made rational sense, to add up to a story not only of whats but of whys. We cannot but want there to have been adequate reasons for why we did (or thought or felt) what we did (or thought or felt)'.[13]

Gardner presents this as part of an 'Aristotelian story' of human beings and their flourishing, and his account is indeed in many ways Aristotelian, notably in the role it gives the emotions as important elements of a rational life. But here as elsewhere his account also has a Kantian flavour, since it emphasises the importance of our character as rational beings, and of treating each other as such; a Kantian tone is also evident

---

[11] Gardner and Shute, 'The wrongness of rape', pp. 29–30. See also Gardner and Edwards, 'Criminal law', pp. 4–5: they also (pp. 5–7) identify other limits on the scope of the criminal law, including rights to privacy and liberty, and 'rule of law' demands for certainty, clarity and prospectivity.

[12] J. Gardner, 'The mark of responsibility', in Gardner, *Offences and Defences*, p. 182 (originally in (2003) 23 *Oxford Journal of Legal Studies* 157): this is what he calls 'basic responsibility'.

[13] Gardner, 'The mark of responsibility', p. 178.

in Gardner and Shute's account of the core wrongness of rape as consisting in the rapist's 'sheer use' of another person,[14] which has clear and explicit echoes of the Kantian prohibition on treating others merely as means.

This is not to present Gardner as a Kantian, since in many ways his account of criminal law, and of human action and responsibility more generally, is profoundly and explicitly anti-Kantian: he was happy to count himself a 'rationalist', who 'stood up for the primacy of reasonableness in life and law',[15] but his rationalism was not Kantian. In particular, as noted, he gave the emotions a central and un-Kantian role in our rational life, since they fall within the realm of reason: they are sources of reasons for action, they are responsive to reason (for we can have reasons to feel as well as to think and to act), and they can be appraised as reasonable or as unreasonable.[16] He also developed a broader critique of Kantian views on 'moral luck' and the place of morality in our lives. A central element of that critique is captured in Gardner's denial of the Kantian claim that 'morally perfect people cannot be morally unlucky in their lives', and his counter-assertion of the Aristotelian claim that 'no amount of moral virtue … ensures that one leads a morally perfect life', because '[o]wing to bad luck, even a morally perfect person may lead a morally imperfect life'.[17] One reason for this is that we can, through no fault of our own, find ourselves in situations in which we cannot but violate a duty, either because it is impossible to fulfil the duty (as when I cannot save a person whom I have a duty to save), or because we face a conflict of moral demands and find that we must (morally) violate one of our duties (as when a parent must break his promise to take his children to the beach, in order to help one of his students who is in urgent and desperate need). In such cases we do wrong, and although we should not be blamed or condemned for it, it nonetheless leaves a moral 'blemish' on our lives; our lives are thus 'damaged'.[18]

Another anti-Kantian dimension of Gardner's view of responsibility is his insistence (partly developing Tony Honoré's work on 'outcome responsibility') that we are responsible not just (as Kant would have it) for our choices or the exercise of our wills (which is supposedly within our control), but for the actual effects of our actions on the world, even when those effects are not, or are not wholly, within our control.[19] This is true not only when we act culpably, intending to bring about some

---

[14] See Gardner and Shute, 'The wrongness of rape', pp. 14–16.

[15] Gardner, 'In defence of *Offences and Defences*', 128.

[16] See also J. Gardner, 'The logic of excuses and the rationality of emotions' (2009) 43 *Journal of Value Inquiry* 315.

[17] J. Gardner, 'Wrongs and faults', in A. P. Simester (ed.), *Appraising Strict Liability* (Oxford, 2005), p. 52.

[18] See e.g. Gardner 'Wrongs and faults', pp. 54, 57; 'In defence of defences', pp. 80–1.

[19] See T. Honoré, *Responsibility and Fault* (Oxford, 1999).

harm or taking a reckless or negligent risk of doing so, and are then held responsible for the harm if it actually ensues, but even when we act in wholly innocent inadvertence: for, Gardner argues, 'the ordinary or basic kind of wrongdoing is "strict" wrongdoing, e.g. hurting people, upsetting people';[20] if I cause injury to another person, I do wrong (a wrong that leaves a blemish on my life), even if I had no reason to believe that I might cause injury.

To say that we are responsible for the actual effects of our actions, and for the wrongs that we commit even if we commit them justifiably or through non-culpable inadvertence, is to talk of our 'basic' responsibility: these are things that we can be called upon to answer for—and that, as rational beings, we must be ready to answer for. If our answer, the account we give of why we acted as we did, is justificatory or excusatory, we can avoid certain kinds of 'consequential responsibility': in particular, we can avoid being blamed, and should be able to avoid a criminal conviction—although we incur other kinds of consequential responsibility, for instance duties of apology and reparation.[21]

The discussion in the previous few paragraphs did not distinguish sharply between moral and legal responsibility—between our responsibility as moral agents in our extra-legal lives and the responsibility that the law, in particular criminal law, ascribes or should ascribe to us. This reflects Gardner's own approach: not just because he wrote about our moral lives as well as our lives under the law, but because he grounded criminal law in morality, both substantively and conceptually. Criminal law should criminalise, that is, identify as criminal wrongs only conduct that is indeed morally wrongful;[22] and it draws its concepts from our extra-legal moral discourse. That is not to deny that, given the institutional character of criminal law, and the constraints that bear on it, it will inevitably diverge to significant degrees from extra-legal moral discourse: but

> specialised legal concepts always depend for their existence on unspecialised everyday concepts to which the law resorts, and in relation to which ... the specialised legal concepts are given their shape. ... [T]he criminal law helps itself to the ordinary

---

[20] J. Gardner, 'Fletcher on offences and defences', in *Offences and Defences*, pp. 141, 150; see Gardner 'Obligations and outcomes in the law of torts', in P. Cane and J. Gardner (eds.), *Relating to Responsibility* (Oxford, 2001), p. 111; 'The wrongdoing that gets results' (2004) 18 *Philosophical Perspectives* 53.

[21] See also J. Gardner, 'The negligence standard: political not metaphysical' (2017) 80 *Modern Law Review* 1, on 'assignable' responsibilities.

[22] Wrongful either in virtue of its pre-legal character, as with so-called '*mala in se*', or in virtue of its prohibition by the law, as with '*mala prohibita*': see Gardner, 'Reply to critics', p. 239. This, as noted above, makes Gardner a kind of 'legal moralist'—but not the kind who thinks that the justifying purpose of criminal law is to denounce or punish moral wrongdoers (see at nn 8–9 above).

concepts of justification and excuse, among many others, in constructing its more specialised concepts.[23]

Thus, although we cannot assume that the law's concepts and doctrines should precisely match those found in extra-legal moral thought, the latter is the essential starting point for analytic or normative discussion of the former.

This brings us finally to a further set of issues in criminal law theory to which Gardner made a distinctive and influential contribution: those concerning justifications and excuses. Theorists used to tell a fairly simple story about justifications and excuses. One way to ward off a charge of culpable, responsible wrongdoing is, on the simple view, to admit responsibility, but to deny that the action for which I admit responsibility was wrong—in other words, to justify my action. The other way to ward off the charge is to admit that the action was wrong or untoward, but to deny responsibility for it—in other words, to excuse it.[24] Gardner comprehensively rejected this view. Both justifications and excuses, he argued, serve to ward off the kind of *consequential* responsibility that consists in conviction and punishment (in criminal law) or in blame (in moral life); but both admit *basic* responsibility for that which we seek to justify or excuse. And neither justifications nor excuses need deny wrongdoing: for what I justify (what requires a justification) might be a wrong.[25]

At least two qualifications are needed. First, to argue that justifications might not negate wrongdoing is to reject the 'closure view', according to which to justify an action is precisely to show that it was not, in its particular context, wrong. As Gardner later made clear, he robustly rejected such a view in relation to justifications outside the criminal law—both in our extra-legal life and in private law; but he thought that the position in criminal law was less clear cut, since some criminal law justifications can be portrayed as wrong-negating.[26] Second, he certainly did not deny that some non-justificatory defences in criminal law negated basic responsibility: the insanity defence is the obvious example. Nor did he argue, outright, that it was *wrong* to class such defences as 'excuses':[27] his concern was, rather, to distinguish those kinds of defence from defences that admit basic responsibility but constitute excuses, rather than justifications.

[23] Gardner, 'In defence of *Offences and Defences*', 112.

[24] See, famously, J. L. Austin, 'A plea for excuses', in his *Philosophical Papers* (Oxford, 1961), p. 124; cited by Gardner in 'In defence of defences', pp. 82–3.

[25] See especially Gardner 'The mark of responsibility'; 'Justifications and reasons', in *Offences and Defences*, 91 (originally in A. P. Simester and A. T. H. Smith (eds.), *Harm and Culpability* (Oxford, 1996), p. 103); 'The gist of excuses', in *Offences and Defences*, p. 121 (originally in (1998) 1 *Buffalo Criminal Law Review* 575).

[26] See Gardner, 'In defence of *Offences and Defences*', 118–19.

[27] See Gardner, 'In defence of *Offences and Defences*', 116.

Gardner's account of justifications and excuses flows from his conception of human beings as rational agents who 'cannot but want there to have been adequate reasons for why we did (or thought or felt) what we did (or thought or felt)':[28] for both justifications and excuses appeal to the reasons for which I acted (or thought or felt) as I did. To put his position very crudely, when I justify my action, I show that I had good enough reasons to act as I did: in the case of criminal law justifications, this involves showing that the law permitted me to attend, and to be guided by, reasons that would otherwise be excluded from practical consideration as operative reasons for action; but the key point in distinguishing justifications from excuses is that I appeal to the good reasons for which I acted.[29] When I excuse my action, by contrast, I do not claim that I acted for good enough reasons. I claim instead that although my action did fall short of what it ought to have been, it was motivated by emotions and beliefs that were themselves justified; and that though in being motivated by those emotions and beliefs I displayed 'human frailty', I nonetheless '*lived up* to the relevant normative expectations, by coping as well as we should expect anyone to cope with a difficult predicament'.[30] Someone who uses defensive force to protect another from attack is justified in what she does, because she acts for a reason (an 'undefeated' reason) for which the law permits her to act. Someone who, by contrast, commits perjury under duress might not be justified in doing so: but he may be excused if he acted out of a reasonable, justified fear of the threatened harm, and 'cop[ed] as well as we should expect anyone to cope' in such a situation.

This brings us back to Gardner's central conception of criminal law, as a rational enterprise that addresses us as responsible agents—'a vehicle for the public identification of wrongdoing ... and for responsible agents, whose wrongs have been thus identified, to answer for their wrongs by offering justifications and excuses for having committed them'.[31] The criminal law's 'public identification of wrongdoing' is a public identification of reasons by which we should guide our actions. As responsible agents, we can then be called (and should be ready) 'to answer for [our] wrongs'—an answering that involves appealing to the reasons for which we acted, and to their relationship to the reasons, identified by the law, that should have guided us. We must hope that if we do commit criminal wrongs (our primary hope, of course, must be that we do not commit them), we will be able to offer a justification, or failing that an excuse, for

---

[28] 'The mark of responsibility', p. 178; see at n. 13 above.
[29] Gardner, influenced by Joseph Raz, developed a sophisticated and subtle account of the different structures and categories of reason that bear on our conduct: see J. Gardner and T. Macklem, 'Reasons', in J. Coleman and S. Shapiro (eds.), *Oxford Handbook of Jurisprudence and Philosophy of Law* (Oxford, 2002), p. 440.
[30] Gardner, 'In defence of *Offences and Defences*', 116.
[31] Gardner, 'In defence of defences', p. 80.

doing so: in offering such justifications and excuses we exercise, and thus assert, the 'basic responsibility' that marks our human agency.

III. Discrimination law

John Gardner never completed an intended general theoretical account of laws against discrimination. Nevertheless, he made a profound contribution to a better understanding of possible justifications for those laws in articles published in the decade commencing in 1989.

Gardner's first major contribution was in the article 'Liberals and unlawful discrimination'.[32] At the heart of this essay is the question why private bodies such as employers and landlords should be required to refrain from exerting any discriminatory preferences with regard to sex and race when entering into contracts with others. Gardner maintained that, although governments can be required to treat all their citizens equally, in a liberal state respect for maximising the freedom of individuals should argue against the imposition of such a duty on private citizens to treat others equally. Such a duty placed on employers, landlords and other private actors should only be legitimate within a liberal political theory, argued Gardner, if it met the normal conditions for state regulation, namely, the 'harm principle' or the requirements of a distributive end-state principle. In brief, the harm principle limits the exercise of state power to prevent one person from harming another. The distributive principle justifies regulation on the ground that it helps to achieve a fairer end-state of distribution of benefits and burdens in society by, for example, progressive taxation and welfare benefits.

Gardner was not the first to notice that the distinction drawn in discrimination law between direct and indirect discrimination apparently corresponds to these two kinds of justification for intervention by the state.[33] Direct discrimination corresponds to the idea that the state should intervene to prevent harm, in this case the deliberate imposition of a disadvantage on the ground of sex or race. Indirect discrimination may be justified as making a contribution to the reduction of inequalities in the distribution of benefits between different groups such as men and women. But Gardner subjected these associations to forensic inspection and revealed their inadequacies. He asked, for instance, in what sense is it a 'harm' in the required sense in liberal theory for an employer merely to decline to offer a job to a woman? And why is it appropriate

---

[32] J. Gardner, 'Liberals and unlawful discrimination' (1989) 9 *Oxford Journal of Legal Studies* 1.
[33] E.g. C. McCrudden, 'Changing notions of discrimination', in S. Guest and A. Milne (eds.), *Equality and Discrimination: Essays in Freedom and Justice* (ARSP Beiheft 21; Stuttgart, 1985).

to require through the law of indirect discrimination a private employer to redistribute benefits such as job opportunities and promotion for the sake of achieving a fairer or more just distribution of benefits in society overall? Gardner also pointed out the inherent tension between these two liberal justifications for discrimination law. The tension is brought out in many contexts, but none more clearly than in calls for positive action (or reverse discrimination). The tension consists in the point that when one ground for intervention may be satisfied, the other almost certainly will not. The case for positive action in favour of minorities may satisfy a principle of end-state distributive justice, but will almost certainly conflict with the harm principle that restricts intervention to proven cases of past inflictions of harm.

Gardner concluded this sceptical account of the adequacy of liberal theories of justification of discrimination law by making a radical innovation in the liberal theoretical perspective. He turned to the perfectionist model of liberalism that had recently been brilliantly articulated by Joseph Raz in *The Morality of Freedom*.[34] On this account of liberalism, state intervention can be justified on the different ground of securing autonomy for all its citizens. Raz stated that: 'The government has an obligation to create an environment providing individuals with an adequate range of options *and the opportunities to choose them.*'[35] Gardner used this formulation to combine in a coherent way both a version of the harm principle and a distributive principle. Failure to provide everyone with an adequate range of options and realistic opportunities to secure those opportunities amounts to a wider concept of harm that can justify state intervention: 'Securing (rather than merely permitting) access to opportunities is a governmental task; and an employer who fails to provide opportunities to a woman, because his criterion of selection disadvantages women, harms her in the sense required by the wide harm principle—he fails to enhance her opportunities in the way that respect for her autonomous agency requires.' On this theory, the government is under a duty to create a society where everyone can enjoy effective opportunities to enjoy an adequate range of options to enjoy a worthwhile life (of their own choosing). That duty justifies the imposition of laws against discrimination on employers because of their key role in the distribution of worthwhile opportunities in the form of jobs and careers.

In a later essay, 'On the grounds of her sex(uality)',[36] Gardner considered the justification for regarding certain grounds for discrimination such as sex and race as impermissible. He recognised that often these grounds for discrimination may be

---

[34] J. Raz, *The Morality of Freedom* (Oxford, 1986).

[35] Raz, *The Morality of Freedom*, p. 418; emphasis by Gardner, 'Liberals and unlawful discrimination', p. 19.

[36] J. Gardner, 'On the grounds of her sex(uality)' (1998) 18 *Oxford Journal of Legal Studies* 1.

forbidden because they are irrational, based on stereotypes and prejudice. But the law normally prohibits these grounds for discrimination even when there may be a rational basis for using them. Gardner considered the suggestion by Wintemute that the grounds for discrimination that are prohibited are either an immutable characteristic or a fundamental choice of the individual.[37] Whilst accepting that these labels fairly describe the prohibited grounds in discrimination law, Gardner made the important argument that in fact both justifications for the identification of prohibited grounds are based on the idea of autonomy. Discrimination on the basis of an immutable characteristic tends, at least if it is a frequent occurrence, to deny us a life in which we can enjoy the freedom to take up a succession of valuable opportunities. Similarly, Gardner argued that discrimination on the basis of fundamental choices such as religion or pregnancy also interferes too much with autonomy.

> There are some particular valuable options that each of us should have irrespective of our other choices. Where a particular choice is a choice between valuable options which ought to be available to people whatever else they may choose, it is a fundamental choice. Where there is discrimination against people based on their fundamental choices it tends to skew those choices by making one or more of the valuable options from which they must choose more painful or burdensome than others.[38]

The reliance on autonomy again permitted Gardner to suggest a more coherent basis for the selection of the prohibited grounds of discrimination. Characteristics do not need to be immutable for them to harm the experience of autonomy and making valuable choices. This justification instead opens up the possibility of extending the prohibited grounds for discrimination not only to sexual orientation and religion, but also more controversial grounds such as having a visible tattoo.

Gardner's essays on discrimination law also offered criticisms of other aspects of the law of discrimination. He subjected the idea that there is a private sphere that should be excluded from discrimination law to critical scrutiny, challenging for instance the persistence of the lawfulness of Gentleman Only clubs.[39] He also argued that the 'but for' test of discrimination adopted by the House of Lords in *James v Eastleigh* with respect to direct discrimination had been misunderstood by its proponents.[40] In the *James* case, the House of Lords had upheld a claim for direct sex discrimination when a woman aged under 65 was able to enter a public swimming pool for free on the ground that she was in receipt of a state pension once aged 60,

---

[37] R. Wintemute, *Sexual Orientation and Human Rights* (Oxford, 1995).
[38] Gardner, 'On the grounds of her sex(uality)', p. 171.
[39] J. Gardner, 'Private activities and personal autonomy: at the margin of anti-discrimination law', in B. Hepple and E. Szyszczak (eds.), *Discrimination: the Limits of the Law* (London, 1992), p. 148.
[40] *James v Eastleigh Borough Council* [1990] 2 All ER 607.

whereas her husband had to pay because he had not yet reached the age of 65 when men qualified for a pension. Using technical philosophical analysis, Gardner insisted that the 'but for' test of direct discrimination necessarily considered not only the outcome of a decision (a difference in treatment of the sexes), but also the reason of the alleged discriminator for the decision.[41] In other words, the test necessarily included the issue of why (i.e. the actual reason) the alleged discriminator had made the decision. In the *James* case, presumably the Council's reason was to provide a benefit to pensioners, not to discriminate on grounds of sex, so, contrary to the decision of the House of Lords, the but for test should have prevented a claim for direct discrimination (though perhaps not one of indirect discrimination).

But Gardner's major contribution to the theory of discrimination law was to reject most of the mainstream theories that sought to justify the law on the basis of various conceptions of equality. American constitutional law had framed the question of the legitimacy of discrimination law in terms of the principle of equal protection of the law. In turn, that legal framework had and continues to have a strong influence on philosophical discussion of the foundations of discrimination law. By reorienting the theory of discrimination law towards freedom or autonomy, rather than equality, Gardner's account was both original and extremely fertile. It influenced many subsequent investigations of the foundations of discrimination law.[42] In particular, it was a major influence on the work of Gardner's doctoral student, Tarunabh Khaitan, in his prize-winning book *A Theory of Discrimination Law*,[43] where many of the more detailed implications of grounding discrimination law in autonomy are worked out and critically assessed. Khaitan makes the useful corrective point, however, that although the ultimate point (general justifying aim) of discrimination law should be regarded as promoting autonomy, the law has the foreseeable and arguably desirable side-effect of increasing equality in society.

IV. Law in general

In his book *Law as a Leap of Faith*,[44] John Gardner assembled with some modifications his principal articles that discussed the nature of law in general. In the Preface to the book, he is quick to deny that he is offering a general theory of law himself. His

---

[41] Gardner, 'On the grounds of her sex(uality)', pp. 181–2.
[42] E.g. H. Collins, 'Discrimination, equality and social inclusion' (2003) 66 *Modern Law Review* 16; S. Moreau, 'In defense of a liberty-based account of discrimination', in D. Hellman and S. Moreau (eds.), *Philosophical Foundation of Discrimination Law* (Oxford, 2013), p. 71.
[43] T. Khaitan, *A Theory of Discrimination Law* (Oxford, 2015).
[44] J. Gardner, *Law as a Leap of Faith* (Oxford, 2012).

purpose is rather to clarify and if possible correct mistakes made by others and to try
to introduce some useful and interesting concepts of his own within a limited compass.
'My remarks about the nature of law in the book, when they are true and interesting,
are just a small sample of the countless true and interesting remarks that could be
made about the nature of law.'[45] He does not seek to avoid proposing a general theory
of the nature of law because he rejects the idea of an essence or inherent nature of
things like law. Nor does he agree with a view that he attributes to Dworkin that a
general theory of law is philosophically uninteresting and of no importance.[46] His
position is rather that law is such a complex phenomenon that it resists the kinds of
simple accounts of the nature of law that tend to form the meat of textbooks on jurisprudence. His contribution is, he claimed, to sort out some of the confusions and
over-simplifications from which theories of the nature of law tend to suffer. Having
recognised that narrow focus of the book, it should also be recognised that much of it
is devoted to an examination of the work of legal positivists such as H. L. A. Hart and
Hans Kelsen with a view to producing what he described as a 'makeover' of legal
positivism.[47] It is possible to view the general direction taken in the book as a restatement of the perspective of legal positivism, which makes many crucial concessions to
critics of legal positivism, though it remains incomplete in its account of the nature of
law.

Gardner argued that all law is made by people, though not necessarily intentionally
or with an awareness of what they are doing.[48] For instance, customary law is made by
the actions of lots of individual actors converging around an approved rule. In Hart's
theory of a legal system,[49] the officials (or senior judges) accept as a matter of practice
a rule of recognition and a rule of change that determine which rules count as laws of
that particular legal system. All these laws, including legislation and customary law,
are 'posited' in the sense that they are made by people. In addition, in harmony with
theories of legal positivism, Gardner accepted that whether a given norm is legally
valid turns on whether it forms part of the system of norms that are identified by their
sources, not their merits. In other words, the identification of the applicable legal rules
depends on how they were made, such as by legislation or a decision of a judge that
has precedential value under the rules of recognition of the legal system. Importantly,
the validity of a legal rule does not depend on whether the standard it adopts is
morally right or generally regarded as such. These are the classic positions of legal

---

[45] J Gardner, 'Fifteen themes from law as a leap of faith' (2015) 6(3) *Jurisprudence* 601, 606.
[46] 'Law in general', chapter 11 in Gardner, *Law as a Leap of Faith*.
[47] Gardner, *Law as a Leap of Faith*, vi.
[48] Chapter 3, 'Some types of law', in Gardner, *Law as a Leap of Faith*.
[49] H. L. A. Hart, *The Concept of Law* (Oxford, 1961).

positivism often identified with the work of H. L. A. Hart, which in turn were developed from the classic formulations of John Austin.[50]

Having identified legal positivism with this narrow set of propositions, often described as the 'sources thesis', Gardner was able to reject many criticisms of legal positivism on the ground that they miss their mark. For instance, the idea that there are moral qualities in the nature of law, famously described by Lon Fuller as the 'inner morality of law' and by others as 'the rule of law' or the justice of general rules in treating like cases alike apparently poses no objection to Gardner's account of legal positivism. As long as conformity to those inner moral standards is not a condition of validity for a law, Gardner argued that legal positivists can accept the existence of these moral qualities of law.[51] For instance, if the moral qualities of law include that it should be clear and only prospective in its imposition of duties, those virtues of law can be acknowledged as its own special moral qualities, without sacrificing the sources thesis. An obscure and retrospective law is valid if enacted in accordance with the rule of recognition, even though it fails to meet the special moral qualities that laws normally possess. While this interpretation is a possible account of legal positivism, there remains the troublesome issue, which Gardner acknowledged,[52] that the stress on the fact that law can be discovered from its sources, with the emphasis on the mechanical nature of this task, seems to indicate the presence of a view among legal positivists that the virtue of the sources thesis is that it makes the law discoverable and its content transparent, values which do seem to tie legal positivism indissolubly to the advancement of a particular view of the moral importance of the rule of law. On this point, however, Gardner insisted that legal positivists need not endorse the idea of the value of tying the nature of law to the ideal of the rule of law, for the theory of legal positivism is merely about the validity of law under the sources thesis and the rejection of any requirement that a law should be morally proper or just. In so far as leading legal positivists such as H. L. A. Hart muddied the waters by linking the sources thesis to the ideal of the rule of law, Gardner dismissed those contributions as 'bungled and preliminary attempts to formulate the sources thesis'.[53]

Having narrowed the theory of legal positivism down to the sources thesis, it then became possible for Gardner to reject other positions that are regularly attributed to legal positivists. It is often said that legal positivists believe that there is no necessary connection between law and morality, but in Gardner's view that is a false attribution.[54] A positivist can believe that law is very much like morality and in general

---

[50] J. Austin, *The Province of Jurisprudence Determined*, ed. Rumble (Cambridge, 1995).
[51] Gardner, *Law as a Leap of Faith*, p. 33.
[52] Gardner, *Law as a Leap of Faith*, p. 26.
[53] Gardner, *Law as a Leap of Faith*, p. 49.
[54] Gardner, *Law as a Leap of Faith*, chapters 2 and 9.

mirrors its requirements, whilst at the same time insisting that conformity to morality
is not a requirement of legal validity (unless perhaps the rule of recognition explicitly
requires for the purpose of legal validity the conformity of a rule with a particular
moral standard as may be the case in some constitutions). It is also said sometimes
that legal positivists are committed to a formalist style of interpretation of legislation
in which one should simply apply the rules, but a particular style of interpretation
does not appear to be entailed by the sources thesis. It would be consistent with legal
positivism for the valid laws to be interpreted according to their literal meaning, their
purpose, or, if available, the intention of the original maker of the law. More generally, as confined by Gardner to the sources thesis, legal positivism does not appear to
require particular stances on any other much debated issues in jurisprudence, or at
least, as Gardner observed, these issues can be treated relatively independently.

> [O]nce one has tackled the question of whether a certain law is valid there remain
> many relatively independent questions to address concerning its meaning, its fidelity
> to law's purposes, its role in sound legal reasoning, its legal effects, and its social func-
> tions, to name but a few. To study the nature of law one needs to turn one's mind to
> the philosophical aspects of these further questions too. To these further questions
> there is no distinctively 'legal positivist' answer, because legal positivism is a thesis
> only about the conditions of legal validity.[55]

Armed with this defence of the theory of legal positivism, John Gardner turned
his attention to various claims about the nature of the central case of law. Here he
maintained the position that indeed there are conceptually necessary connections
between law and morality. One connection, which draws on the work of Raz and
Alexy,[56] is that law by its nature holds itself out as morally binding, even though that
may be a mistake or a pretence.[57] Law always claims moral authority and expresses
itself in the language of rights, obligations and duties. It is possible, of course, that the
law has endorsed a mistaken view of what morality should require, but it claims
nevertheless the moral authority to impose its own interpretation of what obligation
applies to the circumstances. In this sense, legal positivists can maintain their familiar
contention that there can be immoral laws. A second conceptual link presented by
Gardner is that legal reasoning is moral reasoning with one or more legal premises.[58]
For instance, if there is a conflict between two legal norms, their reconciliation must
be achieved by additional legal reasoning that necessarily involves moral norms.
Similarly, if there is a gap in the legal rules with respect to a particular situation, legal

[55] Gardner, *Law as a Leap of Faith*, p. 49.
[56] R. Alexy, *The Argument from Injustice: a Reply to Legal Positivism*, trans. B. Paulson and S. Paulson
(Oxford, 2002); J. Raz, 'Legal validity', in J. Raz, *The Authority of Law* (Oxford, 1979), pp. 154–7.
[57] Chapter 5, 'How law claims, what law claims', in Gardner, *Law as a Leap of Faith*.
[58] Chapter 7, 'The legality of law', in Gardner, *Law as a Leap of Faith*.

reasoning must fill that gap by extending the local rules through additional reasons that are moral reasons. Gardner placed no limits on the kinds of moral reasons that might assist in this kind of elaboration of law.[59] He recognised, however, that as well as ordinary moral reasons, judges must take into account the special moral obligations of their position as officials of the legal system and the distinctive moral qualities of law that Fuller described as the inner morality of law.

V. Tort law and the nature of private law

In his final years, most of John Gardner's published work concerned theories of the law of tort and more general reflections on the nature of private law. Most of these essays were published in a posthumously published collection of journal articles with some additions in *Torts and Other Wrongs*,[60] which was supplemented by further reflections on the morality of the law of tort in the earlier monograph *From Personal Life to Private Law*.[61] The law of tort (or delict) is that part of the law that provides individuals with rights of action to obtain redress for wrongs committed against them that cause personal injury, damage to property and other similar harms. The law of tort is part of what lawyers classify as private law, which includes the law of contract and the law of property. Private law invariably entitles one person (the plaintiff) to bring a claim against another, usually a claim for damages or financial compensation, for a loss that the other person wrongfully caused to the plaintiff—for instance, that wrong might consist of an accident causing personal injury, financial loss by breach of contract or the misappropriation of another's property.

Since the 1970s, a fierce debate had evolved about the nature of the law of tort. The traditional 'moralist' view was that tort law merely provided isolated measures of corrective justice between two individuals. Where a wrong had been identified, on the complaint of the plaintiff, the law required the defendant to pay the plaintiff compensation.[62] In contrast, various kinds of instrumentalist or consequentialist accounts of the law of tort insisted that the purpose of the law should be understood in terms of social and economic goals. One goal might be, for instance, achieving compensation for accidents rather like a system of insurance. Another goal might be efficiency in the

---

[59] J. Gardner, *Law as a Leap of Faith*, p. 192.
[60] J. Gardner, *Torts and Other Wrongs* (Oxford, 2019).
[61] Gardner, *From Personal Life to Private Law*.
[62] E.g. J. Coleman, 'The morality of strict tort liability' (1976) 18 *William and Mary Law Review* 259; J. Coleman, 'Corrective justice and wrongful gain' (1982) 11 *Journal of Legal Studies* 421 (1982), 421; S. Perry, 'The moral foundations of tort law' (1982) 77 *Iowa Law Review* 449; E. Weinrib, 'Toward a moral theory of negligence law' (1983) 2 *Law and Philosophy* 37.

sense of maximising the wealth of society by imposing liability on those who could, at the least cost, avoid the harm caused by accidents.[63] These instrumentalist accounts of tort law were often not so much an account of legal practice, but rather formed the basis of a critique that suggested that tort law was not fit for its social and economic purpose and needed reform, even radical reform including abolition. John Gardner entered the debate by making the unpopular claim that both sides had valid insights, which could even be combined. He then added two important amendments to the traditional moral account of the law of tort.

With respect to the debate between the 'moralists' and the instrumentalists, Gardner argued that all theories should be instrumentalist to some extent. For example, he claimed that everyone should accept that tort law, or private law, should be efficient.[64] Whatever tort law/private law's goal may be, it should achieve that goal as effectively as possible. So he thought that, up to a point, there is no real contest between instrumentalist theories and others and that all theories are instrumentalist.[65] That is not to say he that agreed with the economists on what tort law should be efficient *at*—certainly not wealth-maximisation. But its goal might be, quite possibly, the doing of corrective justice, and, in so far as the doing of corrective justice efficiently triggers issues of distributive justice, the doing of distributive justice as well.[66] 'We should think about which institutional set-up is most efficacious in righting the wrong, least wasteful, and most sensitive to the circumstances of the case.'[67] At the same time, Gardner accepted the emphasis of the moralists on the reasons the law itself gives for judgments with regard to torts as a necessary part of an explanation and justification of tort law. This emphasis is linked to his deeply held view that legal reasoning in private law is a translation of ordinary moral reasoning in a person's life.

One important contribution to the moralist account suggested by Gardner was his justification of reparative duties. Many traditional accounts of the law of tort hold that a tort is a wrong that breached the primary rules that set standards of conduct such as a duty of care, for which a court would grant a corrective justice remedy in the form of damages under a body of secondary rules that were independent of the primary duties of care. Gardner rejected this view in favour of what he described as 'the continuity thesis'.[68] This thesis states that the reasons which grounded a primary

---

[63] G. Calibresi, *The Costs of Accidents: a Legal and Economic Analysis* (New Haven, CT, 1970); R. Posner, 'A theory of negligence' (1972) 1 *Journal of Legal Studies* 1 29.

[64] J. Gardner, 'What is tort law for? Part 1. The place of corrective justice' (2011) 30 *Law and Philosophy* 30 1; and reprinted in Gardner, *Torts and Other Wrongs*, chapter 2.

[65] J. Gardner, 'Tort law and its theory', in J. Tasioulas (ed.), *The Cambridge Companion to the Philosophy of Law* (Cambridge, 2018).

[66] Gardner, *Torts and Other Wrongs*, chapter 3.

[67] Gardner, 'Tort law and its theory', p. 21.

[68] Gardner, 'What is tort law for? Part 1'.

obligation to *x* (or not-to-*x*) continue to demand conformity after the breach of the primary obligation. While the primary obligation may be breached and come to an end (e.g. my primary obligation not to damage your car comes to an end once I've destroyed your car: the car no longer exists, so there can be no obligation not to damage it), the reasons which justified that primary obligation—say, your well-being—continue to demand conformity, and *these reasons* are what justify secondary obligations to compensate. By compensating you, I imperfectly conform to the well-being reason which justified my earlier (now disappeared) primary obligation not to damage your car. I imperfectly comply with this reason by compensating you just in so far as your well-being is restored to the level which it would have been in had I complied with the primary obligation in the first place. In this, he started a disagreement with Ernest Weinrib, whose view is that compensatory duties are a continuation of the *primary* duty itself.[69] For Gardner, what continues is the underlying reason for the primary duty, not necessarily the primary duty itself. His view also contrasts with consequentialist views which locate the justification of secondary duties in the realm of incentives for future conformity with other primary duties. This misses, Gardner argued,[70] the sense in which the secondary duty is grounded immediately in the breach of the primary duty; we already have a reason to compensate when a primary duty is breached, without engaging in a consequentialist weighing-up of whether optimal deterrence would be achieved by now requiring a person to compensate. The obligation to compensate is tied in that way to, and grounded in, what happened in the past.

A second important contribution to the moralist accounts of the law of tort concerned his views on strict liability. Strikingly, John Gardner thought that strict liability was the morally 'primary' or 'basic' position, and that fault liability was something that was a legal add-on.[71] His idea was that in morality we are on the hook for outcomes we produce even without fault. But for various reasons to do with the rule of law, difficulties of allocating causal responsibility, and so on, the law might choose to depart from that basic moral position. Most people start with something like the idea that culpable wrongdoers ought to bear the costs of their wrongs, then do some intellectual gymnastics to bring in pockets of justifiable strict liability. On Gardner's view, the pressing question is how to justify so much *fault* liability when morality has us already on the hook for outcomes produced without fault. Why believe that in morality we are accountable for outcomes not traceable to fault? Part of the idea is that our reasons for action are basically strict in character. We do not merely have

[69] E. Weinrib, *The Idea of Private Law* (Cambridge, MA, 1995).

[70] Gardner, 'What is tort law for? Part 1'.

[71] J. Gardner, 'The negligence standard: political not metaphysical' (2017) 80 *Modern Law Review* 1; reprinted in Gardner, *Torts and Other Wrongs*, chapter 7.

reasons to *try*, Gardner pointed out, but reasons to *succeed* in not producing certain (harmful) outcomes. Indeed, we can only make sense of reasons to try if we have reasons to succeed. If we have reasons to succeed in not producing certain outcomes, then by the 'continuity thesis', we also have reasons to compensate when we do produce those outcomes, so far as compensation will serve as imperfect conformity to those reasons.

VI. From personal life to private law

In some important respects, John Gardner's monograph *From Personal Life to Private Law* brought together his ethical values, his views of what constitutes a good life, his aspirations as a legal scholar and his theories about the nature of law. In the introduction to the book, he explained that his ambition was to show how law, especially private law, is no more than a translation of ordinary personal relations between friends, family, neighbours and colleagues. '[W]hat private law would have us do is best understood by reflecting on what we should be doing quite apart from private law, which obviously entails reflection on the reasons why we should be doing it.'[72] To explore this proposition, he wanted to draw on his personal experiences such as family life and stories from literature to examine those reasons for what we should be doing, with the ultimate goal of shedding light on what tort law and private law more generally are or should be doing. He wanted to do this in a way that might be accessible to the general reader, using anecdotes, literary stories and parables, though in this aspiration he recognised he was only partly successful.

This close linkage between personal life and private law, in which the reasons and concerns are common to both, is linked to his earlier discussion of the nature of law in general, for he argues that private law uses law's moral authority to reach determinate and therefore useful answers about what we should do in circumstances where there is more than one defensible thing to do.[73] Similarly, the law of contract recognises special relationships that people enter into, for the purpose of supporting those relationships, contributing to their availability, affirming their social significance, or emphasising their solemnity.[74] But Gardner is clear that the purpose of private law is not primarily about promoting autonomy in the sense of choices about how we live

[72] Gardner, *From Personal Life to Private Law*, p. 8.
[73] Gardner, *From Personal Life to Private Law*, p. 13.
[74] Gardner, *From Personal Life to Private Law*, p. 46.

our lives. Instead, the purpose of private law is to protect our security, the continuity of our lives and to conserve value.[75]

In all these discussions of theoretical perspectives on law and life, what comes through is a 'brilliant, ebullient mind' blessed with 'an infectious and lively enthusiasm for thinking about how he or you or I might live a life—how we might be able to respond to the opportunities and the necessities it involves, and how we might hold each other responsible in a community'.[76]

Acknowledgements

We are extremely grateful for detailed guidance from Sandy Steel on section V concerning the theory of the law of tort, and from Stephen Shute on section II concerning criminal law. Nicola Lacey FBA read the whole text and offered many suggestions and corrections.

Note on the authors: Hugh Collins is Cassel Professor of Commercial Law at the London School of Economics and Emeritus Vinerian Professor of English Law at All Souls College, Oxford; he was elected a Fellow of the British Academy in 2006. Antony Duff is Emeritus Professor of Philosophy, University of Stirling; he was elected a Fellow of the British Academy in 2004.

---

[75] Gardner, *From Personal Life to Private Law*, p. 231.
[76] T. Endicott, 'John Gardner 1965–2019', https://www.law.ox.ac.uk/news/2019-07-12-john-gardner-1965-2019.

FERGUS MILLAR

Fergus Graham Burtholme Millar

5 July 1935 – 15 July 2019

elected Fellow of the British Academy 1976

by

ALAN BOWMAN
Fellow of the Academy

MARTIN GOODMAN
Fellow of the Academy

Professor Sir Fergus Millar was the outstanding Roman historian of his generation. He was a prolific author whose scholarship covered a wide range of periods, from the Republic to late antiquity, and a wide geographical range, with a particular emphasis on the Roman Near East.

Biographical Memoirs of Fellows of the British Academy, 20, 25–50
Posted 3 November 2021. © British Academy 2021.

F.S.B. Millar

Fergus Millar spent most of his life in England, but he always considered himself a Scot and would occasionally remind his friends and colleagues of his national allegiance, particularly at Burns Night.[1] His father was a lawyer ('Writer to the Signet') in Edinburgh, and Fergus received an intensive education from the age of eight at the Edinburgh Academy until the age of 14, when, shortly before the death of his mother, he was sent to board in the less academic environment of Loretto School. The change of school, exacerbated by the trauma of his mother's death, left him socially isolated, and he spent much of his time at Loretto focussing on school work and golf (at which he excelled). In intellectual terms, Millar complained in retrospect that the move from the Edinburgh Academy, where Latin was taught in traditional fashion with knuckles rapped for grammatical errors, had prevented him from receiving the thorough education which would have made him what he considered a proper classicist, but he progressed well enough to be awarded in 1953 a Minor Scholarship to Trinity College, Oxford.

Studying at Trinity was postponed for two years of National Service in the Navy, where he was taught Russian, and in light of this hiatus in his education, Trinity permitted him to take an accelerated three-year degree in place of the standard Greats course. The shortened course allowed only two terms of Prelims to study classical languages and literature instead of the usual five terms of Classical Moderations, but he excelled in the Ancient History side of Greats under the tutelage of James Holladay, gaining a First in 1958, and he had the self-confidence to apply successfully for a Prize Fellowship at All Souls in the autumn of the same year.

As an undergraduate Millar had been much engaged in student journalism, and it was not inevitable that he would prefer academic life to Fleet Street, where he had been offered a position with the *Daily Mail* prior to his graduation. He had enjoyed studying Ancient History, however, and he embarked on a doctorate on Cassius Dio under the supervision of Ronald Syme. The obvious model for the topic selected was Syme's *Tacitus*, which had been published in 1958, and Syme must have played the most important role in the selection of the subject and its general treatment, but he seems to have had little interest in providing much more than general encouragement. Awarded the Conington Prize in 1962 for the doctoral dissertation, Millar was a prime

[1] We have made extensive use of biographical notes and a list of publications drawn up by Fergus Millar with characteristic thoroughness for the benefit of a future obituarist. No full bibliography of Millar's writings has been published, but most of his papers can be found either in the three volumes of *Rome, the Greek World and the East* , (2002–2006), edited by Hannah M. Cotton and Guy M. Rogers, or in *Empire, Church and Society in the Late Roman Near East: Greeks, Jews, Syrians and Saracens (Collected Papers 2004–14)* (2015). We are grateful to Averil Cameron, Peter Garnsey and Priscilla Lange for reading the memoir and offering valuable insights and information.

candidate for a tutorial fellowship, and in 1964 he moved to The Queen's College Oxford as Fellow and Tutor in Ancient History in succession to Guy Chilver.

Millar immersed himself in undergraduate teaching with enthusiasm, boasting in 1975 that he had never yet had to postpone or cancel a tutorial because of illness. Life was less enjoyable in Queen's than in All Souls because the common room was riven by deep-seated personal animosities (a motivating factor for Chilver's departure to the University of Kent at Canterbury). Initially, his university lectures and his undergraduate teaching as a college tutor were largely confined to the imperial period (then formally designated in the Oxford Greats syllabus as '43 BC to AD 117'). His lectures of the mid–60s on 'Documents of the Roman Empire' were characteristically unshowy and very substantive, giving a clear indication of the direction of travel of his studies on the administration of the empire.

As an Oxford college tutor he thrived in the current pattern of teaching mainly one-to-one or in pairs, although after a decade he might have felt that he needed something different. His tutorial practice was to listen without interrupting to the essay being read aloud from start to finish, taking notes in the course of the reading. He would then correct or comment on specific points, often shoving a copy of a relevant piece of ancient evidence (habitually Cassius Dio) under the student's nose, before broadening the discourse to the context and importance of the subject at hand. Sometimes he would share a draft of one of his soon-to-be-published articles. His style was not meretriciously 'inspiring'; for those with a real historian's instinct the inspiration came from seeing him in action and observing his hard work, attention to evidence, analytical thoroughness and intellectual integrity.

He felt stifled, however, by what he later described as the 'benevolent inertia' of Oxford and the lack of institutional attention to graduate students, which he tried independently to remedy without attracting much support from colleagues. Never shy of giving his views in committee, he muttered 'There you go again' when Peter Brunt, the Camden Professor, said 'No, I don't' in a sub-faculty meeting of ancient historians in 1975 in reply to a complaint that he [Brunt] always said 'no' when any innovation was proposed. Millar accepted an invitation in 1976 to succeed Arnaldo Momigliano as Professor of Ancient History in University College London, even though the new post condemned him to eight years of early morning departures to commute to London from the family home in Oxford.

He found congenial the departmental context of his life in UCL, enjoying being part of an academic community who would meet in corridors and chat over coffee in the common room in the Institute of Classical Studies, at that time still located in Gordon Square, just behind UCL, and he established links with the Department of Hebrew and Jewish Studies, studying Hebrew with Ada Rapaport-Albert. A major achievement in this context was the very inclusive ICS ancient history seminar, for which he drew in all the ancient historians across the University of London, including the Near Eastern specialist Amélie Kuhrt.[2] This was an academic culture which he later promoted with outstanding effectiveness on his return to Oxford.

The syllabus in UCL covered a huge range of Graeco-Roman history from the Archaic period to Late Antiquity and Millar was plunged into teaching periods quite new to him, an expansion of his teaching range in three directions which also represented a significant change in the nature of his personal contact with undergraduates. He took on the lecture course from 404 to 31 BCE, previously given by Arnaldo Momigliano, and that on Archaic and mid-Republican Rome, for which he acknowledged a debt to his colleagues John North and Tim Cornell. His later publications on the Republic were a product of this teaching. Then there was the history of the Empire down to 400 which was the basis of his later publications on Late Antiquity.

If the number of his undergraduate pupils who followed him into academic positions in ancient history was relatively small (only Simon Price, Guy Rogers and the two authors of this memoir), it was a different story after his return to Oxford as Camden Professor in 1984 in succession to Peter Brunt. As was traditional for statutory professors, he gave lectures and seminars open to all and supervised postgraduates but did not tutor undergraduates. He supervised doctoral students (in the days before Masters' courses existed) over a huge timescale and range of topics in Roman imperial history and historiography (theses on ancient authors included Strabo, Josephus and Fronto). He had the knack of encouraging prospective supervisees towards promising and appropriate subjects without pushing or overpersuading them. This generally gave them a feeling of confidence and intellectual freedom (though there were a few cases in which their choices did not work out well and it seemed in retrospect as if he could have been a bit more *dirigiste*, though he never failed to offer generous support and advice). He was certainly meticulous and exhaustive in reading drafts and responding with detailed and substantive comments. Despite occasional references from scholars familiar with other academic cultures and some Oxford precedent (particularly Ronald Syme), this did not lead to the emergence of a 'school of Fergus Millar' – the supervisees and their subjects were far too diverse and heterogeneous. This was surely very much his style and his preference.

Millar's doctoral thesis on Cassius Dio, on whose work our knowledge of much Roman history in the Republic and early Principate depends, was submitted in 1962 and published by Oxford University Press in expanded form two years later.[3]

---

[2] See T.J. Cornell, 'Professor Sir Fergus Millar 1935–2019', *Journal of Roman Studies* [hereafter *JRS*] 110 (2020), 1–3.
[3] *A Study of Cassius Dio* (1964).

It constituted an original and detailed demonstration that Dio's depiction of the late Republic and the rule of Augustus reflected the state of the Roman political system and Dio's understanding, derived from his own political career, of the workings of government in the early 3rd century. Millar was impelled by the genre of a doctoral thesis to cover topics previously treated in the voluminous earlier literature on Dio, but he was more interested in placing Dio himself in the social and political setting of the Greek world under Roman rule during the Severan dynasty than in the traditional exercise of trying to disentangle the sources Dio had collected during the ten years he claimed to have spent gathering material for his history, and Millar's study was widely recognised as a major achievement by 'a historian of stature ... with a deep insight into the rationale of Roman imperial politics'. This interest in the historian's political world was replicated in Millar's later studies of other Greek historians, notably Dexippus (who lived through the 3rd-century invasions of the Greek world), Polybius, and especially Josephus, whose writings Millar regarded as the most important surviving source for the functioning of Roman provincial government.[4]

Already in his decade as a tutorial fellow at Queen's Millar developed intellectually from two chance encounters which took him far beyond the syllabus of Oxford Greats and the concerns of his doctorate. The first was an invitation in 1964 to contribute to the Fischer Weltgeschichte a volume on the Roman Empire up to 284 CE: the series editor did not have any particular author in mind when he came to Oxford to seek a volunteer to fill this gap in the series, but Millar threw himself into the task with energy. The resulting book, *The Roman Empire and its Neighbours*, published in Germany in 1966 and then in England in 1967, was written with striking clarity and reached a wide readership, even if Millar's disarming note in the preface that this was a young man's book, composed at too great a speed, was a hostage to reviewers.[5] The second chance opportunity arose from the arrival in Oxford in 1968 of Geza Vermes as the new Reader in Jewish Studies and an invitation to work as joint editor on the revised English edition of Emil Schürer's *The History of the Jewish People in the Age of Jesus Christ*, a massive task which was to occupy him from 1969 to 1989.[6]

It was while teaching at Queen's and during a visit to the Institute for Advanced Study at Princeton in 1968 that Millar had begun collecting ideas and materials for *The Emperor in the Roman World*, the book for which he was to be best known for the

---

[4] 'P. Herennius Dexippus: the Greek World and the Third-Century Invasions', *JRS* 59 (1969), 12–29; 'Polybius between Greece and Rome' in J.A.T. Koumoulides (ed.), *Greek Connections: Essays on Culture and Diplomacy* (1987), 1–18; 'Last Year in Jerusalem: Monuments of the Jewish War in Rome', in J. Edmondson, S. Mason and J. Rives, eds., *Flavius Josephus and Flavian Rome* (2005), 101–28.
[5] *The Roman Empire and its Neighbours* (1967).
[6] E. Schürer, revised and edited G. Vermes, F. Millar, M. Black and M. Goodman, *The History of the Jewish People in the Age of Jesus Christ 175 BCE–AD 135*, 3 vols. (1973–87).

rest of his career.[7] The book was completed during a sabbatical in 1973–4, and by the time that it was published in 1977, he was already, at the age of 42, established as a major figure in Roman studies. In 1975 he became editor of the *Journal of Roman Studies* and in 1976 he was elected a Fellow of the British Academy.

His inaugural lecture as Camden Professor already prefigured the Carl Newell Jackson lectures given in Harvard in 1987 which appeared (in much expanded form) as *The Roman Near East* in 1993.[8] The Jerome Lectures, delivered in Ann Arbor, Michigan in 1993 and the American Academy in Rome in 1994 and published as *The Crowd in Rome in the Late Republic*, were much shaped by his discussions with Tim Cornell and John North during his time in UCL.[9]

Millar's retirement in 2002 enabled him to embark on a long period of further scholarly productivity, enhanced by a deliberate scaling back of his other commitments following an attack of angina in the late 1990s, presaging the problems that plagued him intermittently until the heart failure which ended in his death. Provided by the Oxford Centre for Hebrew and Jewish Studies, of which he had been a Senior Associate since 1990, with shared office space in the Oriental Institute where he found himself a new academic home which he much enjoyed, and with the benefit of two Leverhulme Emeritus Fellowships and two grants from the Academy for part-time secretarial help, he settled down to full-time research, retiring from all the committee work which he had found so frustrating. He gave the Sather Lectures in Berkeley in 2002–2003,[10] and, irritated by the lack of clear guidance by specialists on which rabbinic texts could validly be used for the history of late-Roman Palestine, he cajoled colleagues into organising a conference at the Academy on the subject and then instigated and produced, with Yehudah Cohn and Eyal Ben-Eliyahu, a *Handbook of Jewish Literature from Late Antiquity*, published by the British Academy for the assistance of historians such as himself.[11] As the number of his studies multiplied, the prospect of putting them all together into a new synthesis faded, but he brought many of his themes together in the Schweich Lectures, delivered at the Academy in 2010 and published in 2013, and the volume of his collected papers from 2004–14, published in 2015, preserves the insights which could have infused such a synthesis.[12] At an event held to celebrate the publication of the latter book, which comes to 807 pages, he

---

[7] *The Emperor in the Roman World* (1977) [hereafter *ERW*].

[8] *The Roman Near East* (1993).

[9] *The Crowd in Rome in the Late Republic* (1998).

[10] *A Greek Roman Empire: Power and Belief under Theodosius II, 408–450* (2006).

[11] E. Ben-Eliyahu, Y. Cohn and F. Millar, *Handbook of Jewish Literature from Late Antiquity, 135–700 CE* (2012).

[12] *Religion, Language and Community in the Roman Near East, Constantine to Muhammad* (2013); collected papers in *Empire, Church and Society* (see note 1). The volume of collected papers ends, characteristically, with an epilogue (pp. 779–801) entitled 'Open Questions'.

stated firmly that, at the age of eighty, he had said all he wanted to say. It was not quite true – he continued to present occasional seminar papers in his final years – but he was content to leave his contributions to scholarship to speak for themselves.

The epicentre of Millar's work in the 1960s and 1970s was meticulous study of the administrative and legal institutions of the Roman empire. This was grounded in exhaustive reading and annotation of documentary and legal sources (above all the *Digest*). It was presaged by his second published article,[13] on the Constitutio Antoniniana, the measure which extended Roman citizenship to virtually all free subjects of the empire in the early 3rd century; he once remarked that this had given him more pleasure than any of his other publications because it provoked fourteen separate refutations. Other early studies of the financial instruments of governance (the imperial *fiscus* and the public treasury [*aerarium*]) remain of fundamental value for their collation and detailed analysis of the sources of evidence and the lines of demarcation between the treasuries.[14] Much of their lasting value lies in his nuanced understanding of the precision of the legal and documentary evidence, alongside and in contrast to the looser and frequently opaque statements in the literary sources such as Tacitus, Suetonius and Cassius Dio.[15] Above all, there is a clear focus on how the complex mechanisms of government worked on the ground across the empire, rather than a Rome-based view of an imperial machine managing by diktat *ex cathedra*. This was a perspective which was conveyed to Oxford undergraduates in the mid–60s though his lectures on 'Documents of the Roman Empire' and it was early manifested in his important article on 'Emperors at Work'.[16]

That article leads in a direct trajectory to his *magnum opus* of 1977, *The Emperor in the Roman World* (with a second edition in 1992). He had originally hoped that Oxford University Press would publish it, but he refused to consider a request from the Press to shorten it and instead took it to Colin Haycraft at Duckworth, who required no cuts. In this book he overtly eschewed comparison with other imperial governmental systems, collecting and citing a huge amount of primary evidence: 'The Millar method is the collection, analysis and organisation of a body of evidence that is never explained *a priori* by a conceptual framework of interpretation.'[17] That in itself was, and remains, an immense resource for the study of the Roman empire and

---

[13] 'The date of the constitutio Antoniniana', *Journal of Egyptian Archaeology* 48 (1962), 124–131.

[14] 'The fiscus in the first two centuries', *JRS* 53 (1963), 29–42; 'The aerarium and its officials under the Empire', *JRS* 54 (1964), 33–40.

[15] See also 'Some evidence on the meaning of Tacitus, Annals XII.60', *Historia* 13 (1964), 180–187 and 'The development of jurisdiction by imperial Procurators: further evidence', *Historia* 14 (1965), 362–367 with the detailed critique by P.A.Brunt, 'Procuratorial jurisdiction', *Latomus* 25 (1966), 461–89.

[16] 'Emperors at Work', *JRS* 57 (1967), 9–19.

[17] S. Benoist, cited and translated by Peter Wiseman in a letter to the *Times Literary Supplement*, 31 July 2020.

its governance, but it provoked some sharp criticisms, the most notorious of which were presented in a characteristically robust review by Keith Hopkins[18] and subsequent debates (to which Millar did not respond defensively or in detail). Prime areas of vulnerability were identified in Millar's statement in the preface 'the emperor was what the emperor did', which he could have modified in the second edition but chose not to, and the assertion that the emperor governed not by being pro-active but only reactive, thus placing the 'petition and response' process at centre stage. That prefatory statement was in truth a hostage to fortune in the sense that it allowed critics to take it as implying that the emperor was *only* what he did, thus ignoring *inter alia* the symbolic, psychological and iconographic perspectives. Nevertheless, as a detailed study of the evidence for what emperors did it is an original and unparalleled piece of work, 'simply the empirical method, testing hypotheses against all the available evidence, the foundation of all scholarship'.[19] Millar himself was clear in his belief that for the historian true originality consisted not in striving to find brilliant new solutions for old problems but in having a point of view and being led by the evidence in developing it.

Some critics were inclined to see his approach as simply sandblasting or machine-gunning the subjects with huge amounts of factual evidence, but this fails to do justice to his appreciation of the multifarious levels and modes in which government and administration were made effective. His massive article on obligations and excuses in the cities of the empire shines an intense light on government by the elite at the local level.[20] This is the devolved administration, the successful operation of which depended on the imperial authority's ability to secure the co-operation and effective participation by those citizens who commanded the major proportion of the local economic and social resources. The undermining of this entente underpinned Rostovtseff's now unfashionable view of the 'decline of the bourgeoisie' and its replacement by elements of the 'lower orders' as a key factor in the evolution of the empire. Here Millar amasses detailed legal evidence to show how specific decisions of emperors could acquire the status of broadly applicable regulations; how and why the increasingly intolerable burdens placed on the local elites could be alleviated by a complex network of exemptions; in effect a divisive process which, along with the growth of a formalisation of status distinctions, ranks and functions in the imperial bureaucratic and military institutions, led to the greater isolation and self-reliance of the 'super-rich' while the burdens for those in the middle ground became largely unsustainable. The very ambitious timescale over which these phenomena are analysed

---

[18] 'Rules of evidence', *JRS* 68 (1978), 178–86.
[19] Wiseman (n.17, above).
[20] 'Empire and city, Augustus to Julian: obligations, excuses and status', *JRS* 73 (1983), 76–96.

has important implications for the ways in which Millar perceived changes in the mechanisms of imperial government over four centuries and the sharp focus on the legal sources inevitably bears on the 3rd and early 4th centuries for which, in comparison with the earlier part of the period, good literary-historical narrative sources are sadly lacking. This renders his use of the documentary and legal sources all the more original and compelling even if the article is to some extent a rebarbative read in the density of detail in its arguments.

'Yet legal writers so central both to the character of Roman culture and (obviously enough) to the "legacy of Rome" have attracted extraordinarily little attention from classicists, from students of Roman historiography, or even from ancient historians, for whom this gigantic body of material represents, or ought to represent, an almost inexhaustible treasure-house of economic and social history, and of ideologies, conceptions and attitudes.'[21] The use of legal evidence and the relationship between Roman and Greek parts of empire were constant and crucial preoccupations. This 1986 article and his return to the subject of Pliny and Trajan, putting correspondence between emperor and governor into context with parallel evidence from legal sources, perhaps represent, if not an explicit defence against the critics of *ERW*, an amplification of his conviction that the legal sources do give us a vivid and realistic picture of how the imperial government actually worked both in the central administration, as an agglomeration of acts of communication in various forms, and at the level of the local civic communities. They also provide prime examples of his ability to perceive and draw the broader significance from crucial nuggets of information in an apparently mundane document.

Analysis of how the principles and practices of administration and law played out in the Greek east, particularly through the spectrum of what we can call imperial bureaucracy or the 'governing class', is critical and this theme is worked out in specific detail in his study of the dossier of Licinius Rufinus, an individual from Thyatira in Lydia (western Turkey) who is commemorated for local benefactions to his city, held high imperial office and achieved prominence in the field of Roman Law and an authorial presence in the *Digest*. This is the 'complex ... process by which the upper classes of the Greek East "became Roman" while staying Greek',[22] and it looks forward to a 'Greek-speaking Roman empire' ruled from Constantinople, a development later examined in great detail in another major book.

---

[21] 'A new approach to the Roman jurists', *JRS* 76 (1986), 272–80 at 272. In this review of the work of Tony Honoré (not without hesitation over his hypotheses) he reads Roman law and particularly the *Digest* as the writings of real people rather than lifeless excerpts from a dry codification.
[22] 'The Greek East and Roman law: the dossier of M. Cn.Licinius Rufus', *JRS* 89 (1999), 90–108.

The emphasis in *ERW* on the reactive mode of government led some critics to observe that he had failed to do justice to the military and imperialistic aspects of the emperor's role. The latter omission Millar himself attempted to repair in an important article on frontiers, wars and foreign relations in which he considered how foreign and frontier 'policies' were formulated, thus also addressing the issue of proactivity in imperial behaviour.[23] This was in part also his response to Edward Luttwak's persuasive and influential book,[24] though Millar was somewhat agnostic on the existence of such a grand strategy and insisted instead on the centrality of transmission of knowledge and communication (much of it concealed from us) in formulating approaches to frontiers and neighbours. No firm conclusions can emerge from the haphazard evidence, arguments from silence are fragile but at least they prevent 'the interpretation of archaeological evidence in the light of naïve assumptions as to information, communication and responsibility'.[25] That comes back in the end to the question of agency and puts the emperor under scrutiny. With very few exceptions (Marcus Aurelius in his *Meditations*, Trajan in his correspondence with Pliny), we can never know what an emperor was thinking.

At the same time as Millar was getting to grips with the workings of imperial government, he sought to understand the multifarious cultures of the Roman provinces in their own right. The process had begun with study of the elite Greek society which informed Cassius Dio's view of Roman history, but for twenty years from the late 1960s he was immersed specifically in the history of the Jews from the Maccabean revolt in the mid–2nd century BCE to the revolt of Bar Kokhba in the 2nd century CE as reviser of Schürer's *The History of the Jewish People in the Age of Jesus Christ*. It was quite remarkable that a Roman historian approaching the peak of his career and committed to a heavy teaching load in Queen's should have chosen to devote himself to the selfless task of updating this classic of 19th-century scholarship which was still much cited despite being hopelessly out-of-date. Millar never explained why he spent so much of his working life on the history of the Jews, and in retrospect he put down his involvement in the Schürer project to the persuasive charm of Geza Vermes, but it cannot have been irrelevant that in 1959 he had married Susanna Friedmann, daughter of a Berlin cantor, and that he had been immersed in reading Josephus in 1961.

The revisers of Schürer took the unusual route of updating the text of the 4th edition of Schürer's history, which had been published in German in 1909, excising redundant material and polemics and adding new evidence and more recent bibliography in order to 'remind students of the inter-Testamental era of the profound debt

[23] 'Emperors, Frontiers and Foreign Relations, 31 BC–AD 378', *Britannia* 13 (1982), 1–24.
[24] *The Grand Strategy of the Roman Empire* (1976).
[25] *Op.cit.* (n.23), 20.

owed to nineteenth-century learning, and by placing within the framework of the finest product of that scholarship the vast accretion of knowledge gained in the twentieth century'. The revisers chose not to mark which material was new, so that the immense effort required to bring some sections up to date is invisible except to alert readers who can see which elements of the final text rely on knowledge acquired since 1909. Millar and Vermes had distinct fields of expertise, but they worked closely together on the first volume (which covered political history), with tasks more clearly divided for the second volume, for which Millar produced an extended survey of the evidence for the Hellenistic cities of Palestine. In the third volume, on which he was working in the early 1980s while at UCL, he took responsibility for the long survey of the evidence for diaspora Judaism. The detailed and painstaking work of revision was constrained by the need to interpret the new material in as neutral a fashion as possible, but the close acquaintance Millar acquired with a vast range of evidence sparked a series of influential articles on Jewish history, starting with an influential re-reading of the background to the Maccabean revolution published in 1978 and a study of the Jews of the Graeco-Roman diaspora between paganism and Christianity in the 4th and early 5th century which originated in a seminar in UCL convened by John North, Judith Lieu and Tessa Rajak. Millar was consistent in his insistence that the Greek and Latin evidence about Jews in inscriptions, Roman law codes and patristic texts deserved to be given equal weight alongside the dominant narrative of Jewish history in late antiquity derived from the rabbinic tradition.[26]

At the same time as Millar delved in detail into Jewish history, he was seeking to make wider claims for the significance of local cultures in the Roman world. A substantial study of language use in Roman Africa, examining the relationship of Libyan and Punic to Latin on inscriptions, was published in 1968, an article on the hellenisation of the cities of Phoenicia in 1983, and in 1997 he wrote an analysis of the ethnicity and language of Porphyry.[27] From the 1980s his main focus was on the Near East, with a series of studies, including his Carl Newell Jackson Lectures, based primarily on inscriptions and papyri. One result of this focus on documents was to emphasise the importance of the spread of use of Greek alongside a family of Semitic languages and scripts in the public self-representation of members of distinct

---

[26] 'The background to the Maccabean revolution: reflections on Martin Hengel's "Judaism and Hellenism"', *Journal of Jewish Studies* 29 (1978), 1–29; 'The Jews of the Graeco-Roman diaspora between paganism and Christianity, AD 312–438', in J. Lieu, J. North and T. Rajak (eds.), *The Jews among Pagans and Christians in the Roman Empire* (1992), 97–123.

[27] 'Local cultures in the Roman Empire: Libyan, Punic and Latin in Roman Africa', *JRS* 58 (1968), 126–51; 'The Phoenician cities: a case-study of hellenisation', *Proceedings of the Cambridge Philological Society* 209 (1983), 55–71; 'Porphyry: ethnicity, language and alien wisdom', in J. Barnes and M.T. Griffin (eds.), *Philosophia Togata II: Plato and Aristotle at Rome* (1997), 241–62.

communities whose cultural affiliations could be quite precisely correlated to specific sub-regions and local areas in specific periods, and *The Roman Near East* contains a series of maps on which the inclusion of geographical features is designed to help considerably with comprehension of the somewhat dense text of the book. Millar himself considered it important to visit the places about which he wrote and felt a sense of contact with the ancient inhabitants of the regions as a result. Whether the spread of the epigraphic habit in the early centuries CE reflected a deeper hellenisation of local cultures is disputable, and (as archaeologists of Roman Syria were quite quick to point out) Millar paid little attention to the cultural significance of non-written artefacts which might be thought to reveal greater continuity than he suggested, but indisputable was his demonstration of the extent of the continuing expansion of direct Roman rule over the Near East down to the 4th century. The 'mental map' he created of the Roman Near East is destined to endure, as is his insistence that study of the Roman empire, even by scholars in northern Europe, should shift eastwards.

Literary evidence for the Roman Near East before Constantine was not plentiful, although Millar made extensive use of Josephus and already in 1993 wrote an intriguing study linking Josephus's depiction of Hagar and Ishmael to the origins of Islam.[28] In 1993 he described the study of the Near East from the death of Constantine to the first Islamic conquests as 'a major challenge for someone else' not least because of the plethora of surviving Christian and Jewish texts in Syriac and Aramaic as well as Greek, but tackling these sources was precisely the challenge he himself took on after retirement, along with a series of novel forays into interpretation of the iconography of mosaics.[29] Characteristic of all this work was an insistence on studying pagan, Jewish and Christian material together, and he took great pleasure in showing how the different academic disciplines which concerned themselves with the late-Roman Near East could learn from each other. For years he fulminated as he struggled to puzzle out the relationship of inscriptions from the same places in different languages when they were included in separate corpora, publishing already in 1983 a call for editors of corpora of inscriptions to publish all the material from one locality in one place – a call which, to his delight, began to bear fruit in his last years.[30] This focus on bringing together sources from very different worlds and perspectives laid him open to criticism for not always fully grasping the complexities of the material studied by specialists in Syriac Christianity, rabbinic Judaism, Arabic epigraphy and the emergence of Islam,

---

[28] 'Hagar, Ismael, Josephus and the origins of Islam', *Journal of Jewish Studies* 44 (1993), 23–45.

[29] *The Roman Near East,* xii; 'Narrative and identity in Near Eastern mosaics, pagan, Jewish and Christian', in Y.Z. Eliav, E.A. Freedland and S. Herbert (eds.), *The Sculptural Environment of the Roman Near East: reflections on culture, ideology and power,* (2008), 225–56.

[30] 'Epigraphy', in M. Crawford (ed.), *Sources for Ancient History* (1983), 80–136.

but he was so fascinated by the discovery of new evidence of all kinds that he was unconcerned if those specialists sometimes claimed that his approach was a bit naïve.

Shortly after he had begun to work on Jewish history, Millar turned his attention also to work on the politics of the Roman Republic which occupied him for about 25 years, with publications spanning the period from 1974 to 2002. At the heart of this work is an attempt to describe and analyse the political character of the Republic as it developed from the later 4th century BCE down to 50 CE (at which point, it can be argued, it ceased to exist in its traditional form). This was hardly an untouched area of scholarship, enriched as it had been by the work of many major 20th-century scholars including Matthias Gelzer, Ronald Syme and Peter Brunt (Millar's Camden predecessor). But Millar wanted to counteract the excessive (in his view) emphasis that had earlier been placed, albeit to some extent modified by others, on the centrality of patron-client relations in political activity and on the character of the political elite as grounded in *nobilitas*, the quasi-hereditary monopolisation of high political office by members of a small and elite group of senatorial families who allowed the admission of 'new men' (like Cicero) into the charmed circle only sparingly.

Millar's approach was to put the *populus Romanus*, the citizen body, at centre stage, arguing that laws, elections and other major political decisions depended on the will and the votes of the citizen body as expressed through their voting assemblies, the class-based *comitia centuriata* which met on the Campus Martius to elect senior magistrates and the *comitia tributa* which met in the forum to attend rhetorical *contiones* and to pass legislation. As far as the character, composition and functioning of the assemblies was concerned this was certainly the most important work since that of Lily Ross Taylor in the 1960s.[31] Millar's method was characteristic. Proceeding on a chronological platform (although the publications were not quite in that order of appearance) with relentless attention to the key items of evidence, he agglomerated a formidable battering-ram of sources and analysis which left no doubt that the role of the *comitia tributa* in particular, and thus the citizen body, was central and effective in political debate and decision-making. This turns out to be true at all periods under scrutiny, though there are differences in the major sources and their understanding and perspectives, for example as between the Greek Polybius (mid–2nd century), Cicero (the major player in 70–50 BCE), and Cassius Dio (a 3rd-century CE derivative account, dependent on earlier sources).[32]

---

[31] L.R.Taylor, *The voting districts of the Roman Republic: the thirty-five urban and rural tribes* (1960) and *Roman voting assemblies from the Hannibalic War to the dictatorship of Caesar* (1966).

[32] See 'The political character of the Classical Roman Republic, 200–151 BC' *JRS* 74 (1984), 1–19; 'Politics, persuasion and the people, before the Social War' *JRS* 76 (1986), 1–11; 'Popular politics at Rome in the Late Republic', in I.Malkin and Z.W.Rubinsohn (eds). *Leaders and masses in the Roman world : Studies in honor of Zvi Yavetz* (1995), 91–182.

The culmination of this strand of Millar's work, which he termed 'a deliberately one-sided contribution', is *The Crowd in the Late Republic* (1998), dedicated to Peter Brunt. Here he deals in systematic chronological order with events of the 70s through to 50 BCE and concludes by asking what sort of 'democracy' might be under the microscope. Naturally, Cicero's activities (mainly the forensic ones because of the subject under discussion) are at the core. Millar, again characteristically and as in much of his whole *oeuvre*, lets the primary evidence speak for itself and rarely dismisses a statement as false or misleading. The evocation of 'popular' politics is vivid and compelling and like others before him Millar sees the unshackling of the powers of the *tribuni plebis* in 70 BCE as the watershed after which radical legislation was put to the legislative assembly frequently and with dramatic effect. For the next 20 years recurrent episodes of legislation, violence and political mayhem presaged the fall of the Roman Republic. For Millar it is the role of the people that is crucial,[33] not the failure of the senate, despite the role of its minority in eventually precipitating civil war, nor the strife between 'military dynasts' (as the so-called 'First Triumvirate' of Pompey, Caesar and Crassus is often described). A particularly robust challenge to traditional views was posed in his statement that 'the widespread notion that the senate was the governing organ of the Roman Republic is not merely misleading, it is straightforwardly false',[34] which does not quite square with an earlier assertion that 'the senate thus exercised a real governmental, even, one might say, parliamentary function in debating the replies to foreign embassies.'[35]

That point aside, none of this was exactly virgin territory for scholars of the late Republic, nor the last word on the subject: Millar himself hoped it would be a stimulus to 'a future political analysis by someone else'. That hope has been fulfilled, for analysis continues and several reviewers have vigorously taken issue with Millar. Why? Moving the spotlight away from senatorial influence and conflict is one factor. Most would accept that 'however hesitant we may be to allow the name of democracy to a system whose structural weaknesses and contradictions were so profound, … any valid assessment of the Roman Republic must take account of the power of the crowd'.[36] That seems persuasive and grounded in the many items of evidence that Millar cites and quotes. But for him 'the *res publica* was a direct democracy not a representative one'[37] and despite the welter of evidence we still know too little about who turned up to vote and how. Does it come down to what we mean by democracy and

---

[33] *The Crowd in Rome*, 123: 'in the 50s major decisions would depend on the votes of the people assembled in the forum.'
[34] *The Crowd in Rome*, 209.
[35] 'The political character of the Classical Roman Republic' (cited in n. 32), 4.
[36] *The Crowd in Rome*, 225.
[37] *The Crowd in Rome*, 209.

does Millar take too little account of the (unseen) effect of other powerful elements in influencing and managing the 'democratic bodies'? What do we make of the fact that democratic laws and decisions had to be implemented by powerful individuals who, as it turned out, could be held to account for their actions only with great difficulty and open conflict. Cicero was not powerful enough to resist exile but the dynasts got away with murder (literally) and one cannot ignore the ways in which the powerful elite (from among whom the most important magistrates and generals emerged, almost without exception) both cared about and influenced the outcome of the reality of popular participation.

This is all very stimulating scholarship and argued with characteristic clarity and cogency. It has not radically changed the landscape of the subject. Millar's final sub-stantive publication on the subject was for him an unusual departure, in the form of a book derived from lectures in memory of an Israeli scholar and friend Menahem Stern, who was tragically murdered in Jerusalem in 1989 during the First Intifada.[38] Here Millar ventured into the (for him, unfamiliar) field of European political thought with a broader readership in mind, analysing the afterlife of perspectives on the char-acter of the Republic through the writings of major thinkers including Machiavelli and Rousseau. Thus it does not bear directly on changing views of the fall of the Republic but it does, in passing, give an important clue to one of the driving forces behind Millar's thinking. As noted briefly in a review by Zetzel,[39] he was really angry about what he regarded as the erosion or failure of 'direct democracy' in later periods and contexts. The relevance of this to his deep and frustrated preoccupation with con-temporary academic politics in universities (see below) was sharply analysed by John North in his brilliant introduction to (one of) Millar's *Festschriften*.[40] Thus, the detailed analysis of democratic power in political systems was not ivory-tower stuff but of fundamental importance for the way modern institutions behave.

By the time he stepped down from the Camden Chair in 2002, Millar had authored six books and edited a further two, and he had published 75 articles as well as a series of major review articles and a large number of reviews, but instead of taking the opportunity to slow down in retirement, he threw his energy into a major re-evaluation of the 'Greek Roman Empire' of Theodosius II in the 5th century CE for the Sather Lectures of 2003. The topic required deep immersion not just in the Roman law codes (on which he had long worked) but in patristic texts and the acts of Church councils, all read in the original languages, which for him constituted a whole new field of

---

[38] *The Roman Republic in Political Thought* (2002).
[39] Online in *Bryn Mawr Classical Review* (https://bmcr.brynmawr.edu/2002/2002.05.31/).
[40] 'Introduction: Pursuing democracy', in A. K. Bowman, H. M. Cotton, M. D. Goodman and S. Price (eds), *Representations of Empire: Rome and the Mediterranean World* (*Proceedings of the British Academy*, 114; 2002), 1–12.

research that continued to fascinate him for the following decade. His technique was to work his way steadily through page after page of dry argument over abstruse theological questions (which interested him little), extracting with delight the glimpses of human interaction, such as the evidence for linguistic coexistence of Greek, Latin and Syriac in 6th century Constantinople, and he pressed enthusiastically for Roman historians to pay more attention to such material by presenting and analysing long extracts in articles in the *Journal of Roman Studies*, and insisting, perhaps too vehemently, on the predominance of Syriac over Greek in many of these documents.[41] The Sather Lectures themselves demonstrated the continuing strength of imperial government in Constantinople as the empire in the West collapsed, the extent to which administration continued to privilege Latin as the language of the central bureaucracy even as it used Greek for communication with the emperor's subjects, and the application by emperors and their entourage of the same methods of control by personal contact and correspondence to issues of ecclesiastical politics and theological dispute through which military strategy and financial administration continued to be mediated as in the early Empire. [42]

It is impossible for scholars to work on any topic from late Republican politics to the cultures of the late-Roman Near East without taking into account Millar's contributions. In terms of method, his influence has essentially been conservative, though his conclusions were not. At a time when many historians sought new insights through sociological, anthropological or political theories, Millar championed the collection and analysis of data from the ancient world as the only honest route to understanding societies so far removed from the preoccupations of the modern historian. He was impatient of pretension, remarking, for instance, in the 1970s that, so far as he could see, the theories of Moses Finley about the ancient economy lacked any substantial base – as he put it, 'the emperor has no clothes'. For Millar, the true task of the historian is to continue digging for what he considered 'real' evidence, by which he meant material produced in antiquity, and he was assiduous in encouraging students and colleagues to engage themselves in the ancient evidence – he never lost the sense of awe that it is possible to make direct contact with the ancient world through an inscription or papyrus or (in late antiquity) literary works in manuscripts written in antiquity and not mediated through medieval copyists like the works of Cassius Dio on which he had first worked. Millar was well aware that this reverence for the evidence could strike some colleagues as naïve, but, after their robust exchanges over *The Emperor in*

[41] 'Rome, Constantinople and the Near Eastern Church under Justinian: two synods of 536', *JRS* 98 (2008), 62–82; 'Linguistic coexistence in Constantinople: Greek and Latin (and Syriac) in the Acts of the Synod of 536', *JRS* 99 (2009), 92–103.
[42] The title of the lectures (*A Greek Roman Empire*) reflected Millar's insistence on the Greekness of the imperial administration despite the importance of Syriac in the ecclesiastical documents.

the Roman World, he found distasteful the playful exploration of the difficulties in interpreting evidence by Keith Hopkins in his last book, *A World Full of Gods* – when asked, soon after its publication, whether he had read it, he replied that he had indeed, and that he was trying hard to forget it. Millar felt that such scepticism undermined the academic profession. He had a strong sense of the value of the hard empirical work on which he felt proper ancient historians should engage, and he dedicated himself to inculcating the same values among his colleagues and students, discouraging cant, promoting the notion of historical research as intrinsically valuable in a civilised society and encouraging a sense of self-esteem within the profession.

Millar's championing of ancient history did not in his case extend to writing for a general audience beyond the readers of the *TLS* or the *London Review of Books.* This was not because he thought such popular history without value – on the contrary, he was himself an avid reader of such histories for other periods – but his interest lay in influencing less the general public than colleagues and students in what he saw as a collective endeavour by historians to get at the truth about the past: his willingness to help and advise younger colleagues, whatever their approach, was legendary, and authors of a great variety of historical studies inserted into the preface of their books their thanks to Millar for his guidance. He made no attempt to woo a general audience by simplifying his presentation of the past, his literary style was too dry to appeal to a wide readership, he never took part in televised history or even radio programmes, and his contributions to understanding the Roman world did not make him a publicly recognised figure as much as his ventures into the public arena in defence of academic freedom. All the more remarkable was the unanimity on his death that he had been one of the greatest Roman historians of the 20th century, a judgement based on his relentless focus on uncovering the past by trying to find out what people in the past said about themselves.

The foundation of all his research was obsessive and chalcenteric reading and note-taking. His reading covered the widest range of types of sources and the preoccupation with government in action at the highest and lowest levels led him to draw on literary works for reflections of the realities of life in the imperial court[43] and the small towns in the Greek east and north Africa,[44] with little attention to genre or authorial intention, whether parody, satire or romance. The severely empirical approach offers a very literal interpretation of the 'facts' with little regard for theory or modelling, and sometimes risks the accusation of being over-literal.[45]

[43] 'Epictetus and the Imperial Court', *JRS* 55 (1965), 141–148.
[44] 'The world of the Golden Ass', *JRS* 71 (1981), 63–75, reprinted in: S.J. Harrison (ed.), *Oxford Readings in the Roman Novel* (1998), 247–268.
[45] Particularly evident in his article cited in n.44, above.

This focus on evidence shaped Millar's distinctive working methods. The foundation of his scholarship for Millar was always the discovery and analysis of ancient evidence. His preferred mode of exposition was to present and discuss ancient sources, allowing voices from the past to speak directly to the reader and he took particular pleasure in presenting data which he thought had been ignored by others. For many years he preferred to do all his research in the Ashmolean Library, arriving early in the morning and establishing himself in one of the seats in the main room near the library catalogue, both gathering material and writing the entire text of books and articles, apparently undisturbed by the presence of other readers. Exercise consisted in frequent excursions to the shelves to extract a new book, taking systematic notes of primary sources from which he compiled extensive card indexes. General books on history, and books for review, he read at home, managing to absorb new books soon after publication with extraordinary speed and in a variety of European languages (he referred to Russian publications in his own writings only on occasion, despite his pride in his competence in the language, perhaps because he felt strongly that references to secondary works should always be in a form which made it easy for readers to chase up, and he was aware that few of his readers would be able to check a source in Russian).

Millar's notable linguistic expertise extended to his ability to converse with European colleagues, and he quite naturally dropped into French, German, Italian or Spanish as required. The same was not true of Hebrew, despite his efforts to learn the language, particularly during his time at UCL, and although he felt he understood the structure of the grammar and, with some help, could puzzle out written texts from antiquity, he made no attempt to speak the language and he employed in his writings a distinctive form of transliteration of the consonantal letters in Semitic languages which had the advantages of representing accurately the original text while requiring no judgement on its vocalisation and demonstrating the similarities between texts in Hebrew and other kindred languages.

Millar wrote with extraordinary facility. He never seems himself to have suffered from writer's block and found it quite hard to understand or sympathise when others did: he advised his graduate students, if they were stuck on a particular problem, simply to write down on the page a note about the issue they could not resolve and to move on to writing the next passage in the expectation that they would be able to go back to fill in the gaps at a later stage. Millar himself never seems to have needed to employ this technique since if he did not know what he thought about an issue he was happy just to put down the evidence he had collected and summarise what in his view it might demonstrate. The result could sometimes be a somewhat clumsy literary style, with a paragraph presenting a cluster of cases which pointed in one direction followed by presentation of a cluster of counter-instances ending with a cautious statement that the precise significance of the evidence is unclear, but Millar saw any lack of certainty as an honest admission of our state of knowledge about the ancient world, about many aspects of which we remain inevitably in the dark.

Everything Millar published was handwritten by him to be typed up by a secretary. Deciphering his crabbed handwriting was by no means straightforward and even Priscilla Lange, who worked with him from 1989 to 2015, sometimes struggled to make any sense of it. For his earlier books and articles the first draft was very close to the final draft, although he allowed himself to rewrite drafts more often as he got older. His reluctance to engage directly with any form of electronic communication, apparently engendered by a traumatic experience with radar equipment during his national service, became increasingly idiosyncratic as the rest of the world changed around him in his later years, and he would write his responses to emails by hand for Priscilla to send on his behalf. He did, however, manage to master email in his final years. He was adamant, with some justification, that his refusal to be drawn into the world of the internet allowed more time for serious reading and for the conversation and discussion from which he was convinced that the best ideas generally arise, but he sometimes expressed bewilderment that he did not know what was going on because information was no longer available on paper and, although he was supportive in principle of the employment of IT in Humanities scholarship, he himself found it hard to adapt to the transfer online of library catalogues and other crucial aids to research.

Millar seems to have felt a compulsion to keep writing. He worked to self-imposed deadlines for completion of projects and did his best to use the same method in joint projects undertaken with others, such as the revision of Schürer, the volume he edited with Erich Segal in 1984 in honour of Ronald Syme, and the *Handbook of Jewish Literature*, although with mixed success since not all his collaborators were as self-disciplined as him. He generally preferred working alone and complained periodically that he was never going to work on a joint project again. He found the tardiness of some colleagues hard to comprehend; he was so appalled by the slow progress in pub-lication of a memorial volume to which he had sent his contribution in good time that he withdrew his article and published it elsewhere, with an outraged footnote to explain what he had done and why.

One related aspect of his academic leadership which has a broader significance than his influence on his personal supervisees was his creation of a culture of seminars and intellectual debate among postgraduates and senior academics. This (in the shape of the Thursday seminar at ICS) was an innovative and distinctive feature of his tenure at UCL and he brought it back to Oxford with him (though on Tuesdays, so as to avoid a clash with the continuing ICS seminar). Predecessors, notably Ronald Syme, had held regular seminars or classes but he (along with others such as Eduard

Fraenkel) was much more magisterial and the classes did not generally feature invited speakers from home and abroad. The Millar style was crucial to the creation of a postgraduate community (a real innovation for Oxford) which was much more inclusive, giving doctoral students the opportunity to rub shoulders with senior established scholars and bounce ideas off them. He had a particular way of introducing a student to an established scholar and making the student feel that the introduction was just as important for the scholar as it was for the student. His initiative on this front on his return to Oxford in 1984 is best described in his own words: 'it emerged that they [*sc*. the graduates] had no information as to who the other graduates were, or what they were studying and most had never seen each other before. They also had no information as to who the members of the Sub-Faculty of Ancient History were, or where they could be contacted. So lists of both were regularly provided, a "work-in-progress" seminar, run by the graduates themselves, was started and still continues; and an extensive (perhaps even too extensive) range of other research seminars grew up.'

There was another, more informal side to this: his relentless insistence on the importance of gathering groups for morning coffee, whether in the Oxford Playhouse, the Oriental Institute or the Centre for Hebrew and Jewish Studies (but not in the Ioannou Centre where he did not find the Common Room congenial enough and in any case sensitively decided to stay at arm's length from the Faculty of Classics in his retirement). Students, staff and especially academic visitors from abroad were encouraged to join in for wide-ranging conversation and exchange of ideas. Along with post-seminar drinks and other faculty social events these were symptoms of serious sociability which were welcoming, inclusive and stimulating and certainly made the Oxford Faculty a magnet for established and aspiring Roman historians. He also encouraged and supported communal activities elsewhere, whether in the annual national Norman Baynes meeting of ancient historians or the Ancient World Cluster at Wolfson College.

He had an extraordinarily wide range of contacts with ancient historians in the UK, many of whom had been his doctoral supervisees, whom he unfailingly supported. Among senior academics, he was close (as far as was possible) to Ronald Syme who had been his doctoral supervisor, but given Syme's personality and the prevalence of laissez-faire supervision in the 1950s there was no sign of personal intimacy. In fact, Millar himself said that the major intellectual and scholarly influence on him came from Peter Fraser[46] after Millar's election to the All Souls Fellowship. 'It was Peter Fraser's deep immersion in, and commitment to all aspects of the wider Greek world … which most profoundly determined my approach.' His general reluctance to engage

---

[46] See Simon Hornblower's memoir in *Biographical Memoirs of Fellows of the British Academy* XII (2013), 137–85.

in formal collaboration with other scholars in research or publication was closely connected to his impatience with what he perceived as dilatory or remiss behaviour on the part of others in getting publications finished. Not a few of us who fell short in this regard received a letter written in that notoriously indecipherable handwriting which appeared to be almost libellous or actionable. Despite this, personal relations were always friendly, civil and humane even when robust disagreement was involved (as with Keith Hopkins). He did have very serious reservations about a few senior ancient historians but he never committed them to print unless in the form of polite debate, disagreement or criticism. The sad exception, which he surely regretted, was the offence unintentionally given to Arnaldo Momigliano by Millar's review of his *Quinto Contributo* in the TLS.[47] Millar thought this was in his own words 'fair, sympathetic and appreciative' but it was not taken as such. Millar was incapable of rancour or deliberate hostility but this marred the end of his period at UCL and was instrumental in his decision to return to Oxford as Camden Professor (where there was no serious rival for the appointment).

Beyond national borders, he fostered and encouraged a very wide range of personal international friendships (far too many to list individually), most particularly but far from exclusively in Spain, Israel, the USA, but also Italy, Germany, France and Russia. The formal testimony to his international standing lies partly in the distinguished named lectures which he was invited to undertake, culminating in the prestigious Sather Professorship at UC Berkeley.[48]

Far from confining himself to the ivory towers of research, Millar engaged vigorously, often passionately with the wider academic world in the UK with, it must be said, mixed results. He was passionate about academic freedom from bureaucratic control and democracy in universities, expressed in a stream of grumpy letters to Vice-Chancellors and other powers-that-be, in articles in the *Oxford Magazine* about the unchecked growth of the 'administration' and other matters. He believed that Oxford and Cambridge could and should have scuppered the introduction of the Research Assessment Exercise in 1986 by simply refusing to participate, a proposition that was never put to the test. He was an elected member of Oxford's Hebdomadal Council (1996–2000) but 'it is best to say only that the role was wholly futile since the Council did not, and had no wish to take counsel for the future of the university.' His effort was also directed towards supporting the Council for Academic Autonomy, a response to

---

[47] 'The Path of the Polymath', *TLS* 28 January, 1977, 99–100, see G.W.Bowersock, 'Momigliano e I suoi critici', *Studi storici* 53.1, 7–24 (we are grateful to Glen Bowersock for alerting us to this).
[48] Carl Newell Jackson Lectures (Harvard, 1987); Jerome Lectures (Ann Arbor, Michigan, 1993); Jerusalem Lectures in History in Memory of Menahem Stern (Jerusalem, 1997); Sather Lectures (Berkeley,2003). In the mid–80s he was invited to consider accepting an appointment as Fellow of the Institute for Advanced Studies, Princeton in succession to J.F.Gilliam but decided against it.

the 1988 Education Act 'which in all essentials nationalised the universities'. He published various arguments in defence of autonomy but neither governments nor Vice-Chancellors paid any attention and the Council was dissolved around 2000. This indicates that, lacking the patience or diplomatic will to negotiate with opposing views, engagement with committee work in this broader academic landscape was not his forte. This may be the one of the reasons why his interest in the Wardenship of All Souls College in 1994 did not bear fruit. But he was for many years an effective and respected voice on the board of Delegates of the Oxford University Press.

He was more effective in relatively routine Faculty and College administration, particularly in roles and on committees relating to postgraduates. Unusually for a Professorial Fellow he took on the post of Tutor for Graduates at Brasenose College with great success and cultivated good relationships and pastoral responsibilities across the whole range of subjects and backgrounds. His most significant contribution to the status and future of the Faculty was his determination to establish the physical presence of the Faculty of Classics (which had by then been reduced from its previous identity as 'Literae Humaniores' by the secession of Philosophy) in the area between St Giles' and the rear of the Ashmolean Museum. This was a really major step. The initial idea was pursued through the so-called three-site strategy adopted by Vice-Chancellor Richard Southwood and the eventual manifestation, as a consequence of two large benefactions (of Greek and Cypriot origin) as well as major input from the national Science Research Infrastructure Fund, came in the form of the Sackler Library (replacing the old Ashmolean Reading Room) and the Ioannou Centre for Research in Classical and Byzantine Studies. It was the latter which he tirelessly campaigned for, with eventual success.

Also on the positive side must be reckoned his contributions to national academic bodies. He was an excellent President and figurehead of the Society for the Promotion of Roman Studies, as well as sometime editor of its prestigious journal and founder of its monograph series. He served on the Academy's Council and various committees. He was an invaluable presence at the executive level of the Academy as its Publications Secretary (1997–2002) and often emphasised the financial success of its operations. The publishing programme flourished under his watch. The series of monographs by British Academy Postdoctoral Fellows – initiated under his predecessor – bore its first fruit and established itself. The British Academy *Review* magazine first appeared (in 1999), providing information about the Academy for a more general readership. And at a time when the Academy Research Projects were the subject of quite hostile internal scrutiny Millar persuaded the Publications Committee to conduct its own review of all the ARP series it published. The Committee produced a clear statement of principle that 'the publication of projects of the character and duration of the existing Academy Research Projects was something that national academies *should* undertake.' Millar also saw through the delicate negotiations with the Fellowship that enabled the Memoirs (originally within the *Proceedings of the British Academy*) to be separated from the Lectures and published in a volume of their own. As the Academy celebrated its centenary in summer 2002, he ensured that its publishing programme played a prominent part – both with its series of Centenary Monographs (see below), and with a display of all the books ever published by the Academy during the Centenary event itself.

Millar also served for several years on the Committee on Academy Research Projects but there was a negative side to this in his often expressed frustration at the Academy's failure to provide financial support for long-term major research programmes, as a counterbalance to the short-term constraints embedded in the Arts and Humanities Board's (later Council) funding priorities. He regarded this as an inglorious and shameful abnegation of responsibility on the part of the BA and an abandonment of one of the key aspects of what an Academy should be.

In his own estimation, the most rewarding role of this kind was in relation to the British School at Rome, as member of the council, vice-chairman and then chairman in which capacities he initiated fundamental changes in effective governance and in 1997 helped to secure, with the support of Robert Jackson MP, a large one-off capital grant from the government, a crucial step in enabling the renovation of the fabric of its iconic building next to the Borghese Gardens.

Millar was accorded exceptional public esteem, which he undoubtedly enjoyed, treating, with justification, the honours bestowed on him as a reflection not of his public roles, in which he had frequently opposed the establishment, but of his outstanding scholarly contributions. He received honorary doctorates from Helsinki, St Andrews, Edinburgh, and the Hebrew University. He was elected a member of the Academia Europaea, a Corresponding Member of the German Archaeological Institute and the Bavarian Academy, and a Foreign Member of the Finnish Academy of Science and Letters, the Russian Academy of Sciences, the American Academy of Arts and Sciences, and the Australian Academy of Sciences. In 2005 he received the Kenyon Medal for Classical Studies from the British Academy, and in 2010 he was knighted.

Such recognition was testimony to the quantity as well as the outstanding quality of Millar's scholarly output. He took for granted that he would continue working and writing until his very last days, still setting off early for work and devotedly attending and participating in research seminars. Work provided an excuse also for sociability, which he took seriously not just for the sake of the education of graduate students but as intrinsic to civilised life. Conversations could frequently veer far beyond the ancient world and remained always congenial even when serious: Millar had strong views on many aspects of politics and society and a strong sense of moral probity, and he could indulge in obsessional correspondence with local and national press on topics which raised his ire (such as damage to the Oxford skyline caused by the University's erection of badly sited high-rise buildings near Port Meadow). But he was not prone to foisting these ideas on others face-to-face except in formal situations when the topic arose, when he was fearless in stating his views with such clarity and passion that he was known to some disconcerted bureaucrats as 'the grumpy professor'.

At work, Millar dressed formally, often wearing a dark blue suit with a blue shirt and red tie, and he was slow to drop the formal habit of addressing students and colleagues by surname, although he was universally known in his later years as 'Fergus'. The formality reflected in part his insistence on the value of the work in which historians are engaged, but it also reflected an instinct to be in control of his surroundings – he was uninhibited in taking action if the lighting in a committee room seemed to him inadequate or if a restaurant was too noisy for conversation. He enjoyed parties and dinners, but the conversations were always the point, ranging over novels, films and sport as well as politics (about which he was uninhibited in express-ing his liberal views with great certainty) as well as ancient history and especially family – his remarkable ability to recall the detailed family circumstances of his wide acquaintance was a product as much of his care for those around him as of his outstanding memory.

Millar contrived somehow to combine this essential seriousness with a huge enjoyment of domestic life in which he immersed himself so fully that he managed to give his three children the impression while they were growing up that he was always a presence despite all the pressures of Oxford college life with evening meetings and the long commute during his UCL days. It was an academic household, with Susanna immersed in her own work on child psychology. In later years Millar was immensely proud of the scientific and medical careers of his children, delighted that they had the freedom to follow their own interests, unperturbed that none of them shared their father's fascination with ancient history.

In retirement Millar continued to follow golf and rugby with enthusiasm and he engineered with Susanna a regular regime of films, seminars and concerts to ensure that they kept as active and sociable as possible. The large crowd of friends who came to celebrate his 84th birthday over coffee when he knew he was already very ill was a testimony to this sociability and his success in reaching out to so many people, and Millar would probably have been pleased that it was these personal qualities of toler-ance, generosity, humanity, integrity and courage which were emphasised in the many obituaries published in the months after his death as much as his contributions to historical knowledge.

Note on the authors: Alan Bowman was formerly Principal and Camden Professor Emeritus of Ancient History, Brasenose College, Oxford; he was elected a Fellow of the British Academy in 1994. Martin Goodman is Professor of Jewish Studies, University of Oxford; Fellow, Wolfson College, Oxford; he was elected a Fellow of the British Academy in 1996.

MYLES BURNYEAT

Myles Fredric Burnyeat

1 January 1939 – 20 September 2019

elected Fellow of the British Academy 1984

by

MALCOLM SCHOFIELD

Myles Burnyeat was a profound and exceptionally influential scholar of ancient Greek philosophy, and an inspiring teacher. He worked especially in epistemology, stimulating revival of interest in Pyrrhonism, and making major contributions to the study of Plato's *Theaetetus*. He published classic studies of Aristotle's ethics and logic. On Aristotle's theory of soul, he took a radical stance emphasising as often a gulf between ancient and modern presuppositions. Latterly he wrote extensively on the *Republic*, and did innovative work on James and John Stuart Mill as Plato scholars. A Russian speaker, with *glasnost* he developed significant relationships with Russian scholars.

Biographical Memoirs of Fellows of the British Academy, 20, 51–74
Posted 3 November 2021. © British Academy 2021.

In 1964 Myles Burnyeat attended a two-hour lecture on Plato's *Theaetetus* by Bernard Williams, given in University College London. That lecture left him 'convinced that in the *Theaetetus* I had found a work of philosophy which would reward a lifetime's study'. It was in 1990 that he published the final fruit of his study of the dialogue and its exploration of the concept of knowledge. His 'introduction' (to a translation by M.J. Levett) was not the jointly composed definitive commentary he and Williams had envisaged in the 1960s: 'The dialogue will always leave you with more questions than you have answered'. Its 'readers are required to contribute more and more as the dialogue proceeds'. Of its three parts, diminishing in length but greatly increasing in difficulty, our job in the first, Burnyeat proposed, is to *find* the text's meaning, in the second to *respond* to it, and in the third to *create* from it a meaning which will solve the problem of knowledge: in short, to engage in strenuous philosophical reflection ourselves. His long discussion of that third section is, as he thought it had to be, extremely demanding, requiring the most attentive precision in appreciation of possible philosophical options, their attractions and drawbacks, while always attuned to the complex large issues at stake – about 'nothing less than the mind's relation to its objects', about 'the powers and prospects of the human mind'. This uniquely imaginative form of 'introduction', which has been described as 'the twentieth century's most influential book on the dialogue', truly is what it claims to be: help (increasingly challenging) for the reader, suggestively open-ended.[1]

By 1990 Burnyeat was a key figure in Classics and philosophy, with a distinguished chair, a global reputation, and an ever-growing list of collaborators and correspondents. Back in 1964 he was just beginning, having arrived in UCL the previous autumn to pursue postgraduate work in history of philosophy with Williams. That *Theaetetus* lecture was one of a number of pivotal moments in his life and career.

I

The life began on New Year's Day 1939, when Burnyeat was born the eldest child of Peter, who ran a ship-provisioning business, and Cherry (née Warburg), a talented potter. His parents had made their home in North Kensington, but after his father joined up, his and his sister Jane's early years were spent in rural Hertfordshire and Essex. In due course, he was sent to Bryanston School in Dorset, where he won a Minor Scholarship in Classics to King's College, Cambridge just before his 17th birthday, and then took his A-Levels the following summer. For the one hour of the week

---

[1] Burnyeat (1990a: xii-xiv, 68, 24); 'most influential book': S. Broadie, 'Laureation', University of St Andrews, 30 November 2012.

not wholly devoted to Greek, Latin, and Ancient History, one of the teachers got Burnyeat's class to read A.J. Ayer's *Language, Truth, and Logic*. 'I was overwhelmed with enthusiasm', he recalled. '*This* was the sort of thing I had been longing for, without realizing it.' He then had one more year of school ahead of him, when he was made Head Boy and captained an undefeated Rugby XV.

Instead of Cambridge immediately, he elected to do his National Service next, in its final phase as it proved. He had already (at his father's insistence) been a Sea Cadet, and was able to serve in the Royal Navy, where he trained and qualified as a Russian interpreter. His parents had put pressure for something more practical. But the route he took was 'the best decision of my life'. These highly enjoyable two years (1957–9) proved transformative. One full year was spent in London. There he was based with other trainee interpreters in an elegant Kensington residence, where the first Aldermaston March was partly organised (he did the full distance), and with theatre sometimes in the evenings – it was the early days of George Devine's Royal Court. But he had been started off in Russian at the Joint Services School for Linguists in Crail, the fishing village a few miles south of St Andrews, before the School of Slavonic Studies (for that London year), with a return to Crail and the final exam at the end. After initial struggles with Russian, for which however his training in Greek and Latin proved an advantage, 'a whole new area of the modern world opened up for me'. His teachers – 'aristocratic White Russians, Baltics, a Pole' – encouraged talk. 'The more, the better, so long as it was in Russian. Life became an endlessly argumentative seminar, on every subject under the sun. And that went on for eighteen months, becoming more sophisticated each week as our Russian grew into ever more subtle thoughts. An education like no other I have known or can imagine.' Others were then sent off to do other things, but he was retained to help with the teaching. Thereafter he joined the Royal Naval Volunteer Reserve, to keep up his Russian, with an annual two-week refresher course and occasional stints as an interpreter. He was retired with the rank of Lieutenant Commander in 1974, after missing a course one year when their daughter Abigail was born to his wife Jane Buckley, a lecturer in education (there followed their son, Jake).

At Cambridge (1959–63) friends observed 'his infinite capacity for detail', and 'formidable powers of concentration and tenacious persistence in pursuing issues to the end', which could mean 'well into, and often right through, the night' (the student intensity never left him: in 1978, he 'stayed in bed, scribbling notes, all day every day', on Walter Burkert's revolutionary study of Pythagoreanism, *Weisheit und Wissenschaft*). In his first year, he discovered from John Raven's year-long introductory course how much 'wonderful philosophy' the ancient Greeks had generated – but was puzzled that no reference was made to any modern philosophers. For Part II he changed to the Moral Sciences Tripos. He had the good luck to be tutored in his last year by Jonathan Bennett, then lecturing on Locke, Berkeley, and Hume, who conducted his teaching as a collaborative research enterprise with his students. Burnyeat felt he was himself as much influenced, however, by the ancient historian Moses Finley, confessedly deaf to philosophy, but a 'wonderful, clever mind'.

It was Finley who perhaps suggested and certainly facilitated (with Ernst Gombrich) a move to the Warburg Institute for graduate work from autumn 1963. Burnyeat concluded after just three days, however, that the Warburg was not the right fit for him – even if Finley had already spotted his interest in philosophy's *longue durée*. Bennett put him in touch with Williams, who duly became his supervisor at UCL, but took up a chair at Bedford College in autumn 1964. Burnyeat was appointed Williams' successor, as Assistant Lecturer, promoted to Lecturer from 1965. He flourished in the UCL philosophy department, and was on good terms with Tony Long in its department of Greek and Latin. Friendships developed particularly with Jerry Cohen, who taught a joint seminar with him from time to time, and with David Wiggins at Bedford College (in 1970 they published in *Tribune* a co-authored article entitled 'Homes before Roads'). With Ted Honderich he co-edited a collection of essays entitled *Philosophy As It Is* (1979). Richard Wollheim, the Grote Professor, was a nurturing Head of Department, and like Burnyeat himself a liberal left member of the Labour Party. Wollheim recommended Lord Reith, appointed Chairman of a Party Commission on Advertising, to enlist his young lecturer as Secretary – and in his first year of teaching Burnyeat found himself ferried round London in Reith's chauffeur-driven Rolls Royce.

His files contained folders for several of the UCL lecture series he gave in ancient philosophy: on the Presocratics, early and middle Plato, Aristotle's ethics, and already Pyrrhonism, destined to become a major preoccupation. After Richard Sorabji arrived in King's College in 1970, they particularly relished the two-hour joint intercollegiate lectures they gave annually, to audiences of a hundred or so ('one of the most exciting circumstances of my career', in Sorabji's words, adding *inter alia*: 'Myles is perhaps the most electric philosopher I have known'). They took turns at the lecturing, with the other posing questions, sometimes tending to the 'gladiatorial' according to Sorabji, to get the students going on serious discussion, even if not all could respond.[2] Then in the later 1970s Burnyeat started giving lectures regularly at the Architectural Association, whose brilliance was recalled nearly forty years later by an audience member. He also lectured for a couple of years in this period at the City Lit, as well as for London's Extra-Mural Panel, until to Sorabji's great regret he departed to a post in Cambridge in 1978.

---

[2] Sorabji (2005: 12).

In those fourteen UCL years he read voraciously as always (his personal library eventually contained 10,000 volumes). He also made notes on virtually every seminar or lecture he had attended or philosophical conversation he had had, deposited in a giant filing cabinet, and meticulously organised. From his earliest days at UCL he was working on research projects, too. One of the first was on the Presocratic thinker Parmenides. He developed a paper entitled 'Parmenides and eternity'. He argued about its claims with myself in the mid–1960s; kept letters about them from Gregory Vlastos (1975) and from Sorabji and Bob Sharples (Long's successor at UCL) of the later 1970s; and shared a 'draft' with Paul Kalligas a little after that time. But he never published it, though he returned to its theme in his contribution to the Festschrift for Sorabji (2005), focused on Numenius, 'the only witty Platonist after Plato himself', in which he ranged over much of the entire ancient Platonist tradition.[3]

Perhaps the most celebrated item in his unpublished oeuvre was a long draft article on Academic scepticism entitled 'Carneades was no probabilist', belonging also to the 1970s and early 1980s, which circulated widely in samizdat form, generated enormous interest, and was often cited. But he was never satisfied with it. The folder housing the drafts contains a covering note anticipating pressure for posthumous publication. He observes that the paper exists in two versions, neither finished; regards it as now part only of the history of a scholarly debate; and refers potential readers to a subsequent published article, for his 'later, less dramatic views of Academic (so-called) "scepticism"'.[4] He became notorious for refusing to rush into publication. He used to say that he could never have even got started in our contemporary academic world. Indeed, although he began what became a long career of book reviewing for the *Listener* (whose demise in 1991 he lamented) and *Times Literary Supplement*, and in due course the *New York Review of Books* and its London counterpart, there were otherwise only four philosophical publications in his first decade of teaching.

These included a first essay on the *Theaetetus*, 'The material and sources of Plato's dream' (1970),[5] and a study entitled 'Virtues in action' (1971), which appeared in a collection of essays on Socrates commissioned by Vlastos.[6] Burnyeat was also invited by Vlastos to spend the autumn term of 1970 in Princeton, where he gave a graduate seminar on Aristotle's ethics. A strong bond was forged between them (he was eventually to edit Vlastos's own posthumously published collected Socratic essays).[7] Such indications of a growing reputation were confirmed by Harvard's invitation for autumn term 1973, replacing G.E.L. Owen, who had just left for the Laurence Chair

[3] Burnyeat (2005a: 143–69; quoted phrase: 144).
[4] Burnyeat (1997a). 'Sceptics' was never a description Academics applied to themselves.
[5] Burnyeat (1970).
[6] Burnyeat (1971).
[7] Vlastos (1993).

in Cambridge. The 1971 article was an elegantly argued and incisively meditated treatment of various attempts by Socrates' interlocutors in the early Platonic dialogues (with reference also to similar moves in contemporary ethics) to explain virtues in terms of features of actions or of powers to perform them, concluding with the importance of giving priority to being over doing in our thinking about what it is to be courageous or generous.

II

A turning point came in the academic year 1974–75, when he took a year's leave, thanks to a research fellowship from the Radcliffe Trust. The year proved astonishingly fruitful. Burnyeat wrote, or in two cases finished off, four major essays, and did the groundwork for three more published papers. Most were on the *Theaetetus*, and most were subsequently reprinted, usually by other scholars in edited collections, sometimes in translation. The earliest was a study split into two for publication, devoted to consideration of 'Protagoras and self-refutation' (1976), which Burnyeat made the first two chapters in his own collected papers.[8] The topic is an argument found in various forms in several Greek philosophers, claiming to show that 'Man is the measure of all things', the doctrine of the 5th-century BC sophist Protagoras, is self-refuting. The first of the paired papers dealt with Sextus Empiricus. It sent the philosophical community two necessary messages, both leitmotifs of Burnyeat's work in philosophy and its history. The twinning with a paper on the *Theaetetus* served notice that later Greek philosophy was as deserving of serious exploration and engagement as were Plato and Aristotle. At the same time Burnyeat's discussion suggested that philosophers might need to realise that their contemporary toolbox of distinctions (here between a proposition and the act of asserting it) might not quite work for philosophy in other eras, despite sophisticated formulations that might look very similar: 'logic at this period had not yet lost its connection with dialectic and disputation'.

The second Protagoras paper was inspired by that Williams lecture of 1964 on the *Theaetetus*. It dealt with the argument that, on the basis of his doctrine that 'Man is the measure' of truth, Protagoras himself must agree that his opponents' contention that that doctrine is false entails that it is indeed false: it refutes itself. The effectiveness and validity of this argument had already been long debated. Some judged it vitiated

---

[8] Burnyeat (1976a & 1976b; quoted clauses: 55, 195); collected essays: Burnyeat (2012) (most of those of Burnyeat's papers mentioned that were published up to and including 1998 may be found in the two 2012 volumes).

by failure to include in its formulations of claims of truth and falsehood the relativising qualifiers with which Protagoras specifies for whom a judgement is true or false. Others had argued: 'No amount of manoeuvring with his relativising qualifiers will extricate Protagoras from the commitment to truth absolute which is bound up with the very act of assertion.' Burnyeat's defence of this latter view was developed in unprecedented depth, with assured command of text and context, and with penetrating exploration of alternative hypotheses about the way the argument works. Perhaps its most distinctive element was his insistence (which he never abandoned) that even relativised truth must be true of a 'world', even if a world special to the individual for whom it is true (as Protagoreanism postulated) – and truth about such worlds is 'truth absolute'. Few readers thought Burnyeat's assessment altogether right, even if headed in the right direction. Some thought it quite wrong. Its stature was from the start unquestioned, and it remains the one essential reference point on its topic.

Next off the drawing board was 'Plato on the grammar of perceiving' (also 1976), tackling a problem – pointed out by Williams in that 1964 lecture – in interpreting the contrast highlighted at the end of Part I of the dialogue between seeing 'with' and seeing 'through' the eyes.[9] The ultimate focus was 'Plato's achievement in arriving at the first unambiguous statement of the difficult but undoubtedly important idea of the unity of consciousness'. What Burnyeat presented along the way was a patient and subtle demonstration of exactly what the 'with'/'through' distinction amounted to and how it helped Plato articulate that idea, performed with what was to be the hallmark of his scholarship: a command equally and inseparably of the philosophical issues at stake and their history, and of the philological, literary, and both detailed and strategic argumentative dimensions of the text in ancient context. The article's classic status was immediately recognised.

Together with his treatment of self-refutation arguments, it established or consolidated perceptions that Burnyeat was becoming a major force among a body of highly talented scholars of Greek philosophy in the rising generation. These were reinforced by the respect and authority he commanded by the weight of the oral contributions he made in philosophical gatherings. He was a loyal, supportive, and approachable figure in groups to which he belonged, even if he could sometimes be fierce with what he regarded as intellectual sloppiness or unpreparedness. In particular, a group started in London by G.E.L. Owen on his return to England drew in colleagues from several institutions. It met monthly on Saturday afternoons in term to work through the central Book Z of Aristotle's *Metaphysics* (and subsequently the

---

[9] Burnyeat (1976c; quoted clause: 49).

following two books). Burnyeat acted as principal note taker, and in due course prepared published versions.[10]

Further products of his Radcliffe Fellowship quickly appeared. One essay pursued self-refutation into the anti-sceptical Epicureanism of Lucretius.[11] Three focused on the *Theaetetus*'s introductory philosophical discussion. They announced the versatility of his ambition, as well as his view of the many kinds of demand Plato makes on readers. Their titles, and the vehicles chosen for their publication, already indicate that variety. 'Socratic midwifery, Platonic inspiration' appeared in a Classics journal, where the subject matter resonates with a number of strains in Greek literature – and indeed concepts such as self-laceration and the operation of unconscious forces in the mind, brought to bear upon themes in Greek poetry and tragedy by modern scholarship, eventually get deployed.[12] 'Examples in epistemology: Socrates, Theaetetus and G.E. Moore', and its placement in the Royal Institute of Philosophy's house journal, indicate determination to contribute to a contemporary as well as an ancient philosophical conversation, accessible to a wide interested readership.[13] Finally, the leading international history of science journal was the home selected for 'The philosophical sense of Theaetetus' mathematics'.[14]

His mind had not been wholly preoccupied with scepticism and the *Theaetetus*, however. The year 1980 saw another publication in ethics: an essay entitled 'Aristotle on learning to be good', a final outcome of the Radcliffe Fellowship. Here he presented a magisterial synoptic account, drawn from many passages scattered throughout the *Nicomachean Ethics*, of the good man's development. This highly accessible paper immediately established itself as a classic study of the topic, more anthologised and translated than anything else he wrote. It remains perhaps the best-known and most read of all his writings.[15]

III

At a conference on Stoic logic in Chantilly organised in September 1976 by Jacques Brunschwig, Burnyeat and Jonathan Barnes took a walk round the water. Their conversation resulted in a colloquium held in March 1978 at Oriel College, Oxford. This became the first of a regular sequence of Symposia Hellenistica, which have done

[10] Burnyeat & others (eds) (1979) and (1984).
[11] Burnyeat (1978a).
[12] Burnyeat (1977a).
[13] Burnyeat (1977b).
[14] Burnyeat (1978b).
[15] Burnyeat (1980a).

much to help generate philosophical work of high quality on the Epicureans, Stoics, and Sceptics. The subject chosen for the occasion was epistemology, and Burnyeat contributed a powerfully argued paper (delivered also in Amsterdam, at the University of Essex, and at several North American universities), asking the old question 'Can the sceptic live his scepticism?' Modern scepticism has typically been scepticism about the possibility of knowledge. Burnyeat's first concern was to make clear that the ancients (like Hume) took belief, not knowledge, to be the more important focus for sceptical questioning. His final conclusion was that Hume was right to answer 'No': to live without belief, as the Pyrrhonist claims he lives, would require him so radically to detach himself from himself as to abolish any possible human life. He was aware that others read Sextus very differently, as distinguishing between dogmatic belief, particularly about matters subject to theoretical investigation, from which the sceptic is free, and belief reflecting a non-dogmatic attitude to experience, which does enable him to live an ordinary life. But he himself saw no basis in Sextus (or indeed otherwise) for a notion of belief cut loose from a claim to truth and from responsiveness to reason.[16]

That issue Burnyeat continued to explore in discussion with others, above all Michael Frede, for some years to come. He and Frede both published further attempts upon it in an edited collection of 1984, and in 1997 they together edited a volume collecting five major published contributions to the debate: both Burnyeat's papers, two of Frede's, and one by Barnes.[17] Burnyeat also at this time commissioned essays by other scholars on scepticism in both antiquity and later philosophy, which he published in an edited collection that included his own 'Can the sceptic?' and a seminal article from 1929 by Pierre Couissin, translated by himself and Jennifer Barnes.[18]

Meanwhile in 1979 he had delivered as a Dawes Hicks Lecture of the British Academy an extended assault on the idea that conflicting appearances give irresistible reason to embrace relativism or scepticism, or resort to sense-data: a notion common in antiquity and especially prominent in Pyrrhonism, but in much subsequent philosophy too, down to Berkeley, Russell, and recently in ethics J.L. Mackie, for example.[19] Then in 1983 came an essay he entitled 'Idealism and Greek philosophy: what Descartes saw and Berkeley missed'.[20] In it Burnyeat made one of his most ambitious and admired attempts, arresting in its originality, to diagnose the sort of thing that makes ancient Greek thought radically different from modern philosophy. The key he proposed there is what he called the assumption of realism. The Greeks never

---

[16] Burnyeat (1980b: 20–53).
[17] Burnyeat (1984); Burnyeat & Frede (1997).
[18] Burnyeat (ed.) (1983a).
[19] Burnyeat (1979).
[20] Burnyeat (1983b).

considered it open to question *whether* there is an 'external world'. All philosophers, even the Pyrrhonists, assumed that the challenge is to explain *how* we access reality, taken to be distinct from our minds – or else (as with the sceptics) to show that we have no reliable means of achieving such access. He argued that a 'decisive shift of perspective' was first achieved by the exposure and questioning of the assumption in Descartes' 'hyperbolical doubt'.[21]

Ancient Pyrrhonism was now attracting more interest among scholars of philosophy than ever before in recent times. But Burnyeat was also developing one of the most important and influential ingredients in his interpretation of the Platonic and Aristotelian conceptualisation of knowledge, in three articles of the early 1980s. First was a provocative paper on Socrates' treatment of testimony before a jury (at the end of Part II of the *Theaetetus*), presented with a reply from Barnes at the joint summer session of the Mind Association and Aristotelian Society in 1980.[22] By 1982 he had a draft of 'a sort of sequel', on Augustine's treatment of learning and teaching in *De Magistro*. The final version, a nuanced, learned essay that gave a masterly treatment of the teasing to and fro of Augustine's dialogue, was delivered in 1987 to the joint session, under the title 'Wittgenstein and Augustine *De Magistro*', as his Presidential address to the Mind Association.[23] In a longer paper focused on the *Posterior Analytics* (1981), Burnyeat had elaborated on the suggestion, widely if not universally embraced, that for Aristotle as for Plato, true knowledge is best interpreted as 'understanding', construed as a synoptic grasp of key explanatory connections. He gave it the indicative title 'Aristotle on understanding knowledge'.[24]

Other articles (1982) turned to matters of logic with a bearing on epistemology. 'The origins of non-deductive inference' preferred Aristotle to the Stoics.[25] 'Gods and heaps' was an innovative study of the non-canonical form of sorites argument deployed by the Academic Carneades against Stoic theology.[26] But for a visit to the University of California at Santa Barbara in January 1983, he composed a short paper in a very different mode. He entitled it: 'Is an Aristotelian philosophy of mind still credible?' A revised version began to circulate widely, and objections to its argument, published as well as unpublished, proliferated. Finally, professing reluctance, he published it in 1992. What had caused a greater stir than anything else he ever wrote was

---

[21] Burnyeat (1982a; quoted phrases: 40). Against 'decisiveness', Richard Sorabji argued that a Neoplatonist style of idealism, with some affinities with Berkeley's, was propounded in antiquity by Gregory of Nyssa: Sorabji (1983: 287–96).

[22] Burnyeat (1980c).

[23] Burnyeat (1987a).

[24] Burnyeat (1981). Indebtedness to Barnes' writings, here and in the following two articles, was warmly acknowledged.

[25] Burnyeat (1982b; quoted material: 203, 238).

[26] Burnyeat (1982c).

his representation of Aristotle's theory of sense perception, claiming inheritance from Philoponus, Aquinas, and Brentano, as involving '*no physiological process* which stands to a perceiver's awareness of colour or smell as matter to form. The most basic effect on the perceiver is identical with an awareness of colour or smell.' His immediate target was the functionalist interpretation of the theory, particularly as proposed by Martha Nussbaum and Hilary Putnam, which as he saw it needed Richard Sorabji's account of the relation between Aristotelian body and soul (very different from his own) as its basis. Once again, he was proposing that the presuppositions of ancient Greek philosophy, despite its richness and sophistication, often set it at a distance from any modern philosophical agenda.[27]

The mid 1970s to early 1980s were undoubtedly the most intensely concentrated and influentially productive continuous period in writing philosophical scholarship (mostly on interconnected epistemological themes) during Burnyeat's entire career. At the same time, he was publishing as many book reviews as ever (including a jewel given the title 'Message from Heraclitus'),[28] and of course teaching, in London, in Cambridge, and (in the early 1980s) in a string of visiting appointments in the USA: at Berkeley, UCLA, and Cornell as well as Santa Barbara (he thrived on synergy). His publication record over that whole period speaks for itself, and indeed spoke to the Fellows of the British Academy, who elected him to their number in 1984.

IV

Burnyeat had moved in 1978 from UCL to a lectureship in the Faculty of Classics in Cambridge. There were obvious pluses and minuses in switching from a philosophy to a Classics department and from London back to Cambridge. A main attraction was the exchange of a solo position in ancient philosophy for membership of a strong clutch of colleagues with a wide range of interests in Greek philosophy and science (Geoffrey Lloyd, G.E.L. Owen, Malcolm Schofield, David Sedley). He was not enamoured of the ethos of the more traditional Cambridge colleges. In 1977, however, Robinson was in its first year of existence as a college. Charles Brink, chairman of the trustees who oversaw its creation, was alerted to the possibility of recruiting Burnyeat to the fledgling College's teaching strength. The move to Cambridge was thus made financially possible by his simultaneous election to a Fellowship and lectureship in philosophy at Robinson. There he relished being part of a small group of Fellows who

[27] Burnyeat (1992a; quoted passage: 15). A sequel appeared soon after, in its final English version as Burnyeat (1995). For the debate: Caston (2005). See further Section V below.
[28] Burnyeat (1982d).

took on the shaping from scratch of a new and less hierarchical collegiate community. He had spacious and comfortable rooms at 5 Adams Road, their tobacco aroma and paraphernalia (including big tailor's scissors) recalled evocatively by Jake. Here he gave his classes and undergraduate supervisions from a battered leather armchair he had brought with him from UCL, along with a no less battered small blue suitcase which housed books and papers in use. The rooms he shared precariously, as an inveterate pipe smoker in that period (later he took snuff), with his memorably enthusiastic mongrel Jenny, whom he carted around Cambridge on his bike in a knapsack. One of his first Robinson students has written:[29]

> Supervisions with Myles were extraordinary … [They] were oases of calm study, the piles of books on the floor, the paper strewn desk, the pipe puffing all adding to the focus, which was wholly devoted to the subject matter, the thinking. To a keen young philosophical mind, his gentle encouragement to go deeper, to find the nuances, to articulate my passion for the subject, and the chance to be guided through the stumbling blocks, produced capsules of time I have never experienced before or since. … He somehow alchemised time itself; each supervision with him gave me access to an infinitely deep pool of knowledge, experience, learning, and profound intellectual pleasure.

Mutatis mutandis, much like time spent reading, talking, and walking with their father experienced by Abigail and Jake.

In 1984 came a further significant change in Burnyeat's academic circumstances, when he became Laurence Professor of Ancient Philosophy in succession to Owen, who had died at the age of 60 two years before. He was by now one of the best-known figures in the field, much in demand on many fronts. Colleagues and enquirers everywhere wanted to discuss philosophical problems with him. For Bryan Magee's BBC2 television series *The Great Philosophers* (autumn 1987), it was Burnyeat with whom the conversation on Plato was conducted. He often gave a talk on the charge of impiety levelled against Socrates. There was invariably a majority vote of 'Not guilty' by audiences at the outset. By the end, the majority verdict was no less invariably 'Guilty' as charged. Burnyeat had argued that the Socrates of Plato's *Apology* patently did *not* believe in his city's gods.[30] He made fewer contributions to the literary weeklies. But 'Sphinx without a secret', his devastating critique in the *New York Review of Books* of Leo Strauss's treatment of Plato and its development into a cult and a political ideology, prompted an indignant reaction from leading Straussians and the support of Gregory Vlastos in the same journal (also privately communicated gratitude from

---

[29] Shea (2020).
[30] Burnyeat (1997b).

some younger scholars in the USA).[31] He reprinted it (like 'Message from Heraclitus', also an *NYRB* piece) in his collected papers. Strauss's reading of the *Republic* was subsequently to be a minor target of a short article, appearing in Wollheim's Festschrift as 'Utopia and fantasy: the practicability of Plato's ideally just city'.[32]

With new institutional responsibilities, his academic life inevitably diversified. He played an increasingly prominent part in the life and work of the Faculty of Classics; and although in later years he might protest that he was a philosopher, not a classicist, it is indicative that when the Faculty could celebrate final completion of its new building in June 1990, it was to Burnyeat that his colleagues turned for the address at the inauguration.[33] In the University at large he was active around this same time, particularly with the logician Timothy Smiley, in opposing with some success introduction of more managerial structures. His main concern, however, was naturally the promotion of the study of ancient philosophy, especially in Cambridge. One might say that he started with himself. Initially he evidently devoted much of his own research time to completion of long-delayed work on the *Theaetetus* book.[34] He fostered a succession of Cambridge PhD students, including Angie Hobbs, Dominic Scott, Thomas Johansen, Melissa Lane, Verity Harte, and Noburu Notomi, today themselves well-known Plato and Aristotle scholars (also supervising for the Open University Barrie Fleet's edition of Plotinus *Ennead* III.6). And he welcomed many visiting practitioners of the subject.

In 'First words', his valedictory talk in 1996, he spoke of what he felt most distinctive about his entire eighteen years in Cambridge:[35]

> It has been a very special experience to have belonged to a group that has met together every week in term-time ..., with a changing population of graduate students and visitors, to explore the entire range of ancient philosophy from Xenophanes in the sixth century BC to Simplicius in the sixth century AD, with all and sundry in between. It made ancient philosophy in Cambridge a continuous adventure into the unknown which was simultaneously a continuous re-education in the known.

Through intellectual example, he often assumed leadership in discussion. Sometimes at the first session of term he would propose a hypothesis, perhaps startlingly far-reaching, about how best to read the text ahead (as for example with the first Plotinus attempted: *Ennead* V.1), which could be tried out in future weeks.

---

[31] Burnyeat (1985).
[32] Burnyeat (1992a).
[33] Burnyeat (1990b); a shorter version had appeared in the *TLS*, 15–21 June 1990.
[34] He also arranged for the publication of Gilbert Ryle's famous unpublished paper 'Logical atomism in Plato's *Theaetetus*', the same year as his own 'Introduction' to the dialogue eventually appeared.
[35] Burnyeat (1997c: 1–2). A footnote listed the remarkable number of texts studied.

In his own work, some earlier preoccupations were taken further. For the 1990 Symposium Aristotelicum, pursuing his interest in non-deductive inference, he composed an authoritative study of the enthymeme and its fate in the history of logic, which made better sense of Aristotle's attachment to its theoretical soundness as an instrument for persuasion than anything in the existing literature.[36] His final contribution to a Symposium Hellenisticum (in summer 1995) saw him returning both to self-refutation and to Carneades and the Academics, in a supple and delicate treatment of decidedly refractory material, entitled 'Antipater and self-refutation: elusive arguments in Cicero's *Academica*'.[37]

Two Platonic dialogues besides the *Theaetetus* came to bulk larger. In 1995 and 1996 he lectured on the *Euthydemus*, Socrates' encounter with eristic sophistry (also explored in the reading group). He saw this dialogue as much closer in its theoretical ambitions and insights to the *Republic* and especially to Plato's later work than was generally supposed. There was eventually to be a publication: an elegant essay entitled 'Plato on how not to speak of what is not' (aptly dedicated to Jacques Brunschwig), which against the *idée reçue* made a powerful case for interpreting the dialogue as already anticipating the key element in the much-admired solution to the problem developed in the late *Sophist*.[38]

Above all, an immersion in the *Republic* began, that from then on became often dominant in his work. Burnyeat had delivered Cambridge's 24-lecture course on the central books of the *Republic* in the academic years 1983–6; and in summer 1984 at the Symposium Aristotelicum he contributed a paper entitled 'Platonism and mathematics: a prelude to discussion' (of the critique of Platonist metaphysics in Books M and N of Aristotle's *Metaphysics*).[39] This was one of the richest of all his writings, wide-ranging, and radical too, in the many challenges it posed for the focus and presuppositions of much modern English language Plato scholarship. 'The choice between an Aristotelian and one of the Platonist accounts of mathematics', he proposed, 'is simultaneously a choice as to which sciences we should take as most fundamental to our understanding of the world and its goodness.' Mathematics and mathematical education were for him integral, not merely psychologically and methodologically preliminary (as was generally supposed in Anglophone scholarship), to the 'grand vision' of the *Republic*. Plato's intimations of the vision culminated, as he saw it, in references to 'the Unwritten Chapter', that nomenclature deliberately echoing Aristotle's mention of 'unwritten doctrines', and establishing contact with

[36] Burnyeat (1994).
[37] Burnyeat (1997a).
[38] Burnyeat (2002a).
[39] Burnyeat (1987b; quoted material: 213, 217).

the Plato of the Tübingen school, usually ignored or dismissed in the Anglo-American literature. There the identity of Good and One, and the mathematical structure of (for example) justice and health, would have been expounded.

From 1989 onwards, Burnyeat was also developing ideas in a quite different area, worked up into talks he was invited to give, often as lectures on named foundations, particularly in the USA (where in 1992 he was elected Foreign Honorary Member of the American Academy of Arts and Sciences). By 1990 he had an illuminating trio for delivery at Cornell and Johns Hopkins, under the titles 'Ancient Freedoms', 'Anger and Revenge', and 'Happiness and Tranquillity'. He repeated them in Buenos Aires and at Notre Dame in 1993, and in 1996 at Berkeley. They met with an enthusiastic reception. But although for a stay at the Wissenschaftskolleg in Berlin during the academic year 2004–5 he proposed to develop them into a book (*The Archaeology of Feeling*: the echo of Foucault signals their intent), together with a fourth on philosophy and physiognomy, other commitments intervened.[40]

The late 1980s and early 1990s were the era of *glasnost*. An exchange scheme was funded (by George Soros) between the Universities of Cambridge and Leningrad. Burnyeat was the first Cambridge academic to seize the opportunity. He made a two week stay in Leningrad in April 1991, after a welcome by a friendly group of Classicists and philosophers. The visit triggered renewal of his passion for things Russian, and delight in discovery that he could still speak the language. He much admired the knowledge of ancient Greek he found there, and the commitment – long sustained in inauspicious circumstances – to studying particularly the Neoplatonists and Plato's *Laws* (on which he had interesting observations). He wrote journalistic pieces about his experiences in *urbs Sancti Petri*, and returned as often as he could, giving lectures and seminars, and joining the editorial board of the new ancient philosophy journal *Hyperboreus*. He conceived a particular regard for the senior scholar Alexander Zaitsev; and he translated for publication an important article on silent reading in antiquity by A.K. Gavrilov (acknowledging help from Irina Levinskaya and his second wife, the poet Ruth Padel), adding a short piece of his own on the topic.[41] He also paid academic visits elsewhere in eastern Europe: to Budapest (1998), Sofia (1999) (both written up in the *TLS*), and Sarajevo (2000), *inter alia* giving seminars on Plato's *Crito*. In 2001, however, tensions within the St Petersburg Classics department impinged on the translation of an article of his own, and he felt he had to sever relations with it. Nonetheless Russia remained on his agenda. In 2003, he visited Siberia with Ruth (investigating tiger conservation) and their daughter Gwen.[42]

---

[40] They will appear in their original lecture form in Burnyeat (forthcoming).
[41] Gavrilov (1997) & Burnyeat (1997d).
[42] Burnyeat (2004a).

V

In the mid–1990s, it was suggested to Burnyeat by Isaiah Berlin and his old friend Jerry Cohen, now a successor to Berlin in the Chichele chair of political theory at Oxford, that he think of applying for a Senior Research Fellowship in philosophy shortly to become available at All Souls. By this time, for one reason or another of a kind familiar to modern academics, he was finding little opportunity for sustained work of his own. He applied, and was elected from 1996. He once described his period at All Souls as 'paradise'.

Work on the *Republic* on a different scale became possible. The magnificent published versions of two responses he made to further invitations to lecture make that immediately apparent. He gave three Tanner Lectures at Harvard in December 1997. 'Culture and society in Plato's *Republic*' was an extended and wide-ranging exploration of a topic never much before pursued in the large literature on its treatment of art and artists (although standard problems of interpretation were examined afresh too). Burnyeat offered a powerful and highly original study focused on the dialogue's concern (not least, as he saw it, in the Cave passage of Book 7) with the insidious effects of culture, its registers and modes of operation, on the shaping of both society and individual psychology. He laid stress – not only by the dedication to Reith's memory – on the contemporary urgency he saw in Plato's insights.[43] 'Plato on why mathematics is good for the soul', presented to a British Academy symposium the following year, elaborated at length on the epistemological and metaphysical vision of the *Republic* first argued for in 'Platonism and mathematics'.[44] These two eloquent essays, written for the interested general reader as much as for students and scholars, constitute a summation of what he thought most important to understand about the dialogue as Plato's greatest work.

Another paper addressed to a wider potential readership had first been developed as a Cambridge undergraduate lecture for a course on Classics in the nineteenth century. This was 'The past in the present: Plato as educator of nineteenth-century Britain'. It was designed to explain the part that Jowett and before him the Philosophical Radicals – heroes for Burnyeat not least for their fostering of the 'Godless College of Gower Street' – played in restoring Plato to the reading and intellectual formation of educated Britons from long general neglect.[45] James Mill has a walk on part only here. But in Burnyeat's 2000 Master Mind Lecture to the British Academy (much of it devoted to the *Republic*), he has a starring role as the rediscoverer of the sceptical

[43] Burnyeat (1999).
[44] Burnyeat (2000).
[45] Burnyeat (1998).

Plato in modern times, counterpoised with Plotinus and the Neoplatonist systematic Plato – with both however seen as philosophical responses Platonic in spirit. Burnyeat's own generous appreciation of Plato's many different meanings for different readers in different eras shines through.[46]

He referred in the printed version to two further pioneering essays of his published at this time. One was a study of James Mill's developing engagement with Plato, and his influence on George Grote as well as his critique of Thomas Taylor.[47] The second was one of the most extraordinary pieces of scholarship Burnyeat ever published. In John Stuart Mill's mention of reading at the age of seven the first six dialogues of Plato in 'the common arrangement', that expression much intrigued him. His article reports the outcome of his comprehensive bibliographical investigation into its likely reference. He explored with the help of many colleagues and librarians the history of publication of editions of Plato from the Renaissance to the end of the nineteenth century (catalogues are given in two appendices), as well as the evidence for Plato editions in the Mill household. His conclusion was that the arrangement was the Stephanus ordering, which John Stuart very probably read in the Bipont edition of 1781–7, and that he must in that case have written 'six' by mistake for 'seven' (if indeed he read all dialogues up to and including the *Theaetetus*). The paper was published simultaneously in three differently appropriate journals.[48]

Burnyeat continued to reflect on the *Republic*. In his Presidential Address to the Aristotelian Society in 2005, he spoke on 'The truth of tripartition', defending Plato's theory of soul (not Plato's arguments).[49] A seminar conducted back in 2001 with Michael Frede, whose presence in Oxford he found one of its greatest attractions, yielded a joint publication after Frede's death: *The Pseudo-Platonic Seventh Letter*. In his section of the book, Burnyeat construed the letter, with striking imaginative power, as a sort of prose drama, designed to show the damage done to the soul by our emotional responses to social pressures of various kinds, as the *Republic* had suggested: 'a major aid for all readers of this difficult text', said Charles Kahn.[50] He also published essays on other dialogues. A study of what he argued should be understood as 'the rational myth' of the *Timaeus* was at once recognised as another classic, which helped fuel increasing interest in the dialogue. Plato, he suggested (noting the concern

[46] Burnyeat (2001a).
[47] Burnyeat (2001b).
[48] Burnyeat (2001c).
[49] Burnyeat (2005b), dedicated to Bernard Williams' memory.
[50] Burnyeat & Frede (2015), reviewed in Kahn (2015). Kahn like some others, however, was unconvinced by Burnyeat's argument for inauthenticity.

with political as well as cosmic order), was thinking of the reasonableness of the practical reasoning in which a supremely good designer would probably engage.[51]

Aristotle, too, consumed much energy in Burnyeat's years at All Souls. He became particularly preoccupied with what he regarded as the neglected problem of how to read a chapter of an Aristotelian treatise, and particularly with the function of cross-references to other parts of the treatise, and to other treatises. He argued that cross-references indicate appropriate order of argument and exposition, and so of reading order. The issue was a prime focus especially of his persuasive interpretation (presented at the Symposium Aristotelicum in 1999) of the function of Book 1 of *On Generation and Corruption* within the corpus – as designed to provide three kinds of foundation for understanding the physical world: physical, conceptual, and teleological.[52] But the problem was no less a concern of three major publications he worked on. First came a return to the *Metaphysics*, after many discussions and seminars devoted to it since Owen's London group. The focus on how to read the work is immediately clear from the title of a short monograph: *A Map of Metaphysics Zeta*, a map (it transpired) not only of its internal structure but of its place within the whole.[53] Recent scholarship had tended to concentrate on the theory of form and substance that Book Zeta was developing, in requisite intensive detail. Burnyeat was suggesting a need to prioritise a wider (in some ways more traditional) perspective. There was disagreement over whether he got right either map or what he was mapping. But many readers found his approach refreshing and illuminating.

Specific Aristotelian chapters were the subject of two long subsequent essays. In the first, devoted to *De Anima* II.5, Burnyeat returned to Aristotle's treatment of sense perception, developing the account first broached in 'Is an Aristotelian philosophy of mind still credible?'[54] He built an authoritative exposition, alert to cross-references, of actuality as a physical alteration – but conceived differently, in order to account for the cognitive accuracy of perception, from the notion as introduced in the *Physics*: what Aquinas (the subject of a further study) conceived as a 'spiritual' but still physical form of change.[55] The other paper, originating in 1995, exhibited formidable command of philological as well as philosophical resources. Here Burnyeat argued that a passage *distinguishing* actuality from change in Book Theta of the *Metaphysics*, often treated as canonical by analytic philosophers, must be misplaced. He judged it, though probably by Aristotle, a 'freak performance'.[56]

---

[51] Burnyeat (2005c).
[52] Burnyeat (2004b).
[53] Burnyeat (2001d), dedicated to the memory of G.E.L. Owen.
[54] Burnyeat (2002b).
[55] Burnyeat (2001e).
[56] Burnyeat (2008; quoted phrase: 276).

There were further essays on Plato and Aristotle, two pieces of detective work on ancient Greek optics, and a sequence of memorable book reviews. He also brought to posthumous publication both Williams' collected papers on history of philosophy[57] and those of his third wife, the Croatian philosopher Heda Segvic.[58] In 2008 he was initiator of a discussion evening at the British Academy on the striking group portrait by Stuart Pearson Wright of its recent Presidents, seated round a table with a plucked chicken (uncooked) sprawled centrally. He himself drew attention to Diogenes the Cynic's similar presentation of just such a fowl to Plato – who had defined humans as featherless bipeds.

VI

Burnyeat had become Emeritus Fellow at All Souls in 2006. In 2007 he was appointed CBE, 'for services to scholarship'. The same year he was presented with a Festschrift, aptly entitled *Maieusis*.[59] In 2012 St Andrews conferred upon him an Honorary Doctorate, a distinction he appreciated the more for its renewal of his earlier link with East Fife; earlier that year two volumes of his collected papers, from his UCL period and the subsequent years in Cambridge, appeared (two more, from his time at All Souls, are following posthumously).[60] Robinson had made him an Honorary Fellow in 2006, giving him a much-valued academic base again in Cambridge. From then on, he was frequently in evidence in College and at the ancient philosophy reading group, while mostly living in Oxford with his devoted partner, the musicologist Margaret Bent.

But there was Alzheimer's in his family. It had afflicted his mother and her mother and aunt before that. Not long after retirement from his All Souls Fellowship, scientific confirmation came of evidence that he too was developing the condition. Decline was gradual. For several years, he was able to continue delivering papers already written, and preparing substantial drafts for new ones. Latterly he became attracted by ancient evidence that the *Republic* contained six books, not ten, with Book 1 probably then ending after Glaucon and Adeimantus had restated the anti-Socratic position. It formed the topic of his short Yamamoto Memorial Lecture at the Symposium Platonicum in Tokyo in 2010, marking his long years of support for Plato scholars from Japan (his first visit was in 1980; this time Gwen came too). He could write

[57] Williams (2006).
[58] Segvic (2009).
[59] Scott (ed.) (2007).
[60] Burnyeat (2012a; and forthcoming).

characteristically generous and insightful notes to friends, and penned a lively sketch of key elements in his own formation in 2012. He even passed a further driving test in 2014. A move to an Oxford care home finally became inevitable, however. He seemed to be content there, with family and friends still finding something of the old Myles in him. He died on 20 September 2019.

In the field of ancient Greek and Roman philosophy the range and fertility of his achievement, his public intellectual profile, and his world-wide impact had been exceptional.[61] The generous help he gave to countless students and other scholars, not least in Japan and Russia, whether starting or established, needs no further comment, nor his enterprise in bringing their unpublished or untranslated or uncollected work to publication. He had provoked thinking on the less familiar and fresh thinking on the familiar, perhaps especially on Aristotle, often combating current views or presuppositions. He opened larger vistas on virtually everything he wrote about. In particular, his publications on knowledge and scepticism, from Heraclitus to Augustine, and on resonances of ancient views about them in modern philosophy, from Descartes and Berkeley to Moore and Wittgenstein, had continually cast new light upon the fundamental problems they tackled, as well as into their own distinctive perspectives. And he was one of the great Plato scholars of our era: in his command of the Greek text, in penetrating insight into its many literary and philosophical dimensions, and in deploying informed attention to the long history of its interpretation over millennia.

One substantial unpublished essay from the 1970s which Myles Burnyeat did decide to include in his collected papers he entitled 'the passion of reason'.[62] His own passionate attempt to understand in historical perspective the philosophising of the greatest minds of the past relied on learning, acuteness, rigour, and patience, but also sympathy, imagination, and openness. The passion was surely what drove him upon that 'continuous adventure into the unknown which was simultaneously a continuous re-education in the known', thinking deeper thoughts and glimpsing bigger pictures than one could oneself.

References

Barnes, J., Brunschwig, J., Burnyeat, M. & Schofield, M. (eds) (1982), *Science and Speculation: Essays on Hellenistic Theory and Practice* (Cambridge).
Berti, E. (ed.) (1981), *Aristotle on Knowledge: 'The Posterior Analytics'* (Padua).
Burnyeat, M.F. (1970), 'The materials and sources of Plato's dream', *Phronesis*, 15: 101–22.

---

[61] The American Leiter Reports posted in a blog (8 February 2016) the result of a write-in poll making him 'the best post-WWII Anglophone scholar' of the subject.
[62] Burnyeat (2012b).

Burnyeat, M.F. (1971), 'Virtues in action', in Vlastos (ed.) (1971), 209–34.

Burnyeat, M.F. (1976a), 'Protagoras and self-refutation in later Greek philosophy', *Philosophical Review* 85: 66–91.

Burnyeat, M.F. (1976b), 'Protagoras and self-refutation in Plato's *Theaetetus*', *Philosophical Review* 85: 172–95.

Burnyeat, M.F. (1976c), 'Plato on the grammar of perceiving', *Classical Quarterly*, 26: 29–51.

Burnyeat, M.F. (1977a), 'Socratic midwifery, Platonic inspiration', *Bulletin of the Institute of Classical Studies*, 24: 7–16.

Burnyeat, M.F. (1977b), 'Examples in epistemology: Socrates, Theaetetus and G.E. Moore', *Philosophy*, 52: 381–98.

Burnyeat, M.F. (1978a), 'The upside-down back-to-front sceptic of Lucretius IV 472', *Philologus*, 122: 197–206.

Burnyeat, M.F. (1978b), 'The philosophical sense of Theaetetus' mathematics', *Isis*, 69: 489–511.

Burnyeat, M.F. (1979), 'Conflicting appearances', *Proceedings of the British Academy*, 65: 69–111.

Burnyeat, M.F. (1980a), 'Aristotle on learning to be good', in Rorty (ed.) (1980), 69–92.

Burnyeat, M.F. (1980b), 'Can the sceptic live his scepticism?', in Schofield, Burnyeat & Barnes (eds) (1980), 20–53.

Burnyeat, M.F. (1980c), 'Socrates and the jury: paradoxes in Plato's distinction between knowledge and true belief', *Aristotelian Society Supplementary Volume*, 54: 173–206.

Burnyeat, M.F. (1981), 'Aristotle on understanding knowledge', in Berti (ed.) (1981), 97–131.

Burnyeat, M.F. (1982a), 'Idealism and Greek philosophy: what Descartes saw and Berkeley missed', *Philosophical Review*, 90: 3–40.

Burnyeat, M.F. (1982b), 'The origins of non-deductive inference', in Barnes, Brunschwig, Burnyeat & Schofield (eds) (Cambridge), 193–238.

Burnyeat, M.F. (1982c), 'Gods and heaps', in Schofield & Nussbaum (eds) (Cambridge), 315–38.

Burnyeat, M.F. (1982d), 'Message from Heraclitus', *New York Review of Books*, 3 May 1982.

Burnyeat, M. (ed.) (1983a), *The Skeptical Tradition* (Berkeley & London).

Burnyeat, M.F. (1983b), 'Idealism and Greek philosophy: what Descartes saw and Berkeley missed', *Philosophical Review*, 90: 3–40.

Burnyeat, M.F. (1984), 'The sceptic in his place and time', in Rorty, Schneewind & Skinner (eds) (1984), 225–54.

Burnyeat, M.F. (1985), 'Sphinx without a secret', *New York Review of Books*, 30 May 1985.

Burnyeat, M.F. (1987a), 'Wittgenstein and Augustine *De Magistro*', *Aristotelian Society Supplementary Volume*, 61: 1–24.

Burnyeat, M.F. (1987b), 'Platonism and mathematics: a prelude to discussion', in Graeser (ed.) (1987), 213–40.

Burnyeat, M. (1990a), *The Theaetetus of Plato*, with a translation by M.J. Levett, revised by M. Burnyeat (Indianopolis/Cambridge MA).

Burnyeat, M. (1990b), 'The importance of Classics', *Cambridge Review*, 111: 120–4.

Burnyeat, M.F. (1992a), 'Is an Aristotelian philosophy of mind still credible? A draft', in Nussbaum & Rorty (eds) (1992), 15–26.

Burnyeat, M.F. (1992b), 'Utopia and fantasy: the practicability of Plato's ideally just city', in J. Hopkins and A. Savile (eds), *Psychoanalysis, Mind, and Art* (Oxford), 175–87.

Burnyeat, M.F. (1994), 'Enthymeme: Aristotle on the logic of persuasion', in Furley & Nehamas (eds) (1994), 3–55.

Burnyeat, M.F. (1995), 'How much happens when Aristotle sees red and hears middle C?', in Nussbaum & Rorty (eds) (1995), 421–34.

Burnyeat, M.F. (1997a), 'Antipater and self-refutation: elusive arguments in Cicero's *Academica*', in Inwood & Mansfeld (eds) (1997), 277–310.

Burnyeat, M.F. (1997b), 'The impiety of Socrates', *Ancient Philosophy*, 17: 1–12.

Burnyeat, M.F. (1997c), 'First words: a valedictory lecture', *Proceedings of the Cambridge Philological Society*, 43: 1–20.

Burnyeat, M.F. (1997d), 'Postscript on silent reading', *Classical Quarterly*, 47: 74–6.

Burnyeat, M.F. (1998), 'The past in the present: Plato as educator of nineteenth-century Britain', in Rorty (ed.) (1998), 353–73.

Burnyeat, M.F. (1999), 'Culture and society in Plato's *Republic*', *The Tanner Lectures on Human Values*, 20: 215–324.

Burnyeat, M.F. (2000), 'Plato on why mathematics is good for the soul', in Smiley (ed.) (2000), 1–81.

Burnyeat, M.F. (2001a), 'Plato', *Proceedings of the British Academy*, 111: 1–22.

Burnyeat, M.F. (2001b), 'James Mill on Thomas Taylor's Plato', *Apeiron*, 34: 101–10.

Burnyeat, M.F. (2001c), 'What was "the common arrangement": an inquiry into John Stuart Mill's boyhood reading of Plato', *Utilitas* 13: 1–32; *Philologus* 145: 158–86; *Apeiron*, 34: 51–90.

Burnyeat, M. (2001d), *A Map of Metaphysics Zeta* (Pittsburgh).

Burnyeat, M.F. (2001e), 'Aquinas on "spiritual change" in perception', in Perler (ed.) (2001), 129–53.

Burnyeat, M.F. (2002a), 'Plato on how to speak of what is not: *Euthydemus* 283a–288a', in Canto-Sperber & Pellegrin (eds) (2002), 40–66.

Burnyeat, M.F. (2002b), '*De Anima* II 5', *Phronesis*, 47: 28–90.

Burnyeat, M.F. (2004a), 'Diary', *London Review of Books*, 19 February 2004: 34–5.

Burnyeat, M.F. (2004b), 'Aristotle on the foundations of sublunary physics', in Haas & Mansfeld (eds) (2004), 7–24.

Burnyeat, M.F. (2005a), 'Platonism in the Bible: Numenius of Apamea on *Exodus* and eternity', in Salles (ed.) (2005), 143–69.

Burnyeat, M.F. (2005b), 'The truth of tripartition', *Proceedings of the Aristotelian Society*, 106: 1–23.

Burnyeat, M.F. (2005c), 'Εἰκὼς Μῦθος', *Rhizai*, 2: 143–65.

Burnyeat, M.F. (2008), '*Kinêsis* vs. *Energeia*: a much-read passage in (but not of) Aristotle's *Metaphysics*', *Oxford Studies in Ancient Philosophy*, 34: 219–92.

Burnyeat, M.F. (2012a), *Explorations in Ancient and Modern Philosophy*, volumes 1 & 2 (Cambridge).

Burnyeat, M.F. (2012b), 'The passion of reason in Plato's *Phaedrus*', in 2012a: 2. 238–58.

Burnyeat, M.F. (forthcoming), *Explorations in Ancient and Modern Philosophy*, volumes 3 & 4 (Cambridge).

Burnyeat, M.F. & Frede, M. (2015), *The Pseudo-Platonic Seventh Letter* (ed. D. Scott) (Oxford).

Burnyeat, M. & Frede, M. (eds) (1997), *The Original Sceptics: A Controversy* (Indianapolis).

Burnyeat, M. & others (eds) (1979), *Notes on Book Zeta of Aristotle's Metaphysics* (Oxford Study Aids Monographs, No. 1, Oxford).

Burnyeat, M. & others (eds) (1984), *Notes on Books Eta and Theta of Aristotle's Metaphysics* (Oxford Study Aids Monographs, No. 4, Oxford).

Canto-Sperber, M. & Pellegrin, P. (eds) (2002), *Le Style de la pensée: Recueil de textes en hommage à Jacques Brunschwig* (Paris).

Caston, V. (2005), 'The spirit and the letter: Aristotle on perception', in Salles (ed) (2005), 245–320.

Furley, D.J. & Nehamas, A. (eds) (1994), *Aristotle's Rhetoric: Philosophical Essays* (Princeton).

Gavrilov, A.K. (1997), 'Techniques of reading in classical antiquity', *Classical Quarterly*, 47: 56–73.

Graeser, A. (ed.) (1987), *Mathematics and Metaphysics in Aristotle* (Bern & Stuttgart).

Haas, F.J. & Mansfeld, J. (eds) (2004), *Aristotle: On Generation and Corruption, Book 1* (Oxford).

Inwood, B. & Mansfeld, J. (eds) (1997), *Assent and Argument: Studies in Cicero's Academic Books* (Leiden).

Kahn, C.H. (2015), Review of Burnyeat & Frede (2015), *Notre Dame Philosophical Review* 2015.11.9.

Nussbaum, M.C. & Rorty, A.O. (eds) (1992), *Essays on Aristotle's De Anima* (Oxford). Reprinted with an appendix (1995).

Perler, D. (ed.) (2001), *Ancient and Medieval Theories of Intentionality* (Leiden/Boston/Cologne).
Rorty, A.O. (ed.) (1980), *Essays on Aristotle's Ethics* (Berkeley & Los Angeles).
Rorty, A.O. (ed.) (1998), *Philosophers on Education: Historical Perspectives* (London & New York).
Rorty, R., Schneewind, J.B. & Skinner, Q. (eds) (1984), *Philosophy in History* (Cambridge).
Ryle, G. (1990), 'Logical atomism in Plato's *Theaetetus*', *Phronesis*, 35: 21–46.
Salles, R. (ed.) (2005), *Metaphysics, Soul, and Ethics in Ancient Thought: Themes from the Work of Richard Sorabji* (Oxford).
Schofield, M. & Nussbaum, M.C. (eds) (1982), *Language and Logos* (Cambridge).
Schofield, M., Burnyeat, M. & Barnes, J. (eds) (1980), *Doubt & Dogmatism: Studies in Hellenistic Epistemology* (Oxford).
Scott, D. (ed.) (2007), *Maieusis: Essays in Ancient Philosophy in Honour of Myles Burnyeat* (Oxford).
Segvic, H. (2009), *From Protagoras to Aristotle* (ed. M. Burnyeat) (Princeton & Oxford).
Shea, C. (2020), 'Memories of Myles Burnyeat', *The Robinson College Record*, 36: 91–2.
Smiley, T. (ed.) (2000), *Mathematics and Necessity: Essays in the History of Philosophy* (*Proceedings of the British Academy*, 103) (Oxford).
Sorabji, R. (1983), *Time, Creation and the Continuum* (London).
Sorabji, R. (2005), 'Intellectual autobiography', in Salles (ed.) (2005), 1–36.
Vlastos, G. (1993), *Socratic Studies* (ed. M. Burnyeat) (Cambridge).
Vlastos, G. (ed.) (1971), *The Philosophy of Socrates* (New York).
Williams, B. (2006), *The Sense of the Past* (ed. M. Burnyeat) (Princeton & Oxford).

Acknowledgements

Main sources used for this memoir, besides Myles Burnyeat's published and unpublished scholarly writings, are his private papers, which contain much autobiographical material (and to which as a literary executor I had access); funeral tributes; obituary notices by Paul Levy, *Daily Telegraph*, 7 October 2019, and Angie Hobbs, *The Guardian*, 8 October 2019; and my own recollections. I am grateful to Margaret Bent and David Sedley for comments and advice on drafts, and to Jonathan Barnes for confirming some details. Richard Fries and Ralph Grillo, friends from Burnyeat's undergraduate days, kindly gave permission to quote from their own reminiscences. The account of his time at Robinson College, Cambridge reproduces material first published in *The Robinson College Record* 36 (2020) 89–90.

Note on the author: Malcolm Schofield is Fellow of St John's College, Cambridge, and Emeritus Professor of Ancient Philosophy in the University of Cambridge; he was elected a Fellow of the British Academy in 1997.

TREVOR DADSON

Trevor John Dadson

7 October 1947 – 28 January 2020

elected Fellow of the British Academy 2008

by

JEREMY LAWRANCE
Fellow of the Academy

Trevor Dadson was a leading expert on the literature and history of the Spanish Golden Age. He is distinguished for his editions and studies of Baroque poets, in particular Bocángel and Salinas, and for broader contributions in bibliography, textual criticism, biography, and the history of books and reading, all based on the discovery and analysis of manuscript, early printed, and archival sources. The latter led to his equally influential work on the local history of Moriscos (forced converts to Christianity after the conquest of Muslim al-Andalus in 1492) in La Mancha up to their expulsion from Spain in 1609.

Biographical Memoirs of Fellows of the British Academy, 20, 75–88
Posted 3 November 2021. © British Academy 2021.

Trevor Dadson, Emeritus Professor of Hispanic Studies at Queen Mary University of London, died suddenly in the early hours of 28 January 2020 in Charlottesville, where he had just begun teaching for a semester as Distinguished Visiting Professor at the University of Virginia. Aged 72, he had taken 'full' retirement in 2017, but that led to no perceptible diminution of activity; in the ensuing two years he had published some fourteen articles and co-edited a volume of essays, as well as an extensive critical edition and two further book chapters still in press.

This reflected the character trait for which he was most renowned among his peers, single-minded determination; but also the unflagging energy and passion of his devotion to his subject, Spanish literature and history. In his entry in *Who's Who* he listed his recreations as 'ski-ing, walking, tennis, reading' (to which one might add playing the piano and a love of music he shared with his son Daniel, a gifted trumpet-player); but these hobbies can have occupied only a small portion of his time. He was a devoted family man, keen on decorating, gardening, and repairs, but even on holiday at the seaside or in the Aragonese Pyrenees the impetus to research never abated; a colleague recalls how he would recount his *après-ski* diversions in Astún (Huesca) ... writing up articles he had 'written in his head' on the slopes.[1] He published almost a page a day for every day of his 48-year career, roughly one book or article every three months; not to mention equally tireless dedication to teaching and—less usual among top-flight scholars—management, not just as Head of School at the University of Birmingham in 1993–97, Vice-Principal for the Humanities and Social Sciences at Queen Mary University of London in 2006–10, and member and then chairman of the UK Higher Education Funding Councils' Research Assessment Exercise panel for Iberian and Latin American Languages in 1992, 1996, and 2001, but also on the editorial boards of various publishers and journals (notably as editor-in-chief of the *Hispanic Research Journal* and, from 2013, Trustee of the Modern Humanities Research Association and founding editor of Legenda's Studies in Hispanic and Lusophone Cultures), as well as President of the Asociación Internacional del Siglo de Oro in 1999–2002, Vice-President of the Asociación Internacional de Hispanistas in 2004–2007 (during which he helped steer the XII Congress back to our shores, at Birmingham in 2005, for the only time since the first at Oxford in 1962), and President of the Association of Hispanists of Great Britain and Ireland in 2011–15 (involving four annual conferences). In all these walks of academic life, and at the many scholarly symposia at home and abroad where he delivered papers or was invited to speak, his presence was familiar and forceful. If Chris Martin is correct in declaring pogonotrophy 'the signature of *gent* embossed on the heavy business card of his own legend', the flamboyant Dadson moustache—of the horseshoe variety, but tending in

[1] Elena Carrera, in a letter to me.

abundance to the walrus, and in defiant sweep to the Pancho Villa—declared that anything worth doing is worth doing 'on a massive scale': the hirsute hallmark of an irrepressible appetite for resolute action.[2]

Born in Tonbridge on 7 October 1947, Trevor took great pride in being a Man of Kent; he grew up in the rural hamlet of Newington on the outskirts of London, surrounded by cherry orchards and hop fields which he would fondly recall harvesting, an idyllic childhood making dens in the woods with his brother Peter and carrying little sister Christina all the way back up the hill from the village on his back.[3] At the age of 11 he won a place at Borden Grammar School in nearby Sittingbourne, where a young Welsh teacher, Mr Davies, fired his lifelong interest in Spanish and his destiny as a 'textbook Englishman' who became a 'virtuoso scholar with Spain in his heart', a fate confirmed by his first visit to the country for a summer course in Jaca at the age of 17: love at first sight.[4] He adopted as his own the school motto *Nitere porro* ('Ever onwards'); after matriculating at the University of Leeds, where he was awarded a first-class degree in Spanish and Portuguese in 1970, he went on to gain a PhD at Emmanuel College, Cambridge in 1974. In Murcia Cathedral on Easter Sunday of 1975 he and María de los Ángeles Gimeno Santacruz, a student of English and German whom he met as a language assistant at Salamanca University two years before, were married. Then, after taking a PGCE at Durham in 1975–1976 and a stint teaching in a Bolton secondary school during which he published two articles on the subject of his thesis, he was appointed in 1978 to a lectureship at Queen's University in Belfast. There he was to remain for twelve years. Despite the tense tribulations of the Troubles, which involved the intervention of the British Army and menacing partition of areas of the city, they were happy and productive: besides the births of two sons, Daniel and Christopher, they saw Dadson's rise from Assistant Lecturer to Head of Department in 1985, Reader in 1986, and Professor of Hispanic Studies in 1988, and the publication of his first four books—a monograph and critical edition springing from his doctoral thesis on the poet Bocángel, and two further editions of Golden Age court poetry—and 27 articles. Nevertheless, when the Chair of Spanish at Birmingham University fell vacant following the retirement of mediaevalist Derek

---

[2] C. Martin, *A Gentleman's Guide to Beard and Moustache Management* (Stroud: The History Press, 2011), Ch. 2 'A Guide to Beard & Moustache Styles', pp. 31–81 (pp. 33, 38).

[3] I am grateful to Christina for these memories , and to Trevor's wife Ángeles for passing them on.

[4] I. Peyró, 'El sabio británico que amaba España' (obituary), *ABC* (Madrid), 2 Febrary 2020, p. 75 <https://ignaciopeyro.es/obituario-de-trevor-dadson-en-abc/> 'un destino tan singular como hermoso: [...] nacido en Kent, llegó a ser un virtuoso del castellano [...]. Un británico de manual, sí, pero con España en el corazón.' In a letter, Trevor's colleague Rosa Vidal too comments that Trevor seemed 'more Spanish than English' in his lack of reserve, openness, and impatience with hierarchy: 'he had no time for the British honour system', she inferred, 'but was extremely proud of his Spanish gong.' Spanish friends all remark that his command of Spanish was exceptional, almost flawless.

Lomax in 1990, Dadson applied and was elected. There he spent fourteen even busier and more productive years, while Ange also taught Spanish in the Language Centre, before finally moving to the chair of Hispanic Studies at Queen Mary University in London's East End in 2004.

The following thirteen years crowned his career. Besides the prominent managerial posts listed above, he published eleven books, three co-edited volumes, and over fifty articles. His achievements were recognised by a Leverhulme Major Research Scholarship in 2012 (his second, the first in 2002), Fellowship of the British Academy in 2008, the award of a Commandership of the Order of Isabel la Católica by King Felipe VI in 2015, and nomination as *Académico correspondiente* in both the Real Academia Española and Real Academia de la Historia (Spanish Royal Academies of language and history) in June and December 2016, a double honour rarely bestowed on a single scholar. Trevor was almost as proud of these distinctions as he was of his childhood award of the Gardening Cup by Newington's Church of England Primary School, or having a street named after him in 2009 in Villarrubia de los Ojos in La Mancha (population 9,800, perhaps 2,500 in 1610) in honour of his *magnum opus* on the municipality's Moriscos. In short, he became one of the best-known scholars in his field, both in Spain and in this country.

The content and character of Dadson's scholarship were underpinned from start to finish by an avowedly positivist, empirical approach. He had no time for literary or cultural theory, of which (despite occasional terms such as 'intertext') he boasted no knowledge and for which he declared a disdain he considered self-explanatory.[5] Not much space was devoted, either, to the niceties of literary critique; even in his work on contemporary Spanish and Portuguese poets and novelists he held fast to the material data of history, biography, sources (classical and Golden Age), and the plain explication of words, images, metre. There can be no doubt he was a genuine lover of poetry, which was the 'authentic matrix' of his academic career from the moment of his first enthusiastic contact with Baroque verse during his undergraduate days at Leeds in the late '60s through the 'inspirational' teaching (as he described it) of eminent scholars Colin Smith and Gareth Davies, and then with Edward M. Wilson at Cambridge, who pointed him in the direction of the obscure Madrid court poet and playwright Gabriel Bocángel y Unzueta (1603–58).[6] On the latter Dadson would continue to publish for

[5] T.J. Dadson, *'Breve esplendor de mal distinta lumbre': estudios sobre poesía española contemporánea* (Sevilla: Renacimiento, 2005), p. 11 'el protagonista es el poema, no el crítico y desde luego no la teoría crítica de moda (de la moda efímera que sea)' ('the subject is the poem, not the critic, and *of course* not fashionable critical theory, of whatever passing fashion it may be', my emphasis).

[6] The phrase 'authentic matrix' is from the editors' 'Introduction' in J. Letrán & I. Torres (eds), *Studies on Spanish Poetry in Honour of Trevor J. Dadson: Entre los Siglos de Oro y el siglo XXI* (*Colección Támesis*, A388; Woodbridge: Tamesis, 2019), pp. 1–13, at p. 9.

the rest of his career, from his first article in 1972 while still a student to one of his latest in 2018,[7] including two lengthy monographs and two even lengthier critical editions—some 3000 pages in all.[8] From Bocángel he was led to the equally little-studied poet and statesman Diego de Silva y Mendoza, count of Salinas, on whom he published almost 2000 pages between 1985 and 2020, with a second volume of his critical edition of the complete works—to judge by the first, a further 1000 pages—still to come. He also wrote five or six literary essays on major Golden Age poets (Garcilaso, Camões, Lope, Góngora) and, as mentioned above, eleven on modern poetry between 1997 and 2011, to the study of which he said he was drawn by attending a conference on Golden Age poetry in the mid-80s at which the presence of some living Spanish poets drew his attention to their often troubled 'dialogue' with their Baroque predecessors (*'Breve esplendor de mal distinta lumbre'*, pp. 9–10).

One thing leads to another. Yet, despite the passion that motivated this impressive output, only a small percentage of it was devoted, as I have said, to what we should call 'poetic' aspects. The vast majority was concerned with textual, bibliographical, and historical matters, and above all with Dadson's deepest and most abiding interest, biography. This in turn led directly to the second 'matrix' of his scholarship, the turbulent history of the Morisco population of New Castile. At the start of his second book on the theme he began by stating that his aim was to 'give voice' to the Moriscos, 'see them as real people, living real lives'.[9] Any reader of his works can be left in no doubt that such microscopic interest in other people's lives, the texture and detail of biographical experience, was the true fuse that drove his research, just as much in literature and the history of books and libraries as in social and political history. All the areas he studied naturally involve wide and complex theoretical debates, and Dadson was never backward in stating outright and undeviating conclusions. Nonetheless, the real focus was not grand theory or the bigger picture but the facts of individual lives; the element of Golden Age love poetry that most fascinated him, for instance, was the

[7] T.J. Dadson, 'Poesías inéditas de Bocángel', *Boletín de la Biblioteca de Menéndez Pelayo*, 48 (1972), 327–57; 'El mecenazgo en el siglo XVII: la familia Bocángel y Unzueta y la casa ducal de Sessa', in G. Laín Corona & R. Santiago Nogales (eds), *Cartografía literaria: en homenaje al profesor José Romera Castillo*, 3 vols (Madrid: Visor, 2018), I, 255–75.

[8] T.J. Dadson, *The Genoese in Spain: Gabriel Bocángel y Unzueta (1603–1658): A Biography* (*Colección Támesis*, A97; London: Tamesis Books, 1983); *La Casa bocangelina: una familia hispano-genovesa en la España del Siglo de Oro* (Anejos de *RILCE*, 7; Pamplona: EUNSA, 1991); (ed.), Gabriel Bocángel, *La lira de las Musas* (*Letras Hispánicas*, 226; Madrid: Cátedra,1985); and (ed.), Gabriel Bocángel y Unzueta, *Obras completas*, pról. L. A. de Cuenca, 2 vols (Madrid: Iberoamericana, 2000).

[9] T.J. Dadson, *Tolerance and Coexistence in Early Modern Spain: Old Christians and Moriscos in the Campo de Calatrava* (*Colección Támesis*, A334; Woodbridge: Tamesis, 2014), p. 1.

poet's love life.[10] His student Javier Letrán has written that what Dadson learned from his supervisor E.M. Wilson was 'scholarly rigour and precision [...] and the incalculable value of trawling original documents in all manner of libraries and archives'.[11] This is entirely true—though Wilson was also an accomplished literary critic—but the image of a dedicated book-worm may evoke a misleadingly dusty notion of the nature of that rigour. For Dadson, archives were first and foremost a source of the lively biographical anecdotes that fired his imagination.

In all he published 18 books (nine monographs, one reissued in an enlarged and revised Spanish translation, and nine critical editions), co-edited seven collections of articles, and wrote some 143 articles, as well as over a hundred reviews and columns for the Spanish and English press.[12] More remarkable than the number of these works is their weight: the books alone comprise almost 9,000 pages, an average of 500 each. As already hinted, this extensive output covers a kaleidoscope not just of topics, but of disciplines; it embraces a full spectrum of the cultural, social, and literary history of Baroque Spain, ranging from textual and critical editions and studies of political and literary figures (Bocángel, Salinas, and his mother the court schemer Ana de Mendoza y de la Cerda, princess of Eboli, the latter in collaboration with New York scholar Helen H. Reed)[13] to bibliography, the history of books, printing, reading, and libraries, and the aforesaid microhistorical examinations of the Moriscos of the Campo de Calatrava (Ciudad Real) from their forced

---

[10] For example, T. J. Dadson, 'La psicología del amor en los sonetos de Filis de Bocángel', in A. Vilanova (ed.), *Actas del X Congreso de la Asociación Internacional de Hispanistas: Barcelona 21–26 de agosto de 1989*, 3 vols (Barcelona: Universidad Central, 1992), I, 863–76; 'Un poeta del amor y los amores de un poeta: Diego de Silva y Mendoza, conde de Salinas (1564–1630)', in F. Cerdán (ed.), *Hommage à Robert Jammes*, 3 vols (Toulouse: Presses Universitaires du Mirail, 1994), I, 299–311; 'El conde de Salinas y Leonor Pimentel: cuando se juntan el amor y la poesía', in J. Andrews & I. Torres (eds), *Spanish Golden Age Poetry in Motion: The Dynamics of Creation and Conversation* (*Colección Támesis*, A340; Woodbridge: Tamesis, 2014), pp. 185–212; 'The Count of Salinas and the Women in his Life', in A.L. Martín & M.C. Quintero (eds), *Perspectives on Early Modern Women in Iberia and the Americas: Studies in Law, Society, Art and Literature in Honor of Anne J. Cruz* (New York: Escribana Books, 2015), pp. 52–71.

[11] J. Letrán, 'Trevor J. Dadson (1947–2020)', *Bulletin of Spanish Studies*, 97:6 (2020), 1051–5 at 1053 (first publ. as 'Trevor J. Dadson, un jinete de luz en la hora oscura', *The Objective*, 8 February 2020 <https://theobjective.com/elsubjetivo/trevor-j-dadson-un-jinete-de-luz-en-la-hora-oscura/>).

[12] The fullest bibliography is Appendix A 'The Publications of Trevor J. Dadson', in Letrán & Torres, *Studies on Spanish Poetry*, pp. 213–26, but they do not list reviews. Three of the books, three co-edited volumes, and 35 articles are in English, two articles in Portuguese; the remainder—75 per cent—in Spanish.

[13] T.J. Dadson & H.H. Reed (eds), *Epistolario e historia documental de Ana de Mendoza y de la Cerda, princesa de Éboli* (Madrid: Iberoamericana, 2013), and H.H. Reed & T.J. Dadson, *La princesa de Éboli, cautiva del rey: vida de Ana de Mendoza y de la Cerda (1540–1592)* (Madrid: Centro de Estudios Europa Hispánica, 2015), as well as five single-authored articles between 1986 and 2016, and one more in press.

conversion after the conquest of Muslim al-Andalus in 1492 up to and beyond the decrees ordering their expulsion from the Spanish empire in 1609–14. Alongside these are also the four collections of essays co-edited with Derek Flitter and eleven articles on 20th-century Spanish poets under Francoism and beyond (six republished, along with two new ones, in *'Breve esplendor de mal distinta lumbre'*); and, with his wife Ange and Birmingham colleague Antony Clarke, a Spanish translation and commentary of the diaries of two 19th-century English women travellers in Spain, Lady Holland and George Eliot.[14]

Despite this breadth, and Dadson's genial claim that his scholarly interests were guided not by design but by the whim of the moment,[15] what strikes one is their single-mindedness. His early articles and books were on the autograph copies, manuscripts, early printed editions, and biographies of Bocángel and Salinas, on both of whom he was still at work at the end of his life. But before long his bibliographical and textual discoveries in these projects led him to consider the momentous Renaissance passage from script to print, and the bearing that the history of early printing had on the diffusion and reception of literature and ideas in that age,[16] and hence its implications for modern critical and editorial practice.[17] This in turn prompted a 600-page

[14] A.H. Clarke & T.J. Dadson (eds), M. de los Á. Gimeno Santacruz (trans.), *La España del siglo XIX vista por dos viajeras inglesas: Elizabeth, Lady Holland (1802–04) y la novelista George Eliot (1867)* (Zaragoza: Institución Fernando el Católico, 2012).

[15] Peyró, 'El sabio británico que amaba España': 'una vida doctoral, según confesión propia, sin más designio que sus inclinaciones'.

[16] For example, T.J. Dadson, 'El autor, la imprenta, y la corrección de pruebas en el siglo XVII', *El Crotalón*, 1 (1984), 1053–68; 'The Dissemination of Poetry in Sixteenth-Century Spain', *Journal of the Institute of Romance Studies*, 8 (2000), 47–56; 'La imprenta manual y los textos poéticos', *Edad de Oro*, 28 (2009), 73–104; *Historia de la impresión de las 'Rimas' de Lupercio y Bartolomé Leonardo de Argensola* (Zaragoza: Institución Fernando el Católico, 2010); 'La difusión de la poesía española impresa en el siglo XVII', *Bulletin hispanique*, 113:1 (2011), 13–42; 'What the Preliminaries of Early Modern Spanish Books Can Tell Us', in G. Sánchez Espinosa (ed.), *Pruebas de imprenta: estudios sobre la cultura editorial del libro en la España moderna y contemporánea* (Madrid: Iberoamericana, 2013), pp. 21–42; '"Poesía que vive en variantes": Antonio Rodríguez-Moñino Revisited', in S. Boyd & T. O'Reilly (eds), *Artifice and Invention in the Spanish Golden Age* (*Studies in Hispanic and Lusophone Cultures*, 3; Abingdon: Legenda, 2014), pp. 54–68; 'La publicación y diseminación de obras de entretenimiento en la España del siglo XVII', in M.J. Pedraza Gracia, Y. Clemente San Román & N. Bas Martín (eds), *Del autor al lector: el comercio y distribución del libro medieval y moderno* (Zaragoza: Universidad, 2017), pp. 69–95; and 'Books, Readers, Readings and Writings in *Don Quixote*', in S. Boyd, T. Darby & T. O'Reilly (eds), *The Art of Cervantes in 'Don Quixote': Critical Essays*, Studies in Hispanic and Lusophone Cultures 27 (Oxford: Legenda, 2019), pp. 11–34.

[17] For example, T.J. Dadson, 'La corrección de pruebas (y un libro de poesía)', in F. Rico (ed.), *Imprenta y crítica textual en el Siglo de Oro* (Valladolid: Centro para la Edición de los Clásicos Españoles, 2000), pp. 97–128; 'La edición de textos poéticos españoles del Siglo de Oro', in J. M. de Bernardo Ares (ed.), *El Hispanismo anglonorteamericano: aportaciones, problemas y perspectivas sobre historia, arte y literatura españolas (siglos XVI–XVIII)*, 2 vols (Córdoba: Cajasur, 2001), II, 1155–70; 'Editar o no editar: ésta es

volume embodying 10 preceding articles on the spread of literacy and reading based on his studies of inventories of private libraries and booksellers' lists,[18] and succeeded by 13 more up to 2016, including fresh overviews and approaches.[19] At the same time the archival sources drew his interest to Bocángel's family and Italian origins, and hence to the community of Genoese bankers and businessmen who played such a prominent role in the economy of the Philippine empire.[20] With the statesman Salinas the ramifications went deeper, extending beyond the poet's noble family to studies of the imperial court, its culture and politics,[21] the administration of Portugal under

[la] cuestión, o cuando el olvido es el mejor regalo para ciertas obras y ciertos autores', in P. Botta (ed.), *Filologia dei testi a stampa (Area iberica)* (Modena: Mucchi, 2005), pp. 335–42; and 'Editing the Poetry of don Diego de Silva y Mendoza, Count of Salinas and Marquis of Alenquer', *Bulletin of Hispanic Studies* (Liverpool), 85:3 (2008), 285–332.

[18] T.J. Dadson, *Libros, lectores y lecturas: estudios sobre bibliotecas particulares españolas del Siglo de Oro* (Madrid: Arco/Libros, 1998).

[19] For example, T.J. Dadson , 'Las bibliotecas particulares en el Siglo de Oro', in V. Infantes, F. Lopez & J.-F. Botrel (eds), *Historia de la edición y de la lectura en España, 1475–1914* (Madrid: Fundación Germán Sánchez Ruipérez, 2003), pp. 123–32; 'Literacy and Education in Early Modern Rural Spain: The Case of Villarrubia de los Ojos', *Bulletin of Spanish Studies*, 81:7–8 (2004), 1011–38.

[20] T.J. Dadson, 'A Genoese Family in Sixteenth-Century Toledo', in C. A. Longhurst (ed.), *A Face Not Turned to the Wall: Essays on Hispanic Themes for Gareth Alban Davies* (Leeds: University of Leeds, 1987), pp. 27–49; 'Pedro Bocangelino: A Genoese Merchant in Sixteenth-Century Toledo', in *La storia dei genovesi*, XI: *Atti del Convegno di studi sui ceti dirigenti nelle istituzioni della Repubblica di Genova, Genova, 29-30-31 maggio–1 giugno 1990* ([Genova: Associazione nobiliare ligure], 1991), pp. 375–400; and see nn. 7–8, above.

[21] T.J. Dadson (ed.), *'Avisos a un cortesano': An Anthology of Seventeenth-Century Moral-Political Poetry* (Exeter: Exeter Hispanic Texts, 1985); (ed.), Alonso de Barros, *Filosofía cortesana (Madrid, 1587)*, 2 vols (Madrid: Comunidad de Madrid, 1987); 'La defensa de Aragón en 1625 y el papel desempeñado en su planificación por Diego de Silva y Mendoza, Conde de Salinas', *Revista de historia Jerónimo Zurita*, 55 (1987), 105–35; 'Un memorial inédito del Conde de Salinas en contra de la política del Conde-Duque de Olivares', *Hispania: Revista española de historia*, 47:165 (1987), 343–48; 'The Duke of Lerma and the Count of Salinas: Politics and Friendship in Early Seventeenth-Century Spain', *European History Quarterly*, 25:1 (1995), 5–38; 'Diego de Silva y Mendoza, Conde de Salinas (1564–1630), y el arte de la supervivencia política', in I. Arellano *et al.* (eds), *Studia aurea. Actas del III Congreso de la AISO (Toulouse, 1993)*, 3 vols (Toulouse: Presses Universitaires du Mirail, 1996), I, 309–17; 'El viejo y el nuevo régimen: los condes de Salinas y Olivares durante la década de 1620', in P. Bolaños Donoso, A. Domínguez Guzmán & M. de los Reyes Peña (eds), *'Geh hin und lerne': Homenaje al profesor Klaus Wagner*, 2 vols (Sevilla: Universidad, 2008), II, 583–99; '"Con haberme vos visto servir, me parece que os he dicho lo que habéis de hacer": la teoría y la práctica de ser noble, según los escritos y la experiencia de Diego de Silva y Mendoza, conde de Salinas', in F. Calvo & G.B. Chicote (eds), *Buenos Aires-Madrid-Buenos Aires: homenaje a Melchora Romanos* (Buenos Aires: Eudeba, 2017), pp. 197–206; '"Um viso-rei que faz trovas". El conde de Salinas, Diego Silva y Mendoza: mecenazgo poético y político entre Madrid y Lisboa', *Atalanta*, 7:1 (2019), 39–68; and with Laura Muñoz Pérez, 'Beyond the Boundaries of Private Spaces: Women and the Spanish Court', *Bulletin of Spanish Studies*, 93:7–8 (2016), 1371–86.

Spanish rule 1580–1640,[22] and relations with England.[23] He also co-edited the papers of a conference held at the Spanish Embassy in London on the tercentenary of the Anglo-Spanish Treaty of Utrecht of 1713 by which Habsburg rule was ended and Gibraltar ceded to the British Crown.[24] This was hosted by his old friend the ambassador and ex-minister Federico Trillo-Figueroa, whom Dadson had taught English as a student language-teacher forty-five years before in Cáceres and given a copy of the works of Shakespeare on which Trillo would write his PhD thesis, published in 1998.

This last example underlines the point: that all these studies, varied as they were, grew from the single seed of his Cambridge days, and from the archival research that he first undertook for his PhD. The latter began with royal and court documents in the national repositories (Madrid, Archivo Histórico Nacional; Archivo General de Simancas) and spread to embrace, from the early 1980s, the Count of Salinas's papers in the extensive archive of his descendants, the dukes of Híjar, deposited in Zaragoza's Archivo Histórico Provincial, and finally local records in the townships of the count's demesnes in New Castile. It was among Salinas's estate papers that he discovered by chance in the late 1990s a bundle of documents about the count's refractory involvement in the expulsion—or rather, three separate expulsions and eventual return—of his 950 or so Morisco tenants in Villarrubia (38 per cent of the population). Struck by the connection with a famous passage in *Don Quixote*, Pt II, Ch. 54 in which Sancho Panza encounters and greets with affection the figure of Ricote, a former Morisco shopkeeper from his Manchegan village making his way back from exile in disguise, he put pen to paper on what he first envisaged as a 20-minute paper, then as a longer article, which soon became five.[25] But the 'problem', as he put it, was the quantity of

[22] T.J. Dadson, 'Conflicting Views of the Last Spanish Viceroy of Portugal (1617–1621): Diego de Silva y Mendoza, Count of Salinas and Marquis of Alenquer', *Portuguese Studies*, 7 (1991), 28–60; 'A Spanish Landowner in Seventeenth-Century Portugal', in T.F. Earle & N. Griffin (eds), *Portuguese, Brazilian, and African Studies: Studies Presented to Clive Willis on his Retirement* (Warminster: Aris & Phillips, 1995), pp. 169–83; 'Portugal, España e Inglaterra en la década de 1620: las maniobras de los condes de Salinas y Gondomar', *Península: Revista de Estudos Ibéricos*, 4 (2007), 23–33.

[23] T.J. Dadson, 'La imagen de España en Inglaterra en los siglos XVI y XVII', in J.M. López de Abiada & A. López Bernasocchi (eds), *Imágenes de España en culturas y literaturas europeas (siglos XVI–XVII)* (Madrid: Verbum, 2004), pp. 127–75; 'Diego de Silva y Mendoza, conde de Salinas, e Inglaterra: una perspectiva desde Madrid y Lisboa', in R. Mª Alabrús *et al.* (eds), *Pasados y presente. Estudios para el profesor Ricardo García Cárcel* (Barcelona: Universitat Autònoma de Barcelona, 2020), pp. 339–51.

[24] T.J. Dadson & J.H. Elliott (eds), *Britain, Spain and the Treaty of Utrecht 1713–2013* (*Studies in Hispanic and Lusophone Cultures*, 8; Abingdon: Legenda, 2014).

[25] T.J. Dadson, 'Literacy and Education in Early Modern Rural Spain'; 'Convivencia y cooperación entre moriscos y cristianos del Campo de Calatrava: de nuevo con Cervantes y Ricote', in P. Civil (ed.), *Siglos dorados. Homenaje a Augustin Redondo*, 2 vols (Madrid: Castalia, 2004), I, 301–14; 'Un Ricote verdadero: el licenciado Alonso Herrador de Villarrubia de los Ojos del Guadiana —morisco que vuelve', in M.L. Lobato López & F. Domínguez Matito (eds), *Memoria de la palabra. Actas del VI Congreso de la Asociación Internacional Siglo de Oro, Burgos-La Rioja 15–19 de julio 2002*, 2 vols (Madrid:

documentation and the fact that, 'as every researcher knows', short works 'inevitably' turn into long ones; and so, like a persistent dog with a juicy bone and unaware, it would seem (he was incapable of irony), of how *un*usual this way of proceeding was, within three years he published his book of 1328 pages (530 of documents) on the Villarrubia expulsions.[26] A second followed in 2014, and a stream of further articles (I count sixteen between 2007 and 2019).

None of this interrupted his continuing work on earlier interests, as we have seen, but it was infused by a new element, absent from the others: a sense of crusade, a desire (as John Elliott wrote in his review of the first book in the columns of the newspaper *El País* on Friday, 21 December 2007) 'not merely to challenge the conventional view' of Christian-Morisco relations, but 'to turn it head-over-heels', or, as Dadson himself put it in the title of a later talk given in Tangier, to 'rewrite history'.[27] He was, of course, in the first place excited by 'the hidden side of the matter, [...] since it dealt with real people with names, jobs, and families, individuals I would soon get to know personally, as if they were still alive' (*Tolerance and Coexistence*, p. 7); if his edition of the complete works of Bocángel had carried the dedication 'For my family',[28] this one was inscribed 'For Villarrubia, and the descendants of the Moriscos who still live there' (p. [v]). But he soon became convinced that his findings about how individual Moriscos of Villarrubia contested the original decree of expulsion in the royal courts and councils, and how, with the not so tacit connivance of their neighbours, they not only contrived to return but also after decades of legal petitioning recovered much of their original property and standing, proved on one hand that the 'Black Legend' of Spaniards as a nation driven by savage fanaticism and interconfessional hatred, subject to the heavy oppressions of Inquisition and state, was a lie; and on the other, that the view of Arabist scholars that many Muslims forcibly converted to Christianity

---

Iberoamericana, 2004), I, 601–12; 'Cervantes y los moriscos de la Mancha', in N. Martínez de Castilla Muñoz & R. Gil Benumeya Grimau (eds), *De Cervantes y el Islam* (Madrid: Sociedad Estatal de Conmemoraciones Culturales, 2006), pp. 135–50; 'Official Rhetoric versus Local Reality: Propaganda and the Expulsion of the Moriscos', in R.J. Pym (ed.), *Rhetoric and Reality in Early Modern Spain* (*Colección Támesis*, A227; London: Tamesis, 2006), pp. 1–24.

[26] T.J. Dadson, *Los moriscos de Villarrubia de los Ojos (siglos XV–XVIII). Historia de una minoría asim- ilada, expulsada y reintegrada* (Madrid: Iberoamericana, 2007), p. 11 'Prefacio al lector'. 'En un prin- cipio, este libro iba a ser una ponencia de unos veinte minutos [...] pasé de preparar una ponencia corta a pensar en un artículo más extenso. [...] Todo investigador sabe que lo que empieza siendo un trabajo corto inevitablemente se convierte en algo más sustancioso [...]. El problema [...] fue la cantidad de documentación.'

[27] T.J. Dadson, 'Reescribiendo la historia', in A. Tahiri & F.-Z. Aitoutouhen Temsamani (eds), المؤتمر الدولي أعقاب الأندلسيين المهجرين والمنصرين في المغرب وإسبانيا والبرتغال / *Los descendientes andalusíes 'moriscos' en Marruecos, España y Portugal* ([Tanger]: Fundación al-Idrisi Hispano-Marroquí, 2014), pp. 71–86.

[28] Bocángel, *Obras completas*, I, p. [5] 'Para mi familia'.

after the conquest of Granada secretly retained their Islamic faith and allegiance was equally a lie. 'Assimilation, coexistence, and tolerance between Old and New Christians in early modern Spain were not a fiction or a fantasy', he stated, for the reality was that 'thousands of ordinary individuals [...] lived in peace and harmony side by side for generations'; and this 'rebalance' of the picture would 'hopefully' place 16th- and 17th-century Spain in 'a new, infinitely richer, and more rewarding light' (*Tolerance and Coexistence*, pp. 11–12).

Historians have pointed out that such claims represent an unwarrantable projection of the evidence from Villarrubia onto the whole empire; to challenge the Black Legend is always a praiseworthy endeavour, but to deny that 17th-century absolutism was brutal—the expulsion of the Moriscos, which in interviews for the local press Dadson did not demur to call 'ethnic cleansing',[29] being a classic case in point—or that 17th-century society (not just Spanish) was cruel and intolerant, too exaggerated a response. That he had in certain respects been carried away was evident in a hasty *TLS* review of L.P. Harvey's *Muslims in Spain, 1500 to 1614*, with the give-away title 'Moors of La Mancha' (possibly not his, but Harvey's book is not about La Mancha),[30] in which he called its account of the persistence of crypto-Islam a 'reductive view', choosing to sideline the Arabic and *aljamiado* evidence on the tortuous grounds that, had such crypto-Muslims existed, it would have provided 'a perfectly coherent justification for the expulsion of the Moriscos between 1609 and 1614'—an argument that provoked a condign response quietly suggesting that perhaps he might learn to read Arabic before venturing such generalisations.[31] Yet, if his 'extreme focus' could sometimes lead him to overstate his case, Dadson always remained capable of debate and friendly engagement with scholars with different views; typically, he would set matters right in this case by co-editing a fine posthumous volume of Harvey's essays on Islam in Spain up to 1614 for Legenda's Studies in Hispanic and Lusophone Cultures.[32] Meanwhile, his basic contention, first adumbrated in a brief essay by Domínguez

---

[29] 'La expulsión de los moriscos fue una limpieza étnica', *Noticias de Almería*, Wednesday, 23 April 2014 <https://www.noticiasdealmeria.com/noticia/18652/>.

[30] *Times Literary Supplement*, 5367 (Friday, 10 February 2006), 28.

[31] L.P. Harvey, 'Letters to the Editor: Fatwas in early modern Spain', *Times Literary Supplement*, 5369 (Friday, 24 February 2006), 15.

[32] L.P. Harvey, *Islamic Culture in Spain to 1614: Essays and Studies*, ed. T.J. Dadson & N. Martínez de Castilla Muñoz (*Studies in Hispanic and Lusophone Cultures*, 17; Cambridge: Legenda, 2019); the author had been a predecessor in the Chair of Spanish at Queen Mary (1967–73). The phrase 'extreme focus' is from Rosa Vidal, who goes on to speak of Dadson's 'immense time and respect for other scholars working from different angles', including hiring herself (an expert on ethno-religious controversy in medieval Spain) at Queen Mary.

Ortiz,[33] then tossed to and fro by critics of the Cervantine passage on Ricote,[34] has provoked fruitful research, a significant measure of assent and corroboration, and fuller and more accurate comprehension of the facts about the expulsion. As for his massive history of Villarrubia's Moriscos, it seems doubtful that another word remains to be said.

This account of Dadson's academic trajectory has sought to explain and put flesh on the bones of my opening remarks about his energy and devotion to his subject. In quantity and quality his research was notable: firmly anchored on the bedrock of unrivalled familiarity with and indefatigable exploration of original sources and archives, but also flashing out vigorous opinions and ideas, and expressed with uncompromising trenchancy and conviction. His critical editions are, to the extent that such a term is meaningful, definitive; the poets and texts he chose are not, perhaps, in the first rank of literary fame and only likely to attract the attention of experts, but it is difficult to imagine anyone in the foreseeable future doing a more complete or reliable job of discovering and editing their poems. One may say the same of his huge compilations of documents on Bocángel, Salinas, the princess of Eboli, and Morisco Villarrubia; they are, in the Thucydidean phrase, κτήματα ἐς αἰεί, *faits acquis à la science* for any expert who wants them. Where I think his works will find a broader, more continuous readership is in the fields of cultural studies: first on court society, where he shed new light on various facets of the complex historical reality such as the role of patronage or the meaning of 'friendship' in court politics, the place of libraries in shaping the self-image of nobility, or of poetry in the mentality of 'courtliness'; and second on the history of books and reading and the strangely anomalous and complicated chronology of the substitution of manuscript by print culture, on which he not only proposed correctives to older views that poetry persisted in being transmitted chiefly in oral or handwritten form, or speculated on the reasons for the scarcity of what we should consider works of literary entertainment in wills and inventories when we know they were a mainstay of the commercial book-trade, but also discussed the implications of the history of their transmission for our critical reading of the texts.

Dadson's personality fully mirrored the brisk energy and character of his scholarship; it was, as many who have written about him recall, a remarkable mixture of life-affirming joviality and steely determination, liveliness and erudition. He did not

---

[33] Antonio Domínguez Ortiz, 'Felipe IV y los moriscos', *Miscelánea de estudios árabes y hebraicos. Sección Árabe-Islam*, 8 (1959), 55–65.

[34] The Cervantine connexion was, as mentioned above, the link that perhaps fired the 'crusade'. Elena Carrera observes that 'Trevor not only loved teaching Cervantes to undergraduates', but 'made a point' of drawing the attention of colleagues from other disciplines to him at seminars. But of his six published essays on him, five were on Moriscos, the other on 'Books, Readers, Readings and Writings in *Don Quixote*' (2019, n. 16 above).

willingly brook procrastination or opposition, but was unfailingly optimistic and positive, dedicated to the success and greater good of the institutions he served, and a staunch friend and mentor. Letrán describes his teaching as 'inspirational [...], quite frankly irresistible', a 'unique recipe' of enthusiasm, knowledge, and intelligence 'blended with just the right amount of sensitivity and good humour', recalling that on one occasion the class, 'even to Trevor's surprise, spontaneously erupted into thunderous applause'.[35] He and Isabel Torres also praise him as a 'loyal' supervisor of postgraduate students, a fact borne out by the number of them who have gone on to academic careers of their own.[36] Colleagues likewise recall his supportiveness and sense of fun.[37] It was characteristic that in the acknowledgements of his English book on the Moriscos he gave pride of place to María Gabriela López Menchi for translating into English 'a number of chapters originally written in Spanish' (we might be forgiven for supposing he could have done this himself) and 'my son Christopher, who read through and edited the whole text for me, improving substantially the English'.[38] He enjoyed company, conviviality, and a laugh; his presence and contributions, in all the many walks of academic life in which he participated, will be much missed.

Acknowledgements
I gratefully thank Trevor Dadson's wife Ángeles Gimeno Santacruz and former colleagues Drs Elena Carrera and Rosa Vidal Doval of Queen Mary University of London for correspondence in which they generously provided the invaluable recollections that are cited in this memoir.

Note on the author: Jeremy Lawrance is Emeritus Professor of Golden Age Studies, University of Nottingham, and Honorary Research Fellow, Faculty of Medieval and Modern Languages, University of Oxford; he was elected a Fellow of the British Academy in 2011.

[35] Letrán, 'Trevor J. Dadson', 1052.
[36] Letrán & Torres, *Studies on Spanish Poetry*, p. 13.
[37] Rosa Vidal notes that he 'always had time to read my work, no matter how pressing my deadline or busy his schedule', and the 'great fun' they had teaching together.
[38] Dadson, *Tolerance and Coexistence*, p. ix. Chris, after degrees in English and Latin-American Studies, is a poet, author of *Twenty-First Century Renderings* (London: Austin Macauley, 2019).

RON JOHNSTON

Ronald John Johnston

30 March 1941 – 29 May 2020

elected Fellow of the British Academy 1989

by

CHARLES PATTIE

PETER TAYLOR
Fellow of the Academy

KELVYN JONES
Fellow of the Academy

Ron Johnston was one of the leading human geographers of his generation, a remarkably energetic, prolific and intellectually curious scholar. He was an early advocate of quantitative geography who took a keen interest in the intellectual development of his subject. He was particularly known for his major contributions in urban geography, political geography (especially the analysis of electoral systems), his passionate use of empirical evidence to evaluate theory and policy, the intellectual history of human geography and the promotion of the discipline.

Biographical Memoirs of Fellows of the British Academy, 20, 89–109
Posted 15 December 2021. © British Academy 2021.

Ron Johnston was one of the leading human geographers of his generation. A remarkably energetic, prolific and intellectually curious scholar, over the course of his long research career he authored 40 books (several of which went into multiple editions, and were widely translated), more than 800 refereed papers, and many more book chapters, reports, and popular pieces. He also edited more than 40 other books. Ron was an early advocate of quantitative geography who took a keen interest in the intellectual development of his subject. In an age of increasingly narrow academic specialism, his interests were wide-ranging, including research on such diverse subjects as world trade patterns, church bell ringing (outside his academic life, he was a well-known and accomplished campanologist, and he claimed his best-selling book was his 1990 *An Atlas of Bells*, written with Graham Allsopp, John Baldwin and Helen Turner) and home advantage in professional football. But he was particularly known for his major contributions in urban geography, political geography (especially the analysis of electoral systems), his passionate use of empirical evidence to evaluate theory and policy, the intellectual history of human geography and the promotion of the discipline.

Born in 1941, Ron grew up in Chiseldon, a Wiltshire village just outside Swindon, where his parents ran the local Post Office. For much of his early childhood, he was raised by his mother and grandparents: his father, serving in the British army, had been captured in the fall of Singapore and spent the remainder of the war as a Japanese PoW. One of Ron's earliest memories was of being introduced to him by his mother in late 1945. Appropriately for a future geographer, Ron retained a sense of identity with his Wiltshire roots throughout his life. This manifested itself in a variety of ways, not least his remarkably inventive ability to find ways of using Swindon as an illustrative example in talks and conversations on almost any subject, and in his life-long (and often unrewarded) support for Swindon Town FC.

Success in the 11+ examination took him to the Commonweal Grammar School in Swindon, where he was a good pupil, even though (much to his amusement in later life) his final pre-sixth form school report declared him to be 'Cheerful but irresponsible'. Maps proved an early fascination, and geography was his favourite school subject. Encouraged by his Geography master, he applied and was accepted to read the subject at Manchester University, beginning his BA there in 1959. While there, he met his future wife, Rita Brennan, a fellow student: they married in 1963.

Ron made his first tentative entry in the academic world in 1962. After graduating in the Department of Geography at Manchester University he attended the Geography Section of the British Association Conference held that year in the city and started his research MA in the department in the autumn. This timing is very important for Ron's subsequent career: geography was in the throes of its 'quantitative revolution'. To begin a research career in these circumstances was very exciting and yet quite limiting. Ron was to exploit the latter quite brilliantly later in his career.

British Geography departments in the 1950s and through much of the 1960s taught a very traditional form of geography based upon the concept of the region, where knowledge about a place, both physical and human, could be synthetically assembled. This regional geography depended on research in systematic geography (specialist knowledge ranging from geomorphology to economic geography). In practice the latter work was conducted largely without thought for subsequent synthesis but it retained an inferior persona. The quantitative revolution that emerged from North America in the late 1950s swept away this way of thinking. Named for bringing statistical methods into research, it was much more than the introduction of new numerical analysis. It produced a 'New Geography', fundamentally re-orientating the discipline from idiographic description of regions to a nomothetic study of spatial organisation.

But the diffusion of these ideas was relatively slow to begin with and this was to create a generational divide. Ron's MA dissertation was on rural towns and their service areas. He was able to build his ideas on previous empirical research in systematic geography but as soon as he started reading the latest literature he found central place theory, a generic way of explaining service patterns. This theory had not been mentioned in his undergraduate course. So here was Ron doing MA research in a completely different way to his erstwhile teachers, now his academic advisors but without relevant knowledge. This is not necessarily a difficult situation, but it is an unusual one: new young geographers reinventing their discipline!

The quantitative revolution came with a very compelling narrative: it was saving Geography as a university discipline by moving it from an art to a science. The old regional geography was not up to the modern task of creating real scientific knowledge and had to be dispensed with. Geography now had a research frontier where journal papers built upon one another, pushing knowledge of spatial organisation incessantly forward. This was the exciting bit – participating in an intellectual revolution. Hence Ron's PhD research (at Monash University) was on the spatial structure of a city, Melbourne, using the theory and methods of factorial ecology, a very popular approach in the 1960s.. Again signalling a key break with the past: regional geography had had little or nothing to say about cities. This was the academic world in which Ron established himself as an up-and-coming and, certainly by the early 1980s, a world-renowned geographer. His new-found reputation was based upon a string of conceptually sound and empirically robust books covering a wide range of human geography: *Urban Residential Patterns* (1971), *Spatial Structures* (1973), *The World Trade System* (1976), *Geography and Inequality* (1977, with Brian Coates and Paul Knox), *Political, Electoral and Spatial Systems* (1979), *Geography of Elections* (1979, with Peter Taylor), and *City and Society* (1980).

Being part of a revolution provides a cloak of certainty over research: quite simply the new way is the right and proper way to do research. But inevitably a new generation comes along to spike this assuredness. Hence in the 1970s the spatial quantitative approach itself came under critical scrutiny and was found to be wanting. Attacked from radical and behavioural perspectives, the now not so new geography was revealed to be positivism, a very narrow view of science. Stripped of its autonomous knowledge assumption with its grand theory-making, Geography like all other knowledge was recognised as a human product of an imperfect world. Goodbye certainty.

Ron's response to this career-threatening development was twofold. First, and quite creatively, he used Thomas Kuhn's theory of scientific revolutions to re-interpret Geography's quantitative revolution. Periods of certainty about the way forward in academic disciplines were paradigms, and revolutions in thought were paradigm shifts from one scientific consensus to another. He used this in his *Geography and Geographers* (1979) to provide a guide to the changes in the way Geography had been practised since 1945. This book is probably Ron's most influential, going into seven thoroughly revised editions (the latter ones with James Sidaway), making Ron the discipline's great chronicler. This was combined with other discipline-defining contributions such as the *Dictionary of Human Geography* (1981, various co-editors with fifth edition, 2009: amazingly, Ron wrote in the order of 740 of the dictionary entries over that period). The *Dictionary* was augmented by an enduring concern for the nature and vitality of his discipline represented by his editing *The Future of Geography* (1985) and *A Century of British Geography* (a British Academy Centenary Monograph, 2003, with Michael Williams). Ron is undoubtedly the most influential geographer of his times.

Second, Ron was much more than a guide to the discipline. His use of Kuhn was a masterstroke: this put the quantitative revolution in its place without totally dismissing it. This enabled him and others to continue doing relevant research by adhering to the specific strong point of the quantitative-spatial approach, its rigorous empirical methods and way of thinking. This inherited toolset was a means to produce relevant and practical research, to continue a vibrant research career. In Ron's case this involved a focusing of the range of his research interests to largely two important public policy matters: elections and their organisation, and inequality and segregation. In both cases his researches had direct inputs to policy-making and practice in Britain. Another outstanding contribution: he showed Geography to be useful outside the academy.

These shifts in Ron's research focus roughly coincided with moves in his academic career between universities. If his Manchester MA and his Monash PhD had fostered his interest in the new approaches, he grew increasingly dissatisfied with some of the work in which he was then engaged. Discussing some of his early work 20 years later, he felt he had done 'lots of little empirical pieces, few of them containing more than a simple analysis of a small data set on a trivial hypothesis'.[1] A move to New Zealand in 1967 to take up a lectureship in Geography at the University of Canterbury (then one of the leading departments in Australia and New Zealand) brought him into the company of a group of congenial and collegial – and research-oriented – colleagues. There, he deepened his interests in theoretical as well as methodological approaches to research and added to his rapidly growing corpus of published work. Promotion came quickly: in 1968, he was made a Senior Lecturer and by 1973 had become a Reader.

Some of the work Ron began at the University of Canterbury was to inform his empirical research for much of the rest of his career. For instance, an encounter with Kenneth Cox's 1969 paper on the neighbourhood effect in voting (which provided a theoretical explanation for why voters might be influenced by the views of fellow residents in their local area, producing communities which tend to vote together) interested and troubled him.[2] Initially sceptical, he set out to disprove Cox's theory empirically. But his analysis confirmed the theory's predictions – sparking his career-long research interest in electoral systems and voting behaviour.

The more radical approaches entering the discipline in the early 1970s also intrigued Ron and seemed to offer a firmer and more wide-reaching theoretical and explanatory footing for his work than the approaches he had encountered up to that point. David Harvey's seminal *Social Justice and the City* (1973) was a particular influence, and when Ron moved back to the UK in 1974 to take up a Chair in Geography at the University of Sheffield, it formed the basis of a new course he taught (titled 'Spatial systems and society' after the then head of department objected to the original title of 'Social justice': Ron taught what he intended regardless). That new, more theoretically informed, approach underpinned much of his subsequent research and writing – not least in *City and Society* (1980, 2nd edition 1984), *The American Urban System* (1982), and *Geography and the State* (1982).

For a period in the late 1970s and early 1980s, Ron combined his existing research on urban social geography and electoral geography with work on the political geography of public policy, researching the geography of government spending and resource allocation in Britain and the USA. Sometimes patterns of resource alloca- tion followed patterns of need: sometimes they were informed more by calculations of potential political advantage for the government or for individual politicians – the politics of the pork barrel. Much of this work is summarised in *Geography and*

---

[1] R.J. Johnston, 'A foundling floundering in World Three', in M. Billinge, D. Gregory & R. Martin (eds), *Recollections of a Revolution: Geography as a Spatial Science* (London: Macmillan, 1984), p. 43.
[2] K. Cox, 'The voting decision in a spatial context', *Progress in Human Geography*, 1 (1969), 31–118.

Inequality, Political, Electoral and Spatial Systems and *The Geography of Federal Spending in the United States of America* (1980). The complex mosaic of local government in the USA also proved a fascination, not least in terms of how the incorporation of municipal areas could be used to define and redefine local government jurisdictions in order to control and segregate populations. This formed the subject of his 1984 book *Residential Segregation, the State and Constitutional Conflict in American Urban Areas.*

It was another Sheffield undergraduate course, on the history of human geography, that spurred Ron's interests in the development of the subject and in its philosophical underpinnings. *Geography and Geographers* emerged from his thinking and preparation for this course, its Kuhnian structure in part an attempt to systematise and explain to students how academic debates moved forward.

Human geography was becoming increasingly diverse in the late 1970s and 1980s as interest in social theory grew within the discipline (a process that has continued apace since then). The relatively simple story of a discipline moving from a descriptive 'regional' focus to a more analytical 'quantitative' one, and then on to a more 'radical' account of social processes, was no longer sufficient. Researchers increasingly followed a range of different paths. Quantitative, behavioural and radical geographers were joined by others drawing inspiration from following humanist, phenomenological, feminist, post-structuralist and other traditions. *Philosophy and Human Geography* (1983, 2nd edition 1986), which also emerged from Ron's 'history of human geography' course, was an attempt to explain to undergraduates how different theoretical and philosophical 'traditions' within geography saw the world, and the consequences that had for the nature of geographical research.

Spurred on by the 'social turn' in the discipline, Ron sought (notably in books such as *On Human Geography* (1986) and *A Question of Place* (1991)) to clarify his own philosophical position throughout the 1980s and early 1990s – both for himself and for others. Anthony Giddens' structuration theory and versions of Roy Bhaskar's critical realism seemed to offer ways forward. People's choices and decisions might be affected by various structural constraints and possibilities. But they were not entirely determined by them either – agency remained important (and could in its turn help reshape and reconfigure the structural conditions). Social structures were not immutable. This was quite a substantial step away from the search for fixed 'universal laws' of society which had driven the early quantitative revolution. But (importantly for Ron) these approaches avoided a drift into a post-modern vision in which only competing interpretations of the world were possible and in which there was no way to adjudicate between rival interpretations. They held on to a notion of a real world which could be researched, and which could be apprehended and understood, even if knowledge remained partial and contingent.

Importantly, too, they stressed the importance of geographical and temporal context in human affairs. Whereas more economistic accounts tended to see people as isolated rational decision-makers, structuration and critical realism (and related approaches) emphasised the situated and relational aspects of life. People were influenced not only by their personal circumstances and views, but also by what was going on around them – in their families, their communities, their workplaces, and so on. Place (as Ron would often say) matters.

That concern with the role of geographical context had underpinned Ron's work on electoral geography since the late 1960s. From the late 1970s on, this became the main focus of his empirical research (bringing with it a growing reputation in international political science to complement his standing in human geography). Three main areas dominated that work: voter behaviour; party campaigning; and electoral redistricting. His 2006 book, *Putting Voters in their Place* (written with Charles Pattie) summarises the main themes of his electoral work after 1980.

As discussed earlier, the neighbourhood effect was an initial impetus for work on vote choice. In the 1960s and 1970s, influential theories suggested that class formed a particularly salient cleavage in the electorate. Working class manual workers, it was hypothesised, would vote predominantly for parties of the left while middle-class white-collar workers and professionals would lean mainly to parties of the right. Ron's analyses of constituency voting trends in British elections during the 1970s and 1980s showed that not only did the geography of the vote in Great Britain follow the geography of social class (the more working class the area, the higher the Labour vote share; the more middle class, the higher the Conservatives' support), but that this class cleavage was not spatially uniform. In particularly working-class constituencies, Labour did even better than might be expected given the national class cleavage. And (*mutatis mutandis*) the same was true for Conservative support in predominantly middle-class constituencies.[3] These patterns were consistent with the predictions of Cox's neighbourhood effect theory. As William Miller (who noticed the same patterns) noted, those who lived together (in the same areas) seemed to talk together about politics – and undecided voters were more likely to be won over to the locally dominant political party than to its rivals.[4]

But changes in politics and society from the mid–1970s onwards meant that social class was becoming a weaker predictor of individual party support. In part, this reflected a generational shift, captured in the famous *Affluent Worker* study in the late

---

[3] R.J. Johnston, 'Contagion in neighbourhoods: a note on problems of modelling and analysis', *Environment and Planning A*, 8 (1976), 581–6; R.J. Johnston, 'The neighbourhood effect won't go away: observations on the electoral geography of England in the light of Dunleavy's critique', *Geoforum*, 14 (1983), 161–8.

[4] W.L. Miller, *Electoral Dynamics in Britain Since 1918* (London: Macmillan, 1977), p. 65.

1960s, which interviewed workers in a car factory in southern England.[5] Most workers leant towards Labour, as class voting theory would suggest. But their motivations differed. Older workers, who had grown up during the Great Depression, tended to support the party based on their class identity. Younger workers in the factory, who had come of age in a period of post-war affluence, also leant towards Labour, but for instrumental reasons. Their support was conditional on the party delivering better conditions. That mattered, as it opened up the possibility they might shift their support to another party, should Labour prove unable to offer continued improvement in living standards. Ten years later, Mrs Thatcher's Conservatives made just such an appeal, aiming their message that 'Labour isn't working' at (among others) aspirational skilled working-class voters.

But the appeal of the Thatcher message was not likely to be spatially even. It had greater resonance in more prosperous parts of the country than in less prosperous areas. And this was exacerbated as regional economic divides began to widen rapidly in the 1980s. That implied a potential for substantial geographical variations in class voting, which (if members of the same class increasingly diverged politically, depending on where they lived) might help account for the weakening effect of class as a predictor of vote at the national scale. But how to show it? Survey data could not pick up fine-grained geographical variations, as national surveys did not have sufficiently large local samples to do so. And while aggregate constituency level analyses could draw on election results and on constituency class profiles from Census data, they could not provide constituency-level measures of class cleavages (such data is not gathered in the UK – or, indeed, in any other democracy). Some other method was needed if analysts were to estimate how the class cleavage varied from place to place.

Conversations with his Sheffield colleague Alan Hay introduced Ron to a possible solution: entropy maximising, an estimation method developed by Alan Wilson of Leeds University. Basically, the approach used known constraints – the national class cleavage at a given election, drawn from national survey data, the election results in each constituency, and (from the Census) the class profile in each constituency – to calculate small 'c' conservative estimates of the class cleavage in each constituency. The results were summarised in *The Geography of English Politics* (1983). The national class cleavage had indeed broken down – but not in the same ways everywhere. In Scotland, Wales and the industrial North of England, working class voters still cleaved to Labour – but so too did increasing numbers of middle-class voters (particularly those working in the public sector professions). In much of southern and suburban

[5] J. Goldthorpe, D. Lockwood, F. Bechhofer & J. Platt, *The Affluent Worker: Political Attitudes and Behaviour* (Cambridge: Cambridge University Press, 1968).

England, meanwhile, things were moving in the other direction, as skilled manual workers increasingly switched their support to the Conservatives.

The insight which helped explain those regional shifts in class voting came from emerging political science research on economic and valence voting. On numerous issues (often termed valence issues), most voters want the same outcomes (prosperity, security and so on), but are often not strongly ideologically tied to particular means of achieving these ends: what matters for them is effective government performance. They punish governments that fail to deliver adequately on these valence issues by voting against them, while rewarding governments that seem to succeed with their support. In the (now infamous) words of Bill Clinton's 1992 Presidential campaign, 'It's the economy, stupid': governments that preside over rising prosperity are more likely to be re-elected, and those that preside over declining prosperity risk being kicked out of office. Ron realised that voters' perspectives on governments' performance would likely be influenced not only by national economic trends but also by what was happening in their localities and regions. And, given the very different economic trajectories of different parts of the UK through the 1980s – deindustrialisation and decline in the industrial heartlands, rapid growth in the service sector south – perceptions of government success or failure might well be very different in different parts of the country. Analyses of elections from the 1980s onwards (originally summarised in his 1988 book, *A Nation Dividing?*, written with Charles Pattie and Graham Allsopp, but further expanded in his studies of subsequent UK elections over the next 30 year) proved the value of this insight.

A clear implication is that particular geographies of electoral support, even if relatively long-lasting, are not immutable – as Ron chronicled in his analyses of the UK's electoral geography throughout the remainder of his career. By the 2010s, his work was analysing declining Labour support in previous 'traditional' heartland areas like urban Scotland (where the SNP has eclipsed Labour) and the industrial towns on northern England – presaging the so-called 'collapse' of the so-called 'Red Wall' of traditional Labour constituencies in the urban Midlands and north of England in 2019, when many of these seats went from Labour to Conservative control.

Increasingly, Ron's electoral work drew not only on ecological data (analysing constituency trends), but also on survey evidence, often combining the two to put individual voters in their local contexts (as in innovative work he conducted on so-called 'bespoke neighbourhoods', linking survey respondents to very local census information).[6] This allowed him to explore neighbourhood effects in greater detail,

[6] e.g. R.J. Johnston, K. Jones, R. Sarker, C. Propper, S. Burgess & A. Bolster, 'Party support and the neighbourhood effect: spatial polarisation of the British electorate, 1991–2001', *Political Geography*, 23 (2004), 367–402.

showing that many voters were indeed influenced by the views of those around them. People whose friends and (especially) families and fellow housemates leaned towards one party were themselves more likely to switch their votes to that party than were those who either did not discuss politics with their peers or whose networks were politically diverse – confirming a key mechanism behind the neighbourhood effect.[7]

Another aspect of Ron's psephological work examined party election campaigning, particularly at the constituency grassroots. When he originally embarked on this work, in the late 1970s and early 1980s, the accepted wisdom in British political science was that the advent of national televised campaigns in the late 1950s had put paid to local campaigning as an effective tool of electioneering. Voters, it was argued, experienced the campaign increasingly through the national media and elections turned on nationally uniform swings. Constituency campaigns, in this view, did little to affect the outcome of elections: at best, they provided a harmless though inconsequential outlet for local party activists' energies, giving them something to do while the serious business of the campaign took place elsewhere. Using information every UK election candidate must declare on how much they spend on their election campaigns as a proxy for campaign effort, Ron challenged this accepted wisdom. In fact, as he showed in publications like *Money and Votes* (1987) and *Money and Electoral Politics* (2014, with Charles Pattie), the harder candidates campaign, other things being equal, the more votes they receive. The effect – generally stronger for challengers than for incumbent candidates and parties in a seat – is not huge. But it is large enough to make the difference between winning and losing in closely fought constituencies. Not surprisingly (and as Ron was also able to show), the major political parties focus their constituency campaigns accordingly, putting more effort into their battles in marginal seats than in seats where they were likely to either win comfortably or stood little realistic chance of winning. When he began work in this area, Ron was one of only a very small number of researchers challenging the orthodoxy that local campaigns did not matter. But that changed as his work made a major contribution to overturning that orthodoxy. Studies of local campaigning are now mainstream in UK political science, and his work on the subject is seen as pioneering.

The third major strand in Ron's electoral work focused on perhaps the most overtly geographical aspect of electoral systems – the definition and occasional redrawing of the constituency map. Party support is not spread uniformly in most countries: parties tend to be stronger in some areas and communities, weaker in others. So how the map of electoral districts interacts with the geography of party support can have an

---

[7] See e.g. R.J. Johnston, K. Jones, C. Propper, R. Sarker, S. Burgess & A. Bolster, 'A missing level in the analysis of British voting behaviour: the household as context as shown by analyses of a 1992–1997 longitudinal survey', *Electoral Studies*, 24 (2005), 201–25.

important impact on the outcome of elections, particularly (though not exclusively) in plurality electoral systems like 'first past the post', used for Westminster elections. Even if no voters change their choices, shifting the boundaries of constituencies can change the election outcome. And there is very unlikely to be just one obvious 'solution' to how a constituency map should be redrawn. Electoral redistricting is an example of the well-known MAUP – the modifiable areal unit problem. In any given redistricting, there is a potentially huge number of alternative ways of redrawing the electoral boundaries, all consistent with legal constraints that might be set on the process (such as requirements on how equal electorates should be). Each different map of districts can create a different election result. In countries where politicians are in control of drawing the map of electoral districts, unscrupulous individuals and governments can exploit this to ensure they increase their chances of winning seats and reduce their rivals' chances – a process popularly known as 'gerrymandering'.

But even where (as in the UK) the responsibility for designing the constituency map is the responsibility of a scrupulously independent and non-partisan body (in the UK, the job is undertaken periodically by Boundary Commissions for England, Scotland, Wales and Northern Ireland) and the political implications of drawing that map in one way rather than another are not allowed to affect the process, redistricting still has political consequences. As a country's population geography changes over time (population grows in some areas relative to others), existing electoral districts become increasingly uneven in size. Voters living in districts with smaller populations have more electoral influence than their peers in more populous districts (which can lead to malapportionment – if one party is especially popular in the less populated districts and its rival is more popular in the more populated ones, the former party gains an advantage). Hence there is a need to review the boundaries of the electoral districts periodically, in order to equalise (as far as possible) their electorates and to counter the effects of population change on parliamentary representation.

However this is done, it is liable to be electorally consequential. In the UK, for instance, population change over much of the post-war period meant that over time northern urban and inner-city constituencies (where Labour tended to dominate) lost voters relative to southern and suburban (and generally more Conservative) areas. As a constituency map aged, therefore, there was a tendency for Labour to gain an advantage relative to the Conservatives, as it took fewer votes to win in a Labour than in a Conservative seat. Periodic boundary reviews, conducted by the independent Boundary Commissions, redressed the balance by allocating more seats to areas gaining population, and fewer to those losing population. So the Conservatives tended to look forward to boundary reviews while Labour tended to fear them.

Understanding the operation and effects of boundary reviews is therefore important. Electoral redistricting was a recurring theme in Ron's research for 40 years, from the early 1980s till his death in 2020, and was the central subject of his final, posthumously published, book, *Representative Democracy?* (2021, with Charles Pattie and David Rossiter). An initial focus was on redistricting as an example of the MAUP. Working as his research assistant in the early 1980s, David Rossiter wrote a computer program which could identify all possible sets of constituencies consistent with some simple but plausible constraints. They were able to show, for instance, that there were over 15,000 different ways of distributing Sheffield's 29 local government wards into the six constituencies the city was entitled to, all of which would have produced coherent seats with electorates within around ±8% of the city average. While most solutions would have resulted in five seats for Labour and one for the Conservatives, this was not true in all cases – and some would have seen the city return three MPs from each party!

When the Boundary Commissions began their Third Periodic Review in 1980, Ron and David Rossiter presented evidence to the public inquiry into the proposals for Sheffield (their alternative configuration of seats was accepted). This led to an approach from figures in the Labour party who (fearing they would lose seats as a result of the review) were planning a judicial challenge to the Boundary Commissions' new seats for the 1983 election. They appeared as expert witnesses in the resulting case. Labour lost. But their reputations as experts on boundary reviews was firmly established among academic election analysts, practising politicians, and members of the Boundary Commissions.

Ron analysed and commented on every UK boundary review between the Third Periodic Review and his death. His 1999 book *The Boundary Commissions* (with David Rossiter and Charles Pattie) is arguably the standard work on the subject. It provided both a detailed history of approaches to redrawing the UK's constituency map from their earliest origins, and a close analysis of the Fourth Periodic Review, which took place in the early 1990s, creating the seats used in the 1997 General Election. All aspects of the review process were analysed: the politics behind the legal frameworks guiding redistricting; the work of the Boundary Commissioners and their teams; the public inquiry process (through which members of the public and political parties attempt to have some influence on the outcome); and the electoral consequences of the revised boundaries which emerge from the process. This connected with his work on electoral systems more generally, and in particular on electoral bias – the extent to which an electoral system systematically favours one party rather than another and how that is affected by boundary reviews (the subject of 2001's *From Votes to Seats*, written with Charles Pattie, David Rossiter and Danny Dorling, and 2021's *Representative Democracy?*).

This was not only an academic, but also an applied interest. Ron served for two years as a Deputy Electoral Commissioner for the Boundary Committee for England (overseeing redrawing local government and ward boundaries). He was a trustee of the McDougall Trust (a charity promoting the public understanding of electoral democracy) and a member of the Law Commission's Advisory Group on Electoral Law Reform. And he advised the Boundary Commission for Bermuda on redistricting when a new electoral system was proposed there in the early 2000s. When the Conservative party began to consider legislating to revise the rules governing UK boundary reviews prior to the 2010 election, Ron was one of the experts the party called on.[8] Several aspects of the 2011 legislation (which still – with minor amendments – governs the process in the UK) can be traced to his work and advice. But he also identified potential flaws in the new legislation, and gave frequent evidence to parliamentary committees and to other bodies during (and after) the passage of the Bill on ways in which some of the more disruptive aspects of the new rules could be mitigated – effort recognised by the Political Studies Association when it named him its Political Communicator of the Year in 2011. He was respected and trusted by all sides of the debate, and was invited to give evidence again in early 2020, when new legislation slightly amending the rules was due to go through parliament. Sadly, he died shortly before he was able to do so.

Ever energetic and curious, Ron was not just an intellectual historian and psephologist par excellence, for he also found time to pursue other research interests into his later career. He developed an interest in the politics of the environment and of global crisis, and in particular the challenges created by the need to find solutions to global problems in a world in which states were key actors. How would it be possible to co-ordinate global efforts to deal with environmental damage on a global scale? What was to prevent some states 'free riding' on the efforts of others, to the potentially disastrous detriment of all – a dilemma famously captured in Garrett Hardin's concept of the tragedy of the commons. As ever, a string of books and papers emerged – notably *Environmental Problems* (1989, 2nd edition 1996), and the edited collections *A World in Crisis?* (1986, with Peter Taylor; 2nd edition 1989) and *Geographies of Global Change* (1995, with Peter Taylor and Michael Watts: 2nd edition 2002). It was in this area that Ron taught a final year course in the undergraduate programme at Bristol, seeing it as fulfilling a need for students who had chosen to undertake a combined programme of human and physical specialisms.

In the new millennium, Ron renewed his interest in residential segregation, a research area which had formed an important part of his early career (in his second

---

[8] In 2010 Ron co-authored two British Academy policy reports on electoral issues: Simon Hix, Ron Johnston & Iain McLean with Angela Cummine, *Choosing an Electoral System*; Michel Balinski, Ron Johnston, Iain McLean & Peyton Young with Angela Cummine, *Drawing a New Constituency Map for the United Kingdom*. See also Ron Johnston & Iain McLean, 'Individual electoral registration and the future of representative democracy', *British Academy Review*, 19 (2012), 58–60.

book, published in 1971, *Urban Residential Patterns*, he had examined in detail the work that had been done on the differentiation experienced by urban sub areas). With Jim Forrest and Michael Poulsen (friends and colleagues from his Antipodean days), he worked on discrimination against migrant groups and the development of ethnic and racial segregation in cities in Australia, the USA, the UK and elsewhere. Joined by colleagues in Bristol (including Kelvyn Jones, David Manley, Richard Harris and Simon Burgess), he extended that to look at the effects of residential segregation on segregation in schools and on educational performance. This work was in part concerned with the development of new quantitative techniques to assess the changing degree of segregation and to do so at multiple scales simultaneously.[9] This brought a range of new insights including overturning the long-held 'stylized fact' that the greatest segregation was to be found at the smallest scale.[10] This research was also used to challenge political statements arguing against Trevor Phillips (a former head of the Commission for Racial Equality) that the UK is 'sleep walking to segregation', finding that ethnic residential segregation in London for example is decreasing, and they disputed that Muslim ghettoes are developing in British cities, and that Australian suburbs are being 'swamped' by Asians and Muslims. They also deployed this methodology to assess the degree of electoral segregation in the form of polarisation in the USA, finding that presidential elections were increasingly ones of local landslides and ever-increasing spatial sorting at multiple scales, with potential deleterious effects on civic engagement.[11]

Ron delighted in getting his hands dirty with detailed empirical analysis. Much of this was quantitative and given the nature of his undergraduate degree was largely self-taught. He openly acknowledged that he had learnt a lot by having to teach techniques to others, and his 1978 *Multivariate Statistical Analysis in Geography: A Primer on the General Linear Model* is, judged by the number of citations, one of the more influential of his books, being reprinted multiple times. At the start of his career, he had to write his own programs (in FORTRAN) to undertake the analyses he wanted, and he remained a wizard at using *SPSS (Statistical Package for the Social Sciences)*. Data preparation and initial analysis was not something delegated to the junior member of the team (indeed there often was not a junior member of the team) and he

[9] e.g. K. Jones, D. Manley, R.J. Johnston & D. Owen, 'Modelling residential segregation as unevenness and clustering: A multilevel modelling approach incorporating spatial dependence and tackling the MAUP', *Environment and Planning B: Urban Analytics and City Science*, 23 (2018), 367–402.

[10] D. Manley, K. Jones & R.J. Johnston, 'Multiscale segregation: multilevel modelling of dissimilarity – challenging the stylized fact that segregation is greater the finer the spatial scale', *Professional Geographer*, 71 (2019), 566–78.

[11] R.J. Johnston, D. Manley, K. Jones & R. Ryne, 'The geographical polarization of the American electorate: a country of increasing electoral landslides?', *GeoJournal*, 85 (2020), 187–204.

delighted in sharing what he had found. We have already covered some of his quantitative outputs in urban and political geography, but he would be stimulated by what he came across in everyday life and therefore made all sorts of telling contributions in all sorts of areas. To take a single example, the Minister of State for Schools had commissioned research to compare whether GCSE results (usually taken at 16) were as good as AS-level results (taken usually at 17) as a predictor of whether students would go on to achieve a 2.1 or above at university, finding that degree performance can be predicted to a similar level of accuracy based on GSCE grades alone. Using a Freedom of Information Request and dogged persistence, he obtained the exact same data on 88,022 students and the re-analysis found missing data, sample bias, poor research design and that one in five students could have their chances to fulfil their potential on a degree course damaged.[12] He was passionate that quantitative methods should be widely taught in geography degree programmes as this would allow students to become better active citizens and that they should be a vital part of any critical geography.[13]

Ron's extraordinary research productivity would have more than filled most normal careers. But somehow he found time to engage energetically in an immense amount of the 'good citizen' work on which academia depends, but which is rarely adequately acknowledged (and which, in these research assessment obsessed times, can even be discouraged). Increasingly from the mid–1970s on, he took on a remarkable range of academic leadership roles while maintaining his prolific research activities. The list of committees he sat on (and often chaired) is dizzyingly long – and Ron was almost invariably a very active and involved participant. Some of that work was aimed at supporting the wider research community of which he was so active a member. Within academic geography, for instance, he played an active role in learned societies in New Zealand (where he was a member of the Council of the New Zealand Geographical Society between 1968 and 1974, during which time he also edited the Society's journal, *New Zealand Geographer*) and the UK (he was first elected as a Councillor of the Institute of British Geographers in 1977). Actively involved in the running of the IBG, he served as its Honorary Secretary (1982–1985), Vice President (1988–90) and President (1990–91), and at various times chaired the Institute's study

[12] R.J. Johnston, D. Manley, K. Jones, R. Harris & A. Hoare, 'University admissions and the prediction of degree performance: an analysis in the light of changes to the English schools' examination system', *Higher Education Quarterly*, 70 (2016), 24–42. Two associated blogs are illuminating and well capture Ron's distinctive 'voice'. https://blogs.lse.ac.uk/politicsandpolicy/statistically-flawed-evidence-on-the-relationship-between-school-and-degree-performance/; https://blogs.lse.ac.uk/impactofsocialsciences/2014/07/30/replicating-government-commissioned-research/

[13] R.J. Johnston, R. Harris, K. Jones, D. Manley, C.E. Sable & W.W. Wang, 'One step forward but two steps back to the proper appreciation of spatial science', *Dialogues in Human Geography* 4 (2014), 59–69. A much-expanded text is to be found at https://www.researchgate.net/publication/261062153

Groups for Urban Geography, Quantitative Geography and for the History and Philosophy of Geography. He also served as Chair of the College of Academicians for the UK's Academy of the Learned Societies in the Social Sciences, and was for many years a member of grants boards and peer review colleges for the Social Science Research Council and Economic and Social Research Council. In the early Research Assessment Exercises (the precursor to today's Research Excellence Framework), Ron was an assessor on the Geography panel, a task for which he was perfectly suited given his extensive knowledge of the breadth of human geography. Between 1976 and 1986, he served on the Joint Matriculation Board, representing Geography in discussions over A-level examinations and syllabi in England. In the late 1980s and early 1990s, he was a member of the Council for National Academic Awards, the body then charged with validating the degrees awarded by English Polytechnics.

A co-editor of the leading journals *Progress in Human Geography* (from 1979 till 2006) and *Environment and Planning A* (1979–2004), Ron served on a number of other journal editorial boards (including *Political Geography Quarterly*, *Electoral Studies*, the *Journal of Elections, Public Opinion and Parties*, *Urban Geography*, and the *Journal of Geography in Higher Education*). Unlike some senior (and not so senior) colleagues, he was also a very frequent referee for a remarkably wide range of other journals. Though requests to review papers were very numerous, he rarely turned them down. A beneficiary of others' peer reviewing efforts, he saw this as a key part of academic work and was often scornful of those who felt they were too busy or important to respond to requests to review but still expected their own work to be reviewed to a high standard. This, he felt, was another tragedy of the commons in the making, and one which potentially undermined the integrity of academic research. He was decidedly not a free-rider, invariably and promptly returning thorough, thoughtful and insightful reviews. He was consistently a *Top Peer Reviewer* as recognised by the *Web of Science*.[14]

Ron was also generous with his time and input. Colleagues and students who asked for advice on their work, their careers, their lives (and there were many) were not turned away. No matter how busy he was, he made time to provide extensive and constructive feedback when his advice was sought: remarkably, this more often than not was sent within a day or two. Over the course of his career, he acted as an external examiner on around 56 occasions (14 outside the UK), and was in demand as an external assessor for other departments and universities (a task he undertook on around 71 occasions, half of which were for institutions outside the UK). He under-took a very sizeable and often unseen workload of assessment for appointments, promotions, fellowships, research grants, prizes and departmental reviews. He never

---

[14] https://publons.com/researcher/496437/ron-johnston/

based his judgements on reputation alone, reading the material and 'outputs' widely before coming to a balanced conclusion.

For much of the 1980s and early 1990s, Ron took on increasingly senior academic management roles. Over the course of his career, he sat on (and often chaired) just under 100 different university committees and sub-committees. A member of the university Senate from his arrival in Sheffield in 1974 till his departure in 1992, he served as Head of Department for Geography in the early 1980s, before becoming a member of the University's Academic Development Committee (the main planning body for the university at the time) from 1982 till 1992 (acting as its chair for much of that time). The 1980s were difficult years for UK higher education in general and for the University of Sheffield. Resources were scarce and pressure was on to do more with less. Opportunities for new investment were few and far between as resources stagnated or even declined. As chair of ADC during such a challenging period, Ron was involved in often difficult discussions with colleagues around the university as budgets were cut and departments restructured. Ron approached this work with patience and humanity, gaining the respect of colleagues throughout the institution – but it was a stressful and difficult time.

From ADC, Ron became the university's Pro Vice Chancellor for Academic Affairs (1989–92), effectively the deputy to the Vice Chancellor. This came with added responsibilities for designing and overseeing the university's strategic plan and of navigating the institution's way out of the cash-strapped 1980s into a renewed phase of expansion. In doing so, he played an important part in making Sheffield a centre of research excellence.

The next obvious move was to become a Vice Chancellor, and in 1992 Ron left Sheffield to take on that role at the University of Essex. The new post brought new opportunities, but also new challenges. While he liked the institution and made many friends there, university administration was becoming increasingly burdensome and frustrating. As the senior manager and the public face of their institutions, Vice Chancellors carry considerable responsibility, but are often more constrained than is generally understood. Inevitably his research output (though still remarkable by normal standards) suffered, to his chagrin. At the same time, the 'diplomatic' aspects of being a Vice Chancellor (representing the institution in the wider world) grew. Increasingly, the strain took its toll. In 1995 he made the difficult decision to step down as VC, taking early retirement from the post.

On appointment to Essex, and with an eye to life after his academic career, Ron and Rita had bought a flat in the Close of Salisbury Cathedral. Having left Essex, they moved there permanently, taking him back to his Wiltshire roots. This was a happy move, with the added bonus of allowing him to joke about being a neighbour of former Prime Minister Edward Heath, who also lived in the Close.

'Retirement' proved a very short-lived experience. Freed from his responsibilities at Essex, Ron was quickly offered and accepted a Chair in Geography at the University of Bristol, home of one of the most important Geography departments in the world. Though he had kept his scholarly career alive throughout the years of senior university management, this brought him back almost full-time to the research work he so enjoyed. He responded with typical energy and enthusiasm, building new research partnerships and friendships. Bristol provided a very congenial and collegial academic home for the remainder of his life (he remained on the staff until his death). The quantitative human geographers and their postgraduates met weekly and he was always there, presenting, critiquing and supporting the work of the group.

Never the tidiest of people and something of an academic hoarder (old books and offprints were rarely discarded, drafts of papers and piles of computer output from projects conducted years before were retained), Ron's office in the Bristol Geography Department was a remarkable sight – and something of a health and safety hazard. A large, high-ceilinged room, it was crammed. Innumerable books stood two-deep on the specially reinforced floor-to-ceiling shelving (and more books were laid on top of those that had been shelved). Every other surface in the room – floors, tables, chairs, filing cabinet tops – was covered in teetering piles of papers, offprints, printouts and notes, often several feet in height. In the middle of the chaos sat Ron, hammering away on his computer keyboard, answering emails, analysing data, writing papers, calling friends and colleagues around the world. He was indefatigable; and he could rapidly put his hands on what you wanted amidst the apparent chaos.

Ron's academic and professional reputation brought a number of prestigious awards. Over the course of his career, he received several of the top prizes available for academic geography. He was awarded the Royal Geographical Society's Murchison Award in 1985 for services to political geography, and the same Society's Victoria Medal in 1990 for his 'contribution to human geography'. He was likewise honoured by the Association of American Geographers (AAG) awarded in 1991 for his 'out-standing contribution to human, political and economic geography and for his work on the history and nature of geographical thought'. Almost 20 years later, in 2010, he also received a Lifetime Achievement Award from the AAG; a very rare accolade for a non USA-based geographer. And in 1999, he was the tenth recipient of the Prix Vautrin Lud, the most prestigious international accolade for an academic geographer and often described as Geography's Nobel Prize. His contributions were also valued outside the disciple, twice winning prizes from the *Market Research Society* for 'Innovation in Research Methodology' (2006) and 'Best paper published' in the society's journal (2019), as well as the previously mentioned Politics/Political Studies Communicator of the Year in 2011,

Ron was awarded honorary doctorates by four universities. Essex made him a Doctor of the University in 1996 and Monash awarded him an LLD in 1999. The Universities of Sheffield and Bath awarded him honorary DLitts in 2002 and 2005 respectively. In 2011, he was appointed an Officer of the Order of the British Empire (OBE) for services to scholarship.

A founding Academician of the UK's Academy of Social Sciences, Ron was elected a Fellow of the British Academy in 1999. Typically, he threw himself into the activities of both organisations. To take just one example, for over a decade he edited the British Academy's *Biographical Memoirs of Fellows*, as well as contributing memoirs for deceased fellow Geography FBAs.[15]

Throughout it all, Ron continued to research and write with undiminished energy and insight. In the last weeks of his life, he was discussing future research plans with colleagues, drafting new papers, completing what turned out to be his final book – and preparing to get involved once again in the public and parliamentary debate around changing the rules for parliamentary boundary reviews. His sudden and unexpected death came as a huge shock to his family and his many friends.

Undoubtedly one of the outstanding figures in modern academic geography, Ron was a formidable scholar, highly esteemed and respected by the many who encountered and benefited from his work. He not only contributed importantly to the many specialist fields in which he worked but he also helped shape how geographers think of their subject and how it has developed. No mean achievements.

But Ron was also a remarkably human (and humane) colleague. Lacking in pomposity, he wore his considerable distinction lightly. A passionate, kindly and warm man, he was generous with his time and his ideas, particularly to younger colleagues, many of whom benefited from his support, mentoring and advice. This was invariably offered with a remarkably light touch, making the recipient feel an equal, and generally leavened with a hefty dose of humour. He was a very convivial (and sought-out) companion at academic meetings and conferences. His penchant for *soto voce* asides, jokes and puns made sitting near him in seminars and committees a risky business if one wanted to maintain a straight face: laughter was rarely far away. He was also remarkable for his willingness to learn from, and to acknowledge his debts to, others, at whatever stage in their careers. And he was a loyal, loved and dependable friend to very many, maintaining close contacts and active, long-running collaborations with many colleagues and former students from all stages of his career. After his unexpected death, many tributes (both public and private) commented not only on his academic achievements and contributions, but also on the loss of a close and valued friend.

---

[15] Ron served on the British Academy's Publications Committee 2005–10.

This memoir has focused largely on Ron's academic career and achievements. But it would not be complete without acknowledging the absolutely central place his family occupied in his life. His marriage to Rita was long, happy and the bedrock to his adult life. He took immense pride in her achievements (prior to her retirement, she held university posts in adult education at Sheffield and Bath) and in those of his children, Chris (now a logistics expert and a company vice-president for Sodexo) and Lucy (a Professor of Psychology and Pro Vice-Chancellor at Murdoch University in Perth, Australia). He is survived by Rita, Chris and Lucy and by his grandchildren and great-grandchildren.

Note on the authors: Charles Pattie is Professor of Geography at the University of Sheffield. Peter Taylor is Director of the Globalization and World Cities (GaWC) research network, Emeritus Professor at the Department of Geography and Environmental Sciences, Northumbria University, and Emeritus Professor at the Department of Geography, Loughborough University; he was elected a Fellow of the British Academy in 2004. Kelvyn Jones is Professor of Human Quantitative Geography at the University of Bristol; he was elected a Fellow of the British Academy in 2016.

JOHN COLES

John Morton Coles

25 March 1930 – 14 October 2020

elected Fellow of the British Academy 1978

by

ANTHONY HARDING
Fellow of the Academy

John Coles was an archaeologist who managed to encompass a large number of fields in his academic life, becoming influential in all of them. While his most lasting achievement is perhaps in what has become known as wetland archaeology, in earlier phases of his career he made a lasting impression on the study of Scottish prehistory, he wrote standard textbooks on field archaeology, the Palaeolithic and the Bronze Age, and he was a pioneer in the study of experimental archaeology. An interest which endured from the early part of his career into his later years was the study of rock art, particularly that in Scandinavia, where frequent study trips to Sweden became an important part of his life.

Biographical Memoirs of Fellows of the British Academy, 20, 111–137
Posted 7 February 2022. © British Academy 2022.

John Morton Coles[1] was born in Woodstock, Ontario, the son of Alice (née Brown) and Jack (John) Coles. His grandfather Edward, always known as EJ, came from Somerset, where the family were farmers. Both of EJ's parents died young, leaving seven children; EJ emigrated to Canada and eventually established a department store in Woodstock, becoming a pillar of the local community. His son Jack, John's father, set up a real estate, insurance and investment firm, for which the young John Coles worked after university. He studied at Victoria University, which is federated with the University of Toronto, graduating in 1952. He was a talented tennis player and represented the university in tournaments; this skill was one which he maintained after his move to Scotland, when he won the Scottish men's singles title in 1957 and the Scottish Tennis Cup in 1959. He also learnt the trumpet and played in the High School band and at university, something which came in handy later on when he was invited to blow on the horns of Bronze Age Ireland.

After graduating he started work for the family firm but soon found this was not to his liking. As he described in his memoir, 'I found myself … working in an office in a small town, and doing things that were of little interest to me, buying and selling'.[2] As a natural 'doer' he found sitting in an office stifling and the work boring. In his holidays he came to Europe and made extensive tours of Britain and the Atlantic seaboard and visited a range of historical and archaeological sites. In 1955 he stopped off in Cambridge on the way home and met Professor Grahame Clark FBA. Clark encouraged him to come to read for the Diploma in Prehistoric Archaeology, which he did over the following two years, attached to Fitzwilliam House, though staying in a flat in town as Fitzwilliam in those days had no college buildings (and only became a full College in 1966).

John has described how he began his studies with no real knowledge or understanding of archaeology, but learnt on the hoof very quickly. His account of the course of study at Cambridge in the 1950s, and the staff who taught it, sheds fascinating – if not always complimentary – light on a famous Department and on well-known scholars (Clark himself, Charles McBurney, Miles Burkitt, and Glyn Daniel). Learning prehistoric archaeology at that time was mostly a question of learning typology, particularly of flint tools, and not of the techniques of field archaeology, in which none of the teachers was very skilled. (This is in spite of the fact that Clark's famous excavation at the Mesolithic site of Star Carr near Scarborough was long regarded as ground-breaking in its approach,

---

[1] A Festschrift for John Coles was published in 1999: *Experiment and Design. Archaeological Studies in Honour of John Coles*, ed. A.F. Harding (Oxford, 1999); a bibliography of his publications up to 1998 appears on pp. 194–8. Through the 2000s Coles continued to publish, mainly on the rock art of Scandinavia (see p. 131). He also edited a number of volumes in this period, contributing articles of his own. Because of the large volume of Coles's output (the 1999 bibliography lists 235 items), this memoir concentrates on the main phases of his career, and his main archaeological interests by topic, rather than attempting to include consideration of everything he wrote.

[2] John Coles, *Yesterday's Man. An Archaeological Life 1955–1980* (Wetland Archaeological Research Project, 2019), 1.

especially in the use of biological information to supplement the inorganic remains dominated by flintwork.) Later, John wrote a concise and authoritative account of field techniques, which remains valuable, the result of his years of fieldwork in Scotland and, subsequently, Somerset (see below).[3]

John concentrated on Palaeolithic archaeology during his Cambridge student years, at the insistence of Grahame Clark. This gave him the thorough grounding in the sites and artefacts of the period, or periods, that enabled him later to write his textbook on the Palaeolithic.[4] His reading and travels had already made him particularly interested in the cave paintings of France and Spain. An interest in prehistoric art became an enthusiasm that lasted throughout his career.

During this time John also went on his first excavation, at Hoxne in Suffolk, where McBurney was keen to investigate a site that was famous through the late 18th-century observations of John Frere, one of the pivotal moments in the recognition of the antiquity of ancient flint implements (soon to be recognised as Palaeolithic handaxes). This was a short-lived project, but John subsequently dug at Wandlebury hillfort near Cambridge (site of the supposed hill figure studied by T. Lethbridge), and – more significant – at the Upper Palaeolithic site of Arcy-sur-Cure in the Yonne *département*. These were the beginnings of a long career in field archaeology.

Scotland

At the end of his Cambridge studies, he toyed with the idea of doing doctoral study on the painted caves of France, but following a meeting and correspondence with Stuart Piggott FBA, in 1957 he decided to move to Edinburgh. He had wanted to study the Picts, but Piggott persuaded him that the Late Bronze Age metalwork of Scotland needed work, so John threw himself into the topic with a vigour which came to characterise all that he undertook. In his memoir he described amusingly how he got access to museum objects in apparently unopenable glass cases, in sometimes dusty museums the length and breadth of Scotland. But he did get access, to large numbers of bronze objects, and their study began his academic career. His first published papers were on some of the bronzes he studied; one, on swan's-neck sunflower pins, necessitated perusal of a wide range of continental material, an early indicator of the thoroughness with which he pursued the topics that interested him.[5]

[3] John Coles, *Field Archaeology in Britain* (London, 1972).
[4] J.M. Coles & E.S. Higgs, *The Archaeology of Early Man* (London, 1969).
[5] J.M. Coles, 'Scottish swan's-neck sunflower pins', *Proc. Soc. Antiqs Scotland*, 92 (1958–9), 1–9.

He later said that the study of bronzes was not 'the most exciting subject I have ever encountered', but having started it he persevered with it, and typically his paper on the Late Bronze Age metalwork of Scotland appeared in the *Proceedings of the Society of Antiquaries of Scotland* in the volume dated 1959–60 (actually appearing in 1962).[6] Not many students can claim not only to have completed their PhDs so swiftly (he actually had to resubmit it, because Edinburgh University required a minimum of two years doctoral study), but also to have submitted them for publication by the end of their study period.

This lengthy paper, essentially a slightly abbreviated version of John's PhD thesis, is a workmanlike account of its subject matter. It starts with a consideration of the Middle Bronze Age background, in terms of both settlement and metalwork. This picture was then supplemented by the arrival of the bronze sword, one of the most characteristic types of the Late Bronze Age. John related the Scottish finds to the wider British picture and to potential continental influences. One of the find types that obviously interested him particularly, and which was to play a part in his later work, was the shield, with splendid examples from Yetholm and Beith. He discusses axes, spearheads, knives, cauldrons and buckets, pins (notably 'sunflower pins', the subject of the paper mentioned above), gold and bronze bracelets, lockrings, dress fasteners, moulds and hoards (with consideration of the possible motives for hoard deposition). Particular attention was paid to the 'Covesea bracelets', named after the eponymous find at the Sculptor's Cave in Morayshire, with their parallels across Britain and the North European plain. These types are then summarised in terms of chronological phases between the 10th and 5th centuries BC (nowadays modified somewhat; subsequent refining of Bronze Age chronology built on such beginnings). A series of distribution maps was followed by an exhaustive listing of the objects.

It is easy to see why John found this type of study less enthralling than the subjects to which he subsequently turned his attention. The work clearly began with the task of assembling all the material, reading whatever had been published on British and continental bronzework, and creating lists and maps. This type of study, while essential and valuable, was alien to his mercurial nature and offered little scope for the lighter touch, at least in terms of publication.

Nevertheless, John was not finished with Scottish metalwork. The Late Bronze Age paper was followed by ones on the Middle Bronze Age[7] and the Early Bronze Age;[8] these appeared after he had left Scotland, but he had collected most of the material during his museum trips in the 1950s. The Middle Bronze Age paper followed a slightly different path from the Late Bronze Age one; each type was first considered individually, followed

---

[6] J.M. Coles, 'Scottish Late Bronze Age metalwork: typology, distributions and chronology', *Proc. Soc. Antiqs Scotland*, 93 (1959–60), 16–134.

[7] J.M. Coles, 'Scottish Middle Bronze Age metalwork', *Proc. Soc. Antiqs Scotland*, 97 (1963–64), 82–156.

[8] J.M. Coles, 'Scottish Early Bronze Age metalwork', *Proc. Soc. Antiqs Scotland*, 101 (1968–9), 1–110 (appeared 1971).

by a consideration of 'industrial traditions' (essentially chronology). Lists of objects completed the survey. The Early Bronze paper is different again, the result of the fact that the evidence base is different from that for later periods, notably the number of grave finds rather than simply isolated bronzes or hoard finds. The date and context of the earliest metalwork in Scotland had already been a matter of debate, as it was (and is) in England too; not only that, but by the time John moved to consider the earliest metalworking period, metal analysis had become a major topic of interest. While some work had been done on British metals before, it was the work of the Stuttgart programme, Studien zu den Anfängen der Metallurgie, that stimulated new research.[9] These analyses had identified particular metal groups, which appeared to suggest that specific metal types were widely distributed across Europe. This might have made metallurgical sense but it seemed to fly in the face of the archaeological evidence, as a consequence of which a pair of Dutch scholars adopted a different way of looking at the analytical data, which resulted in much more acceptable archaeological groupings.[10] John followed this method, identifying five 'clusters' (so called to distinguish them from the 'groups' used by the Stuttgart team and other scholars), of which four were firm and clear, the fifth (E) more ambiguous.[11] Although the method was only applied to the Scottish material, it appeared to provide believable archaeological results, whereas the Stuttgart method implied that a particular metal type – and thus presumably the metal from a particular metal source – was distributed widely across Europe.

Brendan O'Connor and Alison Sheridan have written about how studies of Scottish metalwork have progressed since John's articles were published. O'Connor was able to use the metalwork groupings established by more recent work, for instance those identified by Peter Northover and now accepted as standard,[12] or the work on copper mines in Ireland by William O'Brien (particularly the identification of the copper used for Beaker metallurgy emanating from the mine at Ross Island, Killarney),[13] and did not discuss how these correlate with John's Clusters A–E. Sheridan was able to point to a number of very significant new finds from Scotland, both in bronze and in gold. Inevitably much has been

---

[9] The first two volumes to appear were S. Junghans, E. Sangmeister, & M. Schroder, *Metallanalysen kupferzeitlicher und frühbronzezeitlicher Bodenfunde aus Europa* (Berlin, 1960); and *Kupfer und Bronze in der frühen Metallzeit Europas* (Berlin, 1968), both of which Coles took into account.

[10] H.T. Waterbolk & J.J. Butler, 'Comments on the use of metallurgical analysis in prehistoric studies', *Helinium*, 5 (1965), 227–251.

[11] A second paper on the topic was published at the same time: J.M. Coles, 'Metal analyses and the Scottish Early Bronze Age', *Proc. Prehistoric Soc.*, 35 (1969), 330–344.

[12] J.P. Northover, 'The analysis of Welsh Bronze Age metalwork', Appendix to H.N. Savory, Guide Catalogue of the Bronze Age collections, National Museum of Wales (Cardiff, 1980); 'The exploration of the long-distance movement of bronze in Bronze and Early Iron Age Europe', *Bull. Inst. Archaeol. Univ. London*, 19 (1982), 45–72.

[13] W. O'Brien, *Ross Island: mining, metal and society in early Ireland* (Galway, 2004).

written, and much found, since the 1950s and 60s, but the basic work that John did remains the starting point for all later investigations.

John was also active in fieldwork during his time in Scotland, and this continued after he moved to Cambridge in 1960 to take up a post as Assistant Lecturer. After taking part in various small excavations, mostly led by other people in the 1950s, he undertook various projects of his own. One of the most significant was the excavation in 1964, together with Derek Simpson, of a round barrow at Pitnacree, Perthshire.[14] This site, one of a considerable number in the Tay valley east of Loch Tay, was expected to belong to the Bronze Age, but on excavation turned out to produce Early Neolithic pottery and a Neolithic radiocarbon date. The turf mound covered an 'enclosure', in reality a roughly rectangular space framed by large stones with large pits at either end, thought to have contained massive timbers; a number of cremations had been placed on the old land surface at the western end. The pits were compared with similar arrangements in Neolithic long barrows from southern England; the real surprise was that such things should have been found so far north on the British mainland, something that has been confirmed by other projects since.

In 1969 he took over a major project at the fortuitously named site of Morton in Fife, just south of the Firth of Tay, an important Mesolithic site, excavating there in 1969 and 1970.[15] He had already investigated the Mesolithic of south-west Scotland in a paper published in a local county journal.[16] Previous work at Morton had recovered flints but the general character of the site was unclear, and some of the material had gone missing. John systematically collected and analysed the stonework, showing where the densest distribution of material lay, demonstrating the existence of occupation areas, some with lines of stakes suggesting windbreaks; hearths; and a midden containing large quantities of bone, shell and other debris. All this suggested that occupation was of a temporary nature, repeated many times, with no more than ten persons present at any one time.

The Morton assemblage was the largest quantity of stonework known from any Scottish mainland site. The analysis showed that a large proportion of the material was retouched or utilised, nearly 20 per cent, much higher than at other Mesolithic sites in Britain. This suggested to John that material was being treated in antiquity in a much more careful manner than at equivalent sites in England. In cultural terms, the Mesolithic industries of southern Scotland were not sufficiently well known or differentiated for the Morton assemblage to be attributed to a particular type or phase, with the occupation of the site probably

---

[14] J.M. Coles & D.D.A. Simpson, 'The excavation of a Neolithic round barrow at Pitnacree, Perthshire, Scotland', *Proc. Prehistoric Soc.*, 31 (1965), 34–57.

[15] J.M. Coles, 'The early settlement of Scotland: excavations at Morton, Fife', *Proc. Prehistoric Soc.*, 37 (1971), 284–366.

[16] J.M. Coles, 'New aspects of the Mesolithic settlement of South-West Scotland', *Trans. Dumfries and Galloway Nat. Hist. and Ant. Soc.*, 41 (1964), 67–98.

lasting anything up to 1000 years. John was able to suggest different types of stonework on different features of the site, presumably of different ages.

Unusually for the time, no less than eleven radiocarbon dates were obtained, from different site features and from the midden. By today's standards the error terms were unacceptably large, but ignoring one exceptionally early date, the rest were reasonably consistent and suggest an occupation of the site across the 6th millennium cal BC, with a couple of outliers somewhat earlier.

From analysis of the bones (mammals, fish and birds), shells and the plant remains (hazelnuts, a few seeds and grasses), John attempted a reconstruction of the likely population of the site, using estimates of human protein requirements in relation to protein availability. This exercise would be considered one usual in the 'New Archaeology' which was becoming fashionable at this time; but John was never a New Archaeologist in the usual sense of the term. Instead, this is surely the influence of Grahame Clark's 'economic archaeology' being brought into play. The practice of sieving to recover small bones and plant remains as well as small pieces of stonework was very much something that John's Cambridge colleague Eric Higgs was developing with his students; the Morton dig was just as revolutionary for the period and area he was researching as the excavations of Higgs in north-west Greece at around the same time, not least in its involvement of specialists to cover aspects hitherto paid little attention.

The Bronze Age

At Cambridge John initially taught a course on the Palaeolithic, but as he explained in his memoir, by mid-career he was involved in the teaching of nine other courses, in whole or in part.[17] He must have had the highest teaching load of any member of staff in the Department of Archaeology, on his estimation around 60 hours per week, which made him particularly annoyed that some of his colleagues appeared to do very little in either teaching or administration. One of the courses that was significant for his research output, other than that on Experimental Archaeology, was that on the European Bronze Age, which a number of students who subsequently became well-known in the discipline took, including the author of this memoir. The single most important outcome of this interest was a book published in 1979 on the Bronze Age of Europe, still the only one of its kind.[18] John covered the north and west of Europe, and Harding the centre, south and east. In retrospect, the extraordinary thing about John's achievement in the book was that it was accomplished

[17] *Yesterday's Man*, 54.
[18] J.M. Coles & A.F. Harding, *The Bronze Age in Europe. An Introduction to the prehistory of Europe c.2000–700 BC* (London, 1979).

while he was extremely busy with his fieldwork in Somerset, quite apart from his teaching duties, as a glance at his publication list during the 1970s shows; he also published his second book on experimental archaeology in the same year as the Bronze Age book.[19] Subsequently John declined further involvement in general studies of the Bronze Age.[20] He was very occupied with the work in Somerset, and by then he was moving on to another focus of research, rock art (see below).

Experimental archaeology

Already during his Scottish period, John was finding that metalwork studies were leading him to other aspects than merely typology, in particular to the reconstruction of particular objects in order to ascertain their function or precise way of operating. This was in effect the start of his interest in experimental archaeology, which he pursued vigorously once he arrived in Cambridge, notably through his important studies of shields and horns (see below). In a paper dated 1966–7 (appearing in 1968) he introduced the topic.[21] In this, John went through some of the most important work that had appeared up to that point, noting especially the work done by Danish scholars on techniques of ancient agriculture and house-building, on cooking in pits by Irish archaeologists, on earthworks (drawing attention to the Overton Down experiment by Jewell and Dimbleby),[22] and to work on artefacts, bringing in his own work on bronze horns and shields (see below). His was not the first article on the topic; the field was begun by an article in 1961 by Robert Ascher, based on American material.[23] But his was the first to take a holistic view of the subject.

John went on to publish two books on the subject, which have dominated the field ever since.[24] Although there are now many groups working in the field, and journals devoted to the topic,[25] none has surpassed the utility of these books. They cover a wide range of material, and are suffused with a breadth of knowledge, combined with gentle humour, that makes them classics in the field, and reading them a pleasure. Chapter 1 of the 1979

---

[19] He finished the writing of *The Bronze Age in Europe* in early 1978 and wrote *Experimental Archaeology* in 1978–9.

[20] He told me in the early 1990s, when I asked him if he was prepared to work on another Bronze Age book, that it was a chapter of his life that was over. He did, however, produce one general article drawing on the 1979 book: 'The Bronze Age in Northwestern Europe: problems and advances', *Advances in World Archaeology*, 1 (1982), 265–321.

[21] J.M. Coles,' Experimental archaeology', *Proc. Soc. Antiqs Scotland*, 99 (1966–7), 1–20.

[22] P.A. Jewell & G.W. Dimbleby (eds), 'The experimental earthwork on Overton Down, Wiltshire, England: the first four years', *Proc. Prehistoric Soc.*, 32 (1966), 313–342.

[23] R. Ascher, 'Experimental archaeology', *American Anthropologist*, 63:4 (1961), 793–816.

[24] John Coles, *Archaeology by Experiment* (London, 1973); *Experimental Archaeology* (London, 1979).

[25] E.g. *Ethnoarchaeology*; *EXARC Journal*; *Experimentelle Archäologie in Europa*.

book covers the theoretical aspects of experimental archaeology, concentrating on the need for correct materials and production methods in reconstruction, the use of ethnography for gaining knowledge of technologies no longer available in the developed world, and the study of function. For the latter, he stressed the importance of manipulation and operation, and environment, as well as repetition (a one-off experiment may produce a particular result, but only if it is repeated many times can legitimate inferences be drawn). He considered questions of cost and time, discussing scaled-down experiments and their problems; he also stressed the need for a flexible approach in order to adapt experiments to unforeseen problems and outcomes.

His interest in the topic had been fired initially through his study of the Late Bronze Age metal shields. A classic study, appearing in 1962,[26] examined the evidence for the date and distribution of Bronze Age shield types. So far so traditional; but John was not satisfied with having established the typological and chronological parameters of the pieces, successful though this was, necessitating a far-reaching study of shields across Europe. After considering the well-known continental types (Herzsprung, Nipperwiese and others), John set the British and Irish examples in a typological framework, and considered their origins. But from there he moved on to consider how the shields were made and how they were used. In this, the survival of a shield in leather, from Clonbrin, Co. Longford, was crucial, as well as wooden formers or moulds from Churchfield, Co. Mayo, and Kilmahamogue, Co. Antrim, and wooden shields from Annandale, Co. Leitrim, and Cloonlara, Co. Mayo. These finds stimulated John to reconstruct the processes by which leather shields were made. Three different ways of treating the leather were attempted; the best turned out to be beating after soaking in cold water followed by impregnation with wax.

John did not attempt a reconstruction of a wooden shield, contenting himself with detailed study of the moulds and surviving shields. He did, however, make a metal shield, of copper, ribbed, and of metal 0.03 cm thick. He then proceeded to see how it fared in combat; pictures of the experimental fighting show John wielding a Bronze Age sword, and one of the Cambridge departmental technicians the shield. To quote him: 'the point of a leaf-bladed bronze sword easily penetrated the metal shield, and a slashing blow cut entirely through the shield, only the wired rim holding the two slices together'.[27] By contrast, in trials the leather shield only suffered minor flexing and no perforation, leading John to argue that the sheet metal shields were ceremonial in nature, and not used for 'real' fighting. While this theory has been challenged in recent years, it remains very plausible for the highly decorated bronze shields, which were surely designed for display rather than

---

[26] J.M. Coles, 'European Bronze Age shields', *Proc. Prehistoric Soc.*, 28 (1962), 156–190.

[27] Coles actually did one of these demonstrations at a lecture at the Society of Antiquaries in 1961: *Yesterday's Man*, pp. 61–2. It is fortunate that the Health and Safety Executive did not exist in those days.

defence. The whole exercise was a model in the conduct of archaeological experiments.

A somewhat similar exercise was conducted the following year, this time with bronze horns from Ireland the object of attention.[28] These splendid objects had long attracted attention, combined as they were with jangly bronze pendants and bell-like rattles known as crotals, thus suggesting the existence of Bronze Age 'orchestras'. In this case, John demonstrated both the typological affinities of the horns, not only in the British Isles but also across Europe, and then discussed how they were made and how they might have been blown. Some of the horns were blown from the end, like modern horns and trumpets, other from the side, rather like flutes. In the case of the end-blown examples, there was typically a flange at the end and a metal tube could be inserted to act as a mouthpiece; the side-blown pieces have nothing to aid blowing which suggests that a mouthpiece of organic material (wood or bone) might have been used (blowing across the hole as with a flute would not create a sufficient column of moving air in the horn). Most modern experiment-ers had added their own mouthpiece (from a modern brass instrument), which helped produce sounds, but this procedure was hardly authentic. John was able to show that the end-blown horns could produce two or three notes, the side-blown ones just one note, and demonstrated these skills in the National Museum in Dublin as well as in the British Museum for a TV show.[29] This recalls the playing in 1939 of a trumpet found in the tomb of Tutankhamun, when James Tappern, a bandsman of Prince Albert's Own 11th Royal Hussars, had played the trumpet for a BBC broadcast, but finding it very difficult had inserted his own mouthpiece, thus producing a range of notes not unlike those of modern cornets.[30] The sounds (which one can hear through BBC iPlayer) are very unlikely to represent what would have been heard in ancient Egypt.

John also considered the extent to which horns might have been blown together; several of the finds occurred in groups, while the Danish *lurs* usually occur in pairs (probably through imitation of horned or antlered animals). Whatever the truth of these matters (which John admitted was unknowable), his enthusiasm for the reconstruction of these ancient objects was infectious.

John himself carried out experimental reconstructions later in his career, notably of structures he had found in his excavations in the Somerset Levels (see below). These included most famously a reconstruction of the Sweet Track, but also other features such

[28] J.M. Coles,' Irish Bronze Age horns and their relations with northern Europe', *Proc. Prehistoric Soc.*, 29 (1963), 326–356.

[29] *Yesterday's Man*, p. 58; *Archaeology by Experiment*, pp. 164–6. One of the first archaeological lectures I myself ever attended was on ancient music given by Coles to the student Archaeology Society in Cambridge, probably in 1967, and included a tape of him playing the horns, having previously pointed out that a 19th century attempt had resulted in the experimenter bursting a blood vessel in his throat and dying.

[30] https://en.wikipedia.org/wiki/Tutankhamun%27s_trumpets and https://www.bbc.co.uk/news/world-middle-east–13092827, last consulted 19 October 2021; *Archaeology by Experiment*, p. 159; *Experimental Archaeology*, pp. 204–5.

as hurdles as used in the Walton Heath (Neolithic) and Eclipse (Bronze Age) trackways.[31] He also tested axes of stone and bronze on a range of native species of wood, to see if different materials produced different traces.

He taught a course in Experimental Archaeology at Cambridge and has described how he would take students outside to try spear-throwing, or to visit West Stow in Suffolk to experiment with hafting stone axes and using them to cut down trees. He also teamed up with Peter Holmes at Middlesex Polytechnic (now Middlesex University, in Hendon, north-west London) to carry out melting and pouring copper and bronze, hammering sheet metal and other activities related to the production of metalwork.[32] He was friends with Peter Reynolds and a great supporter of the Butser Ancient Farm experimental archaeology site which Reynolds founded.

John, in his early article and then in the two books, set out the principles and procedures of experimental archaeology. He pointed out that there are two aspects to the exercise: imitation or reconstruction, and assessment of functional capabilities. He pointed to the difficulty of accurate imitation of ancient technology, given that modern tools and materials are usually different from those used in ancient times, for whatever reason, and that modern experimenters are usually inexperienced and therefore inefficient in production. They are also handicapped by the contemporary cultural environment in which they work. For all these reasons, the various parameters must be strictly controlled. This helps to mitigate the fact that much about ancient technology remains unknowable: he warned against the common problem that many experiments 'fall within the compass of that damning definition of prehistory, the unwarrantable deduced from the unverifiable'.[33] This salutary reminder cannot be reinforced too often.

Somerset and wetlands

In 1962 John was taken by Grahame Clark to Somerset to see work that was being carried on in the peat areas, known as the Levels, by a local amateur archaeologist, Stephen Dewar. Dewar was observing the peat-cutting that was taking place on Shapwick Heath and elsewhere on the Levels, and recording features of interest. Clark was interested in the area because various wooden objects, notably bows, had been pulled out over the years, and he had involved Professor Harry Godwin to investigate the palaeoenvironment of the Levels. Following a series of meetings with all those involved, John started work in 1964 on a

---

[31] J.M. Coles & R.J. Darrah, 'Experimental investigations in hurdle-making', *Somerset Levels Papers*, 3 (1977), 32–38.

[32] I was invited to one of these exercises in the 1980s; it left one in awe of the achievements of the Bronze Age metalsmith.

[33] *Experimental archaeology*, p. 6.

wooden trackway known as the Abbot's Way, with small numbers of students from Cambridge and elsewhere. He brought in Alan Hibbert, then also at Cambridge, to cover the environmental material. This resulted in his first paper on the Somerset material, specifically on the Abbot's Way and the Bell Track, both of which produced Neolithic radiocarbon dates.[34] Although the Abbot's Way had been noted and described before, its extent and precise method of construction had not previously been studied in detail. This paper can justly be described as revolutionary in its findings. Clark had realised that the Somerset Levels had great potential, while Godwin had undertaken significant studies of the environmental context of several fragmentary trackways; archaeologists in Lower Saxony in north-west Germany had already published some of their findings.[35] But the 1968 paper includes detailed plans of trackways along with descriptions of the ways in which the planks and posts were fixed in position. A singular find from the Bell Track was a crude hermaphroditic figurine in ash wood, which John called a 'god-dolly', and which remains the earliest such piece from Britain or Ireland.[36]

The 1968 paper was followed by another in 1970 and a third in 1973.[37] In 1973 the Somerset Levels Project was set up, with a small steering group consisting of John, Geoffrey Wainwright, Alan Hibbert and Bryony Orme. In 1975, John and his main collaborator Bryony Orme started a series specifically for publishing the work done by them and their team on the Levels: the *Somerset Levels Papers*, which continued until the final volume (15) in 1989. In these volumes, annual reports of the work in Somerset appeared, along with studies of particular aspects, for instance woodworking, wood species, individual tracks, conservation and so on. The format of the *Papers* was landscape rather than portrait, to enable easier presentation of trackway plans and pollen diagrams. During the 1970s and 1980s large numbers of papers were produced, both in the *Papers* and elsewhere.[38] A book published in 1986 described for a wider audience the history of the Somerset Project, still one of the easiest places to study the overall picture of the Somerset work;[39] other summarising papers and booklets were also produced, and a small museum

---

[34] J.M. Coles and F.A. Hibbert, 'Prehistoric roads and tracks in Somerset, England: I. Neolithic', *Proc. Prehistoric Soc.*, 34 (1968), 238–258.

[35] H. Hayen, 'Zur Bautechnik und Typologie der vorgeschichtlichen, frühgeschichtlichen und mittelalterlichen hölzernen Moorwege und Moorstrassen', *Oldenburger Jahrbuch*, 56 (1957), 87–189.

[36] J.M. Coles, 'A Neolithic god-dolly from Somerset', *Antiquity*, 42, 275–7; 'Prehistoric roads and tracks I', 256 Fig. 9a-b; B. Coles, 'Anthropomorphic wooden figures from Britain and Ireland', *Proc. Prehistoric Soc.*, 56 (1990), 315–333.

[37] J.M. Coles, F.A. Hibbert & C.F. Clements, 'Prehistoric roads and tracks in Somerset, England: 2. Neolithic', *Proc. Prehistoric Soc.*, 36 (1970), 125–151.

[38] In the final volume of the *Papers* (no. 15), John summarised what they had covered and what the Project had achieved: J.M. Coles, 'The Somerset Levels Project 1973–1989', *Somerset Levels Papers*, 15 (1989), 5–14.

[39] B. & J. Coles, *Sweet Track to Glastonbury. The Somerset Levels in Prehistory* (London, 1986). The volume won the 1986 British Archaeology Book Award.

was set up in a local garden centre. A brief assessment of John's feelings about the success (and potentially the shortcomings) of the Project appears in the last of the *Papers*.

John was not the first to recognise the importance of wooden trackways in Britain or Europe; this study had a history going back to the 19th century, when the Abbot's Way was first recognised, a typical 'corduroy' track composed of planks placed laterally across piles driven into the peat. In Germany trackways had been recognised on the Ipwegermoor near Oldenburg and on other moors in the area;[40] similar things were known from the Netherlands.[41] In Somerset, the work of Arthur Bulleid and (later) Harold St George Gray, starting in the 1890s and culminating in the excavation of the Glastonbury and Meare 'lake villages', was crucial, as were the investigations by Harry Godwin, starting in the 1930s and continuing into the 1960s, when he worked with Clark. John's arrival on the scene led initially to a fuller investigation of the Abbot's Way as well as recognition of other tracks (Viper's, Bell, and the Baker Platform). By 1970 attention turned to a new discovery: the Sweet Track.[42] This remarkable structure, excavated over 12 years, produced not only Neolithic radiocarbon dates but also contemporary artefacts, including a jadeite axe.[43] The construction technique, hitherto unknown, consisted of oblique pegs overlying a longitudinal pole, creating a V shape onto which planks were placed. The wood was predominantly oak and hazel, with ash, willow, holly and smaller amounts of other species. Perhaps most remarkably, tree-ring studies were able to show that the track was constructed in the years 3807–6 BC; with dendrochronology specialists, John and Bryony Coles were able to suggest the dynamics of construction and repair of the track.[44] Continuing John's abiding interest in experimental work, a section of the track was later reconstructed.[45]

This work on the Abbot's Way and the Sweet Track was followed by work on several other trackways, of varying methods of construction. Neolithic tracks were discovered at

---

[40] See note 37.

[41] W. van Zeist, 'Pollen analytical investigations in the Northern Netherlands, with special reference to archaeology', *Acta Botanica Neerlandica*, 4 (1955), 1–8.

[42] J.M. Coles, F.A. Hibbert & B.J. Orme, 'Prehistoric roads and tracks in Somerset: 3. The Sweet Track', *Proc. Prehistoric Soc.* 39, 1973, 256–293.

[43] J.M. Coles, B. Orme, A.C. Bishop, & A.R. Woolley, 'A jade axe from the Somerset Levels', *Antiquity*, 48 (1974), 216–220.

[44] R.A. Morgan, 'Tree-ring studies in the Somerset Levels: the Sweet Track 1979–1982', *Somerset Levels Papers*, 10 (1984), 46–84; J. Hillam, C.M. Groves, D.M. Brown, M.G.L. Baillie, J.M. Coles & B.J. Coles, 'Dendrochronology of the English Neolithic', *Antiquity*, 64 (1990), 210–220.

[45] J.M. Coles & B.J. Orme, 'A reconstruction of the Sweet Track', *Somerset Levels Papers*, 10 (1984), 107–9. This reconstruction was built at the (then) Peat Moors Visitor Centre. Funding for the Centre from Somerset County Council was withdrawn in 2009; the Centre later reopened under the aegis of Natural England with the name Avalon Marshes Centre. The original reconstruction, along with that of a replica house from the Glastonbury Lake Village, was visible until a few years ago but its remains have now (2021) been entirely removed, its place taken by new reconstructed buildings. Sections of the Sweet Track and Meare Heath Track were constructed by volunteers in 2014 in the nearby woods in Shapwick Heath National Nature Reserve.

Walton Heath and Chilton Heath; at the former, the Garvin's track was of brushwood, while the Eclipse, Walton and Rowland's tracks were constructed from hurdles, each hurdle being 2.2–2.5 m long and 0.7–1.4 m wide, and carefully constructed from hazel rods. These tracks belong to the later Neolithic and the transition to the Bronze Age. Running from Edington Burtle to Westhay Meare Island was the Honeygore Track; while at the eastern end there were two superimposed tracks, dubbed Bell A and B, and a platform, the Baker.

Trackway construction continued into the Bronze Age, and fine examples were the Meare Heath, a plank track with two layers of planks laid at right angles to each other, the Viper's track of planks and brushwood, and a number of small lengths of track in Tinney's Ground (mostly brushwood) and elsewhere. These were mostly built on a wet raised bog, which was later (*c.* 700 BC) the subject of a major flooding episode. The story of track building could thus be followed from the early Neolithic, in the early 4th millennium BC, to the middle of the 1st millennium BC. The Coleses were able, on the basis of these interventions in many places in the Levels, and a large amount of palaeoenvironmental work, to create a model of how settlement and subsistence worked in the area throughout later prehistory.

The really significant thing about John's work on the trackways, most of it with Bryony Coles, is not that they were the first to discover or work on them, but that they created a fully worked out plan of study, which enabled them to place the sites in a context of movement and development across three millennia, with some of the tracks being dated to a specific moment in time which can be compared with what is known of other aspects of life and death in prehistory. Of course this work involved many days and weeks of labour in uncomfortable conditions, urgent journeys across southern England in response to reports of new discoveries, and a determination to rescue whatever could be rescued and preserve, through discussion with peat companies and pressure on the heritage organisations, what could not be examined, even fleetingly. In the last of the *Papers*, John summed up what the original intentions of the Project were, and how they achieved them or pointed to future needs. He specifically mentioned the success of the Project in concentrating on organic materials (principally wood), but also the need for continuing predictive surveys of the sort which he and his team had undertaken.

The other thing to mention is the matter of funding: John's early work was done on a shoestring, but he enlisted the support of Geoffrey Wainwright, Chief Archaeologist for what became English Heritage, who was persuaded of the significance of these and other wetlands in England, and assisted with funding to enable work to be done on a much larger scale.

Separate from the work on trackways was that on the Glastonbury and Meare Lake Villages. Only a small excavation was conducted by the Coleses at the Glastonbury site, but John with Stephen Minnitt (Curator of Archaeology at the Museum of Somerset in

Taunton) undertook a comprehensive review of the well-known publication by Bulleid and Gray, which had led to many re-interpretations in the past.[46] This was amplified in the light of the work at Meare, which included both reconsideration of the work by Bulleid and Gray, a small excavation by Michael Avery in 1966 with trial trenches in 1968–69, and some excavation at both western and eastern sites (Meare consists of two separate sites, the western one published by Bulleid and Gray, the eastern one barely published before the Coleses started work).[47] The publication of the material from the old excavations, amplified by that from their own work, has led to a much better understanding of the nature and date of these important late Iron Age sites, consisting of large numbers of mounds, most of them the site of a round house with clay floor and hearth, many times renewed.

John and his team excavated at Meare in 1979 and 1984 (West site) and 1982 (East site), with a long trench between the two sites in 1984 to investigate what lay between them (in essence nothing). Understanding of the West site, where John excavated some 300 m², essentially has to follow from the detailed work they did on the East site and the Glastonbury site; the same problems are basically present with all the Bulleid and Gray sites, as John made clear.

For the Meare East site, where John excavated only 150 m², he undertook an enormously detailed and laborious examination of the old Day Books, sketches and pencil drawings, catalogue of finds, and interim reports, along with the interim report of Michael Avery, combined with the new material from the Somerset Levels Project's work between 1979 and 1986. A detailed account of the 51 mounds was thus produced, with plans and section drawings of most. John was then able to indicate a sequence of deposits on the site, specifying the context of the mounds, with clay floors, ash spreads, hearths and so on. A catalogue of all known finds followed, with specialist reports on glass, pottery, plant remains, animal bones and other biological material. It is the summary and assessment (Chapter 7 of the 1987 report) that gives the most detailed account of John's thinking about the site.

Glastonbury is somewhat different from Meare, both in its archaeological survival and its location: the Meare villages were on the edge of the raised bog, arguably a more difficult location than Glastonbury. For Glastonbury, Coles and Minnitt described the difficulties in

---

[46] A. Bulleid & H.St George Gray, *The Glastonbury Lake Village*, 2 vols (Glastonbury, 1911, 1917); *Sweet Track to Glastonbury*, 156–171; J.M. Coles, B.J. Coles & R.A. Morgan, 'Excavations at the Glastonbury Lake Village 1984', *Somerset Levels Papers*, 14 (1988), 57–62; J. Coles & S. Minnitt, *'Industrious and fairly civilized': The Glastonbury Lake Village* (Taunton, 1995).

[47] A. Bulleid & G. St George Gray, *The Meare Lake Village*, 3 vols (Taunton, 1948–1966) [this is the West site]; J.M. Coles, *Meare Village East: The Excavations of A. Bulleid and H. St George Gray, 1932–1956. Somerset Levels Papers*, 13, 1987; B.J. Coles, S.E. Rouillard & C. Backway, 'The 1984 excavations at Meare', *Somerset Levels Papers*, 12 (1986), 30–57; M. Avery, 'Excavations at Meare East 1966. An interim report and discussion', *Proc. Somerset Archaeol. and Nat. Hist. Soc.*, 112 (1968), 21–39. Interim accounts of the excavations by Gray on the East site appeared in *Proc. Somerset Archaeol. and Nat.Hist. Soc.* between 1933 and 1956–7.

marrying accounts of excavations conducted in the late 19th and early 20th centuries with the available field and artefactual data; in particular the very varied quality of the excavation and recording themselves. In spite of these difficulties, they succeeded in tying in most artefacts to the mounds they came from and in giving a description of each mound, based on what Arthur Bulleid wrote in his 1911 book, supplemented by his notebooks and plans. The structure of the mounds was then examined, based on the plans and section drawings which Bulleid made; they succeeded in producing believable plans of several house-mounds, along with their history of repeated floor and hearth construction. What is more, their examination of the stratigraphy thus revealed showed that there were four phases of occupation on the site, increasing in density from the Early (6 houses, 15 spreads) to the Final, with a *floruit* in the Late (third) Phase when almost every mound was utilised (13 houses, 57 spreads, 6 shelters, and a causeway). But they stress that these are only 'moments' in the life of the settlement, and that not all the structures of any one phase were in use at the same time. The plans that they produced, however, are a very remarkable outcome of their endeavours.[48]

Coles and Minnitt then considered the various models that had been advanced over the years for the form and function of the site. Particular attention was paid to a well-known attempt by David Clarke to understand the nature of the site.[49] The assessment of this model was polite but in the end the critique was scathing: Clarke did not know the material at first hand and evidently misunderstood many of the details presented in the original reports. One remark may illustrate the problem: Fig. 7.1 in their account reproduces Clarke's idea of 'modular units' on the site (his Fig. 21.1), with this caption: 'Clarke's modular unit, in theory. Nothing on the site fits this scheme'.

Coles and Minnitt present their view of the significance and nature of the Glastonbury site following this critique. The basic problem, of course, lies in the inadequacy of the original report, and the previous lack of environmental evidence on which to base an assessment of the situation of the site in its landscape. On the basis of the work done by them and their collaborators, the site can now be seen to have lain in a tree swamp or fen carr, so that it was a 'swamp village' rather than a lake village. A raised bog lay to the west, and reed swamp, sedge fen, fen carr and open water to the east. The landscape was thus viewed as 'concave', the site surrounded by wet ground, and with the arable and pasture areas, and woodland, on the higher ground a little further away.

At the end of the day, the reasons for the establishment of these villages on wet ground is puzzling, given that dry ground is available a few kilometres to the north and the south. They are also rich in artefacts, evidently having access to a range of resources, human and

---

[48] *Industrious*, Figs 4.9–4.12.
[49] D.L. Clarke, 'A provisional model of an Iron Age society and its settlement system', in *Models in Archaeology*, ed. D.L. Clarke (London, 1972), pp. 801–869.

other. The sites are not defended, though their wet location might have served as a deterrent to hostile incursion. One suggestion that Coles and Minnitt put forward is that they
may have served as seasonal markets, at or near the boundaries between different tribal
groupings (the Durotriges in Wessex, the Dobunni in the Severn-Cotswold area, and not
far away the Dumnonii in south-west England).[50]

Other wetland interests

The work in Somerset led to invitations to get involved with wetland archaeology in other
areas of Britain, and to advise on similar situations in other countries, notably Ireland. The
support of Geoffrey Wainwright was crucial in getting projects started in several parts of
England in the following years. John was involved in the Fenland Survey from the beginning, when in 1975 meetings of a committee of which he was chairman discussed threats
to archaeology in the area around the Wash, principally the counties of Cambridgeshire,
Norfolk and Lincolnshire; as a consequence a Field Officer post was established to undertake a preliminary survey of the Cambridgeshire fens. Initial work soon demonstrated the
nature of the threat, as a result of which the Fenland Project was established, funded by
the Department of the Environment, later English Heritage, and chaired by John. It concentrated on survey work rather than excavation; John himself acted as advisor rather than
fieldworker (he was fully engaged in Somerset at the time) though he did conduct one
excavation.[51] The impressive results of this initiative were demonstrated by the end
publication of the project in 1994, a book of which around half was written by John.[52] His
contribution consisted of a chronological survey of patterns of settlement across the
Fenlands, with chapters on the Palaeolithic and Mesolithic, the Neolithic, and the Bronze
Age. Put like that, this does not sound a very demanding task, but in fact these chapters are
highly detailed, taking into account not just important recent excavations such as those by
Francis Pryor at Flag Fen and Ian Hodder at Haddenham, but also older work by Grahame
Clark and others. Each chapter is rounded off with a review of the sites in their environmental context, and an overview of the character of settlement in each period. David Hall
covered the Iron Age, Roman and medieval periods. John then provided a summary
chapter, 'Reflections', which brings together the outcomes of the whole project.

The project identified hundreds of sites, many not previously known; John pointed to
particular areas of great potential, where both more fieldwork and preservation measures

---

[50] The archive of the Somerset Levels Project is held by the South West Heritage Trust in Norton Fitzwarren
near Taunton.

[51] J.M. Coles, B. Orme, J. May & N. Moore, 'Excavations of Late Bronze or Iron Age date at Washingborough
Fen', *Lincs History and Archaeology*, 14 (1979), 5–10.

[52] D. Hall & J. Coles, *Fenland Survey. An essay in landscape and persistence* (Swindon, 1994).

should be considered. He enjoyed introducing quirky features into his writing, and his account of the 'fen slodgers' is a classic example; these were fenland inhabitants who lived by catching birds and their eggs, and taking reeds and rushes, as well as wood, for their subsistence – often contrary to the law. The precarious life of these traditional inhabitants of the fens is sketched, showing us that not everything can or should be reduced to emotionless scientific fact.

The Fenland Survey was succeeded by the Fenland Evaluation Project, which produced a dossier of sites, 148 of which were presented to English Heritage as being of particular importance. Overall, the Fenland work was a remarkable achievement on the part of many people; John Coles acted as stimulator rather than primary researcher, but whether the project could have happened without him is an interesting question.

He helped to set up, and advised, a number of other projects, for instance the Humber Wetlands Project (based in Hull and Exeter), the North-West Wetlands Project (Lancaster), and the Severn Estuary Levels Research Committee (from 1985). His encouragement led to the formation of the Scottish Wetland Archaeology Programme in 1998.

Ireland[53]

John's involvement in Irish wetlands predates the development of the discipline in Ireland, as underscored by his short but impactful 1984 article 'Irish Bogs: the time is now'.[54] His existing friendship with Professor Barry Raftery also played an important role when soon afterwards Raftery was drawn into peatland excavations with the discovery of the Iron Age road at Corlea. John was an adviser and supporter from the outset and the work of the Somerset team was a ready reference as the Irish programme developed. The Coleses visited on a number of occasions and shared their experience and publications.

In 1988 they led an application to the European Science Foundation that brought together teams of young graduates from Exeter, Dublin, Leiden and Aarhus to work and train in wetland archaeology and host exchange visits.

In the late 1980s Barry Raftery campaigned for the establishment of a systematic national survey of industrial peatlands. It led to the formation of the Irish Archaeological Wetland Unit (IAWU), which ran from 1990 to 2005. Even though John was not directly involved with the IAWU, the case studies and bodies of literature from Somerset provided ongoing standards on which to draw. Initially the state funded surveys by the IAWU, but later (1998 onward) the state peat company, Bord na Móna (BnM), reluctantly accepted

[53] I am grateful to Conor McDermott (University College Dublin) for information on this section; with his permission, several of the paragraphs have been adopted from his email of 18 November 2021 more or less unchanged.
[54] *North Munster Antiq J.*, 26 (1984), 3–7.

responsibility for a degree of mitigation through excavation. Later the funding of both survey and excavation was transferred to BnM. John was a member of the Directorate of the Discovery Programme in the 1990s. Earlier he had served as external examiner for the National University of Ireland, working with colleagues in Dublin, Cork and Galway.

One of John's last major roles in Ireland was in 2001 when he was commissioned by *Dúchas* The Heritage Service (the state heritage organisation at the time) to undertake 'An Evaluation of Current Peatland Survey and Excavation Strategy'. This provided a frank and comprehensive review of what had been achieved to date and what remained to be done, with recommendations on future strategy and practice. While not all of these were adopted, there is no doubt that John's Somerset work and wide experience of wetland archaeology throughout the world had a major impact on the situation in Ireland, both in the field and in the classroom.

In 2005 he was elected a member of the Royal Irish Academy. More recently he donated his archive of material on experimental archaeology to the Department of Archaeology at University College Dublin, which is active in the field and runs graduate programmes in the subject. John was also a strong supporter of the magazine *Archaeology Ireland*.

Poland

In Poland, John was in regular touch with Wojciech Piotrowski and the team at the Early Iron Age site of Biskupin, well known for its very well preserved wooden structures, and made several visits there. In 1989 he was asked to become a consultant on wetland matters to the project (which at the time was a part of the State Archaeological Museum in Warsaw). In 1991 he was invited for a longer trip, with Bryony, and advised on the setting up of monitoring tubes on the site, as well as visiting other wetland sites in the area, such as Izdebno, and other parts of Poland, notably Masuria, including the extensive swampy bog area of the Biebrza river basin, and the towns of Łomża and Nowogród on the river Narew and Ciechanowiec on the river Bug, in the east of the country. In 1997 the Coleses were guests of honour at the third Biskupin Archaeological Festival, where John delivered a keynote paper on the problems of wetland archaeology across the world.[55] His last trip to Biskupin was in 2007, at a conference to honour the memory and academic legacy of Grahame Clark. He delivered a paper about Clark and his work, and with Arkadiusz Marciniak edited a volume of the proceedings.[56] A nice spin-off from his Polish connection occurred at the conference in his honour held in Exeter in 1997, when Piotrowski and his

[55] J.M. Coles, 'Wetland archaeology in the 20th century: history and commentary', *Archaeologia Polona*, 35–36 (1997–98), 287–317.
[56] A. Marciniak & J. Coles (eds), *Grahame Clark and his Legacy* (Newcastle upon Tyne, 2010).

Biskupin colleague Wiesław Zajączkowski presented him with a replica Bronze Age sword, to his amazement and pleasure, and the delight of the assembled company.

The Coleses travelled widely as a result of their wetland expertise. In this, the formation of the Wetland Archaeology Research Project (WARP), based in Exeter, was very important, as its newsletter NewsWARP and its regular conferences began to be influential around the world. John was frequently invited to lecture on wetland archaeology, for instance in Florida, in both the US and Canada on the north-west coast of America, and in Japan. Several of these locations later hosted WARP conferences. NewsWARP morphed into the *Journal of Wetland Archaeology*, a respected journal with a wide circulation;[57] John often contributed pieces to NewsWARP.

Rock art and Sweden

As early as the 1960s, John became interested in the rock art that is abundant on the glacially polished rocks of Scandinavia, above all in Sweden but also in parts of Norway and on erratic boulders in Denmark. This interest was part of his lifelong enthusiasm for ancient art, and was stimulated by his long-standing friendship with Bo Gräslund from Uppsala University, whom he knew through his earlier shield studies, and who went with him to some of the locations in Uppland where the art panels occur. The interest had to remain latent while Somerset was his top priority, but even during that period he visited the rock art sites of Scandinavia frequently, including all the major carving areas, and certain ones many times.[58] Much had been written about the art, over many decades, but John soon realised that the published accounts concentrated on the most accessible and obvious art panels, the depictions of which were often unreliable, whereas large numbers lay in inaccessible spots and were unknown to scholars. Thus began a series of visits to Sweden, both the west coast (above all Bohuslän where the most famous sites lie), the east (the province of Uppland), and less frequently the south. These trips were essentially working holidays, undertaken on minimal budgets.[59] Together with Gräslund, and often with Bryony Coles and/or Stephen Minnitt, John would decide on an area to explore on the basis of existing surveys, and set off with recording materials into the meadows and forests, inspecting any rock outcrop they came across. By this low-tech method, large numbers of

---

[57] Now published by Taylor and Francis; the latest number is 20 (2020).

[58] J. Coles, 'A conflict of opinions. Rock carving in Sweden 2003', *J. Nordic Archaeological Science*, 14 (2004), 5–12.

[59] Coles did sometimes apply for funding from the British Academy, in the days when its Small Grants scheme was a welcome source of funding for many scholars; these applications were often successful, though the amounts requested were invariably small.

new sites were discovered, and their location and character made known to the local heritage authorities (notably the rock art museum at Tanum and the Swedish Rock Art Research Archive in the University of Gothenburg).[60] John donated all his rock art documentation to the ATA Archive at the National Board of Antiquities in Stockholm. As well as studying the panels for their content and artistic merit, John was concerned, as he had been with endangered wetland areas, to draw attention to the ways in which some of them were suffering from agricultural and industrial activity, as well as natural processes, for instance acid rain.[61]

Tracings of the art were produced through a range of techniques. Various methods had been used over the years, the most intrusive of which was that of painting the motifs with red paint; the art was thus spectacularly revealed but the method was potentially destructive since as the paint wore away, the rock surface might come away with it; and it was certainly inaccurate, in that it only showed the most obvious and easily defined images as one particular observer saw them at one particular time. Early methods involved simple sketching; later, scholars attempted tracing or rubbing, in both cases by laying soft paper over the rock and attempting to produce an image of the underlying art on the paper. In John's work, the first step was to clean the rock surface using a soft brush, and to set up a gridded recording framework. Images might be highlighted using white chalk and planned using a 1m grid; or they might be rubbed onto 60 g paper using grass or carbon. In all cases the plans were supplemented by photographs. John was at pains to stress that much recording is subjective, and needs to be done in optimal lighting conditions, such as low sunlight or, in some instances, dampness, and that repeated viewings are essential.[62]

The task of making some sort of sense of all these images was, and is, a daunting one. Previous scholars, for instance Mats Malmer, had attempted to categorise the motifs,[63] and in his first Bohuslän guide book (1990) John did the same, listing thirteen groups of images and giving a rough count of their frequency. Cup marks are by far the most common in the 40,000 plus images known (something in excess of 27,000); of the figurative images the ship is particularly common, and thereby particularly interesting. More detail was added in his later, more lengthy, discussions.

What was it all about? That simple question belies the baffling nature of the art. As John headed a chapter in *Shadows*, the images represent a 'complex simplicity'. At first

---

[60] As well as many articles presenting individual sites, or the problems of survival and recording, two major books were published in the 2000s: *Patterns in a Rocky Land. Rock Carvings in South-West Uppland, Sweden* (Uppsala, 2000), and *Shadows of a Northern Past: Rock Carvings of Bohuslän and Østfold* (Oxford, 2005). Two smaller guidebooks to the art in the east and the west appeared in the 1990s: *Images of the Past: A guide to the rock carvings and other ancient monuments of Northern Bohuslän* (Vitlycke, 1990), and *Rock Carvings of Uppland: A guide* (Uppsala, 1994).

[61] J. Coles, 'The dying rocks', *Tor*, 24 (1992), 65–85.

[62] Discussions of the techniques were presented in *Patterns* pp. 14–24 and *Shadows* p. 5.

[63] M. Malmer, *A Chorological Study of North European Art* (Stockholm, 1981).

glance the images appear unstructured, with the same motif repeated many times over and placed randomly. The technique is simple, and the approach 'minimalist', in that the lines of each motif are simply and economically drawn. But John points out that the subjects are restricted and controlled, with strict parameters beyond which the artists did not stray.[64] The production was 'linear', based on lines created by pecking, sometimes enhanced by grinding; and the lines can be shown to proceed from those creating a basic shape to those designed to enhance the representation of particular motifs. The method of depicting motifs depends on the subject matter: side view for birds, animals and boats, front view for humans, top views for feet or footprints, known as 'footsoles'. The degree to which motifs are conceived as part of a unified piece of art has been much discussed; John was able to show that some complex motifs can only have been created as a group, such as the 'processions' of human figures, or the 'stacks of boats', seen on some panels.[65] Equally important is whether or not a given set of panels were intended to be viewed or experienced together, or as different experiences depending on time and context. It is also the case that panels must have been intended to be viewed from certain viewpoints, e.g. below or above the panel, and at different times of day and night.

Another vital question to be asked is the timescale over which panels were created, in particular the extent to which one can observe chronological depth in them, and evidence of palimpsests. This bears too on the question of whether one or many artists were involved in the work, and the length of time over which they were intended to be used and visible. None of these matters is straightforward, given the medium on which the art is created, and the techniques of creating it.

The other aspect relates to the landscape setting of the art panels, which, as a consequence of isostatic uplift, can be shown originally to have frequently, if not always, lain within sight of water or close to the shoreline.[66] Concentrations of art panels, when not just the consequence of especially active fieldworkers in particular areas, may reflect the importance of special areas that were thus marked out by an abundance of art – particularly true with parts of Bohuslän. These 'major catchments', as John dubbed them, occur in places such as Tanum, Kville or Vitlycke, with art panels widely found across landscapes of around 4–5 km². In addition, what John calls 'minor catchments' show smaller groupings in particular locations, stretching in a line only a few tens of metres long. Pointing out that with sea level change, conditions around bays and inlets must have sometimes been challenging, John allowed himself a moment of unusual subjectivity: 'This was perhaps exactly the place for such an outpouring of emotion in the rocks, to mark the transient

---

[64] *Shadows*, p. 15.
[65] J. Coles, 'And on they went … processions in Swedish Bronze Age rock carvings', *Acta Archaeologica*, 74 (2003), 211–250; 'Bronze Age rock carvings at Häljesta, Västmanland, Sweden: domination by isolation', *Germania*, 79 (2001), 237–271. These matters are also discussed in *Shadows*.
[66] *Shadows*, pp. 100–103.

nature of the land and the sea and to ensure that the ideology expressed on the rocks was captured by the landscape itself, inaccessible to the flow of normality over the drylands and the deep waters'.[67]

Finally John asked himself, and us, what is 'the meaning of it all, or nothing'? 'Can we rely upon a wider scene, an archaeological landscape, as representing a reliable reality?', he asked in the concluding chapter of *Shadows of a Northern Past*.[68] He identifies four areas of life surrounding the art: the story or idea or belief; the griot, holder of ancestral voices and interpreter of traditions; the artist-craftsperson who was empowered to trans-form the rock surface; and the viewers or onlookers, for whom the art represented a means of consolidation of community and cohesion against seen and unseen forces. The motifs obviously had a meaning, though it may have changed with time and context. A motif meant something in itself, but also reflected an association, for instance with boats or particular humans. Figures with arms and armour seem to be involved in some kind of fighting; boats suggest the importance of water-borne movement; animals suggest subsis-tence. Given the other evidence for remarkable social and economic developments in Scandinavia during the period over which the art was created, it would not be surprising to find indications of long-distance contact as represented by images that reflected those found in distant lands to the south.

Unusually for John, he finished his discussion of the art with a 'traveller's tale', a fictitious and personalised account of a lone traveller who brought back stories of distant lands and places. This was a special person, distinct from his home group. He visited wonderful places in southern lands where stone monuments and temples were erected, where people worked with little tangible reward to quarry stone to build, and to create statues and sculptures. He returned home to find the difficult situation of the sea withdraw-ing, creating mudflats where boats could not be launched, and where artists would work to create designs on rock panels. He might tell tales of his journeys and the battles and dis-plays he had seen; his tales would enhance his standing in his native land, and enable him to create new concepts of expression, even new images, which might get transferred into the local art, and encourage the local people to 'absorb new ideas, and develop their own concepts of behaviour and belief'.

'Whether', he mused, 'anyone will wish to accept such an explanation seems quite unlikely to me'. But the rock art attests to an indigenous origin and the emergence, over centuries, of thought and belief systems. 'The fundamental concerns and their symbolic representation on the rocks came to be firmly established in the social consciences and behavioural patterns of the many small congregations of people ... their expressions of desire and commemoration on the rocks were unwavering and were not deflected by

---

[67] *Shadows*, p. 117.
[68] *Shadows*, p. 120.

external ideologies and imagery ... their symbols are those we now encounter on the rocks, a record of endeavour and strongly-held beliefs, now reduced to shadows of a northern past.'[69] These words conclude John's last single-authored book, a remarkable study of a remarkable phenomenon; and a rare excursus into a style of writing that ventured into the subjective and the imaginary.

Personal qualities and appreciation

In his Scottish sojourn, through tennis John met Mona Shiach, a schoolteacher. They married in December 1958 and had four children, born 1959–1966. The marriage ended in divorce, and in 1985 he married his long-time collaborator Bryony Orme (Bryony Coles FBA), with whom he published many articles and several books.

He was elected a Fellow of the British Academy in 1978, and in 1995 he received its Grahame Clark Medal. This was one of many distinctions he received: he was awarded the gold medals of the Society of Antiquaries of London (2000) and of the Swedish Royal Academy of Letters, History and Antiquities (2009), presented to him by the King. He was awarded an honorary doctorate by Uppsala University (1997). He won the European Archaeological Heritage Prize of the European Association of Archaeologists in 2006, being nominated for his work on wetland archaeology.

He served on many national committees, notably as a commissioner for the Royal Commission on the Ancient and Historical Monuments of Scotland; he was an adviser to the Heritage Lottery Fund, on its Historic Buildings and Land expert panel, from when it was established in 1994 until 2004. His notes from the work on that panel show how seriously he took the tasks, and the considerable lengths to which he went to master the sometimes complex briefs involved. He was President of the Prehistoric Society from 1978 to 1982, having served as its editor for many years previously. He was a member of the working group which resulted in the formation of the Institute for Field Archaeologists in 1982 (now the Chartered Institute for Archaeologists). He and Bryony set up the John and Bryony Coles Bursary, established in 1998 and administered through the Prehistoric Society, to fund student members of the Society to undertake foreign travel to deepen their understanding of prehistoric archaeology through fieldwork, museum study or site visits. In 2007 he established the British Academy's Medal for Landscape Archaeology.

As a man he was kind, witty, discreet to a fault, and highly amusing company. He was well read and well travelled; he was a book collector, and with Bryony regularly went to visit second-hand bookshops, especially in Hay on Wye. They had no television; they read and they listened to the radio. Their home in Devon is quite isolated, but they knew all their

---

[69] *Shadows*, p. 128.

neighbours and took part in a range of local activities. They were frequent visitors to John's children in different parts of Britain, or received them at their home.

It is less easy to assign John a particular place in the firmament of major archaeologists in the second half of the 20th century. He was a man of many talents. He was essentially a practical archaeologist. He was perfectly familiar with the theoretical trends that emerged during his career, but he saw them as a means to an end, not an end in themselves. He did not write purely theoretical articles, divorced from the reality of practical work, though he did write about the theoretical underpinnings of, for example, experimental archaeology, and he was well aware of what might be called ideological or cosmological aspects of rock art (in the sense of experiencing the world as the creators of the art did). Indeed, two of the poems that he wrote reflect respectively the view of the carver and the view of the archaeologist observing the art. In 1989 he wrote: 'If the word theory hardly figures on the printed pages of the *Papers*, it is because theory and practice were merged from the first in such a way that they are bidirectionally evolutionary and individually indistinguishable, or so we believe' – a clear statement of where, in his opinion, the true tasks of archaeology lie.[70] In this, his work stands out from that of other big names in 20th-century archaeology; he was essentially an empiricist. He never engaged with 'big theory' as practised by other big names, including some he taught in Cambridge; indeed, if anything he could be disdainful of their approach which can seem arrogant and intolerant of the more practical side of the discipline. He had a great capacity for assimilating information at great speed (witness the breadth of reading evident in his articles) and obviously chose not to go down the theoretical path.[71]

The practical nature of his approach can be illustrated by two simple things: first, when he needed slides for his teaching in Cambridge, rather than waiting for the wheels of departmental bureaucracy to grind slowly into action, he used a photographic stand on which to mount a camera, and simply photographed the images from books and articles that he needed, sending the film off to a company that offered a rapid return of the resulting slides. Second, he had a drawing board and set of pens in his office, and was able to produce rapid but accurate drawings of the plans and other images that he needed for his publications. Simple things, and involving him in work and expense that could have been left to others, but ones that meant he had the results he needed straightaway and in the form he wanted.

[70] *Papers*, 15 (1989), 13.

[71] Many of those he taught went on to successful careers in archaeology; some are Fellows of the Academy. The best-known of his former students is undoubtedly HRH the Prince of Wales; in *Yesterday's Man* (pp. 74–79) John amusingly describes a trip to France in 1968 with Prince Charles and Glyn Daniel to visit the painted caves of the Dordogne and the megalithic monuments of Brittany.

John was a remarkable man, versatile, industrious, thorough, and much loved by those with whom he worked and those whom he taught or advised. He achieved a huge amount through diligence and hard work, never by bullying or unduly forceful behaviour. He could be single-minded in achieving his aims, but always showing by example how things could and should be done. It was to this aspect of his character that Bo Gräslund alluded when, in the opening talk at the 1997 conference in his honour, he remarked: 'John is like a never-ending eruption of new publications and achievements. I bet he finished a fresh article this morning'; and later in the piece: 'Since John has never followed any trends just because they are new, he will never be untrendy. His works are based on so much professionalism, wisdom, experience, intelligence, methodological insight and awareness of the conditions and possibilities of archaeology, that when the archaeology of our time is looked back on in retrospect some hundred years ahead, he will be one of the few who will still be reckoned with and whose influence will still be felt'. And he finished with these words describing John's approach: 'Don't wait, do things now, do it yourself, do it cheap, do it simple, do it thoroughly and do it well'.[72] These words perfectly encapsulate the approach to life and work that John Coles took, and which made him such a dominant presence in the fields in which he worked.

Acknowledgements

I am very grateful to several people who worked with John and knew him well in helping with the preparation of this memoir: first and foremost Bryony Coles FBA, who has checked the accuracy of this account and supplied much information, but also Bo Gräslund, Chris Coles, Conor McDermott, Aidan O'Sullivan, Wojciech Piotrowski, Alison Sheridan FBA and Andrew Fleming.

Note on the author: Anthony Harding is Emeritus Professor of Archaeology at the University of Exeter. He was elected a Fellow of the British Academy in 2001.

[72] B. Gräslund, 'Introductory address', in *Experiment and Design*, p. x.

SUSAN REYNOLDS

Susan Mary Grace Reynolds

27 January 1929 – 29 July 2021

elected Fellow of the British Academy 1993

by

DAVID D'AVRAY
Fellow of the Academy

JOHN HUDSON
Fellow of the Academy

Susan Reynolds was elected to the British Academy after she had worked out a new frame-work for the medieval history of England, France, Germany and northern Italy. The break-through book was her *Kingdoms and Communities in Western Europe 900–1300* (1984); it brought all levels of society together in a synthesis, and was a stunning achievement. Her subsequent *Fiefs and Vassals* (Oxford, 1994) left a generation reluctant even to use the word 'feudalism', and other important contributions continued until not long before she died. In 2001 she was honoured with a *Festschrift* entitled *Law, Laity and Solidarities*.

Biographical Memoirs of Fellows of the British Academy, 20, 139–164
Posted 28 February 2022. © British Academy 2022.

Susan Reynolds

Susan Reynolds[1] was elected to the British Academy in 1993 after she had worked out a new framework for the medieval history of England, France, Germany and northern Italy. The breakthrough book was her *Kingdoms and Communities in Western Europe 900–1300* (Oxford, 1984). Her previous publication record, including the edition of part of a bishop's register[2] and a good book on medieval English towns,[3] was solid enough but *Kingdoms* was of a whole new quality. It brought all levels of society together in a synthesis. For all its limitations (only England, France, Germany and Italy, very little religion) it was a stunning achievement. Her subsequent *Fiefs and Vassals* (Oxford, 1994) left a generation reluctant even to use the word 'feudalism', and other important contributions continued until not long before she died.[4] In 2001 she was honoured with a *Festschrift* entitled *Law, Laity and Solidarities*. Nobody could have foretold all this from her undramatic start.

Susan's father did not go to university; neither did his father, and perhaps nobody had done so at least in the male line. Still she was born into a prosperous upper middle class world, which would have some relevance to her career as a historian. Her paternal grandfather, the son of a greengrocer in south London, had been an office boy in a solicitor's firm. He was gifted and had the chance to work towards qualifying as a solicitor himself, which he did. He rose fast, which paradoxically was bad luck for his daughters. The family moved up in the world to better and better neighbourhoods, so Susan's aunts were never in one place and social milieu sufficiently long to meet a potential husband. They stayed at home and were frustrated. One of the aunts was a gifted Latinist – self-taught? – and coached Susan when she was told she needed to improve her Latin before taking up her place at Oxford. (In the end a threatened exam was quietly forgotten. Susan used to say with her underlying modesty that her Latin was never quite good enough for the purposes for which she *needed* it.) Susan often spoke about her father and his sisters, her aunts; much more seldom about her mother or her maternal grandparents, though she mentioned that her mother's father too was a lawyer. Yet 'mother' was Susan's last word when she died.[5]

This legal lineage no doubt predisposed Susan to be interested in legal history, an interest that grew stronger in her later work. On a personal level she was certainly interested in her father's legal career almost as a slice of social history. He was destined to

[1] The memoir is largely based on many conversations between Susan Reynolds and the authors. See also the interview conducted under the aegis of the Institute of Historical Research on 17 March 2008: https://archives. history.ac.uk/makinghistory/resources/interviews/Reynolds_Susan.html, accessed 10 January 2022.

[2] *The Registers of Roger Martival, Bishop of Salisbury, 1315–1330*, iii, *Royal Writs* (Oxford, 1965), ed. Susan Reynolds.

[3] *An Introduction to the History of English Medieval Towns* (Oxford, 1977).

[4] *Ideas and Solidarities of the Medieval Laity: England and Western Europe* (Aldershot, 1995); *Before Eminent Domain: toward a history of expropriation of land for the common good* (Chapel Hill NC, 2010); *The Middle Ages without Feudalism: essays in criticism and comparison on the medieval West* (Farnham, 2012).

[5] Information from the carer on duty.

follow in her grandfather's footsteps, from a much more advantageous position (though after serving through the First World War). He too was very successful. For many years he ran his law firm without partners. Eventually he took on two bright young men. When, after two heart attacks, he asked them to buy him out, they refused, presumably because they could not afford it, and Susan vividly remembered finding him utterly distraught on the evening in question. He felt he was ruined but that was evidently far from the case. He was good with young children, though – reading between the lines – insensitive or hard to know when she was a teenager. Despite his eventual wish to retire he was clearly a work-aholic, and Susan may have inherited that single-mindedness. It was not so much that she worked Stakhanovite hours, and she always took a long summer holiday (three weeks in France, more on which below), but her academic research became the centre of her life, what made it worth living for her, for all her warm relationships with friends and family. She never married. At one crossroads point she developed passionate feelings for a married man – was 'dotty about him'. Apparently he was also in love with her and told her. She knew she could have said: 'What a coincidence!' and started an affair; instead she said: 'What a pity', and that was the end of it. She knew that if they had gone on to discuss the situation she would have weakened, but she did not want to break up a marriage. From then on, the desire to investigate and interpret History was the fire inside her.

That she would do a degree was apparently taken for granted. Susan's father wanted his three daughters to avoid his sisters' fate and to go to university but not to join the family firm. Perhaps that was the patriarchal mentality of his generation, or perhaps it was because a university degree was still not the normal path to a solicitor's career, so that he had to make a choice for them. At any rate, they all got degrees, one sister from Oxford and the other from St Thomas's Hospital Medical School (University of London) (she became eminent). Susan was on good terms with them and especially with her nieces, who used to play in her bed-sitter when she lodged with one of her sisters and who helped her greatly when she was old and frail. As is common, in her old age she retained vivid memories of her early years.

Her school days were happy enough. There was one girl who mildly bullied her. Curiously, the same girl and Susan regularly went to tea at each other's houses, and the bullying relationship lapsed into a different dimension. Eventually her headmistress learned of the problem from Susan's mother and solved it by asking the most popular girl of the cohort to befriend Susan. The head may also have had a word with the bully. Decades later she and Susan resumed contact, and the girl said it was the first time that she really understood that other people were real in their own right, not just part of her life.

Until and during the early part of the Second World War Susan attended Francis Holland School in London. She and her whole family thought that a German invasion was going to happen. Her well-to-do family had a second residence in Norfolk where they were staying. (Her mother had grown up there as a girl, and had happy memories of it, though her father, Susan's maternal grandfather, another successful solicitor, had parked the family there and only visited at weekends.) Susan vividly remembered a rather pathetic contingent of some forerunner of the Home Guard who were supposed to hold off the invading Germans. Via her mother, who had one of the only telephones in the area, they were given the codeword 'Windmill' to warn them of imminent attack. Susan didn't think much of their chances; when one of Susan's sisters was left alone in the house in Norfolk she did indeed receive such a phonecall and had to go out to the pioneer corps in the middle of the night and say 'windmill' at which they all woke up and swore. Their mother sent the family back to London and a brief spell in North Wales followed – safer from Germans?! Then, in July 1940, her father managed to arrange for his wife and three daughters to go to Canada – Montreal. The family that agreed to take them was not expecting four people, but did their bit. During her time at Dartmouth College in the mid–1980s, Susan was pleased to reconnect with her host family from four decades earlier.[6]

In Montreal, Susan attended an excellent school called 'The Study', where she appears to have been very content. As the fortunes of war changed, a return to England seemed possible and highly desirable, for her father had had a heart attack. A passage was arranged for January 1944, as Susan's mother was the sister of a naval officer: technically not quite a justification but it did the trick. Susan was then sent to school in Wales, Howells School Denbigh. Again she seems to have been reasonably happy, probably because she was sufficiently clever to manage transitions between schools easily, though presumably her Latin was not quite good enough for Lady Margaret Hall, Oxford – hence the catch-up lessons with her aunt. Her interest in History seems to have been sparked by reading romantic novels about the English Civil War period – just as a later generation would be hooked by Tolkien and a still more recent one by 'Game of Thrones'. To judge from a half memory that surfaced when she was dying, she may have supplemented the fiction reading with Dame Veronica Wedgwood's distinguished three-volume history of the English Civil War.[7]

---

[6] Professor G.R. Garthwaite, personal communication.

[7] This came up when Susan could only talk with difficulty. The train of thought was as follows. I had mentioned to her that Lucy Sutherland had been offered the Regius Chair at Oxford before Hugh Trevor-Roper, and commented that maybe the Prime Minister Macmillan (who made the appointment) was better informed than one might think. Or maybe he didn't care, responded Susan. I then mentioned that I had once had a chat with the then Patronage Secretary at a party, and learned that he relied much on Veronica Wedgwood's guidance. Did Susan remember Veronica Wedgwood? I was about to continue talking when she said: When you ask a question, wait for an answer! A memory of how Wedgwood had been important in her life was struggling to the surface. Was it when Susan was already at LMH? No, she didn't think so. A little later she ventured that she may have consulted Wedgwood about university applications, and been told that LMH was a college for ladies. (Susan couldn't remember whether that was meant to be a positive or a negative comment. Given that Wedgwood had been a student at LMH, it was probably positive.) Susan could not remember how she knew this very distinguished amateur historian. (DLd'A)

Susan was an undergraduate at Lady Margaret Hall, Oxford, from 1947 to 1950. Her medieval tutor at LMH was Naomi Hurnard, whose significant contributions to scholarship were lengthy articles on 'The Anglo-Norman Franchises' and a book on *The King's Pardon for Homicide before 1307*. A comparison with Natalie Zemon Davies' much more recent book about French royal pardons (in a later period) would say a lot about historical trends. Hurnard may not have been an inspiring teacher but she got off to a good start with Susan. What is your evidence? – she asked on some point in the first tutorial. Susan mentioned a historian, Maitland no less. That's not your *evidence*, said Hurnard, it's your authority. Later Susan's immense yet critical respect and affection for Maitland would contrast with Hurnard's compulsive efforts at correcting him.

Significant for Susan's later career were tutorials with Lucy Sutherland, the Principal, and an important figure in the Oxford of the day. Not long afterwards Sutherland was more or less offered the Regius Chair of History, but turned it down rather than give up her position as Head of House (at Oxford, unlike Cambridge, it has to be one or the other); Hugh Trevor-Roper then took the job. Later events would prove that Dame Lucy had been impressed by Susan. Lucy Sutherland was a post-medieval historian. Susan does not seem to have been much inspired by the Oxford medievalists of the day or to have remembered a lot about the medieval teaching she received, apart from the tutorials with Hurnard, though perhaps she owed more than she realised from the university's then still very strong focus on medieval history. For medieval history it was, indeed, rather a good day, when a clientele of devoted undergraduates trailed behind K.B. MacFarlane, R.W. Southern was well established, and F.M. Powicke was bringing together a stellar group of intellectual and cultural historians who worked with manuscripts. Great woman scholars were nearby: Beryl Smalley at St Hilda's and Marjorie Reeves at St Anne's. Role models for Susan? There is no sign of it. It says something about the role of the colleges in Oxford, at least in those decades, that the impact of this milieu on Susan's intellectual development seems to have been minimal, at least so far as she remembered.

She graduated in 1950 with a good second (the class was not divided in those days). She did not dare propose herself for doctoral work, or, apparently, think she would be given the opportunity. Later on, she would attribute her sense of being an outsider to the fact that she had not been a doctoral student alongside other future dons. How justified this little chip on her shoulder was is another question: how many of the other medieval dons had been research students together? For Susan's generation, furthermore, the doctoral qualification was less crucial than it would later become. Even those who had doctorates, like Maurice Keen and Beryl Smalley, preferred to be addressed as 'Mr' or 'Miss', as if a doctorate were a slightly shameful thing.

In any case Susan would manage well without one, and obtained what may have been an even better research training thanks to her career path over the next few years. When she was asked by Lucy Sutherland what she wanted to do, she said 'archivist'. As it happens, this was a happy choice.

She took the archive course at University College London (1950–1951). In general it was not excitingly taught but Palaeography and Diplomatic were in the hands of L.C. Hector, a Public Record Office man who was an inspired communicator of those disciplines. He later wrote an outstanding teaching book, *The Handwriting of English Documents*, than which there is no better way into the field. Susan still remembered his instruction on scribal errors: the usual categories but also the joker in the pack, errors due to something unrelated to the text going on in the scribe's mind as he was copying. If she had stayed on for research at Oxford she would have been taught Palaeography by Neil Ker, a great palaeographer indeed but by most accounts an abysmal teacher: one former student remembered how he would write an abbreviation up on the blackboard with one hand and almost simultaneously rub it off with the other. Susan herself would take over the Palaeography teaching of History graduate students in her last years as a don at Oxford, leaving Pierre Chaplais to focus on the teaching of Diplomatic, that is, study of the structure and setting of documents.

To go back to her early career: her research training continued with a brief spell at the Middlesex County Record Office followed by recruitment to the Victoria County History, based at the Institute of Historical Research, University of London. 'Susan was an assistant, not at a tranquil time, but when the VCH's content, design, and research guidelines were being rapidly and extensively modernized under [Ralph] Pugh's new regime, and she played a full and important part … before going on to be editor of the Middlesex VCH herself'.[8] At the VCH her boss Ralph Pugh believed that his staff should also do personal research. He assigned her to work on the writs in the episcopal register of the 14th-century bishop of Salisbury, Roger Martival. Her edition of vol. 3 of the Register, 'Royal Writs', would be published by the Canterbury and York Society in 1965. Editing the highly formulaic writs was an advanced training in Diplomatic as well as in Palaeography. This editorial work together with Pugh's supervision and guidance at the VCH gave her a research training probably superior to anything available in Oxford or Cambridge.

After seven years of this hands-on training, working tranquilly alongside the future General Editor of the VCH Christopher Elrington, she decided it was time for a change. As if sleep-walking into her academic vocation, Susan decided to try teaching – school teaching. For school teaching she had no training. Her first school was an un-academic 'secondary modern' school, Christ Church School, North Finchley. None of the other teachers had a degree, and the common room was tiny. There was no resentment of her, or impatience with her inexperience and the discipline problems that went with it. Susan remembered her fellow teachers with gratitude and affection. They offered sincere congratulations when

---

[8] Christopher Currie, later General Editor of the VCH, personal communication.

she landed a presumably far better-paid job at an independent girls' day school, Queens College Harley St London, founded in 1848 to train governesses. Here she taught from 1960 to 1964. From time to time she would visit her old tutors at LMH.

The urge to do more original research was, however, making itself felt. She planned to do a biography of the Anglican bishop and historian of the papacy Mandell Creighton. At that time Susan was still a believing Anglican. Her faith left her when she was about 40, by her own account because of her habit of questioning everything.

She was already in her early thirties when her professional life took an unexpected turn at which, for the rest of her life, she continued to marvel. Lucy Sutherland, the Principal of her old college LMH, wrote to her – hand-written note – saying that she might be aware that Naomi Hurnard was going to retire, and would Susan like to come to lunch. Susan suspected that Hurnard had not really expected her resignation to be accepted, but if so Hurnard was mistaken. She and the other LMH History tutor Ann Wightman had not spoken to each other for years – one wonders how entrance interviewing was managed – and Wightman and the Principal were on good terms. So a space was created.

It was a different age. A head of house and a tutor could in effect offer a job for life. The lunch was the interview with the appointment board, but it had all been decided beforehand. Susan had mixed feelings about this modus operandi, which belonged to a world about to vanish, but it was certainly a good call in her case. Susan's research would go from strength to strength. It was a slow build-up to world class achievement as a scholar. She already had under her belt the edition of writs in the Martival register. In 1969 an article in the *English Historical Review* exposed the charters of Barnstaple as forgeries. Here she showed real detective flair. The clues were there but previous scholarship had missed them. In 1977 she published with OUP an *Introduction to the History of Medieval English Towns*. While not as exciting as her later books, it was a good monograph in a field previously deadened by Tait's learned but, for many, unreadable *Medieval English Borough*. Susan's study achieved the by no means routine accolade of a positive review in the journal *Annales*, at that time the most important historical journal. Her VCH training may have helped with the research; much of the Middlesex covered by her volume had become part of London, and she had written particularly well on the development of Twickenham. And all that work sowed the seeds of the very different, later, studies for which she is best known. As she says at the start of the Preface to her first volume of collected essays, 'My interest in the collective activities of medieval lay people and the solidarities that underlay them were awakened soon after I started to work on medieval English towns in the mid-sixties' (*Ideas and Solidarities*, p. vii).

Susan was clearly a good teacher, as pupils like Pauline Stafford testify. In an interview given in 2008, Susan commented that 'after about twenty years there I was getting a bit stale, partly because I was more and more interested in the research and therefore spending less and less time on doing new things in teaching. So the teaching got staler.' Yet this was far from the impression one of the authors of this piece got when, in 1982–3, Susan taught him for his Special Subject on 'Reform and Revolution 1258–1267'. Not that the tutorials got off to an auspicious start. The preparatory meeting had to be cancelled because I (JH) was suffering from chickenpox. The first proper tutorial started late, after I limped across the Parks to LMH, having hurt my knee playing rugby. In the second I tried the phrase 'Well, feudal in inverted commas.' No one will doubt which of these three events was the most dangerous. Yet I remember very well the firm and insightful reprimand that when people say 'in inverted commas' they are just avoiding having to work out exactly what they mean. And the tutorials were memorable too for seeing a historian's mind working in a rather different way from those which I had previously observed. Other tutorials had often been characterised by an approach that can best be described as combining the socratic and the contrarian – at their best to wonderful effect … but not always at their best. Here one could see Susan continually turning over in her mind her latest hypotheses – and I rejoiced when she interrupted some statement of mine by saying, 'Stop, let me take down that point, it fits with something that I am arguing.' And all was done with enthusiasm and humanity. As another student writes, 'Apart from looking over one's shoulder for the rest of one's life before saying the word "feudalism", it is Susan's enthusiasm that I remember, having had the good fortune to be tutored by her at LMH [1974–77]. She really did bounce in her chair, eyebrows up and beaming, if she was pleased. She was very kind – students who she felt were flagging before finals were taken out for a country walk and a pub lunch. In spring her room was filled with troughs of hyacinths in bloom, a scent which evoked Susan for ever after.'[9]

No doubt her years as a school teacher helped. As with all new university lecturers, the start was challenging: she was not yet familiar with the bibliography of the papers she had to teach. In Oxford's Collegiate system, furthermore, she had to work to existing course and examining traditions, irrespective of her personal knowledge and interests. To the rescue came Barbara Harvey (prompted by Ann Wightman), who passed her own bibliographies and essay questions over to Susan.

In retrospect on her teaching, Susan criticised two categories of tutorial pupils who came her way at LMH. There were men from well-known public schools taught by confident young male teachers. (To this day, famous public schools often recruit history masters with excellent academic records even if they have no teaching qualifications or experience – a system that seems to work better than it should do.) These gentlemen were unable to let go of what they had learned at school, especially since it was a woman who was subverting their assumptions. Then there were women described on application forms by their head teachers as 'scholarly'. This seems to have been a code-word for hard working and dutiful but uninspiring to teach, because unwilling to talk. On one occasion Susan told two

[9] Kate Currie, personal communication.

of them that if they weren't planning to say anything she might as well go and prepare her supper. Susan must have given lectures but does not seem to have attached so much importance to them as to tutorials. This was in tune with the general ethos of the Oxford History School. Research supervision seems rarely to have come her way. As noted above, in her final years at Oxford she took over the Palaeography teaching of History graduates, and enjoyed this change from undergraduate teaching.

Undergraduate teaching for Susan, as for others, was a predominantly college affair. That may explain what Susan felt to be a problem with the whole milieu, viz., that there was a lack of collective intellectual life. Intellectual leadership by great professors was not Oxford's style. It is true that the retired Regius Professor V.H. Galbraith (and his wife) made Susan very welcome on her return to the university, and she was most grateful for it and for the drinks sociably thrust into her hand. She was aware of R.W. Southern as an admired figure, but does not seem to have had much contact with him. Ernest Jacob, Geoffrey Barraclough (mostly conspicuous by absence it is true), Michael Wallace-Hadrill and Karl Leyser seem hardly to have been on her radar, to judge from her later reminiscences.

Furthermore, according to Susan, it was not done simply to turn up at seminars run by a colleague. One had to ask permission and there was no culture of doing so. In her mind, the contrast with London's Institute of Historical Research, on which more below, was overwhelming. Nor was it easy to find interlocutors with whom to discuss her own research. When the idea of *Kingdoms and Communities in Western Europe, 900–1300* (first edition Oxford, 1984), probably her greatest work, was germinating, she tried to engage Maurice Keen in conversation about it, but he said he didn't know enough. Since his general knowledge of medieval history was very wide, that must have sounded unconvincing, but Keen probably just felt that they were on different wavelengths. It was again Barbara Harvey who came to the rescue by being prepared to listen.

It was probably largely a matter of listening rather than criticising. Susan was herself not the best of listeners, though she wanted to be: but her own train of thought would soon take over, despite her benign intentions and her disarming self-awareness of this pattern. Whether she would have listened long and patiently to Maurice Keen's theories about Chivalry without interrupting is an open question – but in any case she was probably right that such discussions were uncommon in the Oxford History Faculty, despite Susan's theory that dons who had done doctorates together were intellectually close.

Perhaps Susan's approach and interests were not a good fit with the intellectual communities that did exist in her time among the dons. The focus on religious and cultural history, as transmitted in manuscript books, which united the informal group of Beryl Smalley, Marjorie Reeves, Daniel Callus, W.A. Pantin, and above all R.W. Hunt, had no more impact on her than when she was an undergraduate, and, as then, she remained far from the intellectual offspring of K.B. McFarlane. For whatever reason, she felt intellectually isolated.

One matter that did bring fellows of different colleges together was university examining. In her first year after returning to Oxford, Susan only had a college post and salary, but then a university appointment was added to it. Eventually, she took her turn on the Finals examination board: a heavy burden as the Oxford History School had many undergraduates. Her co-examiner was Maurice Keen. In the first year, they disagreed about practically every script. John Cowdrey of St Edmund Hall had to be brought in to re-mark the whole set. In subsequent years, Susan and Maurice Keen's marks were entirely in harmony, so they had learned from each other about examining at least, and clearly got on well personally.

Like a post-captain in the navy of Nelson's day, Susan rose in seniority, and thus she became Chair of the History Board of Examiners. She was not a professor and was warned on all sides to expect trouble from a potentially obstreperous Hugh Trevor-Roper, the Regius Professor, who had returned to the Board that year. His previous stint on it was vividly remembered for his drastic culling of potential First Class degrees, leaving only a handful. But by the time Susan was chair, his zeal or energy had diminished and he did not give too much trouble. Nonetheless he pulled down the class of one candidate who deserved better. Peter Mathias, who had a status close to Trevor-Roper's, took her aside during the lunch hour and proposed that they try to reverse the decision, which they did. Susan seems to have been an efficient chair and she took the trouble to thank the administrators with whom she worked, a gesture that was apparently unusual at the time.

She also played her efficient part in College administration. She noted that those who avoided such duties because of the demands of 'their own work' did not necessarily achieve much with the latter either. Notably, Susan took on the role of Dean, responsible for welfare and discipline. Much later she wondered if she had been as aware as she should have been of problems like mental health among undergraduates. Her approach was firm and brisk, but, given the natural kindness that informed all her behaviour, probably effective. When LMH started to take male students, she went the extra mile to make contacts that would increase recruitment from state schools.

Oxbridge college life and teaching brings with it great satisfactions – a sociable community and close intellectual interaction with the college's undergraduates – but the teaching, in particular, can begin to pall after a couple of decades. The main papers are in the thrall of a collective examining tradition, which is overthrown every couple of generations by acrimonious Kuhnian revolutions but is in general out of the control of the individual tutor who needs to prepare undergraduates for the kind of questions that are 'likely to come up'. After a decade or so, every possible way of answering every one of such questions is all too familiar, echoing endless previous tutorials. At this point, they may start looking for ways to get paid leave or diminish their teaching loads. Susan escaped this mid-life teaching crisis. She had come late to the job, and she retired very early. Born in 1929, appointed in 1964, she left Oxford in 1986.

Two years before, she had published the book that made her famous, *Kingdoms and Communities*. This presented medieval society as structured above all by 'horizontal' groups of people *de facto* similar in status, as opposed to 'vertical' bonds between inferiors and superiors. Though 'Kingdoms' is the first word in the title, an alliterative choice she later regretted, the book is about a wide range of communities: parishes, guilds, urban groups, regional assemblies as well as kingdoms, the feudal character of which she was already dismissing. This original synthesis brought together within a single interpretative framework a whole series of social and political phenomena usually studied separately. Sir Isaiah Berlin once proposed that great history was the kind that found connections between different layers of life. That is exactly what Susan did in *Kingdoms and Communities*. She also broke down the barrier that tended to separate British from 'Continental' history. England, France, Germany and Italy were studied together. The traditional medieval syllabi of English universities had tended to segregate English from 'European' history and the strong historical schools of Germany, France and Italy had tended to leave England out of the picture, and indeed also each other (except that German and French scholars treated Italian history as part of their remit). To master the very different historiographies, Susan had to learn German, essential for all but the most specifically English medieval history and sometimes for that too. She could have stayed where she began, in English history, but she broadened out. The protection of Continental history in Bantustan 'General History' papers may have pushed her in that direction. She had to teach it at Oxford. Many a medievalist has done that, however, without doing original research on regions across the Channel. It is a sign of Susan's professionalism that she took the trouble. The book also gave evidence of her reading in social theory, especially anthropology. The writing was crisp and clear. Reading it for the first time I (DLd'A) missed my stop on the London underground, I was so engrossed. Reviews were enthusiastic. Susan was like a different person in this book. Until then a massively powerful intellect had been half concealed. In her mid-fifties, it revealed itself, confident and assured. After *Kingdoms and Communities* her election to the British Academy (in 1993) was a natural thing.[10]

Not long after the appearance of *Kingdoms and Communities*, Susan retired from Oxford, perhaps just in time to save her from getting tired of the conservative syllabus. She spent a year (1986–7) teaching as a visiting professor at Dartmouth College in the USA, and found it stimulating, though problems with the heating system of the house she had exchanged for a year for her London flat nearly spoiled it as the brutal North American winter began. She liked the students (at the same time noting their well-to-do provenance) and enjoyed co-teaching an introductory course on medieval and early modern Europe. For their part, the students and faculty took to Susan. One of the latter told us that

---

[10] Famous and successful though she was, Susan still had difficulty in placing articles in leading journals, as she disarmingly volunteered in her IHR interview. She was also frustrated in her desire to write a book about Nationalism.

Dartmouth students are leery of visiting faculty classes, but not Susan's. ... Susan valued the History Department's culture of openness, commitment to world and comparative history, and the range of interaction on campus in seminars and the continuing of lively discussions off campus on social occasions. We all quickly learned the value of her deep knowledge and critical eye. Her culinary skills were often shown at dinners on North Balch or at faculty potlucks. She delighted in pitching in on friends' projects whether academic or not ... And after 1987, Susan would return to Hanover often on her way to conferences and lectures, or to give one here.[11]

Susan told the Administrator of her department (after helping in the manual labour of lugging and laying rocks to build a walkway to the administrator's house!) that her period at Dartmouth was one of the best times of her life.[12]

Clearly Susan felt very much at home with American scholars, and she built up warm friendships. Ralph Pugh had introduced her to the University of Michigan legal historian, Tom Green, in 1979 as she already wanted to visit the United States and she duly went in 1980. The visit included Ann Arbor, the home of the University of Michigan, and she returned there about half a dozen times up to the early 21st century. She would stay for four or five days, bulding up connections to PhD students, some of whom she would also see when they visited London. Her connections were primarily with History but she also developed friendships with members of the Law School. Bruce Frier describes her as the most delightful dinner companion he has ever encountered, her conversation full of her fascinating observations on subjects such as the differing colour and stance of the green man on British pedestrian crossings, the white man on US ones. Another of these friends, the scholar of Icelandic law, William Ian Miller, recalls flying her in his small plane from Ann Arbor to the medieval conference at Kalamazoo: 'you cannot imagine the danger we were in on that little flight ... in conditions way more demanding than my skill level could manage, though somehow I did. She did not even get the least bit queasy as we banged around and the plane was in turbulence just about at the limits it could safely handle, but instead she continued her flow of talk without interruption.' She was also a regular visitor to Santa Barbara, California, where she again delighted in the intellectual company of the doctoral students whilst not in the least modifying her usual choice of garb, despite Californian weather and informality.

In 1987, on her return from Dartmouth College, she committed to making London her full-time working base – 'retirement' seems decidedly the wrong word. This was a wonderful period for her and for the London medieval scene. She had always been happiest doing research in the British Library and the Institute of Historical Research, and had regularly returned during university vacations to the very nice flat she had kept since 1962 in Lennox

[11] G.R. Garthwaite, Emeritus Professor at Dartmouth, personal communication.
[12] Gail Patten, as reported by Cecilia Gaposchkin (personal communication).

Gardens. In fact the IHR was a great continuity in Susan's life, going back to her time with the VCH which was based there. She enjoyed the Common Room's social facilities, and the opportunity of meeting, and discussing ideas with, both contemporaries and younger scholars, to whom she never adopted a *de haut en bas* attitude. Having left Oxford, she could now work in London full-time and she made the most of it. She regarded the BL as distinctly superior to the Bodleian, and rejoiced in its relative efficiency by comparison with her earliest experiences, when books were often declared to have been lost in the war even if published after 1945. She attributed the transformation to the appointment of a qualified librarian to run the library, though the explanation may be more complex than that. At any rate it was paradise for her, both before and after the move from Bloomsbury to St Pancras.

Similarly, she found deep intellectual satisfaction in the 'Wednesday Seminar' on early medieval history (up to *c.* 1300) in the IHR. The IHR seminars did not 'belong' to any particular London college, and medievalists from all colleges and from outside the University and London could attend with the minimum of formality. The IHR was (and is) common intellectual and scholarly ground. The Wednesday seminar was entering a golden period, partly of course due to Susan's regular presence. Around the time she moved to London full-time, Michael Clanchy and his wife moved down to London, and he too was a regular attender. Adding these stellar medievalists to the existing group around Janet Nelson, John Gillingham, and Wendy Davies made the seminar for a while one of the most exciting in the world. Susan always spoke, very confidently but, even when contradicting, always kindly and benignly. Papers by some of the best medievalists in the Anglophone world (and France) were amicably discussed. Questions and discussion were followed by socialisation, in a pub or, latterly, in the common room of the Institute. Those who wished then went on to an inexpensive dinner, usually at Olivelli's in Store Street. Susan revelled in the intellectual cameraderie that she felt she had missed in Oxford, with its close college communities which brought together scholars from different disciplines but separated workers in the same disciplines

As indicated above, 'feudalism' was already sidelined in *Kingdoms and Communities*. Before that book had come out, E.A.R. Brown had published an influential indictment of the concept in a major *American Historical Review* article (1974). Susan and Peggy Brown now made contact personally. Susan met Peggy on arrival in England, holding a copy of Marc Bloch's *Feudal Society* (which both were implicitly subverting) to identify herself. Susan held Peggy in high regard ('one of the important figures in my field of research', she said in her IHR interview, complimentary language from her somewhat critical lips) and hoped for a joint book, but in fact Peggy Brown's inclinations turned more and more to articles full of insight about the late Capetians, and close study of the relevant documents. Susan for her part had moved away from manuscript research, though a clever essay on Magna Carta noticed a copyist's mistake that suggested that by the late 13th century nobody was reading the small print numbers in the document.

During this time Susan was building up to her monumental *Fiefs and Vassals*, which appeared the year after her election to the British Academy. Its reviewer in *Revue Historique* (Elisabeth Nortier) described it as 'un grand livre, un livre iconoclaste'. The icon that it set out to break was the very notion of feudalism. The field of battle was the same as for *Kingdoms and Communities*, and indeed had been pre-figured in it: '"feudalism" and "feudal" are meaningless terms which are unhelpful in understanding medieval society' (*Kingdoms and Communities*, p. 9). Now Susan set out to use medieval evidence to demolish conclusions and assumptions held by historians like Marc Bloch (*Feudal Society*), Ganshof (*Feudalism*), and indeed Maitland, whose *Domesday Book and Beyond* had argued for feudal elements in Anglo-Saxon society. Susan was unafraid of attacking giants.

Her attack had destructive and constructive elements. She argued that still influential ideas about the early medieval development of fiefs and vassalage were a product of early modern legal writing, drawing on the 12th- to 13th-century north Italian compilation known as the *Libri feudorum*. Likewise, the forms of relationship to which the terms 'fiefs' and 'vassals' have commonly been applied developed in the context of governmental bureaucratisation and the growth of academic legal scholarship from the mid–12th century. Such changes, and changing interpretations, were concealed by continuity in terminology, but not in concepts or phenomena. The constructive element was, first, to allow proper understanding of the vertical, lordship relationships that formed part of medieval societies but should not be taken to define them, and, second, to integrate these relationships with the horizontal ones that had been set out in *Kingdoms and Communities*, along with another type of vertical relationship, that of government.

What then of her target and her method? For many decades, schoolchildren had been taught that 'feudal society' could be summed up in a sort of diagram showing barons below kings, knights below barons, and peasants below knights. It was certainly time to try to pull the carpet from under any assumption that medieval society could be represented in any such simplistic way. It is also true the words 'feudal society', 'feudal', 'fief' and vassal had been employed sloppily, without sufficient thought. Susan liked to apply to her historical analysis the distinction between 'words, concepts and phenomena', taken from Ogden & Richards' famous book *The Meaning of Meaning*. Her belief that historians tend to use words unthinkingly was surely salutary. To Susan's delight, in 2021 Robin Fleming dedicated a book to her as the person who taught her and historians generally to 'mind their language'. The words-concepts-phenomena schema has its limitations. It needs a further distinction between the concepts of the people studied, everyday modern concepts, and the special concepts created by scholars for analytical purposes. Susan was certainly aware of the need to draw that distinction, but she did not clearly see past phenomena as involving concepts: she automatically classified 'concepts' and 'phenomena' as mutually exclusive, though she would backtrack on this when challenged informally in later life. It might have diminished her polemical zeal if she had thought of 'feudalism' as a social system working together with other social systems – those 'horizontal' bonds, loyalty to a monarch, etc. – and as a system which was as much mental as physical, one kind of reason that could be given, alongside other reasons, for doing this or that. 'This or that' in England included allowing the man from whom one held land to pick husbands or wives for marriageable sons and daughter before they reached the age of majority. The traditional explanation in terms of a feudal logic makes perfect sense of these marriage rights, which the barons of Magna Carta treated with a light touch because they wanted to retain them over their own vassals.

Susan was aware of the problem for her thesis and glossed over it like a brilliant barrister passing rapidly through a weak point in the case.[13] Likewise, the book does not address the issue of whether other words that it is happy to use might not be subjected to similar criticisms as talk of feudalism; is the problem a general one, or is it really the damage that has been done by this particular word that requires the assault upon its use? Why not use it, not as a key to a whole society, but to indicate one among a number of ways of organising social life, alongside gift exchange, community and kinship, sacral kingship, etc.? One may also wonder whether the book's arguments fully reconcile emphasis on the effects of academic law, both upon practice from the mid–12th century and upon later historical interpretation, with Susan's belief, stated most clearly in *Kingdoms and Communities*, that 'what the academics, polemicists, and lawyers wrote articulated and refined the old ideas rather than producing entirely new ones' (pp. lvi-lvii). Might this allow room for the custom stated in the *Libri feudorum* to be a better guide to at least some earlier practice and perhaps everyday (as opposed to merely academic) thought than *Fiefs and Vassals* allows?

However, such criticisms must not hide the tremendous achievements of the book. Firstly, it made scholars think hard about what they had previously tended to take for granted. Secondly, there was a positive contribution that has not been sufficiently noticed. Susan brought understanding of Roman law and its medieval reception into the main-stream of historical interpretation. Hitherto it had been carefully studied by specialists in the field. In the course of arguing that its pervasive influence has obscured underlying and older structures, she showed just how influential it was. Above all, she brought out the later, historiographical significance of the *Libri Feudorum* that became an integral part of

---

[13] *Fiefs*, 368–70, cf. 336. The mental schema is that when you hold land from a lord, he has a right to make sure that it doesn't pass through marriage into the wrong hands, or slip out of his control – the classic explanation that still convinces. Susan seems not to have addressed the further problem of the tenurial emphasis of Clause 14 of the 1215 Magna Carta: 'to obtain the common counsel of the realm for the assessment of an aid … or a scutage, we will have archbishops, bishops, abbots, earls and greater barons summoned individually by our letters, and we shall also have summoned generally through our sheriffs and bailiffs all those who hold of us in chief'.

the Roman law corpus as understood in the later Middle Ages, and thereby drew a much wider range of historians' attention to the *Libri* in their own time. Thirdly, and again a neglected contribution, she suggested similarities in early medieval land ownership over a wide geographical area, for example suggesting that the difference between Anglo-Saxon 'bookland' and French or Italian allod was one of language, not substance. This discussion in turn relates to an effort to get historians to think hard about other casually used terms, such as tenure and property, issues to which she would return in later papers.

Above all, *Fiefs and Vassals* is a pioneering essay in comparative legal history. Comparison was as crucial an element of Susan's work as was her emphasis upon words – and the two aspects were closely interconnected. She argued that comparison could reveal not just differences but also similarities: 'there was much less difference in social and political organization – not least in its collective manifestations – between different parts of western Europe than seems to be generally thought' (*Kingdoms and Communities*, p. 7). Essential for proper comparison was to have more than two comparators: 'bilateral comparisons inevitably tend to polarities' (*Kingdoms and Communities*, p. 8). Ill-informed and crude comparisons of England and 'the Continent' were unhelpful. England might, or might not, be different, but if different, different from what? And how? And why? As she said in her 2008 interview, 'I think comparison is vital. If you find that in your bit of history A leads to B, you assume that it always does – but if you immediately look somewhere else, you find that A leads to C, or to X. ... I think comparisons are vital for history.' As epitomised in *Fiefs and Vassals*, comparison thus disrupts the assumptions of national historiographies and questions traditional interpretations.

During her later years Susan also published a string of important papers. One that appeared between *Kingdoms and Communities* and *Fiefs and Vassals* diverged in subject matter from the trajectory that links them. In her 'Social Mentalities and the Case of Medieval Scepticism', published in 1991, 'she pointed out the various ways in which medieval people might *not* have been straightforward "believers" but might treat various claims about Christian religion with a sceptical eye: the powers of saints, the idea of Hell, the wider theological framework proffered by the Church', to quote John Arnold's summary.[14] John Arnold was to take this line of argument much further, and it had been anticipated by Alexander Murray.[15] Susan was making a wider point, however: as John Arnold puts it, the article was

> not simply about revising our opinion of the religiosity of the middle ages, but is very clearly directed against the idea that people are trapped within mental structures (as she saw the concept of *mentalité*). She was very irritated with the French scholarship of this kind, as similarly with *féodalité*, but on the other hand clearly found its generalisations a

[14] Personal communication.
[15] A. Murray, 'Piety and Impiety in Thirteenth Century Italy', *Studies in Church History*, 8 (1972).

useful foil against which to push. To some large degree the 'mentalité' debate has now moved on – I think the move to microhistory in the 80s (*Montaillou* apart!) did quite a lot to shift the idea of 'governing' mental structures, as in a different way did gender history – but Susan's article was then also fundamental in making the space for a more sustained attempt to think through the extent to which ordinary medieval people simply 'believed', or were in fact capable of active questioning in regard to Christianity.[16]

Numerous important articles by Susan were brought together in two Variorum Reprints volumes. These are in many ways companion works to *Kingdoms and Communities* and *Fiefs and Vassals*. *Ideas and Solidarities of the Medieval Laity: England and Western Europe* appeared in 1995, *The Middle Ages without Feudalism: Essays in Criticism and Comparison on the Medieval West* in 2012. Especially interesting in the first is an unpublished paper on 'The history of the idea of incorporation or legal personality: a case of fallacious teleology.' This was a topic that continued to engage Susan's thinking until her very last months, even though it never produced a full-length study. It allowed her full rein for some of her favourite activities, attacking teleology, arguing that the greatest attention should be given to practice rather than academic writings: 'The hypothesis that I suggest emerges from this survey, incomplete as it is, is that attempting to explain the way that west European law about the rights and responsibilities of collective groups at law by looking for the origin of the modern jurist's idea of legal personality is to fly in the face of evidence about how law changes in practice. It is starting at the wrong end' (*Ideas and Solidarities*, VI.16). The later volume is particularly notable for extending still further the already great geographical range of *Fiefs and Vassals*, from Scotland to the kingdom of Jerusalem. Titles of essays such as 'Secular power and authority in the Middle Ages' also clearly illustrate the ever-broader subjects that Susan was tackling, a broadening that is a defining characteristic of her career from the *Victoria County History* onwards. Other articles form part of a project on nations and nationhood, a subject on which Susan contemplated writing a book.

Further, one of the essays in this second Variorum volume, on 'The use of feudalism in comparative history', seems to go beyond the not quite satisfactory 'words, concepts and phenomena' formula, which glossed over the distinction between 'our' (etic) and 'their' (emic) concepts. She writes that 'It is of course perfectly reasonable for historians both to use their own words and to think in terms of their own concepts, but it is easier to distinguish evidence from interpretation if one distinguishes whether a concept is ours or is that of people in the past' (VI.197). In 'Vocabularies for comparative and interdisciplinary history' (written in 2009–2011) she suggests that 'historical comparisons are also made less useful when words are used as if they unambiguously referred to a single phenomenon although they have been used over the centuries to refer to a whole range of different

---

[16] Personal communication.

phenomena perceived in different ways by historians with different interests and ideas about what is significant in history' (XVII.17). She endorses a plea for a 'common vocabulary' and suggests that we 'might even consider replacing or supplementing' words that have been used in too many different ways 'with generic terms where that would help the reader'. She is in effect proposing that historians construct their own terms of art, à la Max Weber. Like most British historians, Susan did not entirely 'get' Weber, while thinking she did. Downright mistaken is her reference (VII.497) to 'teleological assumptions of growing rationality and European superiority that Max Weber made academically respectable', but in her essay on 'Empires: a problem of comparative history' she seems to come close to adopting his ideal-type method, without using the word: '... looking directly at the variety, not to say confusion, of words and concepts that we have inherited may make it easier to lay both words and concepts aside for the moment and concentrate on deciding what seem to be the most important characteristics of the phenomena with which I think that historians of empires, particularly more modern empires, are concerned' (XV.158). She goes on to construct a well-designed ideal-type: 'If one starts by thinking of what we are interested in as, by and large, relatively large polities that consist of a ruling part (the metropolis) and other parts (colonies or peripheries) that it dominates as a result of military conquest or some kind of political or economic bullying, and that are retained and governed separately from the metropolis rather than being absorbed in it, then one has to note that not all the polities that look likely cases seem to have all these characteristics' (XV.158). Susan then works through a series of political agglomerations asking in which respects the ideal-type she has given applied. She finds many differences, offers explanations, and takes from the Middle Ages an element for her ideal-type that modernists have overlooked: the importance of 'a good deal of voluntary submission' (XV.161). She convincingly states that 'the real argument against comparison is that it is such hard work' (XV.165).

Collections of papers aside, Susan's last book was *Before Eminent Domain*. This pursues her feud against feudalism but into entirely different territory, and in such a way that her 'refutation' of feudal interpretations are of secondary importance (just as they were when she put the *Libri Feudorum* on the map of general medieval history). Eminent domain is the right of governments to expropriate property for the common good, for example by confiscation or by compulsory purchase . Some scholars had traced the origins of this right or claim back to feudal concepts. Susan (of course) disagreed. She looked at medieval thinkers, above all academic Roman lawyers, and found that they took the right to expropriate for granted without any invocation of feudalism. If they gave a justification, it was the common good or common utility, but the right was grounded in Roman law anyway. Susan's research instinct led her far beyond the confines of the Middle Ages, however, to Grotius, the 17th-century Dutch thinker who played a central role in the shaping of the idea of international law. For Susan, Grotius not only invented the concept of eminent domain, a new name for an old concept, but also developed an entirely original rationale for the right. He grounded it in social contract theory. In a theory which has since then become commonplace (so that nobody worries about its totally mythical character) there was originally no private property. Private property and the right to it were a consequence of the social contract to submit to a government and its positive laws. Given that origin, the government could naturally override property rights.

When that book appeared Susan was over 80. She was 86 when her remarkable chapter on 'Society: hierarchy and solidarity' was published in the *Cambridge History of the World*, vol. 5. She argued that 'assumptions about hierarchy and solidarity were apparently similar everywhere'. It is an astonishingly bold analysis of concepts that apply very generally to the period 500–1500, across world history. In her mid-eighties, Susan became still more impressive as a historian.

In her 2008 interview, Susan stated: 'I think that historians are not interested enough in historical method and how you prove something or don't prove it. Karl Popper, disproving things and so on. I remember at one stage I got very fussed about this and I couldn't find anything to read on historical reasoning. … what I was interested in was historians thinking harder about what they're doing. You could call it theory, but I wouldn't want to go into what is considered theory now.' We may, then, reflect more broadly upon Susan's own historical method. Some well-known aspects have already been mentioned. There is the emphasis upon words and the relationship of word, concept and phenomenon, along with the connected concern with teleology and national historiographies: 'Differences of vocabulary became differences of concept when they began to be explained by lawyers and historians brought up within their separate national traditions' (*Kingdoms and Communities*, p. 8). There is the return to the sources, and their language: 'It seemed better to try to understand the ways medieval people perceived their communities – the meanings they gave to them – by using their own words, and the circumstances in which they used them, as a guide to their concepts, rather than by starting from modern words and concepts' (*Kingdoms and Communities*, pp. 332–3).

There is also an emphasis upon practice, as a subject for study in itself and as a way into the practical ideas of people at the time, and thence to the relationship between practice and theory, notably the importance of practice in the development of theoretical or academic ideas. In the Introduction to the second edition of *Kingdoms and Communities* Susan reflected:

> Not that I thought the book was only about activity. I meant it also to be about ideas: that is, the ideas of lay people about the rights and activities of groups, but I thought that these could best be explored through the evidence of their activities. … New ideas were only slowly worked out to justify or resist new practices of government and law which were themselves made possible by economic and social changes. (pp. xii-xiii)

And at the end of the book she had concluded that 'it looks ... as if new practice evoked new theory, not the other way round' (p. 332). Despite her conviction that the emergence of academic law and professional lawyers made a major difference to thinking, to records, and to practice, even then she prioritised practical ideas: 'Intellectuals are not the only people in any society who think ... Intellectuals, even if they write in their society's vernacular and have access to ample technologies of popularization, surely do not have as big an effect on their societies' values and assumptions as their societies' values and assumptions have on them?' (*Kingdoms and Communities*, p. lvii). Sensible, one might say commonsensical, ideas should not be mis-interpreted as lofty theories: 'Using the metaphor of a person or body is not the same as working out a theory of corporations in general as fictitious persons' (*Ideas and Solidarities*, VI.8). We feel that for Susan common sense mattered both in the past and in historical writing, common sense that, of course, involved thinking hard.

Not surprisingly, therefore, Susan's work always showed a preference for record sources, especially those that could be taken to reveal lay activity. Particularly in *Fiefs and Vassals* she expressed concern about projecting from the more extensive records of ecclesiastical activities onto lay activities. But more generally she was devoted to returning to the primary sources, and to thinking about them and the people and activities that they recorded.

And once she had read widely in the sources and the secondary literature, and thought hard about them, she would come up with her case, to be presented in lawyer-like fashion. The style of her writing contains phrases resonant of the court room, a statement beginning 'I suggest that ...' being followed by sustained reasoning and evidence based on acceptance of that hypothesis (e.g. *Before Eminent Domain*, p. 3). And the range of types of arguments employed would be familiar to the barrister, or to the scholars of the *Libri feudorum* whom she brought fully to our attention. She drew distinctions, she produced analogies, she gave narrow or broad significances to particular words, concepts, and phenomena, sometimes narrowing the definition of a word whilst broadening the scope of the associated phenomenon, or vice versa. The forms of argument might sometimes evoke worries in the reader, even if the reader did not identify the rhetorical forms she was using: the presentation of possibilities as mutually exclusive alternatives when they might co-exist (e.g. *Fiefs and Vassals*, pp. 382, 470); the rejection of a theory concerning the significance of a phenomenon sliding into a rejection of the significance of that phenomenon itself (e.g. *Before Eminent Domain*, p. 54). Yet if such might be presented as weaknesses, they were in fact what created the very vigour of the arguments, their value along with their basis in the sources.

Of course, not all the ideas in her writings were contained in the initial argument or arguments that she was seeking to prove. As she wrote in *Kingdoms and Communities* (pp. 9–10) 'Other ideas emerged as I worked, some of them quite unexpected but deriving, as it seemed to me, from the primary sources which I read.' However, she then tellingly reasserted the centrality of the core points of her case: 'Although all these [further] arguments confirm and extend my original propositions, they were not formulated, at least consciously, for that reason, for I was prepared to argue the original propositions without them.' And like a barrister, once her brief on one matter was argued, the focus turned to a new case, with the previous one often disappearing from view.

These characteristics go along with her ever increasing interest in the history of law. In *Kingdoms and Communities* the tone is almost apologetic, with worry being expressed about misunderstanding as to the autonomy of law from economic, social religious and political forces, and with justification being provided in terms of the available source material (p. 12). By 2008, when interviewed, she was saying 'And then there's law, which I've always been interested in and am more closing in on. ... This expropriation for public good was not meant to be a book, but it got a bit big and so it's going to be a short book', which indeed was published as *Before Eminent Domain*. Tellingly, and rather differently from many who come to law from other areas of history, her focus was less disputes, more transactional law, and records of transactions involving property or rights were central to so much of her work: 'The law that was applied, in both north and south, is to be deduced for the most part rather from grants to individuals and from more or less laconic reports of individual cases, than from general statements' (*Kingdoms and Communities*, p. 16). Her explorations then broadened further. There is the interest, manifest particularly in *Fiefs and Vassals*, on the developments in academic law. And there is the consideration of the effect of the shift from non-professional to professional law, prominent in *Kingdoms and Communities* and most fully discussed in an article on 'The emergence of professional law in the long twelfth century', published in *Law and History Review* in 2003 and reprinted in *The Middle Ages without Feudalism*. There she examined the effects of the revolution in scholarly law upon legal practice, expounding upon favourite issues such as what happened when words were adopted from Roman law with a limited or different grasp of the concepts, and applied to very different social situations.[17]

Such were the sorts of large questions in which Susan delighted and which took her into what might be referred to as much as Historical jurisprudence as legal history. It is significant that she cited Sir Henry Maine with approval when considering the nature of pre-professional law: 'Law between the tenth and early twelfth centuries was the undifferentiated, indeterminate, and flexible law appropriate to a society that was for many practical purposes illiterate (if not strictly preliterate), and it must be understood in those terms, not in the terms of later professional or academic law. In the words of Maine: "The distinctions of the later jurists are appropriate only to the later jurisprudence"' (*Kingdoms and Communities*, p. 13). She was happy both to identify clear turning points and to make

---

[17] Thanks to Alice Taylor for discussing this point.

brave and broad generalisations: 'It is the nature of custom that it presupposes a group or community within which it is practised. Any statement of law will therefore be made in some sense on behalf of the community, and government is likely to involve some kind of consultation with it' (*Kingdoms and Communities*, p. 21). Some of her contributions in this field are well recognised, such as her discussions of the relationship of technical to other meanings of words and her emphasis on the fluidity of signification. Others merit much greater recognition and much further consideration, for example the suggestion in *Fiefs and Vassals* that many phenomena that law before *c.* 1150 had treated as *variations* in custom or practice came thereafter to be treated as *exceptions* to rules, without the phenomena themselves having changed.

In these ways Susan was also drawn into trying to identify the elementary ideas within both pre-professional and professional law, and the different nature of those ideas before and after a period of great legal change. Particularly in the earlier period, elementary ideas might well be unstated, or only formulated as particular cases arose: 'Given, however, that the boundary between criminal and civil wrongs is never all that simple to draw, it is not surprising that there is no statement in the surviving records of where it ran. If anyone had needed to make the distinction, he would have drawn it in a way that made sense for one particular place, time, and case' (*Kingdoms and Communities*, p. 20). And in the world of professional law, degrees of abstraction differed between systems: 'The character of the Common Law training clearly had a vital influence on the law of corporations that resulted. The culture of the Common Law did not encourage theorizing' (*Ideas and Solidarities*, VI.15). Throughout, she was worrying away at broad jurisprudential categories, be it the separation of legal rules from other social norms in *Kingdoms and Communities* or her 2012 essay on 'Assembly government and assembly law', or 'property' in *Fiefs and Vassals*, or 'freedom' in her last years. And as ever she enjoyed refining her ideas through argument, in conversation with friends or with figures from the past:

> Oh, yes, Maitland. Now, I'm writing a little book on a subject in which he was completely wrong, but it doesn't matter, I think he was a frightfully good historian. ... He had terrific historical imagination. ... he worked very closely on documents and on a pretty narrow field most of the time – English medieval law – but he infused this imagination about how it worked into it, so I think he was a very good thing. (2008 IHR interview)

Though legal history remained a central preoccupation into Susan's mid-eighties, in her last years she was increasingly preoccupied with the history of racial attitudes, and frustrated that she was no longer up to writing on the subject. Her ideas were very clear. There was no clear idea of race until slaves were brought from Africa to North America. Previously, there was no clear black-white distinction, only a spectrum from deep brown in the mediterranean to lighter shades further north. Slaves and their masters really looked different. The abolition of slavery finished the job: now that the descendants of Africans were no longer legally inferior, they had to be regarded as racially inferior to keep them down. That affected America before England. Only when African American GIs were stationed in the UK was there an awareness of colour, though initially the African Americans were regarded as nicer. Mendel's discoveries also came into Susan's interpretation, but we never got that aspect of her argument quite straight. At the age of ninety, Susan could not be expected to keep up with the burgeoning scholarly literature on race in history, but she could not help thinking hard about it, intellectual to the end that she was.

In July 2021 Susan took a turn for the worse. She fell out of bed during the night and had a fever. She was taken to University College Hospital where visitors found her very confused. After returning home she began to recover but was very weak, and bedridden. Her mind was still all there. To a visitor on 15 July she was able to say of a distinguished medievalist that he was 'not a very good historian' – so she hadn't gone soft. At another visit on 23 July she said that she could do better than 'I think therefore I am' by arguing 'I worry therefore I am'. She added that her worries were not too serious. For a while she had hallucinations, perhaps as a result of medication, that she had been kidnapped, but allowed herself to be reassured by being told frankly that her mind was playing tricks on her. On 27 July she could no longer talk easily but the mind was still working. She talked of Maitland: the best historian but still limited: he wrote only English history, only legal history. She talked affectionately of Pierre Chaplais, a well-loved Reader in Diplomatic at Oxford and member of the British Academy's Section H8 (Medieval Studies), and his work in the war for the resistance. She thought this made life difficult for him in France after the war because former collaborators resented what he had done. Amazingly, she was not focused only on her own past. She asked one of the authors of this memoir what had drawn him to History, and what he was currently working on – this when she was dying.

Susan had a great gift for academic friendship. Dame Janet Nelson rang her every other day in her last years. Michael and Joan Clanchy went out of their way to visit her before the Covid restrictions came down, even though travel was already physically difficult for them. Janet Loengard tells us that

> Toby Milsom [the historian of law] said to me one day a little more than fifty years ago, 'You should know Susan Reynolds' and promptly arranged for us to meet. And meet we did and have been meeting ever since. Susan has stayed with me in New Jersey and once lectured most splendidly to my students on the Fonthill Dispute. I was not at her annual houseparties in France because they were in August and I was in England from mid-June to late July, but I did get to the last one, in Northumberland (the Alnwick/Annick one!) Most of the time we met in London, and by letters and email and the phone, where we argued happily for hours over nation/state and especially eminent domain, because I work in medieval English property law. Susan is the only person I know who could tell me that I was wrong, why I was wrong, and that in some cases I might be right, leaving both of us contented and happy to be together.

Jonathan Jarrett wrote in his medieval blog that

> Certainly, what I mainly remember Susan for is interest and kindness. Quite early on we bonded somewhat over being the only two people in England whom each other knew to have thought about what the people called *Hispani* in the legislation of the Carolingian rulers actually were, in terms of status; but I used to make a point of chatting with Susan whenever I was in the IHR and saw her, partly in the hope of some delicious *bon mot* that could be quoted later, I admit, which I was not the only one collecting, but also because it was always interesting to talk with her and because she was always happy to be interested.

Susan was a well-rounded person with a great gift for friendship and collective sociability. This was especially in evidence at her house parties in France. At one of these she told John Arnold that she wrote a lot about 'community' but was not very good at it herself. He comments that

> what I think she meant was that she liked to be *in charge*. Anyone who went on holiday with Susan knew what that meant: we were to take it turns to cook, tomatoes must always be skinned before being used in salad, we must all drink the cough-syrup-like Ambassador aperitif before dinner and so forth. And Susan could certainly be very fierce. My wife Victoria can remember thinking that Susan was the first person she had seen who really did stamp her foot in anger, the context being an occasion when Susan's older sister Vicky was stacking the dishwasher 'in the wrong way!' But – but – as 'in charge' as Susan was, for those who went to Ver, the point was that it was actually rather relaxing to know who was supposed to be doing what, when; and that Susan's in-charge-ness in fact made community possible for us. We were able to get along precisely because she provided a frame in which we could. And because we all loved her, we all came to realise ways in which we, sometimes quite disparate folk, could in fact get along with each other.[18]

Tom Green remembers how Susan developed friendships through shared interests with the non-historian partners of the medievalists who joined her on these holidays. Children were very welcome. She was enthusiastic with them, and firm in her views about them and about proper parenting; she said that the only thing for which she could not forgive Maitland was that he did not send his daughters to school.

She loved literature, perhaps above all the novels of Trollope which she continued re-reading into her final year. And she at times had literary aspirations of her own. In a perhaps unguarded moment in a tutorial, she revealed that as an undergraduate she had written a Shakespearean history play on the fate of the sons of Simon de Montfort after his death at the Battle of Evesham. She was vigorous in her politics. On entering Buckingham Palace for an event to mark the octocentenary of Magna Carta she remarked in her quietest, chandelier-shattering whisper, 'I wonder if they know that I am a republican.'

---

[18] Personal communication.

Susan's funeral was a roll-call of many of the country's greatest medievalists. Words from the address by Dame Janet Nelson sum up Susan's impact on her fellow scholars.

> I first met Susan at one of the seminars at the Institute of Historical Research but our friendship was forged over the years when we both regularly attended the Early Medieval Seminar. Susan loved this seminar and our presence in a field still dominated by male historians seemed to attract many women to the group. Susan was an outstanding teacher: she had a way of drawing women out and encouraging them to participate fully in the lively discussions that she enjoyed so much. Of course, our main bond was our shared passion for medieval history. Susan was always ready to discuss thoughts and ideas, sharing her knowledge and insights and coming up with difficult questions. I have been so grateful to her for helping me refine and develop many ideas over the years.

So many people can say the same.

Acknowledgements
We would like to thank John Arnold, Robert Bartlett, David Bates, Peggy Brown, Carmem-Maria do Carmo M. Silva, Christopher Currie, Kate Currie, Robin Fleming, Bruce Frier, Cecilia Gaposchkin, Gene R. Garthwaite, Kate Gavron, Tom Green, Martha Hayward, Jonathan Jarrett, Andrew Lewis, Bill Miller, Jinty Nelson, David Palliser, Gail M. Patten, Lucy Peck, John Sabapathy, Felicity Spencer, Pauline Stafford and Alice Taylor for help of various kinds.

Note on the authors: David d'Avray is Emeritus Professor of History at University College London; he was elected a Fellow of the British Academy in 2005. John Hudson is Bishop Wardlaw Professor of Legal History at the University of St Andrews; he was elected a Fellow of the British Academy in 2016.

W. EDGAR YATES

William Edgar Yates

30 April 1938 – 10 March 2021

elected Fellow of the British Academy 2002

by

RITCHIE ROBERTSON
Fellow of the Academy

W.E. Yates, always known as 'Gar', was a distinguished scholar of German and particularly Austrian literature, and one of the foremost specialists on the work of the great Viennese comic dramatist Johann Nestroy.

Biographical Memoirs of Fellows of the British Academy, 20, 165–178
Posted 15 March 2022. © British Academy 2022.

W.E. Yates, always known as 'Gar', was born in Hove on 30 April 1938. He was an only child. His father, Douglas Yates (1898–1955), was Reader in German and Head of the German Department at Aberdeen University (a Chair of German was established only later). His mother, Doris Goode (1901–90), trained as a history teacher and later taught children of kindergarten age. After their marriage on 4 March 1924, Douglas and Doris Yates moved to Breslau (now Wrocław in Poland), where Douglas had a post as *Lektor* in English. There he gained his doctorate in 1928 with a dissertation on Grillparzer.[1] His appointment at Aberdeen followed in 1930. Gar spent his boyhood there, in his parents' large bungalow at the Bridge of Don and at their second home, a large house called Craigmore at Birnam, near Dunkeld in Perthshire.

Gar's youth, however, was overshadowed by his father's illness. Douglas Yates had joined the army during the First World War when he was still under age. The lingering effects of a wound sustained in the trenches took the form of a neurological disorder which led to progressive paralysis. He retired early from his Aberdeen post about 1945, having completed the first part of a critical biography of Grillparzer which was published in 1946.[2] Gar was intensely devoted to his father. To ease the strain on his mother (herself suffering from arthritis) of tending an invalid, he was sent to boarding-school at Fettes College in Edinburgh, to which he won a Foundation Scholarship that paid all his fees. When at home in the holidays he spent many hours with his invalid father, talking with him and holding his hand to steady the tremor that was among his symptoms. His own monograph on Grillparzer, published in 1972, not only conveys his own deep and lasting interest in Austria's great dramatist but is an act of filial homage to his father, who died when Gar was seventeen. His mother lived on until May 1990.

Fettes, with its emphasis on sports, particularly rugby, was probably less than congenial to the relatively unathletic Gar, but he benefited from outstanding teaching in modern languages given by Dick Cole-Hamilton. Gar was enduringly grateful to Cole-Hamilton and remained in touch with him till his death in 1992. It was to Cole-Hamilton's enthusiastic and effective teaching that he attributed his own success in gaining an Open Scholarship to Emmanuel College, Cambridge, to read French and German.

Before going up to Cambridge, Gar was obliged to do two years' National Service. He was assigned to the Royal Army Service Corps and stationed – fortunately, when one recalls that a war against Communist guerrillas was going on in Malaya – at Hounslow in West London. Here, as a second lieutenant, he established a reputation for efficiency and also, having time on his hands, managed to pay many visits to the West End theatres and the Royal Festival Hall, the start of a lifelong love of theatre and music.

[1] Published as *Der Kontrast zwischen Kunst und Leben bei Grillparzer* (Berlin: E. Ebeling, 1929).
[2] Douglas Yates, *Franz Grillparzer: A Critical Biography*, Volume I (Oxford: Basil Blackwell, 1946).

At Cambridge Gar benefited from a wide-ranging syllabus that aimed (and still aims) to give broadly equal emphasis to literature, history and thought. Part One of the Tripos was intended to bring undergraduates' linguistic knowledge up to a high standard so that they could easily explore a variety of challenging subjects in Part Two. In the latter, Gar especially enjoyed a course on Austrian literature of the 19th and early 20th centuries. When he undertook a PhD, his subject was Viennese popular comedy and its reception by more literary Austrian dramatists from Grillparzer to Hofmannsthal, under the supervision of F.J. Stopp (1911–79). Although Stopp's professional title was Reader in German Renaissance Studies, his interests extended much more widely; his books included a study of Evelyn Waugh, with whom he shared a devotion to Roman Catholicism.[3] More pertinently, he was also Germanic Editor of the *Modern Language Review*, a position Gar would later hold. Gar recalled him as a demanding supervisor; at all events, under his supervision Gar completed his thesis within three years, a feat much rarer then than it is now.

Gar's research required him to spend some time in Vienna, using the Theatersammlung of the National Library. We have a glimpse of him at this time in the autobiography of his friend Edward Timms, who for a spell shared his lodgings in the Strohgasse in the Third District of Vienna. Edward, who was then writing his Cambridge PhD thesis on Karl Kraus, was talking to the elderly satirist Friedrich Torberg, who wanted him to write an article about Kraus: '"What can *you* write about?" he asked, when Gar joined us at the Café Sacher. "About everything," Gar replied. "That's not enough!" was Torberg's riposte. The spirit of the coffeehouse was thriving still, and I returned to my typewriter inspired.'[4] Gar was clearly not overawed by a distinguished writer, who in turn had a reply ready for a self-confident young man.

During his doctoral studies, on 6 April 1963, Gar married Barbara Fellowes, likewise a Cambridge graduate in Modern Languages, whom he had known since they were both in their first year. Barbara read French and Spanish at Newnham. Her family name was originally Fuld; her parents had come to Britain in 1936 as refugees from Hitler's Germany. A distant relative – appropriately, in view of Gar's academic interests – was the once famous dramatist and critic Ludwig Fulda (1862–1939), who not only wrote comedies of his own but also translated those of Molière. Barbara would become a schoolteacher and eventually Head of Languages and Director of Sixth Form Studies at St Margaret's, a girls' independent school at Exeter which closed in 2012. She and Gar have two sons: Tom (born in 1971) read Modern Languages at Durham University and is currently Director of

---

[3] F.J. Stopp, *Evelyn Waugh: Portrait of an Artist* (London: Chapman & Hall, 1958).
[4] Edward Timms, *Taking up the Torch: English Institutions, German Dialectics and Multicultural Commitments* (Brighton: Sussex Academic Press, 2011), p. 91.

Corporate Affairs for the Quality Assurance Agency for Higher Education and QAA's Company Secretary; and Paul (born in 1975) read Music at Emmanuel, wrote a PhD on the song cycle in 19th-century France, did a law conversion course and is now Counsel at the international law firm Freshfields Bruckhaus Deringer and heads its global pro bono practice.

In 1963, while still working on his thesis, Gar was appointed to a lectureship in German at Durham. Barbara obtained a teaching post in the nearby town of Spennymoor. Gar immediately plunged into heavy teaching duties. He was required in his first year to give lectures on Hölderlin and in his second on 16th-century literature; the latter subject was new to him. At the same time as working up these lectures and getting through a demanding teaching load, Gar managed to complete his thesis. He met these challenges with the efficiency and industry that would characterise all his subsequent academic work. During his time at Durham he wrote two substantial academic monographs, *Grillparzer* and *Nestroy*, both published by Cambridge University Press in 1972.

This research achievement, supported by many articles and conference papers, earned Gar the Chair of German at Exeter University, which he took up in 1972. He simultaneously became Head of Department, and found that a good deal needed to be changed. There were no German-speaking *Lektoren*. The undergraduates were not required to spend a year abroad. Gar changed all that. He secured *Lektoren* with the help of the Austrian Institute (now the Austrian Cultural Forum) in London, whose director, Bernhard Stillfried, was tireless in stimulating British interest in Austrian culture as a counterweight to the dominance of Germany. Stillfried's energy in supporting a series of rewarding academic conferences on Austrian subjects, and in helping with the foundation of the yearbook *Austrian Studies*, is still remembered with gratitude.[5] Under Gar's predecessor, Henry Garland, what would now be called a research culture was not encouraged. Gar strongly encouraged his colleagues to write articles and monographs. At a time when ingrained prejudices were still common, he was entirely gender-blind in appointments and promotions, and he always treated his loyal secretary, Gisela Fischer, with the respect befitting a fellow-academic. His colleague of many years, Lesley Sharpe, writes:

> As a new appointee at Exeter in 1981 I found Gar to be an exemplary mentor. He embodied the all-round academic who combined research, teaching and administration to the highest standards and with total commitment. Though his involvement with the Nestroy edition was growing rapidly, his scholarly work was not pursued at the expense of his teaching, which remained inspirational. He was generous with his time and expertise in commenting on my research on Schiller, though it was not central to his own interests. He also introduced

---

[5] On Bernhard Stillfried (1925–2011) and his work, see the volume edited by Ilona Slawinski and Joseph P. Strelka, *Viribus Unitis. Österreichs Wissenschaft und Kultur im Ausland: Impulse und Wechselwirkungen. Festschrift für Bernhard Stillfried aus Anlaß seines 70. Geburtstages* (Bern: Peter Lang, 1996), to which Gar contributed 'Nestroy zitiert Grillparzer. Zu Nestroys Anspielungskunst' (pp. 539–46).

me to reviewing for the *Modern Language Review*, of which he was Germanic Editor at
the time.

It was inevitable that Gar's conspicuous abilities should draw him into administration.
Not only was he Head of Department from 1972 to 1986, but from 1980 to 1983, at the
invitation of the Vice-Chancellor, Harry Kay, he became Chairman of the Academic
Development Committee, the University's main planning committee. This was the era
when, under Margaret Thatcher's premiership, severe cuts in higher education funding
threw many institutions into disarray. The responsibility Gar assumed was an unenviable
one, but colleagues felt that he enabled the University to steer a humane and judicious
course. From April 1986 to September 1989 he was Deputy Vice-Chancellor. Lesley
Sharpe recalls:

> When that period of major administrative work in the university was over, Gar remained
> an influential figure, fully engaged with developments within a rapidly changing environ-
> ment. One particular moment stands out in my memory. Sometime in the mid–1990s, as
> the audit culture was taking hold and people spent much time trying to formulate their
> aims and objectives, the senior management at Exeter produced a document that was a
> kind of mission statement. Staff were invited to a large auditorium for an open meeting to
> discuss it with the Vice Chancellor. Early in the meeting Gar stood up and pointed out,
> calmly but forcefully, that there was no mention in the document of any academic values;
> he then gave a superb, concise statement of the primary function of a university to pursue
> research and scholarship to the highest standards.

At the same time Gar took on many duties outside the University. From 1980 on he
was a member of the committee of the Modern Humanities Research Association. The
MHRA's work in supporting academic research deserves to be more widely known than it
is. In some respects it fulfils the role that in other countries is performed by an academy of
sciences such as the Akademie der Wissenschaften in Austria (where *Wissenschaft* com-
prehends the humanities quite as much as natural science): it finances long-running projects which even an academic publisher would shy away from, and it supports a string of
journals. Thanks to the financial acumen of its long-term Honorary Treasurer, Roy Wisbey
(who had been Gar's supervisor in his first year at Cambridge, but then moved to the Chair
at King's College London), its healthy position freed it from worrying about the profitabil-
ity of its enterprises in the short term.

The MHRA's journals include the *Modern Language Review*, which has a General
Editor and a team of editors responsible for particular language areas. Gar was its Germanic
Editor from 1981 to 1988 (succeeded by Alan Bance, and later by Lesley Sharpe and then
myself). I remember how he commissioned my first academic reviews, and how, when I
had been (I now think, unnecessarily) negative about a rather slight collection of essays on
Kafka, he accepted the review with the words 'Still, the truth must be told'. In one of the

many warm tributes to Gar that Barbara received after his death, Andrew Barker, who retired in 2010 as Professor of Austrian Studies at Edinburgh University, wrote:

> Gar was exemplary not just in the standards he set in his own work, but in the specific help he gladly gave others. At the outset of my career – he was then Germanic Editor of the *Modern Language Review* – he published an essay of mine without requiring me to alter a word. This, of course, I took as a terrific compliment. He also wrote me a cover-note, outlining his own disagreement with everything I had written, but emphasising nevertheless the need to publish the piece.[6]

Gar remained a member of the MHRA Committee until 2015. He was also a member of the Council of the English Goethe Society from 1984 to 2009, General Editor (with Hans Reiss) of the monograph series British and Irish Studies in German Language and Literature, published by Peter Lang, and a member of the Advisory Board for *Austrian Studies*. His intense involvement with academic life in Vienna will be described following a survey of his own academic achievements.

The two books Gar published in 1972 immediately established him as an authority on two great Austrian dramatists, Franz Grillparzer (1791–1872) and Johann Nestroy (1801–62). Both writers are still somewhat under-appreciated. The understandable bias of *Germanistik* towards Germany as opposed to Austria (and Switzerland) means that Grillparzer can too easily be dismissed as an Austrian epigone of Weimar Classicism, while Nestroy, as a comic dramatist, can fall victim to a prejudice that only 'serious' literature really counts. It would be juster to see Grillparzer as a major contributor to the series of tragic dramas that make 19th-century German-language literature so markedly different from its French and English counterparts, and to apply to Nestroy the words of Lessing's comic heroine Minna von Barnhelm: 'Kann man denn auch nicht lachend sehr ernsthaft sein?' ('Can't one also be very serious while laughing?')[7]

The study *Grillparzer: A Critical Introduction* complements and extends the earlier book by Douglas Yates. The father's book, in keeping with the critical assumptions of the early 20th century, asks how its subject's experiences, especially his emotional entanglements, are transmuted in his earlier dramas. The son's book, in accordance with later approaches to literature, separates the life from the works. It opens with a 35-page chapter, 'Grillparzer's Life', a strictly factual, chronological account, which has not yet been superseded (strangely, there is no full-scale biography of Grillparzer in any language), and thereafter focuses on the plays, presenting them in thematic groups along with necessary historical information. Gar emphasises how important it was for Grillparzer to write in Vienna, a city with a living theatrical tradition, where, apart from the hazards of censorship, his plays were sure of reaching the stage. There is a temptation to play him off against

---

[6] I thank Andrew Barker for permission to include this paragraph.

[7] Gotthold Ephraim Lessing, *Minna von Barnhelm oder Das Soldatenglück*, Act IV, scene 6.

Schiller, who wrote not for a metropolitan audience but for provincial theatres first in Mannheim and later in Weimar. Among Grillparzer's many strengths, such as psychological subtlety and frequent lyricism, much is made of his plays' intrinsic theatricality, their unfailing expression of meaning through bodily actions and visual effects. Grillparzer's theatrical, i.e. visual, language is contrasted, perhaps unfairly, with 'the rhetoric of Schiller'.[8]

Although the companion volume, Gar's study of Nestroy, is outwardly a rather slim volume (175 pages of text, plus appendices), it condenses a vast amount of information not readily available even in German, and offers a judicious interpretation and evaluation of Nestroy's work.[9] It places Nestroy in the tradition of the Viennese *Volkstheater*, dating from 1711, the year in which Josef Anton Stranitzky established his company in the newly built Theater nächst dem Kärntnertor, just outside the walls which at that time still surrounded the inner city. Popular comedy specialised in three genres: the magical play (*Zauberstück*), descending ultimately from the visual effects of Baroque theatre; the 'local play' combining satire and morality in the portrayal of contemporary manners; and parody, whose targets included Shakespeare (transplanted to Vienna in *Othellerl, der Mohr von Wien*) and Grillparzer (whose *Sappho* was parodied as *Sepherl*, a Viennese contraction of 'Josephine'). All three genres were adapted and enriched by Nestroy, a gifted actor and prolific dramatist, whose witty language often reveals philosophical depth. Nestroy himself, whose stage presence was legendary, played the lead role, always a character with both practical and linguistic resourcefulness. He deserves to stand alongside Molière and Ben Jonson as a master of supremely intelligent farce, and alongside Heinrich Heine and Georg Büchner as a leading socially critical writer of his time. This study, based on minute familiarity with his eighty-odd plays as well as his theatrical context, gives full attention to his linguistic ingenuity, his satirical techniques, and his creative adaptation of other texts: Nestroy often adapted French or English originals (making even a dramatised version of *Martin Chuzzlewit*), and comparisons here reveal much about Nestroy's working methods. Gar also examines Nestroy's radicalism, which mostly had to be damped down because of Metternich's censorship, but flourished in 1848 when the censorship was lifted. Although Nestroy clearly sympathises with the Viennese revolutionaries in his play *Freiheit in Krähwinkel* (which could be freely translated as *Revolution Comes to Sleepy Hollow*), he satirises their excesses as much as he does the misgovernment of the authorities. More broadly, his plays invite sympathy for honest working people and for social underdogs, while mocking the political rhetoric adopted by self-serving careerists. Altogether, *Nestroy* is an admirable introduction to this dramatist, and although the critical edition of Nestroy's works has added enormously to our knowledge, this study still has no

[8] W.E. Yates, *Grillparzer: A Critical Introduction* (Cambridge: Cambridge University Press, 1972), p. 43.
[9] *Nestroy: Satire and Parody in Viennese Popular Comedy* (Cambridge: Cambridge University Press, 1972).

counterpart in any language. In 1975 it was awarded the J.G. Robertson Prize by the University of London.

Gar's work on Austrian theatre extends far beyond Nestroy, though he also published a survey of Nestroy criticism[10] and the first thorough biography of Nestroy.[11] In 1992 he brought out a study of two more recent dramatists, Arthur Schnitzler (1862–1931) and Hugo von Hofmannsthal (1874–1929).[12] The emphasis falls mainly on their comedies: Schnitzler's light but far from lightweight dramas of the 1890s and 1900s, along with his tragicomedies of antisemitism, *Professor Bernhardi* (1912), and of marriage and infidelity, *Das weite Land* (1911); Hofmannsthal's Mozartian comedies *Der Schwierige* (1921) and *Der Unbestechliche* (1923). Rather than engage in negative criticism, Gar largely ignores Schnitzler's dull attempts at serious drama (e.g. *Der einsame Weg*, 1904) and Hofmannsthal's later plays where his conservative agenda is disturbingly apparent (though the tragedy *Der Turm*, 1925, which won the admiration of Walter Benjamin, might have rewarded more attention). The theatrical and biographical setting is explained in ample detail, but with a light touch. The biographical materials here are particularly rich: Hofmannsthal's correspondences with contemporaries have been published mostly in separate volumes; Schnitzler's letters have been collected, but the great event in late 20th-century Schnitzler scholarship was the publication in ten volumes of the diaries he kept from 1879 till shortly before his death in 1931. The diaries at first caused disappointment because so many of the entries are mere jottings such as 'Nm. Spz.' (i.e. Nachmittag Spaziergang – 'Walk in the afternoon'); somebody told the editors 'You are editing a telephone directory'[13]; but the patient reader, as Gar pre-eminently was, finds abundant fascinating material.

This body of knowledge is also manifested in *Theatre in Vienna: A Critical History, 1776–1995* (1996), which runs from Stranitzky's arrival in Vienna in 1711 to the reign of the controversial German director, Claus Peymann, at the Burgtheater in 1986. It covers both the Burgtheater, which from 1810 was Austria's national theatre for spoken drama, and the commercial theatres in the suburbs where popular comedy flourished. Opera and operetta are also considered, as are the varying roles played by official censorship before and after 1848. The last few pages are a fine example of Gar's firm but diplomatic judgement. He gives due space to the arguments for and against the iconoclastic approach introduced by Peymann, a striking example of the state-subsidised *Regietheater* (director's theatre) common in German-speaking countries; but the arguments against (commercial

[10] *Nestroy and the Critics* (Columbia, SC: Camden House, 1994).
[11] *'Bin Dichter nur der Posse'. Johann Nepomuk Nestroy: Versuch einer Biographie* (Vienna: Lehner, 2012). The nearest counterpart, Walter Schübler's *Nestroy: Eine Biographie in 30 Szenen* (Salzburg: Residenz, 2001), is excellent as a more popular and selective account, but hardly a rival.
[12] *Schnitzler, Hofmannsthal and the Austrian Theatre* (New Haven and London: Yale University Press, 1992).
[13] This comment ('Sie edieren ein Telefonbuch') was reported to me when I visited the Austrian Academy of Sciences, where the diaries were edited, in the mid 1990s.

misjudgement, excessive reliance on political support) weigh most heavily, especially when Gar deplores Peymann's 'relative neglect of the Austrian classics' and, 'when productions have been attempted, their unsympathetic character'.[14] Anyone who has absorbed the whole book will be able to contrast Peymann with Karl Carl (the name is also written Carl Carl), a gifted director who was also a hard-headed and sometimes unscrupulous man of business and whose fortune was founded on recognising and promoting the talents of Nestroy. These books, like all of Gar's academic work, manifest his altogether exceptional command of detail and his distinctive style – clear, firm, free from redundancy – which was not only intellectually but also aesthetically pleasing.

In view of his pre-eminence in the study of drama and theatre, it is easy to forget Gar's equally distinguished publications on poetry. The main outcome was his book *Tradition in the German Sonnet* (1981),[15] which shows a minutely detailed knowledge of even the most obscure byways of German poetry. German poets adopted the Petrarchan sonnet and rejected the Shakespearean model. Sonnet-writing first flourished in the 17th century, discussed in a chapter whose major figure is Christian Hoffmann von Hoffmannswaldau (1616–79), then sank into disuse till the late 18th century, when its enthusiastic revival was called a veritable 'Sonettenwut' (sonnet mania). Well-known practitioners such as Goethe, Heine and Mörike receive due attention, but so do less-known poets who subscribed whole-heartedly to classical ideals and produced many series of sonnets, notably August von Platen (1796–1835) and the Viennese Josef Weinheber (1892–1945). Analysing the appeal of the sonnet, Gar finds it first in the challenge presented by its exacting formal demands, second in its appeal as an image of formal order and thus a symbolic defence against chaos: it is no coincidence that the sonnet flourished during such upheavals as the Thirty Years War and the Napoleonic Wars.

These conclusions are developed in some remarkable articles that make one wish Gar had written more about poetry. They include a sympathetic appreciation of the work of Weinheber, a poet who since his death has been under a cloud because of his membership of the Nazi Party and because his classical odes, elegies and sonnets can easily seem rather arid. Gar focuses on the sonnet 'Blick vom oberen Belvedere', which describes the view from the upper Belvedere palace northwards across Vienna to the distant hills of the Wienerwald, with Baroque churches to right and left and the medieval spire of the Stefansdom in the centre of the prospect. He shows how the poem not only exemplifies formal order but evokes a townscape which is itself an ordered achievement.[16] In another, he traces Mörike's development from a Romantic reliance on inspiration to a classical

---

[14] *Theatre in Vienna: A Critical History, 1776–1995* (Cambridge: Cambridge University Press, 1996), p. 240.
[15] *Tradition in the German Sonnet*, British and Irish Studies in German Language and Literature, no. 4 (Bern: Peter Lang, 1981).
[16] 'Architectonic Form in Weinheber's Lyric Poetry: the Sonnet "Blick vom oberen Belvedere"', *Modern Language Review*, 71 (1976), 73–81.

aesthetic derived particularly from the later Goethe.[17] Together with his work on Grillparzer, this article finely illustrates Gar's sensitivity to the art of the Biedermeier period (1815–48). Often decried as unambitious and provincial, the best Biedermeier works carry on the aesthetic outlook and also the ideal of humanity ('Humanität') powerful in German literature and thought of the late 18th century. Gar formulated these ideals in his inaugural lecture, *Humanity in Weimar and Vienna: The Continuity of an Ideal*, and explored them also in a little-known article on Paul Celan's early poem 'Die Krüge'. With extensive reference to Hölderlin, he shows how Celan's paradoxical image of jugs drinking at a table transforms the traditional conception of poets as vessels of inspiration or memory, and comments on his rejection 'of that optimistic classical view of the human condition, of the conception of the poet-prophet as a divine vessel'.[18] These concise and rich publications suggest much about the personal values of a modest scholar who shunned the use of the first person singular.

Gar may be best remembered, however, for a scholarly monument of a different order: his leading part in the critical edition of Nestroy's works: Johann Nestroy: *Sämtliche Werke, Historisch-kritische Ausgabe* (Vienna, 1977–2012; abbreviated as HKA). When this edition was first planned in the 1970s, it was expected to contain seventeen volumes: fourteen of texts and three of documentation.[19] In the end there were thirty-eight volumes of text and seven further volumes, including Nestroy's letters and a volume, *Nestroy im Bild*, containing visual representations of Nestroy (who survived into the age of photography). At first the project made only halting progress, but at a meeting in Vienna in January 1992 Gar and Walter Obermaier (then in charge of the manuscript collection of the Wiener Stadt- und Landesbibliothek) were added to the team of General Editors, and the pace quickened, not least thanks to Gar's energy in spurring on the editors of individual volumes.

At the same time the project became more ambitious, in keeping with the complexity of reproducing Nestroy's texts.[20] Only seventeen of Nestroy's plays were published in his lifetime, and those editions were inaccurate and unreliable. The editors needed therefore

---

[17] 'Mörike's Conception of an Artistic Ideal', *Modern Language Review*, 73 (1978), 96–109.

[18] 'Mythopoeic allusion in Celan's poem "Die Krüge"', *Neophilologus*, 65 (1981), 594–9 (p. 599). Cf. Hölderlin's 'Buonaparte': 'Heilige Gefäße sind die Dichter, | Worinn des Lebens Wein, der Geist | Der Helden, sich aufbewahrt' – 'Poets are holy vessels | In which the wine of life, | The spirit of heroes, is preserved': Friedrich Hölderlin, *Selected Poems and Fragments*, trans. Michael Hamburger (London: Penguin, 1998), pp. 4, 5.

[19] See W.E. Yates, 'Prospects of Progress: Nestroy Re-edited', *Journal of European Studies*, 9 (1979), 196–205 (p. 198).

[20] This account is drastically summarised from W.E. Yates, 'Das Werden eines (edierten) Nestroy-Textes', in W.E. Yates (ed.), *Vom schaffenden zum edierten Nestroy. Beiträge zum Nestroy-Symposium im Rahmen der Wiener Vorlesungen 28.–29. Oktober 1992* (Vienna: Jugend & Volk, 1994), pp. 11–30.

to work from Nestroy's last fair copy (*Reinschrift*). In reconstructing its genesis, they had to begin with the *Vorlage*, the prior text which Nestroy adapted. Nestroy made drafts and sketches, but first of all he made a detailed scenario. All these are valuable as a guide to his intentions. From these Nestroy developed the play and wrote out a fair copy. But the play's genesis did not end there. The fair copy had to be submitted to the censor. Nestroy would circle expressions to which the censor might object and add inoffensive variants above the line. When the play was performed, the original expressions could be restored. The HKA aims to print the drafts as fully as possible, without making the edition unwieldy and unusable. In many cases it also includes, in a tiny font, the entire text of the *Vorlage* (e.g. John Oxenford's *A Day Well Spent*, the basis for *Einen Jux will er sich machen*). Explanatory notes are also required, especially for expressions that would be unintelligible outside Austria. All this imposed a tremendous amount of work on the editors (including the difficulty of deciphering Nestroy's notoriously illegible handwriting), especially since they aimed to complete the edition by 2001, the bicentenary of Nestroy's birth. At one stage a timely archival discovery suggested that he might have been born in 1802, thus permitting delay; but this proved false, and the leeway was not required. All but two volumes, held up for particular reasons, appeared by the deadline.[21] Supplementary volumes and an index followed, so that the whole undertaking was finished in 2012.

Gar himself edited or co-edited eight volumes of texts, comprising twelve plays, plus the two supplementary volumes. He recruited a number of British scholars to the editorial team: his Exeter colleague John McKenzie, Peter Branscombe (Professor of Austrian Studies at St Andrews), and Louise Adey Huish, who has contributed the following reminiscence of working with Gar:

> Gar Yates was a dedicated and generous colleague, who welcomed me into the Nestroy project with immense warmth in the early 1990s, after I had listed Nestroy as a research interest in one of the UK registers of Germanists. It probably helped that I had experience of reading Ludwig Tieck's 'unchristliche Hand', as I was initially set to work on the manuscript of *Die Verhängnisvolle Faschings-Nacht*, which existed mainly in exuberant pencil shorthand. Gar and I pored over our respective photocopies of the manuscript, he in Exeter and I in Oxford, until I came up with a more or less credible version of the play from jottings, gobbets and allusive shorthand. Gar's knowledge of Nestroy's autobiography, and the historical and literary context in which he operated, was encyclopaedic; and yet he had a knack of making the flattering assumption that you knew all these things too (but had momentarily forgotten them). In those days before email the letters would fly to and fro – mine to him usually answered by return of post, in exhaustive detail, and with humorous asides which made the sometimes disheartening process entirely palatable. At the same time, he had an eagle eye for detail, and would never allow the merely approximate to

pass, without at the very least raising a quizzical eyebrow, or offering (with apparent humility) the answer you knew you had been looking for all along.[22]

One may well wonder how Gar found time for all his activities, which continued after his retirement from the Exeter Chair in 2001. He joined the Council of the Internationale Nestroy-Gesellschaft, based in Vienna, in 1986, and was its Vice-President from 1997 onwards. He edited the journal *Nestroyana* single-handed from 1992 to 2001, and jointly with Ulrike Tanzer from then till 2009. He was also Vice-President of the Shakespeare Society of Vienna from 1992 to 2002 (the *Sonnet* book contains a substantial chapter on translations of Shakespeare's sonnets). He organised numerous conferences on Austrian theatre, some in Exeter and others in Vienna, and helped to edit the proceedings.[23]

In addition, Gar took seriously his responsibilities towards the local community in Exeter. In 1986 he joined the Board of Governors of Exeter School, within walking distance of his and Barbara's house at 7 Clifton Hill, and in 1994 he took over as Chair, a role he retained for fourteen years. He remained as Vice-Chairman until he stood down from the board in June 2011. He was also Chairman of the Finance and General Purposes Committee from 1994 and a member of the Academic Committee from 2004. A posthumous tribute to his work from the Board of Governors notes:

> Gar clearly recognised the difference between governance and management and was always supportive of the school's staff, providing guidance, encouragement and both physical and conceptual resources. He prized intellectual curiosity and academic rigour and he was a superb chair of meetings, as well as a punctilious recipient of official paperwork.

This combination of efficiency and humanity was recognised by many colleagues, especially younger academics who received his praise at conferences and were encouraged to publish their papers. He combined an incisive manner and distinguished presence with warmth and humour. He made it a private rule to do at least a little bit of academic work every day: editorial work, in particular, lent itself to gradual and incremental completion. But the centre of Gar's life was undoubtedly his family. At one time his study contained a small snooker table, and he was always ready to be interrupted at his work to play snooker with one of his sons (also a valuable occasion for father-son bonding). Since then the snooker table has been replaced by a handsome rocking-horse, and his four small grand-children had similar licence to interrupt him in order to ride on it. He and Barbara were devotees of music (she had introduced him to opera during their student days, and he was

---

[22] I thank the Rev. Louise Adey Huish for this contribution.
[23] For example, W.E. Yates and John R.P. McKenzie (eds), *Viennese Popular Theatre: A Symposium* (Exeter: Exeter University Press, 1985), which included Gar's essay 'Nestroy, Grillparzer, and the feminist cause' (pp. 93–107); and (his own favourite) W.E. Yates, Allyson Fiddler, and John Warren (eds), *From Perinet to Jelinek: Viennese Theatre in its Political and Intellectual Context* (Bern: Peter Lang, 2001).

particularly fond of Mozart and Richard Strauss). They entertained generously, drawing on a cellar that featured mainly French and Austrian wine.

Gar received many honours, notably the Österreichisches Ehrenkreuz für Wissenschaft und Kunst 1. Klasse (2001) and the Ehrenzeichen der Stadtgemeinde Schwechat in Silber (2005). Schwechat is a town on the south-eastern outskirts of Vienna where a conference on Nestroy is held every year; Gar attended regularly and delivered twenty papers between 1976 and 2013. In 1995 he was elected a corresponding member of the Austrian Academy of Sciences, and in 2002 he became a Fellow of the British Academy. In 1998 he was honoured with a Festschrift, a volume of *Austrian Studies* edited by Lesley Sharpe and John McKenzie, on the theme of the Austrian comic tradition – the subject which he had done more than anyone else to put on the academic map.

Acknowledgements
I owe warm thanks to Barbara Yates for talking to me in detail about her husband's life and for giving me a copy of a 13,000-word autobiographical essay, headed 'Apologia pro vita mea', that he wrote probably in 2013. I also thank Lesley Sharpe for her reminiscences of Gar as a colleague, including her contribution to the present memoir.

Note on the author: Ritchie Robertson is Emeritus Schwarz-Taylor Professor of German, at the University of Oxford. He was elected a Fellow of the British Academy in 2004.

WILLIAM ST CLAIR

William Linn St Clair

7 December 1937 – 30 June 2021

elected Fellow of the British Academy 1992

by

RODERICK BEATON

Fellow of the Academy

Born in London to Scottish parents and brought up Falkirk, Stirlingshire, William St Clair embarked on his career as an independent scholar while working as a senior civil servant in Whitehall. After publishing a series of landmark biographical studies relating to Romanticism and the creation of modern Greece, he left the civil service to take up research positions successively at All Souls College, Oxford, Trinity College, Cambridge, and the University of London. His scholarly interests encompassed the history of publishing and reading practices in Britain since the invention of printing, women's studies, the history of slavery, and the custodianship of cultural heritage, exemplified by the notorious case of the 'Elgin Marbles' or 'Sculptures of the Parthenon'. He was an early champion of Open Access publishing and a co-founder and Director of Open Book Publishers.

Biographical Memoirs of Fellows of the British Academy, 20, 179–199
Posted 24 May 2022. © British Academy 2022.

Among the rollcall of Fellows of the British Academy in recent years, the name of 'Mr William St Clair' stood out. He never took a doctorate or held a teaching post at a university, and was always proud to call himself an Independent Scholar. His entry in the *Directory of Research and Expertise* for the School of Advanced Study, University of London, lists his research interests as: 'Archaeology, Classics, English Literature, History of art, History of the book, Romanticism'.[1] During a lifetime in which fields of professional academic specialism tended to become ever narrower, St Clair, on the contrary, chose to tread a very different path, inspired perhaps by the Enlightenment ideal of the all-round man of learning. To achieve the success that he did, in several senses 'against the grain' of his times, required extraordinary resources of personality: tenacity, persistence, a forensic attention to detail, and above all a strong moral conviction.

Irmgard Maassen, his co-editor on one of his projects, writes that 'He was intellectually fearless – he needed to be as he often came to the topics he wrote about essentially as an outsider.' Others who knew him at various times in his life and worked alongside him have recalled his bearlike quality (both in physique and manner), a stubbornness that could be exasperating, but also his many acts of kindness and generosity, particularly towards younger scholars and the graduate students with whom he came into contact at Oxford, Cambridge, and London.[2] A prolific biographer himself, St Clair also reflected sceptically on the nature of biography as an art, and 'used to insist that the truth of a life is likely to lie beyond the testimony of archives and documents'.[3] Anyone attempting to write a memoir such as this has been fairly warned!

Early life and civil service career

William Linn St Clair was born in London on 7 December 1937. His father, Joseph, was an engineering draughtsman who at the time was representing a group of Scottish foundries. Joseph was an enthusiastic follower of art and ballet, and back in his native land a keen mountaineer. William's mother, Susan Bow, was an English teacher, with a degree from the University of Glasgow. Shortly after the outbreak of the Second World War the family moved back to Scotland, where the young William St Clair attended schools near Glasgow and Falkirk before he became a day boy at the prestigious Edinburgh Academy.

---

[1] https://research.sas.ac.uk/search/fellow/158.
[2] See the website of Open Book Publishers: https://blogs.openbookpublishers.com/in-memoriam-william-st-clair/.
[3] Irmgard Maassen, personal communication. See also the volume on the nature of biography commissioned as part of the centenary celebrations of the British Academy: Peter France and William St Clair (eds), *Mapping Lives: The Uses of Biography* (Oxford: Oxford University Press for the British Academy, 2002), and especially the chapter by William St Clair, 'The Biographer as Archaeologist'.

An only child for the first ten years of his life, St Clair became the eldest of three with the arrival of his twin brothers, David and John. When their father died of cancer six years later, he became to some extent the head of the family at the age of sixteen.

From Edinburgh Academy, St Clair won a scholarship in classics to St John's College, Oxford, where he rowed for the First VIII and also made his first visit to Greece, the country that would figure so largely in some of his best known books. From university he went straight into the British civil service, bypassing the postgraduate study that would increasingly become a prerequisite for an academic career in the decades to come. Declining a position in the Scottish Department of Agriculture and Fisheries (known pejoratively as 'Ag and Fish'), St Clair negotiated a more prestigious alternative as Assistant Principal in the Admiralty. His brother David recalls:

> He spent time in Whitehall, at the Admiralty naval headquarters in Bath, the naval base Portsmouth, and at sea in many types of naval vessels including an aircraft carrier. During a stay in Portsmouth when he got to know the officers they allowed him for fun to be photographed transferring by breeches buoy between two destroyers dressed in senior civil service garb that included wearing a bowler hat and carrying a large rolled up umbrella. He served as Private Secretary to successive Civil Lords of the Admiralty in Conservative and Labour governments.

It was during his time at the Admiralty that St Clair married Heidi Fischer, with whom he had two daughters, who survive him. After the Admiralty was merged into the Ministry of Defence in 1964, St Clair took on a new role reviewing British defence arrangements for the Labour government led by Harold Wilson during the last years of empire. His duties took him frequently to Germany, and farther afield to Aden, Malaya, Borneo, Singapore, and Hong Kong. Secondment to the Foreign Office (from 1968 the Foreign and Commonwealth Office), as First Secretary from 1966 to 1969, gave him responsibility during the dispute with Spain over the status of Gibraltar, and latterly saw him briefly serving in the Paris embassy.

In 1969, St Clair moved to HM Treasury, with the grade of Principal, and was promoted to Assistant Secretary in 1974. In this role he was involved in devising and implementing the Prices and Incomes Policy of the Conservative government of Edward Heath. The previous year, he had separated from his wife, but there was no divorce; although many close relationships would follow, St Clair seems never again to have wished to take on the commitments of marriage.

Of his brother's subsequent career at the Treasury, David St Clair writes:

> In 1978, he was head of Industrial Policy Division and helped to devise and operate the Callaghan/Healey industrial policy aimed at reviving British competitiveness in manufacturing. He was also Treasury member of the Monopolies and Mergers Panel, and of several industrial National Economic Development Committees (NEDC). By 1979 St Clair was

head of the Treasury Overseas Aid Division and his career appeared to be going from strength to strength. However when the Thatcher government came to power things changed. St Clair had a degree in Classics from Oxford and as such was looked upon as a relative amateur. ... 'We admire your intellect but not your commitment', was what he was told.

In 1982 he was semi-sidelined into what at the time was considered a position of low prestige in the Treasury. As head of the Superannuation Division, he was responsible for the Principal Civil Service pension scheme and for Treasury supervision of the other public service pension schemes. He unexpectedly enjoyed this assignment and during this period became interested in policy evaluation with a view to improving and professionalising decision making within the civil service in general. In 1985 he was made deputy head of a Cabinet Office/Treasury joint management unit, charged with improving policy analysis and evaluation across government. In 1988 he was promoted to Deputy Under Secretary and was able to attend the Top Management Programme restricted to those potentially promotable to the highest civil grades. His promotion coincided with the publication of a booklet that he wrote for HM Treasury. Using his well honed literary skills he produced a booklet that was easily readable and accessible to all grades of management. It was highly influential and was translated into several languages, including French, Arabic, and Turkish. In 1990 he was promoted to Under-Secretary with responsibility for Treasury control of the civil service and shortly thereafter published his second practical manual for civil service managers.[4]

It was at this time, in his mid-fifties, that St Clair suddenly developed severe coronary angina. Quadruple heart bypass surgery in 1992 was successful. But as his brother recalls, at that time the life expectancy for someone with the condition was about ten years. This seems to have been the moment for St Clair to take stock of his life and decide his priorities for the time remaining to him. Shortly afterwards he took early retirement from the civil service to embark full-time on his career as an independent scholar (an independence, in his case, underwritten by a generous pension).

Writer and independent scholar

Earlier in the same year, St Clair had been elected a Fellow of the British Academy, on whose Council he would serve from 1996 to 2000. He was already the author of four acclaimed books, a prolific book reviewer for publications such as the *Financial Times*, the *TLS*, and the *Economist*, and a prominent member of PEN International. He had been elected a Fellow of the Royal Society of Literature in 1973, of the Huntington Library in California in 1985, and as a Visiting Fellow at All Souls College, Oxford, in 1981–2. Once

[4] William St Clair, *Policy Evaluation: A Guide for Managers* (London: HMSO, 1988); *Executive Agencies: A Guide to Setting Targets and Judging Performance* (London: HMSO, 1992).

he had left the civil service, affiliations at prestigious research institutions followed one another: as a Fellow of All Souls from 1992 to 1996, of Trinity College, Cambridge, from 1998 to 2006, and thereafter until his death, as a Senior Research Fellow in the Institute of English Studies, part of the School of Advanced Study at the University of London.

St Clair's parting with public administration was a protracted affair, however. From 1991 to 1998, alongside his academic affiliation, he acted as consultant to the Organisation for Economic Cooperation and Development (OECD). His role was chiefly to advise on strategic planning, resource allocation and budgeting, performance measurement, and evaluation. On a visit to Turkey on behalf of the OECD, he had a narrow escape after being arrested by local police while photographing a Kurdish refugee camp in the southeast of the country. Although he was interrogated for several hours, the officers did not think to search his car – in which he was carrying a comprehensive list of Turkish writers imprisoned for political reasons, that had been entrusted to him by PEN International, on whose Writers in Prison Committee he was serving at the time. It was one instance when the collision between St Clair's role as a public servant and his service to literature could have brought him into real danger.

It was through his involvement in PEN that St Clair became a friend of the American playwright Arthur Miller, whose biography he offered to write. The two men corresponded and met frequently between 1992 and Miller's death in 2005. Miller was fully in agreement with the plan for a biography, on condition that it must be posthumous. Miller's third wife, the Austrian photographer Inge Morath, had also known St Clair well and had been supportive of the project. But Morath died three years before Miller, and the playwright's literary executors decided not to grant St Clair the access to his subject's private diaries that had been promised. In the words of his brother David, 'St Clair always claimed the diaries were not essential for him to continue writing the biography; but most of the momentum was gone and he reluctantly did not pursue it further.'

William St Clair remained fully active until his death, in Oxford, on the afternoon of Wednesday 30 June 2021. His last book was in the final stages of preparation for press; with the relaxing of restrictions imposed by the Covid-19 pandemic, he was looking forward to travelling to Greece to receive an award for his work on the Greek Revolution of the 1820s. In November he had been due to give a keynote lecture at the University of Edinburgh at a conference that I was co-organising. Ten days before he died, he wrote to me a long email, asking for details of the arrangements, and sharing his latest thoughts about the publication of his book and how his new work could best be presented to a live audience in Edinburgh.

Contribution to scholarship

Biography: Romanticism, Greece, and beyond

St Clair's career as a writer, biographer, and historian seems to have begun almost by accident, with an advertisement in *The Times*. Mrs A.C. Langland, of Abingdon, had inherited the papers of a 'great-grand-uncle' and was seeking someone interested in acquiring them. Her relative turned out to be Dr Philip Hunt, who as a young clergyman had been engaged by Thomas Bruce, Seventh Earl of Elgin, as his private secretary during the latter's service as HM Ambassador to Constantinople from 1799 to 1803.[5] And so was born *Lord Elgin and the Marbles*, St Clair's first book, published in 1967.

At heart, in its original form, at just over 300 pages, this was a biography. Its subject is a minor figure on the fringes of the British Romantic movement – a Scottish nobleman with a chip on his shoulder, congenital syphilis, an unbending sense of honour and his own dignity – and far too little money to encompass his grand schemes. Starting out with an ambition to use his embassy to the Ottoman empire as an opportunity to benefit 'the progress of the Fine Arts in Great Britain' by bringing back drawings of Greek antiquities to be found in Ottoman lands, Elgin moved on to the notorious removal of a large amount of sculpture from the Parthenon and other ancient temples that had been built in the 5th century BC to adorn the Acropolis of Athens. Later known as the 'Elgin Marbles', and later still as the 'Sculptures of the Parthenon', these monuments of the highpoint of ancient Greek art would end up being sold in 1816 to the British Museum, where they have remained, as the subject of controversy, ever since.

Subsequently, St Clair would return to the topic of this first book and also become an activist in the campaign for the restitution of the sculptures to their original home in Athens. But in 1967 his focus was firmly biographical. His treatment of his flawed subject is penetrating, but always evenhanded. And as well as being a blow-by-blow account of all that Elgin set in motion and that his agents did in Athens in his name, *Lord Elgin and the Marbles* is a fine exploration, not just of its biographical subject, but of the multiple ways – mostly unforeseen by Elgin himself – in which the ambassador's controversial actions did indeed have an impact in Great Britain and throughout Europe: not by influencing practice in the arts and crafts, but in establishing the reputation of the sculptors of 5th-century BC Athens at the very pinnacle of European artistic achievement.

From one tarnished and troubled individual on the fringes of British Romanticism, it would not be long before St Clair would move on to another. If Elgin had been, in the eyes

---

[5] William St Clair, *Lord Elgin and the Marbles: The Controversial History of the Parthenon Sculptures* (Oxford: Oxford University Press, 1998), p. ix (preface to the 1st edition of 1967).

of many, a thief and a plunderer, Edward John Trelawny (1792–1881) was, as St Clair's subtitle has it, *The Incurable Romancer*. An incorrigible liar, fantasist and self-publicist, Trelawny would outlive all his contemporaries to write two (often contradictory, as St Clair points out) memoirs of his time spent in the company of the great Romantic poets of the 'second generation', Percy Bysshe Shelley and Lord Byron. St Clair is forensic in pursuing the facts and the reality of the man beneath the many layers of self-fashioning – often in characteristically acerbic style. But, as a good biographer should, he never loses the focus on his subject, and never simply debunks him either. One of the achievements of this eminently readable, and still largely definitive, book is to secure a place for the picturesque and charismatic wannabe Romantic poet in the company of his more famous peers. In St Clair's reading, *Records of Shelley, Byron and the Author* (1878) by E.J. Trelawny comes to seem in its own right a belated achievement, as well as an apologia, of the Romantic era.

Trelawny appeared in 1977. Before that, St Clair had broadened his canvas considerably, while still keeping within the timeframe of the Romantic period and the geographical space of Greece, where some of Trelawny's most famous exploits also took place. *That Greece Might Still Be Free: The Philhellenes in the War of Independence* is, in a sense, a group biography, with a cast of approximately 1,200 – the number of volunteers who set out from all over Europe and from the United States of America to take part in a revolutionary war that began in 1821 and ended with international recognition for Greece as a sovereign state a decade later. St Clair was risking moving into a crowded field when he published this book in 1972; the respected University of London historian Douglas Dakin had published *British and American Philhellenes During the War of Greek Independence* in 1955; *The Philhellenes* by the prolific C.M. Woodhouse, himself a decorated war hero who had served in occupied Greece during the Second World War, had appeared only three years previously. The achievement was all the more remarkable in that, unlike those authors, St Clair, on his own frank admission, did not read modern Greek.

It may have helped that in the early 1970s Greece was in the grip of the military dictatorship of the 'Colonels'. The modern country was frequently in the news; indeed interest in contemporary Greece across Europe and North America seems to have peaked during those years. As well as being repressive at home, the 'Colonels' promoted a brash and naive version of nationalist exceptionalism in their propaganda and public statements. This provided St Clair with the perfect target for the acerbic irony of which he was a master. The heroic themes trumpeted by the regime in Greece became fair game; the author's revulsion at the many excesses committed in the name of liberty is plain to see. A recurrent theme is that Greeks were as often responsible for horrific atrocities as their enemies the Turks and Muslim Albanians. For this reason, the book was not welcome at the time in Greece; indeed a Greek translation was not commissioned until 2020. On the other hand, it was well received by its intended readership; Woodhouse generously paid tribute to a 'melancholy story [told] with sardonic relish and lucid scholarship'.[6]

Part of what makes this book such an enduring classic is its unwavering focus on the foreign volunteers who are its prime subject. St Clair knew very well that the story of the Greek struggle for independence had been told many times already, as indeed it also has been since. The Greeks, whose revolution it was, are in a sense secondary. As he had done with Elgin previously, and would with Trelawny later, St Clair gets under the skin of the perceptions, the expectations (often cruelly falsified by events), and above all the motivations and responses of so many different individuals, of different nationalities, ideologies and backgrounds, who risked everything to fight in a war and for a cause that was not even their own. One of the most poignant aspects of the book, and one that links it closely with the biographies that chronologically frame it, is the author's unswerving exposure of the assumptions that brought many of his protagonists into the field. Again and again he highlights the unbridgeable gaps that separated classically educated youths, straight out of northern universities, from the realities of an inter-confessional war of extermination on the ground. Once again, the biographical subjects are not simply debunked – but once again, too, just as in the more conventional biographies of Elgin and Trelawny, the contradictions that made their experiences so often tragic are mercilessly exposed.

St Clair's most ambitious foray into the genre of biography was published while he was still at the Treasury, in 1989. *The Godwins and the Shelleys* has the subtitle, *The Biography of a Family*. And the author delivers on his promise. Framed by the eight decades of the life of William Godwin, the prolific radical thinker and author of *An Enquiry Concerning Political Justice* (1793), it tells the closely interwoven stories of Godwin himself, of the early feminist Mary Wollstonecraft, who died giving birth to their daughter, the future Mary Shelley in 1797, and the short and tempestuous life of Percy Bysshe Shelley. Once again St Clair's gift for meticulous archival research is matched by close focus on the documented actions, thoughts and experiences of his subjects, from whom he also exercises a consistently sardonic distance.

St Clair had begun to reflect critically about the nature of the biographer's task. Not only, he realised in the book's final chapter, was he following in the footsteps of Mary Shelley, the author of *Frankenstein*, who in later life had shaped the biographies of her father and her husband for posterity, but his task had actually been to undo precisely what she had done; as he put it, 'Mary Shelley ... broke the link between the ideas and the lives. In 1831 she had written a memoir of Godwin without mentioning Shelley: in 1839 she wrote her notes in [sic] Shelley without mentioning Godwin'.[7] It was William St Clair who

---

[6] C.M. Woodhouse, review, *The Observer* cited in William St Clair, *That Greece Might Still Be Free: The Philhellenes in the War of Independence* (Cambridge: Open Book Publishers, 2008 [1st ed. London: Oxford University Press, 1972], front matter.

[7] William St Clair, *The Godwins and the Shelleys: The Biography of a Family* (London: Faber, 1989), p. 392.

had painstakingly reassembled the whole picture. In the process he had also teased out a complex skein of ideas and behaviours that linked the radical wing of Enlightenment thought in Britain in the 1790s with the most explosive manifestations of Romanticism, in *Frankenstein* and the visionary and political poems of Shelley two decades later.

Three densely documented appendices to *The Godwins and the Shelleys*, probably skipped by most readers, simultaneously hark back to St Clair's rigorous training on the job as a senior civil servant and anticipate directions that his scholarship would take in future. Decoding the record of his sexual relationship with Mary Wollstonecraft that Godwin kept in his journal during their year together before their marriage, St Clair trains the spotlight on intimate details that had previously been literally unmentionable in a serious, scholarly biography – but also on attitudes and practices related to sex and birth control at the time. It may well have been while he was working on the lifestory of Mary Wollstonecraft, author of *A Vindication of the Rights of Woman* (1792), that William St Clair became, himself, in his own distinctive way, a champion of modern feminism.

A second appendix, a bibliographical essay on the 'advice books' for women which proliferated during the decades covered by the biography, takes this topic further, and lays the foundation for what was to become a major editing and publishing project a decade later. A graph which plots the number of such books published in each five-year period from 1780 to 1825, relative to the price of government stocks during the same years, has the title (which may or may not be tongue-in-cheek): 'Women: Indicators of changing anxiety levels among the threatened groups'. Rarely can the routines of HM Treasury have found such an inventive application in the field of literary and social studies! And the final appendix, 'Shelley and the pirates', looks forward directly to what would become St Clair's next writing project, as it explores in detail the publishing practices of the time and their impact on the way that Shelley's work came to be received by the reading public.

Conduct literature

The 'advice books' into which St Clair had tapped in investigating the background to the proto-feminist writings of Mary Wollstonecraft turned out to have been the tip of a very large iceberg indeed. *Conduct Literature for Women I, 1500–1640*, edited by William St Clair and Irmgard Maassen, was published in six volumes in 2000; the companion set, also in six volumes, covering the period 1640–1710, two years later. The sum total of just under 5,000 printed pages was priced at the time at just under £1,000. It was not lost on the editors that this exorbitant cost was prohibitive for all but the largest libraries – a realisa-tion that was to have important consequences later. Consisting mostly of facsimiles of original, rare editions (some complete, some excerpted) with a wealth of contextual mate-rial supplied by the two editors, this huge undertaking came to fruition too early to benefit from digital publication – of whose potential St Clair would become a vigorous champion in the last years of his life.

Conduct literature, as defined by his co-editor, Irmgard Maassen, encompasses a wide range

> of admonitory and instructional genres – among them marriage and funeral sermons, household manuals, treatises on education, but also chapbook verse and satire. Advising on apparel and comportment, talk and taste, piety and leisure, household affairs and reading for all walks and ranks of life, these texts are, on account of their overtly ideological nature, a prime source for studying historical constructions of identities and class and gender relations.[8]

On her collaboration with St Clair on this project, Maassen writes:

> We first met in 1996, at a Romanticism conference in Duisburg, Germany, where he gave a talk on the reception of Byron, and I on the anxiety of reading in Mary Wollstonecraft. He took an interest – he was quite in the habit of taking an interest in other people's work, and was always tremendously generous with his wide-ranging knowledge and encouragement of younger scholars. His readiness to share in others' work, I think, provided him with the intellectual exchange and stimulus he did not, as a scholar working outside the university, get through the more mundane business of teaching.
>
> As it turned out, William had on his overflowing shelves (and in storage somewhere up in Golders Green) what was easily the largest collection of English conduct books for women in the country. ... Hunting down the texts for the edition was immensely enjoyable – William would dive into the gloom of old libraries as if in his native element, to emerge triumphantly wielding a new piece of relevant information, which more often than not led to another heated conversation over a dinner getting cold. [St Clair] was one of the most stimulating intellectual companions one can hope to meet, interested in new perspectives and ideas, witty in conversation, refreshingly and surprisingly unstuffy.

On the significance of this project in relation to St Clair's other scholarly work, Maassen concludes:

> [H]is interest in conduct literature for women may, at first sight, strike one as a bit unexpected. But no-one writing about the Godwin-Shelley circle, as he had done, can remain unsympathetic to feminist concerns. William wore his feminism lightly, and with a disarming degree of self-irony, but it was an integral part of his enlightened, atheist rationalism. His interest grew directly out of his book-historical research: conduct titles were plentiful, often came in large print-runs, were frequently excessively (depressingly, from a feminist point of view) long-lived and highly intertextual ... . They provided excellent examples for the way such advice migrated through different formats for different readers. They also contained lots of fascinating paratexts that shed light on marketing strategies.

---

[8] Irmgard Maassen, 'Whoring, Scolding, Gadding About: Threats to Family Order in Early Modern Conduct Literature', *Journal for the Study of British Cultures*, 9/2 (2002), 159–71.

All this feeds directly into the materialist, cultural-economic key concern of William's [next book], *The Reading Nation*: how the accessibility of books, their longevity, pricing and licensing shaped the reception and mentalities of reader constituencies.

'The political economy of reading'

If his work on the conduct books grew out of the first two appendices to *The Godwins and the Shelleys*, St Clair's magnum opus, *The Reading Nation in the Romantic Period*, published in 2004, assuredly grew out of the third. Weighing in at more than 700 pages, with thirteen appendices taking up more than a third of the total, and illustrated by numerous tables and reproductions of engravings from rare editions, this has been described as 'the kind of book that few academics are able to write anymore: a massive compilation of material, based on years of archival work, that thoroughly transforms knowledge about a topic of widespread interest'.[9] The author's aim is nothing less than 'to develop a political economy of texts, books, reading, and mentalities'.[10] St Clair was not, of course, the first to examine the practices of publishing, dissseminating and (so far as this is recoverable) reading, and in this way to open out the discussion of literature from the production and the product to its consumers and the intermediaries whose activities make the connection possible. Conceptually, St Clair's project has much in common with 'Reception Aesthetic' or the 'reader-response theory' associated with the German theorists Hans Robert Jauss and Wolfgang Iser; but in his case the formidable intellectual underpinning that lies behind it owes more to the empirical traditions of the British civil service than to theoretical hermeneutics. Rigorous, data-driven, and far-ranging in its scope, *The Reading Nation* tells the story, and provides the evidence to prove it, of the mechanisms that brought the ideas and the imaginative visions of a tiny elite into the consciousness of average Britons from the time of the first printed books in the 16th century to the Victorian period.

On this book, and its relationship to *The Godwins and the Shelleys* as the two chief pillars of St Clair's contribution to studies of Romanticism, Sir Drummond Bone writes:

> both [these books] share William's insistence that meaningful explanations are testable on the one hand ('there is no way of determining impact on opinion by looking at inputs alone'),[11] and a driving energy aimed at social justice, and particularly social justice for women, on the other. If he was in some ways a man of the sixties – the 1960s that is – there is no doubt that for him the sexual revolution should only be based on a revolution in women's place in society. And his involvement in open access publication has its roots too in the effects of the copyright law and the publication industry on the education of those

---

[9] Andrew Elfenbein, review in *Victorian Studies*, 47/3 (2005), 457–9.
[10] William St Clair, *The Reading Nation in the Romantic Period* (Cambridge: Cambridge University Press, 2004), p. 451.
[11] St Clair, *The Godwins*, p. 510.

without the social or economic freedom to choose. So if Godwin was 'scornful of the "fictitious rules of decorum"', William likewise with Wollstonecraft made openness a major theme of the campaign for equality, and so has no qualms in giving a detailed account of Godwin's sexual relationship with Mary. And this leads him on to manuals of sex education and so to manuals of female conduct and we are heading towards not only publication study but the editions of those conduct books to come. ... His conclusion is pointed: '... women were evidently a problem ... during the revolutionary and romantic period' – a problem that is, for the male hereditary landed authority.[12]

Perhaps surprisingly, in coming to that conclusion about women, William quotes Foucault approvingly. 'Surprisingly', because he was not a 'theory' supporter, in the sense of the term used by English Literature academics. He was actually less disturbed by the deconstructionists than by the new historicists, and less disturbed by the originals than by their followers who seemed to reduce everything by the application of ready-made framework 'explanations'. This considerable irritation was one of the motivations behind *The Reading Nation* – there was a real desire to base cultural explanations on data which could in turn be used to test these explanations. 'Can we begin to model the links between texts, books, reading, changing mentalities, and wider historical effects? ... If we could ... understand how certain texts came to be made available in printed form to certain constituencies of buyers and readers, we would have made a good start in narrowing the questions to be addressed in tracing ideas'.[13]

We note the vocabulary of 'modelling', and the care in differentiation of 'text' and 'book'. Out of the wealth of data on publication he brings together, the pirate publishers emerge as the heroes of the anti-establishment revolution. The myriad of pirated editions of *Don Juan* for example make it 'the Galapagos Islands of literature' in the Romantic and indeed Victorian period. 'The argument that intellectual property is a privilege granted for a limited period in order to reward and encourage innovation that is valuable to the society that grants it is as valid today as it was in Adam Smith's time ... [but it should be granted] with eyes open to the public interest in the likely consequences'.[14] Here we see William's insistence on the primacy of the social. This massively 'academic' and fact-driven study, has in fact a clear reformist goal. Both these books – I use the term advisedly! – are aimed at 'changing mentalities'.

Something, it may be added, which had once upon a time been the stated aim of the authors of the *Encyclopédie*, that foundational set of texts for the European Enlightenment.[15]

---

[12] St Clair, *The Godwins*, p. 509.

[13] St Clair, *The Reading Nation*, pp. 1, 7.

[14] St Clair, *The Reading Nation*, p. 451.

[15] *Encyclopédie, ou Dictionnaire raisonné des sciences, des arts et des métiers* (Paris, 1751–1772), 5.642 ('changer la façon commune de penser') (Diderot). Available online at http://enccre.academie–sciences.fr/encyclopedie/.

Anatomy of the transatlantic slave trade

The last of his books that St Clair saw through to publication was, at first sight, another unexpected departure. Once again, it grew, in part at least, out of a chance occurrence, and would soon far exceed the scope of its simple beginnings. The genesis and significance of *The Grand Slave Emporium: Cape Coast Castle and the British Slave Trade* (2006), published a year later in the US as *The Door of No Return, The History of Cape Coast Castle and the Transatlantic Slave Trade*, are explained by David St Clair:

> Around 2000 Cambridge classics don, Mary Beard became general editor of Wonders of the World, a new mini-series to be published by Harvard University Press, USA. She invited a number of experts to write no more than 50,000 words on a famous building or monument. Buildings included the Treasury of Atreus at Mycenae, the Temple of Jerusalem, the Alhambra, and St Pancras Station. Mary invited St Clair to write about a famous building. While the obvious choice would have been the Parthenon, Mary had already lined it up for herself. Although Cape Coast Castle in Ghana (west Africa) had been designated a UNESCO world heritage building, its history at the time was little known outside specialists in the field of African and international slavery studies. St Clair agreed to write on the castle. Its heyday as a centre of the British slave trade was a period familiar to him, namely the 18th and early 19th centuries. It was an inspired choice.
>
> One of about sixty forts spanning the Ghana coast, Cape Coast was the African headquarters of the British slave trade for nearly 150 years until the legal trade was abolished in 1807. It was out of the dungeon and through 'the door of no return' that Africans passed on their way to the waiting slave vessels. Although the castle appeared forebidding to all who approached it by sea, surrounded by breakers and cannons pointing seawards, in reality it was poorly fortified. It was a key link in a multinational global trading network that 'From the mid-fifteenth century to the late nineteenth century [carried] over 11 million people born in Africa ... across the ocean. About 3 million were taken by ships belonging to British merchants and those of British settlers in North America and the West Indies'.[16] The entire records of Cape Coast Castle were removed and taken to the British National Archives shortly after the slave trade was abolished. Largely forgotten, the records, ledgers, letters and notes bleached by the sun or stained by salt water offer glimpses of people and events as they happened on an almost daily basis over a period of a hundred and fifty years.
>
> From these immense archives St Clair derived most of the source material for his book which soon became too long to include in Professor Beard's mini-series. It allowed him to draw a vivid and authentic picture of the British officers, men and women that formed the small garrison of the fort. He describes the high death rates, boredom, and life both inside and outside the fort.

---

[16] William St Clair, *The Grand Slave Emporium: Cape Coast Castle and the British Slave Trade* (London: Profile, 2006), p. 3.

Unsurprisingly, nowhere does the book describe the thoughts and feelings of the human cargo passing through the dungeons of the 'Grand Slave Emporium'. Comprehensive records were kept but only in the form of numbers of slaves confined and waiting in the castle and numbers and dates of embarkation on which awaiting ships, their tonnage and nationality. The slaves themselves were voiceless. After the slave trade was abolished, St Clair tells how the castle became a staging post for the British empire's inroads into the West African interior.

Even in this unlikely setting, St Clair's penchant for the rebellious literary spirit of the Romantic movement, and for gender issues, found an outlet, as he pieced together the story of the poet Letitia Landon, who was briefly married to the Governor of Cape Coast Castle, where she died of an overdose of prussic acid in 1838. This story would later become the subject of a full biography of the poet known by the 'genderless three initials L.E.L.', who had briefly become 'the darling of what Disraeli called silver fork society' and died in disgrace, at the age of 36, in this desolate outpost of British colonialism.[17]

Champion of causes

St Clair was never involved in formal politics; but once he had left the civil service he made good use of his newfound freedom to take up public causes on which he felt strongly. And he was a man of strong opinions, which he was never shy of expressing publicly.

The 'Elgin Marbles' / 'Parthenon Sculptures'

In 1983 a vigorous campaign for the return of the sculptures that Lord Elgin had taken from Athens in the first years of the 19th century was mounted by the Minister of Culture in the socialist Greek government of Andreas Papandreou that had been elected two years before. Melina Mercouri was not only a committed socialist; she was a world-famous actress (especially for her role in the 1960 film *Never on a Sunday*) and a much loved, charismatic public figure in Greece. Her impassioned speeches at the Oxford Union and at UNESCO made headlines around the world. Oxford University Press rushed out a new paperback edition of *Lord Elgin and the Marbles*, with photographs of Mercouri and some of the newspaper coverage of her campaign on the back cover. In a brief new epilogue to the book, St Clair gave an outline of the newly revived controversy about the future of the 'Marbles'. And he concluded:

---

[17] Lucasta Miller, *L.E.L.: The Lost Life and Scandalous Death of Letitia Elizabeth Landon, The Celebrated Female Byron* (London: Penguin Random House, 2019).

It is evident that Lord Elgin's aims were, from the beginning, honourable; that he obtained as much legal authority for his operations as it was possible to do in the disordered circumstances of the time; and that the Parthenon sculptures would be in a far worse state today if he, or someone else, had not removed them.[18]

This might have been the end of the matter. But St Clair was not done with the sculptures, or with the Parthenon, the building that more than any other stands, in the eyes of many, as the emblem of classical Greek civilisation and its artistic achievements. He would return to them again and again until the end of his life. The second edition of his book had not long been published before he was trying to fill in gaps in the story – which was becoming no longer the biography of Lord Elgin, but rather about the fortunes of the sculptures. Almost at once, it seems, St Clair had begun to question the assertion he had made in the final sentence of his book, with such seeming confidence and certainty.

The very next year, in 1984, he embarked on what would prove to be a long-drawn-out battle by correspondence with officials at the British Museum. It was known that in 1938 and 1939 Lord Duveen, the donor of the gallery in which the Parthenon sculptures are still displayed today, had ordered the cleaning of their surfaces, using methods which had not been authorised and were contrary to accepted practice. St Clair now sought access to the museum's records, to find out exactly what had happened. The responses that he received convinced him that the Museum was determined to cover up damage to the artworks in their care, that had been far more serious than anyone had ever admitted.[19] Returning to the case after a decade, St Clair was finally given full access in 1996 – and set about with gusto to reveal what he considered to be a major 'scandal'.

The result was the third edition of *Lord Elgin and the Marbles*, now with the added subtitle, *The Controversial History of the Parthenon Sculptures*. Published in 1998, the new edition was almost a hundred pages longer than its predecessors, and included three new chapters devoted to the fate of the sculptures since Elgin's time. By now, St Clair's faith in the British Museum's custodianship had been shattered; he had also, in the meantime, unearthed further documentary evidence that cast doubt on the claimed legitimacy of Elgin's actions, in his dealings with the Ottoman authorities in Constantinople and Athens. The third edition includes, in an Appendix, the surviving text of the *firman*, or decree, that gave permission for the removal of 'some stones' from the Acropolis of Athens, along with evidence to show how far Elgin had exceeded the terms set out in that document, and what appeared to be bribes that he had paid to the local governor. St Clair was now ready to take up the cudgels on behalf of the campaign for restitution of the sculptures to Greece –

---

[18] William St Clair, *Lord Elgin and the Marbles*, [2nd edn] (Oxford: Oxford University Press, 1983), pp. 275–6.

[19] For St Clair's own account, and extracts from correspondence dated 1984 and 1995, see St Clair, *Lord Elgin*, 3rd edn, pp. 306–8, 389–90.

principally on the grounds, trenchantly set out in the final sentence of the new edition: 'Now that the British Museum's stewardship of the Elgin Marbles turns out to have been a cynical sham for more than half a century, the British claim to a trusteeship has been forfeited'.[20]

After the book was published, with its explosive twenty-fourth chapter, the 'scandal' of the way the sculptures had been treated while in the care of the British Museum, and its implications for their future custodianship, erupted in the British and Greek press. In hopes of clearing the air, the Museum organised a conference, open to the public, which was held on 30 November and 1 December 1999, and attended by some three hundred delegates.

First to speak was St Clair, who in the meantime had followed up the new edition of his book with a long article, supported by some fifty-five cited documents, in which he pressed home his claims about the seriousness of the damage to the sculptures and the culpability of the Museum, both at the time and since, in systematically trying to conceal the whole episode from public view.[21] The Museum's case was put by Dr Ian Jenkins, the Senior Curator with responsibility for the sculptures, who explained in more technical terms what had happened in 1938–9, while excusing neither the act of cleaning nor the later cover-up. Several Greek experts also spoke. By all accounts the occasion was conducted courteously throughout, until the final session. When the Press Counsellor at the Greek Embassy, Nikos Papadakis, took advantage of the question and answer session to object to a satirical piece that had been published that morning in the *Daily Telegraph* by the columnist Auberon Waugh, he was abruptly told to stop speaking. At the same time – it is not clear for what reason – St Clair was informed that he would no longer be welcome at the dinner hosted by the Museum's Director, Dr Robert Anderson, that evening. Tempers flared. The meeting ended without any conclusions, let alone consensus, on the subject at hand. Eventually, after several acts of mediation, St Clair did attend the dinner, still furious at the way in which the Greek Press Counsellor had been treated.

Relations between St Clair and the British Museum remained frosty for some time, and he never wavered in his newfound support for restitution of the 'marbles' to Athens. But at least at the personal level, it seems that he and Ian Jenkins (who would predecease him by seven months) retained, or regained, something of the mutual respect that seems fitting for two scholars of great distinction who, despite their differences, shared a passion for many of the same things.

The case for restitution continues to be pressed from many quarters, including by successive Greek governments and by pressure groups in the UK and other countries. But the story of the cleaning of the sculptures and the attempts to cover it up has not, in the long

---

[20] St Clair, *Lord Elgin*, 3rd edn, p. 336.
[21] William St Clair, 'The Elgin Marbles: Questions of Authenticity and Accountability', *International Journal of Cultural Property*, 8/2 (1999), 391–521.

run, played a crucial role in these campaigns. These have rather tended to focus on the legality of Elgin's acquisition and methods, and on the aim to unify the surviving sculptures from the Parthenon, that for more than two hundred years have been separated in Athens, London, and museums in several other European cities. The fullest account of the cleaning, its nature, its consequences, and the extent to which the sculptures can be said to have been 'damaged', is to be found in the paper which Jenkins published after the British Museum conference, and runs to sixty-five printed pages.[22]

Open Access publishing

His research for *The Reading Nation* had provided St Clair with a deep understanding of the social and economic processes that for hundreds of years had enabled the dissemination of knowledge and ideas through the medium of the printed word. His own experience of publishing with England's longest-established and most prestigious university presses, as well as with 'trade' imprints, caused him to think long and hard about the future of academic publishing. By the early 2000s, the possibilities for electronic publishing were beginning to be appreciated, first of all by the science community, and latterly in Humanities and Social Sciences. These were the early days of the debate about 'Open Access', as it has come to be known since that time. St Clair could see that the internet would quickly become the equivalent, for the new century, to what inexpensive chapbooks and unlicensed 'pirate' editions had been in the 18th and 19th. He had demonstrated that it had been those cheap editions that had by far the greater reach in transmitting ideas (from the age-old to the revolutionary) to the mass of the British population. And the need for something similar in our own time was becoming acute, as he saw it, particularly when the price of academic monographs was rising exponentially and their print runs were being cut back in almost equal proportion. The fact that many of the highly priced monographs that resulted had been very poorly sub-edited convinced St Clair that academic publishers were outrageously cutting their costs at the same as pushing up their prices and, seemingly deliberately, narrowing their market. Might it be possible to devise a business model that would simultaneously allow free access to readers on the internet and generate sufficient income to cover costs and ensure a high-quality product?

In 2007, in Cambridge, husband-and-wife team Rupert Gatti, an economist and Fellow of Trinity College, and Alessandra Tosi, a specialist in Russian literature, had embarked on a project of their own to establish an Open Access publisher for the Humanities and Social Sciences. Open Book Publishers (OBP) began life as a legal entity in 2008, and began to make its first, cautious approaches to potential authors. One of those was St Clair, whom

---

[22] Ian Jenkins, *Cleaning and Controversy: The Parthenon Sculptures, 1811–1939*, Occasional Paper no. 146 (London: The British Museum, 2001).

Gatti had already met during the former's fellowship at Trinity. A close personal and working relationship was quickly formed, and by the end of that year St Clair had joined Gatti and Tosi as co-founder and Chairman of Directors of the new enterprise.

The business model was quickly hammered out, with each of the three contributing expertise: Gatti on the technical and financial side, Tosi managing the day-to-day business, including acquiring manuscripts and commissioning assessments (there was to be no cutting of corners when it came to peer review), and St Clair advising on strategy and recommending particular projects. The first of these, offered up as the 'guinea pig' for the entire venture, was St Clair's own second book, *That Greece Might Still Be Free*. This had long been out of print, and the rights had reverted to the author. The new edition was essentially a reprint of the old, but with much new visual material added, taking advantage of the possibilities afforded by the new medium. (I had only recently met St Clair for the first time, and felt honoured to be invited to contribute a preface.)

Since then, OBP has published some 250 titles, all available to read online and download in multiple formats free of charge, and to download in ebook and printed editions for a price. On the experience of working with St Clair, Alessandra Tosi writes:

> What characterised our collaboration throughout were the stimulating and free discussions we managed to have until the very end. William always spurred us to push ahead and think outside the box, take risks, and challenge the status quo whenever it was deemed right to do so. His moral compass and disregard of received opinions on the one hand, and his enthusiasm and courage on the other have been at the core of OBP from our first encounter in 2008, until our very last one in June 2021. I'll always remember our last meeting in our garden after months of Zoom encounters: the warmth in William's eyes and the sheer energy of his vision will sustain us into the future.

From his first engagement with OBP, St Clair became a passionate advocate of Open Access publishing in general, and more particularly of the business model that he and his co-directors had pioneered. He appeared frequently – and often combatively – in panel discussions on the subject, including one held at the British Academy in 2012.[23] In the meantime, the Open Access debate has moved on; the big academic publishing houses and the government agencies that sponsor academic research in the Humanities and Social Sciences in the UK, the EU and elsewhere, have developed a huge, bureaucratic industry around the regulation and financing of Open Access publishing in different forms. The simplicity of the vision that St Clair shared with Gatti and Tosi has much to recommend it, in the more complex hybrid environment of academic publishing that has grown up since they set up OBP. Simplicity, forthrightness, and a no-nonsense, practical approach to complex problems, as well as the 'moral compass' remembered by Tosi, were the hallmarks of St Clair's commitment to those causes that were dear to him.

---

[23] https://www.thebritishacademy.ac.uk/events/open-access-new-future-academic-publishing/.

Swansong

During the last two decades of his life, St Clair returned to the subject of the Parthenon and the antiquities of Athens for what he conceived as a single, monumental study. As the years went by, it grew and grew. Starting from diplomatic documents preserved in the National Archives, Kew, that had previously been overlooked, and with assistance from Professor Edhem Eldem of Boğaziçi University, Istanbul, who was able to furnish him with translations of Ottoman sources, St Clair embarked on an elaborate counter-argument to that of Elgin and his supporters, who had argued that the removal of the sculptures in the early 1800s had 'saved' them from destruction, either by the Ottoman Turks, or during hostilities when Athens and its Acropolis changed hands no fewer than three times in the course of the Greek Revolution (1821–33). From this nucleus, the study gathered momentum and accumulated material in the manner of snowball.

It had been St Clair's intention to publish it during the two hundredth anniversary of the outbreak of that revolution, in 2021. But by the summer of that year, it had grown too large to be easily accommodated in a single volume. Its author had moved beyond his earlier focus on either biography or Romanticism; his subject this time was the Parthenon itself – or more precisely the architectural and sculptural monuments of the 5th century BC that had been created to adorn the Acropolis of Athens. In essays and lectures while he had been working on the book, St Clair had begun to develop a concept of 'viewing' to match that of 'reading' that he had explored in *The Reading Nation*.[24] In the new book, which he rather wonderfully described as 'a history of conjunctures of consumption', he discusses the many contrasting, overlapping, and self-contradictory ways in which different categories of viewer, and many different individuals of many different backgrounds and nationalities, had viewed those monuments from the 17th century to the present – with the lion's share going to the period immediately before, during and after the Greek Revolution of the 1820s. By the time of his death, St Clair had extended this novel approach all the way back to the time when the monuments had first been built.

Who Saved the Parthenon? A New History of the Acropolis Before, During and After the Greek Revolution, edited by David St Clair and Lucy Barnes, was published by Open Book in spring 2022, to be followed shortly afterwards by the shorter *The Classical Parthenon*, in which the last of the chapters to be written are presented by the editors as a self-contained work, aimed primarily at readers more interested in the classical period than in its modern reception.

---

[24] William St Clair, 'Imperial Appropriations of the Parthenon', in John Henry Merryman (ed.), *Imperialism, Art and Restitution* (Cambridge: Cambridge University Press, 2006), pp. 65–97; William St Clair, 'Looking at the Acropolis of Athens from Modern Times to Antiquity', in Constantine Sandis (ed.), *Cultural Heritage Ethics: Between Theory and Practice* (Cambridge: Open Book Publishers, 2014), pp. 57–102, the latter based on the 2012 annual Runciman Lecture at King's College London.

At the time of writing, it would be foolhardy to predict for which of his many qualities, interests, and achievements this remarkable man and scholar will be most remembered. His life and work ranged across fields and types of scholarship which have little intrinsically in common, and whose practitioners more often than not are likely to be unknown to each other (as indeed was the case with those who have assisted in compiling this memoir). A significant portion of his life was spent far from academia. And yet it must have been his background in the upper echelons of the British civil service, and the aptitudes he had honed there, that equipped William St Clair to become the polymath, forensic seeker after facts and their underlying causes, and champion of rationalism and ethical values, that he became in later life. Indeed, one way to appreciate his life and work as a whole might be to see him in the company of some of the great figures of the 18th-century Enlightenment (Edward Gibbon, perhaps, most of all) that he admired so much.

Acknowledgements
I am grateful to the following who have helped me immeasurably in compiling this memoir, and in several cases have given me permission to quote extensively from the information they were kind enough to provide: Sir Drummond Bone, Lesley Fitton, Marion Hobson, Irmgard Maassen, James Rivington, John St Clair, Alessandra Tosi, and most of all David St Clair, Emeritus Professor of Psychiatry at the University of Aberdeen.

Note on the author: Roderick Beaton is Emeritus Koraes Professor of Modern Greek & Byzantine History, Language & Literature, King's College London, and Chairman of the British School at Athens, one of the British International Research Institutes (BIRI) supported by the British Academy. He was elected Fellow of the British Academy in 2013.

CHRISTOPHER TAYLOR

Christopher Charles Taylor

7 November 1935 – 28 May 2021

elected Fellow of the British Academy 1995

by

CHRISTOPHER DYER

Fellow of the Academy

Christopher Taylor spent his working life in the Royal Commission on Historical Monuments of England, of which he became Head of Archaeological Survey in 1980. His academic achievement was to record and interpret the earthwork remains of medieval sites. He was a thoughtful surveyor, who integrated the results with information from other sources, and became a leading figure in the study of past landscapes. He contributed to a sequence of inventories published by the RCHME, but also published many articles in journals, chapters in edited volumes, and books aimed in part at the general reader. His achievements were widely recognised, notably in the award of the British Academy's Landscape Archaeology Medal in 2013.

Biographical Memoirs of Fellows of the British Academy, 20, 201–221
Posted 30 June 2022. © British Academy 2022.

I

Christopher Taylor was an innovator and leader in the field of landscape history (also called landscape archaeology), who had strong connections with universities, but was throughout his career a civil servant, employed by the Royal Commission on Historical Monuments of England. The Commission, as it was widely known among archaeologists, was established in 1908 to compile inventories of 'monuments', to provide the means of selecting those worthy of preservation. The commissioners were a distinguished group, including leading scholars, and the grand name suggested a prestigious organisation, but it was not generously funded. The investigations of the staff developed in a predictable way: as they progressed from county to county the range of 'monuments' to be listed expanded from the original emphasis on standing buildings to include sites mainly below the ground. An ever wider range of techniques were applied to the recording of sites, including, for example, aerial photography. The descriptions became more elaborate and time consuming. The first county, Hertfordshire, was completed in two years (1908–10). One of the volumes of the multi-volume survey of Dorset published in the 1970s had taken twenty years. A culture of confidence, combined perhaps with some complacency, developed among a mainly male staff. They put an emphasis on accurate and complete coverage of sites, without a realistic goal of completing the inventory. They prided themselves on their professionalism, but did not always offer new staff thorough training and a 'job description'. The Commission ceased to compile county inventories towards the end of the 20th century, embarking on a series of specific projects, and in 1999 the Commission was absorbed into English Heritage. Within the organisation Taylor worked purposefully and effectively. He set himself challenging deadlines, and by dint of hard work and a systematic approach kept to schedule while maintaining a very high standard of recording. He contributed substantially to a dozen inventory volumes, of which some were produced single handed or with one assistant. At the same time he was teaching in various capacities, and maintained a flow of articles and books which gave him a strong academic reputation. It was appropriate that he should be elected to the British Academy, where he was one of small but significant group of Fellows who were not on the staff of a university.

II

Like many scholars of his generation Taylor came from lower middle class parents who had no previous experience of higher education.[1] His father repaired and maintained agricultural machinery in the countryside around the family's home in Lichfield in Staffordshire. He made occasional comments about the rural landscape which his son later remembered as his first contact with the subject. Taylor's enterprising mother opened a shop in the centre of Lichfield, called 'Nurseryland', selling goods for infants and small children. In 1935 when he was born the family lived in a terraced house outside the town centre, but subsequently they moved to more spacious accommodation above the shop. Taylor's mother was especially ambitious for her son, and he gained a place at the small local grammar school, King Edward VI at Lichfield. After unpromising results at the age of 16 she encouraged him to enter the sixth form, where both history and geography engaged his interest. He was attracted to the local university, the University College of North Staffordshire, later Keele University, because he was reluctant to specialise in a single subject. The degree course extended over four years (1954–8 for Taylor) to accommodate a Foundation Year. This introduction to the full range of subjects taught in the College was welcomed by Taylor, who threw himself into a formidable programme of reading, as well as enjoying the whole university experience. He went on to take a degree in history and geography, with a history syllabus covering a long chronology of mainly political British history, and a geography programme which tended to be deterministic in line with then current thinking.

He encountered very little archaeology at Keele, and developed an interest in the subject on his own initiative. During the summer vacations of 1956 and 1957 he worked for Staffordshire County Council on the early stage of a Sites and Monuments Record (though it was not given that name). He copied out information from the card index of archaeological sites compiled by the Ordnance Survey, and then used this information to begin a recording system in Stafford. Though this was in some ways a routine administrative exercise, he noticed the distribution patterns revealed in the record cards. For example, why did so many Bronze Age finds come from the heavy clay soils and extensive woodlands of the county, which according to deterministic thinking were inhospitable environments for early settlers? Also during the summer vacations, Taylor responded to an offer of summer placements for students advertised by the Commission. He spent time with the Commission's team at Salisbury, and was hooked by the

---

[1] For his early life an especially useful source has been C. Taylor, 'A Driving Lack of Ambition: the Making of a Landscape Historian', an unpublished memoir, kindly made available to me by Stephanie Taylor.

introduction they provided to the planning of earthworks. He obviously made an impression on them, which helped when a post later became available. Meanwhile, he felt the lack of a formal qualification in archaeology, and signed up for a two-year diploma course in West European Prehistory at the Institute of Archaeology in the University of London. This was also a useful alternative to National Service, which he was anxious to avoid. The London course followed a rather traditional syllabus, but he encountered some new developments, such as environmental archaeology in the form of the analysis of animal bones. He passed the diploma exams, but also acquired an antipathy for excavation, confirming a view gained from visits to sites in Staffordshire. This persisted, so he was committed to archaeology, but preferred to practise it above the ground.

III

Taylor was appointed to a post in the Commission in 1960, and immediately was immersed in a year of intense recording of sites in west Cambridgeshire. He used his experience with the Commission as a student, and was working alongside a more senior colleague, but he was also training himself in methods of survey. He embarked on the project with completion in view, as he intended at the end of the year to marry, and move to Salisbury where he was to be employed in the long term. Surveying sites, and writing up the results for inventory volumes was to be Taylor's main activity for the next three decades, but for him it was not a tedious routine, as he found surveying earthworks in the field intensely enjoyable and rewarding, and that pleasure remained throughout his life.

After the initial year in Cambridgeshire, Taylor was pursuing two parallel careers. His official job and main source of income was working on the inventory volumes, but that task did not satisfy his curiosity and ambition to interpret the evidence fully. The Commission was publishing high quality works of reference, based on painstaking research, which carried a great deal of authority. The organisation expected its investigators to interpret the monuments and sites they recorded, but without too much expression of opinion. The preference for factual and objective approaches was shared with other bodies dealing with the past, such as the Ordnance Survey and the Victoria County History. The survey of each site was expected to provide a date, identify its function, and trace any visible changes. A consideration of the wider significance of the evidence risked controversy, and required comparison and perhaps even speculation, which took up valuable space in the publication.

The published inventories did not name a particular author or authors on the title page, though the commissioners' report thanked those responsible. Staff were free to advance discussion of their work in journals and books under their own names, written in their own time, and Taylor took full advantage of this. An example was the village of Culworth, which features in the fourth volume of the inventory of Northamptonshire. This showed that the modern village plan is formed from two streets, different in character, which meet at a triangular green. It was suggested that the green had once been rectangular, and might have been the original village site, before the streets developed, or it could have been a market place, as the lord of Culworth was granted a royal charter for a market in 1264. This was written by Taylor in about 1979, and appeared in the inventory volume in 1982. Also in 1982 Taylor published an article in the journal *Landscape History* under the title. 'Medieval Market Grants and Village Morphology', in which Culworth was cited as one of a number of examples of villages known to have held markets in which space for these occasions was embedded in the village plan, and survived long after the market ceased to be held.[2]

To focus on his Commission work, Taylor's contribution was remarkably productive and worthy of note if it had been his sole activity. The Commission operated from various regional bases. Taylor began with a year at Cambridge, then moved to Salisbury, and after seven years returned to Cambridge. In his first period at Cambridge he contributed substantially to the volume on West Cambridgeshire.[3] He then spent much of the 1960s researching Dorset with the team he had encountered as a student, contributing to four volumes.[4] He went back to Cambridge for a special project on Peterborough, which had been designated as a New Town, with imminent threats to its historic landscape from the expansion of its housing. This survey was completed in 1966–7, and was followed by North-East Cambridgeshire and a section of a volume on Stamford.[5] In the 1970s the Commission decided, with some persuasion from Taylor, to embark on Northamptonshire, its first venture into a midland county. This was Taylor's project, and he produced the first volume entirely on his own, though subsequent volumes benefited from the help of a research assistant, Fran Crowther. Even for two workers the county posed formidable problems, as it was large, with numerous parishes, and many sites of all periods were already known or were to be discovered. Its remote western corners

[2] Royal Commission on Historical Monuments of England (henceforth RCHME), *An Inventory of the Historical Monuments in the County of Northampton*, 4, *Archaeological Sites in South-West Northamptonshire* (henceforth
South-West Northamptonshire, or the appropriate county) (London, Her Majesty's Stationery Office [henceforth HMSO], 1982), pp. 39–40; C.C. Taylor, 'Medieval Market Grants and Village Morphology', *Landscape History*, 4 (1982), 21–8.
[3] RCHME, *West Cambridgeshire* (London, HMSO, 1968).
[4] RCHME, *South-East Dorset* (London, HMSO, 1970); *Central Dorset* (1970); *North Dorset* (1972); *East Dorset* (1975).
[5] RCHME, *Peterborough New Town* (London, HMSO, 1969); *North-East Cambridgeshire* (1972); *The Town of Stamford* (1977).

took a great deal of travelling time from Cambridge. He set himself a target of completing a parish in a week. He was helped to deal with more complex sites by enlisting the help of students who attended training courses at Knuston College, taught jointly with the local Extra-Mural organiser, Tony Brown of Leicester University. These volunteers still came at a price, in terms of the time and energy expended in teaching them surveying techniques. In spite of the problems, and the slow pace of production by the publishers (the Stationery Office), the four volumes of Northamptonshire appeared within a few years of the research.[6]

IV

The inventories that were produced for Cambridgeshire, Dorset and Northamptonshire dealt with all periods, and Taylor was responsible for publishing in them numerous prehistoric and Roman sites, some visible as earthworks, especially in the Dorset chalk country, but many known from crop marks photographed from the air, or revealed by scatters of pottery and flints on the surface of ploughed fields. He was however best known for recording and interpreting the earthwork remains of rural settlements and landscapes of the medieval period, mostly occupied between the 12th and 16th centuries. It is worth setting his thinking in the context of the general growth of understanding of these sites in the second half of the 20th century. When Taylor joined the Commission in 1960 many features of the rural landscapes of the prehistoric and Roman periods were well known and had been studied for decades. Knowledge was not confined to religious sites and burial mounds, but 'Celtic' field systems and linear earthworks were familiar features, the excavated enclosure and building of Little Woodbury (Wiltshire) served as the type site for iron age farms, and hill forts and many Roman villas had been excavated. However, in many ways medieval archaeology was a new subject, which had not been part of the syllabus for archaeology students, and had only just begun to develop an institutional base. The Society for Medieval Archaeology had been founded in 1956, soon after the formation of the Vernacular Architecture Group, and the Deserted Medieval Village Research Group (both in 1952).[7] The most generally recognised rural settlement site, the deserted village, had been discovered by W.G. Hoskins and M.W. Beresford just before and just after the world war, and their distribution over the whole country was established by Beresford's

[6] RCHME, *North-East Northamptonshire* (London, HMSO, 1975); *Central Northamptonshire* (1979); *North-West Northamptonshire* (1981); *South-West Northamptonshire* (1982).
[7] C. Gerrard, *Medieval Archaeology. Understanding Traditions and Contemporary Approaches* (London, Routledge, 2003), pp. 122–5.

book of 1954.[8] Hoskins and Beresford could both see that the irregular mounds, terraces, banks, ditches and holloways represented the remains of a village, especially when the site was surrounded by the ridge and furrow of a medieval field system. However, although air photographs from the inter-war period and some skilful early surveys were revealing coherent village plans, further survey work and selective excavation were needed before these sites could be fully understood. In 1956 Hoskins published plans of seven Leicestershire deserted villages prepared by the Ordnance Survey. His commentary was mainly historical, but he gave brief descriptions of the earthworks, recognising a main street and 'side lanes' (which showed in the plans as holloways), associated with banks and ditches defining property divisions – the tofts and crofts. He seemed unsure of identifying the sites of buildings, though stone foundations were visible on some sites. In five of the Leicestershire examples a moated site, probably in each case representing a manor house, lay within or next to the village earthworks.[9]

The Commission's team working on the inventory of Dorset, who were joined by Taylor in 1961, had to deal with a large number of medieval settlement sites. The deserted villages were outnumbered by the areas of earthworks adjacent to existing settlements, often called shrunken villages. Researchers were gaining confidence in interpreting the different features within the tofts and crofts. Buildings on clay land sites (like the Leicestershire villages described by Hoskins) were visible as house platforms, but in the districts where building stone was available, such as parts of Dorset, the outline of foundations could be planned, including such details as doorways and inner partition walls. The village plan could include boundary banks on the edge of the surrounding fields, and other contemporary features lying near to deserted villages were fish ponds and occasionally mill sites.

In the early stage of archaeological research into medieval rural settlements their importance was thought to lie, not in their origin or development, but in their abandonment. Here had been well-established villages, some of them quite large, and subsequently they had lost all of their inhabitants, or at least the settlement had been greatly reduced in size. To some extent the material evidence was being used to support an historical agenda. The documents showed that the rural population had grown between the 11th and the 13th centuries, and numbers had diminished in the following period in the aftermath of epidemics and a general decline in agriculture. Historians also linked the deserted villages to the known phase of deliberate depopulation of the 15th and 16th centuries, when peasants were removed to make way for sheep pastures.

[8] M.W. Beresford, *The Lost Villages of England* (London, Lutterworth, 1954).
[9] W.G. Hoskins, 'Seven Deserted Village Sites in Leicestershire', *Transactions of the Leicestershire Archaeological and Historical Society*, 32 (1956), 36–51.

As settlements were surveyed aspects of their past became apparent which did not connect so easily with the historical evidence. Some villages had been laid out with regular plans, most commonly with rows of rectangular tofts of equal size along a straight main street. Alternatively the houses fronted on to a rectangular green, or formed a square, or a grid. Analysis of existing villages also revealed their planned origin. We are left with the dilemma of explaining when the plans were made, and who was responsible. Taylor was inclined to suggest a late chronology, with plans being imposed in the 12th century, and to assume that the idea came from the lords of the manor, but recently opinion has moved away from this position. Taylor was insistent on the complexity and variety of settlement, and saw evidence for changes in shape and the mobility of the inhabitants. Some villages showed little evidence for regular planning, for which one explanation might be that an original farmstead expanded with additional houses as heirs settled nearby and developed their holdings of land. In certain regions villages in the sense of large and compact settlements are rare or absent. Taylor found this in Dorset in Blackmoor, a former royal forest, with a number of isolated farmsteads which had developed as land was cleared for agriculture. Much later he examined a settlement pattern consisting of a string of farmsteads at Thurleigh in Bedfordshire. In areas of dispersed settlement there was limited evidence for settlement planning, but still some indications of abandonment, at Thurleigh though not at Blackmoor. [10]

Changes in settlement plan could be revealed by survey, most notably at Bardolfeston, in Dorset, where the street and clearly identifiable houses of the late medieval village were laid across a series of enclosures and boundaries with a different alignment.[11] A decision had evidently been made at some unknown date to redesign the village, but the evidence is entirely archaeological, as no document records such a drastic transformation. That villages were replanned is confirmed by excavations, where boundary ditches and buildings can be found on different alignments in successive periods. Taylor accepted that some village plans could be quite conservative, and he used the street plans and property boundaries of existing settlements as a guide to the layout in the 12th century.

The archaeological evidence, from pottery scatters on ploughed sites, for example, suggested that the desertion of settlements did not occur suddenly, after the Black Death or at the behest of an enclosing lord. People moved away from declining settlements over the 14th and 15th centuries, or indeed the final abandonment stretched into modern times. One explanation for their deterioration was small size and relative poverty which made a village vulnerable.[12] It was sometimes alleged by determinists that marginal land

[10] C.C. Taylor, 'The Pattern of Medieval Settlement in the Forest of Blackmoor', *Proceedings of the Dorset Natural History and Archaeology Society*, 87 (1965), 251–4.; A.E. Brown & C.C. Taylor, 'The Origins of Dispersed Settlement; Some Results of Fieldwork in Bedfordshire', *Landscape History*, 11 (1989), 61–81.
[11] RCHME, *Central Dorset*, pp. 222, 229, plate 183.
[12] C.C. Taylor, *Dorset* (London, Hodder and Stoughton, 1970), pp. 111–21.

(on high ground or in woodland) was most likely to become uninhabited, but a weak village, even with potentially fertile land, was more 'marginal' (in the sense of being liable to collapse) in this period than settlements on heaths or in royal forests.

Surveying the Dorset countryside for the Commission gave Taylor insights into the wider landscape as well as the details of the settlements. He recognised the importance of the advance of cultivation and habitation in the medieval period, especially in the 12th and 13th centuries. One contribution he made to understanding the extent of the area under the plough was to date 'strip lynchets', a feature of chalk country (and elsewhere), which consisted of long terraces cutting into the hill slopes and especially along the side of valleys. These had once been dated to the Bronze Age, but Taylor argued convincingly that they were of medieval origin, forming extensions of the system of plough ridges in the open fields.[13] Constructing them must have been arduous and time consuming, and they indicate the lengths to which medieval cultivators went to maximise the area under crops. At the same time he was critical of the assumption that very large areas of woodland were cleared by the process of 'assarting' in the high middle ages. He argued that the written evidence for the foundation of new settlements was interpreted sometimes with naivety, with the assumption that the first reference to a place dated its origins. The sudden growth in the number of named settlements was the result of the advent of abundant record keeping, and archaeology could sometimes show that the place named for the first time in *c.*1200 had existed for centuries.

There was however a high tide of expanding farmland in the Middle Ages, and Dorset provided an opportunity to observe the consequences for the archaeological record. As a student Taylor had encountered the distinction between the highland and lowland zone that had been advanced by Cyril Fox, believing that early man had settled on high ground and avoided the inhospitable damp oak forests of the lowlands. In Dorset, as Fox knew, the prehistoric hill forts, burial mounds, and linear dykes could be seen mainly on the chalk downs. However, Taylor pointed out that prehistoric sites in the lowlands were invisible because they had been destroyed by the advance of arable farming in the medieval and modern periods. The countryside could be divided between a zone of destruction in the river valleys and the royal forests, and a zone of survival on the chalk uplands. It was beginning to be appreciated in the 1960s that there had been prehistoric settlements in the valleys, for which the evidence has subsequently greatly increased.

When Taylor came to focus his attention on Northamptonshire, he was presented once more with a large quantity of both abandoned and still inhabited medieval settlements. He was well-practised in his observation of earthwork evidence, and was providing interpretations with confidence. He also benefited from the growing research

[13] C.C. Taylor, 'Strip Lynchets', *Antiquity*, 40 (1966), 277–84.

community in Northamptonshire, who were developing new ideas about rural settlement from field-walking, excavation, and the exploration of local topography. True to the tradition of the Commission, most of his writing in the four volumes of the inventory was factual and avoided controversy, but in the introduction to the second volume he did allow himself space to make a series of general statements about rural settlement.[14]

He addressed the then much debated issue of the continuity between the Roman and medieval periods. There was little direct coincidence between sites of the two periods which might suggest that occupation was continuous, or that places had similar functions. However he had indicated the significance of some Roman rural sites which spread over a large area and could have served as exchange centres: 'large non-urban Roman settlements'. One of these lay near Kettering, later to be a medieval small town, and this was the site of a large early Anglo-Saxon cemetery. Less cautious authors might have argued that some of the people buried in the cemetery were the descendants of the inhabitants of the Roman 'non-urban' settlement, and Taylor hinted at this.

He was more certain of the lack of continuity within the pre-Conquest period. The location of settlements that he called 'early Saxon', that is dated by pottery to the period 450–650, were unrelated to the nucleated villages of the 11th century onwards. It appeared that most villages had formed by c.1100, but there was no dating evidence earlier than the 10th century. He doubted the value of the concept of 'daughter' villages, used to explain the existence in some parishes of two nucleated villages, based on the assumption that the smaller village had spun off from the larger when it expanded. He believed that the 'daughters' had formed at the same time as the larger settlements, and both were the products of the same nucleation process in the late pre-Conquest period.

In examining the nucleated villages he emphasised how they were liable to change. He had noticed in Cambridgeshire and elsewhere that some villages consisted of a group of distinct clusters, sometimes called 'ends', and he found further examples in Northamptonshire. He gathered examples together and published them under the title 'polyfocal settlements'. It suggested that large villages could be formed from the merger of a number of hamlets.[15] Stronger evidence for growth in the size of settlements, which he had noticed in his work on Cambridgeshire, was the decision to find new space for housing in an expanding village on arable fields, which he described as 'the movement of villages over their own fields', which might result in the long plots of land on which houses stood retaining the curved shape of the former ploughed strips. Otherwise it was quite difficult to find evidence for expansion – it was easier to establish decline in the form of abandoned streets and house sites adjoining the modern village. Even this apparently direct evidence could be questioned, as it could be the result of a village's inhabitants occupying a new site nearby. Settlement was shifting and mobile.

[14] RCHME, *Central Northamptonshire*, pp. xlvii-liii.
[15] C.C. Taylor, 'Polyfocal Settlement and the English Village', *Medieval Archaeology*, 21 (1977), 189–93.

Finally, ideas which developed from the Northamptonshire work related to the later use of the former village site. As the decay of the village could be slow and piecemeal, an abandoned part of the village might have been cultivated by the cultivators who continued to live there, leaving tell-tale traces of ridge and furrow running across the tofts and house platforms. A striking feature of Northamptonshire villages was that a number were overlain by the earthworks of gardens attached to large country houses. Aristocrats who profited from desertion were likely to have the ambition and means to create gardens on or near to the village site. This tendency had confused some surveyors of village earthworks, who imagined that the terraced walkways and flower beds had been roads and boundaries belonging to the medieval village.

V

By 1980 Taylor had completed programmes of fieldwork in Cambridgeshire, Dorset and Northamptonshire, and the last Northamptonshire volumes were going through the press. He was appointed Head of Archaeological Survey for the Commission, and became responsible for the Cambridge office. His heavier involvement in administrative work increased to a considerable burden when the post of Secretary (the head of the whole organisation) became vacant in 1985 with the departure of Peter Fowler to a university post, and Taylor took charge temporarily.

Soon after he was appointed as Secretary Fowler had proposed that the Commission should concentrate on 'projects'. Taylor became involved in a very successful venture in Lincolnshire, where the Commission had not previously been much engaged. The county had been slow to set up a systematic recording of 'Sites and Monuments', later to be known as the Heritage Environment Record. Work on Lincolnshire was being managed by a single member of staff, Paul Everson. To begin a more systematic approach a section of countryside running across the county to the north of Lincoln was selected, and Everson worked with Taylor and Chris Dunn to examine rural sites. Some of the settlements were exceptionally well-preserved and from them complete village plans could be recovered, but the survey also revealed a shocking amount of damage, mainly from modern agriculture. [16]

Also in the 1980s Taylor was developing his interest in historic gardens, which had been given a strong stimulus from the discovery in Northamptonshire of examples of the 16th to the 18th centuries. More medieval garden designs were being recognised, and the most influential of these was at Bodiam in Sussex. Taylor visited the site by accident,

[16] P.L. Everson, C.C. Taylor & C.J. Dunn, *Change and Continuity. Rural Settlement in North-West Lincolnshire* (London, HMSO, 1991).

outside the area with which he was most familiar. The castle itself, built in the 1380s to a perfectly square plan with round corner towers, was regarded as characteristic of the late phase of medieval fortifications. It was designed to be both impressive and pleasing, but until Taylor and Commission staff analysed the surroundings it had not been realised that the building was set in an elaborately designed landscape. Visitors in the Middle Ages approached on routes which gave them impressive views and even created the sensation of the castle rising out of the ground.[17] The published results had an impact on castle studies which were turning away from military analyses of these buildings. Castles were being perceived as attractive residences, with gardens and adjacent parks, providing a pleasurable environment in which women participated. Bodiam became a shining example for those seeking to compose a revisionist social and cultural history of castles.

Taylor was partly responsible for changing perceptions of moated sites which were much more plentiful than castles. They were houses, many of them manor houses and other high status buildings, surrounded by a wide, water-filled ditch. They were conventionally regarded as defensive, with a purpose of protecting the house and its inhabitants from thieves or raiding parties. When he first encountered them in number while surveying west Cambridgeshire, Taylor decided that their purpose must have been to display the status of the owners. He later elaborated the idea and gave it a cultural dimension by arguing that the water in the moats could have had a decorative function, and might sometimes have formed part of a garden layout.

VI

While Taylor from 1960 onwards was researching and writing for the Commission's inventory volumes, he was also engaged in a self-generated academic programme. This was often closely related to his official duties, but not a requirement. He did not fit this work into periods of relative calm in compiling the inventories: his most productive academic years, between 1973 and 1979, coincided with the demanding period of the Northamptonshire inventories. To some extent the Commission volumes fed his academic work, as his contributions to the inventories stimulated ideas, and he was also able to exchange views with colleagues, to their mutual benefit, as would have been the case in a university environment among academic colleagues. Later in life he recalled lively discussions with Collin Bowen, Desmond Bonney, Paul Everson and others. Taylor's publications were clearly regarded favourably by the Commission,

[17]C.C. Taylor, P. Everson & R. Wilson-North, 'Bodiam Castle, Sussex', *Medieval Archaeology*, 34 (1990), 155–7.

which allowed him access to materials awaiting publication, and it also gave permission for illustrations from Commission volumes to be reproduced. It was presumably recognised that books with a wide circulation by a member of the Commission staff would be good for the organisation's reputation.

Although Taylor's own publications contain many references to sites and settlements in Cambridgeshire, Dorset and Northamptonshire, he familiarised himself with other parts of the country, by travelling widely, reading, especially the periodical literature, attending conferences, and speaking to researchers of all kinds. His curiosity began at home, by investigating the history and archaeology of the villages in which he lived. On his marriage in 1961 he was located near Salisbury at Whiteparish, in the wooded southern tip of Wiltshire, not far from the New Forest. The theme of the article that resulted from his research was the expansion of a dispersed settlement pattern in a woodland environment, much of it in the 12th and 13th centuries. This coincided with similar findings by historical geographers in other English regions.[18] He later came to believe in general that the importance of forest clearance (assarting) in that period had been exaggerated, leading him to suspect a longer chronology for much dispersed settlement.

He moved in 1967 to Whittlesford in the valley of the Cam in Cambridgeshire. As he accumulated evidence about the village, and as thinking about rural settlement was revised over the decades, he was able to formulate hypotheses and then discard them. He wrote a paper for a *festschrift* in honour of Maurice Beresford and John Hurst, tracing the accumulation of evidence and changes of view, as a lesson in the need to adapt interpretations in the light of new knowledge and thinking. He used maps and documents, carried out field walking, and recovered pottery from building sites. He found evidence for a planned market place and a phase of polyfocal growth, ideas which had originated in other village studies. But after a series of reconstructions of Whittlesford's evolution, all of which had to be revised, he was left in a state of uncertainty.[19] Although the results were inconclusive, the process was satisfying for him, and interested his readers. The long timescale of the Whittlesford investigation contrasted with the need when preparing an inventory volume to research and reach conclusions on each village in a week.

A further spur to his 'parallel career' came from his teaching of adult education classes. In his early years in the south-west he was employed by the Extra-Mural Department of Southampton University to conduct evening classes in a succession of

[18] C.C. Taylor, 'Whiteparish: A Study of the Development of a Forest-Edge Parish', *Wiltshire Archaeological and Natural History Magazine*, 62 (1967), 79–102.
[19] C.C. Taylor, 'Whittlesford: the Study of a River-Edge Village', in M. Aston, D. Austin & C. Dyer (eds), *The Rural Settlements of Medieval England* (Oxford, Blackwell, 1989), pp. 207–27

Dorset villages, and he also contributed to day schools where he encountered other specialists in the archaeology of the region. He formed a congenial relationship with Tony Brown of Leicester University's Extra-Mural department, and over the years he became a regular tutor of day schools and training courses at Knuston Hall in Northamptonshire. He taught because he thought that it was important to inform the public about research, but also because it was enjoyable. Teaching connects especially closely with research when adult students are involved. They are confident enough to ask challenging questions which require thoughtful answers, and they bring to the classes specialist knowledge and personal experience so that learning becomes a process of mutual exchange. Encountering adult students showed Taylor that the relatively new subject of landscape history lacked the reading matter that adult students would appreciate. Books on landscape would also be useful for teaching undergraduate students, and for interested members of the public who did not attend formal classes. He began in 1970 with a general account of the landscape of Dorset, which belonged in a series inspired by Hoskins. It followed a template for the series, with a first chapter on the prehistoric and Roman periods, followed by three chapters on the countryside in the Middle Ages, and then through the modern period, with a last chapter on towns. These were popular illustrated books of 200 pages, which gave little scope for detail or elaboration of argument, but Taylor's experience with the Commission shone through and gave the book depth and authority. It was soon followed by another in the same series on Cambridgeshire.[20] He followed these broad surveys of specific counties with thematic books addressing the interests of landscape historians in general and adult students in particular, with an eye to helping amateur researchers. *Fieldwork in Medieval Archaeology* was explicitly aimed at the 'part-time archaeologist', but it must have had a wider readership. It showed how to plan earthworks without sophisticated equipment, gave advice on interpretation, with appropriate examples, and demonstrated the use of supplementary information, such as documents, especially maps.[21] 'The general reader with an enquiring mind' was intended to take an interest in *Fields in the English Landscape*, and it clearly had a general appeal as it was reprinted three times. It provided a clear and systematic overview, using mainly map and earthwork evidence, of fields from prehistory into modern times, with chapters on both enclosed and open fields of the medieval period.[22] Similar qualities are found in his *Roads and Tracks of Britain*, which treated them as elements in the landscape rather than just as long distance channels of communication. He made the simple but important point that an open field system needed a close network of access routes so that cultivators could reach their strips.[23]

[20] Taylor, *Dorset*; C.C. Taylor, *The Cambridgeshire Landscape* (London, Hodder and Stoughton, 1973).
[21] C.C. Taylor, *Fieldwork in Medieval Archaeology* (London, Batsford, 1974).
[22] C.C, Taylor, *Fields in the English Landscape* (London, Dent, 1975).
[23] C.C. Taylor, *Roads and Tracks of Britain* (London, Dent, 1979).

His most important and influential book, appreciated by academics and students as well as the 'general reader' was *Village and Farmstead*.[24] Like the fields and roads books it covered a long time span, and devoted a good deal of attention to the late prehistoric and Roman settlement patterns, delivering the strong message that large areas were being settled and farmed, even in regions which had previously been regarded as under exploited because of environmental constraints, such as heavy soils. He thought that a population of 5 million was possible at the peak of the Roman province's development, a figure that was comparable with the numbers in the 13th or 16th centuries. He was also aware of the likely organisation of the Roman countryside into estates, which echoed cautiously the theory of continuity of boundaries and units of land management between the pre-medieval and medieval periods.

In his chapters on the Middle Ages he reiterated and strengthened arguments that he had been making in earlier writings, both for the Commission and in his own publications. He warned against too strong an emphasis on nucleated villages, which were not the predominant settlement form of the period. Large villages had grown at quite a late date within the medieval period, with most villages being associated with pottery dated after 1000. A large midland village which had been extensively excavated at Faxton in Northamptonshire seems to have formed in the 12th century. He identified the various processes that led to nucleation, such as agglomeration by which the family occupying a single farmstead settled its offspring nearby, leading over the generations to a cluster of peasant farms. Polyfocal settlements reflected expansion in stages, by which hamlets established within a short distance filled the gaps with new settlers and could then appear as a single settlement with a complicated plan. The pottery scatters indicating small settlements from before the 9th century found in the fields around nucleated villages suggested a 'balling' of settlement by which people moved from hamlets and farmsteads to congregate in the central village. Taylor's new statement on nucleation put much evidence on planning. He was insistent that planned villages were more numerous than we had appreciated, because the original core, often a street with rows of houses, was buried in a settlement that had grown into a loose cluster. He assumed the importance of the lords of manors as agents of settlement change. His work on polyfocal villages found that the original foci of settlement belonged to different lords, again suggesting links between settlement forms and lordship.

In examining the subsequent development of villages he was anxious to emphasise their tendency to change, as in his previous writings. These included expansion over former fields, encroachment of houses on the village green, and the addition of new streets. Market places and greens might be added, and most radical of all developments,

---

[24] C.C. Taylor, *Village and Farmstead. A History of Rural Settlement in England* (London, George Philip, 1983).

part of a village might be abandoned because the inhabitants were relocating to an adjacent site, along a road that was increasing in importance, for example. He reiterated the view that the loss of population in the later medieval and early modern periods was often gradual, and that small villages were most likely to be deserted.

In the same year as *Village and Farmstead*, 1983, Taylor's *The Archaeology of Gardens* was published,[25] followed by much more on gardens in the succeeding thirty years. This was a new subject, in the sense that archaeologists discovered gardens in the 1970s, and Taylor had led the way. Earthworks which had been thought to mark the site of buildings, roads for carts and livestock, fishponds, or even Civil War fortifications were now seen to have been walkways, terraces, flower beds and water features. This was not just the result of greater skill in earthwork interpretation, but also a shift from assuming that earthworks should be explained in functional, practical and economic terms, to the idea that they reflected a culture and society that valued beauty, leisure and pleasure. Especially influential was Taylor's reconstruction of the garden, a pleasure ground, attached to the residence of the bishops of Ely at Somersham in Cambridgeshire.[26] Gardens changed with the aesthetic preferences of successive period. Medieval gardens tended to be enclosed, and often included water-filled features, such as ponds and moats. The more elaborate Renaissance designs of the 16th and 17th centuries had a more formal and geometric layout, with such features as prospect mounds. In the late 18th century the new taste favoured extensive grassland and many trees in landscape parks, and the earlier symmetrical flower beds and terraces were abandoned.

Taylor's numerous shorter pieces of writing, ranging from comments on individual sites to wide overviews, interconnected with his books and his contributions to the inventories. Reference has already been made to significant articles on strip lynchets, polyfocal settlements, village market places, dispersed settlements in Blackmoor and Bedfordshire, Bodiam Castle and designed landscapes. His papers on Whiteparish and Whittlesford have also been mentioned. He wrote nine other articles generalising about the relationship between Romano-British and medieval settlements, and the nucleation of villages, both subjects debated generally from the 1960s onwards. There were 15 articles about gardens, five on moats, four discussing deserted villages, and three about fields.

Some articles dealt with subjects which did not feature prominently in his other writings. For example in 2004 he demonstrated field evidence for a deer course associated

[25] C.C. Taylor, *The Archaeology of Gardens* (Princes Risborough, Shire, 1983)
[26] C.C. Taylor, 'Somersham Palace, Cambridgeshire : a Medieval Landscape for Pleasure?', in M. Bowden, D. Mackay and P. Topping (eds), *From Cornwall to Caithness* (Oxford, British Archaeological Reports, 209, 1989), pp. 211–24.

with a Derbyshire park.[27] This was a sport rarely mentioned in documents, in which deer were pursued along a designated course. Taylor also became involved in urban archaeology, in a place where he had lived, his home town of Lichfield. He argued that its territory had originally been focused on a Roman town at Wall, and that the medieval town owed its existence to the regular plan of streets next to the cathedral which had been devised by a bishop in the 12th century.[28]

The fenland, a very special landscape which offered a contrast with the chalk uplands of Dorset had a profound impact on Taylor when he worked on north-east Cambridgeshire, and in later years he returned to write more about fenland villages. His article on Reach discussed its role as an inland port, accessible by the network of waterways across the fens. He traced the process by which Burwell fen was drained in modern times, which included the use of a pumping station, a technology which clearly fascinated him.[29] When Joan Thirsk edited a general book on the English landscape Taylor was persuaded to contribute a chapter on fenlands which enhanced the whole volume.[30] To demonstrate his versatility, he was impressed at a conference by a presentation by Catherine Clark on the literary concept, very relevant for landscape historians, of the *locus amoenus* (ideal place). She quoted from a 12th-century poem written in praise of Downham in the Isle of Ely, a village well-known to Taylor, who was inspired to write an article connecting Downham's medieval landscape with the poem.[31]

A feature of Taylor's method was that he was conscious that new data or fresh thinking might reveal the fallibility of previous conclusions. His Whittlesford paper showed how hypotheses were rendered obsolete by new evidence. A number of his papers included second thoughts on previous writings, and one on Somersham and Pampisford was entirely devoted to the revision of previous publications.[32] He would disarm those attending his lectures with self-deprecating comments, which were not displays of modesty, but a demonstration of the scientific method, by which hypotheses were tested against the evidence. Perhaps he was revealing a mischievous streak,

[27] C.C. Taylor, 'Ravensdale Park, Derbyshire, and Medieval Deer Coursing', *Landscape History,* 26 (2004), 37–57.
[28] C.C. Taylor, 'The Origins of Lichfield, Staffordshire', *Transactions of the South Staffordshire Archaeological and Historical Society,* 10 (1968), 43–52
[29] C.C. Taylor, 'Reach, Cambridgeshire: a Medieval Port and Market', in A. Longcroft & R. Joby (eds), *East Anglian Studies. Essays Presented to J.C. Barringer* (Norwich, Marwood, 1995), pp. 267–75; C.C. Taylor, 'The Drainage of Burwell Fen, 1840–1950', in R.T. Rowley (ed.), *The Evolution of Marshland Landscapes* (Oxford, Oxford University Department for External Studies, 1981), pp. 158–77.
[30] C.C. Taylor, 'Fenlands', in J. Thirsk (ed.), *The English Rural Landscape* (Oxford, Oxford University Press, 2000), pp. 167–87.
[31] C.C. Taylor, '"A place there is in which liquid honey drops like dew". The Landscape of Little Downham, Cambridgeshire, in the Twelfth Century', *Landscape History,* 31 (2010), 5–23.
[32] C.C. Taylor, 'New Work on Old Sites: Somersham and Pampisford Revisited', *Proceedings of the Cambridgeshire Antiquarian Society,* 97 (2008), 121–36.

suggesting that some of his fellow scholars took themselves and their pronouncements rather too seriously.

Taylor was very conscious of the origin and development of the subject that he practised, and the debt that we all owed to the 'founders'. He revered in particular the mentor who helped him in his early days in Dorset, Collin Bowen, and he later wrote in his honour. He encountered Hoskins in his early days, and grew to know him better later in life. He paid his respects to the great man by providing material for a second edition of *Fieldwork in Local History*, and devoted considerable care to preparing a sumptuous new edition of the *Making of the English Landscape* in 1988. This was published with comments by Taylor which modified, corrected or supplemented Hoskins's original text.[33] It resembled medieval manuscripts for which a commentary on the main text was provided in glosses in the margins. Taylor enjoyed working with others, both in the field and in the study. Most of the inventories to which he contributed were team efforts, or with at least two investigators working together. The collaborative nature of his work is clear from the number of his academic publications which were jointly authored. His first wife, Angela, taught geography in schools and at degree level, and in the years before her premature death in 1983 she researched a doctoral thesis on the effects of the Ice Age on the landscape. Taylor joined her in the search for local pingos. Stephanie, who became his wife in 1985, edited publications in the Cambridge office of the Commission, and worked with him on his later publications.

VII

Taylor earned the respect of those who read his works or heard him speak. In addition to the adult education students who he had taught since the 1960s, and the recruits to the Commission who were trained by him, the archaeologists at Cambridge welcomed him as a teacher of undergraduates and a supervisor of doctoral students. Some of those students who were influenced by him went on to become well-known authorities, who were very ready to acknowledge their debt to him.

In his later years former trainees, students, colleagues, and admirers of his contribution honoured him with written tributes. Few academics are presented with three *festschriften*, yet these came in succession in the late 1990s.[34] One was compiled by the staff of the Commission, and the others reflected the admiration for him in the wide research

[33] W.G. Hoskins, *Fieldwork in Local History*, 2nd edn (London, Faber and Faber, 1982); *The Making of the English Landscape*, new edn (London, Guild Publishing, 1988).
[34] K. Barker & T. Darvill (eds), *Making English Landscapes* (Oxford, Oxbow, 1997); P. Everson and T. Williamson (eds), *The Archaeology of Landscape* (Manchester, Manchester University Press, 1998); P. Pattison, D. Field & S. Ainsworth (eds), *Patterns of the Past* (Oxford, Oxbow, 1999).

community both in universities, and in the various branches of the public archaeology service. He received an honorary doctorate from the University of Keele, and as well as electing him a Fellow, the British Academy awarded him in 2013 the John Coles Landscape Archaeology medal.

He did not relish serving on committees, but a succession of organisations were anxious to enlist his advice as a wise councillor or as a prominent scholar to represent them as President. He was connected in various capacities with the Society for Landscape Studies, the Moated Sites Research Group, the Medieval Settlement Research Group, the Nene Valley Research Committee, and Institute of Field Archaeologists. Societies and others organising conferences would often invite him to speak, and he was very ready to do so, which meant that a wide circle of those interested in landscape or settlements, both professionals and others, were familiar with his very effective presentations.

What was the importance of his contribution to the study of past landscapes? The subject had made a slow start, because although the seminal work of Hoskins, *Making of the English Landscape*, was published in 1955, the great surge of interest came in the 1970s, and Taylor played a major part along with a cohort of archaeologists and geographers, with some historians and place-name scholars. The new urgency reflected concerns for understanding the environment, and the need to protect what remained of the English countryside. The scope of research needed to be broadened, and some scholars were willing to embrace kindred disciplines. There was also a widespread enthusiasm among the non-academic public for a subject that showed that their everyday surroundings could be treated as historical evidence. When the Society for Landscape Studies was founded in 1979 by a group of researchers based in Yorkshire some doubted the wisdom of such inexperienced enthusiasts taking on the management of a Society promoting an important discipline. The new Society's success was aided by his support, as Taylor was already widely respected as a leading advocate of the subject.

Taylor had new ways of seeing the landscape, and was capable of conveying the excitement of his vision to the scholarly community and a wider audience. He could visit a field in Northamptonshire and appreciate that the uneven surface had been a planned garden of the 16th century. He could then go on to connect the garden to a particular aristocrat, and understand how the design of the garden belonged to a general cultural movement. The garden was abandoned when formal designs went out of favour, and perhaps the elite family declined or moved its residence, and the space reverted to agricultural use. Detailed survey might then reveal that before the garden was designed the land had formed part of a medieval settlement.

He advocated an ideal of studying 'total landscapes', meaning that instead of focusing on individual features or periods, the whole landscape should be taken into account, from prehistory until the present day. In order to unlock the sequence of events that made up landscape change, researchers should attempt to embrace as many disciplines as possible, including geology, geography, history, and place-name studies. The landscape should be set in the widest possible context, which could bring to bear the political and cultural background as well as the usual economic, agrarian and environmental circumstances. The landscape should not be analysed in static terms, with too much emphasis on enduring features, but as dynamic and in constant development. This was an ambitious ideal which required a wider range of knowledge and skills than most individuals possess. Many would want to add to Taylor's checklist a wider social dimension than he normally deployed. He was very ready to attribute change in the medieval period to the lords of manors, without strong evidence, but devoted much less attention to the country people who lived in villages and farmed the fields. His approach would also have gained from a comparative European dimension.

He was anxious to find ways of explaining change. He was wary of giving authority too much respect, and repeating established perspectives without critical examination. He believed in advancing hypotheses, testing them, and if they did not work abandoning them. He reserved a special scepticism for the pervasive determinism that he encountered in his youth. He showed constantly that geology, soils and climate did not control human behaviour. We cannot divide the land into favourable and unfavourable zones, and expect to find that people lived and farmed according to these variables. He pointed out that distribution maps were often used to justify these ideas, but they were flawed – they showed where the evidence survived, in the case of those that demonstrated that prehistoric people lived on chalk hills but not on the clay soils of the lowlands. Or they reflected where archaeologists had searched. He set out a view of a flexible past that was in constant movement, that was not easily explained, especially by single causes. He was content sometimes to accept that we do not know the answers.

Acknowledgements
Paul Everson and Stephanie Taylor provided invaluable biographical and bibliographical information. Paul Stamper gave much advice.

Note on the author: Christopher Dyer is Emeritus Professor of History in the University of Leicester, who has published works on the social and economic history, the landscape history and the archaeology of medieval England. He was elected a Fellow of the British Academy in 1995.

MICHAEL HOWARD

Michael Eliot Howard

29 November 1922 – 30 November 2019

elected Fellow of the British Academy 1970

by

HEW STRACHAN
Fellow of the Academy

Michael Howard was a military historian who established war studies as a fit subject for university study. He founded the Department of War Studies at King's College, London in 1962. In 1968 he returned to Oxford, where had read history, to take up a Fellowship at All Souls. He was appointed Chichele Professor of the History of War in 1977 and Regius Professor of Modern History three years later. On his retirement from Oxford in 1989 he became the first Robert A. Lovett Professor of Military and Naval History, finally retiring in 1993.

Biographical Memoirs of Fellows of the British Academy, 20, 223–244
Posted 30 September 2022. © British Academy 2022.

Michael Howard

On Michael Howard's 70th birthday, 29 November 1992, his successor as Chichele Professor of the History of War, Robert O'Neill, organised a large dinner in the hall of All Souls College, Oxford. As Howard rose at the end of the meal to respond to O'Neill's birthday greetings, he looked round the room at the assembled company. It included colleagues and admirers, but his speech specifically named those who could be called his disciples and the institutions to which they now belonged. They had taken war studies to some new seat of learning and then propagated them. Michael Howard's somewhat grand manner makes it tempting to use the vocabulary of imperialism but, given that he had no progeny of his own, that of family might be more appropriate. They were his offspring, and he derived both pleasure and self-satisfaction from their success.

Almost single-handedly Michael Howard had put the study of war in the United Kingdom on a new footing after 1945. This made him an innovator, leaving a legacy perpetuated not only by his pupils – and by many others whom he influenced and supported – but also by the institutions he created or helped to create. At the same time, however, as the All Souls dinner suggested, he embodied a set of older traditions, which he embraced and which in part also explained his ability to effect change without disruption. That continuity was evident in three ways.

First, he believed that war was best understood through the perspective of military history. After the use of nuclear weapons in 1945, some thinkers were persuaded that history could no longer provide precedents for understanding what was likely to follow. In the 1950s other disciplines, pre-eminently political science and international relations, secured a foothold in what began to be called strategic studies and which went on to develop a literature of its own which challenged the historical approach to comprehending war that had ruled the roost since Clausewitz. Howard saw strategy not as a subject in its own right but as an amalgam of other disciplines. Today, the range and depth of the literature in both military history and strategic studies has become too vast for one person to embrace them 'in width, in depth and in context', to use Howard's words.[1] He was therefore the last of the old. His more traditional route into strategic studies gave a breadth and humanity to his work which few who followed him could emulate. In this respect, his own success in establishing strategy as a proper subject of enquiry effectively ensured that he was *sui generis* – an impossible act to follow.

Secondly, his roots in history, when combined with a broad education across the humanities, made him a fluent and accessible communicator. A fondness for drama at school and at university gave him the ability to enthral an audience. He valued clear prose just as he eschewed jargon. He knew the value of wit, especially irony, and he was a master of the dismissive one-liner. He could sometimes seem too Olympian to those

[1] 'The use and abuse of military history', a lecture delivered to the Royal United Services Institution in 1961 and reprinted in Michael Howard, *The causes of wars* (London, 1983), p. 197

who toiled in the foothills of more detailed research. However, the results had a clarity which commanded attention which extended far beyond academe. As his standing grew, so did the respect accorded his judgements. He was a public intellectual in ways more characteristic of historians of the first half of the 20th century than of those at the close of the millennium.

Thirdly, he was among the last of the major students of war who had himself served in uniform. Spenser Wilkinson, appointed the first professor of military history at Oxford in 1909, had been a military correspondent for national newspapers, but all Wilkinson's successors until 2001 were soldiers at some stage in their lives, so perpetuating a belief that only those who had seen war could also comprehend it. Michael Howard had served with 3rd Battalion, the Coldstream Guards in the Second World War, and won an immediate Military Cross for his courage and leadership in taking 'the pimple', a hill north of Salerno, in 1943. In the words of the citation in the *London Gazette*, he 'charged the Spandau positions, killing and wounding some of their crews and putting others to flight'.[2] The experience shaped not only his own understanding of war and of armies but also his appreciation of others who wrote about combat with the empathy of experience. Before Howard, Britain had produced outstanding naval and military historians who were not sailors or soldiers, most obviously gentlemen scholars like Julian Corbett and John Fortescue, but they were exceptions. Most who wrote about war had also seen it or had at least served in the armed forces. Since Howard, professional academics have dominated the subject despite never having fought or even served.

Michael Eliot Howard was born in London on 29 November 1922, the third son of Geoffrey Eliot and Edith Julia Emma Howard (*née* Edinger). His father's family were Quakers and manufacturers of pharmaceutical and industrial chemicals; his mother's were originally German Jews, who had settled in London before the First World War. His father had turned to high church Anglicanism and his mother's family had converted to Protestantism. Howard embraced his father's faith, but these diverse religious inheritances made for a fruitful and principled mix when his son faced the ethical conundrums of conflict. Richard Crossman, the Labour politician, was a cousin on his father's side, and Geoffrey Elton, born Gottfried Ehrenberg and to become Regius Professor of History at Cambridge when Howard held the equivalent chair at Oxford, on his mother's. The Howards lived in some style in Ennismore Gardens, were conveniently close to the museums of South Kensington, and had a house in Ashmore in north Dorset. Michael's catholic tastes in music (Mozart especially) and art (he possessed a fine Ivon Hitchens) came from his mother.

[2] Quoted by Michael Brock, 'Michael Howard's contribution to historical studies', in Lawrence Freedman, Paul Hayes & Robert O'Neill (eds), *War, Strategy and International Politics: Essays in Honour of Sir Michael Howard* (Oxford, 1997), p. 295.

He was lucky to escape the worst brutalities of inter-war English preparatory schools, as he readily acknowledged in *Captain Professor* (2006), his memoir which is particularly engaging in its account of his early life and wartime experience. He went to board at Abinger Hill at the age of nine. The school taught its pupils through projects rather than formal classes. Each boy could set his own timetable; discipline was relaxed but maintained, and Howard thrived, reading voraciously and beyond his years. He went on to Wellington College in Berkshire, historically the most military of the English public schools. Howard was more an aesthete than an athlete (although he could run fast): his parents chose it for the usual reasons – because other members of the family had been there and because his father thought, or so his son concluded, that it would knock some sense into him. It did. There were enough inspirational teachers for Howard to be introduced to choral music and opera, to art and design, and to an outstanding history master, Max Reese, to whom in 1961 Howard dedicated his first significant book. By the time he left Wellington Howard had decided he wanted to be a history don and Reese's instruction in the Tudors and Stuarts, the staple of so many school history syllabuses until the 1980s, got him onto the first rung of the ladder with an open scholarship to Christ Church, Oxford. There he was taught by, among others, Keith Feiling, J.M. Thompson and A.J.P. Taylor.

Howard's university career, like that of many of his contemporaries, was derailed by the Second World War. The First that he had gained in 1941 before he went off to fight was followed on his return by a poor Second, acquired in 1945 after a further four terms, too much acting and other understandable postwar diversions. He failed the All Souls prize examination and was turned down for the Studentship (i.e. Fellowship) which had been dangled before him at Christ Church.

Like others, he found that, although the war had effectively closed one route, it had opened another. Howard was not an obvious soldier: 'too precious' in his own later self-description. However, service in the Officers Training Corps at Wellington and Oxford acquired purpose, when set against the background of Munich and then war itself; it was even moderately up to date. When he was at Christ Church, it was effectively compulsory for those deferring their call-up. Both the adjutant and sergeant major of the Oxford OTC were in the Coldstream Guards, and the former suggested that Howard might find the regiment congenial. He did: he was attracted to its uniform and its regimental slow march was composed by Mozart. When he was commissioned in the Coldstream in December 1942, he found himself in a mess of kindred, if patrician, spirits. For the best part of two years, between July 1943 and May 1945, he fought his way up the west side of Italy, beginning at Salerno, south of Naples, passing through Florence, and then swinging via Bologna to the Adriatic coast to finish at Trieste. On the way, he experienced fear and discomfort, he was twice wounded, he succumbed to malaria and jaundice, and he suffered personal loss as others were killed. He also found another side of himself. He showed considerable personal courage and learned to lead. Although he had no intention of staying in the army, he was pleased at the war's end to be Captain M.E. Howard, MC. 'Those of us who served in the armed forces and enjoyed at least the advantages of youth, health and comradeship', he was to write in 1992, 'were in many ways the lucky ones, although it did not always seem so at the time.'[3]

He remained loyal to his regiment for the rest of his life. The Coldstream reciprocated by asking him to assist John Sparrow, the future Warden of All Souls, who was writing the regiment's Second World War history. Howard accepted and finished what Sparrow had barely started. The book was published in 1951. Disappointment at Oxford, recurring if diminishing bouts of malaria, postwar austerity lived out in the parental home, and struggles with his own sexuality dented Howard's self-confidence. He was ambitious and competitive but uncertain whether he would fulfil the hopes he had invested in himself. In 1947 he secured an assistant lectureship in history at King's College London and was required to teach modern European history, so putting to one side his ambition to work on the Tudors and Stuarts. It was not Oxford, and the young former Guards officer did not get on with his head of department, C.H. Williams. In 1953 King's threw him a lifeline. Persuaded by Sir Charles Webster and Lionel Robbins, it decided to revive the teaching of military studies, which had been entrusted to Major-General Sir Frederick Maurice in 1927 but had lapsed. Howard was the internal candidate for a lectureship in 'military studies' and got it on the strength of the Coldstream history. He then asked for a year's sabbatical in order to learn about the study of war, spending it in Vienna. He returned with a renewed sense of purpose.

What became the Department of War Studies at King's did not exist in 1953, not least in the eyes of Williams. He continued to regard Howard as a member of the History Department and increasingly despaired of his pursuit of what he saw as journalism at the expense of scholarship. Howard did not agree and threatened to resign in 1959, when Williams refused him permission to accept J.R.M. Butler's invitation to write the fourth volume in the *Grand Strategy* series of the official histories of the Second World War. The Principal of King's supported Howard and he got a readership in 1961, his own department in 1962, and a chair in 1963. Even then the department was a pale shadow of what it was to become. When he left in 1968 he had only two academic colleagues – another military historian (Brian Bond) and a Quaker specialist in contemporary strategy (Wolf Mendl). It was, however, the only university department for the subject in the country, and the principal centre for military history outside the Department of War Studies at the Royal Military Academy Sandhurst. Not least because the department's resources were so exiguous, but also because Howard believed that those who studied war first required a firm grounding in a traditional undergraduate academic discipline, it

---

[3] Michael Howard, 'Obscenity without illusions', *Times Literary Supplement*, 10 April 1992.

focused its attentions on postgraduate teaching, both for research degrees and for the pioneering taught MA in War Studies. In his promotion of the subject, Howard had to proceed warily, all too conscious of the academic hostility it could provoke.

Howard was clearer about what 'war studies' were not than what they were. They were not operational military history and they were not designed for the education of the armed forces (although that had been Maurice's brief in 1927). War studies at universities should be eclectic. They included military sociology, the laws and ethics of war, and war's place in international relations. They were underpinned by what came to be known as the 'new' military history, which treated war as part of 'total history' and placed it in its political and social context. Howard's vision may have lacked a tight definition but it was broad and above all open. This was not a closed subject designed only for those in uniform.

As Howard made clear in a report on professional military education which he and Cyril English wrote in 1966 for the Defence Secretary, Denis Healey, he was all in favour of officers being sent to universities but so that they could develop a different and broader understanding of war than they would acquire in military academies; the latter taught potential officers 'to operate under stress, to obey, and to know the right answers – and to assume that there is a right answer'.[4] The Howard-English report recommended that officer cadets from all three services should have one year of professional training at single-service colleges, and then go to a joint Royal Defence College for a further year of academic education. Howard was reported to be the likely head of such a 'national defence university', which would have been located at the Royal Naval College Greenwich, but the report was shelved. Not until 2001, when it created the Joint Services Command and Staff College, did the Ministry of Defence accept the principle of 'jointness' and elevate education alongside training.

In other words, war for Howard was too important to be left to the generals. The latent threat of a nuclear exchange presented by the Cold War made it an appropriate subject of study for every responsible citizen. His London base in the Strand, in the heart of the metropolis and within walking distance of Westminster, Whitehall, the BBC and Fleet Street (still then home to the national newspapers), gave him physical access to the levers of power and influence. Here his focus was not on the past but on the present and whether there would be a future. In 1957 he acted as rapporteur for a group of defence experts, who believed that the division of Germany and the Soviet domination of eastern Europe were unsustainable. They met at Chatham House to consider how to reduce the military tensions in Europe. The establishment of NATO in 1949, Howard wrote in the resulting Penguin Special, *Disengagement in Europe*, 'was as salutary for Europe as

[4] Michael Howard, 'The officer class', *Times Literary Supplement*, 9 May 1975.

a plaster cast for a broken limb'.[5] Western Europe had now recovered from the fractures of the Second World War, but there seemed to be few paths towards its demilitarisation which would not be productive of instability. The conclusion to the book, published in 1958, stated the problems but had no clear recommendations.

Howard was not alone in his sense that current defence dilemmas, precisely because they were so intractable, required sustained attention. Although still comparatively junior, he was simultaneously involved in another, larger and somewhat grander discussion group addressing the limitation of war in the nuclear age. It asked him to chair a committee to look at what should follow the publication of its report. The answer was an independent body to address military issues in the same way that Chatham House addressed foreign affairs. Called the Institute (later International Institute) for Strategic Studies, it was established in 1958 thanks to a grant from the Ford Foundation, secured by Denis Healey, then shadow minister of defence. Howard took at least some credit for the appointment of its first director, Alastair Buchan, also an Oxford historian and the defence correspondent of the *Observer*. Buchan became a close friend, staying with Howard in London during the week, and in 1960 secured a grant to enable Howard to go on an eye-opening six-week tour in which he met all the major figures in US strategic studies and sang for his supper with a talk on British defence policy.

Howard had achieved a great deal by force of personality and by cultivating connections outside the confines of the academic profession, but he also needed a big book to cement his standing as a scholar in the academic world and to convince his peers that military history mattered to history more broadly defined. When the Royal United Services Institution weeded its library of its historic collections, Howard offered to buy a tranche of its 19th-century volumes on military history and theory, many in French and German, as the nucleus of the King's library in war studies. He then concluded that, as a result, he should write a book on the Franco-Prussian War. Much studied between 1871 and 1914, it had been neglected since, and there was no up-to-date one volume treatment. Apart from the French military archives at Vincennes, Howard confined himself to published sources: the Prussian military archives were largely destroyed in 1945 and those that had survived were effectively inaccessible in Potsdam. In 1961 *The Franco-Prussian War* was produced to a high standard by Rupert Hart-Davis, not only the book's publisher but also its principal editor. It remains in print, and – although it has never been translated into French or German – its status is undiminished. It addresses the theory and practice of war, but it does so through glancing reflections and not in a full-frontal assault. As a result, it never loses its narrative flow, sustained in lucid prose. It spoke to a general audience but also won over his professional colleagues. It appealed at three academic levels: for historians of France, here was the foundation of the Third Republic;

[5] Michael Howard, *Disengagement in Europe* (Harmondsworth, 1958), p. 89.

for historians of Germany, it embraced not just the country's unification but the first step in the story of German militarism; and for military historians the book gave the subject a good name with those who were not. The reviews were enthusiastic and it won the Duff Cooper prize for non-fiction.

Before *The Franco-Prussian War* was finished Howard had accepted Butler's invitation to write the fourth volume of the *Grand Strategy* series, covering the year from August 1942 to September 1943. The book had already had two false starts and, when Howard undertook the project, he laboured under two misapprehensions. The first was that, according to the terms of the 50-year rule, the archives which he was consulting would remain closed until 1992. The 1966 Public Records Act reduced the period of closure to 30 years and those for 1942 were opened in 1972, the year in which his volume was published. Secondly, unbeknownst to him, the papers which he consulted had been weeded of any reference to signals intelligence. Two years after Howard's *Grand Strategy* appeared F.W. Winterbotham published *The Ultra Secret*, which revealed that Britain had been reading German signals and that the flow of information had become particularly significant from 1943. Much of Ultra's value was more tactical and operational than strategic, and it could be argued that knowledge of Ultra might have clarified more than it would have altered what Howard wrote.

The book addressed the run-up to the Anglo-American conference at Casablanca and its conclusions for British strategy in the Mediterranean. In particular, it established how preposterous were suggestions that D Day might have been launched in 1943. It had two important intellectual consequences for Howard himself. First, it made sense of a war which he had experienced as a subaltern: he now saw it from top down, as well as bottom up. To those who questioned the necessity of the Italian campaign, he responded that 'the Germans had to be fought somewhere in 1943, and the fall of Mussolini made it inevitable that it should be Italy'.[6] Secondly, he had had to engage with grand strategy in practice. His subject was a coalition war waged in several theatres. On the opening page he defined grand strategy as 'the mobilization and development of national resources of wealth, manpower and industrial capacity, together with the enlistment of those of allied and, when feasible, of neutral powers, for the purpose of achieving the goals of national policy in wartime'. The book won him the Wolfson Prize in 1972, and in the same year he wrote and presented a television series for the BBC on grand strategy in the Second World War. Bow-tied and Tayloresque, he lectured his audience, aided by an electronic map which could be as erratic in its portrayal of military manoeuvres as one chalked onto a blackboard.

By then Howard had left King's for Oxford. *The Franco-Prussian War* established his own reputation as a military historian and that standing in turn gave gravitas to the

---

[6] Michael Howard, 'Blunders at Anzio', *Times Literary Supplement*, 6 September 1991.

nascent war studies department: it had become hard to imagine one without the other. But the load which Howard had created for himself as an official historian and public intellectual, as a departmental head and (from 1964) Dean of the Arts Faculty, was heavy. He was the governor of three public schools and a trustee of the Imperial War Museum. To Alastair Buchan, he seemed 'a tired and overburdened man, a consequence of his high sense of public duty'.[7] Howard's very success meant that the literature in military history and strategic studies, boosted in 1966 by what amounted to the simultaneous opening of the British public records for both world wars, was expanding exponentially in ways that meant he needed time to read and to think. The opportunity came in the form of another of Denis Healey's initiatives. In 1966 the Ministry of Defence established five-year lectureships in defence studies in the expectation that those universities which hosted them would take on their funding thereafter. Howard gave evidence to the committee which proposed the scheme, which was of a piece both with what he had achieved at King's and with the thrust of the Howard-English report. Oxford was offered a Fellowship in Higher Defence Studies to be held at All Souls College.

In November 1966 Howard applied for the post, prompted by Healey, Max Beloff and probably by John Sparrow, now the Warden of All Souls. His familiarity with British defence, and the individuals who drove it, stood in his favour, but he lacked the expertise in American politics and in the technologies of nuclear weaponry possessed by Laurence Martin, who two years earlier had returned – after nearly a decade in the United States – to the professorship of international politics at Aberystwyth. Moreover, as All Souls was already host to the Chichele Professorship in the History of War, it had no need for a second military historian. Howard was due to depart for a term's leave at Stanford and Harvard in early December 1966, and chafed at the college's inability to make up its mind before he left. It asked the two candidates (each of whom seems to have been aware of the other's application) to explain how they would contribute to the PPE syllabus and to outline their current research projects. Howard became petulant: he was not sufficiently familiar with the PPE syllabus to know what approach to defence studies would best work and he had 'no specific "research project" to submit'. Privately he protested to Sparrow that both he and Martin were 'established scholars whose achievements are on the record' and he failed to see what could be achieved by 'this rather humiliating performance', which 'is disagreeably reminiscent of the first scene in *Lear*'.[8] He sailed for America in December with the situation still unresolved.

All Souls appointed a committee which took advice from Buchan and concluded that, while Howard was 'of greater intellectual distinction', that point was 'outweighed

---

[7] Alastair Buchan to the Warden of All Souls, 1 December 1966, in Michael Howard file, All Souls. All the following references are to papers in the same file.

[8] Howard to the Warden of All Souls, 30 November 1966; Howard to John Sparrow, 1 December 1966.

by the fact that Prof. Martin represented an approach to Defence Studies which was as yet unrepresented in Oxford, and indeed was under-represented in this country by comparison with the United States'.[9] The College accepted the committee's recommendation in favour of Martin in January 1967. Although Howard seems to have anticipated the possible outcome, he was still deeply disappointed – 'not', he wrote to Sparrow, 'because of the comforts or pleasant surroundings, for I know how many serpents inhabit that Eden, but because I had hopes of setting up a serious school there'.[10] He was keen to quit King's and talked of seeking employment in the United States. But then 'the unexpected happened'.[11] Martin turned down the job. It was not tenured, and neither the Ministry of Defence nor the college could guarantee its extension; nor was there provision for any salary increments, a significant consideration for a family man. With Martin out of the equation, All Souls formally offered the post to Howard in March. He accepted but on condition that he be free to honour his obligations to King's by taking it up in October 1968, not 1967.

Howard found the episode bruising at least in part because he had forewarned both his superiors and (it would seem) his colleagues that he might be leaving King's for Oxford before he sailed for America – and so before All Souls had reached a formal decision. Moreover, he had already suggested a game of musical chairs, in which Martin would succeed him in the Department of War Studies.[12] In practice, this is what happened but in reverse order. Howard's departure created the vacancy at King's, which Martin filled because Martin had turned down Oxford. Howard returned to Oxford, and finally arrived at All Souls, so opening what proved to be a particularly productive phase of his career.

His reputation as a lecturer meant that he had been asked to give the Lees Knowles Lectures at Cambridge in 1966. He devoted them to a consideration of the Mediterranean strategy in the Second World War, so developing some of the themes which he addressed in the *Grand Strategy* volume. They were published in 1968. In spring 1971 he gave the Ford Lectures in British History at Oxford and they too resulted in a book, *The Continental Commitment: the dilemmas of British defence policy in the era of two world wars*, published in 1972 and as a slim Pelican paperback in 1974. Pithy and succinct, it described a British defence establishment caught between the global responsibilities of imperial defence and the security needs of an archipelago off the coast of north-west Europe. In

[9] Report of Research Fellowships Committee, All Souls, 21 January 1967.
[10] Howard to John Sparrow, 27 January 1967.
[11] Sparrow to Howard, 14 February 1967.
[12] Howard to Norman Gibbs, 22 November 1966; for Howard's own account of what happened, see Michael Howard, *Captain Professor: a life in war and peace* (London, 2006), pp. 195-6; Brian Bond, *Military Historian: my part in the birth and development of war studies 1966-2016* (Solihull, 2018), p. 34, recalls the confusion at King's.

1914 and in 1939 it could not maintain one without addressing the other. It recognised that its empire and maritime strategy, given that its principal sea lines of communication passed through the Channel to the rest of the world, depended on the balance of power in Europe. Twice in the first half of the 20th century, Britain had had to put a major army on the continent – and after the Second World War it had stayed there. *The Continental Commitment* remains, fifty years on, the best introduction to its subject.

Formally speaking the book's coverage ended in 1942 but its context was also topical. 'It is now only rarely that we catch a faint, Curzonian echo', Howard wrote in his concluding paragraph, 'that our true frontier lies on the Himalayas'.[13] Even an echo was enough to affront him. He had been appalled by British policy in the 1956 Suez crisis and, in an article for *International Affairs* in 1966, he said that Britain would have to withdraw militarily from east of Suez. Denis Healey came to the same conclusion in the following year and in January 1968 the prime minister announced that Britain would be out of Singapore, Malaysia and the Persian Gulf by 1971. The age of empire was over, and in *The Continental Commitment* Howard described the decision to maintain British armed forces in Europe as 'final' and 'binding'.

Howard's continentalism became an article of faith. It reflected not only the views of the Labour government but also the Europeanism of its Conservative successor in 1970 – and the strategic assumptions of the British Army of the Rhine. In 1974 Howard delivered the Neale Lecture in English History at the invitation of University College, London. Its title, 'The British way in warfare; a reappraisal', took direct aim at Basil Liddell Hart, who had popularised the phrase in 1931-32. Liddell Hart asserted that British strategic practice, developed and tested over three centuries, had rested on maritime power and that the army's role was to conduct amphibious operations to support Britain's European allies at peripheral points distant from the main theatre of war. Scarred by the experience of the First World War, Liddell Hart opposed the formation of a mass army, the use of conscription and the thinking of the army's general staff. In the 1930s he called for a 'limited liability' in Europe and so linked himself with appeasement – and during the Second World War, despite his own liberalism, he had called for a compromise peace with Hitler.

Howard's lecture denounced Liddell Hart's *British way in warfare* as 'a piece of brilliant political pamphleteering, sharply argued, selectively illustrated, and concerned rather to influence British public policy than to illuminate the complexities of the past in any serious or scholarly way'.[14] The criticism was warranted but that did not soften the impact of an attack on somebody whom Howard later described as 'one of the kindest

---

[13] Michael Howard, *The Continental Commitment: the Dilemma of British Defence Policy in the Era of Two World Wars* (Harmondsworth, 1974), p. 149.

[14] Howard, *The causes of wars*, p. 172.

people I have ever met'.[15] Although Liddell Hart had never held a full-time academic job, by the time he died in 1970 he was regarded as Britain's leading military historian and strategic thinker. He had supported Howard early in his career, inviting him to stay, giving him the run of his library, and introducing him to the Military Commentators' Circle, a dining club over which he presided. Liddell Hart agreed to Howard's suggestion that in due course his books and papers should be transferred to King's College London to found the Liddell Hart Centre for Military Archives. In 1965, Howard had edited a *Festschrift* in his honour called *The Theory and Practice of War*, and after Liddell Hart's death in 1970 he orchestrated the appointment of his official biographer. But there was more to Howard's attack than apparent *lèse majesté*; it also revealed his reluctance to engage with the role of sea power in national policy, which had not disappeared and regained vitality as British defence looked beyond Europe after the end of the Cold War. Howard recognised that Liddell Hart had plagiarised the British way in warfare from Julian Corbett's *Some Principles of Maritime Strategy* (1911), but the point remains that maritime strategy and naval history remained blind spots for Howard – or almost so.

The exception was another work of synthesis, one which found its roots in the Radcliffe Lectures given at Warwick University in 1975. *War in European History* (1976) included naval warfare, although it had more to say about warfare on land. It is a forcefully written summary of accumulated reading with a chronological sweep to match, beginning with the 'wars of the knights' and ending with 'the nuclear age', and all encompassed within 165 pages. It quickly found its way on to undergraduate reading lists.

In the same year, a much-longer running project came to fruition, the publication of a new translation and edition of Carl von Clausewitz's *On War*. The idea had been put to Howard by one of his doctoral pupils at King's, Peter Paret, from whom he said that he had learnt so much that it would have been 'impertinent' to call himself his supervisor. Paret was almost coeval with Howard and, like him, had served in the Second World War. In 1962 Paret persuaded Princeton University Press to commission a full English-language edition of all Clausewitz's works in six volumes. Given that there is no modern scholarly German edition, that smacked of hubris and so it proved. But Howard and Paret persevered and in 1974 Princeton issued a fresh contract for a translation of *On War* in isolation.

Howard had first read Clausewitz during his sabbatical in Vienna in 1953 and he claimed to re-read it every year. There were then two English-language editions, both based on the second, corrected German edition of 1853, and after 1908 the better-known of the two, by J.J. Graham, was issued, like the original German edition of 1832–34, in three volumes. In the English-speaking world Clausewitz had acquired a reputation for

---

[15] Howard, *Captain Professor*, p. 154.

being both obscure and militarist, and had only begun to be elevated to his current standing as the most important writer on war in the aftermath of the Second World War. In
1943, Edward Mead Earle's *The Makers of Modern Strategy* contained an outstanding
chapter on Clausewitz by Hans Rothfels and the whole book was studded with references
to *On War*. Significantly, when Princeton University Press decided to commission a new
edition of what had become a canonical text, it asked Paret to edit it. Howard had a
strong influence on Paret's selection of topics and authors, and Howard himself
contributed a chapter on the doctrine of the offensive before 1914.[16]

Howard responded to Clausewitz as one soldier to another, a point he made explicit
in his brief essay on Clausewitz, published in Oxford's *Past Masters* series in 1983. He
therefore hoped that soldiers would read him, an objective which the more convoluted of
Clausewitz's sentences could thwart. Howard and Paret's *On War* is much more fluent
than either of the two previous translations or the original German. It removes ambiguity
by turning passive constructions into active and by breaking long sentences into short.
The apparent bulk was reduced by its publication in one volume, not the original three.
It uses modern military vocabulary, such as 'total war' and 'operations' (to denote the
level of war between tactics and today's understanding of strategy), which were not
familiar to Clausewitz. Howard aligned tactics, operations, strategy and policy in a clear
hierarchy which suited the use of war in western democracies. He equated Clausewitz's
concept of 'absolute war', a Kantian ideal in book I of *On War* but a reality manifested
by the French Revolution in book 8, with the threat of all-out nuclear exchange. Above
all, he stressed the relationship between war and policy, inserting the adjective 'political'
at points where it is not present in the text to suggest that it is the book's dominant theme.
From that he was able to stress Clausewitz's openness to limited war, given that it is
policy which determines the scale of the objectives which war is required to pursue.
Howard's concentration on the present in his version of *On War* could take it in directions which reflected Clausewitz's ambition to write something of universal validity but
which could arrive also at destinations far removed from his immediate preoccupations
– his nationalism, his hatred of France and his readiness to see war as an existential act
which could usurp policy. Howard had fashioned a Clausewitz for the Cold War, adapted
to liberalism and to containment.

It worked and the timing was impeccable. The US army was digesting its defeat in
Vietnam. In 1982 Colonel Harry G. Summers used *On War* as a tool to critique American
conduct of the war. The Clausewitzian framework of Summers's *On Strategy* set a
precedent in strategic studies that others have subsequently followed, and in departments

---

[16] Howard's role in Paret's edition of *The making of modern strategy from Machiavelli to the nuclear age*
(Princeton: Princeton University Press, 1986) is covered by Michael Finch, *Making makers* (Oxford
University Press, forthcoming).

of international relations as much as in military academies. *On War* became a text that transcended time and place, rather than a reflection of the Napoleonic Wars which had so dominated Clausewitz's career. Its sales surprised Princeton University Press and delighted Howard. Between 1976 and 1981 it was adopted by all three US War Colleges. Today, when English-speakers reference Clausewitz, they are more often citing Howard and Paret's *On War* than Clausewitz's *Vom Kriege*.

Michael Howard regarded the close examination of a complex text which *On War* required as the most pleasurable and rewarding exercise of his career. It was also his last big book. He was only 54 when it appeared and he hoped to write a study of Lord Esher, the *deus ex machina* of pre-1914 defence, but it never appeared. Henceforth his output centred on essays, derived very often from lectures, where the spoken word transferred easily to the printed page. Their range, chronologically and conceptually, remained formidable, but there was no major project to match the scale of the Franco-Prussian War, the *Grand Strategy* volume or the translation of Clausewitz.

If there had been, it would have been his involvement in the official history series on intelligence, which was commissioned in the wake of Winterbotham's *The Ultra Secret*. Howard was asked to address not signals intelligence – a bigger task and one given to F.H. Hinsley, who had been in naval intelligence – but deception. Although deception exploited signals traffic, it also used spies and double agents, which added to the attractions of the work. Thanks to Howard's former Christ Church tutor, J.C. Masterman, who in 1972 had published *The Double-Cross System*, more of this story was already in the public domain. Howard completed his book, commissioned in 1972, in 1979, but the Prime Minister, Margaret Thatcher, withheld its publication. The immediate reason was the exposure as a former Soviet agent of Anthony Blunt, the Keeper of the Queen's Pictures and a wartime British intelligence officer. However, another seems to have been a lingering prejudice against homosexuals and a fear that they were vulnerable to blackmail: Blunt was gay and Howard was open about his own sexuality when he was vetted before undertaking the task. A decade elapsed before *Strategic Deception in the Second World War* was published in 1990, and by then too much of what it had to say was either familiar or had been covered by others who had had access to the same sources for its reception to be anything other than muted.

The foibles of official history were not the major block to effective publication over the decade after 1976; more serious were the teaching and administrative demands of Oxford University. In 1977 Norman Gibbs, also an official historian, retired from the Chichele Professorship of the History of War. He had been in post for 24 years and in Howard's judgement had 'sat on his chair'.[17] The potential subject matter had developed

---

[17] A.L. Rowse, *Historians I have known* (London, 1995), p. 185; for the context, see Hew Strachan, 'The study of war at Oxford 1909-2009', in Christopher Hood, Desmond King & Gillian Peele (eds),

exponentially since the Chichele chair's establishment in 1909. The two world wars had added to the content of military history and the Cold War had multiplied the disciplinary inputs to the study of war. Gibbs had grown the subject in terms of doctoral pupils, but not by co-operating with those who taught international relations nor by recognising the opportunities inherent in strategic studies. The electors faced a choice between Howard and Piers Mackesy, a Fellow of Pembroke and author of three studies of British strategy in the reign of George III, as well as a mainstay of undergraduate teaching in military history. They plumped for Howard.

Because the chair carried a Fellowship at All Souls, the appointment allowed him to stay put, to engage as much or as little with undergraduate teaching as he wanted (in fact he wanted to more than he needed to), and to use the opportunities the college provided for public engagement with government and international security. In 1969 he had set up a student-led society, the Oxford University Strategic Studies Group, for which he acted as senior member (to satisfy proctorial requirements) and principal mentor. His influence enabled the group to attract distinguished speakers on a weekly basis to address current issues in international relations. He became a member of the Common Room at St Antony's, home to 'area studies' in Oxford, and he introduced strategic studies to undergraduate and postgraduate studies in PPE and to the Masters' degree in international relations established by his old associate, Alastair Buchan, now the Montague Burton Professor of International Relations. Buchan died suddenly in 1976, only five years into his tenure, but he was succeeded by another kindred spirit, Hedley Bull. Together Bull and Howard worked to secure funding for a readership in international relations in Buchan's memory, filled by Adam Roberts in 1981.

By then Howard was no longer Professor of the History of War. His period as Chichele professor, despite the post's embodiment of everything in which he was interested, was the shortest of all its incumbents in the 100-plus years of its existence. But his impact outlived his tenure. He already had twelve doctoral pupils by the time he was appointed in 1977. Many of those he taught as graduate students went on to careers not as academics but as practitioners, including several Defence Fellows (another Healey innovation) who would reach four-star rank in the armed forces. He had taken the history of war firmly into the field of contemporary affairs, a point reflected in the draft advertisement for his successor. Although the Chichele Professor of the History of War was appointed to the Faculty of Modern History (as it was then), his teaching obligations lay more in politics and international relations.

In 1980 Howard was elevated to the Regius Professorship of Modern History, with a Fellowship at Oriel. Thanks not least to his predecessor, Hugh Trevor-Roper, this was a

---

Forging a discipline: a critical assessment of Oxford's development of the study of politics and international relations in critical perspective (Oxford, 2014), pp. 204–21.

post with a public profile commensurate with Howard's reputation and it was in the gift of a prime minister, who – despite the rebuff over the history of deception – still consulted him. He knew that he was not the obvious choice of the faculty and so had to earn credibility with his colleagues. Since the Regius Professor served on almost every faculty committee and was expected to take more than his fair share of administration, he did not have to strive to prove himself a good citizen, but he did feel that he should show his commitment to a broader understanding of history than he had done of late. He used lectures to make evident his appreciation of the past as much as his understanding of its relationship to the present. Although he was not expected to teach undergraduates, he was now in an undergraduate college, 'a good county regiment in the front line' as he put it, and he enjoyed the stimulus of direct engagement with them which All Souls had not provided.[18] The problem was that he could not also slough off his pre-existing commitments.

His move to the Chichele chair in 1977 had – fortuitously for Howard – coincided with the ending of the Ministry of Defence's funding for the All Souls Fellowship in Higher Defence Studies. Whereas other universities honoured their obligation to the Ministry of Defence, Oxford did not. So it was down one post in the field. A second, the Chichele chair itself, was then frozen for financial reasons. Everything that Howard and others had built up was threatened by these two vacancies. Rather than permit that to happen, Howard continued to teach international relations. It was an outrageous load and an indication of Oxford's capacity to behave in dysfunctional ways. As chairman of the Faculty of Modern History, he requested that the Chichele chair be filled, but his rational explanations of the need went unanswered until 1987, when Robert O'Neill, the Director of the International Institute for Strategic Studies, was appointed.

Howard was now 65, the standard age for retirement, and given the punishing burden loaded on him by Oxford that is what he might have done. He did not. Paul Kennedy wrote to him from Yale, saying that the university was aiming to fill a new post, the Robert A. Lovett Chair of Military and Naval History, and wondered if Michael Howard could suggest whom the university might encourage to apply. Howard replied that he rather fancied the job for himself, and so in 1989 he took up residence in New Haven for four years. This was a period of rapid change, not continuity, with the end of the Cold War, the collapse of the Soviet Union, and the potential dismantlement of the security architecture with which Howard had become familiar, and which to some extent he had help shape. Howard regarded those who tried to make sense of what was now going on, in order to shape the future or even to grasp the present, as 'shooting at a moving target'.[19] He kept abreast by returning to regular book reviewing. In 1991 he damned Martin van

---

[18] Howard, *Captain Professor*, p. 208.
[19] Michael Howard, 'Shooting at a moving target', *Times Literary Supplement*, 14 March 1992.

Creveld's fashionably iconoclastic *On Future War* not just for its misreading of Clausewitz but also for falling into the trap of seizing 'upon an ephemeral trend' and projecting 'it into the future'.[20] Howard's interests may have moved away from deepening military history to widening the understanding of war, but his apparent conservatism still took refuge in his core discipline. 'It is the task of historians', because they have neither access nor knowledge as to how events will turn out, 'to explain, not to predict', he wrote in January 1993. 'They are like interpreters of a very long sentence in German, only at the very end of which will they know what the verb is going to be.'[21]

Away from the university, New Haven is not the most pleasant part of Connecticut but Howard found the experience liberating, and not just because he had put university administration behind him. He was now determined to integrate his life more fully than before. He and his partner, Mark James, a teacher, had lived separate lives during Oxford terms, with Howard residing in college and James at their joint home in the Old Farm in Eastbury, close to Hungerford. Despite the transformation in public attitudes, Howard was of a generation that had learnt to be wary of others' responses to gay relationships. However, Michael insisted that Mark accompany him to the United States, and the openness which the move enabled was a source of relief and strength to Howard. In 2006 they entered into a civil partnership.

Back in Eastbury, Howard remained engaged with the study of war, the state of the world and news of who was doing what almost to the end of his life. Supported and energised by his near-neighbour, Max Hastings, and by a stream of visitors from the worlds of military history and strategic studies, he continued to keep up to date, to read *Foreign Affairs* and to be ready to comment – until increasing deafness made it hard for him to keep track of conversation. He built a library, a portrait of Clausewitz hanging on its wall, adjacent to the two cottages that made up his and Mark's home.

In 1977 he had been invited to give the Trevelyan Lectures at Cambridge and he chose to devote them to *War and the Liberal Conscience*, the title of the book which followed in 1978. Howard later said that the lectures were the first time in which he had engaged with the Enlightenment and its legacy for the ethical and legal justifications for war. This was self-deprecating nonsense. He had never forgotten his Quaker forebears, and his induction into war studies as the Cold War intensified created an urgency to his thinking around the problems of war and peace. In 1958 that imperative spawned an offshoot of the Institute for Strategic Studies specifically designed to address the morality of nuclear weapons, the Council on Christian Approaches to Defence and Disarmament (CCADD). With nuclear deterrence a dominant factor in international relations, Howard also joined a group headed by Herbert Butterfield, the historian and Master of Peterhouse,

---

[20] Michael Howard. 'Famous last screams', *London Review of Books*, 5 December 1991.
[21] Michael Howard, 'Winning the peace', *Times Literary Supplement*, 8 January 1993.

which included Martin Wight, the Christian pacifist credited with founding the 'English school' of international theory. When Howard addressed his Cambridge audience in 1977, he was already poised to succeed Alastair Buchan as Vice-President of the CCADD, and in January he delivered the lecture it had organised to honour Wight's memory. Wight had realised that the challenge for Christians 'in a world of evil' was, Howard pointed out, to 'face the fact of evil'. His central premise was that 'the appropriate response of the political moralist to the world of power must therefore be not to condemn but to enlighten'.

His reading of Hobbes, Grotius, Vattel, Rousseau and Kant left Howard seized of two ideas. First, while he respected pacifism in its various manifestations, he rejected its idealism. As a historian as well as a veteran, he knew that war was a reality of international affairs and that those who went off to fight were not necessarily dupes but could be intelligent young men who thought the cause was right – as he reminded congregations on successive Remembrance Sunday sermons in the 1980s. He saw his own service in the Second World War as part of 'the last and greatest service that the British Empire was able to render to mankind'.[22] That did not mean that humanity was relieved of the moral responsibilities imposed by nuclear weapons or by war. So, secondly, there was a need to find ways to contain and limit war. For him the best instruments for achieving this were the state, which, by establishing the monopoly of force, had the potential to use it wisely, and the armed forces, whose professional training should teach them to employ violence with discipline and restraint. Nuclear weapons had not abolished war, for all Brodie's hopes after 1945, but they behoved states to learn how to use it in limited ways. In 1959 Howard had questioned the British decision to acquire an independent nuclear deterrent and instead favoured strong conventional forces for limited war below the nuclear threshold. In 1980 the radical historian, E.P. Thompson, devoted much of a pamphlet opposing Cruise missiles to a personal attack on Howard for allegedly trying to make nuclear war thinkable. Provoked to respond in tones which were both authoritative and condescending, Howard pointed out that nuclear weapons were not an end in themselves, but a means to defend the political freedoms from which Thompson himself benefited.[23] In 1984 he wondered whether nuclear war 'would produce the total holocaust so often predicted', reminding the CCADD of 'the horrors through which mankind had already passed'.[24] It was here, as a writer in the liberal tradition on war, that Howard best emulated Liddell Hart.[25]

---

[22] Michael Howard, 'Kingdom of the dead', *Times Literary Supplement*, 8 March 1996.

[23] E.P. Thompson. *Protest and survive* (Campaign for Nuclear Disarmament, 1980); Michael Howard, 'Protest and survival', *Encounter* 55:5 (November 1980), 9-14.

[24] 'Reflections at the CCADD Conference at Maryknoll Seminary, N.Y.', 3 September 1984.

[25] See Basil Liddell Hart, *The Revolution in Warfare* (London, 1946).

War and the Liberal Conscience was followed by two edited books. The first, *Restraints on War: studies in the limitation of armed conflict* (1979), was derived from lectures delivered in Oxford in the same term as the Trevelyan Lectures. Howard's own opening chapter attacked the 1977 Additional Protocols to the Geneva Convention for giving belligerent status to insurgent forces in civil war. 'The principle that only "legitimate authorities", states and their agents, have the right to make war and to claim protection in war, has been the basis of the whole system of rational, controllable, interstate conflict', he declared. Although he acknowledged that the system favoured the *status quo*, it had helped to build 'a just, peaceable and orderly society'.

The second edited book, *The Laws of War: constraint on warfare in the western world* (1994), developed this idea of state self-control through the prism of law. It was a product of Howard's time at Yale. As the United States enjoyed its 'unipolar moment', he shared in the sense of optimism. But he cautioned against taking such benefits for granted. He carried into the post-1989 world thoughts that had crystallised in 1984, reflected in the Alfred Deakin Lecture of that year and in addresses to the CCADD.

The principal quality required of statesmen as they considered the problems of international security was prudence. As a layman of faith, Howard urged Christians to respect 'the prudential calculations' on which statesmen based political decisions. Their object was not peace itself but the creation of an international order from which peace, fragile and inherently vulnerable, might emerge. To be effective, that order had to be based on existing circumstances, not on a utopian vision. Peace, he warned, 'is not to be brought about by the creation of any "new order"; if only because, in our infinitely diverse world, there is no consensus on what the new order should be'. Rather, peace 'can only come about as the result of a just ordering of relationship[s] between nations … and that ordering can be maintained only by a process of constant adjustment to take account of the myriad developments and changes, each replete with opportunities for friction and conflict, which occur every day all over the world'.

Howard, who listed weeding among his recreations in *Who's Who*, likened the maintenance of peace to 'the same kind of constant hard work as the maintenance of a well-tended garden'. By 2001, such gardeners were in short supply. In 1984 the threat of nuclear weapons had contributed to stability, but now their role was less clear. Howard's worries about peace multiplied, Cassandra-like, in proportion with those inclined to take *Pax Americana* for granted. The European ideal was vested not in its geography but in its peoples, their diversity and the institutions which they planted. The latter, he told the alumni of the Woodrow Wilson Center in 1996, needed 'manuring, training, and sometimes drastically pruning of dead or diseased wood'.

Horticulture was only an analogy. As Edward Luttwak observed in 2000, 'It is always as a historian that Howard writes, not as a philosopher or social scientist, for his own way of understanding war and peace owes little to phenomenological speculations and much to sequential constructions'.[26] Luttwak was reviewing *The Invention of Peace*. Another essay derived from a lecture, it took a broad sweep of history to argue that peace was not a normal condition simply 'to be preserved', but – partly because war was of greater antiquity – it had to 'be attained'. The historical illiteracy of America's response to the 9/11 attacks in the very next year appalled Howard but did not surprise him. He had already warned in 1998 of the myth-making which exaggerated the threat a renascent Islam posed to the west.[27] In 2001, by treating terrorists as belligerents, the United States implicitly gave them legal rights, when it should have treated them as criminals. 'The global war on terror' was a logical absurdity. Its interventions overthrew the international laws that the United States had helped to put in place, and instead opened a field of conflict which had no logical end. Howard took no pleasure in being right (although he did allow himself some sense of *Schadenfreude*), but in 2002 he added an epilogue to what he had written and called it *The Reinvention of War*.

At that 70th birthday dinner in All Souls, Michael Howard had been presented with a *Festschrift* with a suitably capacious title, *War, Strategy and International Relations*, edited by Lawrence Freedman (one of his most distinguished pupils), Paul Hayes and Robert O'Neill. He was already laden with honours, and more would follow. All three of his Oxford colleges elected him to honorary fellowships. The Royal United Services Institute awarded him its Chesney Gold Medal in 1973. He was made a Fellow of King's College London in 1996, and in 2014 King's established the Sir Michael Howard Centre for the History of War, which sponsors an annual lecture in his name. He was given honorary doctorates by Leeds and London. He was appointed CBE in 1977, knighted in 1986, made a Companion of Honour in 2002, and added the Order of Merit in 2005 (the first person to be both OM and CH since Churchill, he would proudly say). He died on 30 November 2019, the day after his 97th birthday.

Acknowledgements

Michael Howard left a full account of his life, *Captain Professor: a life in war and peace* (2006), and a shorter one called 'A Professional Biography', written in 1991, of which copies are held by the British Academy and All Souls College, Oxford (Mil.Hist.KK.16). I am grateful to the Warden and Fellows of All Souls for permission to study the Michael Howard papers in the College's possession and to Gaye Morgan for her guidance and help. David Skaggs wrote 'Michael Howard: military historian and strategic analyst' as a dissertation for the US Army War College in 1983 and summarised his findings in *Military Affairs* 49 (1983), pp. 179-83. Three of Howard's students, Professor Sir Lawrence Freedman, Professor John Gooch and the Earl of Wemyss and March, have

---

[26] Edward N. Luttwak, 'Peace in and of our time', *Times Literary Supplement*, 6 October 2000.
[27] Michael Howard, 'The past's threat to the future', *Times Literary Supplement*, 7 August 1998.

given me the benefit of their memories and impressions, for which I am very grateful. Professor Brian Holden Reid is writing an authorised biography and until it is complete Michael Howard's papers, held by King's College London, are closed. However, Brian Holden Reid published a preliminary assessment in the *Journal of Military History*, 73 (2009), 869-904, and he has made several suggestions for improving this text. The late Professor Geoffrey Best helped more than he realised when he gave me a sheaf of Michael Howard's reviews and lectures. For fuller accounts of specific aspects of Howard's writings, see Hew Strachan, 'Michael Howard and the dimensions of military history', *War in History*, 27 (2020), 536-51, and 'Michael Howard and Clausewitz', *Journal of Strategic Studies*, 45 (2022).

Note on the author: Sir Hew Strachan is Wardlaw Professor of International Relations at the University of St Andrews. He was elected a Fellow of the British Academy in 2017.

Biographical Memoirs of Fellows of the British Academy (ISSN 2753–6777) are published by
The British Academy, 10–11 Carlton House Terrace, London, SW1Y 5AH
www.thebritishacademy.ac.uk

JAMES CRAWFORD

James Richard Crawford

14 November 1948 – 31 May 2021

elected Fellow of the British Academy 2000

by

MARTTI KOSKENNIEMI
Fellow of the Academy

GERRY SIMPSON
Fellow of the Academy

James Crawford was, at various points in his career, the Whewell Professor of International Law at the University of Cambridge, Director of the Lauterpacht Centre in Cambridge, and holder of the Challis Chair in International Law at Sydney University. He was an immensely productive and influential scholar (his most important contributions are his books on state responsibility and the creation of states) and a prodigious and admired litigator. Latterly, he served as a Judge at the International Court of Justice from 2015 to 2021.

Biographical Memoirs of Fellows of the British Academy, 20, 245–264
Posted 30 September 2022. © British Academy 2022.

James Crawford

James Crawford was born in Adelaide, 'a not very large capital city' (as he put it himself) in South Australia, and he spent his entire early life and undergraduate student days there before becoming a lecturer in International Law at the University of Adelaide Law School. The eldest of seven siblings, he seems to have lived a conventional and happy middle-class life in Adelaide (his parents were a nurse and a Labor Party-supporting company director), though his 'very intellectual' maternal grandmother was only the second woman to graduate in law from Adelaide University.

But if the city was then known for being parochial (nowadays it hosts one of Australia's biggest literary festivals), the young James was keenly aware of the national and international politics of the time. He was an undergraduate (1966-71) during the Vietnam War and participated in a handful of protests against it. The end of his studies in Australia coincided with the end of decades of conservative administration in 1972 and the election of the Whitlam Government (its campaign slogan was 'It's Time'), and the years of 1972-75 are remembered as salad days for a reconstructive, redistributive and progressive politics in Australian political life. There were major legal changes in this period, too (a new Family Law, the ending of conscription and, in government circles, a much keener interest in international law and diplomacy).

James emerged out of this with an LLB along with a BA in International Relations, History and Literature and, among his numerous honours, he was the recipient of the Bundley Prize for English Verse (this, perhaps, inspiring a later poem about Mr Kadi in the *European Journal of International Law*) as well as other prizes in law and English. It doesn't require much, then, to imagine James as an eminent English or History don. Indeed, his submissions to the International Court of Justice (ICJ) many years later – peppered with witty literary allusions – very much bear the imprint of these early interests.

One of his teachers at Adelaide was a fellow South Australian, John Finnis, and it is thought that James pursued further study at Oxford with Finnis's encouragement though without the aid of a Rhodes Scholarship, which he was awarded and then obliged to relinquish after marrying in his final year at Adelaide. In Oxford, he worked under neither Finnis nor Dan O'Connell (a fellow antipodean and the new Chichele Chair), but instead gravitated towards Ian Brownlie. It was Brownlie who first advised him against tackling the creation of states as a PhD topic (too large a subject) but then subsequently agreed that perhaps James could pull it off (of which more later).

On his return to Australia, he consolidated his reputation and career at Adelaide Law School, moving swiftly through the academic ranks, completing and submitting his doctoral dissertation and becoming a professor within nine years of joining the Law School.

He became – of course – a leading figure in Australian international law, something recognised by the Australian Government when it awarded him the Companion of the

Order of Australia in 2013. This early part of James's career coincided with a rich period
for law and diplomacy inspired partly by Eli Lauterpacht's tenure as the Legal Adviser
to the Australian Government on International Law and the ensuing dynamism among
the Australian international law cohort. J.G. Starke, Don Greig, Ivan Shearer and Henry
Burmester were active at that time, and the Australian scene was already one in which
there were regular exchanges between the diplomatic and foreign affairs service, and the
world of international legal academia. James – deeply respected in government circles
– was instrumental in all this. As a result of his growing reputation, James was then
appointed to a three-year position at the Australian Law Reform Commission in Sydney,
where he was commissioned to write a groundbreaking report on Aboriginal Customary
Law. In 1984, he returned to Adelaide to take up his Chair in international law, before
being lured back to Sydney for the Challis Professorship in International Law in 1986.
He became the Dean of the Sydney Law Faculty in 1990 (where he no doubt had a hand
in making international law become a compulsory subject for LLB students).

It was at this point, too, that James became much more involved in international legal
practice through two cases each involving an aspect of Australia's postcolonial relations
with its regional neighbours. In *Certain Phosphate Lands in Nauru*, James acted for the
Nauruan Government and against Australia in a dispute over the mining of Nauru's
phosphate reserves during the period in which Australia (and its partners, New Zealand
and the United Kingdom) had exercised a United Nations trusteeship over Nauru.[1] The
preliminary phase of the case was decided in Nauru's favour and eventually settled (for
just over a million dollars). Shortly after this, Portugal instituted proceedings against
Australia in the East Timor case. Again, James was on the winning side with Australia
persuading the court that it could not proceed to the merits of the case (and, for example,
consider in any depth the question of Timorese self-determination) in the absence of
Indonesia, an indispensable, absentee third party.

Just before I (Gerry) arrived in Australia in 1991 as a tyro international lawyer I
received a letter from Professor Hilary Charlesworth (then a lecturer in law at Melbourne
University, now James's successor on the Court) welcoming me to the Law Faculty and
mentioning something about a forthcoming 'International Law Weekend' in Canberra.
This – a predecessor to the now well-established Australia-New Zealand Society of
International Law Annual Conference – had been convened, in an early golden age of
Australian international law, by Eli Lauterpacht in collaboration with various members
of the Department of Foreign Affairs and the Attorney-General's Office. James had
played a leading role in the weekends since his return from Oxford. Meanwhile, I had
just emerged from undergraduate study at Aberdeen (where Dr Catriona Drew – now at
SOAS, and later an examinee of James's when studying at LSE with one of his own

[1] International Court of Justice, *Certain Phosphate Lands in Nauru* (Nauru v. Australia) Reports 1992/1993.

former doctoral students, Professor Christine Chinkin – had pointed out to me in the library a book called *The Creation of States* describing it as a must-read on self-determination). Professor Philip Alston called me up one day and invited me to speak at the International Law Weekend. Philip was on my panel and tore into my 'theory of secession' mercilessly, and justifiably. By the time the questions came round I was convinced my career was in tatters. But by far the worst thing was that this whole fiasco had happened in front of the legendary Professor James Crawford who I hadn't yet even met. But then James raised his hand and defended my (probably indefensible) paper with such generosity and robustness that I began to think perhaps the paper had been a triumph.

Of course, scores of people have stories like this about James's energy, attentiveness and generosity. After he left Australia again in 1992, James took up the Whewell Chair of International Law at Cambridge, and in 1997 succeeded Sir Eli Lauterpacht as the director of the recently founded Lauterpacht Centre. Along with his talented academic colleagues and hard-working administrative staff, he established a centre of excellence for the study of international law. An extraordinarily large number (over 60) of doctoral students (many of them now themselves prominent international lawyers) studied under James at the Lauterpacht Centre. Professor Douglas Guilfoyle has spoken with great warmth and wit about James the supervisor in a published eulogy. Meanwhile, others have spoken of his prodigious energy, his work ethic, his intellectual discipline – emails would fly in from all over the world at all times of the day or night. This was a period, after all, in which James also was becoming a leading litigator in the field and had revived, as co-editor, the *Cambridge Studies in Comparative and International Law* series (arguably the most prestigious series of monographs in international law), while at the same time acting for several years as Faculty Chairman of the Cambridge Law Faculty.

James was also and perhaps principally, of course, a scholar of distinction. He received the Hudson Medal for non-American contributions in international law, and for a number of decades his work in the field carried enormous weight and authority. He would not have described himself as a legal theorist and at no point did he set down his 'concept of law', at least not in any explicit sense. In a way, then, he was a 'rigourist', someone who appreciated the virtues of legal positivism, and married that appreciation to an acute eye for detail and an extensive knowledge of the operation of international law as a legal system embedded in a world of diplomacy and states.

His two signal contributions to the academic field are his books on, respectively, the creation and responsibility of states, and they are unlikely to be readily surpassed.[2]

---

[2] Lesley Dingle's interview with James, published by the Squire Law Library and a very useful source of information for this obituary, lists 92 journal articles, 82 book chapters, and 14 books (these included – aside from his works on statehood – the eighth edition of Ian Brownlie's *Principles of International Law* and his Hague Lectures, published as *Chance, Order, Change* (2018).

The Creation of States, published in its first edition in 1977, is already a monumental piece of scholarship but it could have been and became (in its second edition) much longer. Completed under the supervision of Ian Brownlie (whose line about theory being a 'bank of fog on a clear day' had been a greater curse on the study of statehood than the targets of this aphorism, the declaratory and constitutive theories themselves), it is described, by Brownlie, as a 'fairly reduced version of a substantial text'. The substantial text was James's draft doctoral dissertation at Oxford and that text, too, had been whittled down for submission prior to being examined by Maurice Mendelson and James Fawcett. Here, then, we already have evidence of its author's industry. (Little wonder the thesis was so long. James even makes the decision to include a concluding section in which he takes up matters such as extinction and reversion that might seem incidental to the creation of states (in that phrase's strictest sense)).

Brownlie's Foreword begins with the sentence: 'A major study of the creation of States has long been wanted'. Public international law is understood in its commonplace textbook iterations as the law regulating inter-state relations, and yet perhaps the state itself had been, at this point, a little taken for granted. This was certainly Crawford's intuition as he set about writing his first book. States created international law but did international law go about creating states (and if so, how)? If we return to the Foreword again, we have Brownlie saying that there has been a 'reserve in the face of material which is said to be "political" and, therefore, not a proper subject of legal analysis'. This idea – indeed, those quotation marks – haunt the pages of the original book. Of course, as James himself points out, statehood has been neglected but hardly ignored entirely. Writers have tended to come to the question at an angle (Marek on identity) or they had disposed of it as part of a larger treatise (think of Lorimer's obsessive taxonomising).

Very often, it had been considered as part of a discussion of recognition (in Hersch Lauterpacht's study, most obviously). James takes on the question of recognition right from the off. The constitutive theory (with recognition at its core) 'does not correspond with state practice' (Preface). 'On the other hand' [and this may be one of the most useful phrases in statehood scholarship], '… in this as in other areas … recognition practice … is of considerable importance'. Here we find ourselves in an 'oscillatory' (to repurpose a Nathaniel Berman word) mode. At the end of the Preface is a note to the effect that 'The State is not allocated a sex'. Even this apparently innocuous phrase seems to prefigure a whole world of feminist scholarship on statehood ('Sexing the State' and so on).

But this was a book that may have seemed a bit old-fashioned for its time. By the late '70s, there had already been a large scholarship urging a more expansive view of international legal personality. The human rights treaties (or at least their protocols) offered standing to individuals; corporations were, since *Barcelona Traction,* said to be subjects of international law; decolonisation had more or less taken its course; and the talk was all about NGOs and institutions. Along came James with his 500-odd-page treatise on *states*. And yet, it turned out that like so many old-fashioned thoughts it was ahead of its time. Ten years after publication, statehood, and the methods of acquiring or gifting it, became a very hot subject with the dissolution of the Soviet Union and Yugoslavia. Anyone trying to work out how to think about the personhood of Bosnia, Macedonia, Kosovo, Lithuania or Chechnya might have been very strongly inclined to consult *The Creation of States*.

A great deal hangs on the word 'creation'. It leaves tantalisingly open the question of how, or indeed whether, states are formed in any way legible to law. There are the quasi-religious origin myth associations of the word, for a start. If states are the result of some romantic idea of *Volk*, then what price the Montevideo Convention? In the face of this, James is keen to establish criteria, of course, to support the application of a more fully realised declaratory theory. But again, the watchword is flexibility; in some cases, these conditions will be strictly applied, at other times they will be 'nominal'.

James might be characterised as a pragmatist of the intelligence and formalist of the will. He takes the rules (the law) seriously in order, perhaps, that they be taken seriously elsewhere. States then are not mere facts but nor are they entirely artificial entities. Or at least states are not facts in the sense that chairs are facts, but are facts 'in the sense in which a treaty is fact' (p. 4). This has on occasion, in the international law classroom, prompted a lengthy digression on the question of whether chairs are in fact facts, but what James means is that a territory's stateness can only be comprehended in its material factness through the application of a set of legal norms. This then is how the questions of fact and law are brought into some kind of alliance. According to James, declaratists don't pay enough attention to the rules that govern the creation of states, while constitutivists (one wonders if it was the nomenclature of statehood thinking that Brownlie took such objection to rather than the theories themselves, which seem rather innocuous) overvalue the act of recognition and especially diplomatic recognition. In the end, James is arguing against two different ways of over-elevating 'facts'. In one case it is the material conditions of community that are the target, in the other the fact of cognition or identification by another state or states. In either case, we are all at sea without a legal regime to guide us. Or, to put this another way, the situation is incoherent. This was the case, according to James, in the 19th century when there were no rules governing the creation of states (or the use of force, according to an accompanying footnote): 'formal incoherence was an expression of its radical decentralisation' (this view of the 19th century is questionable and Antony Anghie's early work constitutes an alternative reading).

The book's historical sections are a rather thin gruel. James tells us that Grotius and Pufendorf write philosophy not law, and there are brief capsule descriptions of Vattel and Vitoria. This is followed by a page and half of historical practice (Aragon and Castille, the Union of Scotland and England) and a nod to revolutionary states followed by a summary of the 19th-century position (admission to the society of states was more significant than the possession of what we might call 'bare statehood'). This is all rather throat-clearing (one can imagine a conversation in which Brownlie and Crawford agree that there needs to be 'some history') and it is obvious that James wants to get started on the nitty-gritty of English case-law as rapidly as possible.

The 'modern position' (the book itself, in effect) then begins with the English courts: *The Arantzazu Mendi, Duff Development, Luthor v Sagor, Carl Zeiss Stiftung v Rayner and Keeler* – famous names to those who have taught or written on the 'domestic effects of recognition', but perhaps provincial as an opening gambit on a book about the creation of states. It continues with a redescription of the great debate. Constituvists (the most convincing is Lauterpacht) are prone to, or permit too much, relativism (a state here but not a state there), and too much decentralisation (international law reduced to a 'system of imperfect communication' (p. 20)). In any case the practice does not bear them out. The declaratory theory (or at least a declaratory theory that can accommodate a role for recognition) is favoured then with all its flaws. And it is favoured too among writers: 'Brownlie states the position succinctly ...' (p. 22).

But the prospects of such a theory depend very much on the availability of a set of criteria. Are these available? Can they offer certainty and coherence? That is the book's major task (taking up over 140 pages). The Montevideo criteria are of course familiar. In the case of territory and permanent population there are quirks (How permanent is the 'professional' population of the Vatican State? 'What about border states'?), but mostly it is a case of knowing it when we see it.

In the case of 'government', James had the difficult task of working his way around ideas of effectiveness (apparently dominant in this area of law where states had little interest in the virtuousness of a government when it came to assessing statehood) and legitimacy (the increasingly influential claim that statehood might depend on the quality of government). This tangle is approached through the case of the Congo (now the DRC) and an ineffectiveness of government (unable to govern without UN aid, unable to control a breakaway province, anarchic) that does not stand in the way of recognition (the sheer legal power of the decolonisation norm meant independence had to be granted). We are led through this material (often by necessity decontextualised) with a steady and careful hand and the right answer is reached.

There is something about James's early voice that is revealed here. He is always keen to position himself between the extremes of facticity on one hand and otherworldly formalism on the other: neither fact nor law; the chair, always a thing *and* a construct of language and law. I began counting the 'one hands' and 'other hands' in the book (James is like Tevye from *Fiddler on the Roof* but without the anguish). He asserts or defends the autonomy of law from the political realm and then chastises those who cannot appreciate the play of practice and politics in the legal world. A commonsense position of jurisprudential precision and cautious worldliness thus emerges. Maybe this is the voice of the discipline's mainstream; maybe it is the voice of a certain way of doing law, but whatever it is James was a master exponent.

Sometimes, though, the exactness of the categorisations gives the work the feeling of a set of mathematical formulae. In the passages on independence, we are confronted with one of the most ornate numbering systems in international legal scholarship. Falling under Chapter 2 (sub-heading II) we have criteria no 5 (Independence) under which there are four different forms of separate existence (i-iv), one of the forms of which (ii) 'absence of subjection' is further divided into different types of independence (a-c), one of which (a) is formal independence. But there are many factors relevant to formal independence (1-3), one of which 'situations not derogating from formal independence' contains eight (1-8) sub-types. By this time, James's mind has far outstripped any existing numbering system and the reader is reduced to flicking back and forth through the text while keeping score on a proximate sheet of paper. It is all rather marvellous, as if James is determined to capture every last nuance of independence through an unapologetic cataloguing of legal forms. In Borges' (one paragraph) short story, 'On Exactitude in Science', a state comes into existence that can only be mapped by a form of cartography in which the maps are on a 1:1 scale. In the story, what remains of the map are mere fragments left to future scholars and historians. Sometimes, it seems as if James is engaging in a kind of juristic cartography in which everything is mapped. *The Creation of States* may indeed be a fragment of the fully scaled-up map (the original dissertation, or perhaps the unexpurgated first draft of the original dissertation).

In the midst of this mapping, some concepts get very short shrift from him. Sovereignty, for example, keeps popping up uninvited like a barely tolerated second cousin. The reader soon receives the impression that it would be 'preferable' (a very Crawfordian term meaning 'the correct and only reasonable' as in 'the preferable view is …') if the term fell out of usage. It has a 'long and troubled history' (p. 26) and 'the dangers of drawing implications from the term are evident' (p. 27). Alas it obstinately refuses to go away. And so, James, a Canute holding the tide of language at bay, can merely importune against unfortunate usages. Thus, '… it seems preferable to restrict "independence" to the prerequisite for statehood and "sovereignty" for its legal incident' (p. 71). Nevertheless, James did not belong to those international lawyers who were ready to simply throw sovereignty overboard (a position never on the cards anyway). It had 'protected status' as an offshoot of the right of a people to decide on its government and resist external interference. True, sovereignty also protected authoritarian forms of rule. But foreign efforts to import democracy, for instance, had not been encouraging. And increasing functional co-operation had lowered the boundaries of sovereignty so that, for example, the protection originally offered to states by the reservation of domestic jurisdiction under the UN Charter had radically limited its scope. Instead, he wrote in a later essay, new notions such as that of the margin of appreciation, aimed to balance the interests of state governments with individual and group rights under the human rights treaty network.[3]

Decolonisation is confronted more fully in the sections on Statehood and Self-Determination. In 1977, James was still able to say that the relationship between statehood and self-determination was 'to some extent, a neglected problem' (p. 84). In the post-Badinter, post Quebec/Scotland/Catalonia, post-Soviet era, that is no longer the case. Indeed, in 1977, viewed a certain way, the relationship of statehood to self-determination was *the* question of the post-war era. This was what lay at the heart of 'decolonisation'. For James, the issue is self-determination's status as a criterion for statehood. But first, there is a discussion of its status in general international law. As late as 1973, Gerald Fitzmaurice is still calling the principle of self-determination 'juridical nonsense'. James, needless to say, prefers the 'studied ambiguity' of the International Court of Justice's opinions on self-determination. Judges Dillard and Petrén are quoted at great length on this subject, and the gloss on these pronouncements gives us a further glimpse into James's concept of law. There are, as ever, two interpretations. On one hand, it may be that there are too many loose ends, too many textual gaps, so little certainty as to how to apply these so-called principles that the whole field is, if not quite juristic nonsense, then at least *de lege ferenda*.

The other (preferable) view is that a law of decolonisation has emerged with a core of applicable principles and a fuzzy margin of developing norms: a concept of law, then, and one that in the context of a history of post-war decolonisation, it is 'rather late in the day to contest' (p. 100). Elsewhere, the law of self-determination, apart from permitting a certain flexibility in the condition of effectiveness when it comes to newly independent post-colonial aspirant states, can work to prevent a State (the Smith Government's UDI in Rhodesia was the proximate event) coming into being in violation of the norm of self-determination itself (p. 105). James ends his discussion of Rhodesia by saying that '… it can hardly be regretted that a rule which merely ratifies the international position of effective but totally unrepresentative regimes is open to change' (p. 106). This is as close to 'personal opinion' as we get.

Because the law of self-determination is often approached as a law of abnormal relations or through a relationship between normal cases and abnormal instances, *Creation* is a vital resource for those trying to make their way around the question of Taiwan or the Holy See. James is a sure-footed guide in these cases, as he remains heroically focused on the sometimes decontextualised legal position, carefully refusing to get drawn into any Cold War manoeuvring on the disposition of Taiwan. He concludes:

---

[3] James Crawford, 'Sovereignty as a Legal Value', in James Crawford & Martti Koskenniemi, *The Cambridge Companion to International Law* (Cambridge University Press, 2012), 119-22.

'Taiwan is not a State, because it does not claim to be, and is not recognised as such: its status is that of a consolidated local *de facto* government in a civil war situation' (p. 151). On first reading, this seems to de-emphasise the territorial nature of Taiwan and its material and diplomatic position but, in the light of recent shadow boxing in the Gulf of Taiwan, the idea of a civil war situation may seem less artificial than it did in 1977. Elsewhere, there are marvellously elaborate encapsulations of the relationship between The Holy See and the Vatican State, and sometimes-definitive statements of the law of devolution or extinction. Students of international law and politics surprisingly often interested in such questions can, with confidence, be directed towards *The Creation of States* and its technical masterclasses.

At the question mark in the text: Was James one of those mysterious publicists whose work forms part of the legal order? An Article 38 figure invested with law-making authority? His work manifests a certainty (even as early as 1977). His descriptions of the legal rules are invested with the kind of confident omniscience that gives the reader the sense that laws are being given their definitive treatment.

At the ICJ, James had several opportunities to expand on his thinking in *Creation of States*. To take one example, in the Advisory Opinion on *The Declaration of Independence of Kosovo*, he can be read in full flight over five pages on the question of the legality of this declaration. This is James at his barbed and penetratingly witty best. It would be impossible to read this submission in ignorance of the identity of its author. The problem here was a kind of Hohfeldian mix-up on the part of those who thought about independence and secession under international law. How to bring into alliance the apparently (but only apparently) contradictory norms that seem to exist in this area of law? People have a right to self-determination under international law. Yet attempted secessions have often been condemned by states and the UN itself. As U Thant had said in 1970, 'As far as the question of secession ... is concerned, the United Nations attitude is unequivocable. As an international organization, the UN has never accepted, does not accept and I do not believe will ever accept a principle of secession of a part of a member-state'. And acts of secession are often illegal under domestic (constitutional) law (this question may soon be put to the test in the case of Scotland). There is certainly no right of secession under international law (this much was made clear in another case regarding the attempted secession by Quebec in 1994, to be dealt with below). But this body of law led some states to argue before the court that declarations of independence were somehow illegal under international law. James wants to put a stop to this and he does it with a parsimonious elegance. Was the Declaration by the Kosovo Assembly illegal?

'Mr President, Members of the Court, I am a devoted but disgruntled South Australian. "I hereby declare the independence of South Australia." What has happened? Precisely nothing. Have I committed an internationally wrongful act in your presence? Of course not.' (para 5).

One can hear the gears cranking up a few paragraphs later. 'Mr President … it is said that declarations of independence are, as such, unlawful. Historically, they were the main method by which new states came into existence. Since when, and by what legal processes, have they been outlawed?' (para 9). This sets James off on an Article 38 hunt for prey he knows does not exist. Sure enough there are no treaties and no relevant state practice and no general principles. What of the doctrine? The leading jurists are in unanimous agreement (Frank, Abi-Saab, Chinkin, Pellet). 'All the experts agreed' (para 18). The textbooks, too, speak with a single voice. 'Malcolm Shaw – to take a random example – says …'.

This of course is one of James's little jokes, because Professor Shaw has just spoken for Serbia arguing that declarations of independence are illegal. The quotation from Shaw's leading textbook goes as follows:

'There is, of course [there is, of course], no international legal duty to refrain from secession attempts: the situation remains subject to the domestic law'.

James, rather over-egging it, not only puts the whole part of the quote in italics but he repeats the offending and clinching phrase in square brackets. It is a little unnecessary then for him to end the discussion by saying: 'I particularly like the phrase "of course".' Of course he did. The whole submission is an exercise in legal analysis that is both ice-cold and yet full of sentiment. A very Jamesian combination. Needless to say, the Court followed this line of reasoning in its final judgement.

Statute of ICC

Two further great contributions to international law came about as a result James's becoming elected as member of the United Nations International Law Commission (ILC) in 1992, a specialist body of 34 members, elected by the UN General Assembly every five years. Established in 1947, the ILC was intended to become a centre for the 'codification and progressive development of international law'. Though the members were to act in principle as independent experts, they are elected strictly following the regular UN practice of regional representation. As an Australian James was elected in the slot reserved for the WEOG (Western European and Others) group.

His first assignment in the ILC was to finish the drafting of the proposal for a statute of the future International Criminal Court (ICC). The proposal had been on the UN's agenda ever since the organisation had begun to elaborate the so-called 'Nuremberg principles' in 1947. But any meaningful development on the topic had been prevented owing to the Cold War. However, the political situation had changed by the early 1990s when civil war and ethnic violence in the Balkans and in Africa led to the establishment by the UN Security Council of two ad hoc international criminal jurisdictions of

Yugoslavia in 1993 and Rwanda in 1994. This led the General Assembly to request the ILC to produce a draft treaty for the statute of a permanent international criminal court. In 1994, James became the Chairman of the Commission's working group on the matter. From that position he was able to direct the finishing of a draft statute with his customary diplomatic skill and with astounding speed (in a UN context) already at the very same session.[4] The draft became eventually the starting-point for the work of the diplomatic conference that adopted the Statute of the International Criminal Court in 1998. Following the original draft, the court was set up by a treaty and it would try crimes of individuals only. The contentious question about the existence and treatment of 'State crimes' – left out of the draft statute – was to occupy James extensively in his later work on State responsibility. The Court was to have jurisdiction over international crimes laid out in specific treaties – namely the 1948 Genocide treaty as well as the 1949 and 1977 Geneva Conventions on the laws of armed conflict. Much of the ILC draft would eventually be incorporated in the Rome Statute of 1998. The Court began its operations in 2002 with 60 ratifications, and now directs its operations from its headquarters at The Hague.

State responsibility

Having finished the draft statute for the ICC, James received perhaps the most massive task of his career. The item of the responsibility of States had been on the agenda of the ILC since 1948, but its career went into the early years of the League of Nations. The Commission had initially limited its treatment of the subject to injuries to aliens, until in 1969 the Italian Roberto Ago had expanded it to all the breaches of international law's substantive obligations. The theoretically complex topic involved widely diverging doctrinal positions and a heterogenous practice. Although it had been slightly narrowed by separating the question of environmental liability from it, subsequent rapporteurs had treated it with perhaps excessive ambition for systemic coherence. When James became the rapporteur in 1997, his instructions were to finish the topic in four years – an almost inhuman task he carried out by focusing intensively on parts where agreement was possible and setting aside the most controversial themes, above all the question of crimes of State (Draft Article 19). The final draft codified customary laws scattered in diplomatic practice and doctrine on issues such as attribution of responsibility and its consequences, as well as a theme of especial interest at the time, namely collective reaction to especially serious violations of international law.

---

[4] See James Crawford, 'The ILC's Draft Statute for an International Criminal Tribunal', 88 *American Journal of International Law* (1994), 141-2, and *Yearbook of the International Law Commission*, 1994 vol II, 26-87.

James went to work with enthusiasm and determination. With respect to attribution, the outcome was that a state would be responsible for all the acts of its organs, including normally their *ultra vires* acts. No subjective 'guilt' on the part of the organ was required, though a broad standard of due diligence might sometimes be relevant – a consideration of eventually great relevance in determining if a state bore responsibility for acts of terrorists operating from within its territory. Nor would actual damage be required as a condition of responsibility. A breach of an obligation was sufficient to bring about a duty to compensate or provide some other type of suitable redress.[5]

Apart from polishing the draft, James's principal achievement was to develop the notion of *erga omnes* obligations – obligations owed to 'the international community as a whole', an item sometimes mentioned in case-law and doctrine, but so far without systemic authority. The hardest nut to crack was that of 'state crimes' – a theme that had accompanied ILC debates since the adoption of the Nuremberg principles. While many states, and perhaps a majority of jurists supported the idea that a state might commit a crime – one typically thinks of aggression or genocide – serious doubts had been voiced against the idea of a collective crime and its place in an essentially delictual concept of international responsibility. The very notion of punishing a state seemed objectionable to many. Through skilful manoeuvring, James was able to finalise article 48 of the draft – what he himself identified as his 'single most important contribution … to international law' – in a way that aligned the *erga omnes* notion with the more well-known concept of breaches of peremptory norms (*ius cogens*). The result was that rarest of things in the law between sovereigns – namely normative hierarchy. There would now be obligations of such importance that every state would be entitled to invoke a breach against them even if they themselves had suffered no direct injury. James himself gave the example of the 2012 case at the ICJ between Belgium and Senegal where the International Court of Justice had briefly characterised the obligations under the 1984 Torture Convention as so important that their violation may be invoked by every party to the convention.[6] Belgium would thus be in its rights to claim that Senegal had violated its obligations by failing to bring proceedings against Chad's former dictator Hissene Habré, present in the country.[7] The idea of 'invocation' was a novelty that allowed James to engage all states parties to a convention or every state in the case of a customary rule of an *erga omnes* character to be concerned of serious violations, even if a matter was not of direct interest to them.

[5] On fault and damage, see further James Crawford, *State Responsibility. The General Part* (Cambridge University Press, 2013), 54–62.

[6] Biography of James Crawford, Squire Law Library, Eminent Scholars Archive, prepared by Lesley Dingle and available at https://www.squire.law.cam.ac.uk/eminent-scholars-archivejudge-james-crawford/biography-judge-james-crawford

[7] International Court of Justice, *Questions relating to the Obligation to Prosecute or Extradite (Belgium v. Senegal)*, Reports 2012, paras 68-9.

In this way, every state was turned into a guardian of international legality. They would even in some cases be entitled to take countermeasures against the violator.[8]

The Draft Articles on Responsibility of States for Internationally Wrongful Acts were provisionally accepted by the UN General Assembly in 2001 and have become an often-referenced source on this hugely important part of international law. No attempt has been made to fulfil the original ambition to turn these articles into an international treaty. The text has instead remained a kind of restatement of this part of the law, as James himself preferred. Going by way of a treaty conference might have opened up carefully drafted compromises. Failure of a conference would have left the world in a worse place than agreeing to regard the draft articles as a competent, UN-endorsed statement of the customary content of this branch of the law.

Human rights and self-determination

James had also a keen interest in human rights law and he was an active participant in debates over of the work of human rights institutions – especially of the role and substance of the human right to self-determination, as noted above. He shared the worry of his Australian colleague, Professor Philip Alston, that the proliferation of human rights institutions, especially at the universal level, had not been matched with the increase of resources and personnel, so that the treatment of periodic reports and individual communications was often disappointingly superficial. Attention was on countries that were ready for constructive debate and rarely on countries with the greatest problems.[9] This was a systemic problem that brought to surface the relative hypocrisy of states in human rights matters where they had so utterly failed to put their money where the mouths were often loudest. James was never one to condone such hypocrisy, and least of all when it came from countries closest to him.

As described above, James had demonstrated his interest in the important but ambivalent notion of self-determination already in the *Creation of States*. This became, of course, one of the fighting notions in the post-Cold War turbulences from Eastern Europe to the Balkans in the 1990s. But the New Continent would not stay aside. The question of possible secession of the province of Quebec had come up already in the 1980s but had failed to attain majority support of the Canadians. Legal consultations at the time had concluded that the right of self-determination provided no automatic right of

---

[8] As explained in James Crawford, *Brownlie's Principles of International Law* (Oxford University Press, 2012), 580–4.

[9] See e.g. James Crawford, 'The UN Human Rights Treaty System: A System in Crisis?', in Philip Alston & James Crawford, the Future of UN Human Rights Treaty Monitoring (Cambridge University Press, 2000), 1–12.

secession. Having won a provincial election in 1994, the *Parti Québecois* put forward a new proposal for independence. The federal government then initiated a 'reference' to the Canadian Supreme Court, requesting its opinion on 'is there a right to self-determination under international law' that would entitle Quebec to secede? Upon the government's request, James prepared a detailed report on state practice on unilateral secession. There he stated what was probably the majority view at least among Western scholars that, while international law did support the ending of colonial regimes, the same could not be said of non-colonial situations such as Quebec. Being able to use the extensive survey of practice he had collected in the *Creation of States*, he showed that it had been a 'common feature' in post-1945 state practice that 'such attempts have gained virtually no international support or recognition … even when other humanitarian aspects of the situation have triggered widespread concern and action'.[10] In a conclusive statement at the end of his report, James observed that there had been not one non-colonial situation after 1945 where a territory would have received independence owing to the force of the self-determination principle alone. 'In fact, no new state formed since 1945 outside the colonial context has been admitted to the United Nations over the opposition of the predecessor state'.[11]

But matters were different in colonial cases, of course. Acting as Australia's counsel in the *East Timor* case before the ICJ, James insisted that the fact that the court did not, in Australia's view, have jurisdiction (because a third state was involved, Indonesia, that had not consented to it), did not at all mean that the East Timorese were deprived of the right of self-determination. On the contrary, Australia fully recognised that the East Timorese did enjoy the right of self-determination – a position eventually also taken by the court, while it nevertheless declined subject-matter jurisdiction for the very reason invoked by Australia.[12] Another colonial self-determination situation concerned the fate of the Chagos islands, originally a part of the archipelago of Mauritius that had been administered as a non-self-governing territory by the United Kingdom until 1965. At the time of independence, the UK had severed the islands from Mauritius in order to lease them to the United States as a military base; inhabitants were forcibly removed. This aroused huge protests in the UN at the time, but the UK action came under legal scrutiny only in 2010 in the context of its having declared a 'Marine Protection Area' (MPA) around Chagos in a way that could be challenged by arbitration under the UN Convention on the Law of the Sea.[13] In his extensive and at times angry pleading before the Arbitration

---

[10] Report by James Crawford, 'State Practice and International Law in Relation to Unilateral Secession', in Anne Bayefsky, *Self-Determination in International Law: Quebec and Lessons Learned* (The Hague: Kluwer, 2000), 31-61, 53.

[11] Ibid. 57.

[12] International Court of Justice, *East Timor* case (Portugal v. Australia), Reports 1995, 102 (para 29).

[13] Permanent Court of Arbitration, *Chagos Marine Protected Area Arbitration* (Mauritius v. United Kingdom), 2015. https://pca-cpa.org/en/cases/11/

Tribunal, James had little difficulty to show the utter illegality (not to speak of the imperialist arrogance) of severing Chagos from the rest of Mauritius. Any 'consent' by Mauritian leaders, referenced by the UK, had been vitiated by duress. UK negotiators, James showed, had cynically exploited the country's economic dependency to severe a part of it to lease that part (and especially the largest island, Diego Garcia) to its Cold War ally, the US. The tribunal did not have jurisdiction on all of the claims, but it unanimously followed James – the declaration of the MPA was illegal owing to the original illegality of the act of severance. In the end, the principal issue came to the ICJ in the form of a request of an advisory opinion by the UN General Assembly in 2017. Though member of the court at that time, James was compelled to recuse himself owing to his earlier involvement in the case. But he must have been satisfied with the Court's agreement with the arguments he had earlier made; the UK's continued rule over Chagos islands was 'a wrongful act entailing [its] international responsibility'.[14]

Other case-law

James developed very extensive practice as counsel, in later years usually as lead counsel, to altogether 29 cases before the International Court of Justice – including some of the most important cases in recent international legal history. It is impossible to review his activity in an exhaustive way here. Perhaps we can note, however, that he often and quite characteristically argued for an evolutive understanding of international legal obligations in view of present-day needs and concerns. He was also frequently found on what most observers would regard as the 'right' side of history, especially in such politically important cases as the advisory opinions on the use and threat of *Nuclear Weapons* (1996), *Palestine Wall* (2004), and *Kosovo's Declaration of Independence* (2010). Acting as counsel for the Solomon Islands in *Nuclear Weapons*, one of the initiators of the case, he argued from the strategically formulated position that the intention was not to put the whole post-war system of nuclear deterrence on trial. The initiators had not intended to undermine the great powers' defence policies or the nuclear non-proliferation system. Only an *actual* threat or use of such weapons was at issue. The law prohibited the indiscriminate killing of civilians. Surely it could not remain silent when such killing was threatened or committed by nuclear weapons. As part of his elegant and powerful performance, James cited the refusal by Dylan Thomas to mourn the death of a child by fire in London – 'After the first death, there is no other' – thus inviting the judges to reflect on the incomprehensible magnitude of killing by nuclear weapons. *Palestinian Wall* (2004)

---

[14] International Court of Justice, *Legal Consequences of the Separation of Chagos Archipelago from Mauritius in 1965* (Reports 2017).

gave James the opportunity to make the classical point that the fact of a case having *political* dimensions did not prevent and had never prevented the court from pronouncing on its *legal* aspects. It had been perfectly within the General Assembly's powers to request an advisory opinion; after all, the Palestinian question had been on the Court's roster of cases from a time preceding the establishment of the State of Israel. In the case concerning the *Unilateral Declaration of Independence of Kosovo* (2010), referred to above, he found himself in a situation where all sides were using his *Creation of States* to argue their respective positions. It was with unrivalled authority, therefore, that he demonstrated that international law 'of course' had nothing against such declarations. They were only of concern to the domestic legal system. If in *Nuclear Weapons*, the Court left a small opening for 'extreme circumstances ... in which the very survival of the State would be at stake', in the latter two cases, the court eventually took the position represented by James.

Unsurprisingly, James would frequently be entrusted with environmental cases. In the *Nauru* case, referred to above, he argued against Australia that its obligations regarding the protection of Nauru's natural resources survived the termination of the 1947 trusteeship agreement.[15] In a 2014 case against Japan's whaling practices he insisted on the need to understand and interpret the relevant 1946 convention in view of present-day needs for the conservation and recovery of whale populations.[16] In his first case as lead counsel, the *Gabcikovo-Nagymaros Dam* case (1997 Hungary v. Slovakia), he integrated great amounts of complex technical data in his pleading on the environmental effects of the planned water diversion project on the Danube. His interest in scientific and technical aspects of his cases was demonstrated by his skilful employment of statistics and other empirical data that were often at the heart of his cases. In the *Southern Bluefin tuna* cases (Australia & New Zealand v. Japan, 1999, 2000), for example, both at the interim measures stage in the International Tribunal on the Law of the Sea (ITLOS) as well in the subsequent Arbitral Tribunal, he based his argument about the reasonableness of the applicants' position on complex and sometimes disputed scientific projections on the development of Southern Atlantic tuna stocks.

Environmental problems were also raised in the *Land Reclamation* case (Malesia vs. Singapore, 2003) where James assisted Malesia to seek from the ITLOS provisional measures against Singapore's construction works the Straits of Johore. The main issue was delimitation – the first such case brought to the tribunal. What James decided to label Singapore's 'land grab at sea' would seriously prejudice the future delimitation of the countries' respective maritime territories. The court did grant interim measures, calling upon Singapore not to act 'in ways that might cause irreparable prejudice to the

---

[15] International Court of Justice, *Certain Phosphate Lands in Nauru* (Nauru v. Australia) Reports 1992/1993.
[16] International Court of Justice, *Whaling in the Antarctic* (Australia v. Japan), Reports 2014.

rights of Malaysia or serious harm to the marine environment'. The case was eventually terminated by agreement. In the *Delimitation of the Maritime Boundary in the Bay of Bengal* (ITLOS, Bangladesh vs. Myanmar, 2011), James used to good effect the old principle from the North Sea continental shelf cases (1969) that using the equidistance line would have cut off Bangladesh from large areas of the bay; equitable principles were to be used to determine each riparian's share of the shelf and its resources.

In a case concerning the fate of a Russian vessel *Volga* (2002) apprehended by Australia for its allegedly illegal fishing activity, James was again putting forward conservation concerns as the justification for what the ITLOS would eventually regard as excessive conditions for the release of the vessel and its crew. Where the rules regarding prompt release, he argued, were intended to protect freedom of transit and navigation, here the issue concerned neither the one nor the other, but the operation of regional fisheries agreement. Although the ITLOS showed sympathy towards conservation concerns in its judgment, it decided the case by following the detailed procedures in the 1982 UN Convention on the Law of the Sea Law of the Sea for release of vessel as against the deposit of a bond it determined.

James is likely to have been, perhaps alongside Alain Pellet from Paris, the most widely used litigator at the ICJ and other international tribunals, often collaborating with colleagues from the Matrix chambers he joined in the early 2000s. The biography with the Squire Law Library lists his involvement in the stunning number of 135 cases. But of course, this is unsurprising. One would wish to have him on one's side – not least in order to avoid having him as adversary. James would always be a good choice, in part owing to the extreme thoroughness of his pleading, but also partly owing to the lightness and literary manner that disguised the sharpness of his attacks invariably on the adversary's most vulnerable points. When he found his 'old adversary and friend' Alain Pellet on the opposite side, as he did in *Bay of Bengal*, for example, he would remark on 'his best hard-boiled manner' and address him with a paraphrase from W.H. Auden: 'Law, says [Professor Pellet] as he looks down his nose, speaking clearly and most severely … Law is the Law'. We receive a glimpse of his style from that same case where he referenced Sherlock Holmes and Mr Watson, reminisced on Alexander Pope's lines, and compared Myanmar counsels' effort to minimise the *North Sea* cases (on which Bangladesh relied) with an effort to suggest that Claudius was really just a bystander in Hamlet – 'all he did was kill Hamlet's father, usurp the throne and married Hamlet's mother'. He knew how to address his audience in an entertaining fashion – though sometimes forgetting that his audience consisted also of sometimes elderly non-native English speakers so that the president was frequently obliged to invite him to speak a little more slowly.

*

When did James sleep? This was an utter enigma for colleagues. We would receive messages from him by email at any time of the day, often in the very early hours of the morning, always with an informally formulated but extremely pertinent response to whatever the question or the concern we had expressed. He was an altogether admirable colleague. But his professionalism went beyond technical knowledge and subtle pleading; it was supplemented by personal qualities that were immediately visible for those who came to know him. Sands is right to remember him as 'direct, subtle and fearlessly independent'.

The energy with which James worked not only with his cases but also with his doctoral students was likewise legendary. Students were repeatedly struck by the rapidity with which he responded to questions about draft chapters in a thesis or other tricky points along the way to a doctorate. The seriousness with he took students' concerns, as well as his accessibility and informality, earned him, as countless reminisces from his students testify, their unabated devotion. There was love on both sides, however – James having regarded the interactions he had with his students as 'the most significant thing in [his] academic career'.

Note on the authors: Martti Koskenniemi is Emeritus Professor of International Law, and Director of The Erik Castrén Institute of International Law and Human Rights at the University of Helsinki; he was elected a Corresponding Fellow of the British Academy in 2014. Gerry Simpson is Professor of Public International Law at the London School of Economics; he was elected a Fellow of the British Academy in 2019.

Biographical Memoirs of Fellows of the British Academy (ISSN 2753–6777) are published by
The British Academy, 10–11 Carlton House Terrace, London, SW1Y 5AH
www.thebritishacademy.ac.uk

ANDREW BARKER

Andrew Dennison Barker

24 April 1943 – 22 July 2021

elected Fellow of the British Academy 2005

by

J. L. LIGHTFOOT
Fellow of the Academy

Trained as a philosopher, Andrew Barker entered the field of ancient music when it still had very few inhabitants. His translations of ancient theoretical treatises on harmonics made available, for the first time in English, a large number of difficult and demanding texts, but above all he drew out their philosophical implications, showing how they contributed to ancient debates about perception, definition, and scientific methodology. His translations and exegeses both enriched the field and enlarged it, and his collaborations with colleagues—especially in Italy, which became an important part of his life—created and fostered international networks that transformed the study of ancient music.

Biographical Memoirs of Fellows of the British Academy, 20, 265–294
Posted 12 October 2022. © British Academy 2022.

ANDREW BARKER

Andrew Barker was born 24 April 1943, in Egginton, South Derbyshire, to Edwin and Nancy Barker (née Daldy). He had an elder brother George, and twin younger sisters, Frances and Judith. His brother (known to close friends and family as Aldus) became a distinguished conservationist, who joined the Nature Conservancy Council, first as Warden of Old Winchester Hill in Hampshire, and eventually the NCC's chief urban expert.

His parents were Low-Church Anglicans. His father held a position in the Church Civil Service and worked for the YMCA. In connection with his job the family moved while Andrew was still an infant to Terwick Rectory, near Rogate, West Sussex, which they rented for a peppercorn. His home life was religious—grace was said before meals—but in later life Barker had no religious faith, and his funeral was conducted by a humanist celebrant. The Rectory's more enduring legacy was its rural location, where Andrew and George collected insects, beetles (the source of George's nickname) and butterflies. One summer they caught an unusual blue butterfly and wrote to the relevant national authority reporting that they had seen a Mazarine Blue. The reply they received was dismissive. The butterfly was on the edge of extinction; they could have seen no such thing. They wrote back with a picture of the distinctive spots they had observed, and received a much more respectful reply. It was never officially confirmed, but this may have been the last ever sighting of a Mazarine Blue in the United Kingdom; they are now considered to have been extinct in the UK for decades.

Nancy put her son forward for a scholarship at Christ's Hospital, which he attended, first the Prep School, then the main school, between 1951 and '62. At school, where he was an exact contemporary of the philosopher Christopher Rowe, nothing spoiled his character as a model pupil—not even a visit to a pub on the edge of the South Downs during an exercise with the Combined Cadet Force which, had it been discovered, would have risked instant expulsion. Butterfly hunting continued—though it was later succeeded by distaste for the sight of beautiful creatures pinned to a board. His teacher in advanced Classics, who coached the sixth form for Oxbridge scholarships, was D.S. Macnutt, who set crossword-puzzles for the *Observer* under the name of the Grand Inquisitor Ximenes, and would compile clues while the boys were working at their Greek and Latin translations. Barker's parents and sisters having moved to Geneva for a few years during his mid teens, he began visiting Italy on family holidays, and he spent some of his extra year in the sixth form, during which he served as Senior Grecian (Head Boy), improving his Italian. This was the beginning of his affection for that country.

He followed his elder brother to The Queen's College Oxford, where he read Literae Humaniores (1962–6). His Mods tutor was J.D.P. Bolton, whose book *Aristeas of Proconnesus* came out in the year Barker came up; his Greats tutors were Fergus Millar (for both Greek and Roman History),[1] Brian McGuinness (himself a Wittgenstein expert) for Plato and Aristotle, and Jonathan Cohen for logic. This was Millar's first year at Queen's (for the first term he still gave tutorials in All Souls) and, he claimed, the best ever. Contemporaries remember Barker's efficiency in tutorials, how he got to the point. He sang, sometimes, but not as much as he would do later.

In 1966 he was awarded a scholarship to study philosophy at the still-young Australian National University in Canberra. An attempt at self-reinvention underlay the move, apparently, but what that meant in practice was a return to his old love of natural history, with a doctorate entitled 'Evolution and Explanation'. Though he took advice from biologists, and included the occasional empirical illustration (the inevitable fruit-fly), it is very much a philosophical thesis, concerning modes of explanation in a system that is both unfalsifiable and unpredictable; it was supervised by John Passmore, whose wide philosophical interests extended to ecology, and Robert R. Brown, who worked in the social sciences and philosophy of mind, but had competence in natural science. Alongside his academic work, Barker was also pursuing and developing his interests in music. It was through them that, soon after his arrival, he met his first wife, Susan, a talented soprano. He eventually returned to England accompanied by Susan, pregnant with his first son, Jonathan, born in 1970. A second son, Nicholas, followed in 1972.

On his return from Australia in 1970 he joined the School, shortly afterwards renamed Department, of Philosophy in Warwick as its Ancient Greek specialist (the University had only started admitting students five years previously). His appointment was probably connected to a strong commitment to the history of philosophy on the part of the founding Professor of Philosophy, Allen Phillips Griffiths ('Griff'). Indeed, ancient philosophy had enormous coverage on the syllabus at the time, and he had near-complete autonomy over course content. He taught a compulsory course on Ancient Philosophy for single-Honours first years, and popular Honours options on Presocratic Philosophy and Greek Ethics. He also taught across faculties. By the time he arrived, Warwick's Philosophy department had moved from the Arts to the Social Studies Faculty, while the Classics department, which was founded later, was located within Arts. But Barker, who remained with the philosophers, was able to build a good relationship between Philosophy and Classics. He taught students on the Philosophy with Classical Civilisation course and Philosophy and Literature joint degree, the former of which he helped to create, despite a distaste for the administration which the complicated set-up entrained. An acrostic concealed on one year's general essay paper spelled out a word not wholly supportive of the Warwick bureaucracy; as for his attitude to authority, one question asked the students, 'Is the Vice-Chancellor a substance?'

---

[1] Bowman & Goodman (2021), p. 28 (on Millar and the Queen's years).

The Warwick years were punctuated by a stint teaching ancient philosophy in Cambridge (1976–8). It was a three-year lectureship in the first instance. There was enough of a possibility of renewal to make it worth buying a couple of cottages in Sturton Street and investing some effort in converting them (the first but by no means the largest of his property-conversion projects). But there was also enough chance of *non*-renewal for Warwick to hold his position open—Griff was keen to retain him—and he duly returned when less-than-encouraging noises were made before the expiry of the probationary period. The marriage to Susan having come to an end in 1975, Barker moved to Cambridge with Jill, a friend from Australia who was now in Britain. They married in 1978, and would have three children together: Michael (1977); Kate (1979); Will (1988).

Although it was so short, the move to Cambridge was the very opposite of abortive, for it was during this time that he discovered his vocation. What apparently started it was that G.E.L. Owen invited him to give a talk in his first term at Cambridge's B Club, expecting, presumably, a paper on ancient philosophy. The date happened to be set for St Cecilia's Day. But 22 November drawing closer, and no title being forthcoming, Owen informed the apprehensive invitee that he was going to publish the title as 'Heavenly harmony'—thereby obliging the speaker to learn about the subject whether he liked it or not. He did like it, clearly. These forced beginnings must be what underlie the Preface to the first volume of *Greek Musical Writings* (1984c, p. xi),[2] where he credits Owen with first stimulating his interest in ancient music and encouraging his first investigations. Recollections of that talk are that it was simple, unscripted, and supported by a fairly crude, home-made stringed instrument on which he demonstrated the basics of ancient Greek harmonics, the first but by no means the last of his efforts in this area. When, the following year, on 10 November, he gave a talk on the predecessors of the harmonic theorist Aristoxenus at the Cambridge Philological Society in Michaelmas Term, matters were altogether different. The written-up version, published as 1978a, is a sophisticated piece already with all the historical grasp and theoretical control of the mature Barker.

As his interest in the subject grew, it came to reflect and to be reflected in his undergraduate teaching. In a preface to a later book (2000b, p. vii) he explained that his courses at Warwick had regularly revolved around Platonic and Aristotelian texts on the nature of knowledge and the means of attaining it. The description of the introductory course lays the emphasis on epistemology, metaphysics, and their links to other areas, including the philosophy of science; that on the Presocratics on 'what it is to understand the world's workings, and the methods by which such understanding is to be achieved and its credentials established'. These are exact descriptions of what his musicological writings were working out in a more tightly-bounded domain. He was singing at

---

[2] For ease of bibliographical referencing, a chronological listing of Andrew Barker's writings is provided at the end of this memoir.

Warwick, too, in the University of Warwick Consort founded by Rowland Cotterill, as well as in local groups in Leamington.[3] But not even a musical setting of Kant's Transcendental Deduction from the *Critique of Pure Reason*, performed by the School of Philosophy Male Voice Choir, could conceal from Barker that the Philosophy Department was no longer the place he wanted to be.

If, to misquote Tolstoy, happy departments are all alike, and every unhappy one unhappy in its own way, this particular one was divided between warring camps of analytic and continental philosophers. There was an early drive to promote the teaching of continental philosophy at undergraduate level, in the days before other universities offered the subject; it was popular, and followed by calls to establish it at graduate level too. But not everyone was happy, or convinced by the subject's credentials. Barker negotiated between the two factions, it is true. The bohemian personal style for which he was well known and, by students, well loved (with goats and hens in the huge garden of the family home in Melton Road) belied considerable political astuteness. He mediated delicately between parties by pointing out classical antecedents for each one, while taking sides with neither. Nevertheless, he wanted to leave, and besides, the joys of first year courses on Platonic epistemology no doubt palled when you actually had to mark their work. He wanted to be a Classicist, and saw his opportunity in a job advert for a position in the Classics department in Otago, which was undergoing an expansion in staffing. It put a perhaps merciful end to a year's tenure as acting Head of Department (1991–2), which he conducted, nevertheless, efficiently and fairly, and with the support of both sides of the ideological divide.

His appointment in Otago as Senior Lecturer, in 1992, followed by promotion to Professor in 1995, brought the complement in the department to nine, higher than at any other time in its history. While in Otago he taught the Greek Philosophy paper (in translation, and hitherto co-taught with the Philosophy Department), plus Greek Music papers newly minted to cater to his specialism. A memorable episode was when he was involved in *The Frogs* in the department's annual drama production in 1993. The original 'Ancient Greek' music was composed by the New Zealand composer Anthony Ritchie. Barker acted as 'technical adviser' and consultant on the lyric metres, with practical suggestions about rendering them in modern English for modern ears. Not only this, but he sang the role of Aeschylus as a counter tenor. (Aeschylus, not Euripides, as the extant programme notes confirm. Aeschylus stands for the machismo of Persian War generation, but the alto register suited his parodies of Euripidean lyric, with all its emotionalism and high camp and outrageous melismata. Besides, a cowboy-booted male alto certainly had impact.) Towards the end of his time at Otago cutbacks on staffing appointments

---

[3] The Oken Singers; the Circle Singers, which he even conducted for a couple of years.

had started in response to declining domestic student enrolments. So on his departure back to the UK in 1996 his position was not renewed.

It was to Birmingham that he returned, to a small Department of Classics with only four members (Ancient History was separate). The job was advertised at the level of Senior Lecturer, and he was already a professor, but they were successful in upgrading the position, immediately to Reader, and then a couple of years later to Professor. In the 2001 Research Assessment Exercise, which was less than helpful to the rest of the department, he was, much to his embarrassment, flagged as a one-man centre of excellence. He taught part of the core Greek Poetry course, including Greek Lyric, Pindar, and Hellenistic Poetry, but also optional courses including Early Greek Philosophy, Plato, and more specialised modules in Greek Music. Takers were mainly undergraduates but there were small numbers of graduates too. He was not, and never would be, known for his love of administration (a British Academy Research Professorship held 2000–03 saved him from the prolonged horrors of being Head of Department, although when he was elected to the British Academy itself in 2005 he was a good citizen, and during 2007–11 served on the Standing Committee of his Section, writing judicious appraisals of its applicants for Postdoctoral Fellowships). But perhaps his greatest contribution to the department was to build up its graduate community.

Among his students at this period were David Creese (1997–2001), now at Newcastle, and Zacharoula Petraki (Masters 2000; PhD 2005), now at the University of Crete (Rethymno). He also supported the work of two young Italian scholars of Ancient Greek music, Eleonora Rocconi (University of Pavia) and Antonietta Provenza (Università di Palermo), who came to Birmingham as visiting students (respectively in January 1997, 1998, and in 2005). Students recollected the generosity of his supervisions—weekly, sometimes lasting for hours, during the Masters stage—and the speed and efficiency with which work was returned. He continued to supervise throughout the period of his leave, during which he was working on *The Science of Harmonics in Classical Greece* (2007a), of which he even shared drafts with students—obviously for the sake of their content, but partly, too, as a gentle lesson in method (no, your work does *not* have to be perfect; yes, it is *allowed* to be provisional). You would never down a pint with him at the end of a supervision. He was not that sort of supervisor. You would certainly receive full and frank criticism. But it was never meant to hurt, it was supportive, and above all, apart from overseeing their theses and launching their careers, what he passed on to his students was what characterised his own scholarship, a courteous and generous way of proceeding in which mistakes were forthrightly corrected, but polemic for its own sake had no place.

The all-important Italian connection began in 1985, when he attended a conference at Urbino, the occasion of a controversy (described below) from which great things could hardly be augured. In any case, his spell in New Zealand interrupted his interactions with Europe until his return to Birmingham. It was, however, as a result of Eleonora Rocconi's visit to Birmingham that he was invited back to Urbino by Franca Perusino, head of the Classics Department, for a one week seminar in 1998. A couple of years later he returned to Urbino, and extended the visit to Cremona: *Euterpe* (2002) contains the texts of ten lectures, most of which were given in the course of these visits. A separate connection was formed with Salerno, where he was first invited in 1998 by Angelo Meriani, whom he had met in 1985. Subsequent visits led to the lectures (given in 2001–2) which appeared, translated into Italian, as *La psicomusicologia nella Grecia antica* (2005b).[4] And in the early 2000s Donatella Restani regularly organised a small annual meeting in Ravenna entitled 'Le musiche dei greci' where like-minded scholars could share their interests. These were the first of the annual meetings which were going to become an important part of his professional life.

Meanwhile the Ionian University in Corfu established an International Summer Academy in 2003, and for the 2004 meeting the Pro-Rector and Chair of the Department of Music, Charis Xanthoudakis, on the suggestion of Panagiotis Vlagopoulos, proposed the theme of Ancient Music. Barker was invited to give a seminar on ps.-Aristotle, *Problemata*. Morning seminars were held around the table of the meeting room in the attic of the Villa of Mon Repos, and lectures in the evening in the hall of the Ionian Academy. The Seminars on Ancient Greek and Roman Music would be held, in the same place and format, until the economic crisis brought them to an end in 2011. Several of Barker's later publications were first born as seminar papers given in Corfu,[5] and when the seminars resumed in 2014 in Riva Del Garda, in collaboration with the Arion society co-founded by Tosca Lynch in 2013, other publications arose out of these meetings.[6]

In parallel with all this, during his time in Otago he had founded the International Society for the Study of Greek and Roman Music with its magazine *Skytala Moisan* in 1993. Donatella Restani and Eleonora now suggested to Barker that he should refound this association to draw people together who shared a common interest. It was accordingly established as *The International Society for the Study of Greek and Roman Music and its Cultural Heritage*, subsequently MOISA, in 2006, when Barker was back in Birmingham, and formalised in 2007 as a non-profit cultural association based in Ravenna, in the Department of Cultural Heritage in the University of Bologna. Barker

---

[4] 2010b, on the music of Pan, arose out of a conversation he had with Roberto Pretagostini also in Salerno, in December 2006.

[5] The 2005 meeting, on ps.-Plutarch, gave rise to 2011a, *via* a later conference in Calabria, and ultimately to 2014b, *via* lectures again in Calabria. 2011b arose from an evening lecture (The Guild of the *Technitai* at Teos) in the 2006 meeting, and 2010c was first given in 2007, when the theme of the meeting was women in music.

[6] 2015b (from the Riva Summer School 2014, on ps.-Aristotle, *Problemata* 19); 2017, already given at the Symposium Cumanum in June 2016, was read again in the Riva Summer School 2018, on Dionysius of Halicarnassus.

was its President and continued in this role until 2012. There were MOISA annual meetings from 2006, the last at which he attended in person being 2017. The executive committee of MOISA in 2012 started to think about establishing a journal. Barker approached Brill, who responded positively, and the result was the journal *Greek and Roman Musical Studies* first published in 2013. Barker served as its editor-in-chief until 2017; the last of his editorials appeared in 2016.

By now several Italian universities had courses on ancient music (Cremona, Ravenna, Lecce), in all of which events occurred under the auspices of MOISA, and in 2015 MOISA became affiliated to the Society for Classical Studies in America, thanks to Pauline LeVen, MOISA member since 2008. The influence of these societies radiated outwards, so that it is in no small part due to Barker's commitment and fame that the discipline has grown from niche to one that is thriving internationally. For instance, a huge conference was organised by a MOISA member in 2019 in Brazil, with the intention of setting up a similar society for students of ancient Greek music in South America.

II

The Cambridge talk in 1976 did not immediately displace his work on Plato (1976, 1977a). A philosopher will call these papers perfectly competent, if not epoch-making. But they are interesting, in the light of what follows, as demonstrating a way of thinking and a method. Both are about philosophical arguments: why Plato deployed them at the points he did, what position the speaker is adopting, what positions he is trying to counter, and how successfully he does so, in other words paying close and scrupulous attention to the purpose and adequacy of an argument in its context. These would always be the questions in his later articles on music: what were the author's motives and rationale, how well-formed or deficient is his argument, what objections could defeat it, whether it answers challenges in terms the opponent would accept. It was always about the stakes of adopting a particular argument or viewpoint. Occasional purely philosophical (i.e. non-musicological) papers follow (1995a, 2006b, both on Plato); at Warwick he jointly edited a collection of papers on Plato (with Martin Warner, 1992), for which he wrote the introduction; and at Birmingham he supervised PhD theses on Plato. But really from that point onwards the attention turns almost exclusively to music, which he finds an immediately fertile subject.

It was clear that he had found his vocation. And it was a bold and independent move, because the field was barely colonised in those days. True, there was Winnington-Ingram, who had written a short, concentrated work on mode in ancient Greek music (1936), and edited the longest work of music theory to survive from antiquity, Aristides Quintilianus'

De musica libri tres (1963).[7] Like Barker, he had come to the subject through philosophy, in his case having been stimulated by an article on the scales of the *Republic*.[8] Barker began to correspond with Winnington-Ingram as soon as his interest in the subject became serious, and paid generous tribute to him, 'the master of those who know' (1984c, p. xi; 1989a, p. vi). But from Winnington-Ingram's more forbiddingly musicological publications it is not immediately obvious what the draw of the subject would be. What could make you throw over Plato for a niche subject full of arid mathematics, childish ratios (2:1 [octave]; 3:2 [fifth]; 4:3 [fourth]; 9:8 [tone]), jejune reductions of a system of music already so 'reduced' (because it lacked harmony) in comparison to our own? For that is what the vast amount of evidence for ancient music consists of—not the stuff itself, and not even analyses of it, but simply theoretical texts about the component parts, scalar structures and intervals. What could keep him returning to the same core of texts for the next forty years and more—mainly, parts of the *Republic* and *Timaeus*, the three books of Aristoxenus' *Harmonics*, the nineteenth book of the ps.-Aristotelian *Problemata*, ps.-Euclid's *Sectio Canonis*, and of course Ptolemy's *Harmonics*, and Porphyry's commentary on that? For even this is a limited selection of what is available. There were other writers—apart from Aristides Quintilianus, there were Cleonides, Bacchius, Gaudentius, and the Anonymi Bellermannii. But Barker had little time for those.[9] The sad truth is that these scholastic little textbooks were *even worse*.

   Yet Barker looked into these works and discovered in them a world of possibilities. The name of Martin West will recur a few times in this memoir (whose author is under no illusions that he would have been first choice to write it had he still been alive).[10] The intellectual world which Barker created and into which he drew his readers was more circumscribed than that of West, but it had a comparable richness and coherence. For neither of them was it ever about technicalities, and although Barker spent more time on them than West—invoking his Warwick colleague David Fowler for help with the more austere mathematics—he would sometimes apologise for being obliged to do so, or simplify in the interests of clarity. The intention was never to bamboozle the reader; if anything, there was the contrary risk, that of belabouring simple points. The question was what realities the various ancient theories about music were supposed to model, what one was permitted to infer from them. Everyone agreed that the question was what principles made certain orderings of notes 'harmonious', admissible as music, as opposed

[7] West (1994).
[8] West (1994), p. 581.
[9] 2022a is a translation of and short introduction to Gaudentius, illustrating its derivative character.
[10] Fowler (2018). It was entirely appropriate that Barker should have been asked to give the first Martin West Memorial Lecture in 2017, published as 2018c.

to meaningless noise. But for one school of thought, numerical principles, which said something about the ordering of the cosmos itself, underpinned it, and for the other, music was itself and nothing else.

Barker grasped the implications of Greek music theory immediately. He seems to have conceived the plan of the two volumes of *Greek Musical Writings* (1984c, 1989a) very shortly after developing his interest in the subject. The first volume, which consists of generously-annotated translations of sources on Greek music from Homer to the end of the 4th century, is a useful collection of material in an area that was still relatively unfamiliar. The second, however, which is described more fully below, is a tour-de-force, and makes available for the first time, in collected form, and in English, the core texts whose philosophical ramifications he was the first truly to have grasped. (He may or may not have realised the particular appropriateness of the task in the hands of a Queen's man, for a 17th-century Provost of the college had been instrumental in the very first great edition of ancient music theory by the Danish scholar Marcus Meibom.)[11] After his original insights in Cambridge the next forty years can be seen as an unpacking, with amplifications and increasing momentum—his publications become increasingly copious from the late '80s, and turn into a flood after his return from Otago—but no essential changes of direction.

The first philosophical question is what sound is,[12] and what are the implications of thinking about it in various terms. Barker's first musicological publications go straight to this question, using his characteristic approach of worrying at a short passage to make it meaningful and extract every nuance. In turn he analyses Plato's hard-core stance on Pythagoreans who failed to go far enough (1978b); Theophrastus' attack on the mathematical approach (1977b); and Aristoxenus' counter-position (1978c)—and what, in turn, was wrong with *that* (Aristoxenus' use of arithmetical values—fractions—which the ear can*not* corroborate). This is our first opportunity to discern the pattern that holds good for all his later work, as he returns over and over again to the same material (for instance *Republic* 3 and 7, and the account of the World Soul in *Timaeus* 35 B–37 C), drawing out new implications. The papers become longer and more discursive. For instance, 1991c gives a fuller and richer characterisation of the contrasts between the world-views of Plato and Aristoxenus (a static conception *versus* a dynamic one, in

---

[11] Gerard Langbaine (1609–58) is credited by Meibom in his *Antiquae Musicae Auctores Septem* (Amsterdam, 1652) with help in collating Oxford manuscripts of several of the authors Barker would translate over three hundred years later (Aristoxenus, Nicomachus, and Aristides Quintilianus), and enlisted the aid of another Queen's man, Richard Rawlinson, a fine mathematician, in transcribing a particularly thorny passage of Ptolemy's *Harmonics* (Poole 2018, pp. 9–10).

[12] That is, musical sound. Sound itself received much less attention from ancient philosophers, though there is a treatise *De audibilibus* which addresses the subject. A number of unpublished talks and papers from the end of Barker's career suggest that he was intending to make a more thorough investigation of what little there was of ancient acoustic science; illness, it seems, put an end to the project.

which notes move in a musical space on trajectories governed by rules that it is the task of harmonic analysis to discover), a more urgent sense of the stakes (a conception of music that roots it, not only in the structure of the cosmos, but also in that of the soul, *versus* one in which musicology is its own field, with no spillover to any other), *and* a sterner look at the limits of both of them. 2005a concentrates specifically on Aristoxenus, and presses harder at his use of the metaphor—if it is metaphor—of the dynamic voice as a traveller through space.

The enterprise is an essentially epistemological one. It is about making sense of what we hear. Barker continues to return to the same passages, teasing out more each time. A good example is the passage where Aristoxenus says the perception of music is a matter of both hearing (*akoe*) and the faculty of thought (*dianoia*) (*El. Harm.* 33.6–11, 38.27–39.3). *Dianoia* has to run hand in hand with sensory experience, which supplies merely quantitative data in need of interpretation. Barker first draws attention to this in 1978c, p. 13, but when he returns to it in 1984a, p. 55, the presentation has become more sophisticated (our perceptions *already* grasp more than quantitative data). Seven years later (1991b, pp. 210–11), still more implications are teased out (perception cannot be limited to pitch, volume and timbre, but must have an element of short-term memory to enable us to grasp relations, and must also be trainable). In 2005a, pp. 164–5 the same passage prompts reflections on the difference between a transient performance and a melody that exists in the abstract (like the Marseillaise); and when he finally returns to the topic (2012b) he continues to worry away at the role that interpretative elements, or *dianoia*, must play alongside the absorption of raw data at the moment of experiencing music, and adds further comparisons with other ancient accounts of the perceptual process.

A series of articles explore ancient theories of perception. Different theorists ask different questions. If, for Aristoxenus, the question was about the respective roles of the sense of hearing and *dianoia*, the Pythagorean / Platonist position invites the question how, if sound really is ratio, we are supposed to register and process that (2010a). And since, for Plato, more is at stake—the attunement of our souls themselves to structures in the cosmos of which music is but one, audible, manifestation—the question becomes how music impinges upon our souls, down to and including the very intimate ways we perceive it in our physiology (2000a). An innovative book entitled *Psicomusicologia* (2005b), the outcome of a series of lectures given in the Department of Classics at the University of Salerno in February 2002, brought together texts that reflect on music and the soul. The word was not Barker's own coinage, but he was the first (as he realised) to bring the evidence of the ancient world to bear under this heading: as far as Classics was concerned, this was new. Of this book it has been commented that it anticipates the growing modern interest in music and the mind. Ancient thinkers innocent of neuro-science could hardly frame questions about the brain's processing of music in terms available to us, although they *could* sometimes be startlingly penetrating (how is it, wondered Theophrastus, that we can conform our vocal cords to produce a note of just the desired pitch? (1985)). Rather, when they thought about music and the mind, it was in terms of music's supposed moral dimensions and therapeutic possibilities, and what Barker does in this volume is, characteristically, not simply to assemble evidence, but to penetrate to the method of the writers under consideration and to their philosophical and epistemological implications.

Although reviewers had less to say about it, one of the most interesting aspects of the book is arguably the way it circulates around the use of metaphor. It does not present itself as a systematic or summative treatment, but once again Barker is seen elaborating on the concerns of earlier articles and anticipating later ones. We use metaphor without realising it, when we think of pitches going 'up' or 'down' (vertically, or horizontally along a keyboard); was it, therefore, metaphor, when Aristoxenus talked about the 'place' (*topos*) occupied by pitch (2005a, pp. 166, 172)? Again, can technical language ever be free of metaphor, or are words bound to reflect the baggage—the 'penumbra' of surplus meaning—with which they have been invested since their non-technical, often poetic, ultimately Homeric, instantiations (2014a)? And is this a problem? In retrospect these concerns make sense of what otherwise looks like a peculiarly 'literary' article on Pindar's first Pythian Ode (2003b)—although Barker had, of course, been teaching literary courses, including on Greek lyric for Birmingham. What that showed was the *enabling* potential of traditional associations in poetic language in the hands of a creative poet. But when literary language is pressed into services for which it was never intended, what then? Confusions, question-begging, and unwanted associations, are all possible results, explored in the pages of *Psicomusicologia*. So too, it must be conceded, there are potential rhetorical and pedagogical dividends, and even, sometimes, interesting philosophical implications. At least one ancient theorist, Aristides Quintilianus, was perfectly aware of the insinuation or seepage of meaning from *comparans* to *comparandum*, and appropriated Stoic language to describe the pathways by which the listener's mind was affected (1999). 'On metaphor' is the great work that Barker did not write.

Always it is a matter of punching through technicality—explaining it slowly and generously where need be, but never as an end in itself—to get to the underlying philosophical questions: the history and practice of philosophical argumentation itself (1985, p. 290); matters of definition (2006a; 2009b, pp. 412–16); and how ancient musicologists are placed with respect to ongoing debates and controversies in philosophy at large, for instance the application to ancient musicology of the concepts of form and matter (1991c, p. 155), or the *criterion* or canon of judgement (2009a, pp. 181–2), or the respective roles of logically constructed demonstration and of direct observation (2009b, an article which, by proceeding from an apparently small and footling notice smothered in layers of transmission, to matters of genuine philosophical importance, shows Barker's method at its best). It was Ptolemy in his treatise on *Harmonics* who posed this last question, that of the relative roles of reason and perception, most acutely. Barker first presented a translation of this difficult treatise in the second volume of *Greek Musical Writings* (1989a). The first article devoted to Ptolemy appeared a couple of years later (1991d), but at the same time, he started work on the book that would eventually become *Scientific Method in Ptolemy's Harmonics* (2000b). The intellectual challenge of the *Harmonics* was that Ptolemy had set out to integrate both halves of the project, reason and perception, and had described it in a searching and self-aware way which makes the text a major, if little-studied, text for the philosophy of science. Barker concentrated on its significance for the field of harmonics itself, but showed what was at stake, too, for the *Almagest*, where the issue is precisely the relation between observation and mathematical modelling, and the good faith of the author in the attempt to make recalcitrant real-world data accord with abstract theory.

This was one subject on which, after he had said his say, Barker did not advance in later publications. But he remained fascinated by the instruments with which Ptolemy purports to subject mathematically-constructed systems to empirical proof. He had used some primitive stringed instrument in that fateful Cambridge talk in 1976. 2009c sees him still obsessing over Ptolemy's instruments, and in particular constructing his own version of a device that allows the production of ratios on multiple strings (not just one, as with the monochord) by means of a pivoted bridge. He called it the meta-helikon, after the helikon Ptolemy attributed to earlier theorists. In the article which he devotes to it, he also describes its construction, and if everything so far has sounded so terribly *cerebral*, here you can imagine the fun he had messing about with the glue and drills and plywood and pegs for the gut strings, a mixture of specialist music shops and Home Base, the serious intellectual endeavour of a Fellow of the British Academy and the little boy with a train-set. You can also feel the pride with which he demonstrated it at the Whipple Museum in Cambridge (May 2008) very likely for the first time in 1800 years, imagining, perhaps, Ptolemy's spirit being momentarily distracted from the music of the spheres by the sound of his own instrument.

And again, if it still sounds terribly *philosophical*, there was another aspect to Barker's work, which was its historical dimension—a strand in his work that, if anything, only became stronger over time. You could say that Oxford Greats in his day had twin prongs, philosophy and ancient history (he was taught by Fergus Millar; his tutorial partner was Alan Bowman), and that this was simply the other half of what he had been trained to do. But the truth is that it came out of the same source as the rest of his work. It was driven by the need to find intellectual context—to establish what authors were arguing about, who they were arguing with, what it responded to in the intellectual climate of their time.[13] It took the form of careful source criticism—the recovery of fragments, in the first place, from the contexts in which they were embedded, and, in the second, the identification of the source's own source. The first volume of *Greek Musical Writings* (1984c) was constructed diachronically, although, as one less charitable review pointed out, the decision not to dislimb later texts that quoted earlier sources disabled the reader who was looking for a systematic chronological account. But it contained ideas about the development of Greek music which Barker did not relinquish and would go on to develop—the challenge, in particular, to the idea that the so-called New Music at the end of the 5th century was actually all that revolutionary, as opposed to the result of a long history of experimentation, especially in the genre of the dithyramb, that had been underway for a century at the very least.

Another longue durée view, which he elaborated and nuanced in many publications, was that the Pythagorean/Platonic and Aristoxenic approaches or schools were only ever polarised in the schemes of ideologues and polemicists, and in reality were blurred—and blurred in ways that shifted and drifted over time. One of his most fascinating pieces—1994b, a gem of an article—concerns one individual who mediated between them, the music theorist Didymus who lived, apparently, in the time of Nero. This man, it seems, set out to revivify the 'music of the golden age', to recast Aristoxenus' analyses in the Pythagorean language which was the approved idiom in his day, and apparently demonstrated his results on a monochord which (by bisecting a string at the bridge, so two notes could be produced instead of one) he utilised in a performance-friendly way. In other words, the enterprise undertaken here is all of a piece with the amateurism, conservatism, and artificiality of the embryonic Second Sophistic movement. This piece sees Barker perform a manoeuvre which he was very good at: that is, showing how music, and musicology, both reflects and is reflected in tastes, fashions, and cultural trends of its time. It is another exercise in historical coherence.

This is one of the themes of his only strictly 'historical' book (2014b), which was born of a series of lectures given at the University of Calabria in 2013, where he had been invited by Antonietta Gostoli. Here, with all the Barker hallmarks of careful source criticism and contextualisation, he set out to collect Greek writings on the history of their own music, the history of ancient musicology, which was effectively to open up a new field. He placed sources in their rhetorical, argumentative, and ideological settings, determining their methods, agendas, and biases. The genre of writing is crucial as well—the comedy which seeks merely to raise laughs, without giving the slightest indication of what the author 'really thought'; the specialist monograph, which positions its subject as

---

[13] And, in one case, how their observations even reflect contemporary speech-patterns. He notes an apparent change in the prosody of Greek speech between Aristoxenus in the late 4th century and Ptolemy and Porphyry half a millennium and more later, as implied by what they have to say about sound that remains at a continuous pitch (2014a and 2015a, pp. 41–3).

the product of a bygone age; the lexicon; the collection of learned excerpts. But above all, this fairly slim volume constitutes a very major contribution to the history of taste, and an assurance, if we needed one, that Barker was completely aware, over and above any impression that his austerely theoretical publications gave, that music was a living and dynamic thing—and that it engendered strong opinions. There is a lovely cameo of a group of reactionaries around Aristoxenus who gathered in a kind of surly Eisteddfod to mutter darkly about degenerate modern ways.

Commenting on this volume, some scholars regretted that he did not say more about 5th-century 'performance culture'. But that is well-populated territory; besides, he had already written a series of chronological chapters on the technological changes in the wind instrument known as the *aulos*, and the heady musical and cultural developments which it facilitated in the course of the sixth and fifth centuries (2002b). Barker cannot be accused of overlooking the performative dimension of music, heard music, music in the real world (and his supervisees certainly stress that he was interested in performance and in the Greek chorus). On the contrary, visitors to the large family home in St Mary's Road, Leamington, recall a variety of home-made musical instruments, including a lyre made out of chair-legs to which modern guitar strings were attached, and a splendid playable concert kithara which replicates the image on a 4th-century silver tetradrachm of Olynthos, down to the incised decoration and a ribbon attachment.[14] And yet it remains the case that the theoretical treatises that he studied did tend to steer him away from that general dimension. They failed to represent *real* music in at least two major ways. First, they conceptualised intervals as notes heard simultaneously rather than successively—a strange choice in a musical culture that was all about melody and had no concept of harmony at all. Second, their analyses were static, as opposed to dynamic, which is of course how we experience it as performers or listeners. No-one knew this better than Barker, and it was well within his powers to write in a way that corrects these intellectual artifices. There are a few such essays; one is left wanting more.

The pieces that best represent this approach are the last two essays in the 2002b volume, which talk us through a couple of items in the very small corpus of ancient music that does survive. Reviewers of the first volume of *Greek Musical Writings* (1984c) both friendly and less so had noted the absence of anything about the surviving musical fragments. Now at last we receive minute analyses of (part of) the Delphic paean of Athenaeus and Mesomedes' *Hymn to the Sun*. What is interesting here is the method. West[15] had described Greek music as habitually 'in constant, restless motion', with little repetition of phrases. Perhaps it was an aspect of his perpetual quest for intelligibility

---

[14] Reproduced on the cover of 2007a; for experiments in supporting a kithara during performance, cf. 1984c, pp. 4–14.

[15] West (1992), p. 194.

that led Barker to emphasise, instead, the repetitions of micro-segments in both pieces, or their transformation in recognisable ways, in other words to insist on pattern. In general it was West who sought 'human intelligibility'.[16] But it is Barker here who finds it, and indeed insists that it is still possible to understand the logic of ancient composers' choices, giving unity and coherence to their compositions (2002b, pp. 118, 122).

He has important things to say, too, about ancient performance practice. To return to the point about harmony, while it remains true that it is foreign to ancient music, one of Barker's major contributions was to insist on the practice of *heterophonia*, or accompaniment that did more than simply reduplicate the vocal line.[17] And it is worth mentioning the arcane subject of the *magadis*, because it shows Barker at most tactful—and tenacious. Modern interpretations of the few, opaque, ancient references to this, whatever it is, had tended to take it as an instrument that sounded two notes simultaneously, an octave apart. It was one of Barker's most consistently maintained beliefs[18] that there was no such thing, and even if *magadis* was an instrument name at all, what it and *magadizein* principally referred to was the use of an instrument to 'respond' to a melodic line by way of providing a descant on it (1988a). It was this that ruffled feathers at the Urbino conference of 1985: the author of a recent article on the subject[19] was not best pleased to be told that his instrument never existed, and the conference proceedings tone down what was apparently quite an angry exchange. But Barker not only stuck to his theory; he reinforced it (1995b; 1998), soothing his disputants with civilities as far as he possibly could. He made another intriguing inference (2002b, ch. 6) about ancient performance practice from a passage in Pliny which indicates that ancient auletes could perform the same line in a number of different ways. The Romans codified this in terms of rhetorical style (they *would* ...), but we might see it as more akin to jazz improvisation.

And blind spots? Rhythm was perhaps one. It is true that the vast majority of the music theory that we have is harmonics, and metrics and rhythmics, which are separate branches of music science, are far less well represented. But there is an intriguing excerpt from the second book of Aristoxenus' *Elementa Rhythmica* (translated in 1989a, pp. 185–9), and some chapters in Aristides Quintilianus, and even if Barker did not want to descend to metrical analyses of extracts of Greek lyric or tragedy or comedy, as some reviewers bemoaned, he could still have indulged himself with ratios and laws of combination, perceptible minima and commensurables, rational and irrational sequences, and questions of definition and ontology a-plenty. For whatever reason, he did no such thing. He had hoped for insights from 'the science of ethnomusicology' (1984a, p. 1), but no subsequent publications ever took the comparative turn that is latterly being explored

[16] Lightfoot (2017), p. 288.
[17] 1995b, which contains what is apparently Barker's one and only reference to the *Orestes* fragment (p. 47).
[18] 1982b, p. 268; 1984c, p. 294 n. 169 and p. 295 n. 175.
[19] Comotti (1983).

by ancient musicologists, especially in North America, and with an eye to ancient Mesopotamia.

Despite his interest in the imbrication of music and ethics in ancient thinking, he has little to say about ancient education. Characteristically, what arouses his interest in the subject at all is when it is pitched in the highest of intellectual settings, namely when he reconstructs the context of Porphyry's commentary on Ptolemy's *Harmonics*. This he locates in groups of intellectuals who congregated around a master to hear him expound an acknowledged classic, and perhaps contribute aperçus of their own (2015a, chs 6, 7). (One struggles to banish the thoughts of the students and scholars surrounding Barker in the meeting room in Corfu, expounding texts he knew better than anyone alive. Patience and humility were perhaps less characteristic of Porphyry.) In general, there is a limited interest in social context—but it is largely beside the point to complain when a scholar resolves not to move into an already overpopulated field, especially that of 5th-century performance culture (the symposium gets a mention, but only *apropos* of a discussion of Dicaearchus as musical historian: 2014b, p. 78). Insofar as he wanted to engage with these questions at all, the Corfiote Summer Schools gave him some prompts to do so. Two articles, one on the festivals of Larisa, the other on 2nd-century Teos (2010–11, 2011b) show that he could do Hellenistic epigraphy with the best of them, extracting insights about the place of performers and performance in specific cities, and what it says about their sense of identity and self-promotion. There was little enough to be said, anyway, about the boorish Romans (2002b, chs 6, 7), but there is a surprising, almost antiquarian, article about imperial voice-trainers (2010d).

These contributions are fairly incidental in his larger oeuvre, but they are enough to blunt any criticism that his approach was too 'ideal', too abstract, too intellectual.[20] He had called (2002b, p. 81) for greater integration of the study of music theorists, composers, performers, teachers, instrument-makers, and critics, and he did much, partly through personal example but above all through the facilitating effect of his meetings, summer schools, and conferences, to advance those ends. He well understood that his field was nothing if not multi-disciplinary, and called for an approach which combined linguistic and lexical analysis with historical vision and understanding of the *Realien* of instruments, which includes the evidence of iconography. When Stefan Hagel's *Ancient Greek Music* (Hagel 2009), achieved precisely such a synthesis, uniting 'practical musicianship, historically informed musicology, and sound textual criticism',[21] he read the book in draft and gave high praise even—indeed, especially—to its revisions of Barker's own

---

[20] The allusion in 2007a, p. 4, to American colleagues who chided him for a 'lack of a properly musicological perspective' looks to Jon Solomon's reviews of 1984c and 1989a. But this controversy in fact had its source elsewhere, and Solomon would subsequently acknowledge the unique strengths of Barker's own approach. They are pictured happily together in Pöhlmann (2019), fig. 4.

[21] Mahoney (2010), p. 157.

earlier views. His contributions on the *aulos* stopped short of the instrument's technical structure—though he applied his historical imagination to performance, as in his rather brilliant idea about staging the nightingale in Aristophanes' *Birds* as the official piper of the whole play (2004b, p. 203).[22] But his agenda and method were wholly distinctive and, over the span of his career, undeviating. He firmly placed himself among the musicologists whose interests lay, not primarily in the reconstruction of ancient music-making, but in 'the sciences themselves, considered as modes of intellectual enquiry', where the task lay in seeking 'to extract an intelligible account of the authors' objectives' (2020a, p. 258), one that was both historically grounded and philosophically committed.

His Oxford training had furnished him with the requisite technical skills. In many ways the most impressive of these is the ability to extract sense from ancient prose that technical terms and abstract expressions render opaque to the point of incomprehensibility. In the second volume of *Greek Musical Writings* (1989a) he made many such treatises available in English, several for the first time. He was helped by unpublished materials which Winnington-Ingram, who had planned but never published a translation and commentary on Aristides Quintilianus, had shared with him. But the achievement remains awe-inspiring. Most importantly this volume contained the first complete English translation of the three volumes of Ptolemy's *Harmonics* (there had been a German one by Ingemar Düring in 1934, and there would be another in English by Jon Solomon in 2000). Other English 'firsts' included the surviving fragment of the second book of Aristoxenus' *Elementa Rhythmica*, and musicological extracts from Theon of Smyrna's 'Mathematics useful for reading Plato' (preserving useful excerpts from earlier theorists) and Nicomachus' *Enchiridion*. Aristides Quintilianus was already available, but Barker himself had written a review (1984b) which devastatingly exposed the translation's linguistic failings (this is the most vitriolic thing he ever wrote; apparently he had not foreseen the furore that ensued, but what prompted it was a philological incompetence that was simply beyond the pale). Parts of Porphyry's commentary on Ptolemy already appeared in this volume, but would be superseded in 2015 by a new, complete translation for Cambridge (again, the first complete translation into English—and probably only the second *ever*, after John Wallis' *Porphyrii in Harmonica Ptolemaei commentarius* (1699)).[23] Difficulties with this text go well beyond niceties about the rendering of technical terms. Porphyry's language is compressed and sometimes abstract to the point of impenetrability, and Barker passes over the astonishing feat of rendering

---

[22] Surprising, but not astonishing, to those who knew him: he was not a great theatre-goer, but did visit Stratford from time to time, including after Finals with friends in the White Elephant, his enormous white Daimler.

[23] Though there was an almost simultaneous Italian one with whose author, Massimo Raffa (2016), he exchanged ideas.

it into intelligible English prose (equipped with generous annotations) with characteristic lack of fanfare.

The translation of Porphyry was accompanied, at the prompting of Michael Sharp at Cambridge University Press, by a text and critical apparatus which included emendations proposed in the scholarly literature since the previous edition (Ingemar Düring, 1932) as well as some of his own. He claimed to lack the expertise to carry out any fresh manuscript collations,[24] although textual coherence was of course essential to his commitment to accuracy and intelligibility. He would probe carefully at individual words to establish possible senses and rule out illegitimate ones. Many of his articles, especially the early ones, take the form of talking the reader through an extract, sometimes breaking it down into a series of lemmata in each of which textual and interpretative problems are discussed, leaving, at the end, a sense of calm and clear rationality (1977b, 1978b, 1981a, 1982b, 1987) and of the intellectual context and philosophical stakes. One article talks us through a difficult papyrus fragment which seems to be discussing modulations, that is, compositional manoeuvres in actual melodies (1994c). We have not seen him in this sub-field before, but no-one should have been surprised that the great-nephew of the papyrologist Arthur Hunt was able to propose such convincing restorations. That relationship, in fact, was the reason for the family's connection with Queen's; and one is rather relieved that family history worked itself out thus, rather than the young Barker succumbing, as his mother had once wished, to the lure of Hunt and Hunt Solicitors, LLP.

Some of these close-focus discussions involve quoted excerpts of earlier authors; in such cases, defining the precise extent of the quotation must precede the elucidation of its context. Careful and rigorous *Quellenforschung* extracted fragments of Archytas from Ptolemy (1994a), data about ancient musicians from Aristides Quintilianus (1982b), Heraclides and Aristoxenus from ps.-Plutarch (2009d, 2012a), and teased apart different sources in the pseudo-Aristotelian *Problemata* through their differing conceptions of pitch (2015b). A *tour de force* of source criticism is to be had in the chapter in *Psicomusicologia* on Aristides Quintilianus (2005b, ch. 8), expounding Aristides' view of the therapeutic possibilities of music through the configuration of our souls themselves. Aristides here pulls together a medley of sources including Pythagorean metaphysics, Platonism, Aristoxenic theory, the contributions of grammarians, and solmisation which probably goes back to the practice of music teachers, all in the service of a poetic conception of the descent of the soul through the cosmos as it becomes embodied in us. Barker rises to the poetry with an address to the reader in the style of a 19th-century novel (pp. 154–5)—one of the rare concessions in his academic prose to

---

[24] 2015a, p. 56 (unlike his 17th-century Queen's predecessors: see n. 11). Raffa's Teubner edition (2016) offers a fresh study of the manuscript tradition.

the stylistic lusters that he knew well how to conjure outside of it. At the end, though, he steps back and quietly, dispassionately, tells us precisely why, even as a myth, it will not do.

Reviewers comment repeatedly on the clarity of his writing, and students wanted to study with him on account of it. The word describes his whole project, the pains he took to get difficult material to make textual and historical and philosophical sense. But it also applies to a deliberate accessibility of style. He can and does, of course, play the scholarly game, but even when an essay or a book originated in lectures for specialist audiences the eventual publication is designed to be readable by non-specialists; Greek is translated, technical concepts patiently explained. Many pieces are sparsely footnoted, and bear the marks of their oral origin in a chatty style ('we'll come back to it'). But the sparse footnoting also reflects another attitude. Footnotes are often weaponised, and Barker did not do polemic. Or else he simply could not be bothered with the conventional rigmarole, and just wanted to cut straight to the argument (2000b, p. 4).

To repeat: the interests and methods stay constant, and there were certain things he did not change his mind about (such as his low estimation of Aristotle, or at least, of Aristotle's treatment of concordance and dissonance, and why we perceive them both as we do). But on small points, on matters of interpretation, he was extremely ready to change his mind and correct himself. There are countless occasions where he returns to an earlier publication to propose a new translation of difficult Greek, or to disagree with an earlier suggestion, and in one late article (2016a), recanting his earlier view of a difficult passage concerning musical notation, he reflects on the difference between politicians and scholars whose duty to intellectual truth positively requires them to set down their shifts of opinion and correct their errors. The first impression of course is one of intellectual scrupulousness. But equally important is the implication that he conceived of his whole corpus of work as an oeuvre, a single intellectual project which grows and ramifies, but remains 'live' (an interestingly different attitude from that of Martin West, who, with characteristic certitude, said his say, and moved on). And because the work is a corpus that is, as it were, hanging in suspension, always ready to be recrystallised, never definitive, he is characteristically modest in urging his conclusions. These are often provisional, because they have to be. Reviewers were sometimes infuriated by what they saw as hedging (2010b, p. 118: 'Perhaps that is too fragile a hypothesis, and I would not go to the stake for it'; 2012b, p. 311: 'It seems a fairly feeble hypothesis, but I have nothing more illuminating to say about the matter'). But scrupulousness required it, and Barker left posturing and bravado to the politicians.

He was dialoguing with himself and his past views, but also with an increasing number of scholars, continental and transatlantic. The field, he would remark in his later pieces, was much more tenanted than when he had first entered it in the late

1970s,[25] partly with his own students, or younger colleagues whose interests he had fostered. And yet it remains the case even now that there are no Andrew clones. There are ethnomusicologists, organologists, cultural historians, historians of performance, practising performers, and early music specialists aplenty. There are students, too, of ancient harmonics, taking interest in modality and tunings and notation, and there are those who approach the subject from a scientific point of view; and yet the *philosophy* of ancient harmonics, the interface between music theory and epistemology and meta-physics, remains essentially his field. At the same time, he made it all seem so easy, as if, once you have a field and a method, all the rest follows naturally; the absence of any-one to fill his shoes is proof to the contrary. Thought took place at the highest level, was abstract—but never theoretical. He was never waylaid by structuralism, let alone what succeeded it, although at one point he makes an intriguing suggestion that a Vernant-type approach might have some light to shed on the reasons why ancient musicology burgeoned in south Italy, Tarentum in particular (1989b, p. 173).

And despite, or rather because of, the historical contingency of his subject, there is much in his writing that is suggestive about the apprehension of all music, any music. We are so conditioned by the metaphors we use that they seem rooted in reality, but why should music go 'up' or 'down' a scale, or a stave? Our ears are conditioned, too, by the tunings we use; a pianist's ears differ from those of a string or wind player (1984a, p. 61), and, as it happens, equal temperament is the product of a compromise that Aristoxenus could have handled but a Pythagorean would abhor. Aristoxenus—any Greek—would have classified a third as a discord, but we do not, and it turns out, even if only by acci-dent, that Ptolemy's approach to types of ratio involved in concords can handle this better than any other ancient theory (2000b, pp. 81–2). On the other hand, it was Aristoxenus who had the wit to conceive music in a dynamic way; he knew that when we apprehend music it is not as decontextualised sounds in an endless succession of moments, but that we simultaneously process and make sense of it by importing our predictive knowledge of structures and sequences (1984a, p. 62). In the old head-to-head of Aristoxenus and Pythagoras, Barker would not only have resisted taking sides, but would have challenged the dichotomy. His combination, however, of intellectualised music theory with non-standard lifestyle choice—he and Jill did flirt with vegetarianism for a few years, and he once wrote a story for his youngest son about a vegetarian wolf—is suggestive;[26] and Warwick colleagues remember him once winning hands-down a balloon debate in the persona of Pythagoras, complete with home-made kithara.

---

[25] The first edition of Egert Pöhlmann's collection of documents had appeared at the beginning of the decade (Pöhlmann 1970), but those texts on music theory were still inaccessible to anyone without the requisite command of difficult and very technical Greek.

[26] Thanks to Professor Angie Hobbs for this suggestion.

III

There is an image of Barker early at the breakfast table in Corfu with his Oxford Classical Text, never less than polite but clearly not wanting to be disturbed.[27] It is remarkable that the publications never flagged when his life was so rich in so many other ways, with family and 'grounded' things (a series of dogs, not to mention unruly goats, gardening, (re-)wilding, building, DIY, and a sideline as an effective swing bowler), alongside the world of ideas. He seems to have had a serene ability to ring-fence his time. Mornings of vigorous work on home-improvement with sledgehammers were succeeded by quiet time covering dozens of note-pads in a small hand as he worked late into the night. The serenity and concentration that observers noted translated into quiet certitude and self-belief, whose corollary was total impatience with scholarly inadequacy and false pretension.

Natural history and a love of the natural world did not leave him (he was a member of the Green Party). His children recall trips with him collecting wild plants. He goes on a series of day-trips exploring the country around Dunedin (New Year, 1994–5), clambering over rocks, admiring the geology, leaving a series of meticulous written observations of penguins, seabirds, and seals, recalling his time studying evolutionary biology. Some are recorded in watercolours, too, which capture the motion of the gulls and the sharp edges of their wings against the clouds; he was an accomplished painter, not only of landscape and wildlife, but of human subjects as well. In 2000 he and Jill bought a barn in a rural district in Le Chezeau, in the Département de l'Indre, in central France. Two years later they added the farmhouse cottage next door. Restoring the barn, concreting the floor, fixing the plumbing, installing windows and doors and interior walls, was a major project. It was also a bolt-hole. Looking at his career, one can only wonder how family life, children and a burgeoning tribe of grandchildren, squared with such productivity. The barn was part of the answer, even if, at least in the early days, papers had to be written by gas lamp beset with moths. Solitude came readily to one so independent and self-reliant. He would spend months there at a time, driving down from France for his seminars in southern Europe. He wrote letters back to his family calling it a 'desirable bachelor pad', and describing the surrounding countryside, which was not spectacular, but populated with buzzards, red kites, violets—and butterflies, which he continued to observe and document with a naturalist's eye.[28]

Needing to illustrate the Aristotelian concept of matter as it applies to music (that is, sound in quantitative terms, as opposed to the form which supplies its nature, structure,

---

[27] Rocconi & Pöhlmann (2022), 9.

[28] Forty-one species, as he informed an old schoolfriend, trouncing the latter's pathetic claim to have spotted a mere eighteen.

and potential to develop)—he uses dandelions (1991c, p. 150), frogs and buttercups (1991c, p. 155), rose-buds, buttercups—and camels (2005a, p. 183). Kangaroos (2000b, p. 7) were perhaps prompted by the view from his window in the University of Queensland, where he was spending a sabbatical term. Just days before he was taken into Warwick hospital—where he died on 22 July 2021 from broncho-pneumonia, his immune system weakened after years of cancer treatment—he was documenting a cylindrical object with a flaky green integument which turned out to be the nesting-tube constructed by a leaf-cutter bee in a rug on the corner of his bed. He wrote occasional verse and prose with a pitch-perfect ear (what else would one expect?) for literary parody—another partial similarity with Martin West.[29] There are poems that bucket along with Belloc. There is a Chaucer skit. There is an astonishingly accomplished Pope pastiche for Griff's 85th birthday, and even better still, Egert Pöhlmann woke up on his 80th birthday to find a tribute in elegiac couplets (ἄνδρα μοι ἔννεπε, ΜΟΙΣΑ) posted on the MOISA website. There is a brilliant parody in which the Psalmist—Barker, after a bad day in the barn—magnifies the Lord Which hath given us wasps, hornets, brambles, and spared us only Japanese knotweed. Yet he also has a first-person voice of penetrating directness. He contemplates time, old age, and curtailed powers. The poem read out at the funeral consists of a series of plain, sharp observations in free verse concerning the natural world (moths, buzzards, and pelicans), or rather, reflections on seeing it through sharp young eyes and through aged ones.

Above all there was music. He was taught piano by his maternal grandmother, and kept that up in later life. The large Georgian family home in St Mary's Road, Leamington, housed four pianos, a clavichord, and a loaned harpsichord. But he would turn his hand to almost anything capable of producing sound, including bottles and blades of grass.[30] Bagpipes, however—despite a certain transferability between them and the reeded ancient *aulos*—he loathed.

By universal consensus he had a lovely voice, which he first put to good effect in the choir at Christ's Hospital, learning to sing Anglican chant, complete with pointing. He also learned to sight-read, which he did immaculately. Later he recalled with pride how he had progressed through all parts beginning as a treble. Oxford contemporaries recall him singing alto, but it was as a graduate in Canberra that he started to take singing more seriously, both as tenor and alto; his first wife, Susan, herself a fine soprano, coached him on the use of the head voice. During his time in Australia, he and she founded a small *a capella* chamber choir, The University Consort, performing madrigals and mediaeval and Renaissance music. They sang cathedral repertoire in church choirs, and one Good Friday they performed Tallis' Lamentations of Jeremiah during a three-hour vigil at

---

[29] Lightfoot (2017), pp. 290–1.
[30] Rocconi & Pöhlmann (2022), 10.

St Paul's Church, Manuka, out of sight and on their knees—a memorable occasion. They also provided the chorus for an unabridged performance of Purcell's King Arthur, for which the philosophy department built a lifting platform so that Venus could arise from the waves—but put the gearing in back to front so that frantic efforts were required for Venus to move at all. He also performed Schubert and Schumann Lieder. He entered, and reportedly won, a singing-contest in Canberra, where the adjudicator told him he had an excellent lyric tenor voice and had a great future singing in that style. In later life, however, his voice matured downwards and there is a video clip of him singing the Seikilos song in a distinctly baritone register. In a particular performance of Dichterliebe in middle age in New Zealand, he flunked the high A in *Ich Grolle Nicht*, and took the optional lower line Schumann provides, which he would not have done a few years before. The judge was disappointed, but did still award him and his son Michael first prize.

His musical tastes were broad church. He especially loved Monteverdi (whose madrigals and Vespers he sang with the University of Warwick Consort), Bach, Mozart, and Purcell (whom he also sang, accompanied by Michael). It is no particular surprise that a man who wrote extensively about ancient beliefs that music had a therapeutic function, and simultaneously had a beautiful counter-tenor voice and loved Baroque music, loved, and did a beautiful rendering of, Purcell's Music For A While. But his tastes were more catholic than that suggests, and than might have been suggested by his studies of highly rule-bound ancient theory. Whether it was interesting, performed proficiently, and coherent: those were the essential criteria. In later years he particularly came to love Berlioz, and his LP set of *Les Troyens* was well worn. He was always open to new musical experiences, for which the radio was a good source—and yet was able to pitch his concentration at such a high level that the radio would not distract him while he worked. Or else it gave him ideas. An essay on the *Philebus* takes Lucia Popp, who was singing the Queen of the Night while he was drafting the conclusion, as a figure for Socrates' point about the trained instincts of the professional musician, and the potential to achieve excellence even by stochastic means (1996, p. 161). The opening music of his funeral was the sonata for Viola Da Gamba and Harpsichord, BWV 1029. An alternative choice might have been the Art of Fugue, which Bach wrote in open score, without instrumentation, a construct in the theoretician's head—music almost too pure to be heard.

Acknowledgements:
Because the author of this memoir never met her subject, she drew very widely on the recollections of people who knew him across the various stages of his career, and thanks them for their remarkable generosity and trust: Michael, Kate, and Jill Barker; Christopher Rowe; Susan Forster; Alan Bowman; Malcolm Schofield; David Sedley; Rebecca Naylor

(Archivist of the Cambridge Classics Faculty); Penelope Murray; Angie Hobbs; Christine Battersby; Martin Warner; Rowland Cotterill; Robert Hannah; Ken Dowden; Zacharoula Petraki; David Creese; Will Mack; Angelo Meriani; Eleonora Rocconi; Armand D'Angour; Tosca Lynch. She also thanks Will Poole for drawing her attention to the Queen's connection.

Note on the author: J.L. Lightfoot is Professor of Greek Literature and Fellow and Tutor in Classics at New College, Oxford. She was elected a Fellow of the British Academy in 2018.

References

Bowman, A. & Goodman, M. (2021), 'Fergus Millar', *Biographical Memoirs of Fellows of the British Academy*, 20, 25–50.

Comotti, G. (1983), 'Un'antica arpa, la *magadis*, in un frammento di Teleste (fr. 808P)', *Quaderni Urbinati di Cultura Classica*, 15, 57–71.

Fowler, R. (2018), 'Martin Litchfield West', *Biographical Memoirs of Fellows of the British Academy*, XVII, 89–120.

Hagel, S. (2009), *Ancient Greek Music: A New Technical History* (Cambridge: Cambridge University Press).

Lightfoot, J.L. (2017), 'Martin Litchfield West', *Proceedings of the American Philosophical Society*, 161(3), 285–92.

Mack, W. (2021), *CUCD* Bulletin 50. https://cucd.blogs.sas.ac.uk/bulletin/

Mahoney, A. (2010), rev. of Hagel 2009, *The Classical Outlook*, 87(4), 156–7.

Pöhlmann, E. (1970), *Denkmäler altgriechischer Musik: Sammlung, Übertragung und Erlauterung aller Fragmente und Fälschungen* (Nuremberg: H. Carl).

Pöhlmann, E. (2019), 'Fifteen Years of Enquiries in Ancient Greek and Roman Music (2004–2018): The Seminars in Corfu (Greece) and Riva del Garda (Italy)', *Greek and Roman Musical Studies*, 7, 1–20.

Poole, W. (2018), 'A royalist mathematical practitioner in interregnum Oxford: the exploits of Richard Rawlinson (1616–1668)', *The Seventeenth Century*. https://doi.org/10.1080/0268117X.2017.1410216.

Raffa, M. (2016), *Claudio Tolemeo, Armonica: Con il Commentario di Porfirio: Testo greco a fronte: Saggio introduttivo, traduzione, note e apparati* (Milan: Bompiani).

Rocconi, E. & Pöhlmann, E. (2022), 'Tribute to Andrew Barker', *Greek and Roman Musical Studies*, 10, 3–14.

West, M.L. (1992), *Ancient Greek Music* (Oxford: Oxford University Press).

West, M.L. (1994), 'Reginald Pepys Winnington-Ingram, 1904–1993', *Proceedings of the British Academy*, 84, 579–97.

Winnington-Ingram, R.P. (1932), 'Aristoxenus and the intervals of Greek Music', *Classical Quarterly*, 26, 195–208.

Winnington-Ingram, R.P. (1936), *Mode in Ancient Greek Music* (Cambridge: Cambridge University Press).

Writings of Andrew Barker

(1976), 'The digression in the *Theaetetus*', *Journal of the History of Philosophy*, 14(4), 457–62.

(1977a), 'Why did Socrates refuse to escape?', *Phronesis*, 13–28.

(1977b), 'Music and mathematics: Theophrastus against the number-theorists', *Proceedings of the Cambridge Philological Society*, 23, 1–15.

(1978a), 'οἱ καλούμενοι ἁρμονικοί: The predecessors of Aristoxenus', *Proceedings of the Cambridge Philological Society*, 204, 1–21.

(1978b), '*Symphōnoi arithmoi*: A note on *Republic* 531 C 1–4', *Classical Philology*, 18, 337–42.

(1978c), 'Music and perception: A study in Aristoxenus', *Journal of Hellenic Studies*, 98, 9–16.

(1981a), 'Aristotle on perception and ratios', *Phronesis*, 26, 248–66.

(1981b), 'Methods and aims in the Euclidean Sectio canonis', *Journal of Hellenic Studies*, 101, 1–16.

(1982a), 'Aristides Quintilianus and constructions in early music theory', *Classical Quarterly*, 32, 184–97.

(1982b), 'The innovations of Lysander the kitharist', *Classical Quarterly*, 32, 266–9.

(1984a), 'Aristoxenus' theorems and the foundations of harmonic science', *Ancient Philosophy*, 4, 23–64.

(1984b), Review of T.J. Mathiesen, *On music in three books: Transl. with introduction, commentary & annotations* (Yale, 1983), in *Ancient Philosophy*, IV, 255–62.

(1984c), *Greek Musical Writings*, 1. *The Musician and His Art* (Cambridge: Cambridge University Press).

(1985), 'Theophrastus on pitch and melody', in W.W. Fortenbaugh *et al.* (eds), *Theophrastus of Eresus: On his Life and Work* (New Brunswick: Transaction Books), pp. 289–324.

(1987), 'Text and sense at *Philebus* 56a', *Classical Quarterly*, 37, 103–9.

(1988a), 'Che cos'era "la magadis"?', in B. Gentili & R. Pretagostini (eds), *La musica in Grecia: Atti del Convegno internazionale sulla musica greca, Urbino, 18-20 ott. 1985* (Rome: Laterza), pp. 96–107.

(1988b), 'Le fonti della antica musica greca', in F. Berti *et al.* (eds), *Lo Specchio della Musica: Iconografia musicale nella ceramica attica di Spina* (Bologna: Nuova Alfa), pp. 9–17.

(1989a), *Greek Musical Writings*, vol. 2. *Harmonic and Acoustic Theory* (Cambridge: Cambridge University Press).

(1989b), 'Archita di Taranto e l'armonica pitagorica', *Annali dell'Università degli Studi di Napoli 'L'Orientale' / Dipartimento di Studi del Mondo Classico e del Mediterraneo Antico. Sezione Filologico-Letteraria*, XI, 159–78.

(1991a), 'Three approaches to canonic division', in I. Mueller (ed.), Περι τῶν μαθημάτων: *Peri ton mathematon = Apeiron*, 24(4), 49–83.

(1991b), 'Aristoxenus' harmonics and Aristotle's theory of science', in A.C. Bowen (ed.), *Science and philosophy in classical Greece* (New York: Garland), pp. 188–226.

(1991c), 'Plato and Aristoxenus on the nature of *melos*', in C. Burnett *et al.* (eds), *The second sense: Studies in Hearing and Musical Judgement from antiquity to the seventh century* (London: Warburg Institute), pp. 137–60.

(1991d), 'Reason and perception in Ptolemy's *Harmonics*', in R.W. Wallace & B.C. MacLachlan (eds), *Harmonia Mundi: Music e filosofia nell'antichità* (Rome: Edizioni dell'Ateneo), pp. 104–30.

(1994a), 'Ptolemy's Pythagoreans, Archytas, and Plato's conception of mathematics', *Phronesis*, 39(2), 113–35.

(1994b), 'Greek musicologists in the Roman Empire', in T.D. Barnes (ed.), *The sciences in Greco-Roman Society* (Edmonton: Academic Printing & Publishing), pp. 53–74.

(1994c), 'An Oxyrhynchus fragment on harmonic theory', *Classical Quarterly*, 44, 75–84.

(1995a), 'Problems in the Charmides', *Prudentia*, 27(2), 18–33.

(1995b), 'Heterophonia and poikilia: Accompaniments to Greek melody', in B. Gentili & F. Perusino (eds), *MOUSIKE: metrica ritmica e musica greca: In memoria di Giovanni Comotti* (Pisa: Istituti editoriali e poligrafici internazionali), pp. 41–60.

(1996), 'Plato's *Philebus*: The numbering of a unity', *Apeiron*, 29(4), 143–64.

(1998), 'Telestes and the "five-rodded joining of strings"', *Classical Quarterly*, 48(1), 75–81.

(1999), 'Shifting frontiers in ancient theories of metaphor', *Proceedings of the Cambridge Philological Society*, 45, 1–16.

(2000a), 'Timaeus on music and the liver', in M.R. Wright (ed.), *Reason and Necessity: Essays on Platos' Timaeus* (Swansea: Duckworth and the Classical Press of Wales), pp. 85–99.

(2000b), *Scientific Method in Ptolemy's Harmonics* (Cambridge: Cambridge University Press).

(2000c), 'Athenaeus on Music', in D. C. Braund and J. Wilkins (eds) *Athenaeus and his world: Reading Greek culture in the Roman Empire* (Exeter: University of Exeter Press), pp. 434–44.

(2000d), 'Diabolus in musica', *Classical Review*, 50, 168–70.

(2001a), 'Armonia', in *Storia della Scienza*, 1, ed. S. Petruccioli (Rome: Istituto della Enciclopedia Italiana), 909–26.

(2001b), 'Diogenes of Babylon and Hellenistic musical theory', in C. Auvray-Assayas & D. Delattre (eds), *Cicéron et Philodème* (Paris: Rue d'Ulm), pp. 353–70.

(2001c), 'La musica di Stesicoro', *Quaderni Urbinati di Cultura Classica*, 67, 7–20.

(2002a), 'Words for sounds', in C.J. Tuplin & T.E. Rihll (eds), *Science and mathematics in ancient Greek culture* (Oxford: Oxford University Press), pp. 22–35.

(2002b), *Euterpe: ricerche sulla musica greca e romana* (Pisa: Edizioni ETS).

(2003a), 'Early *Timaeus* commentaries and Hellenistic musicology', in R.W. Sharples & A. Sheppard (eds), *Ancient Approaches to Plato's Timaeus* (London: Institute of Classical Studies), pp. 73–87.

(2003b), 'Lullaby for an eagle (Pindar, *Pythian* 1)', in T.W. Wiedemann & K. Dowden (eds), *Sleep* (Bari: Levante), pp. 107–24.

(2004a), 'Theophrastus and Aristoxenus: Confusions in musical metaphysics', *Bulletin of the Institute of Classical Studies*, 47, 101–17.

(2004b), 'Transforming the nightingale: Aspects of Athenian musical discourse in the late fifth century', in P. Murray & P.J. Wilson (eds), *Music and the Muses: the culture of mousikē in the classical Athenian city* (Oxford: Oxford University Press), pp. 185–204.

(2005a), 'The journeying voice: Melody and metaphysics in Aristoxenian science', *Apeiron*, 38(3), 161–84.

(2005b), *Psicomusicologia nella Grecia antica* (Naples: Guida).

(2005c), 'Ptolemy's musical models for mind-maps and star-maps', in C. Cheyne & J. Worrall (eds), *Rationality and reality: Conversations with Alan Musgrave* (Dordrecht: Springer), pp. 1–19.

(2006a), 'Archytas unbound: A discussion of Carl A. Huffman, Archytas of Tarentum', *Oxford Studies in Ancient Philosophy*, 31, 297–321.

(2006b), 'On the receiving end: The hidden protagonist of Plato's *Laches*', in D. Spencer & E. Theodorakopoulos (eds), *Advice and its rhetoric in Greece and Rome* (Bari: Levante), pp. 31–46.

(2006c), 'Music', 'Musical Instruments', 'Sound and acoustics', in G. Shipley, J. Vanderspoel, D. Mattingly & L. Foxhall (eds), *The Cambridge dictionary of classical civilization* (Cambridge: Cambridge University Press), pp. 596–8, 598–9, 835.

(2007a), *The Science of Harmonics in Classical Greece* (Cambridge: Cambridge University Press).

(2007b), 'Simbolismo musicale nell' "Elena" di Euripide', in P. Volpe Cacciatore (ed.), *Musica e generi letterari nella Grecia di età classica: Atti del II Congresso Consulta Universitaria Greco (Fisciano, 1 dicembre 2006)* (Naples: Arte tipografica), pp. 7–22.

(2007c), 'Uses and abuses of comedy in the study of Greek musical aesthetics', *Musica e Storia*, 15, 221–42.

(2007d), 'Aristoxène et les critères du jugement musical', in A.G. Wersinger & F. Malhomme (eds), *Mousikè et aretè: La musique et l'éthique de l'antiquité à l'âge moderne. Actes du colloque international tenu en Sorbonne les 15-17 décembre 2003* (Paris: Librairie philosophique J. Vrin), pp. 63–75.

(2009a), 'Shifting conceptions of "schools" of harmonic theory, 400 BC–200 AD', in M.C. Martinelli; con la collab. di Francesco Pelosi & Carlo Pernigotti (eds), *La Musa dimenticata: Aspetti dell'esperienza musicale greca in età ellenistica* (Pisa: Edizioni della Normale), pp. 165–90.

(2009b), 'Musical theory and philosophy: The case of Archestratus', *Phronesis*, 54(4–5), 390–422.

(2009c), 'Ptolemy and the meta-helikôn', *Studies in the History and Philosophy of Science*, 40(4), 344–51.

(2009d), 'Heraclides and musical history', in W. W. Fortenbaugh and E. Pender (eds), *Heraclides of Pontus: Discussion* (New Brunswick and London: Transaction Publishers), pp. 273–98.

(2009e), 'Adrasto e l'altezza: Un argomento eccentrico e il suo contesto intellettuale', in D. Castaldo, D. Restani & C. Tassi (eds), *Il sapere musicale e i suoi contesti da Teofrasto a Claudio Tolemeo* (Ravenna: Longo), pp. 43–56.

(2010a), 'Mathematical beauty made audible: Musical aesthetics in Ptolemy's "Harmonics"', *Classical Philology*, 105(4), 403–20.

(2010b), 'The music of Pan in Hellenistic pastoral poetry', in M. Silvana Celentano, F. Berardi, L. Bravi & P. Di Meo (eds), *Ricerche di metrica e musica greca per Roberto Pretagostini* (Alessandria: Edizioni dell'Orso), pp. 105–19.

(2010c), 'The Music of the Muses', *Vis: Rivista do Programma de Pós-Graduaçâo em Arte da Universidade de Brasilia*, 9(2), 11–19.

(2010d), 'Phōnaskia per cantanti e oratori: La cura e l'esercizio della voce nel periodo imperiale romano / Phōnaskia for singers and orators: The care and training of the voice in the Roman imperial period', in E. Rocconi (ed.), *La musica nell'Impero Romano: Testimonianze teoriche e scoperte archeologiche = Music in the Roman Empire: Theoretical Evidence and Archaeological Findings* (Pavia: Pavia University Press), pp. 11–20.

(2010e), '*Laws* Paper 1'; '*Laws* Paper 2'. https://conferences.ionio.gr/sagrm/2010/en/proceedings

(2010–11), 'Festivals at Larisa in the second and first centuries BC', *Rudiae*, 22–23(1), 15–27.

(2011a), 'The music of Olympus', *Quaderni Urbinati di Cultura Classica*, 99, 43–57.

(2011b), 'Music, politics, and diplomacy in Hellenistic Teos', in D. Yatromanolakis (ed.), *Music and cultural politics in Greek and Chinese societies, 1, Greek antiquity* (Cambridge: Cambridge University Press), pp. 159–79.

(2011c), 'Aristotle *Politics* Book VIII, Introduction'; 'Aristotle *Politics* Book VIII, Part 1'. https://conferences.ionio.gr/sagrm/2011/en/proceedings

(2012a), 'Did Aristoxenus write musical history?', in C.A. Huffman (ed.), *Aristoxenus of Tarentum: Discussion* (New Brunswick and London: Transaction Publishers), pp. 1–27.

(2012b), 'Aristoxenus and the early Academy', op. cit. pp. 297–324.

(2012c), 'Τὰ μουσικά όργανα στην αρχαία ελληνική γραμματεία', in A. Goulaki-Voutyra (ed.), Ελληνικά Μουσικά Όργανα: Αναζητήσεις σε εικαστικές και γραμματειακές μαρτυρίες (2000 π.Χ.-2000 μ.Χ.) (Thessaloniki: Τελλόγλειο Ίδρυμα Τεχνών), pp. 31–9.

(2013), 'The *Laws* and Aristoxenus on the critera of musical judgement', in A.-E. Peponi (ed.), *Performance and Culture in Plato's Laws* (Cambridge: Cambridge University Press), pp. 392–416.

(2014a), 'Greek musical theorists on the sound of speech', *Annali della Scuola Normale Superiore di Pisa, Classe di Lettere e Filosofia*, ser. 5a, 6(2), 657–79.

(2014b), *Ancient Greek Writers on their Musical Past: Studies in Greek Musical Historiography* (Pisa: Fabrizio Serra editore).

(2014c), 'Pythagorean harmonics', in C.A. Huffman (ed.), *A History of Pythagoreanism* (Cambridge: Cambridge University Press), pp. 185–203.

(2014d), 'Empedocles Mousikos', in A. Bellia, *Musica, culti e riti nell' Occidente greco* (Pisa: Istituti editoriali e poligrafici internazionali), pp. 87–94.

(2015a), *Porphyry's Commentary on Ptolemy's Harmonics: A Greek Text and Annotated Translation* (Cambridge: Cambridge University Press).

(2015b), 'Musical Pitch and the Enigmatic Octave in *Problemata* 19', in R. Mayhew (ed.), *The Aristotelian Problemata Physica: Philosophical and Scientific Investigations* (Leiden: Brill), pp. 226–54.

(2015c), 'Aristoxenus', 'Didymus (3)', 'Porphyry: Porphyry's music theory', in S. Hornblower, A. Spawforth & E. Eidinow (eds), *The Oxford Classical Dictionary*, 4th edn, online version.

(2016a), 'Aristoxenus *Harm.* 2, 49, 1–50, 18 Da Rios: A recantation', in *Greek and Roman Musical Studies*, 4(1), 90–10.

(2016b), 'Tribute to Martin Litchfield West, 1937–2015', *Greek and Roman Musical Studies*, 4(1), 3–9.

(2016c), 'Plutarch, *Quaestiones convivales*, 704 C 4–705 B 6: The Host and the Musician', in A. Meriani, L. Lomiento, L. Bravi & G. Pace (eds), *Tra lyra e aulos: Tradizioni musicali e generi poetici* (Pisa: Fabrizio Serra editore), pp. 15–28.

(2016d), 'Pythagoreans and Medical Writers on Periods of Human Gestation', in A.-B. Renger & A. Stavru (eds), *Pythagorean Knowledge from the Ancient to the Modern World: Askesis, Religion, Science* (Wiesbaden: Harrassowitz Verlag), pp. 263–75.

(2017), 'Dionysius of Halicarnassus on Rome's Greek musical heritage', *Greek and Roman Musical Studies*, 5(1), 63–81.

(2018a), 'Disreputable Music: A Performance, a Defence, and their Intertextual and Intermedial Resonances (Plutarch *Quaest. conv.* 704 C 4–705 B 6)', in A. d'Angour & T. Phillips (eds), *Music, Text, and Culture in Ancient Greece* (Oxford: Oxford University Press), pp. 233–56.

(2018b), 'Greek acoustic theory: Simple and complex sounds', in S. Nooter & S. Butler (eds), *Sound and the Ancient Senses* (London: Routledge), pp. 92–108.

(2018c), 'Migrating musical myths: The case of Euripides and the Libyan *Aulos*', *Greek and Roman Musical Studies*, 6(1), (2018), 1–13.

(2020a), 'Harmonics', in T.A.C. Lynch & E. Rocconi (eds), *A Companion to Ancient Greek and Roman Music* (Hoboken NY: Wiley-Blackwell), pp. 257–74.

(2020b), 'Shifting epistemological perspectives in Ptolemy's *Harmonics*: From the Science of Sound to the Study of Music', in F. Pelosi & F.M. Petrucci (eds), *Music and Philosophy in the Roman Empire* (Cambridge: Cambridge University Press), pp. 131–52.

(2022a), 'Gaudentius, *Introduction to Harmonics*: Introduction and Translation', in A. Motta & F.M. Petrucci (eds), *Isagogical Crossroads in the Post-Hellenistic Age and Late Antiquity* (Leiden: Brill), pp. 205–26.

(2022b), *Psychomusicology and Other Ancient Musicological Writings by Andrew Barker: Edited with Introduction, Bibliography and Indices by Francesco Buè, with a Preface by Eleonora Rocconi* (Leuven: Peeters).

(forthcoming), 'Aristides Quintilianus on the Foundations of Musical Taste' and 'Aristoxenus on Listening to Music', in D. Creese & P. Destrée (eds), T*he Beauties of Song: Aesthetic Appreciations of Music in the Greek and Roman World* (in preparation).

—— & D. Creese (2001), 'Eratosthenes', in *Die Musik in Geschichte und Gegenwart*, 2nd edn, Personenteil 5 (Kassel: Bärenreiter), pp. 399–400.

—— & M. Warner (eds) (1992), *The language of the cave = Apeiron*, 25.4.

Biographical Memoirs of Fellows of the British Academy (ISSN 2753–6777) are published by
The British Academy, 10–11 Carlton House Terrace, London, SW1Y 5AH
www.thebritishacademy.ac.uk

OLIVER BRADDICK

Oliver John Braddick

16 November 1944 – 17 January 2022

elected Fellow of the British Academy 2012

by

DOROTHY V. M. BISHOP

Fellow of the Academy

Oliver Braddick made major contributions to our understanding of the nature and development of human vision, with a particular focus on perception of depth and motion. His elegant experimental designs and theoretical insights have had an enduring impact on the field of visual perception. In a long and productive collaboration with his wife, Janette Atkinson, he developed ingenious new approaches to the study of visual development in babies, which extended to clinical investigations of visual consequences of diseases affecting the eye and brain. He also was an exemplary Professor and Head of Department at two of the premier experimental psychology departments in the UK, University College London (1998–2001) and Oxford (2001–2011).

Biographical Memoirs of Fellows of the British Academy, 20, 295–316
Posted 12 October 2022. © British Academy 2022.

Oliver Braddick

Childhood

Oliver Braddick was the only child of Henry John James Braddick ('Jimmy'), a reader in physics at Manchester University, who had worked under both Ernest Rutherford and Patrick Blackett, and Edith Muriel ('Midge'), a teacher who was also a gifted artist. Braddick had a happy childhood in Didsbury, where his parents, keen members of the Fabian Society, would take him hiking in the local countryside, and on barge holidays on the canals. Under his mother's influence he flourished as an amateur artist and developed a life-long interest in photography. His mother taught modern languages and Braddick soon became fluent in German and French.

Education

Braddick attended school first at the local primary in Beaver Road and subsequently at The Manchester Grammar School, which prided itself on its teaching of maths, physics and chemistry. The school identified his outstanding ability and decided he should do only the minimum number of O-level (ordinary level) exams in order to focus on A-levels (advanced) in double maths, physics and chemistry, equipping him to obtain a scholarship to read Natural Sciences at Trinity College, Cambridge just before the age of 17.

Braddick initially intended to follow in his father's footsteps at Trinity as a physicist, but the field of psychology must be grateful to the Cambridge Natural Sciences Tripos, which required him to take two other sciences. Chemistry was an obvious choice, but after that he had to decide between Mineralogy or Experimental Psychology. Once Braddick had attended a set of demonstrations in the psychology department by the charismatic Richard Gregory he was hooked. The study of visual perception requires a rigorous understanding of physics and biology in attempting to account for the way stimuli that fall on the retina are perceived by the brain as objects with properties such as depth, colour, edges and movement. At this time, Gregory would have been finalising his renowned popular book *Eye and Brain* (1966), which focused on the potential of visual illusions to throw light on this translation, by studying cases where there is a mismatch between what we perceive and what is 'out there' in the world. Braddick decided that vision was what interested him, and after obtaining his BA in 1965, he enlisted as a doctoral student in 1968, supervised by Gregory. In this pre-computer age, Gregory had a knack for creating compelling demonstrations of visual phenomena, one of which used a railway track to present stimuli that could move towards or away from the viewer. This may have stimulated Braddick's interest in the topic of his thesis, which was binocular vision. By cleverly varying characteristics of separation and orientation of stimuli presented to the left and right eyes, Braddick could show there could be dissociation between stereopsis (seeing depth) and binocular single vision (seeing a single object despite viewing with two eyes). A good overview of this early work can be found in Braddick (1979).

Early academic career

After a one-year postdoc at the laboratory of Lorrin Riggs at Brown University in the USA, Braddick returned to Cambridge as a university demonstrator, subsequently being promoted to lecturer and then reader. Between 1969 and 1972, he combined his teaching activities with a research fellowship at Trinity College.

These were exciting times to be a vision researcher in Cambridge. The University had created the Kenneth Craik Laboratory with the aim of bringing together vision researchers from physiology and psychology. The, almost exclusively male, environment included some of the great luminaries of the field, although the hoped-for integration of physiology and psychology could be challenging. Physiologist Horace Barlow believed that to understand vision, one needed to derive computational principles from biological processes, identifying neural units with selective tuning for visual properties such as orientation or motion. Barlow focused on low-level summation and inhibition in the retina, as well as higher-level feature detection ('bug' detectors). In contrast, Richard Gregory regarded visual perception as a problem-solving process: our pre-existing knowledge of the world is used in a top-down fashion to interpret sensory input as evidence for an external object or event. Braddick benefited from exposure to these diverse influences, and aimed to link top-down and bottom-up processes in vision, stimulated by the work of physiologists Fergus Campbell and Colin Blakemore, as well as Barlow.

Gregory departed for Edinburgh in 1967, but the psychology department remained strong in neuropsychology and perception, with the influence of colourful characters such as 'old C' Grindley, one of the founders of the Experimental Psychology Society. He would give popular demonstrations of experiments using a tachistoscope – in those days a standard piece of equipment, used to present precisely timed stimuli. The eminent neuropsychologist Oliver Zangwill was Professor of Experimental Psychology and Head of Department; he had played a major role in recruiting Braddick. Overall, Cambridge in the 1960s-1970s was a magnet for academic visitors interested in vision science, including a memorable visit by Edwin Land, inventor of polaroid film, in a limousine.

Braddick developed an interest in perceptual learning, the notion that experience of particular stimuli can influence how they are perceived. In an early paper that remains highly cited to this day,[1] V.S. Ramachandran and Braddick demonstrated this point using random line stereograms; these are random patterns of lines that vary in orientation, presented to left and right eyes, and identical on the two sides except for a proportion of the dots that are displaced horizontally in one image. When viewed in a stereoscope, the images fuse to give an impression of depth. Ramachandran and Braddick showed how changing the orientation of the elements in the stereogram affected the time it took for naïve observers to learn to perceive depth. This kind of neat experiment, where details of experimental stimuli were manipulated to throw light on the basis of perceptual phenomena, characterised Braddick's meticulous approach. His early papers using stereograms to study the processes of masking[2] and visual motion[3] remain as core sources for vision researchers in current times. His paper on short-range apparent motion was particularly influential; he defined the conditions under which this phenomenon occurred when a stimulus was presented to the same eye repeatedly over a precisely timed interval.

Early work on infant vision

In the early 1970s, Braddick began a life-long collaboration with his future wife, Janette Atkinson, who was then a PhD student supervised by Paul Whittle (and one of the only female graduate students in the Cambridge Department), studying cortical mechanisms using afterimages. Their shared interests and complementary skills made a powerful combination, and from this point on they worked so closely together that it is not possible to separate their independent contributions on their joint projects. The topic that they focused on and made their own was the study of visual development in human infants. This was a bold step. Up to that point, most research on vision had either involved asking adult human observers to report what they could see, or had relied on presenting visual stimuli while recording responses from brain cells in animals such as rats or cats. Babies presented problems for both methods, so the question was how on earth could one obtain reliable data from such young humans, without invading their brains or requiring them to speak.

Despite these difficulties, it was clear that the study of infants had enormous potential to throw light on the extent to which experience shaped perception – a question that was starting to attract the interest of Braddick's colleagues in the physiology department. Notably, Colin Blakemore, an exact contemporary of Braddick, was doing exciting studies that showed experience-dependent plasticity of the visual system in cats.

---

[1] Ramachandran & Braddick (1973).
[2] Braddick (1973).
[3] Braddick (1974).

Around this time, developmental psychologists had been making progress with methods that allowed one to infer the ability of babies to distinguish stimuli by their responses (e.g. by looking preferentially at one visual stimulus rather than another). An encounter with visitor Alan Hein, led Braddick and Atkinson to learn about the work of Davida Teller, who had just started to modify the preferential looking method to measure visual acuity in infants. This was called 'forced-choice preferential looking'. The infant was shown two images, side by side, and an observer (out of sight of the infant, looking through a central peep hole) observed the infant's eyes and head movements. At the end of a timed test period, the observer had to choose which side the infant looked at preferentially. This way, one could demonstrate whether infants are above chance at discriminating between the images on the two sides. Using this approach, Braddick and Atkinson developed an experimental method that used spatial frequency analysis to assess visual sensitivity.

In these studies the infant is seated in front of two displays, matched in average luminance (see Figure 1). One screen shows a uniform grey stimulus, while the other shows a grating (striped pattern), the stripes varying in shade of grey; the side of the grating pattern on the left or right screen is varied at random across trials, and the expectation is that if the grating is detectable, the infant will look more at it (from the general principle that infants prefer to look at something patterned rather than a blank screen).

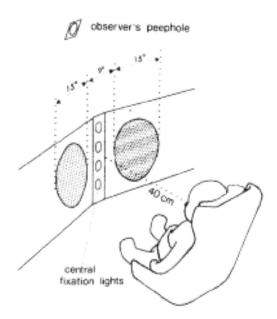

Figure 1. Figure from Atkinson *et al.* (1977), from original drawing by Oliver Braddick (reprinted with permission of the publisher).

The width of the bars of the grating (spatial frequency) is varied, to establish at which level of contrast the infant fails to show a preference as judged by the observer. A challenge is to keep the infant engaged on the task for a sufficient number of trials so that the data is statistically reliable. Fortunately, Braddick and Atkinson had a biddable infant on hand as their first subject: Fleur, their first child, born in 1973, who was 2 months old at the time of the experiment. This single case study was impressive at revealing a contrast sensitivity function that was similar in shape to that normally seen in adults, albeit with poorer sensitivity overall, including poorer acuity than adults. This study, the first measure of contrast sensitivity in an infant, was an important proof of concept in showing that the method of forced choice preferential looking had promise for studying small humans who could not describe what they saw.

Braddick and Atkinson had a sense of fun which could get them into trouble. They added Fleur's name to the list of authors on the *Nature* paper[4] that resulted from this study. Since Janette had retained her own surname, those who only knew of them from the published paper tended to assume that she was a research collaborator, and that Fleur Braddick was Oliver's wife. This led to sharp disapproval, initially, when Braddick and Atkinson booked a joint hotel room for a vision conference. Fortunately, Dick Cavonius enlighted the conference organiser (a strictly 'proper' senior academic professor) as to the correct Braddick family relationships and names.

Braddick and Atkinson went on to run further proof of concept studies using other behavioural developmental methods which they adapted for use with infants. In 1976 they published a paper[5] in which they estimated acuity in infants from the highest spatial frequency at 100 per cent contrast at which a preference could be demonstrated. Again, the challenges of doing this kind of study were substantial: they studied babies lying in a mobile crib, with visual stimuli projected above them. The method used was called 'sucking rate habituation /dishabituation'. The babies wore goggles so that they could view stereoscopic images, and the method measured their rate of sucking on a bottle teat as an index of interest (circumstantial evidence of ability to detect the disparities in the stereoscopic stimuli). Not all babies complied, and there were large individual differences across infants in sucking rates. What is more, the method did not work well for infants who were breast fed rather than bottle fed. Nevertheless, this study needed to be done. It established the value of the method in principle and revealed its limitations. Rather more successful was the visual habituation/ dishabituation method in which the infant is first shown one image of an object or striped pattern over and over again (habituation stage). As the infant becomes bored with the same image each time, looking declines. When the amount of looking reaches a predetermined criterion level, the

---

[4] Atkinson *et al.* (1974): 'Janette Atkinson, Oliver Braddick & Fleur Braddick'.
[5] Atkinson & Braddick (1976).

stimulus image is changed. Here the logic is that if there is a significant rebound of looking time when the new stimulus is presented after the habituation stage, then the infant must at least be able to discriminate the first stimulus from the second new stimulus.

Establishment of the Visual Development Unit

With an informality that would make today's University administrators blench, Braddick and Atkinson 'borrowed' a set of rooms in Trumpington Street from Horace Barlow. The accommodation was not at all suitable for an infant lab, so they set out to redecorate the premises with a jungle mural, turning up with tins of paint and ladders, to create a welcoming and child-friendly environment where the infants could play, feed and sleep, giving the parents a chance to relax. This enabled the infants to be in the best state for testing, usually just before or after a feed or when they had just woken up.

By 1975 they were ready to supplement their behavioural testing method with electrophysiology: averaging the tiny electrical responses from the scalp over repeated presentations of a visual stimulus: this allows one to detect a waveform with a distinctive timecourse, the visual evoked potential (sometimes now called 'visual event-related potential'), whose amplitude increases as the stimulus becomes more visible. They were ahead of their time in recognising the possibilities of what is now known as 'frequency tagging', a method where stimuli of different kinds are presented, with the image reversing at a given rate. The brain response can then be subjected to Fourier analysis, to extract components that are maximal at the same temporal frequency as the reversing stimulus. They were also ready with a new infant subject – Hugo, their second child, who was 6 months old at the time they developed this method. In a ground-breaking study[6] with Laurence Harris (then a student of Colin Blakemore), Braddick and Atkinson showed that visual acuity improved a great deal in the early months of life, and that the visual evoked potential gave data consistent with behavioural methods. This study also provides an early illustration of the flair shown by Braddick and Atkinson in devising methods that ensured babies would be attentive and interested in what could be rather dull tasks: they used a reflecting mirror to superimpose an image of an active face on the stimuli, realising that babies were far more interested in social stimuli than gratings.

A grant from the Medical Research Council allowed Braddick and Atkinson to develop this line of work further, and with research assistant Kathleen Moar they conducted a study comparing contrast sensitivity in three groups of infants, aged 5 weeks, 8

---

[6] Harris *et al.* (1976).

weeks and 12 weeks of age.[7] They demonstrated a steady improvement in contrast sensitivity over the first 3-4 months of life. The large improvement in contrast sensitivity between the youngest group and older babies raised a host of questions about the mechanism. Physiologists working with cats had ascribed improved acuity in young animals to the development of neuronal connections, and it seemed plausible that a similar process may occur in humans. This was of potential practical importance as well as theoretical significance, as it suggested that there may be an early 'critical period' during which it would be optimal to treat amblyopia ('lazy eye'), before neuronal connections had become established.

Nevertheless, it was not possible to be sure how far changes in acuity in the first few months of life were due to neurological rather than optical changes. To answer that question, Braddick and Atkinson adopted a new method similar to that developed by Howland and Howland in the early 1970s, called 'isotropic photorefraction'. A camera is placed so as to measure light reflected from the eye when a small safe flash of light is presented, making it possible to measure visual accommodation and to detect astigmatism and refractive errors (short or long sightedness) at any age. No co-operation is required from the infant, beyond looking at the camera, where an adult would wave an illuminated plastic duck on the end of a pen-torch, saying 'quack, quack', to keep the infant's attention for a few seconds. The method was both robust and rapid, taking about 5 minutes for the whole testing session with the infant.[8] Using this technique, Braddick and Atkinson measured astigmatism in 93 infants recruited from Cambridge Maternity Hospital.[9] They found that many infants under 12 months of age had significant astigmatism, but this decreased to adult levels by 2 years of age.[10] Accommodative error could not, however, account for the poor acuity seen in infants and young children.[11] At this point, it was becoming clear that the work they were doing had considerable clinical as well as theoretical significance, and they made contact with ophthalmologists and paediatricians to develop this aspect of their research. Braddick and Atkinson's third child, Lorrin, was born around this time, in 1977.

In 1979, with research assistant Jennifer French, Braddick and Atkinson studied 97 babies aged between 1 to 10 days using the visual evoked potential method to assess

[7] Atkinson et al. (1977).
[8] At a later stage Braddick and Atkinson, together with Howard Howland and John Wattam-Bell (a student at the time in the VDU), developed an instrument called the 'isotropic videorefractor', which gave images of the infant's refraction, instantaneously, on a video screen. This method avoided the cost of developing photographic images on film and meant that if any of the images were not clear the method could immediately be repeated to obtain a better image.
[9] Howland et al. (1978).
[10] Atkinson et al. (1980).
[11] Braddick et al. (1979).

contrast sensitivity.[12] Results suggested that acuity in these newborns was poor relative to that seen in older infants and adults, but nevertheless adequate to detect features of the mother's face at a close distance. Visual evoked potentials were also incorporated in a clever design that tested whether infants had binocular vision, using correlated and uncorrelated random dot stereograms, in a collaboration with Béla Julesz and other colleagues from the USA.[13] It was the first published study of development of stereopsis in very young infants and showed that most infants had binocular vision by 3-4 months of age.

Alongside the work on infants, Braddick retained an interest in fundamental visual perceptual processes in adult humans. He was fascinated by a central question – how we extract a percept of global motion from many individual motions. He put it so vividly in a later review paper[14] that it is worth quoting in full:

> We are often faced with visual stimuli that have an overall direction of motion but are made up of many diverse local motions. The turbulent but directed flow of water in a stream, gravel being dumped from a truck, or a flock of birds taking to the air, are examples. We also encounter stimui that show motion transparency, in which elements belonging to entities with different motions are interleaved or superimposed – for example a vehicle seen through the gaps in a hedge or fence, or the shadow that a moving object casts on a differently moving surface. (p. 995)

In 1980, he published a highly influential review of visual motion perception – this time, rather than the stereograms used to study binocular depth perception, his focus was on the random dot kinematogram.[15] This stimulus, first developed by Béla Julesz (1971), is a series of matrices, each with random black and white square elements. On successive presentations, some elements in the matrix are repeated, whereas others in the central region are displaced through a specific distance. When the interval between successive stimuli is very brief, this gives rise to a perception of movement of a coherent object, with a boundary between the central moving zone and the static surrounding area. This illusory movement must depend on some mechanism that computes the spatio-temporal relationship between elements. Braddick put forward a two-process theory of apparent motion, with a low-level short-range process that depends on directionally selective neurons in the visual pathway responding to discontinuous stimulation, and a higher-level process that interprets the input as a smoothly moving object. Braddick's logical analysis of the nature of motion perception set a research agenda for years to come.[16] This line of work involved psychophysical experiments of a more traditional kind, with observers

---

[12] Atkinson *et al.* (1979).
[13] Braddick *et al.* (1980).
[14] Braddick (1997).
[15] Braddick (1980).
[16] Braddick (1997); Prins (2008).

being tested in varying parameters over many trials to establish the conditions that influence perception; nevertheless, there is clear interplay between his work on adult perception and the developmental studies.

The Visual Development Unit in Cambridge went from strength to strength during the 1980s, which also saw the birth of Braddick's fourth child, Ione, in 1988. Orthoptist Shirley Anker joined the team, providing invaluable clinical expertise. By this time John Wattam-Bell, a neurophysiologist from Oxford, had also joined, embarking on a productive collaboration with Atkinson and Braddick that lasted for 30 years until his premature death in 2013. As noted above, as a student he had been involved in developing videorefraction methods to replace the more limited photorefraction that was previously in use. One of his earliest papers with Braddick and Atkinson[17] adopted a clever experimental paradigm that used a specific stimulus sequence designed to measure the visual evoked response of orientation-selective mechanisms in the brain. Intriguingly, this response was not apparent in newborns, but could be seen at 6 weeks of age. Bruce Hood, who subsequently became Professor of Psychology at the University of Bristol, joined the Visual Development Unit around this time as Atkinson's postgraduate student, with a particular interest in development of attentional mechanisms.[18]

Alongside these studies of typical infant development, Braddick and Atkinson had also developed a line of clinical research with babies and children who had visual problems with an ocular basis.[19] In 1992, however, they had the opportunity to study two infants (aged 4 and 8 months respectively) who had had surgery to remove the cerebral cortex on one side to relieve intractable seizures.[20] As might be expected, informal observations showed that these infants ignored toys placed in the half-field contralateral to the removed hemisphere, where removal of visual cortex should render them effectively blind, but readily reached for a toy placed in the ipsilateral half-field. Braddick and Atkinson used a fixation shift procedure, where the infant initially sees a central flashing target, which is replaced by a contrast-reversing target to either the left or right of centre. Both infants responded at above chance levels to targets in the contralateral field; i.e., orienting behaviour was evoked by stimuli that cannot have been processed by contralateral cortex. This observation was reminiscent of the phenomenon of 'blindsight' previously described in adults who still oriented to stimuli in a 'blind' visual field, despite expressing no awareness of the stimulus, and it provided evidence that orienting depended on a subcortical route. A further condition was run with one of the children, in which the central flashing stimulus remained on when the lateralised target was presented. This creates a situation where stimuli compete for attention, and performance on

[17] Braddick *et al.* (1986).
[18] Atkinson *et al.* (1992).
[19] Ehrlich *et al.* (1995).
[20] Braddick *et al.* (1992).

Dorothy V. M. Bishop

the contralateral side was much lower in this case. This observation led to development of the Fixation Shift Paradigm as a diagnostic tool. The ability to shift attention when there is no competition is evidence that the infant has developed the subcortical route for orienting, which is typically seen as early as one month of age. The ability to disengage attention from a competing stimulus involves cortical systems, and emerges in typically developing infants around 3-5 months of age. Thus, inclusion of competition and non-competition conditions can be a particularly sensitive diagnostic indicator of neuro-developmental problems. This line of work also made it clear that one cannot study visual perception without studying attentional selection: the brain's perception of an object does not depend just on its physical properties, but also on what other objects are present in the visual field.

University College London

In 1993, Braddick moved to University College London (UCL), together with Atkinson, as professors of Psychology. They maintained the Visual Development Unit in Cambridge, where they were running major screening studies of young infants, but also created a new Visual Development Unit in London. In 1998, Braddick became Head of the Department of Experimental Psychology at UCL.

Braddick's basic psychophysical studies on processes of visual motion perception continued during this period. The use of displays with moving dots allowed one to establish a 'coherent motion threshold'. Figure 2 illustrates the type of stimulus that is used. Most of the dots in the display move at random, but a proportion move coherently in one direction, giving a perception of motion. By varying the proportion of coherently moving dots, one can establish the lower limit for movement detection – typically around 5 per cent in adult humans.[21] This task can also be performed by non-human primates, and it appears to depend on neurons in cortical area V5 (also known as MT). The conclusion is that area V5 is involved in combining information from lower-level motion signals to create a synthesised global motion percept. One point about this task is that the threshold depends on the similarity between the random dots and the coherent dots: if they are different colours, then motion can be detected at much lower levels of coherence. Another point that assumed importance in later work was that one can use a similar task with non-moving stimuli to study coherent form detection, i.e. the detection of a form in a random field, defined by stimulus similarity (e.g. from bars that share the same orientation). This depends on a ventral visual stream, as opposed to the dorsal stream that mediates motion perception.

[21] Braddick (1995).

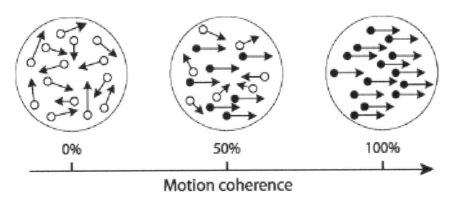

0%   50%   100%

Motion coherence

Figure 2. Schematic diagram of stimuli from random dot motion task. In each frame a proportion of the dots (shown in black) are repositioned with fixed spatial offset, and the remaining dots are repositioned randomly. Figure from Zhang (2012), reproduced under CC BY 4.0 licence.

In 1996, Braddick and Atkinson published two major studies that demonstrated the clinical utility of their approaches to assessment.[22] They had by this time developed videorefraction as a method to accompany photorefraction, making it possible to identify infants with lags in visual accommodation. For their first study, on screening, every infant living in the City of Cambridge over a 2-year period was invited to come for screening using photorefraction. Of the over 3000 infants who were assessed, around 5-6 per cent had evidence of visual problems and were referred for follow-up. In the second study, over 5000 infants were tested with videorefraction around 8 months of age; in this study infants with significant hyperopia (far-sightedness) were randomly assigned to receive spectacles or not, and then followed up at 4 years of age. The first study showed that screening was effective in identifying infants who were at risk of developing strabismus (squint) at 4 years of age, and the second study indicated that this risk could be reduced by providing infants with corrective spectacles. Videorefraction was safer and easier than retinoscopy for testing infants and children, because the testing was faster and did not require the user to be trained in retinoscopy. In addition photo/videorefraction assessed the two eyes simultaneously, so their refractive state could be compared, whereas in retinoscopy, the refractive measures were made sequentially. These studies on early identification and intervention were important, given the evidence that an opportunity to form optimal neuronal connections may be missed if diagnosis is delayed. The videorefractive screening programme was subsequently rolled out in Spain, Portugal, France, Germany and Italy, as well as in the UK.

[22] Atkinson *et al.* (1996).

Subsequently, the children initially studied in the Cambridge screening project provided an invaluable opportunity to look at long-term outcomes of infants with visual problems. A follow-up study of outcomes up to 7 years of age not only confirmed that the screening was effective at picking up visual problems, and early prescription of spectacles could help ameliorate these, but also that children with such problems were more likely to have broader learning difficulties.[23] This study illustrated the value of multidisciplinary working: most studies of infant vision restricted themselves to looking at the function of the eye; by extending the assessment more broadly, Braddick and Atkinson were able to uncover neurodevelopmental interconnections between visual and cognitive functions.

London provided an opportunity for enhanced collaborations with paediatric neurology colleagues, and Braddick and Atkinson developed a new line of research on visual functioning in children with perinatal brain damage,[24] an interesting topic both in terms of identifying clinical needs in these children, and in terms of understanding more about the brain's ability to show plasticity and neural reorganisation in the face of disruption to connections. They also now had opportunity to work with children whose brains had been scanned using MRI, making it possible to relate their visual findings to underlying neuropathology.[25] There developed a rich seam of research with paediatric neurologist Eugenio Mercuri at the Hammersmith Hospital, which also led to a long-term collaboration with Giovanni Cioni, child neuropsychiatrist from the Stella Maris Scientific Institute at the University of Pisa.

Around this time, they also started a research programme on perception in children with Williams syndrome, a rare genetic condition that leads to a distinctive phenotype that includes visuo-spatial weaknesses that seem disproportionate, in relation to their more general intellectual disability and their relatively good speech and language development. Using measures that contrasted different motion and form processing they postulated that children with Williams syndrome had a specific deficit with development of the dorsal visual stream, which encodes spatial relationships and the visual control of action.[26] This was a completely new way of thinking about the Williams syndrome phenotype, which generated clear predictions for future studies. Intriguingly, a similar pattern of selective impairment of coherent motion detection, relative to coherent form detection, was also found in children with autism[27] and a range of other neurodevelopmental disorders.

[23] Atkinson *et al.* (2007).
[24] Mercuri *et al.* (1996).
[25] Mercuri *et al.* (1999; 1997); Ricci *et al.* (2006).
[26] Atkinson *et al.* (1997).
[27] Spencer *et al.* (2000).

One prediction was that measures of form coherence and motion coherence should activate the traditional ventral and dorsal visual processing streams. In 2000, Braddick and Atkinson published a paper showing that, while the tasks activated different brain networks, they did not neatly correspond to the traditional dual stream pathways.[28] The term 'dorsal stream vulnerability' had become an established way of referring to the selective deficits in visual motion processing that were being discovered in a range of clinical conditions, and Braddick and Atkinson continued to use it,[29] but it was clear that the neurobiological basis might be more complex than suggested by this designation.

Braddick and Atkinson were regular visitors to the University of California at San Diego where they taught an annual summer school course. This gave them the opportunity to enjoy seaside life with their young family over the summer, and also to establish strong links with Ursula Bellugi, from the Salk Instiute for Biological Sciences in San Diego, who had a longstanding interest in Williams syndrome. She tried to persuade Braddick and Atkinson to travel the country to do visual testing on a US sample of adults with Williams syndrome, but they suggested a more feasible option would be for them to train Bellugi's research staff in the methods, which is what ensued. This study confirmed persistence of visual motion processing deficits into adulthood in this population.[30]

University of Oxford

In 2001, Braddick took up the Chair of Experimental Psychology at the University of Oxford, a post that entailed acting as Head of Department. This led to the third incarnation of the Visual Development Unit, an area on the ground floor of the Tinbergen Building that was beautifully decorated with a jungle frieze painted by Braddick and Atkinson's adult children. Atkinson officially remained at UCL, continuing to direct the Visual Development Unit there, but also taught courses in medicine and neuroscience, and supervised research and students in Oxford.

In Oxford, Braddick found many eminent colleagues whom he had first known in Cambridge: Colin Blakemore was Professor of Physiology, and Braddick's previous graduate student, Andrew Parker, was based in the same department. In psychology, the former Professor and Head of Department, Larry Weiskrantz had a shared interest in blindsight, as did Alan Cowey, who had done seminal work on visual systems in monkeys. However, the reuinion with these old colleagues was marred by the fact that they were

---

[28] Braddick et al. (2000).
[29] Braddick et al. (2003).
[30] Atkinson et al. (2006).

targeted by animal rights activists. Colin Blakemore had adopted the approach of open dialogue with those opposing animal research, but had at times needed police protection. Alan Cowey was also a particular target for his work on monkeys, and the presence of animal labs at the top floor of the building meant that there were regular protests at the entrance of the building. Initially, the protesters used loud-hailers, which was seriously disruptive to Braddick's research with babies, but eventually an injunction was served which limited the amount and nature of protest that was allowed. Nevertheless, there were at least three incidents of arson affecting members of the psychology department during Braddick's time as Head of Department, though none of them involved anyone who worked with animals. In time, the more dangerous protesters responsible for such incidents were arrested, and life became quieter. Nevertheless, this topic remained a significant source of stress for those working in the department, and in particular for Braddick as Head of Department. He had a strong sense of humanity and fairness, and although he was well aware of the major insights that had been achieved through research on animals, he also was at pains to ensure that any research done in his department was justified and properly regulated.

Braddick had long been interested in visuo-motor interactions, and in Oxford he was able to develop this line of work further, creating a large space for assessment of motor skills. Graduate student Dorothy Cowie experimented with a new method, kinematic markers (luminous patches stuck onto limbs) to study visual guidance of stepping movements,[31] and Marco Nardini led a study on use of landmarks by children and adults to control navigation.[32]

In his year of retirement, 2011, Braddick, with Atkinson, published a masterly review of development of human vision function, drawing on work of the previous 25 years.[33] This illustrates the huge developments in theory and methods that had occurred since they had conducted their first studies on infants, and the numerous clinical applications to both vision and paediatric neurology.

After official retirement and up until his death Braddick continued to work with Atkinson to develop an Italian translation, as well as an iPad version, of their attention battery for young children (ECAB-Early Child Attention Battery).[34] The ECAB was found to be sensitive to perinatal brain injury in a follow-up study of 4-year-olds, conducted in collaboration with Oxford neonatologists.[35] The attentional deficits identified with the ECAB were distinct from generally lower cognitive performance on a standard intelligence test. The same study acted as a pilot trial of the effect of a unique dietary

[31] Cowie *et al.* (2008).
[32] Nardini *et al.* (2008).
[33] Braddick & Atkinson (2011).
[34] Breckenridge *et al.* (2013); Coratti *et al.* (2020).
[35] Atkinson *et al.* (2022).

supplement designed to promote brain development; results were promising enough to justify a much larger trial (DOLFIN), that is being rolled out in 2022.

Another major strand of work focused on clarifying and extending the earlier observations of global visual motion sensitivity in development. The different developmental trends for detection of global motion vs global form had been reliably replicated, with motion sensitivity showing a more protracted course, and frequently being impaired in a wide range of neurodevelopmental disorders.[36] In a study with collaborators in San Diego, Braddick and Atkinson considered brain and behavioural correlates of global visual motion sensitivity in 154 typically-developing children aged from 5 to 12 years.[37] This showed that individual differences in motion sensitivity were not associated with growth of extrastriate visual areas (MT) of the dorsal stream, i.e., those which are involved in initial processing of motion, but were linked to development of specific areas of the parietal lobes, to which the dorsal stream projects, and to structural asymmetry of the superior longitudinal fasciculus.[38] Furthermore, performance on global motion sensitivity showed a specific association with visuospatial and numerical abilities.

Braddick and Atkinson were always interested in the clinical implications of their work, rather than treating research participants just as experimental subjects. This led them to take on the writing of international guidelines for individuals with Williams syndrome from infancy to old age in terms of their visual and cognitive functioning: part of a collaborative effort with 50 medical and scientific experts from around the world. Sadly, Braddick died before this was completed, but Atkinson is continuing this important work.

Braddick as a scientist

Braddick was generally affable, with a leadership style that operated through consensus rather than command. I can remember only one occasion when he was really irritated – unfortunately, an occasion that I unwittingly instigated! In 2017, after Braddick had retired, the Oxford Experimental Psychology Department suffered a disaster when asbestos was discovered in heating ducts. The building had to be evacuated within days, with staff dispersed to temporary locations throughout the city. A year later, most of us moved into a prefabricated building, which would be our home for a few years while the original building was decontaminated, demolished and rebuilt (a process still continuing in 2022, as I write this). The prefab – the Anna Watts Building – was functional but grey

[36] Micheletti *et al.* (2021).
[37] Braddick *et al.* (2016).
[38] Braddick *et al.* (2017).

and anonymous, and I had the idea that we should identify our meeting rooms – currently known only by names such as 2.04 or 1.26 – with pictures of visually interesting psychological phenomena, such as visual illusions, simultaneously making them more memorable and decorative, while providing a psychologically relevant theme. I had assumed Braddick would be enthusiastic about this idea, and so was dismayed to find that he was the only person who responded with strong opposition. It turned out that he had just written an editorial for *Perception*,[39] in which he laid into the study of visual illusions with uncharacteristic venom. The editorial is a masterpiece: in a few short paragraphs, he makes it clear that his beef is with the way people use the 'Wow!' factor of illusions to try to persuade undergraduates that perception is interesting, even though many illusions are still not understood and do not form a coherent topic for investigation. It is perhaps a testament to Braddick's equable personality that he remained friendly with me even though my idea was implemented, and there is now a Müller-Lyer room and an Ebbinghaus room in the Anna Watts building.

In contrast to many vision scientists, Braddick had remarkably wide-ranging interests. He was a believer in interdisciplinary research, and his own research corpus is a testament to the success of that approach, combining insights from physics, psychology, neuroscience, orthoptics, ophthalmology and paediatrics. He and Atkinson were also conspicuous for attending talks well outside their area, and asking thoughtful questions in a way that was stimulating without being hostile. In a wonderfully warm obituary,[40] his fellow vision scientists Peter Thompson, David Burr and Michael Morgan capture it perfectly: 'At so many conferences, be it Vision Sciences Society (VSS), European Conference on Visual Perception (ECVP), Association for Research in Vision and Ophthalmology (ARVO) or specialized workshops, he could be counted on to ask the right question – the question that needed to be answered, rather than the question to show how clever he was.' He would express regret that in recent years, graduate students seldom attended talks outside their specific field of interest, believing that some of his best ideas had come from the novel perspective offered by questions and methods from a different area of psychology. In an in interview about his career, published in *Current Biology* in 2017,[41] Braddick gave the advice: '... remain open-minded to a wider input – make time to find out through seminars and reading what's going on in areas that aren't quite yours. Sometimes going to a seminar that isn't quite your area of research helps you expand your ideas and even move in a new direction.'

[39] Braddick (2018).
[40] Thompson *et al.* (2022).
[41] Anonymous (2017).

Braddick had no ambition to set up a huge research empire. He enjoyed a hands-on approach to experiments, working directly with graduate students and postdocs, rather than being a remote head of the laboratory. He also was an enthusiastic teacher, and many studies had their origins in undergraduate projects, which he and Atkinson continued to supervise despite their seniority.

This attitude to science, pursuing it for its intrinsic interest rather than for any associated glory, and encouraging the next generation of vision scientists, made him a popular colleague. He is fondly remembered not just as an inspirational scientist but also as a fair-minded and hard-working Head of Department in both UCL and Oxford. He was also a good academic citizen, supporting vision research with stints on the editorial boards of Perception, Vision Research and Current Biology, and serving as a trustee for the Association for Research in Vision and Ophthalmology.

Braddick was not one to thrust himself forward, but there was no need for him to do so – his qualities and achievements were evident to all who knew him. He was elected as a Fellow of the Academy of Medical Sciences in 2002, and a Fellow of the British Academy in 2012.

Acknowledgements

I thank Janette Atkinson and Andrew Parker for providing invaluable background information for this memoir.

References

Anonymous (2017), 'Q & A: Janette Atkinson and Oliver Braddick', *Current Biology*, 27, R1–R4.

Atkinson, J. & Braddick, O. (1976), 'Stereoscopic Discrimination in Infants', *Perception*, 5(1), 29–38. https://doi.org/10.1068/p050029

Atkinson, J., Braddick, O. & Braddick, F. (1974), 'Acuity and contrast sensitivity of infant vision', *Nature*, 247(5440), 403–4. https://doi.org/10.1038/247403a0

Atkinson, J., Braddick, O. & Moar, K. (1977), 'Development of contrast sensitivity over the first 3 months of life in the human infant', *Vision Research*, 17(9), 1037–1044. https://doi.org/10.1016/0042-6989(77)90007-4

Atkinson, J., Braddick, O. & French, J. (1979), 'Contrast sensitivity of the human neonate measured by the visual evoked potential', *Investigative Ophthalmology & Visual Science*, 18(2), 210–13.

Atkinson, J., Braddick, O. & French, J. (1980), Infant astigmatism: Its disappearance with age. Vision Research, 20(11), 891–3. https://doi.org/10.1016/0042-6989(80)90070-X

Atkinson, J., Hood, B., Wattam-Bell, J. & Braddick, O. (1992), 'Changes in infants' ability to switch visual attention in the first three months of life', *Perception*, 21(5), 643–53. https://doi.org/10.1068/p210643

Atkinson, J., Braddick, O., Bobier, B., Anker, S., Ehrlich, D., King, J., Watson, P. & Moore, A. (1996), 'Two infant vision screening programmes: Prediction and prevention of strabismus and amblyopia from photo- and videorefractive screening', *Eye*, 10(2), 189–98. https://doi.org/10.1038/eye.1996.46

Atkinson, J., King, J., Braddick, O., Nokes, L., Anker, S. & Braddick, F. (1997), 'A specific deficit of dorsal stream function in Williams' syndrome', *Neuroreport*, 8(8), 1919–22. https://doi.org/10.1097/00001756-199705260-00025

Atkinson, J., Braddick, O., Rose, F. E., Searcy, Y. M., Wattam-Bell, J. & Bellugi, U. (2006), 'Dorsal-stream motion processing deficits persist into adulthood in Williams syndrome', *Neuropsychologia*, 44(5), 828–33. https://doi.org/10.1016/j.neuropsychologia.2005.08.002

Atkinson, J., Braddick, O., Nardini, M. & Anker, S. (2007), 'Infant hyperopia: Detection, distribution, changes and correlates—Outcomes from the Cambridge Infant Screening Programs', *Optometry and Vision Science*, 84(2), 84–96. https://doi.org/10.1097/OPX.0b013e318031b69a

Atkinson, J., Braddick, O., Montague-Johnson, C., Baker, B., Parr, J. R., Sullivan, P. & Andrew, M. J. (2022), 'Visual attention and dietary supplementation in children with perinatal brain injury', *Developmental Medicine & Child Neurology*, 64(3), 340–6. https://doi.org/10.1111/dmcn.15017

Braddick, O. (1973), 'The masking of apparent motion in random-dot patterns', *Vision Research*, 13(2), 355–69. https://doi.org/10.1016/0042-6989(73)90113-2

Braddick, O. (1974), 'A short-range process in apparent motion', *Vision Research*, 14(7), 519–27. https://doi.org/10.1016/0042-6989(74)90041-8

Braddick, O.J. (1979), 'Binocular single vision and perceptual processing', *Proceedings of the Royal Society of London, Series B, Biological Sciences*, 204(1157), 503–12.

Braddick, O.J. (1980), 'Low-level and high-level processes in apparent motion', *Philosophical Transactions of the Royal Society of London, Series B, Biological Sciences*, 290(1038), 137–51. https://doi.org/10.1098/rstb.1980.0087

Braddick, O. (1995), 'Visual Perception: Seeing motion signals in noise', *Current Biology*, 5(1), 7–9. https://doi.org/10.1016/S0960-9822(95)00003-0

Braddick, O. (1997), 'Local and global representations of velocity: Transparency, opponency, and global direction perception', *Perception*, 26(8), 995–1010. https://doi.org/10.1068/p260995

Braddick, O. (2018), 'Illusion research: An infantile disorder?', *Perception*, 47(8), 805–806.

Braddick, O. & Atkinson, J. (2011), 'Development of human visual function', *Vision Research*, 51(13), 1588–1609. https://doi.org/10.1016/j.visres.2011.02.018

Braddick, O., Atkinson, J., French, J. & Howland, H.C. (1979), 'A photorefractive study of infant accommodation', *Vision Research*, 19(12), 1319–30. https://doi.org/10.1016/0042-6989(79)90204-9

Braddick, O., Atkinson, J., Julesz, B., Kropfl, W., Bodis-Wollner, I. & Raab, E. (1980), 'Cortical binocularity in infants', *Nature*, 288(5789), 363–5. https://doi.org/10.1038/288363a0

Braddick, O.J., Wattam-Bell, J. & Atkinson, J. (1986), 'Orientation-specific cortical responses develop in early infancy', *Nature*, 320(6063), 617–19. https://doi.org/10.1038/320617a0

Braddick, O., Atkinson, J., Hood, B., Harkness, W., Jackson, G. & Vargha-Khadem, F. (1992), 'Possible blindsight in infants lacking one cerebral hemisphere', *Nature*, 360(6403), 461–3. https://doi.org/10.1038/360461a0

Braddick, O.J., O'Brien, J.M., Wattam-Bell, J., Atkinson, J. & Turner, R. (2000), 'Form and motion coherence activate independent, but not dorsal/ventral segregated, networks in the human brain', *Current Biology: CB*, 10(12), 731–4. https://doi.org/10.1016/s0960-9822(00)00540-6

Braddick, O., Atkinson, J. & Wattam-Bell, J. (2003), 'Normal and anomalous development of visual motion processing: Motion coherence and "dorsal-stream vulnerability"', *Neuropsychologia*, 41(13), 1769–84. https://doi.org/10.1016/S0028-3932(03)00178-7

Braddick, O., Atkinson, J., Newman, E., Akshoomoff, N., Kuperman, J. M., Bartsch, H., Chen, C.-H., Dale, A. M. & Jernigan, T. L. (2016), 'Global visual motion sensitivity: Associations with parietal area and children's mathematical cognition', *Journal of Cognitive Neuroscience*, 28(12), 1897–908. https://doi.org/10.1162/jocn_a_01018

Braddick, O., Atkinson, J., Akshoomoff, N., Newman, E., Curley, L. B., Gonzalez, M.R., Brown, T., Dale, A. & Jernigan, T. (2017), 'Individual differences in children's global motion sensitivity correlate

with TBSS-based measures of the superior longitudinal fasciculus', *Vision Research*, 141, 145–56.
https://doi.org/10.1016/j.visres.2016.09.013

Breckenridge, K., Braddick, O. & Atkinson, J. (2013), 'The organization of attention in typical development:
A new preschool attention test battery', *British Journal of Developmental Psychology*, 31(3),
271–88. https://doi.org/10.1111/bjdp.12004

Coratti, G., Mallardi, M., Coppola, C., Tinelli, F., Bartoli, M., Laganà, V., Lucibello, S., Sivo, S., Gallini, F.,
Romeo, D.M., Atkinson, J., Braddick, O., Mercuri, E. & Ricci, D. (2020), 'Early Childhood Attention
Battery: Italian adaptation and new expanded normative data', *Early Human Development*, 144,
105013. https://doi.org/10.1016/j.earlhumdev.2020.105013

Cowie, D., Braddick, O. & Atkinson, J. (2008), 'Visual control of action in step descent', *Experimental
Brain Research*, 186(2), 343–8. https://doi.org/10.1007/s00221-008-1320-1

Ehrlich, D.L., Atkinson, J., Braddick, O., Bobier, W. & Durden, K. (1995), 'Reduction of infant myopia:
A longitudinal cycloplegic study', *Vision Research*, 35(9), 1313–24.
https://doi.org/10.1016/0042-6989(94)00228-E

Gregory, R. (1966), *Eye and Brain: The Psychology of Seeing* (McGraw-Hill).

Harris, L., Atkinson, J. & Braddick, O. (1976), 'Visual contrast sensitivity of a 6-month-old infant measured
by the evoked potential', *Nature*, 264(5586), 570–1. https://doi.org/10.1038/264570a0

Howland, H.C., Atkinson, J., Braddick, O. & French, J. (1978), 'Infant astigmatism measured by
photorefraction', *Science*, 202(4365), 331–3. https://doi.org/10.1126/science.694540

Julesz, B. (1971), *Foundations of cyclopean perception* (University of Chicago Press).

Mercuri, E., Atkinson, J., Braddick, O., Anker, S., Nokes, L., Cowan, F., Rutherford, M., Pennock, J. &
Dubowitz, L. (1996), 'Visual function and perinatal focal cerebral infarction. Archives of Disease in
Childhood', *Fetal and Neonatal Edition*, 75(2), F76-81. https://doi.org/10.1136/fn.75.2.f76

Mercuri, E., Atkinson, J., Braddick, O., Anker, S., Cowan, F., Rutherford, M., Pennock, J. & Dubowitz, L.
(1997), 'Basal ganglia damage and impaired visual function in the newborn infant', *Archives of
Disease in Childhood – Fetal and Neonatal Edition*, 77(2), F111–F114.
https://doi.org/10.1136/fn.77.2.F111

Mercuri, E., Haataja, L., Guzzetta, A., Anker, S., Cowan, F., Rutherford, M., Andrew, R., Braddick, O.,
Cioni, G., Dubowitz, L. & Atkinson, J. (1999), 'Visual function in term infants with hypoxic-
ischaemic insults: Correlation with neurodevelopment at 2 years of age', *Archives of Disease in
Childhood – Fetal and Neonatal Edition*, 80(2), F99–F104. https://doi.org/10.1136/fn.80.2.F99

Micheletti, S., Corbett, F., Atkinson, J., Braddick, O., Mattei, P., Galli, J., Calza, S. & Fazzi, E. (2021),
'Dorsal and ventral stream function in children with Developmental Coordination Disorder',
Frontiers in Human Neuroscience, 15.
https://www.frontiersin.org/articles/10.3389/fnhum.2021.703217

Nardini, M., Jones, P., Bedford, R. & Braddick, O. (2008), 'Development of cue integration in human
navigation', *Current Biology: CB*, 18(9), 689–693. https://doi.org/10.1016/j.cub.2008.04.021

Prins, N. (2008), 'Correspondence matching in long-range apparent motion precedes featural analysis',
Perception, 37, 1022–36.

Ramachandran, V.S. & Braddick, O. (1973), 'Orientation--specific learning in stereopsis', *Perception*, 2(3),
371–6. https://doi.org/10.1068/p020371

Ricci, D., Anker, S., Cowan, F., Pane, M., Gallini, F., Luciano, R., Donvito, V., Baranello, G., Cesarini, L.,
Bianco, F., Rutherford, M., Romagnoli, C., Atkinson, J., Braddick, O., Guzzetta, F. & Mercuri, E.
(2006), 'Thalamic atrophy in infants with PVL and cerebral visual impairment', *Early Human
Development*, 82(9), 591–5. https://doi.org/10.1016/j.earlhumdev.2005.12.007

Spencer, J., O'Brien, J., Riggs, K., Braddick, O., Atkinson, J. & Wattam-Bell, J. (2000), 'Motion processing
in autism: Evidence for a dorsal stream deficiency', *Neuroreport*, 11(12), 2765–7.
https://doi.org/10.1097/00001756-200008210-00031

Thompson, P., Burr, D., & Morgan, M. (2022), 'Obituary: Oliver John Braddick (1944–2022)', *Perception*. https://journals.sagepub.com/doi/full/10.1177/03010066221098105

Zhang, J. (2012), 'The effects of evidence bounds on decision-making: Theoretical and empirical developments', *Frontiers in Psychology*, 3, 263. https://doi.org/10.3389/fpsyg.2012.00263

Note on the author

Dorothy Bishop, FBA, FRS, FMedSci is Emeritus Professor of Developmental Neuropsychology, Department of Experimental Psychology, University of Oxford in March 2022. She is an Honorary Fellow of St John's College, Oxford. She was elected a Fellow of the British Academy in 2006.

Biographical Memoirs of Fellows of the British Academy (ISSN 2753–6777) are published by The British Academy, 10–11 Carlton House Terrace, London, SW1Y 5AH www.thebritishacademy.ac.uk

JOHN LUCAS

John Randolph Lucas

18 June 1929 – 5 April 2020

elected Fellow of the British Academy 1988

by

RICHARD SWINBURNE

Fellow of the Academy

John Lucas wrote many books covering many different areas of philosophy. His contributions were often challenging and controversial, opposing contemporary trends in philosophy (both the logical positivist and 'ordinary language' philosophies current when he began to philosophise, and some of the metaphysical theories subsequently current), and opposing contemporary Western secular morality, but usually tentatively and with sympathy for rival views. He wrote much on space and time, on moral responsibility, and on political philosophy; and is well known for his firm advocacy of human free will, based on his argument that Gödel's Theorem has the consequence that human behaviour is not subject to deterministic laws. He also wrote many incisive and amusing essays on academic politics.

Biographical Memoirs of Fellows of the British Academy, 20, 317–334
Posted 12 October 2022. © British Academy 2022.

J. R. Lucas

Life

John Randolph Lucas was born in London on 18 June 1929, into a family of Church of England clergy. His father was a vicar until he became an Archdeacon, and his maternal grandfather was a Bishop; his younger brother, Paul, subsequently became a vicar. His parents, following the practice of many educated but not especially well-off English parents seeking what they regarded as the best education for their children, sent him from an early age to a 'preparatory school' as a border, and then from the age of 13 to a 'public school' (that is, in English as understood outside UK, a private school). Lucas's public school was Winchester College, one of the seven or eight most distinguished public schools, and the most academically orientated of all of them. It was very expensive to send a child to a good public school, and Lucas obtained an entrance scholarship which made this possible. He did not enjoy boarding school life, but was happier at Winchester than at his preparatory school. In the last two or three years at school, students specialised in one fairly narrow area of study; and he specialised in science rather than in languages or history. But he gradually became interested in the foundations of physics and mathematics, and so in philosophy. He obtained a scholarship to Oxford University, and began his life as an undergraduate at Balliol College, Oxford in 1947. He studied mathematics for the examination which all students had to take after their first few terms, but was then allowed to change his course of study to read 'Greats'. Greats involves studying the history of ancient Greece and Rome, and philosophy, including a substantial element of ancient Greek philosophy (principally Plato and Aristotle). As texts were studied in Greek and Latin, and although he had learnt a significant amount of Greek at his preparatory school, he had to spend an extra two terms at Oxford learning Greek before beginning the main course. The central element of undergraduate teaching at Oxford was then (as it is now) the weekly (or sometimes twice a week) tutorial, individually or in pairs with a tutor who is a senior academic. Oxford philosophy in the late 1940s and early 1950s, was much influenced by logical positivism. But for Lucas (as he puts it in a paper about his early life) 'the tenets of contemporary philosophy seemed just too silly to be worth bothering about.' His principal philosophy tutor was Richard ('Dick') Hare, who was highly sympathetic to logical positivism as an account of the meaning of 'factual' statements, and gave an account of the meaning of moral assertions as 'non-factual' but rather 'prescriptive'. But Lucas was looking to philosophy for eternal truths, and so his tutorials with his tutors were battles. He was fortunate to have Bernard Williams as a fellow student at the same stage as himself and claims that the two of them 'used to take pleasure in concerted campaigns to confute our tutors' cherished arguments and force on them a change of mind.' After getting his BA with first-class honours in 1951, he went on to do graduate work at Oxford on a senior scholarship at Merton College, where he then became a Junior Research Fellow. He spent the years 1956 to

1960 in various places other than Oxford – two years as a fellow of Corpus Christi College, Cambridge, a year as a research fellow at University of Leeds, and a year as a Proctor Fellow at Princeton. He returned in 1960 to Merton College, Oxford, where he became a permanent Fellow as well as a permanent Oxford faculty member for the rest of his academic life. John Lucas was very much, and very pleased to be thought as, an 'Oxford man'.

He was also very much a 'family man'. In 1961 soon after becoming a permanent Fellow of Merton College, he married Morar Portal. They had four children – Edward, who became a well-known journalist; Helen, who became a GP; Richard, who became an entrepreneur; and Deborah. Deborah was born with Down's syndrome, and John and Morar cared for her at home with great love. From 1976 they lived in term time in Merton Street, within a few yards of the gate of Merton College. In vacation time, John, Morar, and their family retreated to their home in the West Country (at one period a house near Exeter, at a later period one in Somerset), where John wrote his philosophy. And when John retired in 1996 from his post at Merton College, John, Morar, and Deborah lived permanently in Somerset.

In Oxford John Lucas was very fully involved not merely in his teaching, which he did with diligent enthusiasm and with great care for the welfare of his pupils, but in the political life of the college and university, and more widely in defence of the environment and consumer rights, and in church affairs. He had an ideal of what a university should be like, and he wrote very many witty and provocative articles in successive issues of the *Oxford Magazine* advocating that ideal and many different practical proposals for implementing it, including recommendations for how his fellow academics should respond to various proposals coming from the university authorities. He thought that the university should be run by all its teachers and researchers, and not by its vice-chancellor and a few administrators, let alone by businessmen far removed from university life. Thus for example he favoured the system whereby the vice-chancellor was a tenured Oxford academic seconded from his or her normal duties for two years, and opposed the change subsequently implemented to a system whereby the vice-chancellor who need not be already an Oxford academic was appointed for a much longer period. In the same spirit he argued strongly that the different views advocated in discussions of committees of the University Council should be made public. The extent of his influence is apparent from this incident, which he records in a *Magazine* article some years later: 'There was once a leak from the Hebdomadal Council. The Assessor told her husband, who told my wife, who told me that Monday afternoon had been spent discussing what Lucas would say if various courses of action were adopted, leading to the conclusion that it would be best to do nothing.' He was a strong advocate of well integrated joint BA degree courses between philosophy and some other subject to which it was evidently relevant, and was a keen supporter of the creation of the joint degrees in Mathematics and Philosophy and in Physics and Philosophy.

On first becoming a permanent fellow of Merton College, he was active in helping to oppose the Oxford city plan to build a ring road directly through Christ Church Meadow, which is a large green area in the centre of Oxford, lying between Merton College and the river Thames. This plan, put forward in a car-loving and so road-building era, was of a kind that would never be seriously considered by any planning authority today, in view of the enormous damage it would do to the environment; and even in 1961 the opposition to this plan proved successful. His support for the rights of consumers against large manufacturers was illustrated by his campaign against the terms of the warranty provided by BMC insurers to purchasers of new cars. He noticed that this warranty deprived the purchasers of their normal legal rights to free repair or replacement of products which failed to work satisfactorily. So he bought a single share in BMC, attended its annual general meeting, and made a speech denouncing the company for selling such insurance: and as a result, all car insurers' warranties no longer deprive purchasers of any legal rights. For a time he was a member of the Church of England's Commission on Christian doctrine, and also of the Church's Commission on Marriage and Divorce. In this role he had to defend his very moderate high church religious views both against the then fashionable liberal views of theologians who disliked precise statements of church doctrine, and also against the views of more fundamentalist evangelical theologians. When Robert Runcie, an old friend of his, was Archbishop of Canterbury, he sometimes discussed with Lucas what he ought to say in some speech which he was due to give in the House of Lords or in the Church of England Synod.

Approach to philosophy

John Lucas wrote many books covering many different areas of philosophy; and on the whole supported a fairly common-sense view about them in a conversational style with examples showing sensitivity to different viewpoints, in contrast to many contemporary philosophers who defend hard, precise, philosophical doctrines by hard, precise, philosophical arguments. Anyone whose philosophical education began in Oxford in the 1950s, when 'ordinary language philosophy' began to share dominance with logical positivism, might be expected to begin their philosophical discussion of some topic with an analysis of how its crucial words are used in ordinary language – for example, to begin a discussion of perception with an analysis of how 'it looks red' is normally used, and to begin a discussion of the nature of knowledge with an analysis of how 'know' is normally used. That is certainly a useful way of ensuring that the discussion of a philosophical topic is not a discussion of a topic invented by the philosopher, but rather a discussion of a topic on which non-philosophers are seeking illumination. But it is now generally recognised in the analytic tradition (that is, the tradition which evolved over the last hundred years mainly in Anglophone countries and now far beyond these), that a major task of philosophy is to see what, if any, is the metaphysical foundation for the distinctions made in ordinary language. Lucas often began his discussion of some philosophical topic with a description of how words and sentences are used in ordinary language and the normal beliefs which we express by means of it, before putting forward any recognisably philosophical thesis. Lucas put forward in his British Academy Philosophical Lecture of 1986 on 'Philosophy and Philosophy of' a general justification of this approach, similar to that of Neurath. There are, he plausibly claimed, too few incorrigible truths, from which to reach a world view by deductive reasoning. So, he argued, philosophy must start from whatever beliefs we find ourselves with, and criticise some of them on the basis of others of them, using non-deductive arguments to reach a moderately justified world view. This general approach to different philosophical problems is evident in his *Reason and reality* (PDF file put on the net in 2006, and published as a printed book in 2009). This was a large book containing his final published views on many of the issues of metaphysics which he had discussed previously in separate books and on many which he had not discussed previously. In this book he began his discussion of realism (the issue of what kinds of thing are real) with the remark (p. 220) that 'although the analysis of ordinary language cannot, as was once claimed, give us all the answers in philosophy, it is nevertheless a useful tool; it can save us from bad mistakes.' And so, for example, he endorsed J.L. Austin's claim that 'the meaning of the word "real" is shown in what it is being contrasted with'. But he criticised Austin's choice of examples to illustrate such contrasts, such as the contrasts between 'real coffee' and '*ersatz* coffee', and the contrast between 'real silk' and 'artificial silk', which Austin used in order to suggest that contrast between the real and the non-real was merely a contrast between different kinds of mundane objects and properties. Lucas argued that the disagreements among philosophers about which kinds of entities are real are real philosophical disagreements, and that 'what constitutes reality is revealed by what is denied by various versions of anti-realism – philosophical doctrines denying the reality of some sorts of entity commonly believed to be real'. He distinguished different kinds of anti-realism, denying the existence of different kinds of entity – phenomenalism denies the existence of material objects, behaviourism denies the existence of mental events distinct from their manifestation in behaviour, moral subjectivism denies that there are objective moral truths, and so on. He went on to give different careful accounts of the different marks of reality which would justify us in claiming that some kind of entity is real – for example, that it exists independently of the observer, that statements about it are knowable, that it has causal influence, and so on. And on most of these issues. Lucas took the common-sense view that the entities whose status was disputed are indeed real.

Space and time

In sharp contrast to the 'ordinary language' philosophy of the 1950s, analytic philosophy has now sprouted some extreme metaphysical doctrines, often purportedly dependent on science, of which Lucas has been powerfully critical. One of these doctrines concerns the nature of time. Many philosophers have espoused the 'block universe' view that all moments of time in a sense always exist, and the distinction between past and future is merely a distinction in the point of view from which we view the world, and not a distinction in the world. John Lucas opposed this view, arguing in several books that there is a deep distinction between what has happened and what will happen. His first book about the nature of time was *A Treatise on Time and Space* (1973), a large book which covered many deep metaphysical issues. Lucas followed Kant in approaching the issues of time and space by means of arguments purporting to show that we have to think of ourselves as existing in a time and space of a particular kind, if we are to make sense of our experiences. He claimed, surely correctly, that our conscious experiences have a temporal structure – they are experiences of one state of affairs being followed by another state. He argued that we must think of the before-and-after structure also as governing our interactions with other people. One argument which he gave for this was that we could not have a conversation with another person unless each of us construed the speech of the other as taking account of what the other person had said previously. More generally, we could not make a difference to the world unless we thought of the world being one way to start with and then as a result of our actions subsequently a different way. So there could be neither conversation nor agency unless the same one-dimensional temporal order governed all events; hence the impossibility of backward causation (a cause causing an earlier effect). He argued that 'same cause, same effect' needs to operate for us to be agents making a difference to the world; 'different cause, same effect' would make that impossible, and so – he argued – some form of the second law of thermodynamics would need to operate. He argued that a physical space would make it possible for ordinary objects subject to change to be qualitatively identical (in their intrinsic qualities) but numerically distinct. He analysed P.F. Strawson's claim that there could be different qualitatively identical objects in a purely auditory world, and argued that the features that objects would need to have in an auditory world to make that possible would make the purely auditory world have a spatial character. He went on to argue that if change was to be possible, there must be impenetrable objects existing in a space of more than one dimension. A Euclidean space is simpler than any other space, and so we should assume our space to be Euclidean in the absence of contrary evidence. And he then proceeded to argue for the necessity, at least in a simple and comprehensible universe inhabited by conscious beings, of various other features of space and time – for example Space being three-dimensional, and relations between spatial and temporal intervals being governed by the Lorentz transformations.

This book set the discussions of its topics in the perspective of discussions about them in classical Greek philosophy, Christian theology, the 17th-century scientific revolution, and 20th-century physics. It included, as well as the very general arguments which I mentioned in the previous paragraph, some rigorous mathematics. At a mundane level, the book is impressive in being a large very elegantly printed book containing lengthy extracts in Russian and Greek (almost always translated), equations in red and blue type and complicated lattice diagrams, printed in the pre-digital era when such complicated printing would have been very expensive – how did Lucas persuade the publisher (Methuen) to produce it? At a deeper level, the scope of this book and the way in which it connects many different issues is enormously impressive. Reviewers noted its many insights into issues about which they had not thought. But one very general issue which they raised was that it was not clear how far Lucas was purporting to show that time and space have certain necessary features, how far he was purporting to show that we must think of them as having certain necessary features, and how far it was necessary for it to have certain features in order for us thinkers to have thoughts at all.

Space and time were the major topics of three more of Lucas's books. *Space, Time, and Causality* (1984), was intended as an introduction to philosophy of physics for physics students, and to show them the relevance to their studies of philosophical problems. It does so in a clear way, and could have served as an introduction to philosophy of physics for anyone with a relatively elementary knowledge of physics. It discussed almost entirely issues raised by classical physics, expressing the hope that similar books would deal with philosophical issues raised by Relativity and Quantum theories. *SpaceTime and Electromagnetism* (1990), jointly authored with the physicist Peter Hodgson, showed how the Special Theory of Relativity is a consequence, not merely of certain experimental results, but of imposing on Newtonian mechanics certain conditions of simplicity and symmetry, and of the individuation of particles; and it went on to clarify the philosophical issues raised by Special Theory, especially the issue of how 'the relativity of simultaneity' should be understood.

The Future (1989) describes the complexities and vagueness of much ordinary language use of tenses, and the prospects for a tensed logic which knocks our tensed talk into logical shape – that is, analyses that talk in ways which conform to simple stateable logical rules. Lucas criticised the rule on which most logicians insist, that if a statement is true at one time, it is true at all times. He had two very different criticisms of that rule. His first criticism was that the rule fails to distinguish two different kinds of ordinary language statements about future events, which he called 'predictions' and 'conjectures'. He understood by 'predictions' statements which are true at the time at which they are made if and only if both there is good evidence for them at that time and what they assert subsequently happens, and by 'conjectures' statements which are true if and only if what they claim will happen does happen. It would follow that the former have a truth value which may change as the evidence for them changes. So the meaning of 'it will rain on June 30th' uttered on June 29th would vary dependent on whether it was meant to be a conjecture or a prediction. If it was a conjecture, then it would have been true when uttered on June 29th if and only if it rained on June 30th; and if it was a prediction, it would have been true on June 29th if and only if both it rained on June 30th, and all the evidence available on June 29th strongly supported the hypothesis that it will rain on June 30th. Lucas's analysis of our ordinary use is however subject to the criticism that it seems to confuse what is meant by a claim about the future with what would justify a speaker in asserting it. Lucas had made a similar distinction in *The concept of Probability* (1970), when he used the fact that we sometimes say 'it is true that p' in circumstances when we have what we regard as conclusive reason for believing p, and 'it is probable that p' in circumstances when we do not have what we regard as conclusive reason for believing p, to claim that this contrast in the circumstances in which we use the two expressions reflects a difference in their meaning. He argued that (when so used), these two statements are contraries, and that in their ascription to propositions truth and probability are (p. 12) 'in the same line of business'. His critics however denied that truth and probability are in the same line of business, on the grounds that statements may have different degrees of probability at different times on different evidence and also have truth values (normally supposed to be either true or false); and their probability may change without their truth value changing. So this first criticism provides no good grounds for abandoning the 'if true, always true' rule.

A significant number of philosophers would however agree with Lucas's second criticism of the 'if true, always true' rule, also advocated in *The Future*. He defended the metaphysical thesis that fully to describe how the world really is, we need tensed language as well as tenseless language. Tensed sentences such as 'it is raining now', 'it will rain tomorrow', or 'it rained yesterday', he argued, can be analysed in terms of the operation of an operator – such as 'it is true today' or 'it will be true tomorrow that' or 'it was true yesterday that', on a tenseless sentence such as 'it rains'. Lucas distinguished a sentence type (any utterance on any occasion of words arranged in the same way) from a sentence token (a particular utterance of a sentence type). He then claimed that while tenseless type sentences, if true at one time, are true at all times, token tensed sentences of the same sentence type, if true at one time, may be false at another time. For example, 'it rains on June 30th 1989', if true at one time is true whenever it is uttered; but 'it will rain tomorrow' uttered on June 29th 1989 may be true on June 28th 1989, but false on June 27th 1989. As observers from a timeless perspective, we need only tenseless sentences to describe the world. But, as agents in the world, Lucas claimed, we need also tensed sentences to describe it. For in order to know how to act and react, we need to distinguish what has happened already from what is likely to happen in future. That the danger is past is ground for rejoicing, but that there is likely to be danger in future is grounds for fear. In terms of the way in which this issue is more usually discussed, in order to state everything true about the history of the universe, we need to list the events in its history individuated both by McTaggart's A-series of times in terms of how long ago they occurred or how long in the future they will occur, as well as by the B-series of times in terms of the dates at which they occurred (for example, June 29th 1989, or June 30th 1989). Lucas was not happy with this way of making the distinction, one reason for which was that in his view saying on June 29th 1989 that it will rain tomorrow is not predicating a property (of occurring on the next day) of an event, but operating on a proposition, 'it rains on June 29th 1989', which has a timeless truth value, to make a different tensed proposition; and so he followed others in developing a 'tree semantics' for the truth values of tensed propositions. But he shared with A-series advocates the strong belief that there is an inherent directedness of time, from fixed past to open future, evident to all experience, for example, that the Battle of Hastings occurred several centuries before the Reformation, the former being fixed at a time when it was not yet fixed whether the latter would occur.

Free will and responsibility

Lucas shared the normal view of most of us that humans are morally responsible for many of our intentional actions; and that we can only be responsible if we are acting freely. By far the majority view of analytic philosophers in the 1960s and 1970s was that having 'free will' is simply a matter of acting freely; and that acting freely is logically compatible with being caused deterministically to act as we do. This view, called 'compatibilism' was normally spelled out as the positive doctrine that having free will is simply a matter of not being subject to 'constraint'. Being subject to 'constraint' meant being physically forced unavoidably to do some action, or caused unavoidably to do it by a recognised psychological compulsion such as kleptomania, or threatened with dire consequences if you do not do the action; but merely being caused by your brain state or your psychological condition of a kind not considered an illness to do some action did not, on this then fashionable view, impede your free will. Lucas's book *The Freedom of the Will* (1970) began with a very firm defence of the contrary view, 'incompatibilism', that it is a necessary condition if a human is to have free will, that their actions are not fully determined by any prior causes at all. He acknowledged (p. 15) that to say that an action is 'free' may mean any of the many different things, including 'not being under constraint' in some way. We may indeed often talk of someone who does some action when they are not threatened with dire consequences if they do not do it, as acting 'freely', but there remain issues of whether they are doing it 'freely' in some other sense, and in particular whether they are doing it 'freely' if they are caused to do it by their brain state. And Lucas went on to argue, very firmly, that 'absence of constraint' is not 'the relevant sense of freedom' when we are concerned 'with responsibility'. He argued that there was no justification whatever for claiming that you are unfree if caused to do an action by your kleptomaniac condition, but free if caused deterministically to do an action by some psychological condition which was not considered a mental illness. More generally, he argued (p. 28) that determinism would deprive humans 'of any real say in the course of events' because they would be 'totally dependent on other factors outside their control'. The debate between compatibilists and incompatibilists remains a philosophically vigorous one, but opinions are far more evenly divided than they were in 1970, and Lucas's arguments helped the incompatibilist cause. Although some of his books on other topics show considerable sympathy for rival views and a certain tentativeness about their conclusions, the arguments of this book in favour of incompatibilism are sharp and the conclusions which it reaches are clear, definite, and persuasive.

After arguing in favour of incompatibilism, Lucas devoted the rest of this book, as he had devoted several earlier articles and would devote many subsequent chapters or articles, to arguing that human beings are not (normally) predetermined to perform their intentional actions, and – more positively – do have free will in the sense that makes them morally responsible for their intentional actions. This, he claimed, can be shown by two mathematical and physical discoveries of the 20th century – Gödel's Theorem and quantum theory. He devoted a small part of *The Freedom of the Will* and of *Reason and Reality*, to arguing that quantum theory shows this. In claiming that quantum theory provides good evidence for human actions not being fully determined by their brain states, and so for humans having limited free will, Lucas was one of a fairly small minority of philosophers and scientists who have made the same claim. But Lucas is best known for his claim that Gödel's first incompleteness theorem shows that humans have free will. He sought to prove this in a two-stage argument. The first stage was to show that physical determinism implies the existence of a formal system that models the mind. The second stage was to show by appeal to Gödel's first incompleteness theorem that there can be no such formal system.

The first stage of his argument proceeded from the claim that

> there is only a definite finite number of beliefs which, according to the physical determinist, a particular human being can be said to hold. If this is so, the reasoning of any particular human being can be viewed as a logistic calculus … The beliefs held at the outset are the 'initial formulae' ('primitive propositions', 'postulates' or 'axioms'); and the types of inference drawn by that particular person (whether or not we regard them as valid, sound, or cogent) will be the 'rules of inference'. Thus each human being's reasoning if he can really, as the physical determinists allege, be completely described in physical terms, may be viewed as a proof-sequence in some logistic calculus. (*The Freedom of the Will*, p. 132)

(This idea is reminiscent of J.H. Woodger, *The Axiomatic Method in Biology*, 1937.) By a logistic calculus Lucas meant what would now be more usually called a deductive formal system. It doesn't follow straightforwardly that if some human's reasoning can be described by a logistic calculus, that what the human being will do with the resulting beliefs can also be so described; the calculus would need to show when the human will and when the human will not act on her beliefs. Also, Lucas did not provide a detailed explication of how to read off from a physical determinist's claim to have fully explained a human mind, a logistic calculus, that is a formal system with a precise syntax, which he needs for the second stage of the argument. But, supposing these matters to be resolved, physical determinism implies mechanism.

The second stage of Lucas' argument for freedom of the will was to refute mechanism by his 'Gödelian argument', first published in his paper 'Minds, machines and Gödel' in 1961: 'Gödel's Theorem seems to me to prove that mechanism is false, that is, that minds cannot be explained as machines' (p. 112). By 'Gödel's theorem', Lucas means Gödel's first incompleteness theorem. This proved that in any formal system adequate to prove basic arithmetic of addition and multiplication of the natural numbers, there will always be a well-formed sentence G such that if the system is consistent, then G is not provable in the system, and G is true if and only if the system is consistent.

Lucas argued that if a would-be mechanist puts forward some particular computer programme as 'a complete and adequate model of the mind', then—since a computer programme is tantamount to a formal system—there will be a Gödel sentence for its corresponding formal system which, if the system is consistent, will not be provable in that system; and whose truth is implied by the consistency of the system. (If the system were inconsistent, it could not be a correct model of any actual process.) But in order to claim to know that the system represents all the truths that can be known by some human, the mechanist must claim that the system can prove its own Gödel sentence. Yet Gödel's theorem proves that if the system is consistent, that cannot be done. So the mechanist must accept that that their system has failed to model all that their mind can know. This argument proves weak anti-mechanism, the thesis that there cannot be a computer programme of which we can know that it generates all that some human can know; and in my view this is an important conclusion. But it does not establish strong anti-mechanism, the doctrine that there can be no formal system that generates all that some human can know. Showing that no programmes or formal systems put forward by would-be mechanists could model the mind does not show that no programme or formal system (among the infinitely many unknown to us) could model the mind.

Lucas had another argument for the truth of Gödel sentences , based, not on the claim of a would-be mechanist, but on our understanding of the proof of Gödel's first incompleteness theorem: 'any rational being could follow Gödel's argument, and convince himself that the Gödelian formula, although unprovable-in-the-given-system, was nonetheless – in fact, for that very reason – true' ('Minds, machines, and Gödel', p. 115). This argument would, if correct, have established strong anti-mechanism. However in making this argument, Lucas overlooked the fact that the conclusion of Gödel's first incompleteness theorem, that the Gödel sentence is not provable in the given formal system, depends on the hypothesis that the system is consistent, which is not always known. Furthermore, if this argument were correct, it would imply too much. For the truth of its Gödel sentence implies the consistency of a formal system. So if this further argument were correct, it would establish the consistency of every formal system for which Gödel's first incompleteness theorem is provable. But there are formal systems for which Gödel's first incompleteness theorem is provable whose consistency is unknown – for example Quine's system New Foundations.

There are reasons to doubt that any version of Lucas's Gödelian argument could succeed in proving strong anti-mechanism. One is that there is a theorem by William Reinhardt (1985) that there can be no proof of strong anti-mechanism in the system EA_T (Epistemic Arithmetic with Tarskian Truth Theory), and Lucas's arguments can be formalised in EA_T. Another is that Gödel investigated the implications of his incompleteness theorems for the relationship between minds and machines and was clear that on our present understanding of knowledge and truth, strong anti-mechanism could not be proved outright. Gödel made this point in a paper written in 1951 and only published posthumously, key points of which were published by Hao Wang in 1974 in his book *From Mathematics to Philosophy*, where he reported what are 'in Gödel's opinion ... the two most interesting rigorously proved results about minds and machines'. The second result is Gödel's disjunction: '*either* the human mind surpasses all machines (to be more precise: it can decide more number theoretical questions than any machine) *or* else there exist number theoretical questions undecidable for the human mind.' The first disjunct is strong anti-mechanism, which Lucas claimed to have proved outright from Gödel incompleteness, while Gödel saw that all that could be proved is the disjunction, *either* strong anti-mechanism *or* that there are truths unknowable by human minds. It is puzzling that Lucas did not engage with Gödel's study of the implications of his incompleteness theorems for the relationship between minds and machines.

Alan Turing in his 1950 paper, 'Computing Machinery and Intelligence', had briefly formulated and rejected a version of an argument similar to that of Lucas. Lucas's argument got significant support from Roger Penrose in his books, *The Emperor's New Mind* in 1989 and *Shadows of the Mind* in 1994, in which he argued that Gödel incompleteness shows 'the un-tenability of the viewpoint . . . that our thinking is basically the same as the action of some very complicated computer'. Penrose's argument in the first book, elaborated in the second, is essentially the same as Lucas's Gödelian argument, which has come to be labelled the Lucas-Penrose argument. In *Shadows of the Mind* Penrose propounded a new argument, much more complicated and subtle than the Lucas-Penrose argument, which requires type-free theories of truth and knowledge in which to formalise it, and so is not ruled out by Reinhardt's theorem (see above). Penrose came to his initial idea that anti-mechanism follows from Gödel's incompleteness while he was a graduate student in Cambridge, eight or nine years before Lucas published his seminal paper 'Minds, Machines and Gödel'; and so Penrose's espousal of the Lucas-Penrose argument is not evidence of Lucas's influence. Nevertheless, Penrose's standing as one of the greatest mathematicians and theoretical physicists of his generation testifies to the powerful attraction of Lucas's Gödelian argument.

Lucas's views on the Gödel incompleteness theorems gave him what he considered to be an important scientific foundation for his strong conviction of the (to him) evident sharp difference between humans and inanimate objects. He took further the views which he expressed in an early paper on 'The soul' in his contributions to the two series of Gifford lectures at Edinburgh in 1971-3, given in the form of lectures by Lucas, Anthony Kenny, H.C. Longuet-Higgins, and C.H. Waddington, and discussions between them. These lectures were published in two small books, *The nature of mind* (1972), and *The development of mind* (1973) by Edinburgh University Press. In his contributions Lucas emphasised that humans have conscious experiences and act for reasons, while inanimate objects do not have experiences and do not act for reasons. In consequence he was strongly opposed to behaviourism, the doctrine that all statements about human thoughts and feelings can be reduced to statements about their actual and hypothetical (that is what they would do in certain circumstances) behaviour. But, as with many of the other topics which he discussed, this common-sense approach did not lead to any systematic theory, which in this case would have been a precise dualist theory

Lucas's claim that humans do have free will, and so are morally responsible for some of their actions, led to his discussion in his book *Responsibility* (1993) of the degree of our responsibility for different actions. A consequentialist must hold that we are equally responsible for all the (foreseeable) consequences of our actions and of our failures to act. But Lucas argued that on the contrary, while we are responsible for our actions, we are not responsible for our failures to act – unless there are special reasons why we ought to have acted. He discussed (pp. 45-51) Bernard Williams's example of 'a traveller in South America who comes on a village where a hit squad is about to shoot twenty of the villagers, and their captain says that if the traveller will himself pull the trigger on one of them, the others will go free'. If consequentialism were recognisably true, there would be no dilemma: the best consequence would evidently be obtained by the traveller shooting one of the villagers, given – Lucas assumed – that the traveller reasonably believes that the hitmen will shoot all twenty villagers unless the traveller kills one of them. Lucas argued (p. 51) that 'if the traveller refuses, and the guerrillas carry out their threat, [the traveller] is not automatically and necessarily answerable for what happens. He has not killed anyone. The deaths are due entirely to the guerrillas' actions, not to his inaction.

The chain of causal responsibility is broken by their autonomous action. They do not have to kill the hostages. It is entirely up to them whether they do it or not. The responsibility is therefore theirs.' Lucas acknowledged (p. 48), however, that 'consequences are always relevant, though sometimes not very relevant, and some bad states of affairs are ones we are always under great obligations to avert'. In the rest of the book, Lucas went on to defend various positions on various controversial moral issues. 'In so far as we take pride in what our predecessors have done, and enter into their achievements ... we identify also with the bad things they have done, and make their misdeeds our misdeeds for which we must answer' (p. 77.) In this Lucas shares the morality of many contemporary Western intellectuals. But on other moral issues he is out of line with that morality. Punishment, he argued, should be backward-looking and so retributive (on the basis of past misdeeds), and not forward-looking and allocated on utilitarian grounds of prevention, deterrence, and reform. Likewise, contrary to Rawls, he argues that desert arising from past services is 'an appropriate basis for the just allocation of benefits', though not the only such basis. Sexual intercourse should ideally take place only between married couples. It is a fault of meritocracy that it 'plays down the importance of marriage, the family, and the home' (p. 255).

Political philosophy

Lucas's first book, *The Principles of Politics* (1966) was a large book working out in detail the kinds of political organisation and constraint needed for a society of humans with a nature like ours. To constitute a society humans have to interact with each other and to share some values. But actual humans are imperfect – that is, only partly unselfish, only partly rational, and only partly well-informed. He claimed, plausibly enough, that in their political writings, a few philosophers exaggerated the imperfections of humans, as did Hobbes who regarded humans as entirely selfish; but that more philosophers have assumed that humans are more unselfish, more rational, or more well-informed than they actually are, as did Kant and R.M. Hare. The book went on to work out the consequences of Lucas's account of human nature for the best form of political organisation and the best kinds of limitation of freedom necessary for humans who have the natures they actually have. Society will need laws limiting freedom of its citizens in certain respects and limited punishments of those who break the laws, a recognised process for creating and repealing laws, judges to interpret laws and to determine who has broken which laws and what their punishment shall be, and Lucas analyses the best ways of satisfying such requirements. *On Justice* (1980) was concerned with what makes procedures for reaching decisions just ones, such as the rules that no person should be judge of their own cause, and that all persons should be entitled to equal consideration by the law. Justice is at least in part backward-looking; it punishes or rewards persons for what they have done or what they are like, and not what they would be like if they were punished or rewarded. Hence punishment must be in part retributive. It sends a message to the wrongdoer that society is hostile to him or her for what they have done. But (p. 147) 'justice does not require that there be a rigid tariff' of punishments for particular breaches of a particular law, but it must take account also of the nature and circumstances of the victim and the criminal; there is a place for mercy in the allocation of punishment. Distributive justice, the just way of distributing different goods to different members of society, should take into account many things other than the needs of those members, varying with what the goods are and who the members are – for example, 'I ought to consider my family first in allocating my time and attention, and worldly goods' (p. 166). As in most other areas of philosophy Lucas was hostile to simple general formulae. He devoted a chapter to Rawls's theory that the rational way to organise society is the way all of us would choose if we chose how society should be organised from the standpoint of a previous life, ignorant of which future person we would be in that new society. Lucas argued cogently that this was a confused suggestion, because what sort of a society I would choose to live in must depend on what sort of person I would be in that society; 'I may be, for all I know, a compulsive murderer, in which case I should be far better off if there are no punishments' (p. 193). In ignorance of what sort of a person I would be in that society, there can be no definite answer to which sort of society I would choose to belong. Lucas was similarly critical of the view attributed to Nozick and Hayek that 'the keeping of covenants constitutes the whole of justice, and that the market economy is … of necessity the fairest' form of organisation (p. 214); he pointed out that the only agreement that the weakest can get from the strongest may be unjust. In *Democracy and Participation* (1976) he analysed the advantages and disadvantages of different kinds of democracy and different levels of participation in the decisions of government and their practical implementation; and the strength of different arguments for why citizens have an obligation to obey the law, and the limits to that obligation. *Ethical Economics* (1996) was co-authored by Lucas and M.R. Griffiths, a management consultant. It analysed the moral responsibilities of businessmen to other businessmen with whom they were negotiating, to their employees and to their customers, which form the framework within which they were right to price and market their goods so as to make money.

All of this may be thought to be a deep and detailed exposition of the common sense of many moderately conservative British people of moderate education and moderate means, concerned for their own well-being and that of their family, but sensitive to the needs of others. But it is also one that will make that common sense appealing to others who do not usually share that outlook.

Religion

As an analytic philosopher and a Christian believer, Lucas made an early contribution to 'analytic philosophy of religion', the application to traditional religious claims of the methods and results of the kind of philosophy practised in the analytic tradition. Analytic philosophy of religion began with the publication of two influential collections of essays – *New Essays in Philosophical Theology* (1955), edited by Antony Flew and Alasdair MacIntyre, and *Faith and Logic* (1957), edited by Basil Mitchell, a close friend of Lucas. All the contributors to *Faith and Logic* were Oxford philosophers or theologians, and John Lucas was one of them. His contribution to it was his paper on 'The soul'. He argued that in talking about a person's 'soul' we are talking about their personal qualities and experiences and emotions, their 'inmost self which may long for God' (p. 135). Talk about the soul was useful in emphasising the very real difference between persons and inanimate objects, which he re-emphasised in his Gifford lectures; and it was at this early stage that he vigorously opposed behaviourism, then very influential as a result of Gilbert Ryle's *The concept of Mind*. Lucas claimed plausibly that Ryle's argument depended for its justification on the thesis of logical positivism that the meaning of statement is to be equated with the method by which it can be verified; and he gave powerful arguments for rejecting that thesis. *Freedom and Grace* (1976) is a collection of short papers and occasional sermons delivered on miscellaneous occasions on various issues centred around the tension arising between that human free will in which Lucas so strongly believed and the human condition of self-centredness. They bring to life, in simple non-philosophical language with a sensitivity to the human condition, many associated doctrines of grace, providence, sin, atonement, redemption, and forgiveness. A theme which runs through them is that 'the fundamental reason why I ought to do what I ought to do, is because I love God, and doing what I ought to do is an expression of my love of God' (p. 92). At about the same time Lucas gave a lecture in Durham Cathedral on *Butler's philosophy of religion vindicated* (1978), subsequently published as a separate pamphlet. This defended Butler's non-deductive and to some extent pragmatic defence of Christian theism, directed both against those who claim to have sound deductive arguments for the existence of God, and those who claim to have sound deductive arguments for the non-existence of God. In this lecture, Lucas anticipated the approach of much contemporary analytic philosophy of religion to arguments for the existence of God, although in a more tentative way. Analytic philosophy of religion is much the poorer for the fact that Lucas wrote no systematic treatise on any topic in the philosophy of religion. Nevertheless we have reason for gratitude for those individual chapters or few paragraphs in books of his primarily concerned with other topics, in which he comments on the relation of some view to Christian theology. In particular, in several places in his work on space and time and other writings, he emphatically opposed the long tradition of much Christian theology that God is timeless and changeless. He claims that a God who is a personal agent, as he is always depicted in biblical books, could not know infallibly the future actions of free human agents, and would be able to change his mind, and would be no less perfect for being like this. In this respect also Lucas anticipated subsequent developments in analytic philosophy of religion; many recent philosophers of religion have advocated this temporal account of God, now called 'open theism'. John Lucas's sometimes slightly tentative religious faith was a central element of his outlook on life.

Acknowledgements

I am very grateful to Morar Lucas, for answering many questions on John Lucas's life, and to Tim Horder, a current editor of the *Oxford Magazine*, for providing me with copies of many past articles by John Lucas in that magazine. Very many thanks to John Tassioulas for providing me with an assessment of Lucas's contributions to political philosophy, to supplement my own very limited knowledge of that area of philosophy. I am enormously grateful to Daniel Isaacson for providing me with a long report expounding and analysing John Lucas's many publications of his Gödelian argument, and comparing them with Penrose's arguments against strong AI, and with Gödel's arguments from his incompleteness theorems on the relationship between minds and machines, on a short summary of which my whole discussion of the matter is almost entirely dependent. I am however fully responsible for the selective use which I have made of that summary, and any consequent errors. Isaacson in turn wishes to record his gratitude to Stewart Shapiro for his generous willingness to respond to formulations of these issues.

Note on the author

Richard Swinburne is Emeritus Nolloth Professor of the Philosophy of the Christian religion, University of Oxford. He was elected a Fellow of the British Academy in 1992.

Biographical Memoirs of Fellows of the British Academy (ISSN 2753–6777) are published by
The British Academy, 10–11 Carlton House Terrace, London, SW1Y 5AH
www.thebritishacademy.ac.uk

JAMES HIGGINS

James Higgins

28 May 1939 – 26 September 2021

elected Fellow of the British Academy 1999

by

STEPHEN M. HART

James Higgins is remembered as an outstanding scholar of Latin American literature, Professor at the University of Liverpool (1988), and recipient of the Order of Simón Bolívar conferred by the National University of Trujillo in Peru (2014). He revolution-ised the discipline of Latin American Studies in the United Kingdom and, in works such as *Visión del hombre y de la vida en las últimas obras poéticas de César Vallejo* (1970), *The Poet in Peru* (1982), and *César Vallejo en su poesía* (1989), he consolidated his reputation as the trailblazer of the analysis of Latin America's most important poet, César Vallejo (1892–1938).

Biographical Memoirs of Fellows of the British Academy, 20, 335–355
Posted 28 October 2022. © British Academy 2022.

James Higgins

I first met Professor James Higgins on a cold, rainy evening in Liverpool in the autumn of 1981, a year in from starting my PhD in Cambridge on the life and work of Latin America's 'greatest poet' (James's words rather than mine), the Peruvian César Vallejo (1892–1938). I had travelled up on the train from London to see him and I was daunted by the idea of meeting in the flesh the great Latin Americanist of Liverpool University, James Higgins. Ostensibly my aim was to get some advice on whom I should meet up with in my upcoming trip to Lima, but my real objective was just to meet him. He advised against seeing Vallejo's widow, Georgette de Vallejo who, though still alive at the time, would pass away soon afterwards (1984). He said Georgette would probably try to attack my reputation in the way she had tried to destroy his. I countered that I didn't really have a reputation to lose, but he brushed that off, and advised me to meet up instead with the Peruvian scholar, David Sobrevilla, of the Universidad de Lima. I remain grateful to this day for the advice James gave me at that time. I did eventually meet up with Professor David Sobrevilla in Lima, and it was an important step in my own journey along the path of Vallejo Studies.

James Higgins was born on 28 May 1939 in the small Scottish town of Bellshill in Lanarkshire, Scotland, actually – as it turns out – in the very year that the *editio princeps* of Vallejo's most significant collection of poems was published.[1] The eldest of five brothers, he was a hard-working student and the first of his family to go to university. He read Spanish and French at the University of Glasgow, and completed his teacher training at Jordanhill College of Education in Glasgow (1957–1861). This was when James met the love of his life, Kirstine Atwell. They were soon married and they began their life together in 1962 in Lyon, France, where James took up a post as English Assistant at a Lycée. James and Kirstine lived for two years in Lyon, a period of their life that, as Kirstine recalls, was full of fond memories. During their time there James was invited to interview for the post of Assistant Lecturer in the Department of Hispanic Studies at the University of Liverpool; the interview was successful and he was confirmed in his post by Professor Geoffrey Ribbans, the world-renowned expert on Galdós, Unamuno and Antonio Machado. James and Kirstine moved to Liverpool in 1964. They had two sons, Antony born in Glasgow, and who would one day follow in his father's footsteps and publish a book on Latin America, *Constructing the Criollo Archive* (2000),[2] just a year before his untimely death[3] – and Graham, born in Birkenhead.

[1] *Poemas humanos (1923–1938)*, ed. Georgette de Vallejo & Raúl Porras Barrenechea (Paris: Les Éditions des Presses Modernes au Palais-Royal, 1939), 159 pp.

[2] Antony Higgins, *Constructing the Criollo Archive: Subjects of Knowledge in the 'Biblioteca Mexicana' and the 'Rustication Mexicana'* (Purdue University Press, 2000).

[3] 'In Memoriam Antony Higgins, 1964–2001', *Calliope: Journal of the Society for Renaissance and Baroque Hispanic Poetry*, 8.2 (2002), 95–97.

Not long after his arrival in Liverpool it became clear to his colleagues that James would before long become one of the pioneers of Latin American Studies in Britain. He developed a keen interest in Peruvian literature and in the work of César Vallejo in particular. James's first trip to Peru was on the Pacific Steam cargo ship which departed from Liverpool in January 1967; he was Passenger 13 on that ship,[4] and it was a journey that would transform his life. The six months James spent in Peru were not uneventful. He wrote letters weekly to Kirstine during that period and, in March 1967, he told her about some political difficulties he had experienced. He had been invited to give a talk on Vallejo in the Porras Barrenchea Institute, and the first title he suggested – 'Vallejo's Religious Position'— was rejected. The second title he proposed – 'Vallejo and the Revolution' – was also rejected, as was the third – 'The Indian in Vallejo'. In the end he had to make do with a very innocuous title that could surely not cause offense: 'Vallejo's Concept of Man'.[5] Despite these obstacles, James's time in Peru was enormously productive, and he was awarded a PhD for his thesis on 'César Vallejo's Vision of Man and Life in his Final Poetic Works' at the University of Liverpool in 1968.[6]

James's academic work – showcased in the articles he was publishing at that time – was starting to get him noticed. In the autumn term of 1968, he was invited by Professor Keith McDuffie at the University of Pittsburgh – the author of an excellent thesis on Vallejo that, bafflingly, he never published[7] – to take up Pittsburgh's highly prestigious Andrew Mellon Visiting Professorship. James accepted and he began teaching classes on 19th-century Spanish-American literature and Spanish American Civilisation, working alongside Javier Herrero, the acclaimed *cervantista*, and Robin Carter, a graduate from St Andrews. A highly popular teacher, James was subsequently offered a permanent post as Associate Professor in Pittsburgh, but – though initially tempted – he decided against it.[8]

Two years later his first book came out, *Visión del hombre y de la vida en las últimas obras de César Vallejo* (1970), a highly influential work that revolutionised the field of Vallejo studies. It was the first book to provide meticulously close studies of the style and argument of each of Vallejo's poems. In this short summary I provide some indicators of the originality of Professor Higgins's research. For a more extensive record and summary of Professor Higgins's extensive publication portfolio the reader is referred to the bibliographical essay in the Festschrift volume devoted to James.[9]

---

[4] Kirstine Higgins; email to author, 20 September 2022.

[5] Kirstine Higgins; email to author, 20 September 2022.

[6] Stephen M. Hart, *César Vallejo: Research Bibliographies and Checklists: New Series* (Woodbridge: Tamesis, 2002), p. 159.

[7] Keith McDuffie, 'The Poetic Vision of César Vallejo in *Los heraldos negros* and *Trilce*' (University of Pittsburgh, 1969).

[8] Kirstine Higgins; email to author, 20 September 2022.

[9] 'Bibliography of the Publications of James Higgins', *Studies of Latin American Literature in Honour of James Higgins*, edited by Stephen M. Hart and William Rowe (Liverpool: Liverpool University Press, 2005), pp. 6–10.

Apart from being an excellent scholar not just of Peruvian but also of Latin American Literature, James also managed to act as primary supervisor to a number of PhD students, who have warm memories of his company and support. He became Head of the Department of Hispanic Studies at the University of Liverpool in January 1988, a post he held until January 1997, and he was a founding member of the Centre for Latin American Studies, later the Institute of Latin American Studies, with which he kept close ties throughout his career. Dr Valdi Asvaldsson, who worked alongside James for many years at the University of Liverpool, recalls that he 'was very supportive, always available to have a chat or read drafts of academic work and provide constructive criticism: he would give his honest professional opinion, tell you what he thought was good and where improvements could be made, but he never made you feel as if he was the measure of everything'; he was 'calm, considered, kind and hospitable, a true gentleman with a fine sense of humour'.[10] Núria Triana-Toribio, of the University of Kent, for her part, remembers James as a 'wonderful mentor whose door was never closed'. Though 'a highly influential Latin Americanist (….), he was interested in everything I wanted to discuss with him, Spanish cinema, music, popular culture'.[11] James was especially supportive of his junior colleagues during this period. When Dr Adam Sharman (University of Nottingham) organised a conference on Vallejo, he recalls that James 'was extremely generous with his time (…) He contributed, really, as a favour to a young scholar just starting out. He didn't need to attend the colloquium or to publish in that volume, but he did both. Modest and self-effacing.'[12]

Another of James's colleagues, Mike Thacker, recalls how James worked on the recruitment strategy of the Liverpool department in the 1980s, which proved to be highly successful. He was 'greatly respected by his students, many of whom had been attracted to Liverpool by the strong Latin-American section of the course, which Jim had devised'. Perhaps most importantly, 'Jim was a leader: shrewd and clear-minded, he earned the respect of his colleagues by his manner of running the department (…). A highly competent administrator, he knew how to delegate, and find ways round bureaucratic obstacles. He understood the strengths of his colleagues, valued their contributions to the department, had little time for red tape and made decisions rapidly and without fuss'.[13] But James also had a less conventional side to his character. Roger Wright remembers that James's university office in Liverpool often smelt of cigarettes, even after the time when smoking was strictly forbidden, but there was a reason for this! As Roger recalls: 'put a

[10] Valdi Astvaldsson, 'Obituary: Professor James Higgins', 14 October 2021; https://news.liverpool.ac.uk/2021/10/14/obituary-professor-james-higgins/ (consulted on 1 August 2022).
[11] Email to author, 11 April 2022.
[12] Email to author, 7 April 2022.
[13] Email to author, 13 April 2022.

cigarette in his mouth and sit him in front of a complex piece of Spanish American poetry and he'd explain it in minutes'.[14]

This was, indeed, the genius of James Higgins's literary criticism. Books such as his highly influential *César Vallejo: An Anthology of His Poetry* (1970) show you how Vallejo's poetry works and tease out the literary, cultural and historical ramifications effortlessly before your eyes. Published in the Pergamon Oxford Latin American Series, this book was a model of its kind.[15] Including a brief biography of the Peruvian poet, followed by a discussion of the literary environment in which he moved, the introduction is distinctive in terms of the way in which it analyses each of the poems chosen thoroughly, drawing out the poem's argument and analysing – with great concision and insight – the peculiarity of Vallejo's poetic idiom. This structure allowed James to directly engage with its specified audience – the first-year Latin American Studies undergraduate:

> The modern poem differs from the traditional poem in that, whereas the latter is logical and coherent on both levels, the logic and coherence of the former is that of the poetic emotion and there is no concern that its external representation should be logical and coherent. Hence the relationship between the two levels is not always logically apparent. Often there is no direct reference to the stimulus of the poetic emotion and instead it is reduced to an image that symbolizes its emotional import. Nor is the emotion explained but is conveyed to us by the imagery.[16]

The notes – especially in their careful differentiation in Vallejo's use of archaisms, Peruvianisms, colloquialisms, Gallicisms, technical terms and neologisms, and the inspired translation of particularly difficult passages – are insightful. One of my favourites is his explanation of a particularly obscure word in line 16 of *Trilce* LXXI which describes the to-ing and fro-ing of two lovers: '*ennavajados*, armed with razors. This is a technical term employed in cock-fighting. Cocks often have razors attached to their spurs to increase their effectiveness. Here it can be taken as having the sense of doubly armed.'[17] James was not a great fan of some of the postmodern and postcolonial theories that swept throughout the academy in the 1980s and 1990s. Philip Swanson, the Hughes Professor of Spanish at the University of Sheffield, in his own memoir, articulates James's no-nonsense approach to teaching and knowledge: 'As a teacher, I found Jim inspirational as I did him as a scholar. What really struck me about him was his remarkable economy of expression. He taught and wrote with great economy and precision – he

---

[14] Email to author, 8 April 2022.

[15] 'Introduction', in *César Vallejo: An Anthology of his Poetry*, with an Introduction and Notes by James Higgins (Oxford: Pergamon, 1970), pp. 1–84.

[16] 'Introduction', in *César Vallejo: An Anthology of his Poetry*, p. 35.

[17] 'Notes', in *César Vallejo: An Anthology of his Poetry*, p. 176.

didn't go in for generic commentary or waffle but was able to zone in on the key issue with great precision.'[18]

In subsequent conversations with James after our first meeting in 1981 he told me that – in the academy as much as beyond – everyone seemed to accept that Vallejo was a great poet, but many critics restricted their attention to just a few of the famous poems. James completely revolutionised the field when he began systematically interpreting all of Vallejo's poems, an approach typified by his essay, 'Vallejo en cada poema'.[19] For James the aim of literary criticism was to bring to life the meaning of the poem via a detailed *explication de texte*. Some of the essays he published during this period – such as his study of 'Los nueve monstruos'[20], 'Va corriendo, andando…',[21] 'Y si después de tantas palabras…',[22] 'Un pilar soportando consuelos…',[23] and 'El alma que sufrió de ser su cuerpo…'[24] – are intense and beautifully written close readings of Vallejo's most difficult poems from *Poemas humanos*. James also studied leitmotifs such as the 'conflict of personality',[25] the role played by evil,[26] disillusionment,[27] pain,[28] and (my favourite article of his!) absurdity[29] in Vallejo's oeuvre. His work was particularly insightful about religion; in his essay, 'La posición religiosa de César Vallejo a través de su poesía',[30] for example, James showed how charity and brotherly love were invoked at different stages of Vallejo's writing and, during the Spanish Civil War, essentially re-politicised. Philip Swanson brings out James's skill in this regard pointedly: 'He had, of course, an encyclopaedic knowledge (of Peruvian literature in particular), but he was also a fantastic close reader – I thought he was a brilliant traditional interpreter of literary texts. He once said to me: "There are two types of intellectual – those who make simple things sound complicated and those who make complicated things sound simple." Jim was definitely the latter, and the way he made Vallejo accessible to generations of students was a perfect

---

[18] Email to author 2 August 2022.

[19] 'Vallejo en cada poema', *Mundo Nuevo* (Paris), 22 (1968), 21–26.

[20] '"Los nueve monstruos" de César Vallejo: una tentativa de interpretación', *Razón y Fábula* (La Paz), 2 (1967), 20–25.

[21] '"Va corriendo, andando…"', *Cuadernos del Idioma*, 10 (1968), 119–23

[22] '"Y si después de tantas palabras"', in *Aproximaciones a César Vallejo*, ed. Angel Flores, 2 vols (New York: Las Américas, 1971), II, pp. 263–66.

[23] '"Un pilar soportando consuelos…"', in *Aproximaciones a César Vallejo*, II, 297–300.

[24] '"El alma que sufrió de ser su cuerpo…"', in *Aproximaciones a César Vallejo*, II, 313–21.

[25] 'The Conflict of Personality in César Vallejo's *Poemas humanos*', *Bulletin of Hispanic Studies*, XLIII:1 (1966), 47–55.

[26] 'El tema del mal en los *Poemas humanos* de César Vallejo', *Letras* (Lima), 78–79 (1967), 92–108.

[27] 'El pensamiento y el desengaño en César Vallejo', *San Marcos*, 7 (1967–68), 77–89.

[28] 'El dolor en los *Poemas humanos* de César Vallejo', *Cuadernos Hispanoamericanos*, 222 (1968), 619–31.

[29] 'El absurdo en la poesía de César Vallejo', *Revista Iberoamericana*, 71 (1970), 217–41.

[30] 'La posición religiosa de César Vallejo a través de su poesía', *Caravelle* (Toulouse), 9 (1967), 47–58.

example of that.'[31] For my own part I have always seen James's gargantuan outpouring of criticism on Vallejo from 1966 until 1974 as echoing the extraordinary productivity of Vallejo himself from 3 September until 8 December 1937 when he had just returned to Paris from the battlefields of Spain during the Spanish Civil War, and he began writing the poems that would come together after his premature death as *Poemas humanos* and *Espana, aparta de mi este caliz*.

In 1974 James began a stint as Visiting Professor at the University of Waterloo in Ontario, Canada, in the Department of Classics and Modern Languages. While there he met Professor Jim McDonald, then Acting Head at Queen's University, Kingston, who invited James to give a talk on the work of Vallejo's great rival, the Chilean poet Pablo Neruda. As he told Kirstine: 'Little do they know that I have never given a class on Neruda and until now never read more than a handful of his poems'. Despite this he 'managed to knock up a reasonable lecture' and, as he remarked to Kirstine later on: 'You can talk about anything if you put your mind to it.'[32] This was typical of James's modesty.

It was in his three authoritative works, *Visión del hombre y de la vida en las últimas obras poéticas de César Vallejo* (1970), *The Poet in Peru: Alienation and the Quest for a Super-reality* (1982), and *César Vallejo en su poesía* (1989), that James refined his vision of Vallejo's work in its poetic and historical context. In order to refine the reader's understanding of that context, James chose, for example in *The Poet in Peru*, to portray Vallejo as the North Star within Peru's poetic firmament. In this work he studies Vallejo's work alongside that of five other poets – José María Eguren (1874–1942), Carlos Germán Belli (b. 1927), Antonio Cisneros (1942–2012), César Moro (1903–1956), and Martín Adán (1908–1985) – and he starts from the hypothesis that alienation is the most characteristic trait of 20th-century Peruvian poetry as well as 'all contemporary Western literature'.[33] Though the Peruvian poets share this trait with other western writers, alienation has a special resonance for them since they

> are outsiders who feel themselves out of place in the country and in the world where it has been their lot to live. Yet if theirs has been a painful experience in personal terms, it has been fruitful for poetry. For not only has their disconformity with their world impelled them to write and furnished them with poetic material, but the best of them have embraced their estrangement and have used their isolation to develop a style of their own.[34]

---

[31] Email to author 2 August 2022.

[32] Kirstine Higgins; email to author, 16 September 2022.

[33] *The Poet in Peru: Alienation and the Quest for a Super-Reality* (Liverpool: Francis Cairns, 1982), p. 1.

[34] *The Poet in Peru*, p. 1.

Vallejo's poetry provides the template for this work. His alienation is traced back to his personal experience of homesickness as a 'lonely *serrano* immigrant' in Lima,[35] as well as to his self-distancing from capitalism during the Depression in the 1930s,[36] and this provides a measuring-stick, as it were, for the analysis of this leitmotif in Carlos Germán Belli's work. As James suggests, Belli develops this theme mainly in terms of a rejection of the crassness of Lima's elite in a 'personal style which combines elements derived from Spanish poetry of the Golden Age – a classical or archaic vocabulary; a disconcerting syntax characterised by hyperbaton and ellipsis; the frequent use of reiterative epithet; a predilection for the hendecasyllable and the heptasyllable – with contemporary themes and modern and colloquial language and imagery'.[37] The theme of alienation is seen to veer in a different direction in Antonio Cisneros's poetry via a 'scepticism with regard to utopian idealisations of the pre-Colombian civilisations' of Peru, particularly the Incas.[38]

Balancing this prevailing mood of alienation, however, in the Peruvian poetic tradition is another wave of artistic energy, a 'visionary or neo-mystical poetics in which poetry is conceived as an alternative life style devoted to the passionate pursuit of self-fulfilment'; the visionary poet seeks to 'capture the privileged moment which Pater calls "beatific vision" and Joyce "epiphany", the moment when he is fulfilled by an ecstatic sense of participating in a cosmic harmony'.[39] James finds some evidence of this visionary poetics even in gloomy Vallejo's work, especially in the poems of the 1922 collection, *Trilce*, where there are hints of a 'transcendental state' achieved through art (as in the Venus de Milo statue addressed in Tr. XXXVI), via sex with the beloved, in the unexplained apprehension of life's hidden harmony, and in the ecstatic vision of nature's beauty.[40] Yet it is a foundational structure in the work of poets such as José María Eguren, César Moro and Martín Adán. In Eguren's poetry, for example, this visionary poetics emerges through the veil of French Symbolism with its emphasis on the evocation of an ideal world hidden beneath the objects of the material world, and the messenger of that other world is the poet's alter ego, a figure called 'Peregrine': 'Peregrín cazador de figuras, / con ojos de diamante / mira desde las ciegas alturas'.[41] César Moro, for his part, rejected his native city (Lima, which he famously called 'Lima la horrible', an epithet that stuck) as well as his native language (he only published one collection of poems in Spanish, preferring to publish his poetry in French), and his visionary poetics was

---

[35] *The Poet in Peru*, p. 25.
[36] *The Poet in Peru*, pp. 39–45.
[37] *The Poet in Peru*, p. 46.
[38] *The Poet in Peru*, p. 70.
[39] *The Poet in Peru*, p. 91.
[40] *The Poet in Peru*, pp. 116–122.
[41] *The Poet in Peru*, p. 93.

expressed via his complete immersion in Surrealism. As James notes, Moro joined hands with the Surrealists in seeing the 'artist as a revolutionary waging a campaign of subversion aimed at overthrowing a hated civilisation and liberating the human species', no less![42] In the last chapter of this work, James focuses on Martín Adán whose work differs from that of Eguren and Moro in that he was more of a traditionalist; despite dabbling in some avant-garde techniques early in his life, he devoted the majority of his work to an exploration of the sonnet form, although he did share with these two poets a desire to re-create a super-reality via a 'poetic ecstasy' centred on the allegorical motif of the Rose.[43] *The Poet in Peru* is an excellent compendium of knowledge about the modern poetic tradition in Peru, as guided by the pendulum that swings between alienation on the one hand and a visionary poetics on the other.

A linguist to the core, James was also keen to bring the beauty of Vallejo's poetry to the English-speaking world. His own translation of Vallejo's poetry came out in 1987, and it was complete with a fine introduction along with detailed notes.[44] The distinctive trait of these translations is their linguistic accuracy, the almost physical way in which they cleave to Vallejo's original verse. The original Spanish of one of Vallejo's most famous poems 'Los heraldos negros' runs as follows:

> Hay golpes en la vida, tan fuertes … Yo no sé!
> Golpes como del odio de Dios; como si antes ellos,
> la resaca de todo lo sufrido
> se empozara en el alma… Yo no sé!

James's translation might be too literal for some poetry connoisseurs:

> There are blows in life, so hard… I don't know!
> Blows as if from the hatred of God; as if in the face of them
> The backwash of everything we've suffered
> Had welled up in the soul… I don't know![45]

Other translators have embellished Vallejo's poetry by translating the refrain 'Yo no sé' poetically, but what James manages to conserve in his translation is the colloquial roughness of the Peruvian poet's diction. Vallejo refuses to mince his words. He may be talking via the persona of the Romantic poet for whom the world is a hostile place but Vallejo simply records that some things that happen in life are so bad that it seems like God hates you. And Vallejo just calls them physical 'blows'. James chooses his words carefully. Thus he is able to retain the liquid metaphors with both of the verbs used in

---

[42] *The Poet in Peru*, p. 123.

[43] *The Poet in Peru*, pp. 153–60.

[44] *César Vallejo: A Selection of his Poetry*, with translations, introductions and notes by James Higgins (Liverpool: Francis Cairns, 1987).

[45] *César Vallejo: A Selection of his Poetry*, p. 3.

line 3 and 4 – 'resaca' and 'empozarse' – by translating these words as 'backwash' and 'welled up'. By using these particular words James is able to retain the earthiness and physical disgust experienced by the poet as a result of misfortune. For Vallejo this was not an abstract emotion but something physical and visceral. Vallejo had just heard that his sister had been raped before he wrote the poem, and James's translation manages to capture the feelings of disgust effectively. James's focus upon linguistic accuracy meant that his translations were not vulnerable to the type of critique that other translators such as Clayton Eshleman have been subjected to. Eshleman's *César Vallejo: The Complete Poetry, a Bilingual Edition*,[46] was savaged by the Yale critic, Roberto González Echevarría, with the following words: 'English-language readers of Vallejo will have to make do with what this book offers them, which is quite a lot but, alas, not quite Vallejo.'[47]

James's translations of Vallejo will, indeed, survive the test of time. His English rendition of Vallejo's most famous poem, 'Piedra negra sobre una piedra blanca':

> Me moriré en París con aguacero,
> un día del cual tengo ya el recuerdo.
> Me moriré en París – y yo no me corro –
> talvez un jueves, como es hoy, de otoño.
>
> Jueves será, porque hoy, jueves, que proso
> estos versos, los húmeros me he puesto
> a la mala y, jamás como hoy, me he vuelto,
> con todo mi camino, a verme solo.
>
> César Vallejo ha muerto, le pegaban
> todos sin que él les haga nada ;
> le daban duro con un palo y duro
>
> también con una soga ; son testigos
> los días jueves y los huesos húmeros,
> la soledad, la lluvia., los caminos…[48]

is as clipped and stark as the original Spanish:

> I'll die in Paris when it's raining hard
> on a day that's already lodged in my memory.
> I'll die in Paris – and I'm not running away –
> maybe some Thursday, like today, in Autumn.

[46] *César Vallejo: The Complete Poetry: A Bilingual Edition*, edited and translated by Clayton Eshleman (Berkeley CA: California University Press, 2007).

[47] Roberto González Echevarría, 'Revolutionary Devotion', *The Nation* (21 May 2007), 25–30 (p. 30).

[48] César Vallejo, *Poemas humanos (1923–1938)* (Paris: Les Éditions des Presses Modernes au Palais Royal, 1939); facsimilar edition, edited by César Ferreira (Lima: Universidad Ricardo Palma, 2019), p. 54.

> Thursday it'll be, for today, Thursday, when I prose
> these verses, I've donned my humeri
> with reluctance and never as today,
> for all my long road, have I ever seen myself so alone.
>
> César Vallejo is dead, they all beat him
> when he'd done nothing to them;
> they hit him hard with a stick and hard
>
> too with a rope; witnesses are
> the Thursdays and the humerus bones,
> the loneliness, the rain, the roads…[49]

This translation is deceptively simple. Its almost hidden artistry is epitomised by the slightly awkward phrase 'with reluctance' in l. 7, though this is an inspired rendition of 'a la mala', a Peruvianism intentionally positioned by Vallejo in the middle of the poem, which is the equivalent of 'de mala gana' in standard Castilian (reluctantly). Vallejo, as anyone who reads his poetry will know, often referred to his Peruvian identity in a mock-ironic tone, as occurs most memorably in 'Ello es que…':

> guardar un día para cuando no haya,
> una noche también, para cuando haya
> (así se dice en el Perú – me excuso)
>
> to save a day for when there isn't one,
> a night too for when there is
> (sorry – it's what they say in Peru).[50]

As this passage exemplifies, James's knowledge of Vallejo and Peruvian poetry relied as much on his in-depth knowledge of local idiolects in Peru as anything else.

In many ways it was his study, *César Vallejo en su poesía*, originally published in 1989 and re-issued in 2015, that we find the definitive version of James Higgins's understanding of Vallejo's poetic vision.[51] The prologue to the 1989 edition of the work epitomises James's methodology:

> Este libro obedece a una convicción que ha inspirado todos mis trabajos sobre Vallejo: el major homenaje que podemos rendir al poeta es procurar adentrarnos en su mundo poético. El Vallejo auténtico se encuentra, no en las biografías ni en los libros de tipo general que se valen del escritor para desarrollar teorías personales, sino en los poemas mismos. En las últimas décadas los estudios vallejianos han avanzado mucho, pero aún no hemos hecho más que tocar la superficie de la obra más genial de la poesía de lengua española de este siglo.[52]

---

[49] *César Vallejo: A Selection of his Poetry*, p. 79.
[50] *César Vallejo: A Selection of his Poetry*, pp. 102-03.
[51] James Higgins, *César Vallejo en su poesía* (Lima: Editorial Cátedra Vallejo, 2015).
[52] 'Prólogo 1989', *César Vallejo en su poesía*, p. 14.

This statement is significant for two reasons, first, for its emphasis on the importance of reading the poems themselves, i.e., creating a close reading of Vallejo's work, as well as its expression of James's conviction that Vallejo's poetry was the most significant of the 20th century in the Spanish-speaking world. James's analysis covers the full gamut of the central themes of Vallejo's work, including provincialism,[53] existential crisis,[54] visceral insecurity,[55] urban alienation,[56] the tyranny of biological laws,[57] paradise lost,[58] the poetic search for a super-reality,[59] Vallejo's European experience,[60] the absurdity of life,[61] and the crisis of capitalism sparked by the Wall Street Crash that occurred in October 1929.[62] The extent and depth of Vallejo's expression of a socialist ideology is carefully extracted from four poems, 'Considerando en frío…', 'Hasta el día en que vuelva…', 'Los desgraciados' from *Poemas humanos*, and 'Masa' from *España, aparta de mí este cáliz*.[63] Finally, James picks on three poems ('Salutación angélica', 'El alma que sufrió de ser su cuerpo…' and 'Un pilar soportando consuelos…') to point to the fundamental ambivalence of Vallejo's political positionality in his final collection of poems,[64] and two poems in the final chapter ('Despedida recordando un adiós', from *Poemas humanos* and 'España, aparta de mí este cáliz', the signature poem of Vallejo's Spanish Civil War poems), are explored in terms of Vallejo's vacillation between faith and disillusionment.[65] Chapters 10–13 are arguably the most valuable of this fine collection of essays, not least because they draw out in a lucid and compelling way the causal and necessary connections between linguistic and political ambivalence in Vallejo's work. As a result of Theodor Adorno's famous assertion that 'there can be no poetry after Auschwitz' – aided by poets such as Pablo Neruda and Louis Aragon – the idea has emerged that there is necessarily a juncture when a poet needs to sacrifice artistic complexity on the altar of political commitment. Vallejo's work, however, breaks the Gordian knot linking poetic commitment to rhetorical simplicity, and James Higgins was the first critic to draw this observation out into the open arena of Latin American Studies, seeing it as a sign of intellectual vigour rather than a symptom of political confusion, as had often been the case until then.

[53] Chapter 1, *César Vallejo en su poesía*, pp. 15–19.
[54] Chapter 2, *César Vallejo en su poesía*, pp. 21–36.
[55] Chapter 3, *César Vallejo en su poesía*, pp. 37–44.
[56] Chapter 4, *César Vallejo en su poesía*, pp. 45–60.
[57] Chapter 5, *César Vallejo en su poesía*, pp. 61–74.
[58] Chapter 6, *César Vallejo en su poesía*, pp. 75–88.
[59] Chapter 7, *César Vallejo en su poesía*, pp. 89–110.
[60] Chapter 8, *César Vallejo en su poesía*, pp. 111–124.
[61] Chapter 9, *César Vallejo en su poesía*, pp. 125–144.
[62] Chapter 10, *César Vallejo en su poesía*, pp. 145–160.
[63] Chapter 11, *César Vallejo en su poesía*, pp. 161–180.
[64] Chapter 12, *César Vallejo en su poesía*, pp. 181–198.
[65] Chapter 13, *César Vallejo en su poesía*, pp. 199–208.

In 1990 James was invited to spend a semester as Visiting Professor at the University of Wisconsin at Madison. The teaching regime there, like the weather, was unforgiving. As Kirstine, who accompanied him on this trip, recalls: 'I remember being surprised that everything seemed to stop at 9 pm and it became clear that the 8 am tutorials were the reason for this. We had an apartment in a building on the edge of a frozen lake and the walk to the university was a challenge in the biting wind.'[66] James's stints as Visiting Professor in a number of different universities – he had even spent time as Visiting Professor at the University of Trinidad and Tobago at Port of Spain in 1978 – had served to broaden his interests beyond the study of the poetry of Peru's and arguably Latin America's best poet. We should be wary, therefore, of making the same mistake that Vallejo's widow, Georgette, did when she casually asked James in a conversation with him in Lima sometime in the 1960s why on earth he had decided to focus all of his intellectual energies on her late husband's work. Clearly she was unaware of James's other interests. As noted above, he wrote on other Peruvian poets such as Carlos Germán Belli,[67] José María Eguren,[68] Martín Adán,[69] César Moro,[70] and Antonio Cisneros,[71] but these were not the only Peruvian poets he chose to focus on. He also wrote on Blanca Varela,[72] Sebastián Salazar Bondy[73], as well as novelists and short story writers such as Enrique Congrains Martín,[74] Miguel Gutiérrez,[75] Julio Ramón Ribeyro,[76] the great José María Arguedas,[77] the inimitable Bryce Echenique,[78] and the Nobel Laureate Mario

---

[66] Kirstine Higgins; email to author, 16 September 2022.

[67] 'El mundo poético de Carlos Germán Belli a través del poema "Contra el estío"', in *Literatura de la emancipación hispanoamericana y otros ensayos* (Lima: Universidad Nacional Mayor de San Marcos, 1972), pp. 179–83; 'Carlos Germán Belli: una introducción a sus poesías', *Textual* (Lima), 4 (1972), 59–63.

[68] 'Eguren: alienado y visionario', *Tierradentro* (Lima), 3 (1985), 59–88.

[69] 'La aventura poética de Martín Adán en *Travesía de extramares*', in *Homenaje a Luis Alberto Sánchez*, ed. R. Mead (Madrid: Insula, 1983), pp. 219–317.

[70] 'Westphalen, Moro y la poesía surrealista', *Cielo Abierto*, 29 (1984), 16–26.

[71] 'Antonio Cisneros: la ironía desmitificadora', in *Metáfora de la experiencia: la poesía de Antonio Cisneros*, ed. M.A. Zapata (Lima: Pontificia Universidad Católica del Perú, 1998), pp. 211–43.

[72] 'Blanca Varela', in *Contemporary World Writers*, ed. T. Chevalier (Andover: St. James Press, 1993), 539–40.

[73] 'Sebastián Salazar Bondy', in *Encyclopedia of Latin American Literature*, ed. Verity Smith (London: Fitzroy Dearborn, 1997), p. 748.

[74] 'A Forgotten Peruvian Novelist: Enrique Congrains Martín', *Iberoromania*, 2 (1971), 112–20.

[75] 'Replanteando las relaciones de raza y de género en el Perú: *La violencia del tiempo* de Miguel Gutiérrez', *Neue Romania*, 16 (1995), 247–56.

[76] 'Family History and Social Change in Two Short Stories of Julio Ramon Ribeyro', in *New Frontiers in Hispanic and Luso-Brazilian Scholarship*, ed. T.J. Dadson, et. al. (Lewiston: Edwin Mellen Press, 1994), pp. 517–29.

[77] 'El tema de la *Yawar Fiesta* en la narrativa peruana del 50', in *Homenaje a don Luis Monguió*, ed. J. Aladro-Font (Newark: Juan de la Cuesta, 1997), pp. 233–46.

[78] '*Un mundo para* Julius: The Swan-song of the Peruvian Oligarchy', *Tesserae*, IV.1 (1998), 35–45.

Vargas Llosa.[79] As this list suggests James did not write on writers because they were famous or because they might help him climb the promotion-ladder of academia. He read works for what they were, and he was always ready to voice his considered opinion on them.

An example of James's interest in writers who might be considered off the beaten track is his 1994 study, *Myths of the Emergent: Social Mobility in Contemporary Peruvian Fiction*.[80] In this monograph James demonstrated that his real interest lay not in the set of middle-class writers for whom the lower social sectors 'play a passive role as the raw material' for their fiction, but in the writers from the lower échelons of society who have sought to 'produce fiction reflecting the experience and perspective of the underclasses'.[81] As James went on to suggest:

> [W]hile established middle-class figures like Julio Ramón Ribeyro, Mario Vargas Llosa and Alfredo Bryce Echenique remain the big names in terms of prestige, Peruvian fiction is becoming more representative of the nation as a whole as more plebeian authors, such as Miguel Gutiérrez, Gregorio Martínez, Cronwell Jara and Augusto Higa, begin to make their presence felt on the literary scene.[82]

He studies two novels in this monograph – Miguel Gutiérrez's *La violencia del tiempo* (1991) and Cronwell Jara's *Patíbulo para un caballo* (1989) – and shows how the legitimacy of the Spanish Conquest in Peru is deconstructed in these novels, and thus the marginalised classes are demonstrated to be 'the best in Peruvian society'.[83] In point of fact they are the only class able to 'achieve the ideal of an egalitarian, multiracial Peru',[84] and again we see James's interest in allowing new voices to emerge in Peru's literary establishment which are, to re-quote his words, 'more representative of the nation as a whole'.[85]

Indeed, James was not afraid to ruffle the feathers of the establishment when he saw fit to do so. I remember the occasion when he was invited as part of a delegation to visit the recently inaugurated Cervantes Institute in Stockholm to discuss Vargas Llosa's work. The event occurred on 24 September 2011, and it was clear that the stakes were high since we were informed that some members of the Nobel Prize committee would be in attendance. When the issue of Vargas Llosa's ability to express the wider gamut of

---

[79] 'Un mundo dividido: imágenes del Perú en la novelística de Mario Vargas Llosa', in *Mario Vargas Llosa, escritor, ensayista, ciudadano y político*, ed. R. Forgues (Lima: Minerva, 2001), pp. 267–76.

[80] James Higgins, *Myths of the Emergent: Social Mobility in Contemporary Peruvian Fiction*, ILAS, Monograph Series, No. 19 (Liverpool: Institute of Latin American Studies, The University of Liverpool, 1994).

[81] *Myths of the Emergent*, p. 13.

[82] *Myths of the Emergent*, pp. 13–14.

[83] *Myths of the Emergent*, p. 90.

[84] *Myths of the Emergent*, p. 154.

[85] *Myths of the Emergent*, p. 13.

cultures and races epitomised by the Peruvian nation came up, James stood up and, in a very forthright way, argued that Vargas Llosa was a 'criollo' who – as his novel *La casa verde* (1966) proved – had little interest in or knowledge of the Indian races and their heritage and that it was wrong to use this perspective to look at his work. I had noticed that, just before James stood up, Mario had slipped into the room and I tried to alert James to this fact by a series of nudges, winks and whispers, but it was all in vain. James got into full throttle in his fulsome critique of Vargas Llosa's ideological credentials as articulated by his novels. Vargas Llosa took up the thread of the argument immediately after James finished his tirade, and this led to a lively debate which was keenly enjoyed by the audience – including myself! James told me after-wards that he was grateful for my nudges in his ribs, but he was fully aware of the fact that Mario had entered the room, and that's why he had decided to express his opinion in such a forthright manner!

It should also be said that James occasionally ventured outside the Peruvian ambit with articles on the likes of the Colombian Gabriel García Márquez[86] and the Argentine Jorge Luis Borges.[87] He showed an interest too in popular culture, as evidenced by works on the popular Latin American song, and 'local' Latin American history, as demonstrated by his superb and very readable cultural history of Lima, published in 2005.[88]

James's academic career has been stellar – he became Professor of Latin American Literature in January 1988, was elected Fellow of the British Academy in 1999 and, on his retirement, in 2004, he became Emeritus Professor of Latin American Literature at the University of Liverpool. He was also the General Editor of the *Bulletin of Hispanic Studies* in the late 1990s and early 2000s, and he led the ship through stormy waters with verve and a firm rudder. But James had a fun side too, as the following remembrance by Valdi Astvalsson suggests:

> In 1998, the University of Iceland contacted me to ask if I could form a panel to evaluate the work of two applicants for a lectureship in Hispanic Studies. I asked James if he could help and he immediately agreed. The job included a weekend trip to Iceland, one meeting and a couple of days of sightseeing. I was impressed by James' genuine interest in everything he saw and absorbed with enthusiasm, such as the old centre of Reykjavik, its old harbour, the places we visited on a day trip to the lava fields where the old Althing had been established in the year 1000, the Gullfoss waterfall, the geysers and the green-houses where soft fruit and even bananas are grown. In Reykjavik we also met some members of my family and friends and enjoyed meals and conversation that sometimes

[86] '*Cien años de soledad*, historia del hombre occidental', *Cuadernos del Sur*, 11 (1972), 303–14.

[87] 'On His Blindness: Jorge Luis Borges' "Poema de los dones"', in *Readings in Spanish and Portuguese Poetry for Geoffrey Connell*, ed. N.G. Round and D.G. Walters (Glasgow: University of Glasgow Department of Hispanic Studies, 1985), pp. 98–105.

[88] James Higgins, *Lima: A Cultural History* (Oxford: Oxford University Press, 2005).

went on long into the night. It was clear that all this delighted James and, later, he would often remember this experience with a great smile on his face.'[89]

Shortly after retiring in 2004, James and Kirstine moved to Scotland, where they settled down in a beautiful flat they had bought in an old mansion in the centre of Stirling. As Kirstine recalls:

> James became a member of the Stirling and Falkirk Ramblers. He took delight in discovering walks in the environs of Stirling and beyond. He became a walk leader, keen to share his 'discovered' walks with others. He was not a driver and used his bus pass to explore his native Scotland seeking out new places of interest. He became a master of the bus timetables.[90]

Though he began reading for 'pleasure' during his retirement, 'mainly espionage and light detective stories often with a "medicinal" whisky nearby', as Kirstine remembers,[91] James continued his research on Peruvian literature and, in 2006, he brought out a re-vamped and much extended new version of his acclaimed history of Peruvian literature published originally in 1987.[92] The second edition was in Spanish and – though in the introduction to the volume James suggests that it is not exhaustive – by any reputable academic standard, it *is* exhaustive.[93] It has an excellent chapter on Quechuan literature and cultural production (pp. 15–58), a thoughtful and erudite chapter on the Peruvian chronicles (pp. 61–81), and a highly informative chapter on theatre from the colonial times until the present day (pp. 85–105). He makes the bold decision to call poetry published between 1821 and 1919 'poetry of the republic' (pp. 109–128), thereby junking all the intermediary epithets of Romantic, Modernist, Nationalist, etc., and he does the same with all the epithets such as Realist, Naturalist, *costumbrista* associated with the prose and the novel genre of the same period, which simply become part of the 'prose of the republic' (pp. 131–155). In both cases, James's approach means that he cuts through all the 'red tape' of genre dancing that critics of this period normally indulge in, and he simply analyses each of the significant works – it's a successful formula, and its combination of simplicity and brass tacks sums up the resilience of his approach.

A work of this scope also draws attention to one of the hallmarks of James's work. Similar in this to some extent to the work of Raymond Williams and Terry Eagleton, James's writing is able to tease out the social groups and ideological forces that are at work in the literary works he analyses, and pick on specific events in, say, the novels where the clash of social ideologies or the groups that represent or embody these

---

[89] Valdi Astvaldsson, 'Obituary: Professor James Higgins', 14 October 2021.
[90] Kirstine Higgins; email to author, 20 September 2022.
[91] Kirstine Higgins; email to author, 20 September 2022.
[92] James Higgins, *A History of Peruvian Literature* (Liverpool: Francis Cairns, 1987).
[93] James Higgins, *Historia de la literatura peruana* (Lima: Universidad Ricardo Palma, 2006).

ideologies comes to the fore. It also has the advantage of providing a neat chronological – even developmentalist – structure to the narrative. The book also points to one other feature of James's work: his interest – predominantly – in poetry above all the other genres. Chapter 7 of this work is on Peruvian avant-garde poetry (pp. 159–191), and it is erudite, exhaustive and highly balanced in its assessment. The pages devoted to Vallejo, as one might expect, are particularly powerful (pp. 167–182) and, as a result of being squeezed in with the other poets, Vallejo seems more 'Peruvian' than normal. Of particular interest in this volume are the two completely new chapters dedicated to 'new narrative' (pp. 269–321) in which a new generation of novelists including the likes of Enrique Congrains Martín, Oswaldo Reynoso, Eleodoro Vargas Vicuña, Carlos Eduardo Zavaleta (who was Peruvian Ambassador in the United Kingdom in the 1980s) and Julio Ramón Ribeyro are promoted. The chapter on new poetic voices – including the discussion of works by Javier Heraud (1942–1963), Luis Hernández (1941–1977), Antonio Cisneros (1942–2012), Rodolfo Hinostroza (1941–2016), Marco Martos (b. 1942), José Watanabe (1946–2007), Abelardo Sánchez León (b. 1947), Carmen Ollé (b. 1947), Enrique Verástegui (1950–2018), Giovanna Pollarolo (b. 1952), Eduardo Chirinos (1960–2016),[94] and José Antonio Mazzotti (b. 1961), is authoritative and canonic (pp. 325–357).

But while James continued his research on Peruvian literature, a new literary love of his life developed during this period. Now that he found himself once more in Scotland, James started dedicating his life in retirement to reading Scottish history and literature: one thing he accomplished was to produce and publish a free translation in verse of John Barbour's *The Bruce*.[95] He dedicated this verse translation to his beloved wife, Kirstine.

I managed to prise James out of his retirement on two occasions. The first occurred when I invited him to take part in a debate about the translation of Vallejo's poetry with Clayton Eshleman at the Cervantes Institute in London on 24 April 2006. To set the scene, it should be recalled that James had published his own translations of Vallejo's poems in 1987, as mentioned above,[96] while Clayton had brought out his 'official' translation of the posthumous poems in 1978,[97] which was followed 29 years later by his translation of Vallejo's complete poetic works.[98] The question addressed by the colloquium was: is it possible to translate Vallejo's poetry with perfect accuracy into English,

[94] Stephen Hart, Review, Eduardo Chirinos, *Abrir en prosa: ensayos sobre poesía hispanoamericana*, BSS, XCIV (2017), 559–60.

[95] James Higgins, *John Barbour's 'The Bruce'. A New Translation in Verse* (Bury St Edmunds: Arima Publishing, 2013).

[96] *César Vallejo: A Selection of his Poetry*, with translations, introduction and notes by James Higgins (Liverpool: Francis Cairns, 1987).

[97] *César Vallejo: The Complete Posthumous Poetry*, translated by Clayton Eshleman (Berkeley: University of California Press, 1978).

[98] *The Complete Poetry: César Vallejo: A Bilingual Edition*, edited by and translated by Clayton Eshleman (Berkeley: University of California Press, 2007).

and Clayton said 'yes' and James said 'no'. Fireworks ensued. It was, as you might imagine, a thoroughly entertaining event!

The second occasion occurred when I managed to persuade James to attend the inaugural meeting of the Congreso Internacional Vallejo Siempre which was held in Lima, Trujillo and Santiago de Chuco – the latter is Vallejo's birthplace – on 23–26 October 2014. He gave a paper in this event, 'A Panoramic Vision of Cesar Vallejo's Poetry', which was warmly received by Peru's intelligentsia.[99] James said he was amazed by how many people wanted to shake his hand, get his autograph, even get a selfie with him; he said he felt like a 'movie-star'. In a sense that was exactly what he was, César Vallejo's 'movie-star'. He was awarded the Order of Simón Bolívar by the National University of Trujillo on that occasion – a fitting recognition of his enormous contribution over the years to scholarship on Peruvian literature – but the event that sticks in my mind the most was the guided tour James took me on around various districts of Lima one afternoon during a lull in the conference; I was amazed by the way he drew out a history of the City of Kings before my eyes just by walking down some backstreets in Miraflores and Surco, commenting on the city's architecture, the slope of the mountain ranges, the Pacific lapping on the shore; whenever I dip into his wonderful *Lima: A Cultural and Literary History*, I have the same sense of the personality of the City of Kings emerging in his words.[100]

I persuaded James to give one final address on Vallejo at the Conference dinner to be held at Christ Church Oxford on 14 October 2022, i.e. at the fifth meeting of the Vallejo Siempre International Congress where he would receive an award for life-long dedication to the study of the life and work of César Vallejo, but, alas, it was not to be.[101] Sadly, the UK's most important *vallejista* passed away in the early morning of Sunday 26 September 2021. A couple of weeks earlier, while on his monthly walk in the Scottish countryside with one of his brothers, he fell and broke one of his hips. He was admitted to hospital, where his situation worsened, leading to his death. It was the day before the inauguration of the 4th Vallejo Siempre International Congress held in New York, and many of his Peruvian colleagues were visibly moved when they heard the news. They remembered the time they met him when he first travelled to Peru back in the 1960s. The words Vallejo spoke in his poem 'A mi hermano Miguel: In memoriam' of *Los heraldos negros* (1919) were brought to mind, and are here quoted in James's translation:

---

[99] 'Visión panorámica de la poesía de César Vallejo', in *Vallejo 2014: Actas del Congreso Internacional Vallejo Siempre*, ed. Gladys Flores Heredia, 3 vols (Lima: Cátedra Vallejo, 2014), I, pp. 223–240.

[100] James Higgins, *Lima: A Cultural and Literary History* (Oxford: Signal, 2005).

[101] Kirstine Higgins wrote to me to inform me that she had discovered my letter of invitation to James dated 15 April 2020 among his correspondence, and that she would be happy to receive the life-long award on his behalf (email, 22 August 2022), and the Centre of César Vallejo Studies at UCL along with the Instituto de Estudios Vallejianos in Trujillo have agreed to forward the award to her.

Miguel, you went and hid
One August night, at first light;
But instead of laughing when you disappeared, you were sad.
And your twin heart of those extinct
Evenings has got fed up with not finding you. And now
Darkness is falling in the soul.

Listen, brother, don't be too long
In coming out, alright? Mummy might get worried.[102]

Philip Swanson has, to my mind, distilled what was especially attractive about James – his academic brilliance combined with his humanity and his modesty:

> You will probably, like me, have been with him in Peru on occasions, and you will have seen how venerated he was by members of the Peruvian academy and by a whole range of writers and authors. What was great about him too was how down-to-earth and modest he was. He was in this game for his love of the subject, not for status. He had no airs and graces, and was as comfortable talking to a cleaner or porter as he was to an eminent scholar or writer. He was shy and even awkward in some ways, but was terrific company and knew how to have a good time. I think he was much more admired by students, colleagues and friends than he ever realised. He also had a good life outside of academia and was not blinded by the glamour of success. He loved Scottish literature, walking and family life. And he was very fond of the 'occasional' dram .....![103]

James Higgins is survived by his wife, Kirstine, and his son, Graham, and he will be remembered around the world – and especially in Peru and the United Kingdom – as an outstanding scholar of modern Latin American literature and a true trailblazer of the analysis of César Vallejo's poetry.

Acknowledgements

I take this opportunity to thank those colleagues who have shared their memories of James Higgins for the benefit of this biographical memoir; these include Valdi Astvaldsson, Adam Sharman, Philip Swanson, Mike Thacker, Roger Wright, and especially Kirstine Higgins, who read an early draft of this memoir and made important suggestions and corrections for which I am very grateful.

Note on the author: Stephen M. Hart is Professor of Latin American Film, Literature and Culture at University College London.

---

[102] 'To my brother Miguel In memoriam', in *César Vallejo: A Selection of his Poetry*, with translations, introduction and notes by James Higgins (Liverpool: Francis Cairns, 1987), p. 13.
[103] Email to author, 2 August 2022.

Biographical Memoirs of Fellows of the British Academy (ISSN 2753–6777) are published by
The British Academy, 10–11 Carlton House Terrace, London, SW1Y 5AH
www.thebritishacademy.ac.uk

SIMON GAUNT

Simon Gaunt

4 July 1959 – 4 December 2021

elected Fellow of the British Academy 2018

by

BILL BURGWINKLE

Simon Gaunt was a prolific author and professor of Medieval French and Occitan studies at Cambridge and King's College London. He published outstanding studies on the troubadours, on death and sacrifice in medieval literature, on Marco Polo, on travel and identity, on French literary culture outside France, and on French as a supralocal language at the base of European identity. He established a reputation as being one of the finest revisionary critics of medieval literature, philologists, troubadour scholars, digital humanists, critical theorists, interdisciplinary and multilingual scholars, and queer studies experts of his generation.

Biographical Memoirs of Fellows of the British Academy, 20, 357–382
Posted 28 October 2022. © British Academy 2022.

It is difficult to encompass Simon Gaunt in a single article, of whatever length. He was a London boy, born and bred, and the city always served as his source of gravity. His early years were difficult—the child of an angry divorce, some time spent in care, a stage of economic hardship, several moves and step-parents—out of which he developed early on a strong sense of self, of self-reliance, and a vision of the future that depended solely on his own merits and intelligence. The one truly good thing to have emerged from that period of upheaval were two new stepmothers who were immensely influential and whom he loved dearly, Belinda Graham and Monette Gaunt, the latter of whom, a Martinican Parisian, also inspired a love of French, France, colour, and cuisine. A brilliant student from the start, he ended up in a grammar school which he must have disappointed bitterly when he announced his intention to study at a 'new' university rather than at Oxbridge. He was after a university that matched in look and philosophy his own committed support for widespread public education, with a minimum of emphasis on class and social distinctions. That defiant decision was a harbinger of his lifelong distrust of privilege, of loaded decks, of mediocre education disguised by polished and schooled performance and memorisation skills. And yet, I would describe Simon as a reluctant traditionalist, someone who cared so deeply about the unjustly neglected medieval period and the conveniently overlooked intellectual frameworks that it passed on to modernity, that he was always driven to correct widespread false assumptions when he encountered them, to challenge easy conclusions drawn from dubious evidence, and to call contemporary scholars repeatedly on their own barely masked biases and limitations.

I suppose that none of this is all that surprising coming from a scholar of his generation, a child of the Seventies who had absorbed early on a disdain for back-slapping jingoism, for the widespread post-war mistrust of European and US scholarship, and the ubiquitous political subtexts that passed for objective history during the years of his formative training. Some might find it surprising then that he turned to the medieval period, and specifically to Occitan, as his chosen grazing ground. As a young gay male, he embraced the first liberation movements to rock the UK and turned his attention to the erotic poetry of the troubadours. It is this curious mix of deep respect for history, for linguistic training, for palaeography and codicology, for politically engaged scholarship, and a thorough distrust of some of the institutions that provided some of the best of that training – most notably, Oxbridge and the Russell group – that lies behind some of Simon's best work—not to mention his disdain for the middle-class comforts that provided some students easy access to such training and left others excluded and abandoned.

He showed himself to be, from his earliest publications, a mercurial scholar, a sharp and demanding intellect, and a master of many fields, one whose powers of concentration and determination were, from my experience, unmatched. Little surprise then that the work he left us moves so easily across disciplines, time periods, and languages. The result is a fuller, more diverse, and antagonistic portrait of the Middle Ages than one finds in almost any of the literary scholars who preceded him, those scholars whose works he would have depended upon for his introduction to the field and against whom he took aim. Gone were the certainties about the place of man in the scheme of creation or in the 'feudal' order, the gender roles that had supposedly held sway for a thousand years or more, the national and linguistic boundaries around which most medieval studies were organised, the clear distinctions enthroned in scholarly writing between good and bad, right and wrong, that were shown to be nothing more than mirrors of the period in which their authors were, in turn, educated and wrote. Simon was at his best being the outlier, at speaking and writing at some remove from the orthodox and expected, and at initiating a discussion with a somewhat surprising or even shocking statement that would stun the addressees and move the discussion into new terrain, often one without clear rhetorical boundaries.

As a guide and mentor, he was without equal, and not only as a taskmaster. As one of his PhD supervisees, Alice Hazard, put it, he was 'compassionate and open but the human always came first'. Yet along with this came sometimes brutal honesty and humour. When lockdown arrived in 2020, Alice recounts that when she ran into Simon during one of his last visits to the department, instead of whinging about the inconveniences of internment, as many of us were doing, he laughed and said that maybe the fall of liberal democracy that we had all been hankering after had actually snuck up behind us when we weren't really looking. His final piece of advice was not the avuncular and expected warning to use the time productively but rather an admonition to stock up on porridge. Miranda Griffin, who was taught and mentored by Simon at various points in her career, said this:

> Even after many of us stopped being his students, Simon was also a careful and wise mentor, dispensing devastatingly perspicacious advice even – and perhaps especially – when it hadn't been sought (maddeningly, he was always almost right). Simon was not an unapproachable academic delivering obscure utterances from an ivory tower: his concerns were anchored in the world beyond the university, and he was able to draw on his own experience to help others.

And Emma Campbell, another former PhD supervisee, credits Simon for having brought

> ... medieval literature into dialogue with key concepts in current philosophy and critical theory, as sacrifice, death, ethics, and poetic voice, as well as exploring productive tensions and overlaps between postcolonial studies and medieval texts. One of Simon's extraordinary gifts as a scholar was revealing to others what subsequently appeared to have always been hiding in plain sight.

Despite his love of teaching and his outstanding leadership qualities, which we will get to in a moment, he was probably at his happiest when immersed in a pile of data that needed re-ordering, re-conceptualising, re-presentation—all of which suited him perfectly—and after which he could wipe his hands with satisfaction, then move on to his next challenge. As he once said of himself regarding the arc of his intellectual interests, he began as a philologist and student of rhetoric, moved quickly to the role of prolific and disruptively theoretical reader of medieval literature, a defender and propagator of feminist ideas and gender theory, a critical and queer theorist—a period to which he once referred facetiously as his 'professional queer' phase (his phrasing, not mine)— an early enthusiast of the digital medieval humanities revolution, capped off by a triumphant return to his abiding love, philology. He did all of this, of course, through a great deal of work; he followed a regular regime of discipline, despite his love for an afterhours drink and catch-up. Up early and straight to work was one of his adages, to be followed by gym time at the end of the day and a final bit of fun.

His published work alternated between pedagogical studies that were (and still are) consumed by grateful undergraduates (*Gender and Genre* is still, by any measure, one of the 'greatest hits' of introductory studies to the French Middle Ages, as is *Retelling the tale: an introduction to medieval French literature*), and grand statements on genre and literary history which often had at their base a critique of some of the most noteworthy European medievalists of the 20th century ('French Literature Abroad: Towards an Alternative History of French Literature', 'Genres in motion: rereading the Grundriss 40 years on', and 'Philology and the global Middle Ages: British Library Royal MS 20 D 1'). As I intimated earlier, many of these were the very scholars whose work would have informed his first encounters with French and Latin texts in his early years at Warwick. No one was safe from his critical sights. He became equally well known as a textual scholar unafraid to tackle the classics (Arthurian romance, for example) or the classically difficult and to-be-avoided (the Occitan texts by the poet *Marcabru*, or the hard-to-classify *Daurel et Beton*). He was a critical theorist of the first rank (*Love and death in medieval French and Occitan courtly literature: martyrs to love*), and an intrepid organiser of teams conceptualising data and working through new ways of approaching material, manuscript-driven research on the Middle Ages (*MFLCOF: Medieval Francophone Literary Culture outside France*, and *VOF: The values of French language and literature in the European Middle Ages*). Throughout, a strong contrarian streak already mentioned above surfaces even in his more popularising work – a dissatisfaction with the very bases of the literary history that he had absorbed as student, excessively dependent as it had been upon unexamined assumptions about national character and language use and a flawed notion of the premodern period that owed far too great a debt to the rhetoric of the enlightenment and notions of French *gloire* that were honed during the colonialist era. Summarising Simon's scholarly career, Emma Campbell said that:

'The last two decades of Simon's research thus attempted nothing short of a tectonic shift in scholarly understandings of what French and Frenchness meant in the European Middle Ages, while unravelling the nationalist and colonialist legacies of traditional philology and literary history'.

Warwick proved indeed a very wise choice of university, one for which he always considered himself lucky, for it was there that he met his mentor and role model, Linda Paterson, a brilliant scholar whose career began at a time when women faced considerable hardship in academia, and one who championed historical and palaeographical study and an abiding commitment to the scientific method as necessary components of aesthetic appreciation. Simon lived through the most exciting period of French theory while at Warwick, when the works of Barthes, Derrida, Cixous, Lacan, Kristeva, and Althusser, were being read and taken up by British and American scholars; and university literature courses were being rewritten from the bottom up to reflect the new concerns of psychanalysis, cultural studies, semiotics, and feminism. He was an ardent follower, layering this reading over his solid training in textual scholarship at Warwick, in order to synthesise a new way of reading the medieval as something bold and intellectually challenging, everything but an antiquarian's playground. Linda remembers him as a highly charged undergraduate in a very good cohort, someone who moved effortlessly into research studies and proved, as she put it, 'the ideal graduate student, diligent of course, independent-minded as well as receptive to supervision, a sensitive reader of difficult texts, and his thesis is still an authority world-wide on irony in the troubadours.' They would collaborate on several occasions over the following decades and her deep influence on his teaching and research could be seen even in his final years.

His first book, *Troubadours and irony* (1989), based on the PhD thesis, was indeed an impressive début. Eschewing idealistic 19th-century views of troubadour composition as primarily 'plaintive' and judged primarily on that aesthetic criterion, Simon debunked this as nothing more than romantic bias and claimed that it had led critics directly into the trap of *l'amour courtois*, an artificial and anachronistic descriptive which 'obscured, not only the great variety, but also the humour and vitality, of the corpus' (181). Already in this early work, Simon adopted the persona of the truth teller and righter of wrongs, and the study on irony proved a podium from which to examine the failure of the troubadour singers' public to interpret the songs' diversity and complexity but also the often hopeless readings offered by critics, too tied to notions of hopeless love and spiritual sacrifice, and unable, for one reason or another, to appreciate the double-talk that characterises so much of the poetry. In his brilliant article, 'Discourse desired: Desire, Subjectivity, and *Mouvance* in *Can vei la lauzeta mover*', Simon argued that it was the expectations of 19th- and 20th-century readers that had led to the often cobbled-together editions that editors provided for students and which, in turn, conspired to render the songs more 'courtly' in their modern reception than they had ever been in their medieval transmission.

Irony provided a perfect foil by which to examine the lack of comprehension between reader/listener and poet, and unveil the misinterpretations that ensued between befuddled critic and authorial voice. Once detected—and, as he shows, irony is ubiquitous—it can always be read simply as a stylistic ploy, as it has been by generations of literary and textual scholars, but it could also serve as a tool for the disruption of topoi, of voice, of point of view, of relations of dominance and subservience, and of erotic relations. When poets, working essentially within a courtly environment which demanded a certain adherence to 'courtly' traditions, began to balk early on at those restrictions and to write anti-love songs from within love songs, in deftly rhetorical and musically inventive patterns, then the door was opened to appreciation of ironical love songs and love songs hard to decipher. Many of those songs are now considered the high points of troubadour tradition. Little wonder then that the poets treated in *Irony* are some of the most difficult to interpret in the tradition, including, of course, Marcabru and Raimbaut d'Aurenga.

The other strain that emerges in this first book is theoretical but in a less flamboyant manner than we find in the usage of French theory that would later occupy his thought. Here, the authorities that Simon summons to his side are German philologists, steeped in rhetorical theory and educated in the waning days of a golden age of German romance studies. Erich Koehler is referenced repeatedly for his socio-cultural readings of the medieval court and its strictures; and those Marxist readings, as limiting as they can sometimes be, provided an excellent counterpoint to Simon's own interests in reading troubadours against the grain. Jorn Gruber was equally influential on Simon's early work. In Simon's words: 'Drawing on the notion of Hegelian dialectic, he (Gruber) suggests an awareness of what he calls *das Prinzip der intertextuellen Aufgebung* ("the principe of intertexual sublation"), which involves the simultaneous affirmation, negation and surpassing of another text or texts, [that] is essential if a troubadour poem is to be appreciated properly' (98–101). This interrelation between one text and another, one genre and another, became a hallmark of Simon's thinking, and of course it suited his interest in irony to a tee. The dialogic troubadour genres, the *tenso* and *partimen*, become prime sources for the study but, more importantly, it was the layering of one song upon another, of one poet's voice substituted for another, of one melody serving multiple purposes, that inspired him in his teaching and research, and much of this took root during the writing of the *Irony* book.

He won a Junior Research fellowship at Downing College, Cambridge (1986–88) immediately after the PhD, then a university post and fellowship at St Catharine's College. In all, Simon spent twelve very productive years in Cambridge (1986–1998). The intense style of lecture and supervision pushed his thinking in new directions, and the lectures and papers that he was involved with became infamous within the faculty, popular amongst motivated students, and fed directly into the publications that followed. He also formed there one of the most important intellectual partnerships of his career with his colleague, Sarah Kay, an invaluable intellectual interlocutor for the next 35 years. They, and a circle that formed around them in the late 1980s, and which included visiting scholars as well as PhD students, featuring such participants as Nicky Zeeman, Mark Chinca, Chris Cannon, Elizabeth Edwards, Ardis Butterfield, Rita Copeland, Jane Gilbert, Jim Simson, Gabby Lyons, Ad Putter and many others, served as a springboard for their individual projects and a conduit to the continental theory that was then so influential. Some of the force and originality of their thinking can be found in the special issue volume on *Displacement and recognition in medieval literature* that was published in *Paragraph* 13:2 (1990). This collection stands as a monument to their work during this period and to the fellowship and intellectual rigour that they nurtured and championed.

Simon's next work was indebted both to his experiences within the reading group and the undergraduates who flocked to his lectures and seminars. In *Gender and Genre in medieval French literature*, many of the features of Simon's theoretical, political, and pedagogical interests converged, making it one of the most personal of his works as well as his most influential, at least during the twenty years that followed its publication in 1995. Once, in deflecting praise of the book, he told me breezily that the chapters were nothing more than his notes for the lectures he had given during his first four years in the Modern Languages and Literature faculty. 'Hardly', I responded. While it is true that the chapters more or less follow what was then the lecture list for the first-year paper in medieval French, covering the 12th and 13th centuries—*chanson de geste*, romance, lyric poetry, hagiography, fabliaux—the level of the engagement with the texts, the inclusion of theoretical readings, and the constant underlying examination of the ideological implications of the texts' relations with questions of power, misogyny, domination, gender construction, and sexuality, set it far apart from other such studies. If this was a pedagogical text, as it appeared to be, it was one that challenged most of the assumptions to be found in other contemporary volumes, and one that clearly prided itself on reading the Middle Ages through the prism of contemporary intellectual theory.

The book is explicitly introduced as an intervention in medieval literary studies that would reintroduce ideology into the analysis of medieval texts through the pairing of gender and genre, both of which are, in their own right, ideological productions. Following feminist theorists of the previous decade, Simon argues that the two terms are incontrovertibly linked: gender is one of the most crucial elements of any larger ideological system; and, following Jameson's formulation, narrative is already a socially symbolic act, and genre a means of confronting, dialectically, opposing ideological claims. Highlighting contradictions is the way to approach genre and to unmask its claims regarding uncontested representation of a unified subject or ideological position. Simon challenges two principal generic claims here: one, that masculinist discourse, reliant as it is upon a patriarchal distribution of power, is ever capable of portraying the feminine; and two, that masculinity itself, within that same patriarchal discourse, is monologic, of a whole, entirely consistent with the terms upon which that patriarchy sustains itself. The other assumption under critique is the one that says that medieval authors worked generically, understood their writing and their world as inescapably carved into consistent spheres of experience: war, work, worship, the erotic, the secular and the sacred. What Simon does so magisterially is to confound all of these bases upon which much of the literary criticism he had digested in his school days depended.

Genre, for Simon, is inescapable in medieval texts, though not for the reasons that those before him had mandated. Genres were part of the Latin educational curriculum that authors had been trained in and they pertained to the different ways that texts were received and delivered rather than to their syntactical (form) or semantic (content) classification. Texts that were delivered to large audiences, with musical background accompaniment, demanded a certain form, while others that were read aloud to smaller groups (romance) or sung to a prescribed melody, more or less conformed to expectation. Simon does not debate the fact that genres exist, but contends that their boundaries were far more elastic, and that gender representation is far more crucial to the classification of a genre than has ever been allowed. Jameson's dictum from the *Political unconscious* serves as a war cry: '... the aesthetic act is itself ideological, and the production of an aesthetic or narrative form is to be seen as an ideological act in its own right, with the function of inventing imaginary or formal "solutions" to unresolvable social contradictions (79).'

Over the course of five chapters, Simon uses this argument and its implications in inventive ways to bring the insights of contemporary political theory to medieval literature and to interrogate 12th- and 13th-century texts in the same manner that one might read contemporary fiction or popular journalism. He chose as his topics the *chansons de geste*, romance, the *canso* (Occitan lyric love poetry), hagiography, and the *fabliaux*. The *chansons de geste* (34) (epics) are seen as being as much in dialogue with local power issues, including gender battles, as in sustaining royal or imperial pretensions; masculinity comes off as constructed, feeble, in need of considerable propping up; and the texts are seen as dealing much more with larger continental issues of Christian propaganda and xenophobia than with France itself or the invention of the modern state. Romance is read as multi-layered, ironic, engaged in the construction of an ethos of courtly nobility rather than strait-jacketed by a pre-existing notion of what we later called courtliness. Lyric poetry is seen in the long view, as part of a much longer tradition, extending back through classical and Arabic song, certainly a phenomenon more fully embedded in social history than one might have realised from having read most earlier studies. Occitan is accorded central place in the tradition; French is seen as the handmaiden rather than the bride; and, as one might expect from the author of *Irony*, poetry is less about plaintive idealism and suffering and more about dialogical game-playing, humour, and staged masochism. His take on the saints was, for the time, completely iconic. Saints play a variety of roles in cultural history, sometimes religious but just as often ideological and perversely erotic. Ostensibly celebrations of holy figures' lives, the texts often overdetermine such factors as chastity and virginity; they collaborate in all sorts of unacknowledged political and ideological narratives, and the saintly figures frequently defy Roman Catholic attempts to erase their otherness, their gender ambiguity, their various sins (pride, incest, disobedience), and their rebelliousness against all laws and constrictions from the state that would see them pitted against their God. The *fabliaux* go one step further in bucking enforced social norms. The glee they evince in lying and cheating, in undermining power relations, including gender roles and marriage, in unlawful and non-reproductive sex, set them off to the side of literary history for most earlier scholars as simply an anomaly or a vestige of some sort of pub entertainment or bourgeois coming of age. Simon demonstrates that gender, social class, and economic standing are already in the 13th century relative and constructed, although undermining gender ideology, as they do, never quite stretches to the utopian dream of equity and justice that one might have hoped for. Simon's conclusion—that gender as a theory was already lodged in some sectors of the medieval mind-set; and that gender play and the push to renegotiate the terms on which gender assumptions reigned were clearly articulated in a wide array of medieval genres. This became standard dogma in the decades following *Gender and Genre*, and it is very likely that this text will remain one of the standard introductions to medieval French and Occitan literature for years to come.

It is striking that Simon never wrote another book on the troubadours, having spent so many years working on them, though he did continue to write what are now classic articles on the topic—'Discourse desired: desire, subjectivity, and *mouvance* in "Can vei la lauzeta mover"' (1998) being one notable example. But there is, in fact, an element dedicated to Occitan texts in almost all his work following the *Irony* book; and he did turn almost immediately to a troubadour edition with some of the very best Occitan scholars in the UK as a follow-up. This book, an edition of the notoriously difficult poet, Marcabru—difficult to decipher and interpret, but also difficult in terms of a complex and often contradictory manuscript tradition—was a long-term project involving the editing of the 44 songs, some of which had not been edited since the 1909 French edition. The team couldn't have been better—'the dream team' Simone Ventura called them in a tribute to Simon—and it was an experience that shaped his leadership style for the rest of his career. It involved Linda Paterson, his PhD supervisor and prolific troubadour expert, Ruth Harvey, who had already published much on the poets and specifically on Marcabru, and with John Marshall along as a philological advisor. Some Italian scholars had edited a few of the songs in the decades before the team began work – Aurelio Roncaglia had produced editions of seven songs in the 1950s and '60s, followed by Peter Ricketts (four songs), Lucia Lazzerini (two), and Maurizio Perugi (one) in the decades following – and they often were able to use that material; but the task was so daunting, given the poet's abstruse language, frequently obscure references, and numerous grammatical and versological 'errors', not helped by the complex manuscript tradition, that many continental scholars thought the book would never be finished.

It was, of course; and it was well received, given the task at hand. Linda Paterson recalls the process as one of group training, amusement, and cohesive fellowship. Working with John Marshall was not only an education in itself, it was also very enjoyable, and for Simon, positively inspirational. In his essay, 'Discourse Desired', he cites with evident admiration John's pithy statement from his 1975 book, *The Transmission of Troubadour Poetry*: 'Editors of medieval texts are, as a race, not to be trusted' (11). These are words that Simon would take to heart and they betray a healthy disregard for scholarly doxa that the two men clearly shared. Scrupulously interactive and collegial, each of the three editors would produce a text for the meetings they scheduled with John in London, before which John would, in Linda's words, 'tranquilly rip them to shreds and gradually induct us into the ways of stemma production and philology'. John's critical acuity was apparently matched by his sense of humour and interpretive ease, and his often filthy readings of the texts left them howling. This no doubt helped counter the sting of his always spot-on and invaluable critiques. Long lunches in London following their work sessions not only kept things social and harmonious, they also provided the chance to fill out the contexts of their work more generally as they shared news and gossip about the larger world of Occitan studies.

Marcabru was not only a strident critic of the hypocrisy of courtly manners and the misuse of love songs, he also offered a generally perspicacious view on the changing mores and the clash between Church morality and courtly ethics. Active in the first half of the 12th century (*c.* 1130–50), and certainly well-educated for the time, he was an early practitioner of vernacular poetry and song and gained a reputation as a stern but colourful and often biting moralist. He offered reader/listeners a uniquely Occitan take on the political events of the day, especially the Crusades, then still seen in the glow of the post–1099 victory and just before the debacle of the Second Crusade. The Reconquista in northern Hispanic lands was of particular concern to him and his patrons, especially since his career was spent largely in Gascony and across the Pyrenees. The edition that Simon and the team produced included a complete corpus, based on examination of all the manuscript witnesses, full critical apparatus, copious textual notes, a glossary and commentary on some of Marcabru's more original neologisms, and translations. It also suggests how his songs affected the development of troubadour song, how his versification innovated, and how his work essentially founded a whole line of troubadour aesthetics, such that poets were thereafter seen as following either in the line of Marcabru—signifying a tone and choice of topics—or in the model of more popularly accessible verse from second generation poets such as Jaufre Rudel and Bernart de Ventadorn. The edition remains to this day an indispensable edition for scholarly use. Italian scholars, in particular, had some difficulty with the methodology, largely because it was slightly different from the rigours of the rather strict Lachmannian methodology by which most had been trained, but all agreed that the editorial choices were coherent and largely justified. The editors chose to intervene in the text when necessary for the sake of comprehension, but they declined to correct many of what had been deemed grammatical errors by other editors, arguing that there was no one standard language against which the texts could be compared and no one regional form of Occitan that should prevail. Metrical irregularities were also left intact when possible, as in those cases where it seemed unnecessary to correct them simply to abide by rules and practices that seem to have been erected by scholars well after the 12th century. Some of the songs are even given in two different editions when the differences are so striking as to call for independent consideration of both or where the manuscript versions differ substantially.

In his final years in Cambridge, Simon's work began to turn more to psychoanalysis and to the then newly christened queer theory. Simon's work had always involved questions pertaining to both fields, but his interests turned more explicitly in those directions in the late '90s and continued in that direction after taking up the chair at King's College London. King's inspired him in all sorts of ways—new teaching in a new city (albeit a return home), new lecturing styles, new freer course formats than Cambridge—and his work evolved in relation to that of his new setting, responsibilities, and colleagues. A key essay from this late Cambridge period is 'Bel Acueil and the improper allegory of the Romance of the Rose', which appeared in *New Medieval Literatures* in 1998. In this essay, Simon's rigour and analytical skills are clearly highlighted, of course, but it is the tone that is most striking. A bit sharp, impatient, even sarcastic, Simon has clearly had it with C.S. Lewis and his ilk. Anxious to celebrate allegory but at the expense of Jean de Meung, who never quite plays by the 'rules', Lewis and a host of other critics fail to read the allegory correctly because they arrive at it with their own set of rules and a skewered view of sexuality and, in so doing, they come off as victims of their own heteronormative indoctrination. What is a 'problem' for modern critics clearly wasn't for Jean's highly educated and erudite audience, and in correcting this 'problem'—or at least advising that we ignore it—one might say that they are missing out on all the fun. As Simon makes clear, the equivocation of sex and gender in the *Rose* is part of the allegory; it enables a different sort of allegory; and, as he puts it, 'within the fictional frame, allegory is designed to seduce, to be sexually stimulating' (86) … 'the "literal" (or "proper"?) narrative of the *Rose* inclines towards the homoerotic while the allegorical (or "improper") narrative inclines towards the heterosexual, the neat oppositions that appear to structure the poem become more hopelessly, though wilfully, confused' (91). At the conclusion of the essay, Simon hits home the political charge of his argument as well as establishing its literary sophistication, and he succeeds in claiming for the Middle Ages a central spot in the canon of overlooked queer literary texts at the founding moment of the queer theory explosion:

> The *Rose* may condemn homosexual activity, but its allegorical love plot is articulated through the love story of two masculine figures, while its erotic metaphors are susceptible to a reading that renders them potentially homoerotic rather than heteronormative. The boundaries between the homoerotic and the heteronormative are thus consistently blurred and this would suggest therefore that there are queer impulses at work in the *Rose* … it may not be anachronistic—however unlikely this may seem— to claim Jean de Meun as a queer writer (93).

The apex of Simon's theoretical (primarily psychoanalytical) writings is probably also one of his finest books, *Love and death in medieval French and Occitan courtly literature: martyrs to love*. Shortly after its publication in 2006, I was at a conference in Italy with Simon, when an Italian scholar came up to congratulate him on having finally come back to religion! Not exactly—at least not in the way that the scholar seemed to have been hoping—but the book does delve into the imbrication of troubadour erotic verse and religious sentiment in revelatory ways, especially in the first chapter on Bernart de Ventadorn and martyrdom. Simon may not have been converted but he really was one of the first to take up these questions from a completely original viewpoint following a period of scholarly speculation just before and after the Second World War (De Rougemont *et al.*). The importance of martyrdom, its ubiquity in troubadour love song (*canso*) and in some of the most popular and important French and Occitan vernacular texts of the 12th and 13th centuries, needed attention, especially after a decade of theorising that saw feminist critics decrying the charade of love poetry for men, by men, in which women were dismissed misogynistically. Martyrdom and death, as spectacle and as poetic topoi, became focal points for his analysis: first of troubadour erotic discourse and then of a variety of other high medieval French texts. Simon's account is, of course, quite different from that of most of his predecessors in that he takes on the foremost theme of troubadour song, then expounds upon the language used and the implications it has for philosophy and theology through close reading of texts by Lacan, Derrida, and Agamben. As usual, he strips the question down to its very basics: why, as the model of 'courtly love' was being established in the 12th century, was love seen in ethical terms and so strongly coloured by ascesis and sacrifice? Part of this goes back to Christianity itself, but 12th-century authors began to appropriate and incorporate models of sacrifice and desire that had once been associated almost exclusively with religious discourse and practices, and out of that discourse they constructed an alternative ethical space in which salvation and redemption may be sought through a passionate attachment to another human being, rather than to God (10).

The imbrication of martyrdom, or threatened martyrdom, with death and sacrifice in secular texts—or at least not overtly religious texts—is seen as very much part of a deeper seam in Christian thought, and is explicated through (a) Lacan's understanding that sacrifice involves seeking proof from the desired object that the Other (*le dieu obscur*) desires (us) in turn, and (b) Derrida's statement that the 'gift of death' is the only way in which an individual can become truly responsible, in giving away the one thing that only we can ever really give. For Simon, Lacan offered a theory of the subject that was grounded in desire and renunciation, and he found that model best enunciated in what he and others of his time called 'courtly love'. Far from being a solipsistic exercise, however, Lacan's theory of the subject is intersubjective, dependent upon how other subjects, through their use of language, have constructed our own desires. Derrida's emphasis on secrecy is also a crucial contribution to the theorisation of this sacrificial ascesis. One's sacrifice must always remain unspoken, so as not to enter into public discourse, into the symbolic order. To speak of ethics, in other words, is already to risk being unethical. How ethical can the ascesis, renunciation, and sacrifice, even martyrdom, of the troubadour be, when the whole sacrificial ritual has been staged for his own benefit?

Two contrasting configurations are set side by side in this book as an answer to that question, and we follow them and the responses they elicit through troubadour *cansos*, the romances of Chrétien de Troyes, the Prose *Lancelot*, *Flamenca*, the Tristan legends, and the *Lais* of Marie de France. On the one hand, we have the classic courtly lover who claims to welcome death by love as a form of martyrdom and a way of proclaiming his ethical superiority, or, alternatively, by imposing it on the lady whom he has essentially created in that act. On the other, there is the lover, often a woman or queer man, who actually carries through on the threat to, as Simon would say, paraphrasing Lacan, traverse the fantasy, 'triumphantly challenging the symbolic order by refusing to give up on their desire, however inappropriate this may seem' (210). In the closing lines of the book's conclusion, Simon evokes Stendhal's *Le rouge et le noir*, and the death of Mme de Renal as a final, poignant example. Acknowledging that she may perhaps be the one truly ethical character in the book, having died shortly after the execution of her young lover, Julien, Simon concludes: 'In the modern, as well as the medieval period, this is what good heroes and heroines do. In this book I have tried to explain why' (216).

After 2007, and Simon's lengthy recovery from a first cancer diagnosis at the age of 47—his next book is dedicated to the four physicians he credited with having saved his life—he turned his attention more fixedly to philological and 'global' topics, including French outside of France. I believe that he did so with a greater determination than ever to make a mark and ascertain that what needed to be said got said, while he still had the time. One important review essay from this same period (2009) captures, I think, Simon at his most trenchant and imperious ('Can the Middle Ages be postcolonial?'). It took the form of a review article of nine recent works on the postcolonial Middle Ages, published between 2000 and 2007. Simon took this opportunity to express what it was that so annoyed him about English Studies scholars' insistence on spotting postcolonial topics in the Middle Ages—something that he himself might have done as well and would do in later years—but only through an English lens, focusing on English language writing, and concerned almost exclusively with nascent nationhood and the development of a modern English identity. As a romance language scholar, Simon found this approach far too insular, far too self-important, tinged with a touch of navel-gazing. Although he admired many of the individual essays in the three collected essays volumes, he took issue with several of the presuppositions governing the arguments; and in others he decried the lack of a truly comparative approach that would weigh both languages or cultures equally. His exasperation comes across perhaps most evidently in this statement (167): 'For the Middle Ages of all periods, we need to move outside the Anglophone world if our own intellectual moves are to avoid uncannily replicating the very colonial gestures we seek to critique' (167); and in a final section, entitled 'Postcolonial Futures for the Middle Ages?', Simon more or less maps out his research agenda for the decade to come:

> I have implicitly been sketching here a blueprint for postcolonial medieval studies: they need to work outside the framework of a single literary tradition, since few texts in the Middle Ages were produced solely within the context of a single literary tradition; they need therefore to work across different languages in the Middle Ages; they thus need to return to manuscripts and/or to revise the canon, rather than rely on critical editions produced in the tradition of modern national literary histories that is bound to occlude important evidence of cultural contact and hybridities. But postcolonial medieval studies also need theoretical sophistication in that the insights afforded by postcolonial theory give us a better understanding of how 'Europe' came into being, how it related to the rest of the world, and how the medieval history of contact between Europe and Asia or Africa is in fact an important element of the longer history of which colonialism and post-colonialism are part. (172)

How fitting, then, that for the next major project following his recovery Simon turned to Marco Polo's *Le devisement du monde*, one of the best known and very few medieval texts still read and republished regularly since its appearance in the late 13th century. Not only is it a text that raises all sorts of alarm bells when approached with naïve postcolonial readings, its textual history, one of the most complicated in the vernacular tradition, forces the scholar to confront its linguistic sources, its genre, its author, its language(s), and its place in the history of travel writing, along with the usual postcolonial issues of power, identity, hegemony, and nationalist literary history. Most of these issues were elided, according to Simon, by earlier studies, to one degree or another, and he dedicated four years of intensive research to the writing of this book, which appeared at Oxford University Press in 2013. As we might have expected, Simon takes on most of the earlier critics and translators of the *Devisement* in order to re-establish what he considers the real originality of the text and its place in literary history; but, in doing so, he also demonstrates that its originality does not extend to its being the first factual account of travel through the Mongol empire. As he readily admits, several others had done that before Marco Polo, though to differing degrees and with limited success. Nor is it an exposé or condemnation of non-Christian mores, a tale of distressed Christians adrift in pagan seas and cultures, or a monument to French or Italian or even Latin prose historiography. In typical Simon mode, he carves away accrued critical commonplaces and nationalist allegiances to bring to light the text's convoluted, and therefore crucial, status as a work that challenges so much of what has been said about medieval writing.

He first turns to the language of the earliest manuscript in order to establish that the text was written in a form of international French—in this case, Franco-Italian—and that the subsequent and almost immediate translation of the text into French, Italian, and Latin was only the beginning of its problems. As each national language translation appeared, the text suffered one sort of modification or another, with editors chastising the original language as not sufficiently French or Italian, or others modifying the details or attempting to discipline the narrative to make it fit within a particular genre or to suit a particular audience. The fact that it is written in two narrative voices was often over-looked, for example, with Rusticiaus (Rustichello), as he is originally referred to, and Marco as complementary speakers, sometimes fused, often difficult to distinguish one from the other. With so much information lacking on the actual conditions under which the text was composed—probably in a jail in Genoa in which both figures were being held—it is hard to get any sort of solid grasp of the text, and Simon relegates any attempt to present a definitive reading as doomed and quickly relegated to the arena of cultural fantasy. Yet it was exactly that slipperiness that attracted him in the first place; that, plus the opportunity to unwrite a history of the text as it had developed in critical circles and in the public imagination and to flex his own philological muscles in reviewing the complicated manuscript history.

Critical theory is, unsurprisingly, at the forefront of the project, in particular Derrida's notion of the *monolinguisme de l'autre*, that language that is both mine and never mine and gives rise to fruitless efforts to monitor and legislate it from every angle. In this case, the previous editors demonstrated their own blindness, or intellectual limits, in essen-tially rewriting a text which evades the systems of the two decipherable languages in which it is written, and, in the process, he deconstructs the notion of a language belong-ing to any one people or territory. Simon is interested both in the linguistic forms ('the fundamental ambivalence of first-person pronouns') that the two narrative voices adopt in order to convey this story of global travel, and in the literary form that that hybrid voice and language take on the page. In his final two chapters, he moves to particular instances in the text which betray the authors' clear-sighted vision of cultural phenomena that differ greatly from the Christian world from which the Polo family have sprung. Kublai Khan displays elements of religious tolerance; marvels are not described as fearful and diabolical but as curiosities worth examining and as variations on phenomena known in Venice and Lombardy. Paper currency and cannibalism, both of which might have been viewed with suspicion and horror, are described in terms that display an understanding of different value systems at work in different cultures, even though they might be condemned as incompatible with Venetian mores; and even Islam is seen on a sliding scale. From a distance it can be evaluated not as an antithesis of all that is Christian but rather as a faith that shares some elements with Christian worship; while up close, once it seems about to intrude into political spaces under the control of the Church, it is condemned as an enemy force, avid for conquest, equivalent to, though more virulent for certain than, any foreign military presence who would threaten Christian well-being. Again, we see the political side of Simon's scholarship taking the lead here, both in the choice of topic and in the way it is treated. Without having to spell it out as a critical intervention in the field of postcolonial studies, Simon makes it very clear in his conclusion that he takes the text to be: 'factual', i.e. a recording of lived and observed experience; instructive, especially in its difference from other such accounts, such as the later text by Mandeville; and admirable in its restrained and relatively comparative viewpoint. As Simon puts it, rather pithily: 'Marco Polo embraces the uncanny with alacrity' (180); he never advocates wiping out difference or returning to educate the unenlightened. Furthermore, Simon argues that it is clear throughout the narrative that Marco Polo was 'irrevocably altered by his encounter with difference, becoming a marvel as well as a purveyor of marvels, a stranger if you will' (181).

The experience of writing this book, especially just after his recovery from cancer treatment, was no doubt transformational for Simon; and his final eight years—the book was published in 2013 and he died at the end of 2021—were dedicated to taking forward many of the ideas he had developed in its writing. He emerged from the experience with a revised reading methodology and a blueprint for his future research. These included such dicta as: read from the manuscript before the printed edition, and do not trust textual scholars who display no literary sensitivity or literary scholars who eschew the dirty side of medieval production, who overlook or misrepresent how littered with pitfalls is the path from written folio to polished and published tome. Just before the cancer diagnosis in 2006, Simon and I had been discussing putting in an application for a major AHRC grant, though the specifics—collaborators, topic, timetable—were still to be settled upon. That plan lay dormant for the two years of his recovery, but by 2008 he was back on track and ideas were flowing, most of which eventually came to fruition. Jane Gilbert joined us shortly thereafter, and we settled on a multi-institutional grant which would require a heavy dose of digital humanities expertise, a huge amount of stamina from trained palaeographers and codicologists, and a PhD student willing to work in this area. The four-year award was one of the largest granted to that date for a humanities project, and was shared by King's College London (Simon), University College London (Jane) and Cambridge (myself). Nicola Morato was hired in Cambridge to handle the north-south track of manuscript travel and to take a major role in working on the manuscripts of *Guiron le courtois*, the *Prose Tristan*, and the *Histoire ancienne*, though in point of fact the whole team collaborated on all of the manuscripts. Dirk Schoenaers, in London, handled roughly the east-west track and most of the manuscripts from the *Lancelot*, the *Roman d'Alexandre*, and the *Roman de Troie*. Huw Grange joined the team when Nicola moved on to a lecturer position at the Université de Liège, and David Murray took up the PhD position for a project on the mobility of lyrics in medieval Europe, in terms of translations, multilingualism, and *contrafacta*, across several different language areas. A large amount of the funding was spent on the very large and complex database.[1]

The topic was, of course, intended to be polemical, in the sense that at its heart it questioned the ways in which nationalisms and language ownership had represented the manuscripts of the six traditions in major collections, and how literary scholars and art historians had often colluded in discussing these manuscripts, sometimes simplifying the story of their production and travel. The individual textual witnesses of the prose traditions on which we concentrated were often identified by their holders or libraries as being French, or Italian, or English, without acknowledging that the language utilised in the narratives is not necessarily a sign of where they were composed, for whom they were composed, or whether, or for how long, they remained within a single linguistic domain. Simon had laid the groundwork for the project in several papers that were published just before and during the running of the project, and which reflected his thinking in the years leading to its formulation and final submission in 2010: 'Can the Middle Ages be postcolonial?' in *Comparative Literature* in 2009; 'Genres in motion: reading the *Grundriss* forty years on' in *Medioevo romanzo* in 2013; and 'Towards an alternative history of French literature' in *interfaces: a journal of medieval European literatures*, in 2015. In the earliest, from *Comparative Literature*, he makes the following statement:

> ... the volume *Medioevo Romanzo e Orientale: il viaggio nelle letterature romanze e orientali*, a 789-page book published in 2006, with more than 40 papers from a conference held in 2003, almost all concerning Oriental travel on the part of Europeans, indexes just three references to Said (two in the same paper) and no references to Bhabha, Robert Young, Gayatri Spivak, and so on. One might conclude either that

---

[1] https://medievalfrancophone.ac.uk

postcolonial theory is an exclusively Anglophone concern and largely anachronistic for medievalists, or that the Italian scholarship recorded in this volume (largely devoted to philology in the broadest sense of the term) is so seriously retrograde and blinkered as to be of no interest to Anglophone scholars with postcolonial theory. But surely there is a cultural gap here that is crying out for exploration. Likewise, might not both parties have something to learn from enacting a few cultural encounters of their own, rather than simply studying those of the past? (173)

His final two projects took up those last two sentences and he subsequently aimed to involve and engage with as many Italian scholars working on manuscripts and travel as possible. In the last article mentioned, from *interfaces*, he essentially transmits the thesis driving both projects:

> What would a history of medieval literature in French that is not focussed on France and Paris look like? Taking as its starting point the key role played in the development of textual culture in French by geographical regions that are either at the periphery of French-speaking areas, or alternatively completely outside them, this article offers three case studies: first of a text composed in mid-twelfth-century England; then of one from early thirteenth-century Flanders; and finally from late thirteenth-century Italy. What difference does it make if we do not read these texts, and the language in which they are written, in relation to French norms, but rather look at their cultural significance both at their point of production, and then in transmission? A picture emerges of a literary culture in French that is mobile and cosmopolitan, one that cannot be tied to the teleology of an emerging national identity, and one that is a *bricolage* of a range of influences that are moving towards France as well as being exported from it. French itself functions as a supralocal written language (even when it has specific local features) and therefore may function more like Latin than a local vernacular. (25)

Yes, indeed; and the MFLCOF project set out to address those questions. Firstly, as was intimated earlier, it traced the movement of the six chosen prose romances down two axes: one stretching from England, across the Picardy, the Low Countries and Burgundian lands; the other from the Low Countries, through France, Occitania, what is now Italy, and onward to Cyprus and the Latin Kingdom. The emphasis is on movement, adaptation, travel, and the development of a textual tradition as a result of that movement and travel. Rather than seek 'ideal textual objects' ('Genres', 36), that are trustworthy and as close as possible to an original scripted text, we should be looking at the variants that emerge through cultural mixing, movement, and the passage of time. The way to do this is obviously by consulting manuscript witnesses of the texts, not relegating all the additions, subtractions and variations to a section of 'variants and errors', essentially punishing them for their inability to remain true to an earlier and purified version that will thereafter be memorialised in an exemplary, often imaginary, critical edition. The final point that Simon emphasises is that the movement of these six traditions almost never originates in Paris but far more often from the provinces or enclaves where French is spoken, understood, or mixed with local languages, and sometimes even far further afield—from the Veneto, the Latin Kingdom, the Peloponnese, which were, generally speaking, non-French speaking lands. A remarkable number of these traditions seem to have taken root in the Low Countries or in what is now Italy, and some of them, even when they do seem to have been first composed in Picardy, are taken up and copied with more enthusiasm in Italy (*Roman de Troie*) or in Acre (*Histoire ancienne*).

Over the course of the four-year project, with added time for the preparation of publications, the team met all its deadlines and goals, including an almost complete database, which can be updated, and a repertoire of some 600 manuscripts which convey some complete or partial version of the six textual traditions. Scholars can also find library information, a brief description of the holding, information on where the manuscript was likely composed and to where it later travelled, and folio numbers indicating the precise location where the text or passages from the text are to be found in the manuscript. It also featured: a very successful exhibition on the earliest vernacular French manuscripts in the University of Cambridge library and colleges, curated by Nicola Morato;[2] a book of essays based on international conferences on the topic held in Cambridge and London (*Medieval francophone literary culture outside France: studies in the Moving Word* [2019]), edited by Nicola and Dirk; and a final volume by myself, Jane and Simon on the implications of the topics and questions covered, *Medieval French literary culture abroad* (2020). We were after answers to questions, not all of which could be answered, but which all have implications for larger questions about how literary history is written. Why were francophone texts composed outside of France; where and when? How do the form and focus of texts change as they migrate? What is the cultural freight of non-standard and hybrid forms of French? Does the use of French in any way suggest a cultural identity?

There was no break for Simon at the conclusion of the four plus years of MFLCOF and the publications that followed. The project had barely 'wrapped' when Simon's next proposal was approved by the ERC (European Research Council) under the European Union's Horizon 2020 research and innovation programme.[3] A logical continuation of the MFLCOF investigation, the TVF project (The Values of French) was a bit more narrowly focused, less comprehensive, and, frankly, though equally or more ambitious, in some ways more manageable. Still enquiring into the status and meaning of language usage—in this case, once again, French outside of France—Simon wished to produce,

---

[2] https://exhibitions.lib.cam.ac.uk/moving-word/
[3] https://tvof.ac.uk

alongside a stellar team of scholars including Simone Ventura, Maria Teresa Rachetta, Hannah Marcos, Luca Barbieri, Natasha Romanova, PhD student Henry Ravenhall, and a team of information experts, a digital edition of two manuscripts of the *Histoire ancienne*, the earliest European, encyclopaedic, vernacular 'world' history, begun in either 1208 or *c.* 1230, depending on which textual scholar you choose to follow. Not only was this text central to the formation of 13th-century Western Christian identity, it was also the text from which Chaucer and Christine de Pisan, among others, read an extended account of the Trojan war and incorporated it into their own works. Of the 68 extant manuscripts (the team cite 98 manuscripts that are known to have existed, some of which have now been lost or destroyed), four of the earliest and in some ways most important were composed in Acre, capital of the Latin Kingdom in the three decades preceding the fall of Jerusalem in 1291. The first chosen by the TVF team is the copiously illuminated manuscript, Paris, Bibliothèque nationale de France f. fr. 20125, which also served as the base manuscript for the existing partial editions published before the project began. This manuscript is thought to be very close to the original composition since it contains the moralisations that were excised in later versions. The other, London, British Library, Royal 20 D 1, is the earliest known manuscript of the so-called 'second redaction', made in Naples in the 1330s. Just as BnF f. fr 20125 reflects crusading energies, composed as it was between the Fourth and Fifth Crusades, and very likely in Acre, BL Royal 20 D 1 reflects another time and place: Naples, at the apex of its imperial ambitions, when its holdings spread across the Mediterranean to Jerusalem, the Peloponnese, and Sicily.

The TVF project was particularly noted, as one might expect given its funding source, for its European orientation. A regularly scheduled international seminar, in which many French and Italian scholars presented alongside British, American, and other European scholars, met in London three times a year, over the course of five years, to discuss and evaluate findings. Many of the PowerPoint presentations that were delivered are still available on the project website.[4] A major conference followed in 2019 ('Narrating history across languages in medieval Europe'), and the major outputs were the semi-diplomatic and interpretive editions of the two manuscript versions, both of which are available on the website.[5] Each is lemmatised, i.e., each word is linked with the corresponding lemma, or entry, in the DEAF (*Dictionnaire étymologique de l'ancien français*), thus facilitating comprehension and text searching. In the view of Tom Hinton, a former PhD supervisee, and Karen Pratt, a colleague and fellow medievalist at King's:

[4] https://tvof.ac.uk
[5] https://tvof.ac.uk/textviewer/?p1=Fr20125/interpretive/section/3

In many ways this final project encapsulated several of Simon's scholarly concerns: the importance of reading texts in manuscript, the benefits of collaborative working, and the problematic nature of borders (textual, generic, linguistic, or political). Furthermore, the innovative use of Digital Humanities in both MFLCOF and TVOF makes these projects important in themselves beyond the valuable outputs they have produced; they will stand as models for future DH-facing work on medieval language and literature.

Simone Ventura, who was responsible for the linguistic seam of the project, and who worked closely with Simon during the five years of the project and even beyond, to the last months of Simon's life, has said that as the leader of the project, Simon was always in the forefront, doing it all – transcribing, computer-tagging, marrying 'the historical with the digital humanities, bringing them into sometimes reluctant contact. The results were, as always, rock-solid'. Courage, persistence and perseverance were among the traits that Simon embodied, according to Simone, and that particular blend led to a smooth and very productive research experience for the team and for those following it from the outside. Simon knew that he was very ill during the last phase of the project and, though he and all his supporters were optimistic about the prognosis for his treatment, it is unclear how Simon's work might have developed post-myeloma, had he been given that chance. Simone, who worked with him most closely during those last months, emphasises that everything in the last decade of Simon's life pointed toward a continued and even more intensive meditation on history and the role that medieval history has both played, and not played, in the construction of modern European identity. This question dominated in all three of the major outputs post–2010. The *Devisement* book confronted the historical with deconstructive questions, and Simon's work on the text illustrates how history and theory have always worked together and must remain in constant dialogue. The two data projects underline the fact that history and facts are not to be feared and interpretation is essential to both. French prose romance is as much a historical genre as it is a literary one, and to pull these domains apart in the name of disciplinary purity more or less guarantees a skewed version of both.

I have been concentrating on Simon the scholar here, to the detriment of his other endeavours. As a teacher, he could be imperious and utterly charming, persuasive, demanding, and endlessly supportive, and he taught at all levels of the curriculum, right to the end. When Simon was department head, according to his colleague, Nick Harrison, all the department's members benefited from his energy and care, and some of those colleagues have admitted that Simon was the single most influential person of their career. Never a grandee amongst his peers, he was always willing to take on whatever work needed doing, and doing it efficiently and meticulously. Nick described him as 'inspirational and fervently loyal … and the most efficient person on the planet'. Karen Pratt, a fellow medievalist in the department, said that:

On his arrival as Head of Department and Professor of French Language and Literature at King's College London, he totally modernised the French Department, making sure that quite senior colleagues got the promotion they deserved. He introduced more team teaching and thematic courses into the syllabus, thus assuring the survival of Medieval French studies within wider, sometimes theoretical, contexts.

Miranda Griffin, from Cambridge, wrote that:

Simon was as interested in learning from his students as he was in teaching them. His enjoyment of teaching was part of what made him such a brilliant lecturer and supervisor: in Simon's lectures you always knew you were in for a good time, as well as learning more than you'd imagined. I know that many of his former students reading this will have their own vivid memories not just of his exposition of French literature, but also of the times he listened to what was happening in their lives, and offered thoughtful, practical support.

He served for many years as head of department at King's and then moved into the position of Acting Head of Arts and Humanities at a crucial moment, a move that was not really of his choosing but one that he relished nonetheless. According to Evelyn Welch, who had been appointed vice-president in 2013, the School of Arts & Humanities was in an uproar about the move to Kingsway when she arrived. No matter whom she spoke to about the background information needed to get to the bottom of the grumbling, she was always referred back to Simon as the institutional memory bank, someone whose knowledge and advice could be trusted. When she approached him about acting as Head of A&H, it was only with great reluctance that he finally consented, and with a list of prerequisites in hand, primary amongst which was the demand that he be part of the process that would name his successor. She described Simon in the job much as almost all his colleagues would describe him: wise, rigorous, fair, warm, caring, and fierce when he wanted and needed to be. In his short time in post, he instituted major changes that affected the well-being of the staff: convenient bike racks at the new site, on-site showers, social spaces, a professorial pay framework, leading to a thriving school and department that were both devoted to equity.

All of the traits that had been recognised by his PhD supervisor at the very start of his studies—an amazing sense of responsibility and a strong social conscience were singled out by Linda Paterson—were recognised when in 2015 he accepted an invitation to serve as a fellow of King's College London, and when in 2017 he became a fellow of his previous place of employment at St Catherine's College, Cambridge. He also gave freely of his time on behalf of the profession and scholarly societies. He served as President of the UK Society for French Studies between 2006 and 2008, during which time he updated many of their procedures and sought links with other societies at a time when the Arts and Humanities were under attack. His insight and intellectual generosity shaped the disciplines of medieval studies—in part through service to the International

Courtly Literature Society and French studies—by integrating them more firmly within other, larger, disciplines. Service on two REF panels over the course of a decade further cemented his reputation as a scholar who stands by his word and never fails to do his bit. In addition, he contributed to his discipline through his support of the AUPF/AUPHF (Association of University Professors and heads of French), and served as a distinguished visiting professor at universities in the United States and Europe, at Oregon in 1998, Wisconsin in 2014, Verona in 2017, and UC Berkeley in 2019.

He was deeply committed to LGBTQ+ issues and had spent decades insisting on equal representation and justice, from manning the phone lines for an Aids charity during his time in Cambridge, to helping institute Queer@King's when Bob Mills had joined him in London. The conference they helped organised, 'Queer Matters', with colleagues in English, History, Classics, and American Studies, was at that time the largest such gathering of its kind in London; and, as Bob Mills put it, it attracted 'a who's who' of queer studies, featuring almost 400 participants and 200 speakers, from five continents and over thirty countries. Queer@King's is still sponsoring a regular interdisciplinary seminar series called Queer Discipline, and is now part of a major research centre that is still thriving. Two more symposia were organised with Simon's help, 'Queer Pedagogy' in 2006, and 'No future together' in 2007. I participated in all of these ventures and consider them highlights of my time in Cambridge. Simon ceased to write explicitly on queer theory in his final decade but it imbued all of his work to some degree, and, to quote Bob Mills one final time: 'being a medievalist with Simon around was *always* an unalloyed queer pleasure'.

But Simon was never all work and no play. He loved music—Dalida and Dolly as well as the opera he listened to quite compulsively in his last years. He loved his families, especially his sisters Vanessa Gaunt and Sarah Westlake and nephew Ti, Phil and Joel and Leah Gouget-Levy, Mark Treharne, his beloved partner of over 37 years, and that rock of Gibraltar and angel from above, Manish Modi. He travelled—India and Sri Lanka as well as Italy, Marcilhac-sur-Célé, and Wales; and when Manish, trying to reassure him as he was about to undergo his last treatment, asked what their next trip would be, Simon responded—in one of his final utterances—'Australia'. He loved his students and his colleagues at King's and the bustle of London. He could scope out a good cocktail bar or fish restaurant from miles away, and always appreciated a lively wardrobe, a good dance club, and a new musical discovery. How perfectly fitting that at the two memorial services I attended, the programmes were so eclectic, including: Berlioz's 'Le roi de Thules', 'Hope there's someone' by Antony and the Johnsons, 'As tears go by' by Marianne Faithful, and the funeral closed with Abba's 'Dancing Queen'. The King's memorial service—thanks to all those who organised that moving event—featured the *Adagio* from Schubert's String Quartet in C, Jaufre Rudel's 'Quan lo rius', and closed with Shafqat Amanat Ali's 'Didaara' ('Stand by me').

I will close with two final reminiscences from Simone Ventura and Nick Harrison, colleagues and friends with whom Simon was particularly close, and which capture some of the inherent qualities that endeared Simon to those who knew him. The last word we will leave to Simon.

Simone Ventura picks out Simon's performative qualities as one of the things that he will most miss. His 'clear, elegant, and witty' voice were part of what Simone calls Simon's 'parole': 'The vocal performance was important; performance was part of the message. Theorists have lost a pragmatist and a visionary and philology has lost a profound and provocative interlocutor. He was a committed and radical theorist but a figure who demanded truth in data'. And Nick Harrison lauds Simon's sense of balance:

> To share the world of academic work with someone is to share a lot. On the one hand, Simon struck a balance between working and doing other stuff – travelling, sustaining diverse friendships, going out to eat, watching films and listening to music, and bunking off occasionally at conferences. On the other hand, I think he viewed academic work, at least in its good moments, or at its core, as a vocation that inspires and deserves enormous commitment, and also as a realm of sociability, a realm of conversations and shared enthusiasms that bring people together in enduring ways. Work was far from being his whole life, but he put all of himself into his work, and working with Simon was a lot of fun. He was my colleague, and he was my friend.

Finally, let us go back in time to 1996, and listen to Simon, brimming with confidence and youthful wisdom, on how he saw the future of medieval literary studies. Over the course of the 25 years that followed, he certainly contributed more than his share to the critical recuperation and textual editing project that he was calling for in this statement; but I also know how deeply this mattered to him. With his commitment to education and his insistence that history resides in the complex meshing of data, matter, movement, artistry, and interpretation, he knew that manuscripts are bearers of histories that rarely get excavated and I hope it would please him to know that this call to arms would stand as his final word:

> Medieval texts can, of course, be recuperated for feminist readers (or queer or postcolonial readers for that matter) without their being re-edited, but who knows what new texts, or new versions of old texts, await rediscovery? Scholars seeking to revise or challenge conventional views of the Middle Ages cannot afford to rely on existing editions: they need philology as much as they need theory'. (106, 'Discourse desired')

Acknowledgements
I have borrowed freely from memoirs, memorials, and private communications that were generously shared with me in the months following Simon's death. I would particularly like to thank Simon's sisters, Nessa Gaunt and Sarah Westlake, his nephew, Ti, Manish Modi, Linda Paterson, Simone Ventura, Nick Harrison, Sarah Kay,

Liz Guild, Ruth Harvey, Luke Sunderland, Alice Hazard, Tom Hinton, Karen Pratt, Emma Cayley, Evelyn Welch, Bob Mills, Emma Campbell, Miranda Griffin, Peggy McCracken, Nicky Zeeman, Emma Dillon, Emma Wilson, Lily Robson, Emily Butterworth, Jo Malt, Nick Hammond, Dot Pearce, Phil and Joel Gouget-Levy, and the Quartet Toldrá, many of whom contributed to the Celebration of Simon's life at King's London Chapel on 16 June 2022.

Writings of Simon Gaunt cited in this memoir

S. Gaunt, *Troubadours and Irony* (Cambridge: Cambridge University Press, 1989).

S. Gaunt *et al.* in *Displacement and recognition in medieval literature*, special issue of *Paragraph*, 13:2 (1990).

S. Gaunt, *Gender and genre in medieval French literature* (Cambridge: Cambridge University Press, 1995).

S. Gaunt, 'Discourse desired: desire, subjectivity and mouvance in "Can vei la lauzeta mover"', in J. Paxson & C. Gravlee (eds), *Desiring discourse: the Literature of love, Ovid through Chaucer* (Selingsgrove: Sequehanna University Press, 1998), pp. 89–110.

S. Gaunt, 'Bel Acueil and the improper allegory of the *Roman de la Rose*', *New Medieval Literatures*, 2 (1998), 65–93.

S. Gaunt, R. Harvey & L. Paterson (eds), *Marcabru: a critical edition* (Woodbridge: D.S. Brewer, 2000).

S. Gaunt, *Retelling the tale: an introduction to Medieval French Literature* (London: Duckworth, 2001).

S. Gaunt, *Martyrs to love: love and death in Medieval French and Occitan courtly literature* (Oxford: Oxford University Press, 2006).

S. Gaunt, 'Can the Middle Ages be postcolonial?' *Comparative Literature*, 61:2 (2009), 160–176.

S. Gaunt, 'Genres in motion: rereading the *Grundriss* 40 years on', *Medioevo romanzo*, 37:1 (2013), 24–43.

S. Gaunt, *Marco Polo's Devisement du monde: narrative voice, language and diversity* (Cambridge: D.S. Brewer, 2013).

S. Gaunt, W. Burgwinkle & J. Gilbert, *Medieval francophone literary culture outside France* (2014). https://medievalfrancophone.ac.uk.

S. Gaunt, 'French literature abroad: towards an alternative history of French literature', *Interfaces*, 1 (2015), 25–61.

S. Gaunt & K. Pratt (eds.), *The Song of Roland and other poems of Charlemagne* (Oxford: Oxford University Press, 2016).

S. Gaunt *et al.*, *The Values of French* (2017). https://tvof.ac.uk.

S. Gaunt, W. Burgwinkle & J. Gilbert (eds), *Medieval Francophone literary culture abroad* (Oxford: Oxford University Press, 2020).

Note on the author: Bill Burgwinkle is Emeritus Professor of Medieval French and Occitan at the University of Cambridge, and Emeritus fellow at King's College, Cambridge.

Biographical Memoirs of Fellows of the British Academy (ISSN 2753–6777) are published by The British Academy, 10–11 Carlton House Terrace, London, SW1Y 5AH www.thebritishacademy.ac.uk

ROGER LONSDALE

Roger Harrison Lonsdale

6 August 1934 – 28 February 2022

elected Fellow of the British Academy 1991

by

JAMES McLAVERTY

Roger Lonsdale was pre-eminent as an editor of 18th-century English literature, the scholar who for many of us changed the 18th century. In his two anthologies, *The New Oxford Book of Eighteenth-Century Verse* (1984) and *Eighteenth-Century Women Poets: An Oxford Anthology* (1989), for which he read and evaluated all 18th-century verse, he rescued forgotten voices and introduced us to a culture more diverse, practical, and wayward. Earlier distinguished editions of Gray, Collins, and Goldsmith (1969), Beckford's *Vathek* (1970), and John Bampfylde (1988) were followed by a final, prize-winning, four-volume edition of Johnson's *Lives of the Poets* (2006).

Biographical Memoirs of Fellows of the British Academy, 20, 383–409
Posted 8 November 2022. © British Academy 2022.

Roger Lonsdale

Roger Lonsdale was born on 6 August 1934, and brought up in Hornsea, a Yorkshire seaside town, fifteen miles from Kingston upon Hull. His father, Arthur John (1894– 1977), worked as a manufacturer's agent (1910–59), at first for the Hull Oil Manufacturing Company and then independently. His mother, Phebe (1904–2004), née Harrison, looked after the children and the home. Roger had an elder brother, Martin, and a younger sister, Elspeth. The family were Methodists: regular chapel-going was part of Roger's early life and his early poetry was influenced by Nonconformist theology and hymns.

With the outbreak of the Second World War, Roger, his mother, and his sister were evacuated to Scotland, an event that generated in him a new awareness and his first pre-served writing.[1] On 26 June 1940, they set off for Ormsary, part of the estate of Sir James Lithgow (1883–1952),[2] a hamlet on the shore of Loch Caolisport on the south-west coast of Scotland, looking across the sea to Islay and Jura. Roger went to the local school, where he was remembered by his teacher Etta Cameron as a brilliant but sensitive little boy, a child whose eyes filled with tears when they sang a folksong about a baby lost while gathering blackberries.[3] In a move that was to become characteristic, Roger started to record his new surroundings: 'Roger H. Lonsdale's History of Ormsary In the hand-writing of R.H. Lonsdale. Stories, which happened in his time. Also pictures of Ormsary.' The future scholar is already present in the careful list of residents, which includes 'Mrs Lonsdale Dairymaid'.[4] In his second year at Oxford Roger wrote a poem, 'This Boy Saw Islands', that was at least partly about his Ormsary experience, capturing a sense of alienation and of engagement with the rawness of nature.[5]

The Lonsdale family was reunited in Hornsea on 17 April 1943. Roger then went to Hornsea Council School, but he passed the new eleven-plus examination and moved to Hymers College, an independent, Head Masters' Conference, school in Hull. His career at Hymers (1945–52) was distinguished: editor of *The Hymerian* (1950-2), secretary of both the Music and Debating Societies, Under Officer of the Combined Cadet Force, Head of Brandesburton House, Woodhouse Essay Prize 1951, Prefect 1951–52.[6] At his final sports day he won the 880 yards and the shot, and finished second in the mile and

---

[1] For information on this and other episodes in Roger's life, I am grateful to Nicoletta Momigliano for access to his typed versions of his diaries and letters. As they are private, I refer to them, rarely, as 'Diaries and Letters', with the date.

[2] His son, Sir William (1934–2022), Roger's exact contemporary, was at Lincoln College with him as an undergraduate, but they were never close friends.

[3] Probably 'A Fairy Lullaby (I Left My Darling Lying Here)'. 'Diaries and Letters', 20/4/43 [letter of 20/1/75].

[4] 'Diaries and Letters', preceding account which begins with 26/6/40.

[5] 'Diaries and Letters', 20/4/43, Appendix.

[6] See the notice by Edward Wilson, https://www.oldhymerians.com/news/fondly-remembered/265/265-Roger-Lonsdale-OH-1945-. Wilson was a Fellow of Worcester College Oxford and a member of the English Faculty.

the long jump. He did not continue his athletics career—when he volunteered for the 880 yards in Lincoln's 'Cuppers' team, he was told they had already recruited the Commonwealth champion[7]—but in his final term at school he played cricket for the first eleven, and cricket remained an enduring enthusiasm, though as a spectator. He always remembered with regret going to see the Australians at Scarborough in 1948, and, having promised his father he would be home early, feeling bound to leave the ground, just as Bradman began his innings. He was academically successful at A-level in 1951 (the exams were introduced that year) and secured a place at Lincoln College Oxford in April 1952.[8] The only disruption to his academic success seems to have come from his devotion to Sibelius. Hearing Sibelius in his early teens, he was enraptured, taken from himself into another world. Sibelius became such an important focus for his life that it led to neglect of his school work and the school had to intervene to reset his priorities. His achievements as a sixth-former show the problem was resolved, but he remained devoted to Sibelius (with Mahler a major addition) all his life. Until his final years, he would go to orchestral concerts in London, was a Friend of the Philharmonia, and even went on tour with them. Music in general, including 18th-century music and modern music, remained, like sport, an enduring commitment.

Before going up to Oxford, Roger did his national service in the RAF. His initial training was at Padgate, where he found neither the haircuts nor the meals as bad as he had feared. Russian courses were full, but he was sent to Hornchurch for Air Crew Selection. There his great strength in aptitude tests was his Maths, and, though he did less well in coordination tests, he was quickly selected as suitable for air crew as navigator or engineer, declining the latter. After being successful in interviews and tests at Cranwell, Roger was sent on to Jurby, Isle of Man, for Officer Training. He found flying a new and very enjoyable experience, though he worried about leadership training. He became an officer on 4 February 1953, missing the Sword of Honour by two marks, and was sent to RAF Bishop's Court, near Belfast, for navigation school, before being posted as a navigator on No. 1 Squadron at RAF Flying College, Manby in Lincolnshire. He took well to life in the RAF, combining a full programme of academic reading (including *The Lives of the Poets*, *The Anatomy of Melancholy*, Shakespeare, Wyatt, Surrey, Sidney, the metaphysicals) with his duties, which included serving as first navigator on an important trip back from Keflavik to Manby. He left the RAF with more sorrow, he said, than he had felt on leaving school.[9]

---

[7] Derek Johnson, who also won the silver medal at the Melbourne Olympics in 1956. This incident came to represent for Roger something of the glamour of Oxford.

[8] He had been disappointed not to get into Christ Church in December.

[9] 'Diaries and Letters', 1/9/54.

II

Roger Lonsdale went up to Lincoln College, Oxford on 6 October 1954. The English tutor at Lincoln was Wallace Robson (1923–93). Robson had been a supporter of F.W. Bateson (1901–78) in the founding of *Essays in Criticism*, and later held chairs at Sussex (1970) and Edinburgh (1972). Roger's tutor for Old English was Joan Turville-Petre (1911–2006), with whom he came to have an uncomfortable relationship. Roger was a keen cinema-goer and wrote for her an essay comparing *Beowulf* with the film *Shane* (1953). Both works follow the pattern where a hero enters a society, cleanses it of a threat, and then leaves. Such a comparison would raise no eyebrows today, but Turville-Petre was shocked ('I don't know what you're trying to do here', she is reported to have said, 'but please don't do it again'). The matter was raised with his other tutors at Lincoln, but with no consequences. Outside his scholarly writing, Roger liked to flavour his learning with contrarian spices: he would wonder whether Aphra Behn was an actual person (had she ever been seen in the same room with Dryden, for instance?), insisted that Pope's *Dunciad* was on a topic of major importance, enjoyed blaming Wordsworth for Coleridge's failed career as a poet, applauded Mrs Norris as the only sensible character in *Mansfield Park*, and acclaimed Mr Casaubon the real hero of *Middlemarch*. This spirit played a part in his undergraduate career, as it continued to do in later life in private conversation

A development with more long-term significance than the disagreement with Mrs Turville-Petre was Roger's being sent to Bateson's tutorials in Corpus Christi College in Hilary term 1956, while Robson was on leave. Bateson was something of a renegade in the English Faculty. The editor of the *Cambridge Bibliography of English Literature*[10] and the founding editor of *Essays in Criticism*, he was an advocate for removing compulsory Old English from the Oxford syllabus, and, though deeply committed to historically informed criticism, sceptical of the claims of the new bibliography and opposed to old-spelling editions (particularly sparsely annotated ones). The 'Critical Forum' section of *Essays in Criticism* enabled Bateson to work out his positions in argument with some of the finest critics of the time and his role in these debates was probably more influential than the example of his criticism.[11] Roger found him an immensely stimulating tutor because he was such a challenging one. I have the sense that in later life he was often

---

[10] *Cambridge Bibliography of English Literature*, 5 vols. (Cambridge: Cambridge University Press, 1940–57).

[11] See Valentine Cunningham, 'F.W. Bateson: Scholar, Critic, and Scholar-Critic', *Essays in Criticism*, 29 (1979), 139–55. Although Bateson regarded himself as an inferior critic to Leavis (see e.g. his 'Editorial Postscript: F. R. L. and *E in C*: A Retrospect', *Essays in Criticism*, 28 (1978), 353–61), it is questionable whether his influence on English studies has not been greater. A monograph on Bateson and the Batesonians is much to be desired.

responding to an internal Bateson. At an early meeting, Bateson told him his essay was very well written and suggested he might get a job on the *TLS*—in the context, Roger was sure, an insult. Later a comment that an essay was mainly hot air 'really stung me but made me work even harder'.[12] However, he took to Bateson's historically informed criticism and, when he was scheduled to return to Robson, asked to stay with Bateson. He graduated with First Class Honours in 1957, in a distinguished year that included Gillian Beer, John Carey, and Peter Dronke; Roger's friends Christopher Ricks and Martin Dodsworth had graduated the previous year.

During his time at Oxford, Roger felt a vocation to be a poet.[13] He had written poetry from the age of thirteen, at first comic but moving on to nature and religious themes. During his period in the RAF there had been little time for poetry, but Oxford led to membership of poetry societies and a circle of friends with a commitment to writing: Bernard Donoughue, Dennis Keene, Peter Ferguson, John McGrath, Bernard Bergonzi, Judith Spink, and Marilyn Butler.[14] Perhaps Roger's most popular poem (he describes it in his notes as his mini-'hit') was 'The Other Lords':

> The other lords all fell in lust
> With ladies waiting round the court,
> Committed love, a sin that must
> Remain for me a haunting thought.
> I knew no words for love to trust
> Affection that declines to sport.

> I served the King, stood at his side;
> And when his murderers came, disguised
> With hood and mask, I might have cried
> Alarms of treason. Yet, surprised,
> I knew no words; the good man died.
> Stuck through with knives, I fell despised.

> Risen to heaven, I came on throngs
> Praising with harp and blended voice.
> Yet how could I feel good among
> Such unrehearsed yet perfect noise?
> I knew no words of those rare songs
> That angels sing as they rejoice.

---

[12] 'Diary and Letters', 23/1/1956.

[13] I am grateful to Nicoletta Momigliano for access to Roger's typescript account of his poems, 'RHL Poems', and for giving me access to his collection of contemporary poetry magazines. Unpublished poetry is printed by kind permission of Professor Momigliano.

[14] There is a reflection of the group of poets in Judith Grossman (née Spink), *In Her Own Terms* (New York: Soho, 1988). Roger is the model for Jeremy, a relatively nice character in a world in which niceness is in short supply. Roger and Judy Spink edited *Oxford Poetry* (Eynsham: Fantasy Press, 1959) together.

Lonely in paradise is each
Who must have silence as his state.
Better than any lord should teach
These souls some method to relate
Occasions to a style of speech:
The power to seem articulate.[15]

The poem is in Roger's later, ironical style: words about having no words. It is metrically accomplished, and although some of its word play ('fell in lust'/'committed love') might seem bald, its concern with failure of speech engages persuasively with issues of love and commitment. Like many of his poems of this period, 'The Other Lords' remains within its chosen metaphor, while inviting the reader to interpretation. An earlier poem, 'Image of Water', in which a man of 'great compassion' rescues fish from the sea, where he thinks they must have been bored, only for them to die in their new element (*Lincoln Imp*, Hilary 1955) offers easier interpretation, as it was written only a few months after Roger had arrived in Oxford.

Roger was elected president of the Critical Society in Trinity term 1957 and was chosen, with John McGrath, to be editor of *departure*, a magazine for which he persuaded Philip Larkin, whom he had met while he was using the library at Hull, to contribute a poem, 'Pigeons'. But the Oxford poetry scene was changing and, although Judith Spink had been appointed the next editor of *departure*, it was discontinued. In 1958 Roger moved to America as James Osborn's research assistant, and, preoccupied with scholarship, stopped writing poetry. But one of the unpublished poems he wrote there, dated 24 August 1959, is one of his most successful:

Song

Learn, lover, to withstand
The violent imprecision
Of lover turning friend:
Better that love should end
With sharp derision,
Than haunt old rooms to find –
To pack and unpack more –
What must be left behind.
Avoid her eyes, and stand
Impatient at the door.[16]

[15] Text from Roger's typescript. Printed in *Lincoln Imp* (Hilary, 1956); *Isis* (24 October 1956); *Oxford Poetry 1956* (Oxford: Fantasy Press, 1957).
[16] Text from Roger's typescript (New Haven, 24/8/59). Roger's published poems are 'The Aviator Observes the Gulls' (*The Mitre* (1953)); 'Image of Water' (*Lincoln Imp*, 16:1 (Hilary, 1955)); 'Aubade' (*Lincoln Imp*, 15:6 (Hilary, 1956), *Oxford Poetry* (1956)); 'The Others', later 'The Other Lords' (*Lincoln Imp*, 16:1 (Hilary, 1956),

There is a new, stripped-down maturity, and directness of statement. Roger himself attributed his drying up as a poet not only to his new academic career but to the problematic influence of Larkin. He was fond of saying that he had been put off by Bateson's describing him to his face as 'the poor man's Larkin', which Roger thought 'a bit cruel'. But Bateson was possibly led to this comment by Roger's own concern about his relation to Larkin. Certainly, Roger's Oxford poems are not in any obvious way like Larkin's. There is no observation of the natural or social world, to be transformed by later understanding, nor is there an attempt to create a consistent, reflective poet's voice. Roger says in his notes that he admired 'Larkin's more wistful mode in short meditative lyrics' – exactly how he would have liked to write, if he could—but his problem seems to have arisen from admiration, rather than imitation, of Larkin.

Roger's review of Robert Conquest's important anthology, *New Lines*, in *departure*, 4:10 (1956), 18–20, reveals much about his developing taste in poetry at this time, a taste that was in some measure to sustain him in his role as anthologist. The poems were those of 'The Movement': Conquest himself, Kingsley Amis, Donald Davie, D.J. Enright, Thom Gunn, John Holloway, Philip Larkin and John Wain. Roger congratulates the poets on their 'vitally necessary reliance on basic intellectual structure'. The best of the poetry in the anthology, he finds, is not retreating from extreme emotions but defining them more clearly. Thom Gunn is praised for his technical accomplishment, but 'Larkin's poetry, more than that of any other in this book, has the capacity for gaining our confidence, for successfully integrating the colloquial, for centring a poem on an everyday situation and letting it work out its own implications, simply and unpretentiously, without being either naive or vague'. These are some of the qualities Roger was later to look for in assessing 18th-century verse.

After graduating, Roger began work in October 1957 on a BLitt at Oxford, taking on some Workers' Educational Association lecturing in Banbury from February 1958. Herbert Davis (1893–1967) was his supervisor, and Roger retained a vivid memory of one of his early supervisions. Davis had a room in the New Bodleian (he taught bibliography there), and, visiting him, Roger found himself grabbed and bundled out of the building by his supervisor. He had wandered in while smoking a cigarette, something strictly forbidden in the Bodleian, and Davis was appropriately horrified. Roger was making progress with his thesis,[17] but on 24 April 1958, he received a message from

---

later *Isis* 1280 (24 October 1956) and *Oxford Poetry* (1956)); 'The Witnesses' (*Isis* 1288, 30 January 1957); 'Actaeon' (*Lincoln Imp*, 17 (Trinity, 1957), and *Isis* 1304 (23 October 1957)); 'The Gates' (*Isis* 1301 (13 June 1957)), 'Loss' (*Isis* 1310 (4 December 1957), *Oxford Poetry* (1957), *Universities Poetry 1* (1958)), 'Poem' or 'Considerations' (*Oxford Magazine*, 76:13 (20 February 1958), *Oxford Poetry* (1959)); 'Sympathy' (*Oxford Poetry*, (1959)). The *Lincoln Imp* is misnumbered.

[17] Roger's initial topic is unclear, possibly the relation of Coleridge to 18th-century poetry. Roger had, as he thought, made new discoveries, though Davis was sceptical.

Bateson that was to reshape his academic career: 'An American scholar-millionaire –
J.M. Osborn of Yale – is looking for a research assistant to help him finish off an edition
of the Spence Anecdotes (of Pope etc). $3600 p.a. for 2 years and post in Yale English
Dept. I think this might suit you. Come and see me Monday 11 a.m. Job to start Sept.
F.W.B.'[18] After an interview with Osborn at the Mitre a few days later, Roger was given
the job at Yale, which, he noted to his parents, was 'the most high-powered English dept.
in the world'.[19]

III

Roger left for Yale on 15 August 1958. At New Haven, his role went beyond Spence's
Anecdotes to assisting with a range of Osborn's projects.[20] James Marshall Osborn was
a literary historian and collector of manuscripts, as well as a Holstein cattle breeder.
After an early career in investments in New York, he moved with his wife, Marie-Louise
(née Montgomery) to Oxford, where he took a BLitt. In 1938 he went to Yale as a
Research Associate and remained there for the rest of his life. He became an Adviser to
the library on 17th-century manuscripts in 1954 and started transferring his own manuscripts (over 47,000 items) to Yale in 1963, becoming their first curator. By 1958 he had
already acquired an impressive range of manuscripts, including that of Spence's
Anecdotes, which he had bought from the Duke of Newcastle in 1938, the composer
Thomas Whythorne's autobiography (which, because it could not be taken from the
country, he donated to the Bodleian), and a large collection of papers on Charles Burney
and his family. Roger would work on all these, but his own research was to be devoted
to the Burney papers and to constructing an account of the career of Charles Burney.

Roger made a good early impression on Osborn, not least through his impressive
recall of his reading. On his plane journey to the States he had read *An Apology for the
Life of Mr. Colly Cibber* (1740), and as a result he was able to supply Osborn immediately with a reference he needed concerning Lord Halifax and subscription. A more
significant instance came later, when Osborn was reading to Roger from a book of lute
songs, and Roger recognised one of the lyrics, by William Elderton, as supplying the

[18] 'Diaries and Letters', 26/4/58. For an account of Osborn, see René Wellek's introduction to *Evidence in
Literary Scholarship: Essays in Memory of James Marshall Osborn*, ed. René Wellek and Alvaro Ribeiro
(Oxford: Clarendon Press, 1979), pp. v–xv. Osborn (1906–76) had a long association with Bateson. He had
contributed a section on 'Literary Historians and Antiquaries' to Bateson's *CBEL* (ii. 892–932). Before the
opportunity to work at Yale arose, Bateson had hoped to find Roger a job at Reading.
[19] 'Diaries and Letters', 1/5/58.
[20] Joseph Spence, *Observations, Anecdotes, and Characters of Books and Men*, ed. James M. Osborn, 2 vols.
(Oxford: Clarendon Press, 1966). Osborn acknowledges initial help from Mrs Theodore G. Rochow, A.J.V.
Chapple, and Roger Lonsdale, but says his greatest debt is to Slava Klima and John Barnard.

four lines of Benedick's unidentified song towards the close of *Much Ado About Nothing*
(V. ii). In considerable excitement Osborn published his finding in *The Times* of
17 November 1958, p. 11, acknowledging that Roger had recognised the lines when they
had been read to him. The discovery caused excitement in Yale and Oxford, and Roger
was widely congratulated on it.[21]

Roger's work for Osborn began with the first English autobiography, that of Thomas
Whythorne, the Elizabethan composer (1528-95), which had been transcribed by the
previous assistant, A.J.V. Chapple. Roger collated the transcript with the 'new orthographie' of the manuscript and compiled the index.[22] In collating the two texts letter by
letter, Roger had to teach himself a difficult Elizabethan hand, but it was the sort of
detailed work he enjoyed.[23] Later, when Osborn published his modern spelling edition,
he thanked Roger for helping with the modernisation and reading the volume in proof.[24]
He also worked on Spence's anecdotes, as in a general way on Osborn's other manuscripts, but his personal interest was in the Burney manuscripts, which he had a major
role in cataloguing.

In the evenings and at the weekends, Roger made progress with his own thesis on the
literary career of Charles Burney, and early in 1959, he spent ten days in the Berg
Collection of the New York Public Library, working on their Burney manuscripts. It was
as a result of this visit that his name is found attached to an unlikely publication, *Famed
for the Dance* ..., to which he contributed a short essay on Burney's reminiscences of
John Weaver, the dancing master.[25] At the Berg he met Professor Joyce Hemlow, the
author of the biography of Fanny Burney, and at her invitation he visited McGill
University in Montreal, the centre of a major Burney project, in 1959. Professor Hemlow
would have liked him to join them at McGill, but there were also suggestions that he
should stay on at Yale to teach. Roger very much enjoyed his time at Yale and spoke
warmly of the kindness he had experienced there. He was particularly pleased to meet,
through Bateson's introduction, W.K. Wimsatt, whose *Verbal Icon* (1954) Roger much

[21] By Helen Gardner among others. Christopher Ricks sent Roger a parody of the *Times* article instead. Osborn
also tells the story in 'Neo-Philobiblon', *The Library Chronicle of the University of Texas*, 5 (1972), 15–29.
[22] *The Autobiography of Thomas Whythorne*, ed. James M. Osborn (Oxford: Clarendon Press, 1961), p. vii.
[23] Roger's training for the Oxford BLitt is something of a mystery. As he amusingly recalled in his retirement
speech to the English Faculty in 2000, he failed the bibliography exam, even though his supervisor, Herbert
Davis, taught bibliography, but whether he should have taken Reggie Alton's palaeography classes and learned
secretary hand is unclear.
[24] *The Autobiography of Thomas Whythorne: The Modern Spelling Edition* (London: Oxford University Press,
1962), p. vi.
[25] 'Dr Burney, John Weaver, and the *Spectator*', in Ifan Kyrle Fletcher, Selma Jeanne Cohen, and Roger
Lonsdale, *Famed for the Dance: Essays on the Theory and Practice of Theatrical Dancing in England, 1660–
1740* (New York: New York Public Library, 1960), 59–61. Roger's first publication was 'Dr. Burney and the
Integrity of Boswell's Quotations', *Papers of the Bibliographical Society of America*, 53 (1959), 327–31.

admired and who turned out to be an amiable companion.[26] Nevertheless, Roger was set on returning home at the end of his two years with Osborn, and in early 1960 an opportunity fell in his way.

The A.C. Bradley Fellowship at Balliol was the only research fellowship at Oxford devoted to English. It had been both fortunate and unfortunate in its most recent holders: brilliant literary scholars, they had not stayed long. Christopher Ricks, appointed in 1957, had moved to the tutorial fellowship at Worcester College in 1958; John Carey had succeeded him in 1959 but moved to Keble in 1960. Both Ricks and Carey were in contact with Roger about the Bradley Fellowship, which he decided to apply for, returning to Oxford in May 1960 to be interviewed and appointed to the post. Osborn allowed him to leave early and stay in Oxford, working in the Bodleian. The fellowship freed up more time for Roger's own research, and he was encouraged by a new supervisor, L.F. Powell (1881–1975), the editor of Boswell's *Life of Johnson*, who was to become a good friend. He submitted his DPhil thesis, 'The Literary Career of Dr. Charles Burney (1726–1814)' successfully in May 1962.

As a research fellow at Balliol, Roger took on significant teaching and examining responsibilities, working with John Bryson (1896–1976), the tutorial English Fellow, and in December 1960 he was made Junior Dean. Bryson was due to retire in the autumn of 1963, and when in early 1962 Roger applied for the English Fellowship at Wadham, there was consternation in Balliol that someone who had already attracted the attention of Yale and McGill would go the way of Ricks and Carey. Roger had already got as far in the application process as having dinner with Sir Maurice Bowra and the Wadham Fellows, when at a meeting of the Balliol governing body on Wednesday, 24 January, he was pre-elected to the Balliol English Fellowship that would become vacant when Bryson retired in eighteen months' time.[27] Roger withdrew his application to Wadham. He was to remain in post at Balliol until 2000.[28]

IV

A revision of Roger's thesis, *Dr. Charles Burney: A Literary Biography*, was published by the Clarendon Press in 1965.[29] Percy Scholes, the musicologist, had published a

---

[26] Bateson sent Wimsatt one of Wimsatt's own books to sign and give to Roger ('Diaries and Letters', 31/1/59).
[27] 'Diaries and Letters', 25/1/62.
[28] There was a proposal in 1971, initiated by Philip Larkin, that he should apply for a chair at Hull. But I doubt Roger took the idea seriously.
[29] It was published without quotation from the Berg manuscripts Roger had worked on during his vacation from Osborn. Professor Hemlow persuaded him to exclude them, a matter for regret.

biography in 1948, and that in part explains Roger's emphasis on the literary.[30] For Roger, as for Burney's daughter Fanny, the great achievement of Burney's life was the move from being a 'mere' musician to being a man of letters, patronised by the Court and a member of Samuel Johnson's circle. Much new manuscript material had become available since Scholes's biography: approximately 1,500 letters, plus scholarly note-books, and 150 fragments of Burney's 'Memoirs'. Roger's biography digests this new material and constructs a lucid narrative without rivalling Scholes's attempts to recreate the 18th-century music scene. He faced throughout, however, the problem that Burney, though a very pleasant companion, was always likely to strike the reader as a dull man leading a dull life (making his living through private music tuition until he was seven-ty-eight). Fanny Burney's life of her father, *Memoirs of Doctor Burney*, 3 vols (London, 1832), had resolved the problem by making her father a secular saint, but Roger's view was that Burney, a charming man and anxious to please, was ambitious for literary fame and prepared to be a touch ruthless in his attempts to attain it. Although all Burney's life is dealt with thoroughly, particularly his unhappy childhood, Roger takes the peaks to be the major publications, and much of his research was directed at tracing how these successes were achieved. The achievements are taken to be *The Present State of Music in France and Italy* (1771), *The Present State of Music in Germany, the Netherlands, and the United Provinces* (1773), and *A General History of Music ... Volume the First* (1776), *Volume the Second* (1782), *Volume the Third* and *Fourth* (1789). Two works representing Burney's other major interest, astronomy, are also given appropriate attention: *An Essay towards a History of the Principal Comets* (1769), and 'Astronomy, an Historical and Didactic Poem', written between 1796 and 1801 but never published. Roger's respectful treatment of Burney is never more impressive than in his handling of this twelve-book poem, which Burney was fond of reading aloud to his friends and acquaintances at every opportunity. After a frank verdict from his friend Lady Crewe (which included a refer-ence to '*crabbed chapters* ab^t *parallaxes*'), Burney abandoned it and destroyed it. Roger comments, 'The realization that for years he had been boring his friends in the belief that he was entertaining them must have been humiliating to one whose ambition in life was always to please.'[31]

For the major works, Roger was able to create elements of narrative tension through an account of the difficulties with which the research was conducted, and of the pains and frustrations in getting the books through the Press and favourably reviewed. When

---

[30] *The Great Doctor Burney: His Life, His Travels, His Works, His Family and His Friends*, 2 vols (London: Oxford University Press, 1948).

[31] *Dr. Charles Burney*, pp. 403–4. Roger quotes two surviving passages from the poem, the first from the Osborn collection. Although he concludes we need not regret its loss (Burney did not find a place in Roger's Oxford anthology), he agrees with Fanny Burney that it provided her father with purpose and entertainment, possibly distracting him from depression (p. 405).

The Present State of Music and France and Italy came out in 1771, Burney persuaded his friend William Bewley to take it on for the *Monthly Review*, and looked over Samuel Crisp's notice of it in the *Critical Review*. Some very determined detective work on a letter to Crisp, reading through Fanny Burney's black-ink deletions, revealed that Burney had not only contrived the review but also read it in manuscript and suggested softening some rare elements of criticism.[32] As Roger shows, Burney took a similar interest in reviews throughout his career. Burke's favourable notice of *The Present State of Music in Germany, the Netherlands, and the United Provinces* (1773) in the *Annual Register* was an independent exception and helped draw Burney into contact with Johnson's circle, with Johnson praising Burney as '*one of the first writers of the age* for travels'. Roger, tracing conversations unrecorded in Boswell's *Life*, notes the change from Johnson's response to Burney's first tour, when he said he could not be bothered with 'fiddles and fiddlestrings' (*Dr. Charles Burney*, p. 129). Roger's biography is innovative in its treatment of Burney's relation with Johnson, printing for the first time two touching accounts of Johnson's death (*Dr. Charles Burney*, pp. 286–7).

When it came to Burney's *History of Music*, Roger had to cope with problems even more serious than Fanny Burney's deletions. Burney had received significant help, especially with this first volume and its preliminary Dissertation, from his friend Rev. Thomas Twining (1735–1804). Their letters, or extracts from them, were in the British Museum Library and the Osborn collection, unpublished and often difficult to reconstruct. Roger seamlessly presents a record of this vital partnership, even though it has to be reconstructed from five different groups of documents.[33] Bringing the extracts together reveals a substantial collaboration, remarkable for its academic intimacy: 'Let us slap down our Thoughts as they come, without the Trouble of seeking or arranging them. ... I seem *inside-out* with you & inclined to tell you every secret of my Life' (*Dr. Charles Burney*, p. 135). Tracing the detail of their exchanges, Roger is able to convey much of Burney's conception of his *History* and explain its success.

Roger's sympathetic tolerance of the Burney family breaks down only when he comes to reflect on Fanny Burney's dealing with her father's 'Memoirs' by substituting her own. Charles Burney had started writing his 'Memoirs' in 1782; he had covered his life to 1766, with some material going up to 1806. When Burney died, Fanny took on the duty of editing the 'Memoirs', which were contained in twelve notebooks, but she ended up burning them, all but a few fragments. She had no desire to be reminded of her family's humble origins and thought her father's 'frankness about many celebrated personalities would be dangerous' (*Dr. Charles Burney*, p. 439). She decided instead to

---

[32] *Dr. Charles Burney*, p. 109. Roger claimed to be able to read the deletions at the rate of around three lines an hour, using a magnifying glass.

[33] Roger lays out the details and shelf marks in *Dr. Charles Burney*, p. 134, n. 1.

publish her own *Memoirs of Dr. Burney*. Her book had been subjected to a severe review by John Wilson Croker in the *Quarterly Review* in 1833, but she had been defended by Joyce Hemlow in her biography.[34] Roger's forensic examination of Fanny Burney's practice reveals dishonesty and vanity. She pretended that only the opening of the *Memoirs* was written before Burney's 1807 stroke, when most of it had been, and she exaggerated the effects of the stroke. She misrepresented a passage on recent invitations as Burney's verdict on his 'Memoirs' as a whole (*Dr. Charles Burney*, p. 442–3). Detailed comparisons of Fanny's *Memoirs* with the scant remains of her father's manuscript showed Fanny moving herself to the centre of the narrative and excluding references to other members of the family (*Dr. Charles Burney*, pp. 449–51). Roger's careful analysis reveals an altogether discreditable performance.

John Wagstaff in *ODNB* describes Roger's biography of Burney as painstaking, which it is, but the careful and detailed attention to manuscript evidence gives a much fuller picture of its subject in a style that combines graceful simplicity with maturity of judgement. It is, as the *TLS* judged, 'a book of exceptional learning and sympathy'.[35]

V

In 1961, before the Burney biography was finished, Roger signed a contract to edit Gray, Collins, and Goldsmith in the Longman Poets series that F.W. Bateson was initiating.[36] The edition was due for completion in two years, but, given the Longman requirements for extensive annotation, that was an unreasonable deadline, and the edition was published in 1969.[37] It provided the complete poems of the three poets (including Gray's Latin and Greek verse, and Collins's drafts, fragments, and doubtful poems). In a lecture delivered in Australia in 1976, Roger had some fun with his work as editor:

> I once believed that any editor who succeeded in producing a whole page of annotation to a single line of verse should be automatically obliged to justify himself before a court of his peers. It was therefore with some despondency that I realised some years ago, when I received the page proofs of my edition of *The Poems of Gray, Collins and Goldsmith* (1969), that I had myself committed precisely that crime and that it was

---

[34] *History of Fanny Burney* (Oxford: Clarendon Press, 1958), p. 462.

[35] R. W. Ketton-Cremer, 'Dr. Burney Sets Out to Please', *TLS*, 22 April 1965, p. 310.

[36] I am grateful to Professor Barnard for information about the date and the arrangements for the edition.

[37] *The Poems of Thomas Gray, William Collins, Oliver Goldsmith*, ed. Roger Lonsdale (London: Longman, 1969); a paperback was issued in 1976. Roger read proof while he was teaching at the University of Virginia. He had exchanged houses and jobs with Irwin Ehrenpreis and was at Charlottesville from January to May 1968. He taught postgraduate classes for Ehrenpreis and for Martin Battestin and found the experience interesting but exhausting.

only after delicate negotiations with the printers that we managed finally to squeeze a second line of Gray's *Elegy* onto the offending page.[38]

The problem for the annotator is the space taken by listing parallel passages, though there is a further problem in understanding what they are. Roger has various words for them: borrowings, echoes, reminiscences, imitations, allusions (this last suggesting intended recognition by the reader). In this paper he identifies attitudes evolving through three historical periods. In the first, human experience was regarded as varying little and, therefore, imitation was inevitable and desirable. There had to be what Roger calls 'creative assimilation' with, as Christopher Ricks had put it in the previous set of Canberra studies, 'The Poet as Heir'.[39] The second was a period where originality, individuality, and sincerity became valued; plagiarism, always a problem, became more of a worry for the aspiring author. The third stage, represented for Roger by Eliot's *The Waste Land*, was where failed allusion could indicate the disintegrating culture the poem criticises and where tracing what is lost takes on the burden of a cultural responsibility.

Roger argues that the editor's best response to the problem of parallels is to provide the maximum of information without directing interpretation. His example of a path not to be taken is from a reading of the 'Ode on the Death of a Favourite Cat, Drowned in a Tub of Gold Fishes', by Geoffrey Tillotson, which takes an allusion (perhaps not an allusion) to Helen of Troy as a crucial guide to an interpretation in terms of mock epic.[40] Roger points to complicating echoes, quite as strong, of Gay's *The Toilette*, of Eve's viewing herself in the lake in *Paradise Lost*, of Daphne's appeal to the water deities in Ovid, and of Camilla's pursuit of Chloreus in *Aeneid*, XI. Finally he points out that, although Gray's poem is coloured by mock epic, it is an animal fable with a moral for its reader, something both Tillotson and Samuel Johnson had missed.[41]

Roger's Canberra essay shows us how his edition of Gray, Collins, and Goldsmith works. The echoes he identifies enrich the poem, but they are not all necessary, and they do not dictate a single interpretation. Roger's treatment of Gray's 'Elegy' typifies his approach. The headnote is substantial, fourteen pages long. The evidence for dating,

[38] 'Gray and "Allusion": The Poet as Debtor', in R.F. Brissenden and J.C. Eade (eds), *Studies in the Eighteenth Century, IV: Papers Presented at the Fourth David Nichol Smith Seminar, Canberra* (Canberra Australian National University Press, 1979), pp. 31–55 (31). Roger probably has p. 118 in mind, but there are only two lines on p. 134 also. There is only one line of 'The Progress of Poesy' on p. 168.

[39] R.F. Brissenden and J.C. Eade (eds), *Studies in the Eighteenth Century, III: Papers Presented at the Third David Nichol Smith Seminar, Canberra* (Canberra Australian National University Press, 1976), pp. 209–39. Inevitably I simplify in representing these two Canberra essays, which remain central to the topic of literary echoes.

[40] *Augustan Studies* (London: Athlone Press, 1961), pp. 216–23.

[41] Johnson's criticism, to which Tillotson was responding, is in *The Lives of the Most Eminent English Poets; with Critical Observations on Their Works*, ed. Roger Lonsdale, 4 vols. (Oxford: Clarendon Press, 2006), iv. 181.

1742 or 1746, is represented as inconclusive. The printing of the poem for Robert Dodsley in order to get ahead of the unauthorised printing in the *Magazine of Magazines* is dealt with crisply (the choice of copy-text is good) as is the poem's reception. Roger concludes with an original and sensitive discussion of the two versions of the poem, perceptively arguing that the Eton manuscript version, 'Stanzas Wrote in a Country Church-Yard', presented for Gray too simple an association between the poet and the villagers, and that the final poem is searching to define his own role.[42] Some of these ideas were developed in Roger's 1973 Chatterton Lecture, 'Versions of the Self', an exceptionally clear-eyed and learned approach to this perplexing poet.[43]

The annotation of the *Elegy*, as might be expected from Roger's lecture, is very full. Where possible, as in the opening discussion of the debt to Dante's *Purgatorio*, Gray's own statements or contemporary evidence support the passages cited. Roger is particularly alert to echoes of Petrarch in this poem as he is in the introduction to the 'Sonnet on the Death of Richard West', but he is also aware of the influence of English poetry: Shakespeare, Milton, Dryden, Cowley, Pope, but also near contemporaries such as Warton, Broome, Mallet, and West. One of the changes Gray made to the poem, turning famous classical figures into English ones, is reflected in Roger's identifying fully for the first time the poem's debt to English poetry.

Collins and Goldsmith are not so allusive as Gray, but Roger's approach to his editing was much the same, with appropriate flexibility. That included providing a general account of the conception and publication of Collins's *Odes on Several Descriptive and Allegoric Subjects* (1746), adding to the collation emendations from John Langhorne's enthusiastic edition of the *Odes* (because of the evidence it gave of contemporary reading), and providing notes of Warton's manuscript readings of *Ode to a Lady*. Particular headnotes, for example, that to the 'Ode to Evening', refer back to the general note, leaving themselves free to concentrate on particular problems, such as the poem's relation to the work of the Warton brothers. In annotating the 'Ode to Evening', Roger is again particularly aware of its relation to English poems, drawing attention to lines of the Wartons, but also of Spenser, Milton, Pope, Thomson, and Akenside. There is an exceptionally clear and informative headnote to 'An Ode on the Popular Superstitions of the Highlands of Scotland', where the manuscript had recently been rediscovered by Claire

---

[42] Roger quotes the final lines of the early poem in the right place, at line 72, but it is quite difficult for the reader to get a sense of it. Modern editions, for all their distinction, can be too conservative. The problem was solved by Moses Gompertz in his little edition (London: Philip Holland, 1901) by printing a few pages of facsimile.

[43] *Versions of the Self: The Poetry of Thomas Gray*, Chatterton Lecture on an English Poet (London: Oxford University Press, 1973); also published in *Proceedings of the British Academy*, 59 (1973), 105–23.

Lamont.[44] The poem is then printed from the manuscript with carefully weighed decisions about patterns of indentation.[45]

Goldsmith offered fewer opportunities for the tracing of parallel passages, and what is notable about Roger's treatment of his verse is the neatness with which he deals with matters that might have been contested. The question about the character of the first, 1755, version of *The Traveller*, published in 1764, is dealt with briskly: 'Speculation ... is no doubt pointless', and 'there is virtually no definite information about the progress of the poem' (pp. 622–3). But in this case, compensating for the absence of critical commentary, Roger provides a subtle evaluation of the poem based on T.S. Eliot's insight that Goldsmith has the old and new in 'just proportion'. Roger identifies the poem as belonging to the genre of the Horatian verse-epistle, emphasises the important influence of Addison's *Letter from Italy* (1703), and praises the careful balance and design of the poem (pp. 626–8). In his treatment of Goldsmith's most famous poem, *The Deserted Village*, he is similarly brisk about an old bone of contention: 'It is clear from G.'s own remarks that he considered the problem of rural depopulation to be common to England and his own native country ... The positive identification of the village in question would not have seemed desirable and perhaps not even possible by G. himself' (p. 670). This poem had already been subject to subtle critical investigation, and Roger is content to endorse the view that the poems combined 'elements of purely personal idealised fantasy' with a 'coherent political (Tory) philosophy' (p. 674). Although the textual achievement of this edition is limited, in my view, by Bateson's policy of modernisation, it makes good use of manuscripts, and is unquestionably a critical triumph, enhancing and guiding the reading of three important mid-century poets.

In 1970 Roger followed the edition of Gray, Collins, and Goldsmith, with an edition of William Beckford's *Vathek* in the Oxford English Novels series.[46] In the early 1960s Roger had written two important *TLS* reviews of books on Beckford. In the first, of André Parreaux's, *William Beckford: auteur de Vathek, 1760–1844* (Paris: Nizet, 1960), Roger was sympathetic to Parreaux's textual analyses (and was to follow him in his edition), but not to his attempt to unify the novel into the projection of a myth of the power of bourgeois society: 'Beckford was basically too irresponsible to write a convincing myth of the doomed future of irresponsibility'. The review shows exceptional

[44] 'William Collins's "Ode on the Popular Superstitions of the Highlands of Scotland" —A Newly Recovered Manuscript', *Review of English Studies*, 19 (1968), 137–47.

[45] Roger later edited the Oxford Standard Authors *Thomas Gray and William Collins: Poetical Works* (Oxford: Oxford University Press, 1977), an old-spelling edition with good textual notes and a transcription of the Eton manuscript of Gray's *Elegy*.

[46] William Beckford, *Vathek* (Oxford: Oxford University Press, 1970). This edition was the basis for the Oxford Worlds Classics issue in 1980, which dropped the textual apparatus. Thomas Keymer's new edition in that series keeps the Lonsdale text, with three emendations.

confidence in reading Beckford with responsiveness to his shifting relations to his material, arguing that Parreaux neglects 'the element of parody and burlesque, wild force and brutal comedy, and a barely suppressed giggling by the author at his own naughtiness.'[47] The originality of these readings is somewhat lost in the edition, which has an elegant introduction and an excellent textual apparatus, but distances itself from the naughtiness and giggling which the younger Roger was able to identify, however disapprovingly.

Vathek was followed by a different editing task, volume 4 of the Sphere History of Literature in the English Language.[48] This collection of essays on major writers proved very popular, with a revised edition from Sphere in 1986 and a Penguin reissue in 1993. The contributors were distinguished, with Howard Erskine-Hill contributing a fine opening essay on Dryden. Roger's own essay was on Pope and it offers an impressive and comprehensive account of the 18th century's foremost poet. For many years Roger lectured on Pope in the Oxford English Faculty, and he delighted in telling a story against himself, taken from Leo Bellingham's *Oxford, the Novel*. This version is from his speech at his Faculty farewell dinner:

> A chap gets obsessed with a girl he sees in the Radcliffe Camera, fantasises about getting to know her, etc. etc. Coming out of the Examination Schools one morning he spots her walking just ahead of him up the High and racks his brains for some devastatingly impressive opening gambit. With time running out, he finally blurts out what I hope you will agree is a highly creditable effort: 'Didn't I see you at Lonsdale's lectures on Pope'? Inexplicably, she replies haughtily: 'No. I heard they weren't very interesting.'[49]

The Sphere essay, however, is interesting and original. It begins tellingly, and originally, with Pope's imitation of Spenser, 'The Alley', a poem that combines love of literary tradition with detailed description of slums by the Thames. Roger's eye for such awkward fusions continues in his account of the *Dunciad*, with grandeur glimpsed in the pissing contest and beauty found in Fleet Ditch. An appreciation of the role of earthiness in good poetry is a persistent vein in this essay and remained a constant element in Roger's taste in poetry.[50]

---

[47] 'The mask of Beckford', *TLS*, 10 February 1971, pp. 81–2. In the second review, of Alexander Boyd's *England's Wealthiest Son* (London: Centaur Press, 1962), Roger demolished an attempt to deny Beckford's pederasty, by providing an alert interpretation of a Beckford letter in French ('Baffling Beckford', *TLS*, 2 March 1962, p. 6).

[48] *Dryden to Johnson*, ed. Roger Lonsdale (London: Sphere Books, 1971).

[49] Referring to *Oxford, the Novel* (London: Nold Jonson, 1981), pp. 91–2. The author was Arnold D. Harvey, whose name appears on the second edition (Studley: Brewin, 2012). On his career, see Eric Norman, 'Their Mutual Friend', *TLS*, 12 April 2013, 16–21. The second edition omits the reference to Roger.

[50] A significant essay Roger published at the end of the decade was 'New Attributions to John Cleland', *Review of English Studies*, 30 (1979), 268–90, attributing seven new works to the author of *Memoirs of a Woman of Pleasure* or *Fanny Hill*. This is a good example of Roger's archival work; there are also, for example,

VI

In 1984 Roger startled the literary world with his *New Oxford Book of Eighteenth-Century Verse*.[51] No one would have expected an anthology of this period's poems to have had such an impact. The contemporary reception is captured by the extracts printed with the paperback of 1987: 'a major event ... Enthralling: it enforces a reappraisal of what eighteenth-century poetry is' (John Carey, *Sunday Times*); 'a most readable, most valuable, indeed indispensable collection' (Kinglsey Amis, *The Listener*); 'the voices he has rescued from oblivion are individual, forthright, unpredictable; they speak out of their own experience, and taken together they bring their age back to life with astonishing immediacy' (John Gross, *The Observer*). This anthology even reached politicians, being claimed by Gordon Brown as one of his favourite books (*The Times*, 17 April 2010). But Roger's conception when he began work on the anthology was not of creating a popular book but of undertaking extensive research.[52] Commissioned to prepare the anthology, he decided that he would simply read and evaluate all 18th-century verse. He began by using David Foxon's catalogue, *English Verse, 1701–1750* (Cambridge: Cambridge University Press, 1975), and for the second half of the century he made his own catalogue. Most of his reading was in the Upper Reading Room of the Bodleian Library, but in his acknowledgements he thanks the British Library and eight other libraries. As each poem was read, it was graded. Work on the anthology was completed with the award of a British Academy Readership.

David Nichol Smith's original anthology of 1926 is a charming and learned book. With a nod of appreciation, and an acknowledgement of the editor's duty, Roger began his collection with the same poem, Pomfret's 'The Choice'. But Nichol Smith, for all the sophistication of his introduction, approached his task from the perspective of romantic poetry. What is remarkable for him is that Akenside and Russell foreshadow the lake poets, and that Sir J.H. Moore has the spirit and note of Byron.[53] Roger's taste in poetry, of course, is also that of his era: it reflects the values in his essay on The Movement, particularly his praise of Larkin.[54] He says in his introduction that he 'tried to resist the temptation to include material merely because its style or content might seem to confound familiar generalizations about the period, or because it has purely documentary

---

discoveries of a letter to Pope and a letter from Burke, *Notes and Queries*, 215 (1970), 288, and 227 (1982), 202 respectively.

[51] *The New Oxford Book of Eighteenth-Century Verse*, ed. Roger Lonsdale (Oxford: Oxford University Press, 1984); a paperback, with a different poem no. 304, was issued in 1987.

[52] I am grateful to Jacqueline Norton at the Press, for pointing out that these anthologies are aimed at a general readership, even though they may have academic significance.

[53] *The Oxford Book of Eighteenth Century Verse*, ed. David Nichol Smith (Oxford: Clarendon Press, 1926), pp. x–xi.

[54] *departure*, 4:10 (1956), 18–20.

interest' (p. xxxviii). Nevertheless, his anthology offers a response to a common challenge to the century's poems: 'Where do we find them responding to the agricultural and industrial revolutions, the effects of economic growth, increased social mobility, rapid urban development, changing sexual mores, the impact of British imperialism at home or abroad, or all the social tensions which would erupt in the last decade of the century?' (p. xxxv). Roger's answer is clear: within these pages. He has looked for 'individuality and freshness' and argues that 'when the poet has seen or felt something of his own, naivety or even clumsiness can impart to his verse a kind of immediacy about which conventional criticism and history have found little or nothing to say' (p. xxxviii). The aim is not to subvert traditional accounts of the century's poems but to supplement them (p. xxxvii). This anthology has 552 poems in comparison with Nichol Smith's 450.

There will always be room for dispute about the poems an anthologist chooses from major authors. The arrangement of the poems is chronological, so the decision to divide Pope into two sections was a wise one, though I am baffled by the decision to include the short 'A Hymn Written in Windsor Forest', not at all a bad poem but one Pope never decided to publish in his lifetime. And I regret the omission of Swift's 'A Soldier and a Scholar', one of the most brilliant social poems of the period. What reviewers remarked on, however, and rightly, was the variety of new voices Roger brought forward. Prominent among these were women. Early in the anthology came Lady Mary Chudleigh's 'To the Ladies':

> Wife and servant are the same,
> But only differ in the name ... (p. 36)

And she was followed immediately by Sarah Fyge Egerton:

> From the first dawn of life unto the grave,
> Poor womankind's in every state a slave ... (p. 37)

In spite of Roger's use of masculine pronouns for the poet in his introduction, women, and women protesting against patriarchy, have a voice his selection, with twenty-five women poets represented, almost doubling the number in Nichol Smith.

The collection is striking in escaping the boundaries of politeness. There are poems about labour, most strikingly the extract from Mary Collier's *The Woman's Labour* that he called 'The Washerwoman' (no. 218), which gives details of the work, as well as a protest against it, and Robert Tatersal's 'The Bricklayer's Labours' (no. 189) which similarly traces the work of a day. But the range of material that 18th-century poetry might be expected to have avoided is wide: Jonathan Richardson dreaming of his dead wife (no. 128); John Wright's visit to the province of poverty (no. 138); Edward Chicken's *The Collier's Wedding* (no. 151); Andrew Brice on fear of the bailiffs (no. 155); 'Epitaph on a Child Killed by Procured Abortion' (no. 223); 'Strip Me Naked, or Royal Gin for Ever' (no. 299); a sea-chaplain's petition to be allowed to use the officers' lavatory (no. 315); and poems on boxing (no. 246) and cricket (no. 247). These writers all have something individual to say and find in poetry a way of saying it. Roger concludes on a characteristically humane note, by saying that while Pope would survive his omissions, 'I am more haunted by the lingering memory of some of the totally forgotten men and women whose literary bones I disturbed after they had slumbered peacefully for some two hundred years, who had something graphic or individual to say, however modestly, and for whom I had envisaged some kind of minor literary resurrection, but who necessarily fell back into the darkness of the centuries, perhaps irretrievably, at the last stage of my selection' (pp. xxxix–xl).

Some of these writers, however, were given a second chance in the anthology of *Eighteenth-Century Women Poets* that was published by Oxford University Press in 1989.[55] Here were 110 poets and 323 poems, combined with a more extensive editorial apparatus than Roger had allowed himself in the original anthology. A substantial introduction traces the publication of women's poems throughout the century and each poet is introduced with a biographical essay (often the product of original research) that provides a context for the following poems. The introduction offers an innovative account of its subject, with a perceptive account of the role of the new magazines. As in the first anthology, Roger is conscious of the role of the century's self-anthologising in the collections of Robert Anderson (1792–5) and Alexander Chalmers (1810) which included no poems by women. Roger is perhaps too severe on Wordsworth's negative influence on women's poetry, especially as his revision of the Preface to *Lyrical Ballads* in 1815 included his characteristic praise of Anne Finch, Countess of Winchilsea. Finch does well in this anthology, as does her aristocratic companion Lady Mary Wortley Montagu, but Roger's emphasis in this collection is once again on 'homely writers' who 'had clearly never heard about the requirements of polite taste'. Joanna Baillie (nos. 278–85) is a particular favourite, even though 'the earthiness and vigour' of her first volume (1790) 'were unfashionable and predictably ignored' (p. xxxvi). But poets more expressive of the later century's prevailing sensibility also do well. Charlotte Smith, confined in the earlier volume to 'Sonnet Written in the Church Yard at Middleton in Sussex', is allowed not only a 'Fragment Descriptive of the Miseries of War' but also a cheerful poem on reaching the age of thirty-eight (nos. 237–43), while Mary Robinson, previously excluded, is allotted six poems, including 'The Haunted Beach' (nos. 302–7).

In her valuable review of this 'almost entirely unfamiliar collection of poems' in *The Times* (21 October 1989), p. 36, Julia Briggs recognised 'an extraordinary challenge' to

---

[55] *Eighteenth-Century Women Poets*, ed. Roger Lonsdale (Oxford: Oxford University Press, 1989); a paperback, with corrections and additions, was issued in 1990.

current ways of interpreting 18th-century literature, even though she thought Roger might have been unconscious of it: 'Lonsdale sometimes seems uneasy at the anger, unhappiness, or painful clear-sightedness of his contributors, an embarrassed parent watching his children misbehave. Such hesitations are unnecessary. This is a brilliant and original anthology and, despite its editor's occasional demurs, makes a major contribution to feminist literary studies.' Julia Briggs correctly identified the anthology's potential for supporting a host of courses on women's writing, but she also captured Roger's rejection of a revolutionary stance. I am also conscious of complaints that his anthologies are under-theorised. The claim that he is uneasy about the unhappiness his poems express strikes me as unjust: one of his aims, it is clear from his introductions, and even more so from a review of the poems themselves, was to give voice to that unhappiness. And he expected his material to be taken up by those occupying a radically feminist position. But he also set himself to outline the conditions that gave women the opportunities for self-expression during the century, and saw his anthologies as corrections to the existing accounts of the period's verse and not as a comprehensive rejection of them. He would have seen the request for theorisation as coming from belief in a superior discourse that, like his friend Christopher Ricks, he would reject, sharing with Ricks an admiration for Johnsonian criticism.[56]

Another book, though this time a small one, came out of work on the first anthology.[57] Without knowing the story of John Bampfylde (1754–97), Roger found in his *Sixteen Sonnets* (1778) 'a distinctive and original voice' and included four of them (412–15) in his first anthology. He then started investigating Bampfylde's life, finding he could develop existing accounts through reference to the *Public Advertiser* of 10 March 1779. Bampfylde, perhaps best known as the handsome young man pictured with his friend George Huddesford in Joshua Reynolds's portrait in the Tate Gallery, fell passionately in love with Joshua Reynolds's niece, Mary Palmer, and when she rejected him lost his reason, behaved violently and was incarcerated at the age of twenty-four, only regaining his freedom just before his death. As Roger admits, it is difficult to separate a response to the poems, which were mostly written from retired village life before the relationship with Mary Palmer (though they are dedicated to her), from the sad story of his life. Roger's elegant edition, sharing its admiration of the poetry with Robert Southey, is both celebratory and compassionate. A thirty-five-page introduction precedes the poems, which are followed by textual and explanatory notes. In creating his edition, Roger provided the memorial that Bampfylde's friend William Jackson (1730–1803), the musician, wanted to publish but could not.

---

[56] See especially Christopher Ricks, 'Literary Principles as against Theory' in *Essays in Appreciation* (Oxford: Clarendon Press, 1996), pp. 311–32.

[57] *The Poems of John Bampfylde*, ed. Roger Lonsdale (Oxford: The Perpetua Press, 1988).

VII

In 1987 Roger started work on an edition that brought together his interest in 18th-century poetry with his work on Johnson's circle.[58] Samuel Johnson's *Lives of the Poets* had not received scholarly editing since the three-volume edition by George Birkbeck Hill in 1905.[59] Roger began with the intention of producing a lightly annotated text, signing a contract with Penguin, but soon, with his characteristic thoroughness clicking into operation, the project started to develop into a major scholarly edition that needed four large volumes.[60] The new *Lives* provided for the first time a thoroughly analysed and faithful version of Johnson's text, detailed their composition, explaining and illustrating Johnson's approaches to biography and criticism, and provided an unrivalled level of information about Johnson and about the eminent poets themselves. There is a touching parallel between Lonsdale and Johnson himself, for whom the *Lives* were also a late project that slowly grew in importance.

Roger's introduction, at 185 pages, might stand independently as the best critical account of the *Lives*. It traces how what started as a simple task grew into a major exercise in literary history. As Roger fully recognises, the *Lives* started as a booksellers' project, renewing copyright in a major collection, and with this context, he is not embarrassed, as Birkbeck Hill had been, to acknowledge and thoroughly investigate Johnson's sources (notably the *General Dictionary, Historical and Critical* and the *Biographia Britannica*) and his assistants (John Nichols, George Steevens, and Isaac Read). He provides a pioneering analysis of Johnson's reluctance to engage in primary research, and points to Johnson's belief that the major essays should be written out of the copiousness of his own information and the vigour of his intellect. As in the life of Burney, Roger creates narrative tension through Johnson's struggles to realise his conception. Early in the enterprise Johnson accepted 'judicious celebration of the national heritage' (i. 104) as part of his assignment. English poetry, he would argue, had moved from barbarism and roughness to elegance and refinement in the work of Dryden and Pope, who had combined comprehensiveness with vigour. Roger sets out Johnson's opposition to the conflicting view of the Warton brothers (i. 150–3; iv. 238–40), and, more provocatively, reveals that Johnson struggled with doubts about the validity of his own account. Time and again Johnson has to qualify the praise that he wants to bestow. In the criticism of Dryden and Pope, for example, he finds it difficult

---

[58] Samuel Johnson, *The Lives of the Most Eminent English Poets; with Critical Observations on Their Works*, ed. Roger Lonsdale, 4 vols. (Oxford: Clarendon Press, 2006).
[59] *Lives of the English Poets*, ed. George Birkbeck Hill, 3 vols (Oxford: Clarendon Press, 1905).
[60] Discussion with Penguin began in March 1987, with the contract signed later that year. After Roger signed a contract with Oxford for a major scholarly edition in 2004, discussion with Penguin about use of the material continued. The contract was finally cancelled in 2008.

to identify a major poem to praise, and the success of English poetry comes to lie in translation.

The annotation of the *Lives* is copious and notable for its alertness to matters of doubt or debate. Each section begins with information about composition, the writing of the life and its progress through the press. In 1997, under the guidance of Michael Suarez SJ, 'once my student and, finally, my best critic and mentor' (i. vi), Roger had gone to New York to work on manuscripts and proofs in the Berg Collection and the Pierpont Morgan Library. They are the subject of valuable discussion (i. 175–9) and inform the commentary at many points. The accounts of people and events are, as one might expect, exceptionally thorough, and the commentary also provides detailed reflection on Johnson's critical positions and explanations of his vocabulary. In annotating the negative discussion of the metaphysical poets in the life of Cowley, for example, there are notes on imitation (Aristotle, Dryden, Dennis, Jones), nature (Boyle), wit (Welsted, Trapp, Pope, Pythagoras), affection (the 'pathetick' in Shakespeare), sentiment, the sublime (Milton, Longinus), and generality (Reynolds) (i. 323–31), all generously illustrated by references to other lives and to Johnson's essays in the *Rambler* and elsewhere. For the scholarly reader the volumes have three appealing appendices: 'Sequences of Johnson's Poets'; 'Some Early Periodical Reactions'; 'and 'Spelling and Capitalization in the *Prefaces* and *Lives*', a witty survey of the many failures to impose consistency on the Johnson's text.

Roger's edition of Johnson's *Lives* was received with exceptional enthusiasm. In a learned and critical review, Robert Folkenflik, himself the author of a major study of Johnson as biographer, judged it 'not just the best edition of *The Lives of the Poets*' but 'the best edition of any text of Johnson's, ever' and 'an education in eighteenth-century literature and culture'.[61] It was awarded the MLA Prize for a Scholarly Edition, 2005–6. Subsequently, the long-anticipated Yale edition was published in three volumes (2010), with more detailed treatment of the text but significantly less offered by way of introduction and commentary; it sits alongside rather than displaces Roger's edition in the admiration of Johnsonians.[62]

---

[61] '"Little Lives, and Little Prefaces"? Lonsdale's Edition of Johnson's *Lives of the Poets*', *Age of Johnson*, 19 (2009), 273–82 (273 and 282). Folkenflik's study is *Samuel Johnson, Biographer* (Ithaca: Cornell University Press, 1978).

[62] *Lives of the Poets*, ed. John H. Middendorf, 3 vols. Yale Edition of the Works of Samuel Johnson, vols 21–3 (New Haven: Yale University Press, 2010). A subsidiary title page credits the editors of individual lives: Stephen Fox (Milton), J.A.V. Chapple (Dryden), James L. Battersby (Addison), James Gray (Savage), James E. May (Young). Robert DeMaria Jr. revised the whole edition. Roger was required to resign from the board of the Yale Johnson when it was found he was editing the *Lives* for Penguin. F.P. Lock offered a perceptive and sensitive comparison of the two editions in the *Johnsonian News Letter*, 62 (2011), 41–5, with which I would largely agree, though modernization is always a problem for the textual value of an edition.

By this point, the distinction of Roger's work had received many acknowledgements. He had served as Delegate to Oxford University Press from 1977 to 1987. In 1989 he was elected a Fellow of the Royal Society of Literature. Oxford promoted him to Reader in 1990 and then to Professor in 1992. He was elected to the British Academy in 1991. To celebrate his sixtieth birthday (though the volume appeared two years later), Alvaro Ribeiro SJ and James G. Basker published a festschrift ('To Roger Lonsdale, Scholar, Mentor, and Friend'), *Tradition and Transition: Women Writers, Marginal Texts, and the Eighteenth-Century Canon* (Oxford: Clarendon Press, 1996), with eighteen essays by distinguished pupils, and in 2007 his work was celebrated at a session at the British Society for Eighteenth Century Studies in Oxford.

Roger retired in 2000. He had been a Fellow of Balliol (first as a Research Fellow) continuously for forty years, and had served as Vice-Master 1978–80. He remained in Oxford, where he lived with his second wife, Nicoletta Momigliano, who had been a Research Fellow at Balliol and was to become Professor of Aegean Studies at Bristol University. Roger had first married Anne Mary Griffin (née Menzies), Senior Scholar and Lecturer in Chinese at St Anne's College, who, after their divorce (1994), became President of New Hall, Cambridge. They had two children: Charles, currently Deputy Director of the Conflict Prevention Centre, Organisation for Security and Co-operation in Europe, Vienna; and Kate, Senior Research Fellow, School of Earth and Environment, University of Leeds. In retirement, Roger continued to spend time with his books. He had started collecting antiquarian books on his return from Yale in 1960 and began to keep a catalogue of them in the summer of 1963. At first he concentrated on Burney, then Johnson's circle, and then Gray and his associates, before branching out into the 18th century in general. He bought from catalogues and from the bookshops then available in Oxford: Blackwell's, the Turl, Thornton's (just across the road from Balliol), and Sanders. He was generous in lending books to friends, but cautious about selling to other collectors. The collection is now being sold by his friend Christopher Edwards. Roger also continued his love of watching sport, in which he was often joined by Nicoletta, who showed a capacity for enjoying cricket, happily facing the challenge of translating 'silly mid-off' and 'deep mid-wicket' into Italian. He persevered in the fondness for smoking cigarettes that alone had regularly interrupted his dedicated reading in the Bodleian's Upper Reading Room, but was willing to spare the time necessary for attending the Oxford Restoration to Reform and Bodleian Literary Manuscripts seminars. He enjoyed meeting young people who knew his work (for example, the Burney scholar, Lorna Clark, and the Cleland scholar, Hal Gladfelder), but most of all he liked learning something new and different. He fell ill at the Johnson Conference at Pembroke College in 2016, and from that point his health, including his memory, began to fail. He was cared for with selfless energy by Nicoletta and continued nearly to the end to be an amused and amusing companion. He died peacefully at home on 28 February 2022.

Roger Lonsdale engaged in literary scholarship of rare quality. For predecessors, he would have pointed to Sir Harold Williams, with his edition of Swift's poems in the 1930s, or to the editors of individual volumes of the Twickenham Pope, but even some Twickenham volumes came to be the work of teams. His own edition of Gray, Collins, and Goldsmith falls in with a pattern established by the magnificent Longman volumes of Milton and Tennyson by his contemporaries Alistair Fowler, John Carey, and Christopher Ricks, but what is extraordinary is the intellectual power, dedication, and stamina that led him to go on to do so much more editorial work, including his two anthologies and the *Lives of the Poets*. In an age when teams worked to tight deadlines (or were supposed to), he worked alone, setting his own standards (those of us who tried to help by venturing suggestions often falling short), and took the time the task required. Kindly, compassionate, humorous (colleagues speak often of his self-deprecating humour), he nevertheless judged independently and severely. It was that combination of personal generosity and academic severity that made him, as Robert Folkenflik put it, 'a scholar's scholar'.[63]

Acknowledgements
Unlike the object of desire in *Oxford, the Novel*, I attended, and enjoyed, Roger Lonsdale's Pope lectures in the English Faculty, in the late 1960s, but I first met him in 1984 at a Johnson conference at Pembroke College, Oxford. After a similar conference in 2010, we started to meet once or twice a week, and I had many opportunities to discuss his research with him. In compiling this memoir, I have received the most generous help from Roger's widow, Nicoletta Momigliano, who has made his unpublished diaries and other materials available to me. I am grateful to her for corrections and for advice. I am also grateful to John Barnard for helping me to understand what it was like to be one of James Osborn's research assistants, and to Martin Dodsworth, one of Roger's closest Oxford friends, who kindly shared information about Roger's early career, and passed on further information from Christopher Ricks. There is a dazzling account of Roger by Seamus Perry in the *Balliol College Record* (2022), followed by a witty Tribute by Professor Ricks, pp. 140–7. Edward Wilson, who had been Roger's colleague in the Oxford English Faculty provided an admirable memoir for Hymers College,[64] and I am grateful to Mrs Jenny Richardson at Hymers for further information. Among Roger's other friends, Claude Rawson, Michael Rossington, Adam Rounce, Michael Suarez SJ (who kindly read through this memoir for me), and Abigail Williams have at various times generously shared with me their insights into his personality and career.

.

---

[63] In the review of the *Lives of the Poets* cited above, p. 273.
[64] https://www.oldhymerians.com/news/fondly-remembered/265/265-Roger-Lonsdale-OH-1945-

Note on the author: James McLaverty is Emeritus Professor of Textual Criticism at Keele University.

Biographical Memoirs of Fellows of the British Academy (ISSN 2753–6777) are published by
The British Academy, 10–11 Carlton House Terrace, London, SW1Y 5AH
www.thebritishacademy.ac.uk

PETER LINEHAN

Peter Anthony Linehan

11 July 1943 – 9 July 2020

elected Fellow of the British Academy 2002

by

MALCOLM SCHOFIELD

Fellow of the Academy

FRANCISCO HERNÁNDEZ

With his first book, *The Spanish Church and the Papacy* (1972), Peter Linehan revolutionised the study of relations between church and state in Spain in the high middle ages. His magnum opus, *History and the Historians of Medieval Spain* (1994), covering a vast temporal span, showed, among other things, that medieval chronicles were historical artefacts written not to 'tell the truth', but to present as such the particular agendas of the powers that be. Perhaps his greatest legacy will be the two massive collections of documents and pontifical diplomatic studies included in his *Portugalia Pontificia* (2013) and *España Pontificia* (2023).

Biographical Memoirs of Fellows of the British Academy, 20, 411–432
Posted 11 November 2022. © British Academy 2022.

I

Peter Linehan (b. 11 July 1943) was brought up in East Sheen, in a firmly Catholic household. His father John was a brokerage clerk and his mother Kathleen a primary school teacher. His grandparents had come from Ireland in the early part of the century, his mother's parents from Co. Meath, his father's from the city of Cork. He was the second of three children, with Mary his elder sister (b. 1939) and Christopher his younger brother (b. 1946). Peter's education began at the Sacred Heart primary school in Roehampton, opposite what is now its university. In due course, he won a scholarship to St Benedict's School, Ealing, a monastic foundation. He wrote of his time there:[1]

> I was rather often punished; indeed, I was just about the most regularly beaten boy. This was not because I was the most feral. It was because I was one of the most noticed. This was a distinction I was later to find helpful when dealing with undergraduate offenders as Dean of St John's. The school had excellent history masters, of whom C.S. Walker made the greatest impression on me. Amongst those who would go on to make a mark as medievalists were Edmund King, David d'Avray and Peter Biller.[2] King had been admitted to St John's Cambridge in 1960, and I followed him there as a minor scholar at my second attempt in 1961, the first member of my family to go to university.

His Tutor at St John's was to be Ronald Robinson, wartime bomber pilot and historian of the scramble for Africa, who became a 'chum'[3] and something of a role model,[4] and his Director of Studies, F.H. Hinsley, subsequently Master of the College, whose war had been spent intelligence gathering at Bletchley Park.[5] Medieval supervision was provided in College, 'admirably' by Edward Miller,[6] and less to his consistent satisfaction by Geoffrey Barraclough.[7]

Peter had not as an undergraduate envisaged continuing with research until, with another First in Part II of the History Tripos following the same result in Part I, he decided on a late change of direction. He had become intrigued by Spain and its 20th-century history when visiting the country in summer 1959 while still at school. The Cambridge History Faculty had no expert in that field, so he was sent to Raymond Carr in Oxford as supervisor, with Herbert Butterfield, the Cambridge Regius Professor,

[1] This quotation, as with all others in this section unless indicated to the contrary, is taken like much of the other biographical material from Peter Linehan's 'Autobiography', an unfinished and unpublished fragment.
[2] See Biller, *The Measure of Multitude. Population in Medieval Thought* (Oxford, 2000), p. viii.
[3] As in the dedication of Linehan, *The Ladies of Zamora* (Manchester, 1997).
[4] Obit. (Linehan), *The Independent*, 25 June 1999.
[5] Obit. (Linehan), *The Independent*, 19 February 1998.
[6] Obit. (Linehan), *The Eagle* (2001), 80–86; also (with Barbara Harvey), *Proceedings of the British Academy*, 138 (2006), 231–56.
[7] Obit. (Linehan), *The Eagle*, 70 (1985), 48–50.

keeping a close and frequent eye on him. Despite striking an abidingly happy rapport with Carr, nothing else much in that first term of postgraduate work (Michaelmas 1964) went particularly well. 'More to the point however', as he himself put it, 'I had spent long enough in Spain's 1930s to discover that there was very little prospect of my or anyone else's discovering anything worth discovering while Franco and his system remained in charge.'

Accordingly, having taken various medieval options in the Tripos, he switched to the Spanish Middle Ages. He had consulted Christopher Cheney, who was 'cautious', and Walter Ullmann, 'who knew nothing at all about medieval Spain', but – he guessed – would let him get on with things as he himself wanted. And indeed 'Ullmann proved an excellent supervisor, ever ready to put the goad to me when it was needed.'[8] One book on the subject he came across was the *Iglesia castellano-leonesa y curia romana en los tiempos del rey San Fernando* (Madrid, 1945) of Demetrio Mansilla Reoyo, by then bishop of Ciudad Rodrigo. He wrote to Mansilla, who advised that for monasteries and parishes there were plenty of institutional and liturgical issues to work on, although papal material was much better known. Nonetheless he made his start on microfilms of papal registers recently acquired by Cheney. 'The combination of a sense of being at the coal-face of medieval research with access to things like teapots, decent beer and proper pipe tobacco made these some of the happiest research times of my life.'

Towards the end of 1965 he put in a short dissertation for Cambridge College Research Fellowships. He was elected in May the next year at St John's. In August he set off for Spain. There:

> I spent the next seven months or so either in Madrid or driving my mini around the provinces, seeking, and sometimes securing, admission to cathedral archives from Santiago and Urgel in the north to Córdoba in the south (not excluding a brief excursion to Braga, preliminary to my later longer involvement on the Portuguese front).

Terrorism was returning to Spain at this time. On one occasion in Zamora he had a brush with security police suspicious of his 'investigaciones'. When obstacles to research in Madrid itself became too difficult, he escaped to the provinces, where again he met what he perceived as suspicion and incomprehension. With more experience, he could interpret such a reception as often enough 'merely a preliminary gesture which leads before long to most generous assistance and co-operation'.[9] Toledo supplied a favourite example:

> Toledo cathedral, repository of most of the materials essential for an understanding of

---

[8] With Brian Tierney, he would edit a Festschrift in Ullmann's honour: *Authority and Power: Studies presented to Walter Ullmann on his 70th birthday* (Cambridge, 1980). It was a matter of continuing sadness to him that Ullmann was later to fall out with him, as had frequently occurred with Ullmann's former doctoral students.

[9] P.A. Linehan, *The Spanish Church and the Papacy* (Cambridge, 1971), pp. x-xi.

the history of medieval Christian Spain, was an obvious alternative centre. Here though there were other problems in store. … On my first visit, D. Juan Francisco [the archivist] informed me that the archive was open for an hour a day (excepting feast-days) and then proceeded to request me to provide translations of a batch of letters and to get me to admire the postage stamps he had harvested from his correspondents' unavailing envelopes. And so the precious hour passed, documentless.

But help was at hand. On leaving the archive:

I fell in with a cleric who had been working there. … He revealed himself as a doctoral student at the Gregorian University, Rome. I invited him to join me for lunch in the local bar: no great Lucullan blow-out in 1966 but the standard Francoist repast of noodle soup, fried hake and an orange, I guess. Still, it did the trick, for as I was about to sample the blackish wine my companion reached into a pocket of his soutane and fished from it an enormous key which he placed ceremoniously beside his fork, explaining that it was his 'invariable custom' to return to the archive in the afternoon to read his breviary. Would I care to accompany him? *Would* I?' ...

Thereafter as often as Peter returned to Toledo, the same pattern repeated itself without variation, '*all as if always it was happening for the first time* …'

Back home he had to think it all out and write it up. After completion of the PhD thesis his position at St John's was converted from 1969 into a teaching Fellowship and College Lectureship in History, Edward Miller having departed to a chair in Sheffield in 1965. The thesis had already been awarded a major University prize (Thirlwall with Seeley Medal), and the revolutionary and hugely influential book based on his research (see Part II below) appeared in 1971. 1971 was also the year of his marriage to Christine Callaghan, who had been the editor for his book at Cambridge University Press. They set up home in Impington, a village just north of the city, where their three children – Gabriel, Frances and Samuel – were brought up, and where they entertained friends, students and scholars from the continent with a crackling fire in winter, leisurely Sunday lunches in the garden in summer, and lavish pre-graduation suppers there too for graduands and their families.

Peter was to remain at St John's to the end of his days, as a College don in an old style. There he was tireless in pressing upon those in office forcefully (if not altogether successfully) issues on which he felt strongly, such as tourist control (or its absence). His rather oblique contributions to the deliberations of the Governing Body, on the other hand, might sound more like mild scholarly observations addressed to a seminar. His participation in the work of the History Faculty was limited. He enjoyed strong friend-ships with some of its members, who held him in high regard, and particularly latterly was to become a generously supportive unofficial mentor sought out by research students with medieval interests neighbouring on his own. But for whatever reasons, applications for University Lectureships were unsuccessful. At subsequent stages, attempts were made unproductively to secure a senior position for him. His only University appointments were first as an additional Pro-Proctor in 1973, which resulted in his successfully prosecuting the University for underpayment (he conducted his own case and was awarded £304.15 with costs), and then as Senior Proctor in 1976–7, greatly appreciating and appreciated by his 'bulldogs', with the highlight a presentation at the Palace of a Loyal Address on the occasion of the Queen's silver jubilee, followed by a leisurely and convivial progress homewards. More incognito he penned dispatches by Mercurius Cantabrigiensis (a fictive local 17th-century Protestant divine), which appeared in the *Spectator* in 1975–6 and occasionally in later years in the *Cambridge Review*.

For St John's he was efficient and effective in administration. He relished the role of Secretary to Group 3 of the examinations for Cambridge colleges' entrance scholarships from 1974 until their final demise in 1986. In College itself, he served as Director of Studies in History from 1977 to 1987 (and in 1996–97), Tutor from 1977 to 1997, and Tutor for Graduate Affairs from 1983 to 1997. Under his aegis, the numbers of women research and other graduate students, first admitted upon 'co-residence' in 1981, quadrupled. By 1988 St John's was one of the colleges most sought after by applicants for postgraduate study. He was particularly attentive to the provision of accommodation for graduates, and was largely responsible for the conversion of their annual summer lunch in Hall into a buffet for families in the Fellows' garden, complete with bouncy castle and children's entertainer.

Despite such commitments, the medieval history of the Iberian peninsula continued to absorb much of Peter's time, energy and boundless sharply-focused curiosity; he returned regularly to Spain, with or without his family, latterly Portugal too. His phenomenal rate of production of research publications never slackened (see again Part II), and he was also in demand as a never bland book reviewer, for national broadsheets and weeklies as well as for learned journals.[10] In 1993 his magnum opus, *History and the Historians of Medieval Spain*, appeared; further books and articles followed rapidly, ranging in tone and character from the racy *Ladies of Zamora* (1997) to the monumental two volumes of edited documents *Portugalia Pontificia* (2013).[11] He had served as principal organiser of the Seventh International Congress of Medieval Canon Law (held in College) in 1984, taking his habitual pleasure in the quirks of academic and clerical behaviour, and as co-editor of the *Journal of Ecclesiastical History* from 1979 to 1991 (he subsequently chaired its board, one of the several journal boards of which he became

---

[10] He was himself an avid reader of daily and weekly papers, with the *Daily Telegraph*, and not only but in particular its obituaries, specially to his taste.

[11] To be followed by a posthumously published collection of similar Spanish material, *España Pontificia*. He often hosted a postprandial seminar (Magnus Ryan and Patrick Zutshi with himself) which rotated between their three colleges, whose help he would sometimes seek in making sense of the documents he was currently tackling. Or he would call on the expertise of Michael Reeve in palaeography and plausible Latin.

a member). He frequently gave invited lectures and seminar presentations in Britain (notably the Birkbeck Lectures in 1999), on the continent, and occasionally in the USA. He facilitated appointment of a good number of his European colleagues as Visiting Scholars of the College. He himself was offered but declined the chair of medieval history at Leeds in 1994, thereby incidentally avoiding many of the mounting horrors of modern academic bureaucracy, for which – as for airports – his fierce loathing never abated. Honours came his way, notably with election to Academies in Siena (1988) and Madrid (1996), and to the British Academy (2002).[12] A final accolade was award of an Honorary Doctorate by the Universidad Autónoma de Madrid (2018), followed by a particularly happy private occasion when its contributing authors presented him with a Festschrift.[13]

Peter had been asked to produce a new College History for its quincentenary in 2011. He duly persuaded an expert team of authors to write chapters on the centuries on which they were authorities. One or two of the contributors originally assembled found themselves having to withdraw, and for the 20th century he ended up composing the bulk of the account himself, a witty exercise in micro-history relatively light on broader developments in education. His narrative was founded on his medievalist's capacity to extract illumination and entertainment from a huge volume of disparate mostly archival material – whose custodian, the College Archivist Malcolm Underwood, he held in highest regard. He was able to present a copy of this handsomely produced volume to Her Majesty Queen Elizabeth, when she visited the College for its celebrations that summer.[14]

After his venerated St John Fisher (martyred by Henry VIII in 1535), his modern hero proved to be the gentle E.A. Benians, Master of Fisher's college from 1933–52: pioneering and well-travelled imperial and commonwealth historian with worldwide contacts especially in Asia and America, who 'stood for the casting off of provincial shackles', who had 'a genius for friendship' with young and old alike – and who had dedicated his life to the College. That sounds rather like Peter himself. While to Benians 'a degree of remoteness forever attached',[15] with his established colleagues Peter's own persona tended to the studiedly world-weary. His conversational forte was the unexpected one-liner fired instantaneously. There were circumstances when he did froideur, but he would go the second or third mile for someone who needed it, and younger or more temporary members of the community recognised undemonstrative friendliness.

[12] Where he was very soon taking up the cudgels with wonted vigour against a perceived threat to the continued funding of the Medieval Latin Dictionary project.
[13] Francisco Hernandez, Rocío Sánchez Ameijeiras, and Emma Falque (eds), *Medieval Studies in Honour of Peter Linehan* (Firenze, 2018).
[14] P. Linehan (ed.), *St John's College, Cambridge: A History* (Woodbridge: Boydell, 2011).
[15] Quotations on Benians from Linehan, *St John's College, Cambridge*, 442, 515, 514.

His smile was characteristically mischievous, while his face would light up with a broad grin when encountering an old friend.

Soon after his period as a Tutor was over, he had become the College's Dean of discipline (1999–2010), exercising the role vigilantly, firmly, idiosyncratically, and enjoyed more than feared. He knew what was going on, or with his clientele maintained the inscrutable bluff that he knew. Penalties, occasionally bizarre, were customised to fit offences. He had a soft spot for the more colourful of the miscreants, and dispensed his customary hospitality to the good-hearted among them. Many of his old pupils kept in touch with him. In his rooms one might sometimes encounter them enjoying a glass of Rioja with him on visits to Cambridge, as also younger scholars from the continent who came to draw on his knowledge, wisdom and support. But his concern was not restricted to his pupils or young academics. For many members of the College support staff, too, in his eyes the institution's bedrock, he had a particular affection, translated into action for any in trouble.

He had increasingly seemed to have become part of the fabric of the College as his portly figure made a stately progress through its courts. His health declined however in his 70s, and after cardiac arrests in the first months of 2020 he died two days short of his 77th birthday (9 July 2020). He had remained steadfast in his Catholic faith and attendance at mass. A Latin requiem mass, attended under Covid–19 restrictions only by family and close friends and colleagues, was celebrated for him later in July in the College Chapel before cremation.

II

Peter's first book, *The Spanish Church and the Papacy* (Cambridge, 1971), an offshoot of his PhD dissertation of 1968,[16] made a splash. The novelty of its claims and the mass of previously unknown archival records used to support them astonished everyone, but it raised a few eyebrows. Father Robert I. Burns SJ, whose work on the diocese of Valencia in the 13th century had appeared four years earlier,[17] warned that 'the relations between the several Iberian kingdoms and the long series of thirteenth-century popes would require expertise in a combination of local contexts probably beyond that of any living scholar',[18] and described Monsignor Demetrio Mansilla's *Iglesia castellano-leonesa y curia romana en los tiempos del rey San Fernando* (completed by 1938, but not printed until 1945) as 'a monumental *effort* toward such a goal'. The implicit

---

[16] *Reform and Reaction: the Spanish Kingdoms and the Papacy in the Thirteenth Century.*
[17] *The Crusader Kingdom of Valencia: Reconstruction on a Thirteenth-Century Frontier*, 2 vols (Cambridge MA, 1967).
[18] Review in *Catholic Historical Review*, 61 (1975), 69–71.

comparison is worth pursuing. Mansilla had attempted to assess the political, economic, and ecclesiastical effect of papal policies during 1217–52 on the kingdom of Castile-León. To that end, he had culled the 'Castilian-leonese' items found in the fourteen volumes (9–23) of the Vatican Registers from the pontificates of Honorius III (1216–27), Gregory IX (1227–41) and Innocent IV (1243–54), as well as sundry Vatican materials also related to the reign of Fernando III (1217–1252). As is well known, the registers contain chancery *copies* of papal letters, which, in this case, had already been indexed, if not published in full.[19] In his review of the book, Professor Julio González welcomed the Roman cache, but missed the many *original* letters, ecclesiastical and lay, preserved in Spanish archives and absent from the Vatican Registers.[20]

True, Mansilla continued to gather 'Spanish' papal letters from the Vatican, and, in 1955, published 567 items spanning from 965 to 1216;[21] ten years later he issued his volume on Honorius III, with 640 letters.[22] In 1968, with his PhD thesis completed, Peter provided an *addendum* of 69 original items from 41 Spanish archives, which Mansilla had missed (items and archives), and located another group of 62 *original* letters, whose texts Mansilla had reproduced from old *copies* or modern secondary sources.[23]

But publishing documents, and to do it as accurately and comprehensibly as possible, is, of course, only the first step towards understanding their wider historical significance. Looking back to the preceding century from the height of 1971, Peter could rightly remark that no one had provided any general perspective of the 'possibly humdrum history of the thirteenth-century Spanish Church',[24] just as he was about to offer his own version and to challenge the subject's expected dullness.

He had begun his research in the waning years of Franco's Spain, when he was still deeply interested in the Civil War, a subject for a PhD thesis which he had abandoned as impossible at the time, but whose knowledge coloured the way he saw local authorities, be they police, civil servants, or canon-archivists. Despite cool or hostile receptions,[25] he left no document unturned as he went all over Spain, hopping from archive to archive, collecting the sort of materials Julio González had found wanting in Mansilla's survey. As Williell R. Thomson put it: 'Linehan has unearthed an enormous mass of arcane rescripts, charters, and inventories in Spanish and Portuguese archives. Anyone acquainted with the painful procedures that block even admission to those collections

[19] Pressutti (1888–1895), Auvray (1896–1908), and Berger (1884–1921).
[20] *Hispania*, 6 (1946), 304–8. As many as 70% of all papal letters went unregistered under Honorius III: Jane E. Sayers, *Papal Government and England During the Pontificate of Honorius III (1216–1227)* (1984), p. 67.
[21] *La documentación pontificia hasta Inocencio III* (Rome, 1955).
[22] *Documentación pontificia de Honorio III* (Rome, 1965).
[23] 'La documentación Pontificia de Honorio III (1216–1227): unas adiciones a la regesta de don Demetrio Mansilla', *Anthologica Annua*, 16 (1968), 385–408.
[24] *Spanish Church* (1971), p. 2.
[25] Cf. 'History in a Changing World', St John's College Hull Lecture 1992, pp. 8–9.

must applaud his success. Of almost fifty archives assaulted, only Lerida withstood his entreaties.'[26]

The hostages taken were mercilessly interrogated. Beyond rank and number, Peter not only extracted information about their administrative niches and political allegiances, he also exposed the contradictions between their actions and the religious and secular values they claimed to share with European Christianity, defining in so doing the character of a 'frontier' culture in the western fringes of the western world. The resultant picture was shockingly new but entirely convincing, fleshed out with overwhelming footnoted detail. He was not only interested in the wider legal (customary, canon and common law), economic, and socio-cultural implications of his archival materials, he was infinitely curious about the small, often-enigmatic symbols and scribbles inscribed in the backs and folds of letters, especially papal letters, which he carefully copied, and which would eventually allow him to identify the clerks who made the chancery run: the scribes, *taxatores*, *distributores*, and, most specially, the *procuratores*. He was particularly interested in the latter, the proctors who were present at the Curia 'to get and to receive bulls' on behalf of individuals and institutions, and whose importance in the development and functioning of the Papal Chancery had been shown by Rudolf von Heckel in 1924, disregarded by Mansilla in 1938/1945, and was also being studied from English materials by Jane E. Sayers, another of Ullmann's disciples.[27]

Peter's observations on curial procedure and personnel, derived from Spanish sources and put forward to great effect in his first book,[28] would be much amplified later in several innovative articles on proctors and curial procedure published in 1979, 1980 and 2019.[29] The chancery's inner working continued to fascinate him for the rest of his life, as may be seen in his brilliant piece on '*Fiat A*: the earliest known roll of petitions signed

---

[26] Review of the *Spanish Church and the Papacy*, in *The Journal of Interdisciplinary History*, 3/4 (1973), 768–70: 769. In 2010, the Lleida archive claimed to have 'about 9000 parchment documents', of which 5226 had been classified. Source: https://ca.wikipedia.org/wiki/Arxiu_Capitular_de_Lleida

[27] Jane E. Sayers, 'Canterbury Proctors at the court of *Audientia litterarum contradictarum*', *Traditio*, 22 (1962), 311–45. *Eadem*: 'Proctors representing British interests at the papal court, 1198–1415', in Stephan Kuttner *et al.* (eds), *Proceedings of the Third International Congress of the Medieval Canon Law, Strasbourg 1968* (Città del Vaticano, 1971), pp. 143–63: 143. Both articles reprinted in Sayers, *Law and Records in Medieval England. Studies on the Medieval Papacy, Monasteries and Records* (London, 1988), Pt. III and IV.

[28] *Spanish Church* (1971), pp. 280–90.

[29] 'Proctors representing Spanish interests', *Archivum Historiae Pontificiae*, 17 (1979), 69–123; 'Two unsealed papal originals in Spanish archives', *Archiv für Diplomatik*, 25 (1979), 240–55; 'Spanish litigants and their agents at the thirteenth-century papal curia', in *Proceedings of the Fifth International Congress of Medieval Canon Law, Salamanca 1976*, ed. Stephan Kuttner and Kenneth Pennington (Vatican City, 1980), pp. 487–501. Repr. in Linehan, *Past and Present in Medieval Spain* (1992). With Patrick N.R. Zutshi, 'Found in a corner: the activity of proctors in the papal chancery in the first half of the thirteenth century', in *Le discret langage du pouvoir: les mentions de chancellerie du Moyen Âge au XVIIe siècle*, ed. Olivier Canteaut (Paris, 2019), pp. 195–232.

by the pope (1307)', of 2007,[30] and, most notably, in his monumental surveys of original papal letters, the *Portugalia Pontificia* of 2013,[31] and the posthumous *España Pontificia*,[32] both of which are crucial contributions to the study of the later medieval papacy, its relations with the Iberian kingdoms, and the evolution of the papal chancery, by itself and in relation to the history of Spain and Portugal. In fact, later in life he often returned to the topics sketched in his first book, so that an extended survey of its contents may be used as an initial guide to his prodigious historical output.

Its main protagonists are the Papacy, the Spanish Church, and the kings of the four peninsular kingdoms—although focusing mostly on Castile and Aragon. Expanding on Bishko's idea of the Spanish *Reconquest* 'as a frontier movement in the authentic American sense',[33] Peter presents Spanish laymen and ecclesiastics as *frontiersmen*, with 'their contempt for distant authority—papal authority included—and their peculiar institutions [… such as] clerical concubinage' (p. 2). The directives of the Fourth Lateran Council of 1215 ('the most important single body of disciplinary and reform legislation of the medieval Church'[34]) had little effect on them. The lower clergy kept their concubines and refused to pay for distant crusades — their own *Reconquista* had taken enough out of them. Their leaders were worse: the saintly King Fernando III was a predator of the Church's income, and for the famous archbishop Rodrigo of Toledo 'peculation preceded reform'.[35] The view cherished by earlier ecclesiastical historians of a harmonious co-operation between the Papacy, the Spanish Church and the monarchs was shattered, shown to be a baseless myth.

The reception of papal legates, nuncios, and collectors, representatives and manifestations of Roman authority, is examined in three chapters (2, 3, and 9). They include two exemplary case studies, exposing the tension between ideal and praxis which Peter was so good at portraying. The first two of this trio deal with Cardinal Jean d'Abbeville's legation in 1228–1229, a figure absent from Mansilla's book. A former Parisian master, Abbeville attempts to impose the Lateran reforms in Castile without regard to local

---

[30] (with P.N.R. Zutshi) 'Fiat A: the earliest known roll of petitions signed by the pope (1307)', *EHR*, 122 (2007), 998–1015. Repr. in Linehan, *Historical Memory and Clerical Activity in Medieval Spain and Portugal* (2012).

[31] *Portugalia Pontificia. Materials for the history of Portugal and the Papacy 1198–1417*, 2 vols (Lisbon, 2013).

[32] *España Pontificia. Papal Letters to Spain 1198–1303* (Washington: Catholic University of America Press, 2023).

[33] 'The Castilian as plainsman: the medieval ranching frontier in La Mancha and Extremadura', in *The New World Looks at its History*, ed. A.R. Lewis and T.M. McGann (Austin, 1963), pp. 47–69; repr. in Charles Julian Bishko, *Studies in Medieval Spanish Frontier History* (London, 1980), IV, p. 47.

[34] *Spanish Church* (1971), p. 4, quoting S. Kuttner and A. García y García.

[35] Ibid, p. 7.

conditions and with greater rigour than originally intended; he is 'an academic out of his depth'[36] and his dictates, even if quoted for a long time, become dead letter as soon as he leaves.[37] But he does have some success in Aragon, where he finds a competent assistant in Ramón de Penyafort OP (compiler of Gregory IX's *Liber Extra* [1234]) and a devout follower in Pere de Albalat: of whom more shortly.

Other papal envoys are depicted in chapter 9: the nuncios sent to collect crusade subsidies, and one of the legates, Pietro, bishop of Rieti, directed by Nicholas III to chastise King Alfonso X's abuse of the Church. As in the case of Abbeville, the bishop of Rieti's voice was heard in 1279 and forgotten by 1280. But his list of charges, partially known from a previously printed Vatican register, was used most effectively by Peter to highlight the tensions between King and Church. After his book was published, Peter discovered a twenty-page booklet related to the same legation and compiled in Alfonso X's Court. Preserved in Toledo's Archive, it contains two Latin memoranda of charges against the king, an abbreviated Spanish translation, and answers to some of those charges, intended to placate Nicholas III, all of it published and brilliantly analysed by Peter in the Ullmann Festschrift of 1980.[38]

After Abbeville's intensive but failed mission, whose paper trail from Coimbra to Girona Peter will follow in a paper published in 2001,[39] he turns his attention to Pere de Albalat, archbishop of Tarragona (1239–51), the subject of chapters 4 and 5, and 'the greatest reformer in the thirteenth-century Spanish Church', practically unknown to Spanish historians until then. Albalat was the author of a disciplinary treatise, also discovered and published separately by Peter,[40] who shows how the archbishop implemented Abbeville's reformist agenda as well as he could, but how much was lost when he died and was succeeded by his rival, Benet de Rocabertí, as archbishop in Tarragona.

The next three chapters (6–8) are dedicated to the economic interaction between Church and Crown. They 'are stiff reading, but they contain Mr. Linehan's most original contribution to his subject', according to Evelyn Procter.[41] Fifty years later they have become so successfully embedded in the current historiography of medieval Spain that it is hard to imagine the revolutionary impact they had in 1971. In 1971, Peter began by juxtaposing the 18th-century regalist image, still prevalent amongst

---

[36] Ibid, p. 48.

[37] Ibid, pp. 50–3.

[38] 'The Spanish Church revisited: the episcopal *gravamina* of 1279'. Repr. in Linehan, *Spanish Church and Society, 1150–1300* (1983).

[39] 'A papal legation and its aftermath: Cardinal John of Abbeville in Spain and Portugal, 1228–1229', in *A Ennio Cortese. Scritti promossi da Domenico Maffei*, ed. I. Birocchi *et al.*, vol. 2 (Rome, 2001), pp. 236–56. Repr. in Linehan, *Historical Memory and Clerical Activity in Medieval Spain and Portugal* (2012).

[40] 'Pedro de Albalat, arzobispo de Tarragona y su *Summa septem sacramentorum*', *Hispania Sacra*, 22 (1969), 1–22. Repr. in Linehan, *Spanish Church and Society, 1150–1300* (1983).

[41] *History*, 57 (191) (1972), 417.

leading mid–20th-century Spanish historians, of an affluent medieval Spanish Church and Papacy, with the laments of 13th-century Castilian bishops who had sacrificed much to underwrite the conquest of Andalusia (as Mansilla began to show[42]) and expected a payback, but, when the time came, they got practically none. Then, things got worse. After the economy of the annexed territories started to collapse by 1250, the king requested further funds from the papacy, and Rome helped with Castilian cash. King Alfonso was granted a third of the Church's tithe (*tercias*) for three years, a period the king and his successors extended by two hundred more.

The dynamics of medieval Spanish history had never been exposed so convincingly and starkly. The papacy saw the kings as defenders of the faith in the frontier with Islam, and tolerated there what they would not accept closer to home. Meanwhile, the bishops had no political power in Castile and the Aragonese were not much better off. This view of the Spanish medieval kings, as de facto masters of the Church, supported by massive archival evidence, has not been surpassed since it was presented more than fifty years ago.

But the most innovative section of his book was probably chapter 7, which deals with the pattern of indebtedness that plunged many peninsular churches into poverty. A multitude of little-known financial documents issued by the papal chancery, Italian bank-lenders, and local borrowers, reveals that state of affairs. King Alfonso X blamed the bishops for ruining their churches with their trips to, and prolonged sojourns at, the Curia, but Peter shows that 'it was the king who drove them into the hands of bankers by refusing to allow them to take funds with them out of the country' (p. 138). The best documented and most complex case is that of Gonzalo Pérez, known as *Gudiel*, notary and chancellor to King Alfonso and to his son, Sancho IV (1284–1295), successively bishop of Cuenca, Burgos, and Toledo. Peter offered a preview of his debt-ridden career in 1971, and would return to it with a short article in 1993, and a long book, published in co-operation with F. Hernández, in 2004.[43] His 1993 article appeared in a collective book on *The Growth of the Bank as Institution*, and was heralded as an significant contribution to our understanding of how, already by the 13th century, credit had become one of the motive forces of economic life, 'as [Linehan] reveals a politico-financial interlacement which, starting from Spain, unravels through Italy and through France, involving kings, popes and Florentine bankers, with, at its centre, a cultivated bishop of Toledo plunged into debt'.[44] His case is not atypical. What is unusual is the sheer volume of records related to him that have survived, including a large cache of documents and drafts of letters, hidden before 1971 and uncovered by the present writer while participating in the

---

[42] *Iglesia castellano-leonesa* (1946), pp. 52–8.

[43] *The Mozarabic Cardinal* (Florence: Galluzo, 2004).

[44] *The Growth of the Bank as Institution and the Development of Money-business Law*, ed. Vito Piergiovanni. (Berlin, 1993), p. 5.

reorganisation of the Toledo Cathedral Archive (1979–1983).[45] It was after the discovery was shared with Peter that he generously suggested the idea of writing the already mentioned book on *Gudiel*.

Back again to the 1971 book: King Alfonso's actions and policies are shown to be the root cause of the economic crisis facing the Castilian Church (chapter 8). And yet the bishops stood by the king whose creatures they were and whose exactions they suffered in silence, and only became vocal when asked by Rome to support yet another crusade, as they did in 1262/63.[46] Such selective grievances, amplified by Voltairean regalists in the 18th century and by anticlerical historians in the 20th, are thus placed in their proper context.[47] By the end of the 13th century the political situation changed, but the bishops' situation did not (chapter 10). Most had abandoned King Alfonso expecting better from his rebel son, Sancho IV (1284–1295), only to discover a new master no better than the old. Peter presents three of them as case studies. *Frater* Munio of Zamora, Master-General of the Dominicans in 1285, deposed for unspecified reasons by Nicholas IV in 1290, and made bishop of Palencia with Sancho's backing in 1294, was recalled to Rome by Boniface VIII after Sancho's death in 1295, and resigned again in 1296, staying in Rome, where he died and was buried in 1300. Peter demonstrated that his removal in 1290 had been related to a riotous sex scandal involving the Dominican nuns of Zamora, and uncovered a wonderful tale with wide social and historical implications, which he would later develop into his most popular book, *The Ladies of Zamora,* of 1997, translated into French, Portuguese, and Spanish. On the other side in that tale, as told back in 1971, was the bishop of Zamora, Suero Pérez, a stern prelate who served King Alfonso, initially supported rebellious Sancho, but soon fell out of favour. He would also become the protagonist of another book, written in collaboration with José Carlos Lera Maíllo, archivist of Zamora Cathedral.[48] The last of this group is Juan Ibáñez, bishop of the frontier diocese of Jaén, elected in 1283 and immediately denounced for his ignorance of Latin, but defended by King Sancho, who placed loyalty above literacy and kept him in place.

Peter went on to examine the relations with the Curia during the 13th century's final years. Two hitherto overlooked Vatican registers, insightfully unpacked by him, reveal the activities of papal collectors, how they got far less than they hoped for, and how they

[45] We published one of those documents in '*Animadverto*: a recently discovered *consilium* concerning the sanctity of King Louis IX', *Revue Mabillon*, 5 [66] (1994), 83–105.

[46] Ed. Eloy Benito Ruano, 'La Iglesia española ante la caída del Imperio latino de Constantinopla', *Hispania Sacra*, 11 (1958), 3–20: 813. Peter offers emendations to this edition.

[47] Peter had already published some crucial supporting documents in 1970: 'The *gravamina* of the Castilian Church in 1262–3', *EHR*, 85 (1970), 730–54. Repr. in Linehan, *Spanish Church and Society, 1150–1300* (1983).

[48] *Las postrimerías de un obispo alfonsino. Don Suero Pérez: el de Zamora* (Zamora, 2003).

often spent more than they got as they trudged across the harsh geography of Portugal, Castile, and Aragon. They received no help from the bishops, subservient to kings; while the kings treated popes, their letters, and legates with barely disguised disdain.[49] Finally, Peter completes his picture of the Spanish Church by looking at the flow of clerics who hastened to the Curia 'as flies to the jampot' (p. 254). They went to request benefices, to appeal elections, to act as proctors, to be confirmed as bishops, and often spending money borrowed on the security of their churches. A few, very few, became cardinals of the Roman Church and paid attention to national and family interests, keeping an eye on proctors and Chancery business, and piling up benefices on their friends and relations. Peter concludes (p. 324): 'Despite the eloquent assurances of the eighteenth-century regalists [...], papal nuncios did not succeed in bleeding Spain white. Instead, they encountered in both king and clergy the attitude that the Roman Church was a Welfare State to be sponged on but not contributed to.' The situation became endemic. In the 16th century, it was (p. 330) 'due in large part to [saint] Fernando III that [King] Felipe II could be described in 1566 as "the greatest prelate in ecclesiastical rents that there is in the world, after the pope."'

The *impact* of the book was not immediate in Spain. Aside from the fact that English was not too widely known there by 1971, the book was written in Peter's idiosyncratic style, witty, learned and packing a maximum of significance in a minimum of words. Teo Ruiz calls it 'thick description',[50] Roger Collins sees it as 'demanding, but [...] always free of jargon and the baleful influence of "theory" in its manifold forms.'[51] Some of us enjoy it, others don't.[52] For a non-native speaker of English, Peter's prose was not easy to grasp ... until 1975, when his book was translated into Spanish. Bishop Mansilla read the translation and was not pleased; but university students loved it. Suddenly ecclesiastical history was sexy in Spain, and PhD candidates, who had avoided the field like the plague unless they were men of the cloth, began to enter that field.[53] Professor Carlos de Ayala explains how he and 'the young [Spanish] historians who were in the university during

[49] These same Vatican registers would be at the core of an important article published a decade later by Peter on the same topics: 'The Church, the economy and the *reconquista* in early fourteenth-century Castile', RET, 43 (1983), 275–303. Repr. in Linehan, *Past and Present in Medieval Spain* (1992).
[50] Review of *At the Edge of Reformation, Church History*, 89:2 (2020), 443–4: 444.
[51] *Speculum*, 96:4 (2021), 1200.
[52] Joseph O'Callaghan: 'Mr. Linehan's flippant style is irritating and creates unnecessary obstacles to the reader's willingness to accept his judgments as sound and objective', *Speculum*, 51 (1976), 335–6.
[53] For example: Juan Manuel Nieto Soria: *Las relaciones monarquía-episcopado castellano como sistema de poder (1252–1312)* (U. Complutense, Madrid, 1982); Ana Arranz Guzmán: *Cortes medievales castellano-leonesas: participación eclesiástica y mentalidades religiosas*, (U. Alcalá de Henares, 1988); Iluminado Sanz Sancho: *La iglesia y el obispado de Córdoba en la baja edad media (1236–1426)* (U. Complutense, Madrid, 1989).

the decisive years of the transition [to democracy (1975–1978)] were enchanted by it [Peter's book], with its wide open view of history and its interdisciplinary dimension, hostile to thematic overspecialization.'[54] The history of the Spanish Middle Ages would never be the same again.[55]

The new political climate helped. Following Franco's death, editions of medieval documentary collections began to multiply like mushrooms after a storm. The fifty Spanish provinces had regrouped into seventeen autonomous regions (1979–83) and subsidised any historical projects that would potentially prop up their identities with as-old-as-possible written proof. With a different agenda, Peter was way ahead of them. In 1975, twelve years before León's wealthy cathedral embarked upon the systematic publication of its medieval records—the volume corresponding to 1230–60 only appeared in 1993—he brought out his masterful study of the economic tensions experienced by that church during the second half of the mid–13th century, combining once again unpublished documents from León and the Vatican.[56]

After León, Segovia. In 1980 and 1981 Peter produced three important articles on the Church of Segovia. First he edited and contextualised the previously unknown and crucial *acta* of a synod held there in 1166, when a bishops' assembly imposed feudal practices which may have saved Castile as an independent kingdom. Equally important was Peter's detailed identification of a major work of medieval canon law[57] which was included in the 12th-century manuscript where the *acta* are found.[58] Although Peter's earlier work already displays his grasp of canon law, this is his first important contribution to a field which he will enrich both as editor of the *Proceedings of the Seventh International Congress of Medieval Canon Law, Cambridge 23–27 July 1984*,[59] and with further personal contributions, culminating in the legal texts *(consilia)* edited and annotated as appendixes in his *At the Edge of Reformation* of 2019. In the two other articles

---

[54] 'Profesor Peter Linehan (1943–2020)', *Anuario de estudios medievales*, 50:2 (2020), 895–905: 896.

[55] Writing in 1992, Peter noted that 'when I first tentatively suggested that perhaps the Spanish Church had not profited to the extent that it was alleged to have profited from the Christian victories of the thirteenth century, I was quite properly taken to task. Yet by 1982 this extraordinary thesis was being peddled as orthodox opinion, which was chastening.' Preface to his *Past and Present in Medieval Spain* (Aldershot), p. ix.

[56] 'La iglesia de León a mediados del siglo XIII', *León y su historia III* (León, 1975), pp. 11–76. Repr. in *Spanish Church and Society, 1150–1300*. Cf. José Manuel Ruiz Asencio, *Colección documental del Archivo de la Catedral de León. VIII. (1230–1269)* (León, 1993); J.M. Ruiz Asencio and J.A. Martín Fuertes, *Colección documental del Archivo de la Catedral de León. IX. (1269–1300)* (León, 1994). The texts from Appendices 9 and 10 transcribe Archivio Segreto Vaticano, *Collectoriae*, 397, ff. 85v–87v and 113v–153.

[57] The *Panormia*, attributed to Ivo of Chartres. Cf. *Panormia* Project, dir. Bruce Brasington and Martin Brett. https://www.wtamu.edu/~bbrasington/panormia.html [2015–09–02].

[58] 'The Synod of Segovia (1166)', *Bulletin of Medieval Canon Law*, 10 (1980), 31–44. Repr. in Linehan, *Spanish Church and Society, 1150–1300* (1983).

[59] *Monumenta Iuris Canonici* C/8 (Vatican City, 1988).

on Segovia, Peter refined the definition of a 'frontier' diocese beyond Burns' and Thomas F. Glick's proposals, and offered as proof and illustration two hitherto unpublished 13th-century surveys of Segovia's diocese, local Doomsday books preserved in the British Library.[60]

By 1982, Peter had decided to change tack, from medieval manuscripts to printed books. He explained the decision ten years later:

> In view of the coincidence of English school holidays and Spanish archivists' vacations, by then I had reconciled myself to a future with the published records of the Spanish past and to the study of how our understanding of that past has developed over time. The results of that enquiry, originally intended as a brief study of revisionism in the Spanish medieval camp since the death of General Franco, are about to be published by the Clarendon Press as *History and the Historians of Medieval Spain*.[61]

But while working over the next decade on that 'brief study of revisionism', he also continued to produce a rich crop of articles, some related to that study, others not. Pride of place amongst the latter should be given to his extraordinary excursion into 20th-century English historiography, 'The making of the *Cambridge Medieval History*'.[62]

Then came *History and the Historians* itself. There is no better brief description than the one offered by the publisher, with some assistance no doubt by the author:

> This is a study of medieval Spain and its historians, from the chroniclers of the middle ages to the revisionists of the post-Franco era. The history of medieval Spain has long been perceived as a tale of original sin followed by a long-drawn-out process of atone-ment. *History and the Historians of Medieval Spain* traces the development of that perception. It is a formidably researched tour de force which reveals history in the making during the eight hundred years which separated the end of the Roman period from what is now described as the birth of the modern state. In the differing aspirations of the inventors of the past both then and now – from the restoration of Toledo's Visigothic hegemony in the 1240s to the feudalization of medieval Castile and the sacralization of its kings since the death of Franco – an underlying sense of purpose emerges. In their contest for control of the present through mastery of the past, and the expression of their local loyalties, the historians of the seventh to the fourteenth centuries

---

[60] 'Segovia: a "frontier" diocese in the thirteenth century', *EHR*, 96 (1981), 481–508; 'A survey of the diocese of Segovia (1246–7)', *Revista española de teología*, 41 (1981), 163–206. Both in *Spanish Church and Society, 1150–1300* (1983).

[61] Intro. to *Past and Present in Medieval Spain* (Ashgate, 1992), p. vii. He had already moved that way when he wrote 'Religion, nationalism and national identity in medieval Spain and Portugal', *SCH*, 18 (1982), 161–99. Repr. in *Spanish Church and Society, 1150–1300* (1983).

[62] *Speculum*, 57 (1982), 463–94. Repr. in *Past and Present in Medieval Spain* (1992). The most prominent articles from this period are also reprinted in the same collectanea and in Linehan, *The Processes of Politics and the Rule of Law* (2002).

and the authors of the *False Chronicles* in the early 1600s have their counterparts in the contemporary Spain of the *autonomías*.

This time, the book's *impact* was immediate and lasting. In fact, the words Peter had used to describe the effect of Jean d'Abbeville's legation in 1228–1229 could be applied to himself in 1993: '[…] he hit the place like a tornado and decades later fragments of the old order dislodged by him were still floating down to earth.'[63] In the most detailed and thoughtful review of the book, Professor Ladero Quesada says: '[…] it is possible to predict that the book will have many readers in this and future centuries: medievalists will simply not be able to do without it.'[64] Twenty years later, the same prediction was taken up by a reviewer of *Historia y los Historiadores*, the translation published in 2012.[65] Down the road ten more years yet, Carlos de Ayala says: 'If one had to choose a work of historical research that would serve as *the* handbook for medieval Spanish studies, this would be it, no doubt.'[66] As for Peter's impact in Spain itself, Ayala also points out that peninsular historians working up to the time it was published had either accepted medieval chronicles as reliable sources of 'facts' or rejected them as secondary sources, useful only to 'illustrate' charter-based evidence. Peter showed that they are historical artefacts written not to 'tell the truth', but to present as such the particular agendas of the powers that be (and are therefore liable to be modified as those powers change, becoming new versions meant to serve them)—an insight equally applicable to modern historians.

So, that is how Peter faced eight centuries of narratives as well as the modern constructions based on them. In his review, Brian Tate said of Peter: 'What is important is his stance of perennial questioner of longstanding assumptions. He not only explains why the assumptions should be rejected but asks why they are adopted in the first place.'[67] And, of course, he was also interested in *who* was responsible. The *cui bono* principle served him well. That is how, for example, he identified the clerical *mafia* who falsified the chronicles to promote Toledo's interests. He had denounced them in his 1988 article on the 'Toledo Forgeries'[68] and now he returned to the topic with a vengeance. It is just one case amongst a legion of others. The Augean task of cleansing false chronicles and their descendants, all the way to the 20th century, was not accomplished in a day, but the result was well worth it.

---

[63] See p. 422 n. 39 above.

[64] '[…] se puede predecir que el número de sus lectores será grande, en éste y en los siglos venideros, porque es una obra cuyo conocimiento va a ser imprescindible para los medievalistas', in 'Una reflexión y algunas observaciones sobre nuestra historia y nuestra historiografía'medievales', *Medievalismo*, 4 (1994), 199–205: 199.

[65] F. Abad Nebot, *Espacio, Tiempo y Forma. Serie III, Historia Medieval*, 27 (2014), 555–58: 558.

[66] *Anuario de estudios medievales*, 50:2 (2020), 895–905: 897.

[67] *Journal of Ecclesiastical History*, 46 (1995), 136–9.

[68] 'The Toledo forgeries *c*.1150-*c*.1300', in *Fälschungen im Mittelalter: Internationaler Kongress der Monumenta Germaniae historica, München, 16.–19. September 1986*, vol. 1 (Hannover, 1988), pp. 643–74. Repr. in *Past and Present in Medieval Spain* (1992).

Commenting on *History and the Historians*, R.A. Fletcher, who was Peter's boon companion when both were research students in Spain, said:

> There is an enormous amount of learning and reflection tucked away here on such widely different subjects as the non-participatory architecture of Visigothic churches (pp. 47–8), and the desirability of study of the writings of Alvarus Pelagius OFM, bishop of Silves, who has been 'significantly less well served than his lavishly indulged contemporaries Marsiglio of Padua and William of Occam' (p. 560). [...] This splendid book deserves to be widely read.

It was. Like his *Spanish Church*, *History and the Historians* inspired a new generation of young scholars who were going through the grind of the Spanish university system and saw that book as a revelation, a difficult text that, once cracked, revealed a new and fresh vista of their past. They were also interested in meeting the author, and many made the pilgrimage to Cambridge to meet the congenial Englishman who could teach them how to look at the history of their own medieval past.

As *the* expert in that field, he contributed substantial surveys on Spain in *The Medieval World*, a collaborative work he edited with Janet Nelson,[69] and in *The New Cambridge Medieval History.*[70] In 2008 he also published *Spain, 1157–1300. A Partible Inheritance*. This work, part of the Blackwell History of Spain, is not your usual survey, but a typical Linehan product. It is erudite, iconoclastic, and witty, perhaps too witty for the translator in charge of a Spanish version, who failed so badly that the printed result had to be retired from the marketplace.

Finally, unfortunately finally, Peter published *At the Edge of Reformation* in 2018. Although it incorporates results from Peter's fruitful 'Portuguese' decade leading to the *Portugalia Pontificia*, the book has roots that go back much further. In 1975, at the same time as the Spanish translation of his first book was issued by the Pontifical University of Salamanca, Peter published a piece that was surprising even for him: a long text recording the historical arguments in favour of Scottish independence prepared to be used in the negotiations with the English held at Bamburgh in 1321.[71] The document appears in the miscellaneous notebook, or *zibaldone*, compiled by one Pedro de Casis, who was King Alfonso XI' s agent in Avignon during the 1340s. Preserved nowadays in

---

[69] 2001, second, expanded edition in 2018.

[70] 'Spain in the twelfth century', in vol. IV.2, *c.1024-c.1198* (2004), pp. 475–509; 'Castile, Portugal and Navarre in the thirteenth century', in vol. V, *c.1198-c.1300* (1999), pp. 668–99; and 'Castile, Portugal and Navarre in the fourteenth century', in vol. VI, *c.1300-c.1415* (2000), pp. 619–50.

[71] 'A fourteenth-century history of Anglo-Scottish relations', *BIHR*, 48 (1975), 106–22. Cf. E.L.G. Stones, G.G. Simpson, *Edward I and the Throne of Scotland 1290–1296, an edition of the record sources for the Great Cause* (Oxford, 1978); G.S. Barrow, *Scotland and its Neighbours in the Middle Ages* (London, 1992), pp. 14–15.

Córdoba Cathedral (ms 40), the manuscript was being catalogued at the time by Antonio García y García, Peter's friend at the Pontifical University.[72]

Peter used the notebook again in the 1987 colloquium on the 'Genèse médiéval de l'Etat Moderne: La Castille et la Navarre (1250–1370)'. Commenting on the royal coronation oath's promise 'not to alienate the kingdom's goods' (*de non alienando bona regni*), as reported by Álvaro Pais *c.* 1340, Peter rejected the view that it was intended to guarantee ecclesiastical properties, as argued by Álvaro himself. On the contrary, Peter read it as a pledge to defend and recover previously alienated crown rights, even if they had been gifted by earlier monarchs to the Church. Such was also the regalist advocate's view at the Vincennes Assembly of 1329, whose proposal eventually became known at the Castilian Court, since it was included in Pedro de Casis' *zibaldone*. Nevertheless, events thwarted 'progress' towards the Modern State. The seeds of the Modern State may have been planted in Castile and Navarre during 1250–1370, as the colloquium organisers implied, but come 1370 they were a very long way from yet flowering.[73]

In 1993 Peter reopens Pedro de Casis' notebook at the end of *History and the Historians*. After rereading the Vincennes regalist proposal and other potentially revolutionary pronouncements, which culminate in the last page of the manuscript with verses predicting the Papacy's demise and 'Caesar's' triumph, Peter looks at what actually did happen afterwards and observes that, once more, events in Iberia did not conform to reformist expectations, and that 'despite the claims made on behalf of the Modern State to a foundation date at about this time, again the old order held.'[74] Reformation would have to wait.

In *At the Edge of Reformation* (2018), Peter contemplates the story of that frustration as it played itself out during the first half of the 14th century in Castile and Portugal. The central issue of Alvaro Pais' coronation oath was *inalienability*, an essential attribute incongruously claimed at the same time by Church and Crown. The Church's rights and titles were ancient and firmly based on canon law, but they had been progressively eroded by two factors: by the privatisation of assets by priests, archdeacons, and bishops, who in turn bequeathed them to their concubines' children; and, secondly, by royal annulment of previous kings' grants, which could include whole cities and their hinterlands, as in the case of Braga, whose archbishop claimed sovereign rights over the city and whose king, Afonso IV (1325–57), would have none of it. Full sovereignty was also incompatible with papal appointment of foreign prelates to cities in the king's domain. Alfonso XI of Castile (1311–1350), Afonso IV's son in law and the 'Caesar' who would displace the

[72] Antonio García y García, F. Cantelar Rodríguez, M. Nieto Cumplido, *Catálogo de los manuscritos e incunables de la Catedral de Córdoba* (Salamanca, 1976): Ms 40, with 289 items (pp. 45–98), §211.5, p. 79.
[73] 'Ideología y liturgia en el reinado de Alfonso XI de Castilla', in *Génesis del Estado moderno: Castilla y Navarra (1250–1370)*, ed. A. Rucquoi (Valladolid, 1987), pp. 229–43.
[74] *History and the Historians* (1993), p. 663.

Pope according to Pedro de Casis' *zibaldone*, held those same points of view. But, as already anticipated by Peter in 1993, the future they expected never materialised. The Black Death, universally regarded as God's punishment for a Europe errant in the eyes of God, no doubt had a dampening effect on the *esprit laïque* which had surged in Vincennes and the Castilian Court before 1350.

Peter's five appendices illuminate with enthralling detail his book's main topics. The first three contain archbishop Gonçalo Pereira's elaborate defence of his lordship over Braga and the favourable judgement given by Avignon. The papal Camera's rejection of the demands of relatives of an Italian archdeacon of Toledo, who had claimed a sizable part of his properties as their inheritance on the (demonstrably false) grounds that they were his private property before becoming archdeacon, is edited as appendix iv. Finally, we see Alfonso XI elevated to a level equal or even superior to the pope in bishop Bernat of Huesca's extravagant sermon preached at Avignon in praise of the king after his capture of Algeciras in 1344. But all that promise comes crashing down when he dies of the plague six years later at Gibraltar. And so, Peter ends:

> For all the superficial resemblances between Iberia in the 1340s and Henry VIII's England two centuries later regarding the monarchs' matrimonial problems, and despite [...] the loutish brutality of peninsular Thomas Cromwells and the rest of it, the process of cutting free from Avignon was destined to remain altogether as complex as that of leaving the European Union.[75]

Peter gave new life to ecclesiastical history in Spain, taught two generations of Spaniards how to read their chronicles and history books, recreated worlds within the world of medieval Spain and Portugal, and has left behind his most durable and lasting contribution to scholarship: the two massive collections of documents and pontifical diplomatic studies included in his *Portugalia Pontificia* (2013) and *España Pontificia* (2023).[76]

Acknowledgements
Malcolm Schofield, author of Part I, is grateful for information and comments from David Abulafia, Peter Clarke, Peter Goddard, Christine Linehan, Michael Reeve, George Reid, Magnus Ryan (from whose address at the memorial service for Peter Linehan held on 5 March 2022 some phrases and observations are borrowed with thanks), Robert Tombs, and Patrick Zutshi. Francisco Hernández, author of Part II, is also grateful for information and comments from Carlos de Ayala, Miguel Ángel Ladero, Rocío Sánchez Ameijeiras, and Malcolm Schofield.

---

[75] *At the Edge of Reformation* (2018), p. 167.
[76] As mentioned above. For a detailed description of *Portugalia* see A. Paravicini Bagliani's review in *JEH*, 68 (2017), 583–4.

Note on the authors: Malcolm Schofield is Fellow of St John's College, Cambridge; he was elected a Fellow of the British Academy in 1997. Francisco Hernández is Distinguished Research Professor at Carleton University, Ottawa, and was elected Corresponding Member of Spain's Real Academia de la Historia in 1996.

Biographical Memoirs of Fellows of the British Academy (ISSN 2753–6777) are published by
The British Academy, 10–11 Carlton House Terrace, London, SW1Y 5AH
www.thebritishacademy.ac.uk

GEORGE STEINER

Francis George Steiner

23 April 1929 – 3 February 2020

elected Fellow of the British Academy 1998

by

EDWARD HUGHES
Fellow of the Academy

BEN HUTCHINSON

George Steiner was the very archetype of the European intellectual. Born in Paris in 1929 to Austrian parents, he fled with his Jewish family to New York in 1940, barely escaping the Shoah. He went on to become a deeply influential literary and cultural critic, holding the Chair of Comparative Literature at the University of Geneva as well as numerous Visiting Professorships across the world. Among his many landmark studies are *After Babel* (1975), *Grammars of Creation* (2001), and *The Poetry of Thought* (2011) – all of which convey Steiner's conviction that the humanities express the best, but are incapable of hindering the worst, of humanity.

Biographical Memoirs of Fellows of the British Academy, 20, 433–452
Posted 13 December 2022. © British Academy 2022.

What good are writers in destitute times? Anyone who even attempts to answer Friedrich Hölderlin's question in the context of the 20th century must reckon with the work of George Steiner. Others have arguably been more influential in shaping the discipline of comparative literature, but no one has embodied it quite so flamboyantly: famously trilingual, ferociously high-cultural, Steiner was the very archetype of the European intellectual, unyielding in his conviction that the humanities express the best – but do not necessarily hinder the worst – of humanity. By turns intimidating and engaging, perspicacious and pompous, Steiner challenged us to keep up, to range more widely, to aspire to a quasi-Olympian manifesto of the mind – *citius, altius, fortius* – beyond our ambient mediocrity. In an age of popular culture, Steiner remained, unapologetically, 'elitist'.

That the term now comes quarantined with quotation marks was not the least of his preoccupations. When someone dies at the age of ninety, it is inevitable that their achievements should seem a thing of the past, and so it is with Steiner: the age not just of Europeanism, but also of elitism, seems ever more to have ended with the 20th century. Such elegies, however, already characterised Steiner's own engagement with the cultural canon, fatally compromised as it was, in his view, by the black hole of the Holocaust. If Steiner became a leading tenant of what György Lukács described as the 'Grand Hotel Abyss' of the post-war German intelligentsia – 'a beautiful hotel, equipped with every comfort, on the edge of an abyss, of nothingness, of absurdity' – he was in good company.[1] As obituarists were not slow to point out upon his death in February 2020, Steiner equalled the likes of Theodor Adorno, Leo Spitzer, and Jean Starobinski in both linguistic range and intellectual ambition.

That Steiner can be mentioned in the same breath as such figures owes much to the unusual circumstances of his childhood: the son of Austrian parents, he received a classical French education in a modern American setting. Above all, of course, Steiner was Jewish, a cultural identity without which his work would have been – quite literally – unthinkable.

Childhood and education

George Steiner was born in the Parisian suburb of Neuilly-sur-Seine on 23 April 1929. His parents were Jewish immigrants who, in 1924, had left Vienna where Steiner's father, Dr Frederick George Steiner, already in a senior position in the Austrian Central Bank, was wary of a deep-seated anti-Semitism. Steiner would later reflect

---

[1] György Lukács, 'Preface', *The Theory of the Novel*, tr. Anna Bostock (Cambridge MA: MIT Press, 1971), p. 22.

that his mother, Else Steiner (née Franzos), remained 'Viennese to her fingertips' and that his father never felt at home in French financial and political circles.[2] He observed that, although an investment banker, his father's 'innermost passions' were for reading and languages and intellectual history. This in turn shaped the advice given to his son, namely that he should pursue scholarship: 'I would rather that you did not know the difference between a bond and a share', is how Steiner records his father's steer in his autobiographical *Errata: An Examined Life*. 'I was to be a teacher', mused Steiner, reminding his reader that 'the word *rabbi* simply means "teacher"'.[3]

Growing up trilingual (German, French and English), Steiner was a pupil at the Lycée Janson-le-Sailly in Paris's 16th arrondissement in 1940 when his father, in New York on an economic mission on behalf of the French government, secured its permission for his family to visit New York. The young Steiner, his sister Lilian, and their mother left from Genoa as the German army invaded France.[4] Most of the remaining Jewish pupils at Janson-le-Sailly would die in the Holocaust. Writing in *Language and Silence* (1965), Steiner would look back on the plight of children he had grown up with and who had perished. He argued that although he had been in America at the time of the war, 'in another sense I am a survivor, and not intact. […] The black mystery of what happened in Europe is to me indivisible from my own identity. […] An accident of good fortune struck my name from the roll'.[5]

In New York, Steiner studied at the Lycée Français in Manhattan. The school hosted occasional lectures given by French intellectuals in exile at the time, among them Claude Lévi-Strauss, Jacques Maritain, and Étienne Gilson. Stimulated by these talks, the young Steiner felt the early stirrings of intellectual life. He was one of a group of three pupils who received a weekly class in Ancient Greek from Jean Boorsch, who lectured in French Literature at Yale. He would later see Boorsch, aloof and magisterial, as the teacher who drew him into 'the magnetism of philology'.[6]

Steiner was acutely aware of the tense atmosphere of the Lycée, which remained *pétainiste* until the middle of 1944 and then rapidly switched to supporting De Gaulle. He would later describe the school as being 'a cauldron', with the children of Vichy officials sitting alongside pupils who were refugees from Nazism. Two pupils in the year above him who had lied about their age managed to get back to France to join the

---

[2] George Steiner, *Errata: An Examined Life* (London: Phoenix, 1998 (1997)), p. 9.

[3] See *Errata*, pp. 11–12.

[4] 'Memoranda', in *Steiner* (Paris: Éditions de l'Herne, 2003) ed. Pierre-Emmanuel Dauzat, pp. 402–5 (p. 403).

[5] 'A Kind of Survivor', reproduced in *George Steiner: A Reader* (New York: Oxford University Press, 1984), pp. 220–34 (p. 220).

[6] *Errata*, p. 123.

Resistance and were killed by the Waffen-SS in the Vercors.[7] While the syllabus was very traditional, the young Steiner welcomed the emphasis placed on high literature. Yet, as he would later recall, his introduction to the world of Racine's *Bérénice* ('that most flawless of tragedies') was inseparable from news of Nazi atrocities reaching the Lycée.[8] As Steiner observed, Bérénice's line of farewell, 'Pour la dernière fois, adieu, Seigneur', gave him his 'first and lasting grasp of the tenor of death'.[9]

Following the cessation of hostilities, Steiner went on to study in a rollcall of leading anglophone universities: Yale, Chicago, Harvard, and Oxford. His time at the University of Chicago was especially formative. Under Robert Maynard Hutchins's progressive leadership, Chicago offered students younger than the usual college age – as well as many returning GI's – a broad, fundamental education across the arts, history, and philosophy, an education that was particularly propitious for someone of Steiner's incipient interests. Many years later, Steiner would happily recall the 'passionate electricity of spirit' in post-war Chicago,[10] with its wide range of subjects and (what we would now call) interdisciplinary ethos. None of the institutions where he later studied or taught could match this; all of them, it seems, were measured against it. Steiner would be forced to recreate such formative intellectual ambition in his own writing.

After graduating with his BA in 1948, Steiner took an MA at Harvard in 1950, upon completion of which he moved to Balliol College as a Rhodes Scholar. His time in Oxford culminated in the rejection of his doctoral thesis on account of its cavalier attitude to academic research: footnotes, references, and bibliography were all missing, to the extent that the *viva voce* examination resembled nothing so much as 'the battle of Waterloo'.[11] (Despite this, Steiner's doctoral thesis formed the basis for his most important early work, published by Faber in 1961 as *The Death of Tragedy*.) Between 1952 and 1956, Steiner was employed as a member of the editorial staff of *The Economist*, in which capacity he was sent to interview the notoriously irascible Robert Oppenheimer at the Institute for Advanced Studies in Princeton. Oppenheimer, implausibly, took a shine to the young journalist, offering him a fellowship on the spot on the basis of a chance discussion about Plato and philology.[12] After several happy years on the East Coast – among others, serving as Christian Gauss Lecturer at Princeton from 1959 to 1960 – in 1961 Steiner returned to the UK and was appointed to Churchill College, Cambridge.

The connection with Churchill College was to form a central plank of Steiner's

[7] *Errata*, pp. 27–8.
[8] *George Steiner: A Reader*, p. 22.
[9] *Errata*, p. 31.
[10] George Steiner, 'An Examined Life', in *George Steiner at the New Yorker* (New York: New Directions, 2009), pp. 316–24, here p. 317. See also *Errata*, ch. 4.
[11] George Steiner, *Entretiens avec Ramin Jahanbegloo* (Paris: Le Félin, 1992/2009), p. 51.
[12] For Steiner's recollection of this encounter, see *Entretiens avec Ramin Jahanbegloo*, pp. 55–60.

academic career. Taking up his Fellowship in 1961, the year in which Churchill welcomed its first undergraduates, Steiner was one of the Founder Fellows of the College as well as its Director of English Studies. One undergraduate applicant wishing to study History recalls being advised to read English instead, 'and not miss the chance of being taught by our remarkable new Fellow from America'.[13] Yet Steiner was to be unsuccessful in his application for a University lectureship in English at Cambridge in 1969 – a controversial outcome thrown into relief by the international acclaim he subsequently enjoyed and by the many Visiting Professorships that came with it, including at Princeton, Stanford, Yale, and Harvard, where he held the Eliot Norton Professorship of Poetics.

Steiner regarded Churchill College as his haven, as a source of great support during times when he felt sidelined elsewhere (his papers are today held in the Churchill Archives Centre). During his tenure of posts abroad, he was able to avail himself of the College's category of 'Extraordinary Fellow' which did not bring with it a requirement to be living in Cambridge. He held this role between 1969 and 1996, thereafter becoming an Emeritus Fellow.

In the early decades of Churchill College, Steiner's national and international profile singled him out as the most visible of its Fellows on the Humanities side. As one long-standing Churchill Fellow informed the authors of this obituary, Steiner was a formidable and imposing presence in the College and 'somewhat proprietorial, in the manner of a village elder, in instructing neophytes on the true essence of the Founders' intentions'.

Another Founder Fellow at Churchill was C.P. Snow, the scientist and novelist whose 1959 Rede Lecture at Cambridge (subsequently published under the title 'The Two Cultures and the Scientific Revolution') aroused considerable debate. Steiner was a friend of Snow's and energetically promoted the College's commitment to science and technology. He led a group of Churchill Fellows to hear F.R. Leavis's controversial riposte to Snow in the Richmond Lecture at Downing College in 1962 and then staged a walkout from the event. Writing in *Language and Silence* (1965), Steiner complained of 'parochialism and retrenchment from reality' in England's academic establishment and expressed frustration at the narrowness of the Cambridge English degree, pressing the case for comparative studies as a counter to 'chauvinism and isolation'. Recalling Steiner's style of teaching in the 1960s, one of his Churchill undergraduates remembers how 'in supervisions, his enthusiasms were stunning and global. He had several characteristic words of emphatic praise: a given text was "prodigal", or presented valuable "difficulty", or had immense "possibilities" or was even "peregrine". English works must surely be understood in their European context. How could we appreciate Hardy's

---

[13] Richard Holmes, 'A Teacher of Genius, an Intellectual Star: Remembering George Steiner', *Churchill Review* (Volume 57A), 2020.

Tess of the D'Urbevilles without having "at least some sense of" Flaubert's *Madame Bovary*, or Fontane's *Effi Briest*? Besides, the question of cultural translation ("to carry across … but also to carry back") was crucial.'[14] Steiner's comparatism also extended beyond the field of literary study. He saw in linguistics and the theory of communication a fruitful terrain, 'intermediate between the arts and sciences, a terrain bordering equally on poetry, on sociology, on psychology, on logic, and even on mathematics'.[15]

For some of his students, Steiner's withered right arm (which he had been born with) was part of his aura as a teacher. One of them recalls him holding up a first edition of the *Lyrical Ballads* in his right hand and telling his lecture-theatre audience that this little book had changed the course of European literature. (Steiner would elsewhere reflect that his mother, refusing to let him be left-handed, insisted that he learn to tie his shoe laces, a maternal lesson in overcoming life's challenges.)

Towards the redefinition of culture

For all the subsequent acclaim, for all the Visiting Professorships and Honorary Doctorates that piled up over the years, it is fair to say that Steiner continued to feel embattled and resented throughout much of his career, a generalist in an era of specialists. Underlying such resentment – beyond the standard suspicion of comparative literature as a discipline that encroaches, by definition, on numerous highly defended territories – was the sense that Steiner was just a bit too dazzling for Anglophone ears. Such dazzle was, of course, the very essence of the Steiner sound. The magisterial tone, the cosmopolitan content, the assumption that the reader was as intimately familiar with the history of European literature and philosophy as he was: it all went to form the 'aura' of his work of criticism. 'I take comparative literature to be, at best, an exact and exacting art of reading, a style of listening to oral and written acts of language'.[16] In pursuit of such exaction, names were dropped like confetti, sprinkled from such a height that at times they inevitably missed their target. But Steiner was interested in big pictures, not small incisions. His lapidary name could not have suited him better: to steiner was to pass judgement from on high, to set in stone an imperious, almost impersonal verdict on our human, all too human failings. The rhetorical tics, the opacities and *ex cathedra* proclamations – recurring formulations such as 'there is a sense in which…' that artfully combine both certainty and uncertainty – were part of Steiner's project: to re-enchant culture with metaphysical pathos.

---

[14] The authors are grateful to Richard Holmes for sharing this memory.

[15] *George Steiner: A Reader*, pp. 32–3.

[16] George Steiner, 'What is Comparative Literature?', in *No Passion Spent: Essays 1978–1996* (London: Faber & Faber, 1996), pp. 142–59, here p. 150.

Theology underpinned his aesthetics; even before he explicitly addressed it in *Real Presences* (1991), Steiner had long implicitly argued that genuine creativity presupposes some form of belief in God. In the words of the novelist A.S. Byatt, Steiner was a 'late, late, late Renaissance man, […] a European metaphysician with an instinct for the driving ideas of our time'.

Yet God, scandalously, had abandoned Europe in the 1940s. From his earliest work onwards – *Tolstoy or Dostoevsky* (1959), *The Death of Tragedy* (1961) – Steiner's vision of the human condition was decidedly postlapsarian. By the time he gave the T.S. Eliot Memorial Lectures at the University of Kent, published as *In Bluebeard's Castle* (1971), he set out to relate 'the dominant phenomenon of twentieth-century barbarism to a more general theory of culture'.[17] How could the Buchenwald concentration camp be located next to Weimar? How could Goethe be harnessed to genocide? Controversially, Steiner argued that the Holocaust represented the revenge of Western culture on those who had submitted it to 'the blackmail of transcendence':[18] the moral demands of Judaism – its monotheistic self-abnegation, its Utopian promise – were simply too much for Christian Europe, quivering in resentment at its own inadequacies. European culture had become complicit, catastrophically, in its own capitulation. The question now was how to justify its continuing purpose: as Steiner's Eliotic subtitle indicated, 'some notes towards the redefinition of culture' were long overdue. If all philosophy is a footnote to Plato, Steiner effectively suggested, then all theology is now a footnote to the Shoah.

Around the same time that he was struggling to re-articulate the relationship between ethics and aesthetics, Steiner's work took a markedly linguistic turn. In 1975, he published the book that many still view as his masterpiece, *After Babel*, a virtuoso study of the power of language – and in particular, of *literary* language – to shape thought. All speech is an act of translation, Steiner argues; any reading of a text is a 'manifold act of interpretation'. Steiner's own readings lend an Empsonian ear to a dizzying range of ambiguities: his epigraphs alone – substantial citations in German, Spanish, and French from Heidegger, Borges, and Meschonnic – suggest the extent of his vaulting ambition. The seeming humility of his subtitle 'Aspects of Language and Translation' stands in contrast to his aim: just as he sought to redefine our understanding of culture, so he seeks to re-establish our grasp of hermeneutics. *After Babel*, unsurprisingly, became a foundational text for the emerging field of translation studies.

At the other end of the spectrum, and to some extent underpinning this study, was Steiner's exploration of the relationship between language and silence. As articulated most obviously in the essays published under this title in 1967, Steiner saw the absence

---

[17] George Steiner, *In Bluebeard's Castle: Some Notes Towards the Re-definition of Culture* (London: Faber & Faber, 1971), p. 31.

[18] Steiner, *In Bluebeard's Castle*, p. 40.

of language – whether in music, mysticism, or mute indigence – as the ultimate guarantor of meaning. Throughout his life, he maintained a strong interest in chess and music, two forms of expression that are pointedly *non*-linguistic. He observed that, like mathematics, chess and music 'are resplendently useless […]. They refuse to relate outward, to take reality for arbiter'.[19] 'The invention of melody', he liked to cite Claude Lévi-Strauss as saying, 'is the supreme mystery in the sciences of man'.[20] For Steiner, the only true response to the contemporary debasement of linguistic expression – to our 'retreat from the word' – is to retreat into silence, or, what amounts to the same thing, into our own 'private language'. That he did not actually take this step (like so many others who have advocated such a course of action) tells its own story about our irrepressibly human need to communicate. Even the non-encounter – Hegel and Hölderlin, Heidegger and Celan – must happen through words.

Geneva

In 1974, Steiner was appointed Professor of Comparative Literature at the University of Geneva, a post which he occupied until 1994. The Chair had first been occupied in the 19th century by Sismondi, a political refugee from Italy who, as Steiner reflected with identitarian relish in a Swiss television interview, 'avait le talent de l'exil' [had a gift for exile].[21] The novelist Michel Butor arrived in Geneva round about the same time to take up the Chair of French Literature. The two appointments were the work of the then Dean of the Faculté des Lettres, Bernard Gagnebin, whose aim, as Steiner later recalled with pleasure, was to position Geneva as a university for Europe, located in a free and tolerant country. In the landmark *Steiner* volume published in Paris in 2003 by the Cahiers de l'Herne, Steiner remembered with immense fondness his teaching routine at Geneva which had begun thirty years earlier. The audience for his weekly lectures on Shakespeare in the aula of the University regularly drew 'les troisième et quatrième âges de la ville' [the third and fourth ages of the city], diplomats working at the United Nations, and visitors from Paris; and Thursday morning was the slot for his seminar for doctoral students and others.[22] Alexis Philonenko, the French Professor of Philosophy who taught at the Universities of Rouen and Geneva, described attending one of Steiner's lectures on Shakespeare and being struck by the rhythm in his diction and the sense of melody in his reading of Shakespeare. He added

---

[19] 'A Death of Kings', reproduced in *George Steiner: A Reader*, p. 174.
[20] See, for instance, George Steiner, *Grammars of Creation* (London: Faber & Faber, 2001), p. 20.
[21] 'Les Grands Entretiens: George Steiner' (1998), RTS, a series of thirteen interviews with Guillaume Chenevière (interview 8: 'Cambridge et Genève', 13 November 1998).
[22] 'Memoranda', p. 404.

that Monique Philonenko (whose English was much better than his) marvelled at the beauty of Steiner's delivery: 'Comme c'est beau!', she enthused.[23]

In the same account of Steiner's Geneva years, Philonenko observed that losing his audience was part of the pain felt by Steiner on his retirement from the University there. In Steiner's own words, teaching was, for him, 'indispensable'.[24] He described his Thursday morning seminar, which ran for a quarter of a century, as having become 'le centre de ma vocation, de mes bonheurs quadrilingues, de mes recherches' [the centre of my vocation, of my quadrilingual happiness, of my research].[25] (Beyond the three languages of his childhood, he had now also acquired Italian.) A number of Steiner's works, beginning with *After Babel* (1975), would be published during his time at the University of Geneva. In a 2011 interview with Juliette Cerf for France's 'Télérama', he reflected on how his multilingualism had helped him to teach and to feel at home wherever he was. Multilingualism, he added, had provided the platform for the writing of *After Babel*. Referring to the 'terrible enracinement' [awful rootedness] of a Maurice Barrès and to the strictures of nationalism, Steiner affirmed his preference for cultural mobility.[26] He wrote of his 'plurality of convictions across borders' and cast himself as 'a grateful wanderer' who 'sought to press on my students and readers (the rewards were greatest in polyglot Geneva) that which is "other", which puts in doubt the primacy of household gods'.[27] (His curiosity about languages could also take a mischievous turn, as when, in an evening lecture delivered back when he was teaching in Cambridge, he playfully recalled having chided his wife for not telling him what language he had used when he exclaimed as she drove into a tree!) Written in English, his books came to be translated into many languages, with a good number of the French translations being undertaken by Pierre-Emmanuel Dauzat. As a cultural location, Geneva had made possible for Steiner 'cette "centralité" polyglotte, ainsi qu'une rencontre et une amitié qui a éclairé ma vie' [that polyglot 'centrality' as well as an encounter and friendship that lit up my life].[28]

The geographical location of Geneva was also much to Steiner's liking. He observed that the mountains were close by and that it was only in or near mountains that he felt 'really at home in my own skin'. He enjoyed mountain-walking and suggested somewhat grandly that with this love came a set of philosophical, musical, and aesthetic choices, that mountains might impart 'a darker, more selective view of man' than the sea and coastal locations.[29]

---

[23] Alexis Philonenko, 'Steiner et la philosophie', in *Steiner* pp. 27–58 (p. 28).

[24] *Errata*, p. 141.

[25] 'Memoranda', p. 404.

[26] https://www.telerama.fr/idees/george-steiner-l-europe-est-en-train-de-sacrifier-ses-jeunes,75871.php; consulted 30 March 2021.

[27] *Errata*, p. 37.

[28] 'Memoranda', p. 405.

[29] *George Steiner: A Reader*, p. 18.

The good postman

While post-structuralism and deconstruction dominated French intellectual thought during Steiner's time at Geneva, he remained resolutely opposed to the methods underpinning modern critical theory. In *Real Presences: Is There Anything in What We Say?* (1989), which would soon be translated into French, Steiner called for the need to 're-experience the life of meaning in the text, in music, in art'. These forms, he insisted, 'relate us most directly to that in being which is not ours'.[30] Alexis Philonenko, for one, viewed *Real Presences* as Steiner's most important book, while also stressing its connectedness with his earlier works: in Philonenko's configuration of his colleague's œuvre, *After Babel* addresses the question of 'Que puis-je savoir? [What can I know?], *Antigones* that of 'What must I do? ['Que dois-je faire?'], while *Real Presences* asks the question 'Que puis-je espérer?' [What can I hope?]. Taken together, the three strands constitute a reflection on what it is to be human.[31]

Sketching an often caustic summary of the post-structuralist stance, Steiner was outspoken, in *Real Presences*, about what he termed 'a universe of games in which semiotic structures and their messages are boundless, often discontinuous chains of differentiation and deferral'. Decrying what he saw as 'the breach of contract with the old ghosts of meaning and meaning-fulness', he characterised as nihilistic the process whereby a painting, a poem, or a piece of music became 'the *pre-text* to and for the commentary'. Forthright in his defence of classical humanism, Steiner was no less categorical about what he labelled 'a democracy of equivocation, [...] the hermeneutics of "do-it-yourself"'.[32] In his 1996 preface to the second edition of his early work *Tolstoy or Dostoevsky*, Steiner squarely rejected the view that critical exegesis might have the same weight as the work of art. As he remarked, literary criticism is 'derivative': Tolstoy and Dostoevsky do not need George Steiner or Jacques Derrida.[33] He remained committed to the idea that criticism must work in the service of the work of art, must stand as an act of love and indebtedness in relation to it, as he underlined on the opening page of *Tolstoy or Dostoevsky*. Advocating a 'politics of the primary', Steiner cautioned against forms of reading and criticism that heralded 'the dominance of the secondary';[34] recalling Pushkin's insistence that it was he, Pushkin, who 'wrote the letters', Steiner cast the critic in a facilitating role. As he remarked with characteristic verve in a 2009 interview:

---

[30] *Real Presences* (Chicago and London: University of Chicago Press, 1989), pp. 49–50, 226. *Réelles Présences. Les arts du sens* was published by Gallimard in 1991 (trans. Michel R. de Pauw).

[31] Philonenko, 'Steiner et la philosophie', p. 40.

[32] *Real Presences*, pp. 124–26.

[33] See Steiner, *Tolstoy or Dostoevsky: An Essay in the Old Criticism* (New Haven and London: Yale University Press, 1996 (1959)), pp. xiii–xiv.

[34] Steiner, *Real Presences*, pp. 6, 7.

'J'ai essayé d'être un bon facteur' [I have tried to be a good postman].[35] In his influential work as a critic (notably for the *New Yorker*, as well as for the *Times Literary Supplement*), Steiner spent decades bringing European post to an Anglophone audience. So successful was he in doing so, indeed, that the correspondence cut both ways: his identification, writing in the *TLS* in 1973, of the 'Suhrkamp culture' of West Germany, became a cliché of the Federal Republic, gleefully marketed as such by the Suhrkamp publisher, Siegfried Unseld. Steiner was a man of letters in several senses of the term.

As a writer of fiction, however, he was arguably less successful. His various short stories and novels – the best known of which, *The Portage to San Cristobal of A.H* (1981), imagined Hitler alive in the Amazon jungle thirty years after the war – struggled with the classic problem of the fiction of ideas, namely, how to avoid strangling the fiction with the ideas. Undoubtedly he also suffered from a general perception (and possibly also self-perception) of Steiner the critic, rather than of Steiner the writer; gamekeepers rarely get a fair hearing as poachers. It remains the case, however, that the fiction was largely deemed too cerebral, at least for an English-language readership more used to novels of society than of ideas.

Such differences in modes of creativity were given sustained consideration in one of Steiner's strongest later works, *Grammars of Creation* (2001). Like several of his best books, it was based upon a series of lectures, and it retains the strengths of the oral form, its dynamism and interrogative address. What does it mean to create? What is the difference between creativity and inventiveness? Here as elsewhere, Steiner is at his best when pursuing such questions into the very sinews of syntax: distinguishing, in a manner that betrays his French education in rhetoric, between the differing etymologies of *creatio* ('engender'), *inventio* ('discover'), and *fingo* ('form'), he argues that grammatical categories such as subjunctives and future tenses testify to the power of the human imagination – and that this power, in turn, is at the heart of the human condition. I create, therefore I am.

This relationship between ideas and their modes of expression – between form and content – recurs as the central concern of Steiner's final major work, *The Poetry of Thought* (2011). Language, one last time, remains his principal object of enquiry: how do writers think, how do thinkers write? The answer, of course, is in words, and Steiner shows, through his customary range of examples from Lucretius to Celan, from Heraclitus to René Char, just how much the limits of our language are the limits of our world. Perhaps surprisingly, the abiding influence is not that of the Jewish exile Wittgenstein, but rather that of the Nazi apologist Heidegger, to whose work Steiner wrote an influential introduction in 1979 in the Fontana Modern Masters series. In this as in other regards,

---

[35] In conversation with Laure Adler, 'À voix nue', France-Culture, a series of five interviews, first broadcast 2009 (episode 2: 10 February 2009).

Steiner was much more a Continental than an Analytic thinker: like Heidegger, he looked back to the Pre-Socratics for advice on Modernity; like Heidegger, he saw language as the expression, not as the inhibition, of meaning. Their politics may have violently diverged, but their vision of the human being as the language animal consistently converged.

Steiner's own politics, if only of the identity kind, were not without their foibles. His notorious dismissal of the USA as little more than a museum, an 'archive of Eden', can be understood in the context of his unrepentant Europeanism.[36] Arguably more problematic is the Western bias of this Europeanism, excluding as it did almost any interaction with literatures or cultures beyond the old continent. Steiner's perspective was also decidedly male, with little room for female voices or achievements. His views on pedagogy, too, were not without controversy, insisting as they did on the fundamentally erotic nature of the teacher-pupil relationship: in his Charles Eliot Norton Lectures *Lessons of the Masters* (2003), for instance, Steiner argued passionately for passion, for the Socratic spark that animates the strongest and most vivid pedagogues. If nothing else, such arguments illustrated the lifelong importance that Steiner accorded to the role of the teacher.

With characteristic expansiveness, Steiner also published, in the year before he turned eighty, the ingeniously titled *My Unwritten Books*, a forum in which a range of subjects that he might well have developed further are mapped out in a series of discrete chapters. One such 'unwritten' work is what Steiner calls his 'animal book': in the chapter 'Of Man and Beast', he writes with intense conviction about environmental degradation and 'catastrophes of climate unleashed by our insensate greed'. Prompting his reader to ponder the 'scarcely examined priority of human eminence', he acknowledges the place of sentimentality and self-indulgence in his description of the family pet, Rowena: human language cannot grasp, he argues, the joy taken in the dog's sleep which 'gives to the house a warm hum, a pervasive pitch of presence'.[37]

Possible dialogues

Steiner's posthumous legacy as both critic and comparatist – the controversies and debates that his work continues to occasion – were anticipated by his reception during his lifetime. The special number of the Cahiers de l'Herne dedicated to Steiner, for instance, was central to the reception given to his work in France, while also drawing in contributions from Italy, England, the US, and Israel. Edited by Pierre-Emmanuel

---

[36] See George Steiner, 'The Archives of Eden', in *No Passion Spent*, pp. 266–303.

[37] *My Unwritten Books* (London, Phoenix, 2009 (2008)), pp. 163, 165, 169.

Dauzat, the 414-page volume set out to capture, in the words of the L'Herne publicity blurb, those strands of Steiner's work '(pedagogical, critical, ethical) that find an immense resonance'. The collection also explores corners of his work that had received less critical attention, among them his reflections on Turner, on Yehudi Menuhin, and on poetry. Dauzat stresses that the aim of the other contributors was neither to flatter nor to denounce.[38] One of the numerous tributes to Steiner's work was from the poet and translator Yves Bonnefoy, who recalled how, when he was younger and visiting Cambridge and the US, he had bought copies of Steiner's early works. Hearing him lecture in London, Bonnefoy had admired his willingness to go against prevailing critical trends, to reject what Bonnefoy's interlocutors in the L'Herne volume called contemporary 'textolâtrie'.[39] But whereas Steiner postulates a link between the creative imagination and what he terms 'a wager on transcendence', 'the wager on God', Bonnefoy set out a different understanding of heightened experience and the idea of presence. For him, 'l'instant de présence [...] nous ouvre [...] l'ici et le maintenant de notre existence' [the moment of presence (...) opens up for us (...) the here and now of our existence].[40] Bonnefoy thus proposes an alternative to the stress on the transcendent to be found in *Real Presences*. 'Le dieu "encore inconnu"', he suggests, 'c'est l'être humain quand il aura pleinement choisi, s'il le veut bien, de s'incarner dans sa finitude' [The god 'still unknown' is the human being when he will have fully chosen, should he so wish, to become incarnate in his finitude].[41]

Two adjacent chapters in the Cahiers de l'Herne volume, one by Bonnefoy and the other by Steiner, draw out their shared interest in processes of translation and cultural transfer. An accomplished translator of Shakespeare, Bonnefoy actively welcomed Steiner's argument that the translations were works in progress. Indeed, Bonnefoy was convinced that a translation could never be seen as definitively completed. For Steiner, Shakespeare's lexicon of 24,000 words formed a polar opposite to the just-over 2,000 words that make up Racine's vocabulary (he frequently reflected on the relatively slight attention paid to Racine in the Anglo-American world, arguing that 'the *spiritus mundi* of English' had failed to accommodate the genius of the French playwright. In a similar way, he argued, the French language had not proved receptive to Elizabethan English).[42] Cleopatra's 'All's but naught!', uttered on the occasion of the death of Antony, is heralded as miraculous by Steiner, while Bonnefoy reflects on the inadequacy of his own rendering:

[38] Pierre-Emmanuel Dauzat, 'Du Juif errant aux *Errata*', in *Steiner*, pp. 9–19 (p. 17).
[39] Yves Bonnefoy, 'Sur la traduction poétique', in *Steiner*, pp. 201–15 (p. 201). Pierre-Emmanuel Dauzat and Marc Ruggeri formulated the questions for the dialogue with Bonnefoy.
[40] Bonnefoy, 'Sur la traduction poétique', p. 203.
[41] Bonnefoy, 'Sur la traduction poétique', p. 206.
[42] Steiner, 'L'Inadvertance du Dr. Cottard', in *Steiner*, pp. 216–20 (p. 219).

'Tout n'est que dérision' – it's more Racine than Shakespeare, he suggests.[43] The collegial dialogue between Steiner and Bonnefoy around what had to be negotiated in the movement between English and French reflected a shared level of deep engagement and seriousness of purpose.

'Impossible dialogues'

The defence of the great achievements of European culture was inseparable from Steiner's intense engagement with the same culture's legacy of barbarism. The inability of the humanities to humanise, as he put it, pointed to a crushing failure which he sought to confront in a variety of ways. A high-profile 2006 roundtable in Paris chaired by Valérie Marin La Meslée provided a forum in which some of these confrontations were explored. The event was jointly organised by the Bibliothèque nationale de France and *Le Magazine littéraire*, which had just dedicated its most recent number to Steiner.[44] He dialogued on that occasion with Dauzat, who reflected that the work which made Steiner famous in France was *Les Antigones*, published in French translation in 1986.[45] As the novelist Linda Lê argued in her tribute to Steiner's work, the ancient Greek *Antigone* does not offer a refuge from time but rather reveals to us something about ourselves.[46]

The June 2006 event at the BnF included a screening of extracts from two earlier encounters in the French media involving Steiner. A 1987 televised discussion with André Glucksmann and others on the subject of the work of Heidegger and his silence on Auschwitz formed the first of these. It was followed by footage from a dialogue between Pierre Boutang and Steiner. Boutang had been a fervent supporter of Pétain during the war and a prominent journalist in those years, writing for the anti-Semitic *Aspects de la France*, the paper of *Action française*. At the 2006 event, Daumat, looking back at the discussion with Boutang, remarked on how measured and patient Steiner had remained as Boutang argued that Pétain should have been accorded the honour of burial with his soldiers. For Daumat, the direct encounter with Boutang, together with the participation in the tense television debate about Heidegger in 1987, reflected in Steiner 'ce besoin de se confronter au proprement impensable' [this need to confront the literally unthinkable]. These appearances on French television show Steiner grappling with the forces of anti-Semitism. They capture him drawn him into what Daumat referred to as 'ces dialogues impossibles que vous avez menés' [those impossible dialogues that you conducted].

[43] Bonnefoy, 'Sur la traduction poétique', p. 213.
[44] *Le Magazine littéraire*, number 454, June 2006, 'George Steiner. La culture contre la barbarie'.
[45] Steiner, *Les Antigones* (Paris: Gallimard, 1988), trans. Philippe Blanchard.
[46] Linda Lê, 'Antigone dans un paysage de cris', in *Steiner*, pp. 148–53 (p. 149).

In the case of the rapprochement with Pierre Boutang, Steiner later acknowledged that the 'closeness' had 'an obvious improbability' about it. 'But the debates we have had, both in public and private', he asserted, 'are among the stellar hours in my life. We share an utter passion for Scripture and the classics, for poetry and metaphysics. We delight in the kind of teaching that is an act of shared love (I have watched Boutang initiate one of his numerous grandchildren in New Testament Greek)'.[47] In another conversation between them which took place in April 1996 and which is reproduced in the Cahiers de l'Herne volume, Boutang and Steiner explored the question of evil, original sin, and the issues of love and justice across the Jewish and Christian traditions. The discussion shows them drawn into intense, earnest debate. Steiner remained keenly aware of his paradoxical relationship with Boutang. Impressed by his scholarly brilliance and confessing to feelings of anger at the ways in which Boutang remained a marginalised figure in France, Steiner wondered how all this squared with what Boutang wrote and did in the 1930s and with what 'his enemies allege, [he did] during the Second World War'.[48]

One of Steiner's most striking 'impossible dialogues' was his response in the 1960s to Lucien Rebatet. A journalist and writer who had aggressively campaigned during the Second World War for French collaboration with the Nazis, Rebatet was sentenced to death in November 1946, having been a leading figure in the virulently anti-Semitic publication *Je suis partout* (his death sentence was commuted the following year). The background to Steiner's meeting with him requires some reconstruction. Rebatet had recorded in a diary entry for 24 October 1963 how he had enjoyed hearing Steiner speak on French radio on the subject of the novel. Paul Flamand, an editor at the Éditions du Seuil, was Steiner's interlocutor on that occasion. Just as Steiner did not shy away on other occasions from declaring his admiration for the novels of Louis-Ferdinand Céline or from looking beyond Heidegger's Nazi past to an appreciation of his philosophy, so, in the radio interview, he argued that Rebatet's *Les Deux Étendards* (1951) was one of the great French novels of the 20th century. Immediately after the interview, Flamand told Steiner that he could have no future in France, having just endorsed in such a public way a work by Rebatet: 'C'est foutu pour vous' [You've blown it], Flamand insisted.[49]

Decades later, Steiner would observe that he had initially been seduced by Rebatet's novel, some of the pages of which carried a Tolstoyan grandeur, and that he now saw that there was much in it that amounted to 'sentimental *kitsch*'.[50] But his praise for Dostoevsky in the 1963 radio interview and his assertion that the *nouveau roman*, then much in vogue in France, represented a thin achievement by comparison was enough for Rebatet,

[47] *Errata*, p. 138.
[48] *Errata*, p. 139.
[49] George Steiner, 8 June 2006 conference at the Bibliothèque Nationale de France.
[50] Steiner, 'Une voix qui surgit de l'ombre', in *Steiner*, p. 100.

who was deeply hostile to contemporary French culture, to be intrigued. Following on from the radio broadcast, he rushed to get a copy of *Tolstoy or Dostoevsky*, a work which he nevertheless found disappointing in ways. Yet Steiner's study confirmed Rebatet in his identification with Dostoevsky as 'l'ennemi du "progressisme"' [the enemy of 'progressivism'].[51] At the end of January 1964, he wrote in his diary that he had received from a contact in England a copy of an article Steiner had written for *The Sunday Times* of 1 December 1963. In it, Steiner restated the view he had put forward in the French radio interview a few months earlier that Rebatet's *Les Deux Étendards* was one of two novels (the other was Louis Guilloux's *Le Sang noir*) that made up 'the most vital French fiction of the last decades'.[52]

An exchange of letters between Rebatet and Steiner followed. Writing to Steiner in January 1964, care of *The Sunday Times*, Rebatet made clear his anti-Semitic, Collaborationist stance in 1940 and how he had 'dans la violence de ces batailles [...] écrit beaucoup de choses outrées, cruelles, que je ne signerais plus aujourd'hui' [in the violence of those battles (…) written excessive and cruel things which I would no longer put my name to today].[53] Steiner's stinging reply, written in French, began with the statement that he was Jewish and that, if there were errors of spelling and syntax in his letter, it was because he had been forced to flee France in 1940 'avant que les tueurs de la Gestapo ou de la milice, dont vous étiez, ne m'eussent tué, moi et les miens' [before the killers of the Gestapo or the collaborationist militia, of which you were a part, might kill me and my family]. He went on to say that he was at pains to point out to his addressee that what 'haunted' him was the failure of culture: 'Si toute notre culture ne fut aucun obstacle à l'inhumain, à quoi bon l'immense labeur de la pensée, de la création artistique?' [If the whole of our culture could offer no resistance to the inhuman, what was the purpose of the immense labour of thought and artistic creation?].[54]

The frank exchange with Rebatet served as a marker of Steiner's resoluteness of purpose but also laid bare his openness and vulnerability. He confessed to Rebatet that, having praised his work in the *Sunday Times* article, he realised he now risked hearing directly from him and being drawn into correspondence. How, Steiner protested, could dialogue be possible between them, before adding: 'Mais aussi, comment peut-il y avoir silence? Je ne sais' [But how, too, can there be silence? I do not know].[55]

Steiner went to visit Rebatet at his home in Paris in March 1964. Forty years later in the Cahiers de l'Herne volume dedicated to him, he summed up his motivation thus: 'J'ai voulu comprendre' [I wanted to understand]. At the same time, he referred to the

---

[51] Rebatet, '"Une rencontre"', in *Steiner*, pp. 101–8 (p. 101).
[52] Cited by Rebatet, '"Une rencontre"', p. 103.
[53] Rebatet's letter of 20 January 1964, cited in Rebatet, '"Une rencontre"', pp. 103–4.
[54] Steiner's letter of 26 January 1964 from Cambridge, cited in Rebatet, '"Une rencontre"', p. 104.
[55] Steiner, cited in Rebatet, '"Une rencontre"', p. 105.

memory of that encounter as a source of anxiety. He reflected that Rebatet's account of their meeting as a cordial affair was wide of the mark. Yet Steiner used his brief recounting of the meeting to make the point that, as on so many occasions in his life and career, he had been confronted in the Rebatet encounter with the paradox that 'l'inhumain' [the inhuman] and 'la barbarie' [barbarity] can generate works of value – in Rebatet's case, his novel *Les Deux Étendards*.[56] Such paradox is perhaps the closest Steiner came to answering Hölderlin's question: what good are writers in destitute times? Despite it all, they bring us meaning and beauty.

Legacy

What is Steiner's own legacy as a bringer of meaning? His work endures as testament to the uses and abuses of culture in a post-modern, post-Holocaust world: his defence of 'difficulty', his 'nostalgia for the absolute' – to cite just two of his further book titles – place him firmly in the modernist tradition of viewing art as existential urgency. Increasingly, however, it feels like this tradition is a thing of the past, largely because it has been superseded by the digital age of instant gratification. By his own admission, Steiner never seriously engaged with the cinema, let alone with the Internet; his was a culture of the book if ever there were one. At the disciplinary level, too, his preoccupations were those of another century, of a period in which the canon of Western culture was largely uncontested.

In this as in many other ways, Steiner most closely recalls that great generation of European comparatists – Erich Auerbach, Ernst Robert Curtius, Leo Spitzer, René Wellek – who did so much to establish the discipline of comparative literature. In an era in which World Literature has emerged as the dominant methodology, their almost exclusively European focus now feels dated. Defiant and indefatigable, even in his lifetime Steiner was akin to the proverbial soldier on an island, still fighting the Franco-German war thirty years after it had ended. Europe has been so thoroughly 'provincialized', to use Dipesh Chakrabarty's term, that it too now risks becoming an archive of Eden. Paradise Lost – 'that squandered utopia', to cite *In Bluebeard's Castle*[57] – could be the title of Steiner's collected works. Writing in *Le Monde* (3 February 2020), Nicolas Weill, while placing Steiner alongside Auerbach, Spitzer, Starobinski, and Roland Barthes, considered the paradox whereby, in an age of globalisation, the death of a polyglot author who saw himself as a nomad should awaken nostalgia for an intellectual tradition that Steiner represented and that was disappearing.

---

[56] Steiner, 'Une voix qui surgit de l'ombre', p. 100.
[57] Steiner, *In Bluebeard's Castle*, pp. 13–14.

For these same reasons, however, Steiner will remain as a tutelary figure, as much symbol as savant. For all that he could come across, like Elias Canetti's Peter Kien, as a 'head without world',[58] it is as the embodiment of comparative literature – of its aesthetic challenge and ethical promise – that he will endure. Like most cultural critics, at heart Steiner was a moralist, forever surprising, to adapt Larkin's phrase, a hunger in himself to be more serious. 'I never considered myself chiefly as a literary critic', Steiner once observed, 'but rather as a critic of culture in general. I have always thought that literary criticism is linked to broader cultural issues and spiritual viewpoints.'[59] Steiner matters because culture matters, because he came to personify the sense that the life of the mind – pretentious and portentous though it may sometimes be – acknowledges no borders. To be a great 'European', as Steiner undoubtedly was, is not just to speak the major tongues; it is to see through these tongues to the common history that binds them. What distinguishes humans from animals, Johann Gottfried Herder suggested in his essay *On the Origin of Language* (1772), is not so much their capacity for language as their capacity for arriving at general reflection (*Besonnenheit*) through language. Few thinkers of the post-war era can be said to have pursued this reflection with as much range and rigour as George Steiner.

George Steiner was married for over sixty years to the distinguished historian Zara Steiner, who was a strong intellectual personality in her own right. They met in London in the 1950s when she (then Zara Shakow) was carrying out research as part of her PhD at Harvard and he was working for *The Economist*. Elected a Fellow of New Hall Cambridge in 1968, Zara Steiner was an authority on international relations in Europe in the inter-war years and the author of two major volumes in the Oxford History of Modern Europe: *The Lights that Failed: European International History 1919–1933* and *The Triumph of the Dark: European International History 1933–1939*. She became a Fellow of the British Academy in 2007. They had two children. Their son David is Professor of Education at Johns Hopkins and is the executive director of that university's Institute for Educational Policy. Their daughter, Deborah Steiner, whom Steiner fondly described in *Errata* as 'an exact and illuminating philologist', is the John Jay Professor of Greek and Latin at Columbia University. Zara Steiner's death came just ten days after that of her husband.[60]

---

[58] See Elias Canetti, *Die Blendung* (1935), translated into English as *Auto-da-Fé* (1946).

[59] Quoted in Mark Krupnick, 'George Steiner's Literary Journalism: "The Heart of the Maze"', *New England Review*, 15:2 (Spring 1993), pp. 157–67 (p. 157).

[60] David Reynolds, 'Zara Steiner, 1928–2020', *Biographical Memoirs of Fellows of the British Academy*, XIX, 467–83.

Note on the authors: Edward Hughes is Professor Emeritus of French at Queen Mary, University of London; he was elected a Fellow of the British Academy in 2019. Ben Hutchinson is Professor of European Literature at the University of Kent.

Biographical Memoirs of Fellows of the British Academy (ISSN 2753–6777) are published by
The British Academy, 10–11 Carlton House Terrace, London, SW1Y 5AH
www.thebritishacademy.ac.uk

CORRIGENDUM

Correction to

'Robin George Murdoch Nisbet, 1925–2013', by S.J. Harrison
Biographical Memoirs of Fellows of the British Academy, XIII (2014), 365–382

On page 376, line 6, delete the words: 'and declined the Regius Chair of Greek in 1960'.